WINSTON CHURCHILL
SOLDIER

THE MILITARY LIFE OF
A GENTLEMAN AT WAR

Douglas S Russell

Foreword by
Sir Martin Gilbert

BRASSEY'S

Dedicated to the Memory of
James Russell and Dorothy Sherman Russell

An imprint of **Chrysalis** Books Group plc

Brassey's
The Chrysalis Building, Bramley Road, London W10 6SP
www.chrysalisbooks.co.uk

Distributed in North America by Casemate Publishing,
2114 Darby Road, Havertown, PA 19083, USA

Douglas S. Russell has asserted his moral right to be
identified as the author of this work

Library of Congress Cataloging-in-Publication Data available

British Library Cataloguing-in-Publication Data:
a catalogue record for this book is available
from the British Library

ISBN 1 85753 364 X

Edited and designed by DAG Publications Ltd
Designed by David Gibbons
Edited by John Gilbert
Cartography by Sir Martin Gilbert

Printed in Great Britain

Contents

List of Maps

Acknowledgements

There are many people to thank for their assistance in the preparation of this book. First among these are The Lady Soames, Sir Martin Gilbert and Richard M. Langworth. Each of them labours in the same vineyard and each has encouraged me and helped me a great deal in my own task. I particularly thank Sir Martin Gilbert for providing his kind foreword and the excellent maps for this book, and for reviewing the manuscript and making many wise suggestions. I owe him a great debt of gratitude for building the rock foundation upon which all contemporary Churchill scholarship rests, the eight-volume biography which Randolph Churchill began and he finished. The biographical volumes and sixteen companion volumes (so far) are indispensable. In this first group I wish also to thank my wife, Sue Feeney, for her patience and support without which the book could not have been completed.

For providing research assistance, photographs, books, sharing their experiences and advice, extending their hospitality to the author and encouraging this project along the way, I wish to thank the following: David Barnard, Terry Brighton, Jean Broome, Chelsey (my muse), Winston S. Churchill, the Winston Churchill Memorial and Library, Paul H. Courtenay, Ray Currie, Nimrod Dix, Sue Farrington, David Eddershaw, John Forster, Vera Gallony, Rodney R. Gander, Rita M. Boswell Gibbs, Donald P. Grant, Ryno Greenwall, Alisdair Hawkyard, T. E. Heathcote, Major Robert Henderson, Captain J. M. Holtby, Gillian Hughes, Major David Innes-Lumsden, William C. Ives, David Jablonsky, Joseph E. Kelly, Carole Kenwright, Nigel B. Knocker, Major E. W. Leask, His Grace the Duke of Marlborough, Derek Marsh, Dr John Mather, Doris Maud, Dr Cyril Mazansky, Colonel Colin H. McVean, Colonel Timothy L. May, James W. Muller, the staff of the National Army Museum and particularly the Reading Room staff, Marianne de Nazareth, T. E. Nicholls, Kevin Northover, Allen Packwood, Edward Playfair, General Philip Pretorius, Judith N. Pugh, the officers and men of the Queen's Royal Hussars, Charles D. Platt, David Ramsay, Philip Reed, Dr Earl Rose, Celia Sandys, Major R. J. Sheldon, B. T. Simpkin, Major Robert W. Smith, Dr P. J. Thwaites, Major P. J. Timmons, the University of Iowa Libraries, Steven Walton, Mark Weber, Caspar J. Weinberger, and Ray Westlake.

For permission to quote, I wish to thank: Anthea Morton-Saner, Curtis Brown, and the estates of Winston S. Churchill and Peregrine S. Churchill for the works of Winston S. Churchill and Lord Randolph Churchill; the Harrow School Archive for school records and publications and the poems and essay by Winston S. Churchill; the National Archives for the Sandhurst Register of Gentlemen Cadets; the Queen's Royal Hussars Association for 4th (Queen's Own) Hussars archive documents; the Queen's Royal Lancers Regimental Museum for 21st (Empress of India's) Lancer archive documents; The Oxfordshire Yeomanry Trust, and Gerald Flint-Shipman for Queen's Own Oxfordshire Hussars archive documents; and the Ministry of Defence Archives for Churchill's army personal file. For permission to use photographs, I wish to thank: David Barnard; Director, National Army Museum, London; Sir Martin Gilbert; Illustrated London News; Doris Maud; Dr. Cyril Mazansky; The National Archive, the Churchill Archive Centre, Cambridge; the Oxfordshire Yeomanry Trust; the Royal Military Academy, Sandhurst; Major General Edmund Hakewill Smith; the Winston Churchill Memorial and Library in the United States, Fulton Missouri.

For seeing the typing, proofreading, editing, production and publication of the book through to completion, I wish to thank Caroline Bolton, Roderick Dymott, Anthony A. Evans, John Lee, Karen Luebke, Stephen H. Muller, Wilma (Shebetka) Porter and Stuart Robertson.

To all of these people credit is due for whatever merit may attach to this book. Any errors of fact, judgment or omission are mine alone.

Finally, I wish to thank my subject, Lieutenant Winston Leonard Spencer Churchill, whom I have come to know and admire over the years. I am glad for the experience of entering his soldier's world and for the pleasure of reading his correspondence, essays, books, speeches and poems. He is a splendid writer and has written about the events I describe in this book in prose much finer than my own. He is the author of many notable quotations and it is appropriate, as I complete this book on his 130th birthday, to end this volume with one I particularly admire. 'Authors are the happy people of the world, whose work is a pleasure. I have sometimes fortified myself amid the vexations, vicissitudes and uncertainties of political life by the reflection that I might find a secure line of retreat on the pleasant, peaceful and fertile country of the pen where one need never be idle or dull.'

Douglas S. Russell
Iowa City
November 30, 2004

Foreword
by Sir Martin Gilbert

D OUGLAS RUSSELL put all students of Churchill in his debt when he published *The Orders, Decorations and Medals of Sir Winston Churchill*. The first edition appeared in 1990, and the revised edition in 2004. It is a model of scholarship and research, which roused in the minds of all who read it a sense of the range and versatility of Churchill's soldiering experiences. This new book goes behind the medals to the fighting itself.

Drawing on Churchill's own accounts, and on the material collected by Randolph Churchill for volume one of the Official Biography – as well as my own efforts in volume three – and on much fascinating material that he has uncovered at Harrow School and in other archives and garrisons on three continents, Douglas Russell presents a vivid picture of Churchill's military activities, from his days in the School Cadet Force at Harrow to his six months as a battalion commander on the Western Front in 1916.

Few if any politicians and statesmen, even in the glory days of the Duke of Wellington, have seen so much action on the field of battle. In modern times, only Churchill's ancestor, John Churchill, Duke of Marlborough – about whom Churchill wrote a four-volume biography – and Napoleon – about whom Churchill wanted to write a biography – surpass his record as a man of action and politics combined.

Douglas Russell and his readers are fortunate that Churchill was at home in equal measure in the roles of soldier and war correspondent. His dispatches from the scenes of action, starting in Cuba in 1895, are exceptionally detailed, thoughtful and dramatic. In the First World War, when he commanded a Scottish battalion, his letters to Clementine portray the daily life, moods and dangers in the trenches of the Western Front, centering around the Belgian village of Ploegsteert, known to the British Tommies as 'Plug Street'.

Between Cuba and Plug Street Churchill saw action in the wars on the North-West Frontier of India, in the Sudan and in South Africa. Douglas Russell travels with us to the war zones, takes us to the barracks and the training grounds, and then to the fighting itself. In the fast-moving pages we see the young Churchill emerge from the hesitant yet always prescient chrysalis of a schoolboy to the fighting man who had no illusions about the brutality of war, and was willing to make the often-savage reality known to a wide audience.

It is important that this part of Churchill's life should have found so keen a portraitist.

Sir Martin Gilbert
January 2005

Introduction

SATURDAY, 30 JANUARY 1965 dawned cold and windy in London. The city, though crowded, was unusually quiet as the nation and the news media focused on the observance of the funeral of Sir Winston Churchill, the former Prime Minister, who had died five days earlier at the age of ninety after a parliamentary career that began in the reign of Queen Victoria and ended in the reign of Queen Elizabeth II. He was, by all accounts, a Great Man, the greatest Englishman of his era and one of the very few in British history to be accorded a state funeral.

At exactly 9.45 a.m. the funeral procession began with the chiming of Big Ben and the firing of a salute by the cannon of the Royal Horse Artillery in St James's Park. Three thousand five hundred soldiers lined the three-mile route from Westminster Hall down Whitehall, past the Cenotaph, No. 10 Downing Street and Admiralty House, through Trafalgar Square, to the Strand, Fleet Street and up Ludgate Hill to St Paul's Cathedral, and thousands upon thousands of spectators stood solemnly in behind them. The procession was a splendid sight, including the mounted Horse Guards in their plumed helmets and red capes, the contingents of the Guards regiments, tall and imposing in their bearskins; and the blue-clad sailors of the Royal Navy who pulled the gun carriage with Churchill's coffin, covered by the Union Jack on top of which was placed his Order of the Garter insignia.

Among the many military units participating in the ceremony that day were a number that the general public would probably not have recognised but whose participation would certainly have gratified Churchill. Lining New Palace Yard were uniformed Officers Training Corps cadets from Harrow School where young Churchill had received his first military training in the mid-1880s as a member of the Harrow School Rifle Volunteer Corps. Marching ahead of the Guards regiments was a detachment from the Royal Military Academy, Sandhurst, which Churchill attended with distinction in 1893–4 before receiving his army officer's commission in 1895. A small Territorial Army detachment led by Major Tim May of the Queen's Own Oxfordshire Hussars took part in the parade representing Churchill's service with them as an army reservist from 1902 to

1924. The pallbearers in the London procession were from the Grenadier Guards, the second battalion of which Churchill had trained with in 1915 in France for combat service in the First World War.

In the middle of the procession and behind Earl Mountbatten of Burma, Chief of the Defence Staff, marched four officers in blue great-coats and red service caps, Majors Murray-Brown, Graham, Troughton and Wood, from the Queen's Royal Irish Hussars, successor to Churchill's own cavalry regiment, the Fourth Queen's Own Hussars, carrying black velvet cushions bearing Churchill's many orders, decorations and medals. Among them were the Spanish Order of Military Merit for Churchill's distinguished comportment under fire in Cuba in 1895; the India Medal for active service on the North-West frontier that nearly cost his life in 1897; the Queen's Sudan Medal representing his participation in the great charge of the 21st Lancers in 1898 which won the regiment three Victoria Crosses but cost them crippling casualties; the Queen's South Africa Medal for combat duty in the Boer War in which he served with conspic-uous bravery as a civilian and as a soldier; and three service medals for a very dangerous six-months' tour of duty as an infantry officer in the trenches of the Western Front in the Great War. The medals were recogni-tion of Churchill's remarkable record as a soldier and war correspondent that in part preceded and in part paralleled his singular career as a politi-cian and statesman.

Churchill's biographers most often write of his long parliamentary career and focus on his great years as Prime Minister during the Second World War, his and Britain's finest hour. None of that would ever have happened if an illness and accident-prone boy had not survived or if Lt Winston Churchill had not by good fortune overcome moments of great danger in combat while serving as an officer in the British army as a young man. While it is rightfully Churchill's life as a statesman, war leader and author for which he is best known and remembered, it is remarkable how early in life he began to assert himself to achieve success and recognition.

'Twenty to twenty-five, those are the years,' wrote Churchill in his 1930 autobiography, *My Early Life*, when he looked back on his life from the five-tiered summit of middle age. It was those very years, from 1895 to 1900, that Churchill served as a lieutenant in the British army seeking 'the bubble reputation even at the cannon's mouth'. During that time he saw combat on three continents, won four campaign medals and a Spanish Order, was mentioned in dispatches, wrote five books, established himself as a capable and popular war correspondent and lecturer, gained international fame as an escaped prisoner of war, and won a seat in Parliament – all before his twenty-sixth birthday. Later and perhaps less well remembered, Churchill served as an officer in the Territorial Army, Britain's military reserve, for more than twenty years and as a front-line infantry officer in combat in the First World War during an interlude in his Cabinet career. In all, his military service spanned almost thirty of his first fifty years and made a lasting impression on him.

Churchill was not universally admired in the army where he had his partisans and detractors. He was criticised as a medal hunter, a self-promoter and a glory seeker who was using the army as a mere convenience for his own political ambitions. It was his early military adventures that made his political career possible. As a young man Churchill set out to become a hero, to make a name for himself in the public's estimation and so follow his interest in war and history to a life of politics and statesmanship. There were many chances to fail and many close calls in the face of danger along the way. That Churchill survived and succeeded in his ambitions is an early measure of his courage and stubborn will that the world came to know so well in the dark early days of the Second World War.

I

A Victorian Childhood

THE FUTURE Lieutenant Winston Leonard Spencer Churchill was born on 30 November 1874 into the privileged world of the English aristocracy, the traditional source of the officer class of the British army. He was a descendant of John Churchill, First Duke of Marlborough (1650–1722), the greatest British general of his era and certainly as great a figure in his day as the Duke of Wellington was during the Napoleonic Wars a century later. Under Queen Anne (1702–14) the duke served as Captain-General, or Commander-in-Chief, of the British army that won a series of decisive battles over the forces of French King Louis XIV and his allies in the War of the Spanish Succession. The victories at Blenheim (1704) on the Danube in present-day Bavaria, and at Ramillies (1706), Oudenarde (1708) and Malplaquet (1709) in Flanders destroyed French hegemony on the continent and assured Britain's freedom from foreign domination. As Winston Churchill wrote in *Marlborough, His Life and Times*: 'He commanded the armies of Europe against France for ten campaigns. He fought four great battles and many important actions. It is the common boast of his champions that he never fought a battle that he did not win, nor besieged a fortress he did not take.'[1]

In 1702 the Queen made John Churchill a duke and awarded him the Order of the Garter, the senior and most prestigious English knighthood. After the battle of Blenheim the Crown conveyed to him the royal manor of Woodstock, a 15,000-acre estate in Oxfordshire. As a further reward, the Queen granted £134,000 for the construction of a country house on the estate to be named Blenheim Palace in commemoration of the duke's greatest victory. The palace was built between 1705 and 1723 at a final cost of about £300,000. A 127-foot-high victory column topped by a six-foot, eleven-inch-high statue of the duke was prominently placed in the grounds. In 1874, the palace was the home of Churchill's grandfather John, the Seventh Duke of Marlborough. Blenheim was and remains an imposing house of immense scale. The building has a front 480 feet wide and with its courtyards covers seven acres. One of its public rooms, aptly named the long library, is thirty feet wide, 184 feet long and two storeys tall. The palace is set in a deer park of some 2,100 acres surrounded by nine miles of seven-foot-high stone walls and flanked by an eight-acre artificial lake designed by noted landscape architect Capability Brown.[2] A grander setting outside those of the Royal Family can hardly be imagined.

Blenheim Palace is symbolic of the place of Churchill's family in English society and history and it was there that Winston Churchill was born. Churchill's father, the twenty-five-year-old Lord Randolph Churchill, was the second son of the Seventh Duke and the Conservative Member of Parliament for the family borough of Woodstock. First elected to the House of Commons just nine months before Winston's birth, Lord Randolph was to have a meteoric career in government, becoming the leader of the House of Commons and Chancellor of the Exchequer at the age of thirty-seven in 1886, but resigning from the Cabinet soon after. He suffered a slow, tragic decline both politically and physically and died on 24 January 1895, too soon to see his son Winston in the uniform of a commissioned officer.

Churchill's mother was an American socialite, the twenty-year-old Jennie Jerome of New York City who had lived in Paris for a number of years and, more recently, in London. Her father, Leonard Jerome was a wealthy businessman, patron of horse racing, formerly the American consul in Trieste and one-time part-owner of *The New York Times*. Just as Winston's father was a member of the hereditary British aristocracy, so it may be said his mother was a product of that class sometimes thought of as the American aristocracy, the wealthy east coast élite. Following the marriage, Mr Jerome provided an annual stipend of £2,000 to the couple; the duke provided a further £1,000 per year. Lady Randolph Churchill, as Jennie was known after the marriage, was a bright light of London society and would later become an important ally for Winston as she used her influence to assist him in obtaining desirable postings in the army.

Churchill's Marlborough grandfather was one of only twenty-seven dukes, and as such ranked just below the Royal Family in order of official precedence. Indeed, the Churchills were one of the few hundred families who controlled both society and government, holding vast estates and wielding great power and influence. Because he was the second son, Lord Randolph did not inherit the title or properties of the duke. His title was a courtesy title only. Aside from politics he had no profession. Although Winston's parents were not themselves wealthy and were often very much in debt, they lived a high society lifestyle.

As Churchill later wrote, he grew up during 'the august, unchallenged and tranquil glories of the Victorian Era'.[3] He was born in the thirty-seventh year of Queen Victoria's six-decade reign and the thirteenth year of her reclusive mourning for her late husband, the royal consort Prince Albert. Society was led by the Queen's eldest son, Albert Edward, Prince of Wales, who succeeded to the throne in 1901 as King Edward VII. The prince's social circle, the Marlborough House set, acquired its name from his London residence in Pall Mall, a house sold by the Fourth Duke of Marlborough to the Crown. Churchill's parents were a part of that set and throughout his life Winston would be acquainted with its members and they with him as he moved within this circle or on its fringe. A number of powerful men who would later exert their influence on Winston's behalf when he was in the army knew him from the time he was a little boy.

The Victorian era of the late nineteenth century is far removed from our own. In 1874 there were no aeroplanes or motor cars, no radios or radar, no photocopy or facsimile machines, no television or motion pictures, no computers or nuclear weapons. The widespread use of the telephone was in its infancy. It is said that when Lord Randolph Churchill installed electric lights in the family home at Connaught Place in 1883, it was the first house in London to be so illuminated. Coal was the primary heating fuel in Britain and its sooty smoke was an ingredient of the infamous London fogs. The principal means of long-distance travel in Britain were the steam railway and the canal boat; the standard conveyance for local and intermediate distances was the horse-drawn vehicle.

Although Great Britain had a population of fewer than thirty-five million at the time of Churchill's birth and was geographically less than half the size of France or Spain, it was the centre of the greatest empire the world has ever seen. The British Empire included Canada, Australia, New Zealand and India. At that time, India included all the territories which make up present-day India, Pakistan, Bangladesh and Sri Lanka. The territory of Upper Burma was annexed to India in 1886 when Lord Randolph Churchll was Secretary of State for India. Britain's possessions on the African continent ran almost unbroken from Egypt through the Sudan, to Uganda and British East Africa, and south to Rhodesia and Bechuanaland to the tip of South Africa. The Mediterranean Sea was secured for Britain in the west, centre and east by its possessions of Gibraltar, Malta and Cyprus. The Suez Canal, Britain's lifeline to India, was owned by a British company. The smaller colonies and possessions of the British Empire dominated the most important of the world's sea lanes from Malaya to the West Indies to the Falkland Islands and provided coaling and victualling stations around the globe to support the Royal

Navy and a vast merchant fleet. British subjects lived, governed, sold their goods and preached their Christian gospel on every continent and in the islands of every ocean. One-fifth of the earth's land mass and one-quarter of its population were ruled from Whitehall in London, the seat of the British government.

The Royal Navy had been supreme and unchallenged in the world since the battle of Trafalgar in 1805 and its far-flung squadrons were present in every sea protecting Britain's interests and commerce, spreading her influence and protecting the United Kingdom behind its floating defensive shield. The British army had not faced a challenge in western Europe since the final defeat of Napoleon at the battle of Waterloo in 1815 and had not been at war with a European power since its conflict with Russia in the Crimean War of 1854–6. Although the Victorian British army was regularly engaged in colonial 'small wars' in the last quarter of the nineteenth century, the First World War was at the time of Churchill's birth still forty years and a world away.

Churchill had a traditional, upper-class Victorian childhood. He was raised at home by a nanny, his beloved Mrs Everest. She was his dearest friend and confidante in his early years and also looked after Winston's younger brother, John Strange Churchill, who was born in 1880. Years later at Harrow School Mrs Everest came to visit for a day and Winston proudly walked down the high street with her and kissed her good-bye in public, an act of some real courage in an age when schoolboys were often ashamed to acknowledge the existence of their nannies.

Winston's parents were very much absorbed in society and politics and were quite distant, both physically and emotionally, from their son. Winston often felt neglected and his schoolboy letters are full of requests that they visit for some school activity, which they almost never did. Nonetheless, all his life Winston worshipped his father, a political force and a real national celebrity in his day whom Winston considered to be a great statesman and role model. He genuinely admired his father and had dreams of serving at his side in Parliament. As early as the age of ten, Winston was corresponding with Lord Randolph about politics and he followed the election returns and the doings of the great personalities of the era.[4] Winston always sought his father's approval but seldom received it. Lord Randolph's aloof and critical nature made Winston's early years very frustrating and lonely indeed. Of Lady Randolph, Churchill later wrote: 'My mother always seemed to me a fairy princess ... She shone for me like the Evening Star. I loved her deeply – but at a distance.'[5] She was very self-absorbed and very busy with her own interests, a whirl of dinners, balls and country house visits with the fox-hunting set. In fact, as a small child Winston saw relatively little of his parents and, to his deep and lifelong regret, never established a close relationship with his father. He developed instead the traits of self-reliance and assertiveness. He later wrote: 'Solitary trees, if they grow at all, grow strong: and a boy deprived of a father's care often develops, if he escapes the perils of youth, an independence and vigour of thought which may restore in after life the heavy loss of early days.'[6]

Like other boys of his, or perhaps any, era the young Winston preferred play to study. Of his first school, St George's at Ascot, he later wrote: 'I counted the days and hours to the end of every term, when I should return home from this hateful servitude and range my soldiers in line of battle on the nursery floor.'[7] He was interested in things military from an early age and in his oldest surviving letters we find a child much taken with toy soldiers, flags, castles and war games. He amassed a large collection of lead soldiers which held an endless fascination for him. As his cousin Clare Sheridan later recalled:

> His playroom contained from one end to the other a plank table on trestles upon which were thousands of lead soldiers arranged for battle. He organised wars. The lead battalions were manoeuvred into action, peas and pebbles committed great casualties, forts were stormed, cavalry charged, bridges were destroyed – real water tanks engulfed the advancing foe. Altogether it was a most impressive show, and played with an interest that was no ordinary child's game.[8]

Winston's toy soldiers were most likely those representing the armies of the Napoleonic era manufactured by the French firms Lucotte or Mignot. Although the final resting place of Churchill's own lead soldiers is unknown, there exists today a similar collection of Lucotte soldiers on public display at Blenheim Palace. These were a gift to the duke in 1935 from Paul Maze, a painter friend of Winston Churchill whom he had first met on the Western Front.[9] The pride of Winston's youthful efforts at collecting, the toy soldiers would later play a key role in real life.

An indifferent student in his early years, Churchill was a lonely and often unhappy boy. He looked inward and found 'the greatest pleasure I had in those days was reading'.[10] From a remarkably young age he developed the habit of reading the newspapers in detail each day. This is probably a trait he received from his parents. His mother later noted in her autobiography:

'In the morning an hour or more was devoted to the reading of newspapers, which was a necessity, if one wanted to show an intelligent interest in the questions of the day, for at dinner conversation invariably turned on politics.'[11] No doubt Winston's interest was due in large part to the fact that his father was often written about in the papers. The loyal son read all that he could find about Lord Randolph and his speeches and remarks that were quoted. Winston followed politics closely, being familiar with many of the great men of the day through his parents and grandparents. There were few important figures of politics, government or society, from Members of Parliament and ministers of state to the heir to the British throne, who did not visit their home for, as Lady Randolph said, 'Our house became the rendezvous of all shades of politicians.'[12]

In addition to newspapers, Churchill read popular adventure stories, a staple for boys of all ages. At nine and a half he 'devoured' Robert Louis Stevenson's *Treasure Island*, a gift from his father. He read novels by H. Rider Haggard who wrote *King Solomon's Mines* and many less remembered stories that featured adventurous Englishmen and Englishwomen in exotic climes. One of Winston's surviving boyhood letters includes a request to his mother for copies of Rider Haggard's novels *She* and *Jess*.[13] The young Churchill was also familiar with the historical novels of G. A. Henty, many of which had a patriotic or military theme. The subtitle of Churchill's 1930 autobiography, *My Early Life, A Roving Commission*, may have come from a Henty title, *A Roving Commission (or Through the Black Insurrection of Hayti)*.[14] Many other Henty titles would have been equally fitting to describe Churchill's life. *By Sheer Pluck, When London Burned, Held Fast for England* and *No Surrender* might all serve to be either the stuff of a young boy's daydreams or a statesman's life.

One book we are certain Churchill owned as a boy is *Routledge's Every Boy's Annual* for 1884.[15] One of a series of compilations of a popular juvenile periodical, the book was full of stirring adventure tales, many with a military or imperial theme. Mixed in with 'A Holiday Trip to Norsemanland' and 'The Telegraph' are 'The Victoria Cross – Rorke's Drift', 'The 13th Light Infantry and the Defence of Jellalabad' and 'The Victoria Cross – Morosi's Mountain', all accompanied by vivid illustrations of red-coated British soldiers in heroic poses or in mortal combat with colourful foes. Such works were all emblematic of the romantic nationalism of late nineteenth-century British popular and political culture which affected newspapers and magazines as well as fiction and which were all a part of Winston's intellectual diet.

'From very early youth I had brooded about soldiers and war,' Churchill later wrote.[16] He made note of military items in his reading of the newspapers and at the precocious age of ten wrote a serious letter to his father discussing, among other things, the battle of Abu Klea on the Nile fought by the Gordon relief expedition in 1885.[17] Thirteen years later, as a lieutenant in the British army, Churchill would himself see active service on the Nile in the campaign to retake the Sudan. When Winston visited Mrs Everest's brother-in-law at Ventnor on the Isle of Wight, the latter told the boy tales of his service in the Zulu War of 1879, of which Winston had seen illustrations in a newspaper.[18]

Although an avid reader, Churchill later described himself at that age as 'at once backward and precocious, reading books beyond my years yet at the bottom of the Form' in school.[19] Whisked off to St George's, an all-male boarding school at Ascot at the age of eight, Winston did not do well at Latin, which was a key subject in the curriculum. He never mastered the classical languages, a signal failure for a schoolboy of that era. 'In all the twelve years I was at school no one ever succeeded in making me write a Latin verse or learn any Greek except the alphabet.'[20] In fact, Churchill did much better in Latin and Greek than he suggests in *My Early Life*. It was his wish to go to university but Lord Randolph decided otherwise. The grammatical structure of Latin seemed beyond his understanding and, in any event, did not compare favourably with his native tongue. 'In a sensible language like English,' he later wrote, 'important words are connected and related to one another by little words. The Romans in that stern antiquity considered such a method weak and unworthy.'[21] Churchill also studied French for a number of years both in school and with tutors, but his workmanlike grasp of vocabulary and grammar unfortunately was not accompanied by a felicitous pronunciation. All his life, when speaking French, he sounded exactly like Winston Churchill speaking English. A modern day educator would perhaps say he had no aptitude for foreign language study. The fact is that Winston was a wilful, stubborn boy not unaccustomed to seeking his own way. Like boys of many generations before and since, he did better at things he enjoyed and found interesting and worse at subjects he did not like, particularly if they required too much study.

After two years at St George's, Winston was moved to a private school at Brighton where he would spend three years and find new academic interests including history, 'poetry by heart' and his favourite pursuits of those years – horseback riding and swimming.[22] He rode as often as three days a week and horses became a central pleasure of his life ever after. Although learning to ride was expected of a boy of his class, it would also have a later military application for Churchill. In addition to his schoolboy studies and sports, Winston found time as a thirteen-year-old to join the Primrose League, an organisation of young Tory volunteers founded by Lord Randolph in memory of Lord Beaconsfield who, as Benjamin Disraeli, had been a Tory Prime Minister. It was a first step in the direction of his political career. The schooling Churchill received at Ascot and Brighton was merely preparatory for his public school education where the sons of the aristocracy were sent before entering university and commencing their careers. Although generation after generation of Churchills had attended Eton since the early 1700s, Winston's parents selected Harrow for him, apparently for health reasons. As a small boy he had suffered the usual childhood illnesses and injuries but had also nearly died from pneumonia at the age of eleven. In March, 1886, he was stricken with that illness and for several days his life was in the balance. At one point his temperature rose as high as 104.3°F before the fever was controlled. His condition was of grave concern. It was reported that the Prince of Wales 'stopped the whole line at [a] levée to ask after him'.[23] Since Eton was located in a low-lying, presumably damp area and not healthy for the young boy's lungs, and Harrow School was on a prominent hill, it was to Harrow that Winston was sent in the spring of 1888.

By the time of Churchill's arrival, Harrow had already been in existence for more than three centuries, having received its Royal Charter from Queen Elizabeth in 1572. The school's brick and stone walls spoke of permanence and excellence. Still one of the premier schools in the United Kingdom, Harrow was at the peak of its prestige at the end of the nineteenth century, standing with Eton and Winchester at the very top. By the time Churchill enrolled at Harrow it had graduated five boys who became Prime Ministers of England: Spencer Perceval (1809–1812), the only Prime Minister ever assassinated; Frederick Robinson, later Earl of Ripon, Viscount Goderich (1827); Sir Robert Peel (1834–5 and 1841–6); George Hamilton Gordon, later Earl of Aberdeen (1852–5); and Henry Temple, later Viscount Palmerston (1855–8 and 1859–65).[24] The Harrow tradition of producing outstanding graduates extended to the military field as well. Many of Harrow's old boys served honourably in the British army and the Royal Navy and six of them had won Britain's highest award for heroism, the Victoria Cross. Today their names are proudly displayed in the old Speech Room with the thirteen Harrovians who were awarded the decoration in later years.[25] It was and remains a school of long and proud tradition.

Harrow School was located in the country north-west of London. A stone marker in the wall near the Vaughan Library states the distance to Marble Arch in London as exactly ten miles. Churchill's parents' home at the time was at Connaught Place, close to Marble Arch. In the 1880s the interval between school and city was filled with farm fields and woods as far as the eye could see.[26] It must have seemed much farther away as Churchill seldom visited London during the term and communicated with his parents by letter.

Winston Churchill arrived at Harrow on 17 April 1888, at the age of thirteen-and-a-half. He would be a student there for fourteen terms over the next three years and nine months. There were approximately six hundred boys in residence at the time; no girls were admitted as students. The tuition was £250 per year. There were three academic terms annually, spring, summer and autumn, with school holidays between sessions. Reading assignments were given for the holiday periods, which Winston usually spent visiting his family or travelling on the Continent.

In May 1888, within a few weeks of enrolling at the school, Churchill joined the Harrow School Rifle Volunteer Corps, forerunner of the Officer Training Corps of the twentieth century. This, as the name suggests, was a voluntary rather than a compulsory activity, and to sign up so soon after arrival indicates that Winston had an interest in the military greater than merely collecting toy soldiers. Here was perhaps a chance to give his boyish dreams of service some tangible form. His service in the Rifle Corps marked the first time Churchill wore a military uniform and received military training.

The Harrow Rifle Corps was founded in 1859 and was affiliated with the Middlesex Regiment whose uniform it copied. The uniform was grey, the facings – collar and sleeve trim bands – were blue. The headgear varied from a brimless hat similar to a hussar's busby with a feather plume in front, to the standard army field cap and forage cap shaped like a round pillbox. Rather than display the badge of the Middlesex Regiment, the corps adopted an insignia of two crossed arrows over a garland wreath which is now the official Harrow School badge. Although he did not write home about it, Churchill certainly wore the uniform of the corps – the first of the many military uniforms he would wear in his long life.

Churchill's classmate at Harrow, Gerald Woods Wollaston, later recalled that the Rifle Corps was not popular with the senior students and was not taken seriously until the 1890s when Harrow master M. C. Kemp, with the support of the head of the school, Nugent Hicks, took steps to improve the programme.[27] Although the corps was not particularly popular, membership rose from fewer than one hundred to more than two hundred boys during Churchill's years and even had its own band for musical occasions.

Each day the boys drilled in the Bill yard, marching to and fro and perhaps dreaming of martial glory like that in the song, written a few years later:

Left! Right!
Young Brown he was a little boy
and barely four foot four,
But his manly bosom yearned to join
the Harrow Rifle Corps.
So he went to see the Serjeant
and he made a grand salute,
And he said, says he, 'I want to be
a Volunteer Recruit.'
Left! Right! Left! Right! Left! Left!
O The H. S. R. V. C.
Tis a gallant sight to see,
As they swing along so gaily with the band;
with the trumpets blowing proud,
And the big drum beating loud,
There is not another finer in the land!
With the trumpets blowing proud,
And the big drum beating loud
There is not another finer in the land!
But the Serjeant shook his martial head, and shed a martial tear,
'You'll have to go away and grow and come another year.'
So off he went with grim intent, and did his best and grew,
And when the year was over he was nearly five foot two.
Then they stuck him in a uniform, and made him learn his drill,
And double hard about the Yard, and up and down the Hill.
'Now by my troth,' the Serjeant quoth, 'If little Brown could grow,
He'd make the smartest officer that ever you did know.'
And grow he did: and on the Range so well he practised up,
A 'bull' he got, with every shot, and won the Spencer Cup.
And when he tried for Sandhurst, he was sure as fate to pass,
For wasn't he a member of the Harrow Army Class?
And now he's in a Regiment a-fighting for the Crown,
And soon he'll be a KCB, and Major-General Brown.
So listen all, both great and small, and may there be some more
To rally round to the bugle-sound, and join the Rifle
Corps![28]

In addition to the drill at school, there were annual inspections held with the Middlesex Regiment in May and a demonstration programme called the 'Assault at Arms' each year featuring exhibitions of gymnastics, fencing, tug-of-war and quarter-stave bouts. Among the special events was the visit of Her Royal Highness Princess Louise, the daughter of Queen Victoria, to dedicate a technical school at Harrow on 14 May 1889. Young Winston, as a Rifle Corps member, served in the guard of honour for the occasion.[29] The most popular activities of the corps were the field days and mock battles, combination camp-outs and military manoeuvres, in competition with other schools. These were held at different parks: Rickmansworth, Althorp or Gorhambury, or at Sandhurst and Aldershot. The latter sites would become familiar to Churchill in later years as a gentleman cadet and commissioned officer. It was necessary to attend a certain minimum number of drill sessions and classes to qualify to participate in the field days. These outdoor programmes were held on average once per term during Churchill's years at Harrow and he was a willing participant. He took part in a field day exercise at Aldershot on 25 March 1889. About ten thousand men and boys from both army units and the rifle corps detachments from thirteen public schools were involved. As Churchill wrote to his father: 'It was great fun. The noise was tremendous. There were 4 batteries of guns in the field and a Maxim and several Nordenfeldts. We were defeated because we were inferior in number and not from any want of courage.'[30] As was typical in such programmes, the mock combat lasted a couple of hours or until all the blank ammunition was expended. This day the exercise was followed by a march past review, a picnic lunch, and return to school in time for tea and a band concert.[31] The field days, however, were not serious manoeuvres as J. W. S. Tomlin, head of the school in 1889 later recalled:

> Sergeant Grisdale, a fine specimen of the old army, used to drill a small squad every morning in the school yard, but very few kept their drills, and the field days, though jolly picnics, were often ludicrous from a military point of view. I remember on one occasion during a sham fight in Cassiobury Park, Watford, a master who was captain of the corps, tying a white handkerchief to the point of his sword, and going out of his company shouting to the enemy who were in close formation about fifty yards off: 'Gentlemen, I maintain that you are all dead men.'[32]

Churchill seemed generally to enjoy the Rifle Corps programme. He wrote to his father in March 1889, 'I have bought a book on drill as I intend going in for the Corporal Examinations next term. I went down to the range on Tuesday and fired away 20 rounds.'[33] In fact, he never rose in the ranks and *The Harrovian*, which regularly reported on Rifle Corps promotions, never listed him as a corporal. Although he enjoyed marksmanship practice, he never made the Harrow Eight which regularly participated in rifle-shooting competitions with army units and teams from other public schools.

At Harrow Churchill was not active in team sports like football or cricket but focused rather on individual sports and activities such as swimming, fencing, shooting and bicycling. He showed pluck and self-reliance in sports which, interestingly, could have real value to a military officer. He would have been a first-rate Boy Scout had they been around then.

Winston's participation in the Rifle Corps was certainly noted by Lord Randolph. In the late nineteeenth century the careers open to young men of Churchill's class were few – the church, the bar, the City (meaning business), the military, or the civil service, including the colonial service. A university education was considered a prerequisite for all but the City and the army. In Churchill's case the selection of a career was made for him by his father after Winston had been at Harrow for only a year. The choice of a military career was, as Churchill later wrote, 'entirely due to my collection of soldiers'.[34] On a June day in 1889, while Winston was on a home visit from school, Lord Randolph came to his room to inspect the remarkable display of toy soldiers. By then the collection included almost 1,500 lead soldiers under Winston's command, complete with an infantry division, a cavalry brigade, artillery and even a transport section financed by Sir Henry Drummond Wolff, a friend of Lord Randolph. Winston's brother Jack was left to command the enemy troops which were denied the use of field artillery because of a rather one-sided treaty negotiated between the boys. Being over five years younger no doubt worked to Jack's disadvantage in the field of juvenile diplomacy. In his 1930 autobiography Churchill described his father's visit:

> He spent twenty minutes studying the scene – which was really impressive – with a keen eye and captivating smile. At the end he asked me if I would like to go into the army. I thought it would be splendid to command an Army, so I said 'Yes' at once: and immediately I was taken at my word. For years I thought my father with his experience and flair discerned in me the qualities of military genius. But I was later told that he had only come to the conclusion that I was not clever enough to go to the Bar. However that may be, the toy soldiers turned the current of my life.[35]

It is clear that Lord Randolph had mistakenly concluded that his son was not of high intellectual calibre and that because of Winston's generally poor grades and low standing in school he was unsuited to attend a university. He did seem to choose a career in which he thought Winston could succeed. Young Churchill had shown a great interest in military matters with both his toy soldiers and his enthusiastic participation in the Harrow Rifle Corps. In any event, we must take Churchill at his word that this is how the decision to send him to the army was made. He later repeated the account in his essay, 'The Dream,' written in 1946.[36] Winston certainly believed this is how his army career began; Lord Randolph left no record. After the meeting with his father, one of the few long discussions they ever shared, Churchill wrote: 'All my education was directed to passing into Sandhurst, and afterwards to the technical details of the profession of arms.'[37] Indeed, at the beginning of the very next school term on 18 September 1889, Winston joined the Army Class at Harrow.[38] He was still only fourteen years old.

The Army Class was an academic programme created to help boys pass the entrance examination for the Royal Military College at Sandhurst or the Royal Military Academy at Woolwich. It was common in the late 1800s for public school boys to study for a period with a private tutor in preparation for the army examination. It was to compete with such 'crammers,' as the tutors were inelegantly known, and so to retain its senior students longer, that the Harrow faculty formed the Army Class. In Churchill's time the class consisted of twelve to twenty-one boys each term and was taught by J. E. C. Welldon, the headmaster, and L. M. Moriarty. Although no record survives of the precise curriculum, it did not focus on military topics at all but rather on the academic subjects likely to appear in the army examinations: mathematics, geometrical drawing, freehand drawing, Latin, French, chemistry and history. The programme included extra classes on some evenings and during holidays, and a recommended list of supplementary reading assignments on examination subjects. The class was thought by some actually to hinder academic advancement in the school even though it prepared students for the civil service examiners who selected candidates for Sandhurst and the civilian branch of government because of the extra work required.[39]

Churchill's teachers decided early on that he should try the entrance examination for the Royal Military College at Sandhurst which trained cadets for the cavalry and infantry. They deemed his skills in mathematics too poor to qualify him for a cadetship at the Royal Military Academy at Woolwich which prepared officer cadets for service in the Royal Artillery and Royal Engineers. The Sandhurst entrance examination consisted of two parts – the preliminary examination and the further, or final, examination. An applicant was required to pass the preliminary before he was allowed to take the further. The score on the further examination would determine not only whether the applicant would be admitted to Sandhurst but whether he would be designated as a cavalry or an infantry cadet. Infantry cadetships were more prestigious and went to those with higher entrance examination scores. The fact that his teachers directed Churchill toward Sandhurst was a reflection on Churchill's relatively poor record as a student or, perhaps, their view of his study habits.

Indeed, Churchill never advanced very far in the school academically. At Harrow a boy was moved up from the lowest form or class to the higher forms according to academic performance based on examination scores and regardless of age. Churchill was never much of a success in written examinations. The marks for Winston's first term at Harrow in the summer of 1888 found him ranked in the fourth form, third remove (or sub-class), ninth out of ten in order of exam results. In other words, he started out one from the bottom of the whole school. Six terms later, in the spring of 1890, he was still in the fourth form. Thereafter he was placed in the 'modern shell,' an academic track or programme featuring modern rather than classical languages. In the spring of 1891, his ninth term, he was examined on the 'Special Sandhurst Class' grouping and ranked fifteenth out of sixteen. The next term he was nineteenth out of twenty-one. Reviewing the bill books, or mark sheets, in the Harrow archives one actually begins to see why Churchill's father despaired of a university education for Winston and why the later enrolment of the young man with a London crammer was considered necessary. Churchill never rose higher than the middle of the Army Class academically and was absent for the examination period in his final term in the autumn of 1892 because of illness.[40] His poor performance was due to his difficulty in sitting for examinations and not to a lack of intelligence or application. He often had a nervous worry about exams that gave him a severely upset stomach. As Harrow Master H. O. D. Davidson wrote to Winston's parents, 'As far as his ability goes, he ought to be at the top of his form, whereas he is at the bottom.'[41]

Although his examination results were not the best, Churchill did record a number of academic achievements at Harrow. During his very first term in June 1888, he won a prize open to the whole school for the recitation of poetry from memory. For the contest he selected Thomas B. Macaulay's *The Lays of Ancient Rome* (1842) from which he recited 1,200 lines without an error to the school assembly in the speech room. This was a remarkable display of memory for a thirteen-year-old boy and an early indication of twin abilities that Churchill was to retain all his life: a good memory and a flair for public speaking. *The Lays of Ancient Rome* is an interesting choice, focusing as it does on a martial theme, the heroic defence of a bridge leading to Rome by Horatius Cocles against the Tuscan army:

When the goodman mends his armour,
And trims his helmet's plume;
When the goodwife's shuttle merrily
Goes flashing through the loom;
With weeping and with laughter
Still is the story told
How well Horatius kept the bridge
In the brave days of old.

One can almost hear young Winston's voice at work. This speech performance shows Churchill's early and abiding love of the English language, the spoken as well as the written word. He loved the sound of it and he loved the speaking of it with his own tongue.

While he excelled in English, Winston never improved in Latin, a fact that formed his views for a lifetime. 'Naturally I am biased in favour of boys learning English. I would make them all learn English: and then I would let the clever ones learn Latin as an honour, and Greek as a treat. But the only thing I would whip them for is not knowing English. I would whip them hard for that.'[42] English was one of Churchill's strongest interests at Harrow and throughout his life. Mr Moriarty said it was remarkable for a fourteen year old boy to show 'such love and veneration for the English language'.[43] Churchill's developing skill in English included writing. He won two 'copies' for papers in history. A copy is a quality piece of work sent to the headmaster by a master and represents a commendation for a particularly good effort. In July 1890, Churchill won a house prize for his poem 'Influenza' which was entered in the headmaster's prize book. The subject was the influenza epidemic that swept through the European continent that year and threatened Great Britain. In twelve stanzas of six lines each, in a well-rhymed metre similar to that of *The Lays of Ancient Rome*, he treats the flu virus as an invading enemy army conquered only by the protection given 'Freedom's Isle' by the English Channel and, finally, by divine intervention. It concluded:

Yet Father Neptune strove right well
To Moderate this plague of Hell,
And thwart it in its course;
And though it passed the streak of brine
And penetrated his thin line,
It came with broken force.
For though it ravage far and wide
Both village, town and countryside,
Its power to kill was o'er;
And with the favouring winds of Spring
(Blest is the time of which I sing)
It left our native shore.
God shield our Empire from the might
Of war or famine, plague or blight
And all the power of Hell,
And keep it ever in the hands
Of those who fought 'gainst other lands,
Who fought and conquered well.[44]

This early endeavour reveals the patriotic outlook and writing skill that were to characterise the later, better known Winston Churchill.

While at Harrow, Winston's literary efforts included a series of letters to the school newspaper, *The Harrovian*. All the articles were critical of the school administration and were signed 'Junius Junior'. Two of the letters, published in December 1891 and March 1892, concern Winston's complaint that the school 'Assault at Arms' programme was not adequately supported. So strong were Churchill's complaints that the editor noted after the second letter, 'We have omitted a portion of our correspondent's letter, which seemed to us to exceed the limits of fair criticism.'[45] The editor was Leo Amery, a sixth-form boy who later served in Churchill's wartime Cabinet. He tried to tone down Winston's letters yet they were still noticed by the headmaster. As Mr Welldon told Amery years later, he called Churchill in for a conference and announced, 'I have observed certain articles which have recently appeared in *The Harrovian* of a character not calculated to increase the respect of the boys for the constituted authorities of the School. As *The Harrovian* is anonymous, I shall not dream of inquiring who wrote those articles, but if any more of the same sort appear it might become my painful duty to swish you!'[46]

Churchill later attributed his writing skill to his Harrow education. Through the efforts of Robert Somervell, Winston, 'got into my bones the essential structure of the ordinary British sentence – which is a noble thing'.[47] One of Churchill's few surviving Harrow pieces is an essay saved for posterity by Mr Somervell and now in the Harrow archives. Written in 1889, the composition was a short story of some 1,500 words on eighteen handwritten pages. Entitled 'The Engagement at 'La Marais', July 7, 1914', it has, interestingly enough, a military theme.[48] Written in the form of a diary of a British army officer serving as a general's aide-de-camp, it tells the story of a fictional battle between British and Russian forces near Kharkov in the Ukraine nearly twenty-five years hence. Speaking Churchill's words, the narrator is of course the very brave hero. At one point he is taken prisoner by the enemy but cleverly manages to escape and return to the British lines. Later the narrator narrowly escapes death when an exploding shell lands on a spot where he had been standing moments before. Both episodes presage actual events in Churchill's own war service in later years. The story shows good skill at dramatic narrative and a fair knowledge of military organisation, tactics and the language of command. It is accompanied by six hand-drawn sketches of the battle as it progresses. It is notable both for reflecting the strong interest in military topics and the genuine imaginative feeling for dramatic prose that would characterise Churchill's later writing as a war correspondent during his army years.

At Harrow Churchill also discovered in himself 'a taste for history which I acquired in [Mr Moriarty's] Army Class'.[49] He often discussed history and contemporary politics with Moriarty and read widely on both subjects. Of the five Harrow lectures that Churchill remembered and which he specifically mentioned in his autobiography, two were about battles, Waterloo in the Napoleonic Wars and Sedan in the Franco-Prussian War. He also took an interest in the American Civil War after meeting Colonel Gourand, an American friend of both Lord Randolph and Mr Moriarty, who had been at the famous battle of Gettysburg in 1863.

At the beginning of the spring term in 1890, Mr Welldon decided to hold Winston back from the preliminary examination for Sandhurst to be held in June because of his weakness in geometrical drawing. Winston chafed at the delay, writing to his father: 'I wish I could get into the army through the militia,' since an enlistment there could be an alternative route to a commission and perhaps an easier one than that of the dreaded competitive examination. Churchill's best friend at Harrow, John Peniston Milbanke, entered the army by this route and may have been the source of Churchill's inspiration for the militia.[50] Churchill thought the Army Class was not adequately preparing him for the preliminary and that at the same time it was holding him back from advancement in the school. 'Harrow is a charming place but Harrow and the Army Class don't agree,' he wrote in a letter to Lord Randolph.[51]

In the event, Churchill studied hard and was allowed to take the preliminary examination in November 1890. Luckily for him, it was the last preliminary for which Latin was an optional subject that he could avoid. He was examined in geography, geometric drawing, algebra, Euclid, French and English essay. For the essay Churchill wrote on a military topic, the American Civil War, a subject about which he had both an interest and knowledge from reading. He had good fortune on the geography question as well. In a curious display of last-minute exam preparation strategy, the night before the test he put the names of twenty-five countries 'into my hat & drew out one with my eyes shut. New Zealand was the one and New Zealand was the very first question on the Paper. I consider that this is luck ... Of course I had learnt all about New Zealand.'[52]

Winston passed the preliminary examination in all subjects, one of only twelve of the twenty-one Harrow exam students to do so. He was the boy from the lowest form to pass, demonstrating again ability above his class standing. The year 1890 ended for Winston on this note of triumph. But the rigours of study for the further examination awaited him.

Churchill still had long months of preparation before the final entrance examination for Sandhurst and the path did not prove easy. But because the decision was already made by Lord Randolph that he should go into the army, Winston had no real choice in the matter. It was the most difficult task to which he had thus far applied his energies. Much correspondence passed between Mr Welldon and Winston's parents and between them and Winston himself about his resistance to the hard work and long hours of study required. Lord Randolph was not too sanguine of Winston's chances, writing to him: 'I understand Mr Welldon thinks you will be able to pass your examination into the army when the time comes. I hope it may be so, as it will be a tremendous pull for you ultimately.'[53] Lady Randolph was more hopeful, writing: 'Winston will be all right the moment he gets into Sandhurst. He is just at the "ugly" stage – slouchy and tiresome.'[54] Winston's schoolboy vision of the military remained unchanged; he still played at war games when on holiday from school and had by then 'graduated from drilling his toy soldiers in Connaught Square to drilling his brother, his cousins and his other "volunteers" ', and continued building forts and holding mock battles.[55] On one occasion he built an operating catapult and targeted passers-by with flying vegetables. None the less, he fought against the considerable academic preparations required with a teenager's stubborn will. At one point, in frustration, he wrote to his mother: 'Really I feel less keen about the army every day. I think the church would suit me much better.'[56] It gives one pause to contemplate this possible direction to Churchill's life.

Mr Welldon tried to persuade Winston's parents to send him abroad for tutoring in French during the school Christmas holiday in 1891 saying, 'I promised Lord Randolph I would spare no effort to get him into the army.'[57] Lady Randolph agreed he should go, writing to her son: 'You are old enough not to play the fool, & for the sake of a few days pleasure, give up the chance of getting through yr exam: a thing which may affect yr whole life. You know how anxious Papa is that you shld go to Sandhurst this summer (1891).'[58] Winston fought back, arguing, 'I am very much surprised and pained to think that both you & Papa should treat me so, as a machine. I should like to know if Papa was asked to "give up his holidays" when he was at Eton' and 'Please do have a little regard for my happiness. There are other and higher things in this world than learning, more powerful agents than Civil Service Commissioners.'[59]

Churchill certainly deserves high marks for the vigour and cleverness of his arguments in a losing cause. Nevertheless, he was overborne by his elders and duly dispatched to France, whence he sent letters to his mother in a self-mocking and cleverly humorous Franglais: 'We arrived at Dieppe où nous partook of de bon café au lait. Le chemin de fer etait très incommode. Pour quatres heures. I waited having nothing to do. Nous arrivames au gare St. Lazare. J'ai déclaré ma boite de cigarettes. But they did not charge me anything nor did they open mon mal.'[60] After a couple of weeks of tuition, Winston wrote to his parents for permission to stay an extra week as a holiday. Lord Randolph sternly denied the request for the reason that a longer stay might cause him to fail the Sandhurst exam to be held that June, 'which I am sure you will admit would be very discreditable & disadvantageous. After you have got into the Army you will have many weeks of amusement and idleness should your inclinations go in that direction, but now I do pray you my dear boy to make the most of every hour of your time so as to render your passing a certainty ... I must say that I hope you will work like a little dray horse right up to the summer examination, only about four months off.'[61]

Returning to Harrow for the spring term of 1892, Churchill continued his academic programme and his Army Class studies and for the first time since the poetry-reading prize achieved a notable success, this time in athletics. He won the school championship in fencing, a sport he had taken up thinking it might be useful in the army. He became, in fact, head of the school fencing team. Neither of his parents was present for the competition. Lord Randolph sent Winston a curt letter upon receiving the news: 'I congratulate you on your success. I only hope fencing will not too much divert your attention from the army class.'[62] He also sent a two-pound reward for the fencing instructor but nothing for his son. In August, Churchill went on to win the public schools fencing championship at Aldershot, defeating boys from Bradfield College and Tonbridge School for the medal.[63] *The Harrovian* noted: 'His success was chiefly due to his quick and dashing attack which quite took his opponents by surprise.'[64] Later, in its review of school athletics for 1892, *The Harrovian* reported: 'Churchill must be congratulated over his success over all his opponents in the fencing line, many of whom must have been much taller and more formidable than himself.'[65]

Winston took the further examination for Sandhurst for the first time in July 1892 and failed. Coming in 390th of 643 candidates, he scored 5,100 marks of a possible 12,000 in an exam for which 6,654 marks were required for an infantry cadetship and 6,457 for the cavalry. He did worst in Latin and mathematics, and best in English composition, placing eighteenth of the 415 boys who took the subject.[66] Both of his Army Class tutors wrote to encourage him to try again at the next examination in November, with much advice on the additional hard work required. Lord Randolph was displeased, noting that Winston's score was 1,500 marks too low to pass and 300 places off the list of candidates who did pass. He confided to his mother, the Duchess of Marlborough, that if Winston failed in his next try, 'I shall think about putting him in business. I could get him something very good.'[67]

By all accounts Winston worked hard that autumn with a view to taking the final examination again at the end of November, the day before his eighteenth birthday. He sat the exam that month and in December left for the Christmas holiday not knowing that his Harrow school days were at an end. While visiting his aunt, Lady Wimborne, at her estate at Bournemouth on 10 January 1893, Winston was seriously injured in a game of follow-the-leader with his brother and a cousin. On a bridge over a small valley he was cornered by his approaching pursuers:

> One stood at each end of the bridge; capture seemed certain. But in a flash there came across me a great project. The chine which the bridge spanned was full of young fir trees. Their slender tops reached to the level of the footway. 'Would it not' I asked myself 'be possible to leap on to one of them and slip

down the pole-like stem, breaking off each tier of branches as one descended, until the fall was broken? I looked at it. I computed it. I meditated. Meanwhile I climbed over the balustrade. My young pursuers stood wonder-struck at either end of the bridge. To plunge or not to plunge, that was the question! In a second I had plunged, throwing out my arms to embrace the summit of the fir tree. The argument was correct; the data were absolutely wrong. It was three days before I regained consciousness and more than three months before I crawled from my bed. The measured fall was 29 feet on to hard ground.[68]

To his physical injuries was added bad news about the Sandhurst exam-ination results a few days later. Success had eluded him again and on 20 January 1893, he received notice of his second failure in the further exam. With a total of 6,106 of 12,000 possible marks he finished 203rd of 664 applicants. He improved his scores in mathematics, English history, chem-istry and geometrical drawing but fared worse than before in Latin, French and English composition.[69] Mr Welldon was of the opinion he would have passed if the admission standards had not been raised and that Winston could certainly pass next time if he worked hard. Churchill was very much discouraged. Lord Randolph took remedial steps immediately. Winston was not allowed to enrol at Harrow for the spring term but remained in London where he 'was relegated as a forlorn hope to a 'crammer.' Cpt. James and his highly competent partners kept an establishment in the Cromwell Road. It was said that no one who was not a congenital idiot could avoid passing thence into the army. The firm had made a scientific study of the mentality of the Civil Service Commissioners. They knew with almost Papal infallibility the sort of questions which that sort of person would be bound on the average to ask on any of the selected subjects. They specialised on these questions and on the answering of them ... Thus year by year for at least two decades he held the Blue Ribbon among the Cram-mers. He was like one of those people who have a sure system for breaking the Bank at Monte Carlo, with the important difference that in a great majority of cases his system produced sucess. Even the very hardest cases could be handled. No absolute guarantee was given, but there would always be far more than a sporting chance'.[70]

The use of a private tutor was in fact not uncommon in Churchill's time. In the 1890s it is estimated that seventy per cent of the candidates gaining entrance to Sandhurst were the products of tutors or crammers.[71] Relieved of his regular school studies, the Army Class obligations and the distractions of sports and other school activities, Winston should have been able to focus all his energies on the obvious task at hand, namely his next attempt at the further examination which was scheduled for that June. Yet he did not seem to others to be giving it his all. Lord Randolph received a series of letters from Captain James about Winston's progress not unlike those written by the masters at Harrow in earlier years.

On 7 March 1893 James wrote: 'I had to speak to him the other day about his casual manner. I think the boy means well but he is distinctly inclined to be inattentive and to think too much of his abilities ... he has been rather too much inclined up to the present to teach his instructors instead of endeavouring to learn from them, and this is not the frame of mind conducive to success.'[72] On 29 April he wrote: 'All the tutors complain that while he has good abilities he does not apply himself with sufficient earnestness to his reading.'[73] By mid-June Captain James finally decided that Winston was working well and should pass on his next try.[74]

Churchill devoted much energy to a subject that did not come easily to him, mathematics. He later wrote of his schoolboy experience with this subject:

> We were arrived in an 'Alice-in-Wonderland' world, at the portals of which stood 'A Quadratic Equation'. This with a strange grimace pointed the way to the Theory of Indices, which again handed on the intruder to the full rigours of the Binomial Theorem. Further dim chambers lighted by sullen, sulphurous fires were reputed to contain a dragon called the 'Differential Calculus'. But this monster was beyond the bounds appointed by the Civil Service Commissioners who regulated this stage of Pilgrim's heavy journey. We turned aside, not indeed to the uplands of the Delectable Mountains, but into a strange corridor of things like anagrams and acrostics called Sines, Cosines and Tangents. Apparently they were very important, especially when multiplied by each other, or by themselves! They had also this merit – you could learn many of their evolutions off by heart. There was a question in my third and last Examination about these Cosines and Tangents in a highly square-rooted condition which must have been decisive upon the whole of my after life. It was a problem. But luckily I had seen its ugly face only a few days before and recognised it at first sight. I have never met any of these creatures since.[75]

On his third attempt at the further examination in June 1893, Churchill achieved what he termed 'a modified success'. With 6,309 of 12,000 possible marks, he ranked ninety-fifth out of 389 candidates and passed into Sandhurst. He had, however, eighteen marks too few and was four places too low for an infantry cadetship. It was only enough to be accepted as a cavalry cadet. Indeed, he placed fourth highest among all applicants on the cavalry list. By virtue of cramming, hard work, luck or previous experience, Winston had improved his marks in all eight subjects. His score on English history was the highest of all the successful candidates. He remained consistent in Latin with only five of the successful candidates doing worse.[76]

What a sublime relief for Winston, his parents and teachers that he had finally made it into Sandhurst. The successful third attempt on the further examination was a critical turning point in Churchill's life. He later wrote that had he failed to gain entrance to the military college:

> I might have gone into the Church and preached orthodox sermons in a spirit of audacious contradiction to the age. I might have gone into the City and made a fortune. I might have resorted to the colonies ... in the hopes of pleasing, or at least placating them; and thus had à la Lindsay Gordon or Cecil Rhodes, a lurid career. I might even have gravitated to the Bar, and persons might have been hanged through my defence who now nurse their guilty secrets with complacency.[77]

It was to be the army, after all, and the cavalry at that. It should be noted that the cavalry, viewed today perhaps as glamorous and prestigious, was in Victorian England only second best after the infantry. It was also by far the more expensive branch of the service because an officer had to equip and maintain himself and his own horses. A private income of several hundred pounds a year was required over and above army pay, a fact that carried great weight with Lord Randolph but little with Winston.

Churchill later recorded his reaction at being accepted into Sandhurst:

> I was delighted at having passed the examination and even more so at the prospect of soldiering on horseback. I had already formed a definite opinion upon the relative advantages of riding and walking. What fun it would be having a horse! Also the uniforms of the cavalry were far more magnificent than those of the Foot.[78]

With the congratulations of Mr Welldon and Duchess Lily in hand and well pleased with his own success, Winston wrote a rather off-handed letter to his father which met with a remarkably stern rebuke. Lord Randolph's reply to Winston in a letter of 9 August 1893 is worthy of quotation at length as it says much about the father and his relationship to his elder son.

> My dear Winston,
> I am rather surprised at your tone of exultation over your inclusion in the Sandhurst list. There are two ways of winning in an examination, one creditable the other the reverse. You have unfortunately chosen the latter method and appear to be much pleased with your success.
> The first extremely discreditable feature of your performance is missing the infantry, for in that failure is demonstrated beyond refutation your slovenly happy-go-lucky harum scarum style of work for which you have always been

distinguished at your different schools. Never have I received a really good report of your conduct in your work from any master or tutor you had from time to time to do with ... With all the advantages you had, with all the abilities which you foolishly think yourself to possess & which some of your relations claim for you, with all the efforts that have been made to make your life easy & agreeable & your work neither oppressive or distasteful, this is the grand result that you come up among the 2nd rate & 3rd rate class who are only good for a commission in a cavalry regiment.

The second discreditable fact in the result of your examination is that you have not perceptibly increased as far as my memory serves me the marks you made in the examination ... You may find some consolation in the fact that you have failed to get into the '60th Rifles' one of the finest regiments in the army. There is also another satisfaction for you that by accomplishing the prodigious effort of getting into the Cavalry, you imposed on me an extra charge of some £200 a year. Not that I shall allow you to remain in the Cavalry. As soon as possible I shall arrange your exchange into an infantry regiment of the line ... I shall not write again on these matters & you need not trouble to write any answer to this part of my letter, because I no longer attach the slightest weight to anything you may say about your own acquirements & exploits. Make this position indelibly impressed on your mind, that if your conduct and action at Sandhurst is similar to what it has been in the other establishments in which it has sought vainly to impart to you some education, then that my responsibility for you is over.

I shall leave you to depend on yourself giving you merely such assistance as may be necessary to permit of a respectable life. Because I am certain that if you cannot prevent yourself from leading the idle useless unprofitable life you have had during your schooldays & later months, you will become a mere social wastrel one of the hundreds of the public school failures, and you will degenerate into a shabby unhappy & futile existence. If that is so you will have to bear all the blame for such misfortunes yourself ...

Your affte father
RANDOLPH S.C.[79]

This letter must have been a crushing humiliation for Winston as he very much prized his father's opinion and tried so hard to win his attention and affection. Winston responded with an apology and a renewed promise of improving his standing with his father by hard work and good conduct, saying: 'My extremely low place in passing in will have no effect whatever on my chance there.'[80] Lord Randolph's letter to Winston was not just a show for his son's benefit but reflected his true feelings in the matter. On 5 August 1893 he wrote to the duchess:

I have told you often and you would never believe me that he has little [claim] to cleverness, to knowledge or any capacity for settled work. He has a great talent for show off, exaggeration & make believe ... He will go up to Sandhurst when for the first time in his life he will be kept in order & we shall see whether he can stand military discipline. If he can he may rub along respectably. I will not conceal from you it is a great disappointment to me.[81]

It would be up to Winston himself to succeed, to be a better student than he had ever been, to prove himself worthy of his father's esteem.

Churchill's mother and grandmother tried to lift his spirits and also to encourage him to apply himself to his studies and to take advantage of his newly won opportunity. J. D. G. Little, Winston's private tutor, wrote to Lord Randolph:

> When he showed me your letter, we had a long talk and he told me a good deal about his views of man and things. He was a good deal depressed; I pointed out to him that in going to Sandhurst he began what was practically a new page in his life; and that such opportunities [for] a completely new start occurred at most but once or twice in a lifetime, and therefore ought to [be] made the most of ... I think he intends to try hard ... His weak point is that he allows the whim of the moment to obliterate his calm judgments and from this point of view I think the discipline of Sandhurst will be useful.[82]

Churchill seems to have taken everyone's advice about Sandhurst to heart and wrote to his father at the end of August just before leaving for his new challenge: 'I am looking forward to going there very much more especially as it gives me an altogether fresh start on a course which is certainly "paved with good resolutions".'[83] To Lady Randolph, Winston wrote: 'I am going to buckle to at Sandhurst and try to regain Papa's opinion of me.'[84] Indeed, Lord Randolph's rebuke may well have had the intended effect of redoubling Winston's resolve to excel in his Sandhurst training. Churchill seemed ready for the challenge and looked forward to being a commissioned officer upon graduation. He was then just three months away from his nineteenth birthday.

As he ended his schoolboy years at Harrow and prepared to begin his studies at Sandhurst, Churchill's character had formed and many of the traits of his personality had already taken hold. He was a very intelligent boy though he did not always focus his attention as others thought he should. He had an ear for the beauties of both written and spoken English and a remarkable memory for facts and verse. He was a highly literate boy, interested in reading, and very attentive to newspapers and politics. He was a good writer with fine English composition skills recognised by his peers and his teachers alike. Clearly Churchill's portrait of himself as a self-made man of little native intelligence is overplayed in *My Early Life*. Many later biographers have concluded that Winston was a dunce who excelled neither in the classroom nor on the playing field. The fact of the matter is that Churchill had a fine brain, a good deal of energy and a belief in his own star even as a boy. A person cannot finesse his way into Sandhurst by his family, fortune or connections. He must earn his place by national competitive examination. Nor can one win a fencing championship without pluck and practice. These things Churchill was able to achieve by virtue of his own abilities and exertions.

Churchill was also a brave boy. Whether it was talking back to teachers, pushing a senior boy into the swimming pool (both of which he did at Harrow), jumping off the bridge at Bournemouth, or pursuing the fencing championship, he was physically fearless. He was also loyal in his friendships. His consideration for his nanny during her visit to Harrow led one of his classmates later to describe it as one of the more courageous deeds he had ever seen.[85] He showed every sign of having a stubborn nature and steely determination to get his way. This was clearly demonstrated when he raised his academic and test-taking abilities to the level required to gain admission to Sandhurst.

It was also during his school years that Churchill found and pursued two of the central interests of his life – the military and politics. He was in the Rifle Corps every term he was at Harrow and participated in drills, mock battles and rifle practice. He pursued and showed ability in the manly arts of marksmanship, fencing and riding. For ten of his fourteen terms at Harrow he was in the Army Class with the avowed purpose of passing into Sandhurst. This was the true focus of his academic endeavours and as such they must be viewed as a success.

Winston was clearly aware of and interested in politics from an early age, a result of his father's position in government and all the great men and events it brought into his life. When only sixteen years old he told his physician, Dr Felix Semon: 'I intend to go to Sandhurst and afterwards to joint a regiment of Hussars in India. Of course it is not my intention to become a mere professional soldier. I only wish to gain some experience. Someday I shall be a statesman as my father was before me.'[86] Churchill possessed not only a strong ego and unbending sense of destiny, he had premonitions of great, even glorious days ahead. In a conversation with his friend Murland Evans at Harrow in 1891, he said:

I have a wonderful idea of where I shall be eventually. I have dreams about it ... Well, I can see vast changes coming over a now peaceful world; great upheavals, terrible struggles; wars such as one cannot imagine; and I tell you London will be in danger – London will be attacked and I shall be very prominent in the defence of London ... I repeat – London will be in danger and in the high position I shall occupy, it will fall to me to save the Capital and save the Empire.[87]

But before he could have any realistic chance of pursuing his political ambitions, there was the army and before the army there was Sandhurst.

Although Churchill was looking forward to Sandhurst he seems not to have looked wistfully back at Harrow. Although he had learned much and reached his main goal, he did not really enjoy school and loathed examinations. He later reflected that his school years formed the only unhappy period of his entire life, writing: 'In retrospect, these years form not only the least agreeable, but the only barren and unhappy period of my life ... I am all for the Public Schools but I do not want to go there again.'[88]

2

The Royal Military College
Sandhurst

CHURCHILL received the news of his acceptance to Sandhurst just as he was setting off on a month-long tour of Italy and Switzerland with his brother Jack in the company of Mr Little of Eton who served as chaperon. That August he enjoyed a real vacation; Harrow and his examination worries were then behind him, and his Sandhurst responsibilities had not yet begun. During the holiday he corresponded regularly with his parents about the practical aspects of Sandhurst expenses and the events of his travels.

One episode from Winston's holiday did not appear in any of his letters but only later in *My Early Life* – he nearly drowned in Lake Lausanne. While swimming with Jack from an unanchored boat, it began to drift away. Striking out hard to catch the craft, 'I now saw death as near as I believe I have ever seen him. He was swimming in the water by our side, whispering from time to time in the rising wind which continued to carry the boat away from us ...'[1] Winston finally regained the safety of the boat and hauled the other boy aboard, but it was an experience he never forgot. It was the third near-death experience of Churchill's early years and perhaps contributed to his belief in his own star which he formed early and carried with him through his army career and, indeed, through his whole life.

Upon returning to London on 29 August 1893, Winston was informed by the Military Secretary at the War Office that an infantry cadetship at Sandhurst was available to him after all since some of the applicants who had been offered a place had decided not to enroll. This would make it possible after graduation for him to join the 60th Rifles, the regiment Lord Randolph had chosen for him. The 60th Rifles was one of the most socially prestigious regiments in the British army. According to General Sir Brian Horrocks:

> It was one of the most exclusive family regiments in the military world. No one could hope to become an officer in the 60th without close family connections, and even then only after most searching inquiries had been made by the Colonel Commandant of the Regiment. It is more difficult to obtain a commission in this Regiment than in any other corps in the army, including the Household Cavalry, Cavalry, or Guards.[2]

This was due in no small part to the fact that its Colonel-in-Chief was the Duke of Cambridge, a cousin of Queen Victoria and Commander-in-Chief of the British army from 1856 to 1895. Lord Randolph was pleased with the news because it coincided with his wishes for his son and, not incidentally, because it would save him £200 a year in expenses after Winston received his commission. 'In the infantry, my father had remarked, "One has to keep a man; in the cavalry a man and a horse as well." This was not only true, but even an understatement. Little did he foresee not only one horse, but two official chargers and one or two hunters besides – to say nothing of the indispensable string of polo ponies.'[3]

The annual tuition at Sandhurst was £150 compared with £250 at Harrow. There was also an initial fee of £30 for equipment and outfit.[4] Lord Randolph agreed to pay the tuition and fees together with Winston's tailoring and haberdashery bills for his many uniforms. He also consented to provide a monthly allowance of £10 which Winston thought would be an improvement on his usual financial arrangement with his parents, which he described as, 'Spend as much as I can get; Get as much as I can.'[5] Financial restraint was but one of the forms of discipline facing the new cadet. It was a challenge he did not meet successfully. Often during his terms at Sandhurst he would write to his mother for funds to supplement his allowance without telling his father.

After his return from the Continent and a three-day stay with his grandmother Frances, the dowager duchess, at her Grosvenor Square home in London, Winston arrived at Sandhurst on Friday, 1 September 1893, to begin his course of instruction – the first real steps of his adult life.

The Royal Military College of Churchill's day did not have quite the long history and tradition of Harrow; its antecedents were only from the eighteenth century. The first Royal Academy at Woolwich was created by the royal warrant of King George II in 1741. Known in the army as 'The Shop', the academy trained cadets for commissions in the Royal Artillery and the Royal Engineers. A further royal warrant in 1799 established a staff training school for serving army officers at High Wycombe which in 1801 was named the Royal Military College. The staff school became the senior division of the college when a junior division was added in March 1802. Called the Royal Military Cadet College, the new division was organised at Great Marlow for the training of cadets for commissions in the infantry and cavalry. The junior division moved to its present location at Sandhurst in 1812 and came to be known over the years before

Churchill's arrival as the Royal Military College Sandhurst or, more simply, Sandhurst.[6] The senior division later moved to nearby Camberley where it became the Staff College Camberley in 1857. It continues its traditional function and has kept its separate identity to this day.

The Royal Military College's home in Sandhurst parish, Berkshire near the town of Camberley is about thirty miles south-west of London. Within the grounds is the junction of the counties of Hampshire, Berkshire and Surrey. In the 1890s it was easily reached from London by the Southern Railway Company line from Waterloo Station with a change at Aldershot.

Sandhurst was and is set in beautiful park-like grounds. The army purchased 450 acres of wooded land as the site for the college from the then Prime Minister William Pitt. A further 400 acres were added by the time Churchill arrived. A contemporary description perfectly captures the setting in the 1890s:

> There are few people who could walk from the village of Camberley through the woods of the Royal Military College without being struck by the beauty of the neighbourhood. For a mile and a half the road winds through a forest of larch, birch and pine, with here and there glimpses of the lake seen picturesquely through the trees until the visitor finds himself at the edge of a large clearing ...
>
> The estate in which the college stands is very extensive, and is from end to end densely wooded. Two beautiful lakes afford facilities for swimming and boating ...
>
> The situation is salubrious, the air bracing, and the sub-soil gravel. In fact, it would be hard to find a spot in any country better suited by nature and adapted by art to the requirements of a military college.[7]

It is a peaceful place more closely resembling a country estate than a military base. As long-term Sandhurst professor John Keegan has written: 'Sandhurst's dreamy parkland, acres of mown lawns, colonnaded vistas, and soft creamy facades are the unlikeliest setting I know or can imagine in which to train young men for war. Classical languages, perhaps, or philosophy, or the fine arts – any of those would be appropriate to that sylvan spot; tactics, strategy, drill, musketry, bloodshed seem to have no place at all amid Sandhurst's bowers and arbours.'[8] It was a setting not unfamiliar to an aristocratic young man accustomed to school holidays at Blenheim Palace and frequent invitations to the other grand country houses of the day. It was nothing like the rough recruit depots which greeted other ranks upon their enlistment in the forces.[9]

Much of the Sandhurst of Churchill's time remains today. The original classroom and dormitory building, now called 'Old College', was completed in 1812 during the Napoleonic Wars. It continues in use as a classroom and administrative centre. The Old College is a grand two-storey building constructed of brick and stucco with an imposing facade facing the main parade ground to the south-east. Its grey-painted walls and white windows present a front of some 900 feet. The Grand Entrance, an immense classical portico at the centre, is supported by eight fluted stone columns with Doric capitals surmounted by a pediment featuring a frieze of the royal cypher of King George III and the reclining figures of Mars, the Roman god of war, and Minerva, the Roman goddess of wisdom. On the parade ground near the building and flanking the entrance steps are six polished brass cannon from the battle of Waterloo which saw Napoleon's final defeat in 1815. Above the Grand Entrance the Union Flag is proudly flown. It was here that Gentleman Cadet Churchill would live and study for the next eighteen months. His room was located on the second floor. The classrooms, company anterooms and mess were on the first, or ground floor.

West of the Old College, and between it and the riding school buildings, is Chapel Square, site of the Royal Memorial Chapel. A rectangular red-brick building in the Italian style, it was consecrated as Christ Church by the Bishop of Oxford in 1879. Tablets and plaques displayed on the interior walls in Churchill's day commemorated the Sandhurst graduates killed in action in Britain's far-flung campaigns of the nineteenth century. They served in Waziristan, India, Egypt, on the west coast of Africa or on ships lost at sea. Forty-five of them perished in the Crimean War (1854–6), thirteen in the Indian Mutiny (1857–9), thirty-six in Egypt (1887–8), twenty-eight in Burma (1885–7), others in the Zulu war, in smaller skirmishes or from illness at places such as the Chittagong Hills, Ambigole, Abu-Fatmeh, Bangalore and Gibraltar.[10] Unknown to Churchill, a number of his classmates would later have their names recorded and their memories honoured in the same fashion.[11] Recon-struction of the chapel begun in 1921 more than doubled its size and changed its shape to that of a cross. Since then the names have been added of the fallen graduates from the wars of the twentieth century including 3,274 who died in the First World War. It remains to this day both a place of worship and a shrine, its plaques an awe-inspiring display in perfect, understated tones.

To the north of the Old College and not far away is another building from Churchill's era, the gymnasium. Completed in 1863, it was built along Palladian lines, with simple symmetrical proportions and a classical entrance between four square engaged columns. The windows are large, allowing for plenty of natural light and easy ventilation. The grey brick and stucco building is topped by a copper-domed, wooden lantern tower. In the 1890s the inside walls of the gymnasium were covered with displays of trophies and weapons, gymnastic equipment and climbing ropes for the physical training of the cadets. Today the groans and cheers and shouts of cadets at their exercise are no longer heard, for the building serves as the Sandhurst library. Open stacks of books on military topics and quiet young scholars studying under the gaze of the busts and portraits of soldiers of old are now the rule in this quiet and dignified hall.

The Sandhurst grounds of the 1890s also included stable blocks and the riding school where Churchill was to spend many hours. There were large outdoor training areas for practical instruction in engineering works, entrenchments and explosives and firing ranges for both rifle and revolver instruction. Bridge building was practised on the two lakes in front of Old College. Ample facilities were provided for sports, including cricket and football pitches, golf links and tennis courts. The vast acreage of the college allowed adequate space for riding, marches, map-making and compass reading excursions, mock battles and tactical manoeuvres.

The young Winston Churchill who arrived at Sandhurst that Friday in September 1893 was eighteen years, nine months old, stood five feet six and seven-tenths inches tall and was of slender build. The first three days at Sandhurst were spent learning the way around the college and receiving issues of uniforms and equipment. Churchill found the arrangements uncomfortable and no doubt more austere than his habitual surroundings. With two other cadets he shared a large room that had neither carpets nor curtains. The room was partitioned for privacy but lacked decoration or hot water. He found the halls of the old college to be draughty and the rooms dilapidated and smelling of tobacco.[12]

The company anterooms were provided, in gentleman's club fashion, with a smoking room and a good selection of newspapers. There were also common rooms set aside for billiards, reading, card games and chess. There was a company butler who announced meal times and a personal servant to handle the menial soldierly chores of shining shoes, cleaning rifles and 'pipe-claying' the dress uniform belt with the soft, white clay used as a whitening and polishing agent. Although Churchill repeated to others the old saying that Sandhurst combines the evils of life of a private schoolboy with that of a private soldier, life was, in fact, not at all spartan. Perhaps the best description of the status of a Gentleman Cadet, or GC, at Sandhurst is that attributed to an earlier era professor who said he is, 'almost an officer and not quite a gentleman'.[13]

The cadet's esprit and youthful sense of fun are reflecting in a popular turn-of-the-century song, 'The Noisy Johnnie,' a portion of which follows:

I am a Gentlemen Cadet, and I live at the RMC,
And many other Gentlemen (cadets) live there with me;
Oh! We're the boys to make the noise, we won't be taken down.
And we cut such a dash when we're out on the mash
   in Camberley or Yorktown.
Our manners at mess are perfect, and our morals, oh so high!
And you always hear us coming with our well-known cheery cry.

CHORUS
Get out of the way, get out of the way,
For the boys of the RMC.
For a very fine lot are we,
As I think you'll all agree.
Hulloh there! how are you?
I'm very well known you see;
So what's bad form in other men
Is very good form in me, in me,
Is very good form in me![14]

In the first letter to his father from Sandhurst, Winston wrote in the hopeful tone of the new recruit in unfamiliar surroundings. After less than forty-eight hours as a cadet he wrote: 'Altogether, I like the life. I am interested in the drill and in the military education I shall receive; and now that the army is to be my trade I feel as keen as I did before I went in for any of the examinations. At any rate I am sure that I shall be mentally, morally, and physically better for my course here.'[15]

That first weekend Churchill was fitted for his uniforms. Ever afterwards Churchill showed a love of uniforms and wore them when occasion dictated. The Sandhurst uniforms were similar in most regards to the standard infantry uniforms of the British regular army. The typical day uniform was a single-breasted frock coat and straight leg trousers of blue serge. These were topped with either a round hard hat in blue cloth with a polished brim called a billed or peaked cap, or an envelope-shaped, soft cloth hat known as a field cap or side cap. Pictures exist of Churchill in each uniform cap. On the billed cap the insignia was the 'RMC' cypher for Royal Military College. The field cap bore the regimental insignia for Sandhurst, a circular brass badge with a Victoria crown above it, and the cypher 'VR' for Victoria Regina in the centre, surrounded by a band containing the college's motto, 'Nec Aspera Terrent,' Latin for 'Nor do difficulties deter.'[16] The blue serge uniform was the daily working uniform for drill, parades and studies and was worn with leggings and laced boots. There was a separate working uniform of serge fatigue jacket, overalls and spurs worn for horseback riding.

Dress uniforms were of two types, mess dress and full dress. Mess dress consisted of an open front, scarlet jacket with dark blue lapels and white piping, a waistcoat and blue trousers. Mess dress was worn for dinners and dances whether on the post or in town. Full dress consisted of a scarlet tunic, blue trousers with a white belt at the waist and a blue helmet topped by a three and one-quarter inch brass spike, fitted on the head with a brass chain-link chin strap. The tunic had white piping on its edges, brass buttons and a blue collar and epaulettes. The full dress uniform was worn for formal parades including church parades and for ceremonial occasions such as graduation and annual inspections. Cadets were allowed to wear civilian clothes only when away from Sandhurst. The one exception was the wearing of white flannels for certain athletic events. Civilian dress and military uniforms were not mixed except when caps and greatcoats were worn with white flannels in inclement weather.

The administrative structure of the Royal Military College was headed by the Commander-in-Chief of the army, His Royal Highness the Duke of Cambridge, who held the title of President but was only nominally in charge. Sandhurst was overseen by a board of visitors appointed by the Secretary of State for War to monitor the financial management of the college and to make an annual inspection, the report of which went to Parliament. The actual commander of the college was the Governor and Commandant, a position held in 1893 by Major-General E. H. Clive who was succeeded in 1894 by Major-General C. J. East CB, a veteran soldier who was wounded in the Indian Mutiny and later served at the siege of Sebastopol in the Crimean War. Second in command was Lieutenant Colonel M. Wynyard, the Assistant Commandant and Secretary, who served both as record keeper and commanding officer of the cadet battalion. The remainder of the military administration included a quartermaster, a riding master, a surgeon and his assistant surgeon and a chaplain. They were supported by regular army officers, warrant officers, non-commissioned officers and privates and also by civilian employees.[17]

The cadet battalion was organised into six companies of approximately sixty men each who paraded, messed and were quartered together. Each company included cadets from all three levels of academic classes. Each was commanded by a regular army officer and supervised by a non-commissioned officer who in Churchill's company was Staff Sergeant Girling. The company sergeant also served as the drill instructor. They were assisted by one or more under-officers, senior corporals or corporals – cadets given temporary rank to assist in administrative duties. Winston was never one of these and appears not to have achieved any cadet rank. Gentleman Cadet Churchill was assigned to Company E which he described as 'the crack company of the battalion'.[18] It was commanded by Major Oswald James Henry Ball of the Welsh Regiment. Ball had been in the army since 1874 but did not see active service until the Boer War in 1899.[19] Churchill described him as 'a very strict and peppery martinet. Formal, reserved, frigidly courteous, punctilious, impeccable, severe, he was held in greatest awe. It had never been his fortune to go on active service, but we were none the less sure that he would have had to be killed to be beaten.'[20] Although Major Ball was not yet a combat veteran, he had important lessons to teach.

On one occasion, Winston left the college to visit a friend in Aldershot without remembering to sign out in the company leave book as was required. When he drove his hired tandem from Sandhurst, who did he pass riding in the opposite direction but Major Ball! He realised at once he had neglected to sign out and planned to make the leave book entry immediately upon his return, doubtless hoping not to be found out by the company commander. When he got back and rushed to the desk to sign the leave book he found to his surprise that Major Ball had already signed the approved leaves list for that day but had headed it with Churchill's name. Churchill later recalled: 'This opened my eyes to the kind of life which existed in the old British Army and how the very strictest discipline could be maintained among officers without the slightest departure from the standards of a courteous and easy society. Naturally after such a rebuke I was never so neglectful again.'[21]

A photograph of Sandhurst's Company E as it existed in 1894 survives to this day and is displayed at the Old College. The five rows of cadets in their blue serge uniforms and field caps, white belts and Lee-Metford rifles at rest stare out with the stern confidence expected of a young officer of the Victorian era. Churchill stands in the next to last row with his cap worn jauntily tilted back on his head but with a serious expression on his face. His eyes look directly at the camera. Of this group of sixty-two cadets with their sergeant and commanding officer, only Staff Sergeant Girling displays campaign ribbons. Soon enough the others would have their chance, however, with the Boer War and First World War not far over the horizon. One of their number, Francis Newton Parsons, would win the Victoria Cross in the Boer War at Paardenberg, South Africa, for rescuing a wounded man under fire.[22]

In the melancholy conclusion of the Sandhurst chapter in *My Early Life*, Churchill wrote that only three or four of his Sandhurst friends still survived in 1930. 'As for the rest, they are gone. The South African War accounted for a large proportion, not only of my friends but of my company; and the Great War killed almost all the others.'[23] This appears to be an overstatement. A review of the available records and the Memorial Chapel plaques at Sandhurst indicates that six men from the 1894 photograph of Company E were killed in action in the Boer War and one in the First World War. Of Churchill's intake of 130 men, eight were killed in action in the Boer War, one in West Africa in 1901 and six in the First World War. Still, ten per cent is no small number even among professional soldiers.[24]

Academically, the Royal Military College was organised into three classes, junior, intermediate and senior for cadets in their first, second and third terms, respectively. Each class had approximately 120 cadets. As the course of instruction lasted only three terms over an eighteen-month period, there were two new classes, or intakes, as they were known, begun each year and two classes graduating. It is correct to refer to Churchill as a member of the September 1893 intake rather than the class of 1894. Class rank upon graduation was determined in relation to the other cadets in one's intake group. The academic programme consisted of only five subjects: fortification, tactics, topography, military law and military administration. Of these, Churchill was especially interested in tactics and fortification, and found the latter 'most exciting'.[25]

In 1894 about five hours each day were spent on these subjects with a third of the time given over to outdoor practical work. A further three hours were assigned to drill, gymnastics or riding.[26] The subject of the fortification class was military engineering. The instruction included lectures and outdoor exercises on explosives, artillery, field guns and ammunition, rifles and machine guns, and the penetration of their projectiles against certain defensive structures. Geometrical drawing was also taught as part of the class. Field fortification included a wide range of practical topics including the construction of obstacles and stockades, defensive fieldworks and entrenchments, bridge building of every type, felling of trees, clearing of fields of fire, and the tactical use of defensive positions. Also part of the subject matter were camping arrangements, bivouacs, field sanitation, camp kitchens and water supply and purification.

Instruction in tactics was based on the army's *Infantry Drill Manual* and was the subject of small unit combat operations. Included in this course were the use of terrain, its effect on tactics and the composition and employment of fighting units. Outposts and reconnaissance were discussed as were the various types of marches, the space and time required for each and their purposes. It was in the tactics class that a cadet studied the characteristics of the three arms of the land forces – infantry, artillery and cavalry – the principles for employing each and their use in combination. Practical work included the placing of sentries and pickets and the attack and defence of small positions using blank ammunition.

Topography is the art and science of map reading and land navigation. In this class the cadets mastered the use of the magnetic compass, the prismatic compass, and the clinometer, a device for measuring the angle or incline of slopes and embankments. They read maps, copied them, enlarged or reduced them and made their own by freehand drawing in the field. They learned to navigate and march with compass and map day or night, in the woods, or across open country. They spent much time sketching, with or without instruments, on horseback or on foot. Maps are basic tools of the soldier's trade and the legendary cavalry sketch board was a constant companion.

The military law course was based on *The Queen's Regulations and Orders For The Army*, the basic code of military conduct for the British army. This constituted training for the future officer as a commander of troops and included the topics of command and discipline, the powers of squadron and company officers, redress of wrongs, crimes and punishments, arrests and investigations. Courts martial were also included.

Military administration, like military law, was a classroom course. These lectures provided the necessary education in the bureaucratic organisation of the military system of Great Britain (including India) and the practical aspects of a company officer's administrative duties. The curriculum was very dry indeed: recruiting, enlistments, pay and allowances, clothing, equipment, quarters, transport and supply, the movement of troops and equipment, military correspondence and the writing of official reports. The course was a reminder, if one were ever needed, that whether on active service or in peacetime the work of an officer commanding a small unit was time-consuming and detail-oriented.[27]

For the 1893–4 terms, those subjects comprised the entire curriculum. There were no traditional academic subjects or foreign languages taught until later years. Military history, for example, did not find a place in the syllabus until 1897. Churchill was eager for information to further his studies:

> So I ordered Hamley's Operations of War, Prince Kraft's Letters on Infantry, Cavalry and Artillery, Maine's Infantry Fire Tactics, together with a number of histories dealing with the American Civil, Franco-German and Russo-Turkish wars, which were then our latest and best specimens of wars. I soon had a small military library which invested the regular instruction with some sort of background.[28]

Letters on Cavalry by Prince Kraft Zu Hohenlohe Ingelfingen (1827–92), was translated into English by Lieutenant-Colonel N. L. Walford, Royal Artillery, and originally printed in *Proceedings of the Royal Artillery Institution*. It was reprinted commercially by Edward Stanford in London, the second edition appearing in 1893. It is written in a conversational tone with twenty chapters denominated as 'letters'. In them Prince Kraft discusses the historical role of cavalry in war and the importance of its use in co-ordination with both infantry and artillery. He provides a detailed review of the mounted branch from organisation, training and provisioning to the battle-related tasks of reconnaissance, covering foot soldiers, raiding in small units, and manoeuvring large units from the approach march to the charge. Much of his advice and instruction is based on the experience of the Prussian Army in the Franco-Prussian War (1870–1) during which the prince commanded the Prussian artillery in the siege of Paris. His key conclusions were that the role of the cavalry had changed in light of the improvements in modern firearms and their effective range and that, 'Cavalry, like artillery, can only expect to obtain the best results if it remains always convinced that it is only an auxiliary arm to the infantry. The infantry is the army, and makes use of the cavalry and artillery.'[29]

The Operations of War, Explained and Illustrated was written by Major-General Bruce Hamley, once the Commandant of the Staff College at Camberley. First published in 1866, it continued in print in successive editions until at least 1907. It was considered a standard work on the business of modern warfare. Churchill found it to be 'a very solid but interesting work'.[30] Its strategic and tactical principles and lessons are illustrated by reference to episodes from the campaigns of history including Jena (1805), Salamanca (1812) and Waterloo (1815) from the Napoleonic Wars, the Metz and Sedan campaigns (1870) of the Franco-Prussian War, and the campaigns in northern Virginia (1861–5) during the American Civil War. It is interesting to imagine young Churchill in his quarters at night studying the retreat of McClellan's Union forces from the Chickahominy River to defend Washington, DC, pursued by the Confederate troops of Stonewall Jackson. Hamley's tome is a ponderous volume in every way (weighing nearly four and a half pounds). Almost 500 pages long, with excellent maps, it offered the gentleman cadet the opportunity to think beyond the subaltern's low horizon.[31]

Another supplement to Churchill's education was the occasional invitation to dine at the Staff College at nearby Camberley where the best and the brightest of the army were training for career commands and staff assignments.

> Here the study was of divisions, army corps and even whole armies; of bases, of supplies, of lines of comunication and railway strategy. This was thrilling. It did seem such a pity that it all had to be make-believe, and that the age of wars between civilised nations had come to an end forever. If it had only been 100 years earlier what splendid times we should have had! Fancy being nineteen in 1793 with more than twenty years of war against Napoleon in front of one![32]

To the classroom military subjects were added the military exercises – drill, gymnastics and riding – as part of the regular training. Drill is what the army calls marching on foot and the handling of weapons on command. It includes standing and moving in formations of different numbers of men and the mastery of different steps and cadences for marching. Churchill later wrote: 'I did not like the drill and indeed figured for several months in the "Awkward Squad", formed from those who required special smartening up.'[33] Drill also involved exercises with the Lee-Metford rifle and the bayonet. Musketry – rifle and revolver firing exercises – was supervised by the NCOs, the masters of the army's *Drill Manual*. Churchill practised with firearms almost every day. He became a fairly good shot – a skill he maintained late into life and of which he was quite proud.[34]

Gymnastics was the name given to physical training of cadets. In addition to calisthenics, it included sword drill and swimming. Although he was a fencing champion at Harrow, Winston seems not to have participated in fencing competitions or team sports at Sandhurst except for company marksmanship contests. In the compendium of sports teams and champions in *Annals of Sandhurst* for the period 1893–4 he is not mentioned. Company E won the championship in the drill competition for two of

Churchill's three terms and he may have been a participant in that achievement.

The daily schedule for the junior term at Sandhurst was a full one. In a 3 September 1893 letter to Lord Randolph, Churchill described it thus:

> Reveille is at 6.30. 1st study at 7. Breakfast 8 – parade at 9.10. Study from 10.20 to 1.50. 2 o'clock luncheon – 3 o'clock afternoon parade (¾ hour); 5 o'clock to 6 Gymnastics. 8 o'clock Mess. So you see there is hardly any time for writing or idling.'[35]

The study sessions comprised classes and lectures. The afternoon parade was not required after a preliminary five-week drill period ending in early October. Morning parade was a requirement throughout the course. Although the days were full, the cadets were free after morning parade on Saturday and all day on Sunday. They were allowed to leave the college on weekends and were granted holiday leaves between terms. Churchill did not have his father's permission to visit London for most of the first term and remained close to Sandhurst on weekends, sometimes riding rented horses at Aldershot.

The biggest challenges for Winston in his junior term seem not to have been academic but physical. The physical training and drill were difficult for him. In his very first week he wrote to his father: 'I like the work - but the physical exertion of one day is so severe that at the end of one day I feel regularly fatigued.'[36] In a letter to his mother two weeks later, on 17 September he said: 'I am cursed with so feeble a body, that I can hardly support the fatigues of the day; but I suppose I shall get stronger during my stay here.'[37] In the field of physical training Cadet Churchill resembled the majority of new army recruits through the ages, leaving behind the relative ease of civilian life and beginning military training. Still, it was a terrific new challenge: on 13 October he wrote again to Lady Churchill:

> Well, I have no news to tell you except that we had to run 3/4 mile with Rifles and accoutrements the other day & I had to be helped off parade by a couple of sergeants at the end of it & have been bad ever since ... I have been to see the doctor & he says there is nothing wrong except that my heart does not seem very strong. So he has given me a tonic & lighter work for a few days.'[38]

That this problem might be related to Churchill's smoking of cigarettes and cigars seems not to have occurred to the doctor or his patient.

Another challenge Churchill battled to overcome was his life-long propensity to be late. 'It is not a bit of good turning up for parade or study punctually. You are bound to be in your place when the bugle sounds. So far I have been ten minutes too early for everything. Public opinion of the College is tremendously against unpunctuality.'[39] His first-term letters to both parents are full of references to how he always arrived early or on time for classes and parades. One cannot help but be amused at Churchill's wishful thinking and creative reportage in light of his later report cards and, indeed, his ability to be late for almost everything.

He sent his parents frequent letters during the first term sharing news which he referred to as 'the RMC intelligence'.[40] He reported on his personal progress and travails but also sought to convey a sense of his new world and his optimism about it. On 28 September, for example, he wrote to Lady Randolph: 'Today we had an adjutants parade of almost the whole battalion & did the new physical drill to music. A very pretty sight. You really must come down one day and see it. We appear to have got on very well & the commandant said that E. Company marched past the best.'[41]

During Churchill's first term at Sandhurst and while he was focused on his studies, the cavalry versus infantry debate with his father seemed to be at an end. By mid-October, 1893, Lord Randolph and the Duke of Cambridge had corresponded and it was agreed on Winston's 'name being down for the 60th Rifles' upon his graduation from Sandhurst.[42] This was, of course, all arranged without Winston's views being taken into account. His preference was clearly the cavalry. On November 20th while on a weekend leave visit to his Aunt Leonie's house in London he met Colonel John Brabazon, an old family friend and the commanding officer of the 4th (Queen's Own) Hussars, a cavalry regiment. 'How I wish I was going into his regiment,' Churchill wrote to his mother.[43]

During the first two weeks of December 1893, Winston completed his junior term examinations and looked forward to two months' leave before the next term began. Part of the holiday, including Christmas, was spent at Blenheim Palace with his Marlborough relatives, part visiting friends, and part in London. While in London he stayed with his grandmother Frances at Grosvenor Square and put his time to good use by taking twelve private military riding lessons from the Honourable Captain Charles Henry Burt, riding master of the 2nd Life Guards stationed at Hyde Park Barracks. This was an indication of the seriousness with which Churchill approached his military education. Riding instruction would begin in the second term at Sandhurst and he clearly wanted to start early to make a better showing.

During the holiday, Churchill received his marks for the junior term which were as follows:

1. Fortification	215
2. Tactics	278
3. Military Topography	199
4. Military Law	276
5. Military Administration	230
	1,198

Conduct: Good, but unpunctual[44]

Explaining the marking system in a letter to Lord Randolph, Churchill wrote: 'The maximum is for each subject 300. To pass you have to get 100 in each subject and 750 on the whole 5 subjects.'[45] With 1,198 out of a possible 1,500 marks this was a very creditable beginning even though the mention of his unpunctuality highlighted the difference between his own and the army's standards of being on time. Lord Randolph's response was characteristically critical, 'He may be quite pleased with coming out eighth. But how about the want of punctuality ...'[46]

During the winter break Winston started anew his campaign to enter the cavalry upon his graduation, this time with the conspiratorial assistance of Colonel Brabazon. Knowing well the strengths and weaknesses of his adversaries in the debate, namely his parents, he began with a letter to Lady Randolph on 11 January 1894. He had clearly given the matter serious thought:

11 January [1894]
Hindlip Hall near Worcester

My dearest Mamma,
I have written to Colonel Brabazon and have stated my various arguments in favour of cavalry regiment. I have asked him to say whether or no they are correct – when he writes to you – but in case he should not state this clearly, I will put them down for you.
1. Promotions much quicker in Cavalry than in Infantry. (60th Rifles slowest regiment in the army.)
2. Obtain your commission (3 or 4 months) in Cav much sooner than in Infantry.
3. 4th Hussars are going to India shortly. If I join before 'Augmentation' I should have 6 or 7 subalterns below me in a very short time.
4. Cavalry regiments are always given good stations in India and generally taken great care of by the Government – while Infantry have to take what they can get.
5. If you want to keep a horse you can do it much cheaper in the cavalry than

in infantry – government will provide stabling – forage – and labour.
6. Sentimental advantages grouped under heading of
a. uniform
b. increased interest of a 'life among horses' etc.
c. advantages of riding over walk
d. advantages of joining a regiment some of whose officers you know. i.e. 4th Hussars.
The first 5 of these reasons I wrote to Col. Brabazon the last I write to you. There you are – now don't ever say I did not give you any reasons. There are 5 good solid arguments ...

With best love and kisses, I remain, Ever your loving son.

WINSTON[47]

It appears he was using his mother as a sounding board, giving himself a practice run before taking the matter up with Lord Randolph who would clearly be difficult to convince. In fact, he did not raise the topic with his father for some months. He was also trying to win his mother over as an ally. In this he succeeded.

During the period before the start of the second term the correspondence between father and son concerned riding, the weather, Winston's being ill for two weeks with influenza and, inevitably, Lord Randolph's continuous advice that Winston apply himself to his work. A letter from Lord Randolph dated 10 February 1894 is typical:

Well now I do hope you will do better this quarter even than you did last. They say a good beginning makes a good ending. But you must keep the standard up & keep raising. This is the critical time at Sandhurst which is now commencing for you. If you get through this time well, the rest will follow more easily. Mind if you do well at Sandhurst & get good reports good positions in the classes & even the good conduct medal you would go to your regiment so much higher in credit & more thought of. So if you feel at times like giving way or falling off 'Don't.' Pull yourself together & keep yourself well abreast & even ahead of those you are competing with. I rather advise you not to come up to London too often. Your mother & I can run down. It does not seem such an awful journey. Lastly take care of your health. Keep down the smoking, keep down the drink & go to bed as early as you can. Well I have written you a regular lecture but it is all sound. The better you do the more I shall be inclined to help you.[48]

Churchill's second, or intermediate, term at Sandhurst began in mid-February, 1894. There were immediate changes in his living arrangements. He now had a room of his own at the college which he planned to furnish comfortably with his mother's help with a carpet, curtains and personal furniture, bedding and pictures. Increased seniority in the military has its privileges.

The course curriculum remained the same as previously but there were unwelcome changes in the daily schedule with extra work – meaning study – required in the evenings and lights out thirty minutes earlier. There was more gymnastics as well but Churchill complained not at all about the physical training as he seems to have benefited from the conditioning he had received the first term. He restricted his complaints to common physical ailments that came and went such as boils on his behind or toothache.

The biggest change in the intermediate term over the junior was the addition of riding to the formal programme. One of Churchill's loves at Sandhurst was horseback riding, which was featured in the last two terms only. 'I enjoyed the riding-school thoroughly, and got on – and off – as well as most.' He wrote later:

> I think I was pretty well trained to sit and manage a horse. This is one of the most important things in the world .... No one ever came to grief – except honourable grief – through riding horses. No hour of life is lost that is spent in the saddle. Young men have often been ruined through owning horses, or through backing horses, but never through riding them: unless of course they break their necks, which, taken at a gallop, is a very good death to die.[49]

Not only did Churchill enjoy riding above all other recreations; he became quite good at it. It was a point of pride for him and his letters to his father that term often centred upon horses. This was an area of common interest as Lord Randolph was devoted to the turf. On 19 February Churchill wrote to his father: 'The riding here is most interesting and I get great "kudos" from the instructors and have been put at the head of the ride. It is quite worth while getting up early to take those lessons [with Captain Burt in London].'[50] The course was not limited merely to learning to ride a horse. Using the army's manual, *Cavalry Drill*, as its text, the riding instruction was conducted by Major Hodgins, the riding master, and included practical military skills:

> All cadets, whether intended for infantry or cavalry commissions, are compelled to learn riding – a most judicious arrangement ... For the first six months he rides twice a week; he is taught to saddle his horse, to ride without stirrups or reins, or bare-back; to leap obstacles, to dismount and mount while his horse is trotting (the former a feat very easily performed by some); and having been initiated into the miseries of the 'single ride' he gradually develops a tolerably firm seat.[51]

Cavalry drill also included instruction in riding in formations of lines and columns with varying numbers of other riders. To the practice of riding and manoeuvring on horseback were added mounted fighting drills with the sabre, the officer's primary fighting weapon.

The riding school at Sandhurst was one of the most memorable experiences for the cadets. Indeed, it was a great leveller. The riding masters were legends and those at Sandhurst were the best of a select fraternity:

> There are many doubtless who still remember, and who still shudder at the remembrance of his Mephistopheles-like form standing in the corner of the school, long whip in one hand and horse-pistol in the other, waiting for a victim. 'Can't you press him into the corner, you, Sir, on No. 22? Give him the spur, Sir! Go on, Sir; go on,' he would drawl out quietly in his strange nasal voice; then came a frantic cut from the whip on the horse's flanks and the discharge of the pistol under his belly, and instantly the whole school was in an uproar, with horses bolting in all directions and pale-faced cadets clutching at the pommel. It was only for a moment, however, for at the shout of 'ride-halt,' each horse pulled up short, and half the riders were left in various graceful attitudes on their horses' necks.[52]

One agreeable aspect of Churchill's months at Sandhurst was the increasing number of social contacts it occasioned with important and socially prominent people in and out of the military. It seemed too that his standing with his father improved once he became a cadet. Lord Randolph not only let Winston accompany him on social occasions to the London theatre but also introduced him to the circle of his horse-racing friends. Importantly, Winston went with his father to social gatherings at the home of Lord Rothschild at Tring where he met all the key members of the ruling Conservative Party. Because of his father's status he was introduced to many important people including Lord Roberts, a Victoria Cross hero of the Indian Mutiny, who was later Commander-in-Chief of the British Army in India during Churchill's service there.

Unfortunately for Winston, the adult friendship he sought with his father never really developed and the period of these increasing contacts coincided with the onset of Lord Randolph's final illness. Churchill had always worshipped his father although his affection was not returned by his cool and distant parent:

> In fact to me he seemed to own the key to everything or almost everything worth having. But if ever I began to show the slightest idea of comradeship, he was immediately offended; and when once I suggested that I might help his private secretary to write some of his letters, he froze me into stone ... Just as

friendly relations were ripening into an Entente, and an alliance or at least a military agreement seemed to my mind not beyond the bounds of reasonable endeavour, he vanished for ever.'[53]

The schedule for the intermediate term started with a parade formation at 6.15 a.m. and included classroom activities, study and practical exercises and drill on the parade ground until lunch in the early afternoon. The midday meal was followed by gymnastics and riding school. There was still no class or duty on Saturday afternoon or Sunday and when his parents permitted him to travel, Churchill visited London or Harrow where Jack was then a student. His father encouraged him to remain at Sandhurst on weekends for extra reading and study. This recommendation countered Churchill's natural restlessness and the temptations of nearby London. But Lord Randolph's reasons were sound. He wrote to Winston on 13 April 1894:

> Now it is no use your telling me there is nothing to do on Sunday ... if you devote on Sunday at least 3 hours of real study. You will have that advantage of extra knowledge over those cadets who take their leave for Saturday & Sunday, or who do nothing all day ... Now all this may seem to you very hard & you may be vexed & say that 'all work & no play makes Jack a dull boy', But it is no use complaining about what I tell you to do, for if you act as I advise you, you will excel at Sandhurst and the sacrifice of your taking your leave so frequently will be amply rewarded, and I be shall ten times more pleased with you than if you resumed your habits of coming to London many times in the term.[54]

Winston did indeed follow his father's advice and applied himself to extra reading some weekends. He also took a voluntary class in signalling for three hours a week. Other weekends he and fellow cadets rented horses in nearby Aldershot and got in extra practice riding cross-country.

A curious episode in the second term tells a good deal about Churchill and his relationship with his parents. One day in April as he leaned over to pick up a stick, he dropped a watch his father had given to him into a stream on the Sandhurst grounds. He immediately stripped down and dived in to fetch it but without success. The next day he had the stream dredged, to no avail. Finally, with the consent of the Governor-Commandant he hired twenty-three soldiers from the Sandhurst infantry detachment to dig a temporary new channel for the stream and borrowed a fire engine to pump out the stream pool. He succeeded in recovering the watch and sent it to the watchmaker in London for repairs.[55] This was a notable demonstration of Winston's ability to determine a solution to a problem and to take command of men to achieve a goal, but it is also a clear reminder of how fearful he was of his father's opinion. Unhappily for Churchill, Lord Randolph found out about the damaged watch and wrote Winston a scaldingly critical letter and a letter to Lady Randolph along much the same lines. To Lord Randolph the lost watch episode was simply more evidence Winston was stupid and unsteady. He was very upset at the waste of the £3 cost of repair. Lady Randolph's letter to Winston about the watch was in a calmer, more caring tone, and highlighted how her relationship to him was on a completely different emotional plane from her husband's.

> Dearest Winston,
> I am so sorry you have got into trouble over yr watch – Papa wrote to me all about it. I must own you are awfully careless & of course Papa is angry over giving you such a valuable thing. However he wrote very kindly about you so you must not be too unhappy. Meanwhile I'm afraid you will have to go without a watch. Oh! Winny what a harum scarum fellow you are! You really must give up being so childish. I am sending you £2 with my love. I shall scold you well when we meet.
>
> Yr loving
> Mother[56]

The episode shows again how Lady Randolph was perhaps Winston's strongest supporter, a role that became even more apparent in later years.

The intermediate term also marked an increase in the contacts Winston had with Colonel Brabazon of the 4th Hussars who were then stationed at Aldershot. Brabazon invited Churchill to spend the weekend of 28–29 April 1894 with the regiment suggesting he might come over with a Captain Julian Byng of the 10th Hussars who was then at the Staff College and also invited to visit.[57] The weekend was apparently the first that Cadet Churchill spent in a regimental officer's mess and it made a great impression on him:

> In those days the Mess of a cavalry regiment presented an impressive spectacle to a youthful eye. Twenty or thirty officers all magnificently attired in blue and gold, assembled round a table upon which shone the plate and trophies gathered by the regiment in two hundred years of sport and campaigning. It was like a State banquet. In an all-pervading air of glitter, affluence, ceremony, and veiled discipline, an excellent and lengthy dinner was served to the strains of the regimental string band. I received the gayest of welcomes, and having it would seem conducted myself with discretion and modesty, I was invited again on several occasions.[58]

Now this was the very sort of thing Churchill was dreaming of: being welcomed by the commander and officers of a smart cavalry regiment with a glorious campaign history. Brabazon liked Winston and for that reason and, perhaps, for his long-standing friendship with Lord and Lady Randolph, began a campaign to recruit Churchill for the 4th Hussars. At one point Lord Randolph complained that it was Brabazon who 'turned the boy's head' about the cavalry. The colonel apparently was in close contact with Lady Churchill as the very day after Churchill's weekend visit she wrote to her son, 'A bird whispered to me you did not sleep in yr own bed last night. Write to me all about it. I am not sure Papa wld approve.'[59] Winston was easily won over by Colonel Brabazon and renewed his own campaign to convince his parents that the cavalry was the best place for him after graduation. Replying to his mother's letter he wrote:

> I had great fun at Aldershot – the regiment is awfully smart ... How I wish I were going into the 4th instead of those old Rifles. It would not cost a penny more & the regiment goes to India in 3 years which is just right for me. I hate the Infantry – in which physical weaknesses render me nearly useless on service & the only thing I am showing an aptitude for athletically – riding – will be no good to me. Furthermore of all the regiments in the army the Rifles is the slowest for promotion. However it is not much good writing down these cogent arguments – but if I pass high at the end of the term I will tackle Papa on the subject.[60]

Churchill always wrote separate letters to his mother and father. Those to Lady Randolph were very open and frank. He often confided in her as if she were his closest friend, which indeed she had become. The letters to his father were more formal, less complaining and, perhaps unconsciously, written to impress his father with his achievements.

Throughout the spring of 1894, Churchill kept up his regular correspondence with his father. It was an oddly unbalanced exchange. Winston usually talked shop in his letters to Lord Randolph, writing about his good performance in the riding school, his extra-curricular reading in Hamley and Kraft and the various reviews and parades that were part of the annual Sandhurst programme. Lord Randolph wrote a series of letters about his own interests – politics and turf racing. What is notable is how often the father's letters include criticism of the son, sometimes over finances, sometimes over study habits, often about trivial matters such as Winston's use of a typewriter or how his son should address him. A letter from Lord Randolph on 19 June 1894 may serve as an example of the tone of his letters to Winston as his own health deteriorated:

50 Grosvenor Square

My dear Winston,
How stupid you are you do not stick to 'my dear father' & relapse into 'my dear
Papa.' This is idiotic ... You will see yr mother on Saturday but you won't see
me as I am going to Paris on the morning of that day.

Yr affte Father
Randolph S. Churchill[61]

Indeed, at that time Lord Randolph was quite unwell with a progressive
illness that affected both his mental and physical abilities. By the end of
June 1894, he and Lady Randolph embarked on an around-the-world
tour, intended, it seems, to shield him from society. Winston was informed
about their plans only the day before their departure. By virtue of a special
request from his father to the Secretary of State for War, he was granted a
brief leave to see his parents off. It was a sad parting as Lord Randolph
'looked terribly haggard and worn with mental pain. He patted me on the
knee in a gesture however simple was perfectly informing ... I never saw
him again, except as a swiftly fading shadow.'[62]

For the balance of the intermediate term, Churchill applied himself to
the busy routine of the classroom and practical exercises in preparation for
the examinations which were held in the second week in July. He was
gaining confidence and worked hard. He wrote to his mother on 10 July:
'I feel I know my subject very thoroughly and am not nervous as to not
getting through. I hope however to pass high as I shall take the opportunity of writing a long letter to papa on the subject of Cavalry. I have been
piling up material for some time and have a most formidable lot of arguments.'[63] The term ended on 14 July 1894, and then began a six-week
summer recess. With his parents away Churchill stayed most of the time
with his grandmother, the dowager duchess at Grosvenor Square. During
the summer he had many social invitations and outings but also took time
for more military riding lessons at the Hyde Park barracks. He spent most
of August touring on the Continent with his former tutor Mr Little and his
brother Jack. They visited the Waterloo battlefield and in Brussels
inspected the American cruiser *Chicago* docked on the Scheldt river.

Although his parents were touring in North America, he maintained his
correspondence with them, as usual writing to them separately. In July he
worked up his courage to write to his father about his desire to go into the
cavalry. This letter does not survive but he described it to his mother in a
letter to her on 22 July:

I have written Papa a long letter on the subject of the Cavalry. I do so hope he will not be angry – or take it as 'freespoken' or stupid. I only wrote what I thought he ought to know – namely how keen I was to go into the Cavalry and how I could not look forward with great eagerness to going with even the best Infantry regiment in the world.[64]

Lord Randolph's reply was unequivocal:

21 August 1894
Hotel Del Monte
California

My dear Winston,
I do not enter into your lengthy letter of the 22nd in which you enlarge on your preference for the Cavalry over the 60th Rifles. I could never sanction such a change. Your name was put down by myself on the Duke of Cambridge's list for one or other of the battalions of that Regiment. The Duke of Cambridge would be extremely angry with you if you were to make any application to him for such a change; His Royal Highness would consult me and I should oppose it strongly. So that you had better put that out of your head altogether at any rate during my lifetime during which you will be dependent on me. So much for that subject.[65]

What a harsh rebuff this must have been to receive. And yet looking back one focuses on the prophetic words, 'at any rate during my lifetime'. For Lord Randolph's health was failing and Winston would never have the opportunity to discuss the topic at length with his father in person. This was indeed Lord Randolph's final position on the matter. It was also the last letter Churchill ever received from his father.

In late August Churchill received his Sandhurst marks for the intermediate term:

1. Fortification	254	[up 39 marks]
2. Tactics	266	[down 12 marks]
3. Military Topography	207	[up 8 marks]
4. Military Law	218	[down 58 marks]
5. Military Administration	195	[down 35 marks]
Conduct: Unpunctual	1,140 [66]	

Although he dropped fifty-eight marks, this was only a five per cent decline and still a very good showing in a grading scheme where the maximum possible was 1,500 marks. His conduct remained unpunctual but was no longer rated as good. Winston seemed satisfied however, writing to his mother on 26 August:

Last time I got 1198 so you see I have lost about 60 marks. This I attribute to the fact that the papers did not suit me quite as well as last time – being rather apart from the notes from which I worked ... I should imagine that it [his place] would be in the first 20 ... It is not so bad, after all out of 140 boys among whom I passed in 90th.[67]

By 4 September 1894, Churchill had returned to Sandhurst for his final, or senior, term which would last until mid-December. The academic subjects remained the same but the hours of class study and practical work were again increased. Most of the morning and early afternoon was taken up by study and class, and the late afternoon by riding, gymnastics and sports. The focus of Winston's interest was still riding, which took on a new importance. He hoped his success in the riding competition might help him convince his father about a cavalry commission. Although he did not raise the subject again with his father it was a recurring topic in his letters to his mother. On 4 September he wrote to Lady Randolph:

The riding has begun also and I am working hard at it. I should like nothing better than to win the riding prize. My only chance of persuading Papa to let me go in the Cavalry is, I feel, to do something of that sort. If I take 'Honours' very high on the list, in passing out or win the Riding Prize I shall broach the subject again but till then the future is very gloomy. At Sandown this year the Duke of C. [Cambridge] spoke to me. He said 'You're at Sandhurst aren't you? Do you like it.' I said 'Yes.' and Col Brab [Brabazon] who was there said 'Going into my Regiment eh.' The Duke said 'Oh I am very glad.' So really he had forgotten all about the 60th.[68]

As the autumn progressed Churchill spent much of his free time riding hired horses with his fellow cadets. He liked nothing better than the kind of cross-country galloping and jumping familiar to those who hunt the fox. The extra practice not only polished his skills for the competition at Sandhurst but also fed the heroic daydreams of the incipient officers.

There might even be a mutiny or a revolt in India. At that time the natives had adopted a very mysterious practice of smearing the mango trees, and we all fastened hopefully upon an article in the Spectator which declared that in a few months we might have India to reconquer. We wondered about all this. Of course we should all get our commissions so much earlier and march about the plains of India and win medals and distinction and perhaps rise to very high command like Clive when quite young![69]

Daydreams aside, his riding progressed and he was considered one of the better riders in Company E.

One of Churchill's favourite memories of his Sandhurst days was of an episode which took place away from the college during his senior term. It had nothing to do with his military training but it tells much about him. The scene was the promenade of the Empire Theatre in Leicester Square in London where during evening and weekend performances young men and women socialised together and, as Churchill put it, 'also from time to time refreshed themselves with alcoholic liquors'.[70] In fact, it was suggested that professional ladies of the evening were well represented among the women present. Mrs Laura Ormiston Chant, a member of the London County Council and an important advocate of both abstinence from alcohol and celibacy among young people, sought to have the council close the promenade and the adjoining bar. The controversy spread to the newspapers with Mrs. Chant's Purity Campaign on one side and a shell organisation styled the Entertainments Protection League on the other. A compromise was reached that resulted in placing canvas screens between the bar and the promenade, a solution that was unwelcome to young university men and also to the men of Sandhurst, Churchill prominent among them. He strongly disagreed with the placement of the screens and the hypocrisy of the prudes.

On 3 November 1894, the first Saturday after the screens went up, Winston was at the Empire Theatre with a number of his fellow cadets. One thing led to another, negative comments about the barricade were followed by a man's cane poking a hole in the canvas and soon the crowd of two or three hundred patrons tore the screens to pieces in a riotous scene. 'In these somewhat unvirginal surroundings I now made by maiden speech. Mounting on the débris and indeed partially emerging from it, I addressed the tumultuous crowd.'[71] 'Ladies of the Empire! I stand for Liberty! Where does the Englishman in London always find a welcome? Where does he first go when, battle-scarred and travel-worn he reaches home? Who is always there to greet him with a smile and join him with a drink? Who is ever faithful, ever true? The Ladies of the Empire promenade!'[72] It was a rousing speech in a humorous vein which was wildly applauded. The crowd poured out into Leicester Square still holding bits of the barricade as prizes of battle. It being very late the cadets made their way back to Sandhurst by train, rented hackney carriages, dodged the gatekeeper and were barely there in time for morning parade.

The episode was reported in the London newspapers and Churchill was worried that his role might have negative repercussions at the college.

Although naturally proud of my part in resisting tyranny as is the duty of every citizen who wishes to live in a free country, I was not unaware that a contrary opinion was possible, and might even become predominant. Elderly people and those in authority cannot always be relied upon to take enlightened and comprehending views on what they call the indiscretions of youth. They sometimes have a nasty trick of singling out individuals and 'making examples'. Although always prepared for martyrdom, I preferred that it should be postponed.'[73]

In the event, no action was taken against him by the military authorities and the matter apparently escaped the notice of his parents who were still abroad. Winston was proud of his prominent participation. He wrote to his brother soon afterwards, 'Did you see the papers about the riot at the Empire last Saturday? It was I who led the rioters – and made a speech to the crowd. I enclose a cutting from one of the papers so that you may see.'[74] Although this was his first attempt at a public speech, he seems to have enjoyed the experience of speaking, the reaction of the audience and the press coverage. In the end the County Council replaced the barricade at the Empire, this time with a permanent wall of bricks and mortar.

He sent his parents regular reports of his progress at Sandhurst but received increasingly less frequent replies that autumn. He received no letters from his father whose health was in rapid decline. On 1 November, apparently for the first time, Churchill learned how truly ill Lord Randolph was. Later that month, Dr Roose, one of his father's physicians in London, was persuaded to tell Winston the truth - that his father was terminally ill and would cut short his trip and return to London. Writing to his mother on 25 November he said, 'I cannot tell you how shocked and unhappy I am – and how sad this heavy news makes me feel ... It must be awful for you – but it is almost as bad for me. You at least are there – on the spot & near him.'[75]

In spite of the devastating medical news, Churchill, his heart set on making a good showing at Sandhurst to satisfy his father, applied himself diligently to both his studies and to riding. The long-awaited riding examination was held on 7 December 1894. It was without a doubt Churchill's finest day at Sandhurst. He described it with enthusiasm in a letter to Lord Randolph:

First of all – all the cadets were examined who pass out this term – 127 in all. Then 15 were picked to compete together for the prize, I was one of those and in the afternoon we all rode – the General, Col Gough [the assistant adjutant-general for Cavalry at Aldershot] of the Greys and Capt Byng 10th Hussars,

Judges – with dozens of officers and many more cadets as spectators. This riding for the Prize is considered a great honour and the cadets take great interest in it.

Well we rode – jumped with & without stirrups & and with out reins – hands behind back and various other tricks. Then 5 were weeded out leaving only ten of us. Then we went in the field & rode over the numerous fences several times. 6 more were weeded out leaving only 4 in. I was wild with excitement and rode I think better than I have ever done before but failed to win the prize by 1 mark being 2nd with 199 out of 200 marks.

I am awfully pleased with the result, which in a place where everyone rides means a great deal, as I shall have to ride before the Duke and also as it makes it very easy to pick regts when the Colonels know you can ride. I hope you will be pleased.[76]

It was no doubt gratifying to Churchill to report such a grand success. How poignant it is in retrospect to know it was Churchill's last letter to his father, who was by then too ill to reply.

Final examinations for the senior term were held in the second week of December 1894. By his own account, Churchill worked hard to prepare for them with the goal of improving his marks. He finished these exams, the last of his lifetime, left Sandhurst on 15 December and went to stay with relatives while awaiting his parents' return to London. He was confident he had done well and continued to lobby his mother by mail about the cavalry.

I finished with Sandhurst very successfully; leaving many friends and numerous acquaintances. The examinations were after all easy and I think it extremely probable that I have obtained honours. Papa will read you a glowing account of my riding examinations.

If I were to go into the Cavalry I should get my commission in about 2 months to 2½ months instead of 6 or 7 months wait for the Rifles.[77]

Lord and Lady Randolph returned to London just before Christmas and it was clear to Winston that his father was in no condition to control the choice of regiments. In fact, the next month was a grim death watch as Lord Randolph lingered, faded and finally died in the early morning hours of 24 January 1895. He was only forty-six years of age. It is not clear what discussions Churchill had with his parents during that last sombre month. Certainly, Winston was determined to enter the cavalry and had the strong encouragement of Colonel Brabazon to seek a place in the 4th Hussars. Most probably Winston had made a convert of Lady Randolph who was of course preoccupied with her husband's condition. In his memoirs

Churchill chose to record that his father was finally won over, recalling, 'After my father's last sad home-coming he could take but little interest in my affairs. My mother explained to him how matters had arranged themselves, and he seemed quite willing, and even pleased, that I should become a Cavalry Officer. Indeed, one of the last remarks he made to me was, 'Have you got your horses?'[78]

It is unlikely that Lord Randolph was aware of Winston's marks for the senior term which arrived in late January 1895. Gentleman Cadet Churchill had done quite well with the following scores:

	Maximum	Churchill
1. Fortification	600	532
2. Tactics	300	263
3. Military Topography	600	471
4. Military Law	300	227
5. Military Administration	300	232
(Marks for the following were awarded only for the senior term)		
6. Drill	200	95
7. Gymnastics	200	85
8. Riding	200	190
9. Musketry	150	105
10. Marks Awarded by Professors	600	446
Totals:	3,450	2,646

Conduct: Good.[79]

This was a good report indeed with improvement in every subject but Tactics where he lost but a percentage point from his intermediate term marks. His exact class standing is a matter of debate among the family historians. Churchill in his autobiography claimed to have passed out of Sandhurst 'with honours' eighth out of 150 saying, 'I mention this because it shows I could learn quickly enough the things that mattered.'[80] In the first volume of the official biography of Churchill which was written by his son Randolph, the class standing is given as twentieth out of 130.[81] A review of the original records at Sandhurst shows the official biography to be correct as to both the number of cadets in Churchill's intake and his rank according to the number of final marks.

There are other statistical and definitional pitfalls in this historical record. The term 'with honours' is really quite meaningless in the matter of Sandhurst grading as there is no honours list or honour roll as such. In Churchill's time at Sandhurst there was only one prize, the Sword of Honour, given to the cadet passing out highest in the order of merit. As explained by the then-Commandant, Major General East, 'The Sword of Honour referred to in para. 22 of Standing Orders is awarded at the end of each term to the under officer who is considered to have had the best influence amongst the cadets generally, and to have exerted himself most successfully in his position as an under officer. In fact to the most deserving cadet, although not necessarily passing out high.'[82] An award for the highest number of marks did not come into being until 1897 when the Queen's Medal was instituted to recognise that achievement. 'The Sword of Honour was for the most deserving cadet, selected not by marks, but by the Commandant's opinion of who was best possessed of those qualities desirable in an officer which cannot be expressed in quantifiable terms.'[83] In Churchill's group the Sword of Honour was awarded to Senior Corporal, Under Officer Howarth Greenley, a cavalry cadet who later took his commission in the 12th Lancers. Greeley had 2,720 marks which placed him highest among cavalry cadets and tenth overall. The highest number of marks was 2,894 achieved by Richard Phillipson Dunn-Pattison who was commissioned into the Argyll and Sutherland Highlanders and killed in action as a captain in the First World War.

We may certainly conclude Churchill passed out of Sandhurst honourably and with very high marks. He had the second highest total of marks for a cavalry cadet trailing Greenley by only 74 marks of a possible 3,450 and was twentieth highest overall. Because he did not have cadet rank as an under-officer he was not in the running for the Sword of Honour.[84] It was, nevertheless, the greatest academic achievement of Churchill's school years and deserving of much credit.

Churchill's three terms at the Royal Military College marked his passage from youth to manhood. He was no longer the lonely, under-achieving schoolboy but was growing in confidence, maturity and independence. He was finally realizing some success in his individual endeavours in academics and riding and had risen in his family's esteem. His forceful personality had finally focused his considerable energy on a practical goal as for the first time his interests and abilities coincided perfectly with his work and his responsibilities. He overcame both a weak body and a poor academic record at public school to gain success and to qualify for an army commission as a second lieutenant of cavalry. In retrospect, he held a favourable view of his Sandhurst experience writing:

To those who enter the College direct from Eton or Harrow or any of our public schools, the life at Sandhurst is a pleasing emancipation, profitable to experience, agreeable to recall. It is a time of merriment and sport, a time of high hopes and good friends, of many pleasures and significant worries – a period of gratified ambitions and attained ideals.[85]

It was nevertheless terribly sad for Churchill that after all his striving to excel at Sandhurst to satisfy Lord Randolph and to build an adult relationship with him, he suddenly and rather unexpectedly was left on his own at the moment of his success. Yet in seeking to please his father Churchill had also served himself well for now he had both a good record of achievement and the skills of an honourable profession – the profession of arms. He looked forward to the world awaiting him. 'It opened like Aladdin's cave.'[86]

3

The 4th (Queen's Own) Hussars

Lord Randolph Churchill was laid to rest at Bladon churchyard near Blenheim Palace on 28 January 1895. His death was a great blow to Churchill who worshipped his father when he was alive and his memory after his death. He later wrote of his father's passing: 'All my dreams of comradeship with him, of entering Parliament at his side and in support, were ended. There remained for me only to pursue his aims and vindicate his memory. I was now in the main the master of my fortunes.'[1] By the time his father died Churchill had placed him on a pedestal from which he was never removed. Even in 1906 when he wrote an acclaimed biography of Lord Randolph which was critical of aspects of his political career, Churchill's filial devotion never diminished. This was so even though during his lifetime Lord Randolph was alternately inattentive to his son's needs and feelings or sternly critical of Winston's every effort in school or at Sandhurst.

If his father had always been Churchill's most constant and severe critic, in Lady Randolph he now found his most important confidante and advocate. After Lord Randolph's death they moved closer than they had ever been. 'My mother was always at hand to help and advise; but I was now in my 21st year and she never sought to exercise parental control. Indeed she soon became an ardent ally, furthering my plans and guarding my interests with all her influence and boundless energy. She was still at forty young, beautiful and fascinating. We worked together on even terms, more like brother and sister than mother and son. And so it continued to the end.'[2] He really could not have had a better friend. Although they sometimes quarrelled and often had their differences about money matters, her support for her son's ambitions never wavered.

Lady Randolph was well thought of in society and her popularity did not diminish when she was widowed. As the American correspondent George W. Smalley explained it: 'Nobody, I think, would describe the American genius as one of repression and reserve, nor did Miss Jerome when she married an English husband cease to be an American with more than the usual American exuberance of nature. It was clinging to Americanism which was one of the secrets of her popularity in England: and among the best people in England.'[3] She remained, even without Lord Randolph, well connected to the people who mattered in the government and the military. She was a woman of great vigour and charm and Winston now became the natural focus of her energies. This would bring immediate benefits to her elder son.

Within only a few days of Lord Randolph's death, Churchill and his mother were conspiring with Colonel Brabazon to get Winston out of his earlier commitment to the 60th Rifles and into the 4th Hussars. At Churchill's urging, Lady Randolph sent a telegram to Brabazon requesting his assistance and advice. By the time he replied on 2 February, Colonel Brabazon had already written to the Duke of Cambridge's private secretary to pave the way for Churchill's request. Brabazon recommended that Lady Randolph contact the duke directly and suggested exactly the approach to take.

> What I should say was that the boy had always been anxious to go into Cavalry, but for certain reasons Randolph put his name down for Infantry. That latterly he completely came round to Winston & your wishes & was anxious he should join my regiment. (Indeed Randolph often said if he was to go into Cavalry he should like him to join under me) you can say there is now a vacancy in the 4th Hussars, that you are very anxious he should not be idling about London and that I personally know the boy, liked him & was very anxious to have him. I should add – which is the case – that Winston passed out very much higher than any of the candidates for Cavalry & hope that the Duke will allow him to be appointed to the 4th Hussars and thus fulfil one of Randolph's last wishes.'[4]

This argument, while not strictly in accordance with the truth either as to Winston's marks at Sandhurst or Lord Randolph's dying wish, was apparently persuasive. On 6 February the Duke of Cambridge wrote back to Lady Randolph (not to Winston) promising to contact the War Office in support of her request and commenting: 'The 4th Hussars is a very good Cavalry Regiment, & Colonel Brabazon an excellent Commanding Officer so I think your selection is in that respect a very good one. I am delighted to hear your son had passed so well out of Sandhurst, a proof that he had made good use of his stay at the College.'[5] The War Office quickly approved the transfer and Churchill was soon on the way to his regiment.

For a Victorian-era officer, joining and being accepted into a regiment was a defining moment in his career as a soldier. Once selected, or 'badged', for a particular regiment he was ever after considered to belong to it. If transferred or placed on detached service he would be referred to as 'late of' his own regiment. It was not uncommon for an officer or another rank to serve his entire career in a single regiment. Five of Churchill's contemporaries – Major William Ramsay, Captain Ronald Kincaid-Smith, Captain Reginald Hoare, Captain Francis Lee and Lt Ian G. Hogg – would command the 4th Hussars later in their careers. Lt Reginald W. R. Barnes would serve as (honorary) colonel of the regiment from 1918 to 1941, when he was succeeded by Churchill. The regiment was the focus of a soldier's identity, pride and loyalty in the army. The ability of a British soldier to fight 'for Queen and Country' was largely based on loyalty to his comrades and regiment. For officers and men alike, the regiment was family; it was home.[6]

The 4th (Queen's Own) Hussars were then stationed at Aldershot in Hampshire. Aldershot camp was known officially in the 1890s as Aldershot district and colloquially by all who served there as 'The Shot' or simply 'Shot'. It was created in 1854 and built up after the Crimean War for the purpose of brigade-scale training and manoeuvres. Located thirty miles south-west of London and eight miles from Sandhurst, it consisted of some 10,000 acres of rolling countryside, a large parcel of real estate anywhere and particularly so in the south of England. By 1898, the facilities at Aldershot could accommodate about ten per cent of the entire British army, 585 officers, 19,647 other ranks and 4,358 horses.[7] It was an ideal facility for the training of cavalry and in 1895 was the home camp of the cavalry brigade which included the 4th Dragoon Guards, the Scots Greys and the 4th Hussars. Aldershot was also the site of grand military reviews and parades for the Queen and for visiting foreign dignitaries. For the state visit of the German Kaiser the year before Churchill's arrival, 12,000 troops were on parade at one time. Churchill would take part in similar ceremonies with his regiment in the years ahead.

The 4th Hussars, of which Churchill became the newest subaltern, or junior officer, that February, had a long and distinguished history and tradition.[8] It had been in existence for more than two centuries, originally formed on 17 July 1685 during the reign of King James II as Berkeley's Dragoons named for its first colonel, the Honourable John Berkeley. It was sometimes known as, 'The Princess Anne of Denmark's Regiment of Dragoons', in honour of the king's daughter, but this title was soon abandoned. After Berkeley inherited a family title the regiment became Lord Fitzhardinge's Dragoons and saw its first combat against the army of Louis XIV in 1692 at Steinkirk in France. It remained in garrison in England during the War of the Spanish Succession (1701–14) and so never come under command of Churchill's famous ancestor, the First Duke of Marlborough. It was not until 1743 that the regiment, then known as Rich's Dragoons for its current colonel, was back on active services. The regiment won its first battle honour during the War of the Austrian Succession (1742–8) at the battle of Dettingen on 27 June 1743, against the French.

In 1788 the regiment was designated the 4th Dragoons during an army reorganisation that numbered the regiments according to their seniority and spelled an end to naming them after their colonels. Also in 1788 the 4th Regiment of Dragoons had the words 'The Queen's Own' added to its title, at the direction of King George III. After a peaceful period of more than sixty years, the regiment was at war again, this time as part of the command of the Duke of Wellington fighting the armies of Napoleon in the Peninsular War (1808–14). In that conflict the regiment won the battle honours of Talavera, Albuhera, Salamanca, Vittoria and Toulouse.[9] It later took part in the First Afghan War (1839–42) winning further battle honours. Perhaps the greatest glory of the regiment's history was won in the Crimean War (1854–6). In the Crimea the 4th was commanded by Lord Paget, and together with the 8th and 11th Hussars, the 13th Light Dragoons and the 17th Lancers, formed part of the Light Cavalry Brigade under the command of the Earl of Cardigan.

At the battle of Balaclava on 25 October 1854, they took part in one of the most famous cavalry actions in the history of the British army, the charge of the Light Brigade, which was immortalised in verse by Alfred, Lord Tennyson. It was a poem known to every school child of Churchill's generation:

> Half a league, half a league,
> Half a league onward,
> All in the valley of Death
> Rode the six hundred.
> 'Forward the Light Brigade!
> Charge the guns!' he said.
> Into the valley of Death
> Rode the six hundred.
>   *   *   *
> Cannon to right of them,
> Cannon to left of them,
> Cannon behind them
> Volleyed and thundered;
> Stormed at with shot and shell,
> While horse and hero fell,

They that had fought so well
Came through the jaws of Death,
Back from the mouth of hell,
All that was left of them,
Left of six hundred.

      *   *   *

When can their glory fade?
O the wild charge they made!
All the world wondered.
Honour the charge they made!
Honour the Light Brigade,
Noble six hundred![10]

The charge was, in fact, a complete disaster in which the British cavalry charged Russian artillery in fortifications at the end of a valley over almost two miles of open ground. As the historian of the 4th Hussars later wrote, quoting Major General Bosquet of the French army who witnessed the charge: 'The Charge of the Light Brigade may have been folly; it was certainly magnificent.'[11] During the engagement the 4th silenced the Russian guns at the end of the valley at a cost of half their number killed, wounded or taken prisoner. Among those captured was Private Samuel Parkes who was awarded the Victoria Cross after his repatriation, the only member of the regiment to be so honoured in its entire history. Parkes's VC was the twenty-second ever awarded and one of nine won at Balaclava that day; he was personally decorated by Queen Victoria on 26 June 1857, at Hyde Park in London as part of the first investiture of the Victoria Cross.[12] The decoration is now in the possession of the regiment and is displayed with Parkes's campaign medals at regimental headquarters. Six Distinguished Conduct Medals were also won by members of the regiment for the battle. The DCM awarded to Private R. Grant together with his four-clasp Crimea Medal is in the collection of the regiment's warrant officers' and sergeants' mess. After the Crimean War and in honor of the battle, the regimental anniversary was always celebrated on 25 October, Balaclava Day.

In August 1861, in a further reorganisation of the cavalry, the regiment was renamed the 4th (Queen's Own) Hussars, the designation it kept until 1958 when it was amalgamated with the 8th King's Royal Irish Hussars to form the Queen's Royal Irish Hussars. That regiment was itself amalgamated with the Queen's Own Hussars (formerly the 3rd and 7th Hussars) in 1993 to form the present-day The Queen's Royal Hussars.

When Churchill joined the regiment, it was in the midst of another very extended period of peacetime service in Great Britain and the

Empire. By 1895 the Crimean War was forty years past and the 4th Hussars' First World War service was almost twenty years in the future. Although the regiment provided a detachment of forty-five men for the failed Gordon Relief Expedition to Egypt in 1885 under the command of Captain Cecil W. Peters and Lt Ronald Kincaid-Smith, it would not see active service again as a unit until 1914. Those of its officers who saw combat in the interim did so on their own initiative on detached service with other regiments.

The 4th Hussars were only a small part of the British army of the 1890s which numbered between 200,000 and 225,000 men, all of them volunteers. The standard term of enlistment was twelve years of which the first seven years were active duty and the last five years were in the reserves. Officers' commissions were issued by the War Office and were open-ended with no minimum period of service required. Less than ten per cent of British soldiers were in the cavalry. There were three regiments of Household Cavalry which were garrisoned in London and at Windsor to protect the sovereign – the 1st and 2nd regiments of Life Guards and the Royal Horse Guards (known as the Blues). There were twenty-eight regiments of cavalry of the line including seven regiments of dragoon guards, three regiments of dragoons, thirteen regiments of hussars and five regiments of lancers. Two-thirds of the army's strength was infantry organised in sixty-nine regiments including three regiments of guards (Grenadier, Scots and Coldstream) and sixty-six regiments of the line. The remaining quarter of the army was serving on staff, in the Royal Artillery, the Royal Engineers or in the several support units dealing with provisions, ordnance, medical and administrative matters. Just over half of the British Army was serving overseas at a given time.[13]

All the cavalry regiments except the Household Cavalry regiments took turns serving overseas in peacetime on a rotating basis. In wartime all the regiments could expect overseas service. Between six and nine cavalry regiments were on duty in India; one to four regiments of cavalry were commonly stationed in Egypt or South Africa.[14] When a regiment moved to India it left its horses behind for the regiment that returned to replace it in England and took over the horses of the returning regiment. The cavalry regiments serving abroad always left a cadre, or depot, of officers and men behind for purposes of administration and recruitment.

Of the cavalry regiments stationed in England during peacetime the half most recently returned from overseas was kept at 'low establishment' of twenty-three officers, forty-five sergeants, and 508 other ranks together with 343 troop horses. Officers' chargers and polo ponies were not included in this count. The half of the regiments in England next expected to rotate overseas were kept at 'higher establishment' of twenty-six officers, fifty-one sergeants, 617 other ranks and 465 troop horses. Often these regiments recruited reservists or men from other regiments to fill their ranks before a tour in India. Out there a cavalry regiment of the line was expected to muster a full compliment of 622 men including twenty-nine officers, fifty-four sergeants and 539 other ranks with 525 troop horses.[15]

A cavalry regiment was typically organised into four squadrons, three active and one reserve, each commanded by a major or senior captain. Each squadron was further divided into four troops, each commanded by a junior captain or a lieutenant. When the regiment left for active service abroad, the reserve squadron remained in Britain as the depot unit. Serving overseas or in wartime, the total number of men in a regiment could vary considerably but the basic structure and organisation remained the same.

The British army was the subject of broad support and prestige in the last quarter of the nineteenth century. These were the years when the British Empire was approaching its zenith, the years of Queen Victoria's jubilee celebration in Great Britain and in British possessions and colonies around the globe. The British Isles had not been threatened since the Napoleonic Wars and, with the exception of the Crimean War, the British army had devoted its energies to policing the Empire and fighting an endless series of relatively small-scale colonial wars. In the sixty-four years of Queen Victoria's reign (1837–1901) the government issued thirty-one campaign medals and scores of clasps commemorating individual expeditions and battles. In contrast, throughout the twentieth century after Queen Victoria's death, thirty-three campaign medals have been authorised including ten for the Second World War alone.[16]

It was a time for national pride of the jingoistic variety and a time for heroes in a way that seems very distant and foreign today. The heroes of the era were the great British imperialists of history such as Clive of India, Raffles of Singapore, Rhodes of South Africa and the great military men like General Charles Gordon of Khartoum; General Sir Frederick Roberts, who was an Indian Mutiny Victoria Cross winner; General Sir Garnet Wolseley; General Sir Evelyn Wood, who won the VC in the first Anglo-Boer War; and General Sir Horatio Kitchener, the victor at Omdurman. Even the common soldier, nicknamed 'Tommy Atkins,' was a heroic figure in the popular press and nationalist, imperialist culture of the day at least during wartime. Rudyard Kipling's prose and poetry about the British army in India had a wide readership as did the periodical *Boy's Own Paper* and romantic, heroic novels with imperial themes. Reaching its peak of popularity was an entire genre of paintings with military themes by such artists as Lady Butler and R. Caton Woodville depicting famous battles and colourful campaigns.[17] Photographs, drawings and illustrations of military uniforms and battle scenes enjoyed a wide distribution in magazines such as *The Illustrated London News* and even as collectable cards in packets of cigarettes. Military music was also popular, often heard in Sunday concerts provided to the public by the regimental bands of the British army. A typical popular song of the period and lifelong Churchill favourite, 'Soldiers of the Queen', is representative.

> Britons always loyally declaim, about the way we rule the waves.
> Every Briton's song is just the same, when singing of our soldiers
> brave
> All the world has heard it, wonders why we sing, and some have
> learned the reason why.
> We're not forgetting it, we're not letting it
> Fade away or gradually die; fade away or gradually die.
> So when we say that England's master, remember who has made her
> so.

> It's the soldiers of the Queen, my lads,
> Who've been, my lads, who've seen, my lads,
> In the fight for England's glory, lads
> Of its world wide glory let us sing.
> And when we say we've always won,
> And when they ask us how it's done,
> We'll proudly point to everyone
> Of England's soldiers of the Queen.

> War clouds gather over every land, our treaties threatened east and
> west.
> Nations that we've shaken by the hand, our honoured pledges try to
> test.
> They may have thought us sleeping, thought us unprepared, because
> we have our party wars.
> But Britons all unite, when they're called to fight
> The battle for old England's cause; the battle for old England's cause.
> So when we say that England's master, remember who has made her
> so.
> It's the soldiers of the Queen, etc.

When we're roused we buckle on our swords, we've done with
    diplomatic lingo.
We do deeds to follow our words, we show we're something more
    than jingo
The sons of merry England answered duty's call, and military duties
    do,
And though new at the game, they show them all the same,
An Englishman can be a soldier too; an Englishman can be a soldier
    too.
So when we say that England's master, remember who has made her
    so.
It's the soldiers of the Queen, etc.[18]

During the nineteenth century the introduction of the telegraph and the
expansion of the mass circulation popular press made news about the
campaigns of the British army widely available to the public in Britain. The
war correspondent was an innovation of the 1800s with Britons in the
forefront. The great correspondents of the day were household names –
George W. Steevens, Edgar Wallace, Richard Harding Davis and Bennet
Burleigh. To these Churchill would eventually add his own name. The
army's victories and losses alike were commemorated in print and in
pictures. The tragic defeats in the First Afghan War, the massacre at the
battle of Isandhlwana in the Zulu War and the death of General Gordon at
the hands of the Dervishes at Khartoum in the Sudan lent both tragedy
and glory to the imperial saga and all were avenged in time by the might
of British arms. It was an era that, for the soldiers of a cavalry regiment, at
least had more in common with the eighteenth century than the twentieth.
The army was small, élite and professional. It was an era before modern
technology and conscripted national armies changed the military profession forever. It was an era when empires were supreme and few could
imagine a world without the grandest of them all, the British Empire.

The self-satisfied military culture of the period was nowhere better
showcased than at Aldershot. As one retired colonel recalled in his
memoirs:

They were good days those in the early nineties in Aldershot ... There was a
glamour which is gone, a romance of dash and colour, an atmosphere of the
beau sabreur, which was part of everyday life ... in the daily walks across the
old Canal, over the Queen's Parade and into the North Camp Gardens we
were kept alive to the identity of every regiment in the station by the gay
uniforms which were met with everywhere and were recognisable half a mile
away, on mounted orderlies busily trotting about with leather dispatch bags,

parties at drill and soldiers. 'walking out' … it was soldiers, soldiers, everywhere … The weekly routine included attendance at Church Parades in the little tin church by the canal bridge, route marches in marching order, sham fights and field days in the Fox Hills, Reviews and Queen's Birthday Parades in all the full dress glories of Ceremonial and on Laffan's Plain. And there was colour, colour, colour all the way.[19]

The last quarter of the nineteenth century was, in the words of the 4th Hussar's historian, 'a golden age. The regiment basked in the ease and security of Victorian plenty. A good cavalry regiment has a sort of polished texture and made a fine show.'[20] Service in England for the 4th Hussars had much of the society ball and the country house weekend mixed in with military duties.

The prestige and reputation of a regiment came partly from its history and partly from the tone created by its commanding officer. Since 1893, the 4th Hussars had been commanded by Lt-Colonel John P. Brabazon, a gentleman Irish landlord with a distinguished service record and excellent connections in society. Brabazon was a man of much experience of active service and also many eccentricities. He was tall and slender, strikingly handsome with his hair parted in the middle and combed straight back. He sported a flowing upswept moustache and a Louis Napoleon style goatee which was not at all in accord with regulations. He made a fine appearance in his tailored uniform with five campaign ribbons on his chest for the Ashanti War Medal (1874), the Second Afghan War Medal (1878–80), the Kabul to Kandahar Star (1880), the Egyptian Expedition Medal (1884) and the Khedive's Star (1884). He had been mentioned in dispatches, wounded in action, and had received a brevet promotion in the field.[21] He was a model Victorian officer.

As Churchill later wrote of his colonel:

From his entry into the Grenadier Guards in the early '60s he had been in the van of fashion. He was one of the brightest stars in London Society. A close lifelong friendship had subsisted between him and the Prince of Wales. At Court, in the Clubs, on the racecourse, in the hunting field, he was accepted as a most distinguished figure … To all this he added the airs and manners of the dandies of the generation before his own, and inability real or affected to pronounce the letter 'R'. Apt and experienced in conversation, his remarkable personality was never at a loss in any company, polite or otherwise.'[22]

Colonel Brabazon's speech affectation was the subject of many anecdotes. Once when he appeared at Aldershot railway station and asked 'Where is the

London twain?', and was told it had already departed, he exclaimed, 'Gone! Bwing another!' His close friends called him 'Brab' and, predictably, the troopers of the 4th referred to him behind his back as 'Bwab'.

Under Brabazon's leadership the 4th Hussars was considered a 'smart' regiment, well regarded for the popularity of the colonel and for their consistently fine performance in parades and inspections. The regiment's informal nickname, however, was attributed to them by someone with a sense of humour. During a tour of duty in India after the Crimean War but still under the command of Lord Paget, an observer noted the rather sloppy showing on the drill field and dubbed the regiment, 'Paget's Irregular Horse'.[24] The regiment's motto 'Mente et Manu', variously translated from the Latin as 'with heart and hand' or 'might and main', was earnest rather than inspiring. The regiment's distinctive brass cap badge is a circle inscribed 'Queen's Own Hussars,' with two sprays of laurel below the inscription. Inside the circle is the Roman numeral IV in silver metal and above the circle is a Queen Victoria Crown. The regiment had its own music as well, a song and both a slow and a quick march. The slow march was of Brabazon's own selection:

> Brabazon was on holiday in Italy in 1890 when he heard a series of 'Litanies of Loretto' in honour of the Virgin Mary. These litanies, dating from the thirteenth century, are used in Italy by the Roman Catholic Church, sung to Latin words. Colonel Brabazon got hold of a manuscript copy of the melodies and later asked Bandmaster E .O. Davies to arrange a suitable slow march for the regiment. This was done and the march was officially approved, with the title Loretto. The transcription was not perfect for performance by a mounted band, but the imperfections were rectified in 1932 by Mr. G.R. Jones, then the Bandmaster. The authorised Quick March, 'Berkeley's Dragoons', is a recent original of composition by Captain C.H. Jaeger, previously Bandmaster of the 4th Hussars and later Director of Music, Irish Guards. The Quick Step was named after the first Colonel of Regiment, and it was authoriszed in 1952.[25]

The present regimental song is a wonderfully succinct self-definition of the hussar spirit both at war and at play with a lyric to which an army chorus can give power:

> I'm a soldier in the Queen's Army
> I'm a galloping Queen's Hussar
> I've sailed the ocean wide and blue,
> I'm a chap who knows a thing or two,
> Been in many a tight corner,
> Shown the enemy who we are,

I can ride a horse,
Go on a spree,
Or sing a comic song,
And that denotes a Queen's Hussar.[26]

Churchill's commission was published in the *London Gazette* of 19 February 1895, with an effective date of 20 February.[27] The *London Gazette* was the official publication for posting of commissions, promotions and honours for the military in Britain. For a new second lieutenant to be 'gazetted' is an important event for on that date commence both his seniority and his pay. Churchill's commission was signed by Queen Victoria and by H. Campbell Bannerman, the Secretary of State for War. The full text read as follows:

Victoria R

Victoria by the Grace of God of the United Kingdom of Great Britain and Ireland, Queen, Defender of the Faith, Empress of India, etc. To Our Trusty and well beloved Winston Leonard Spencer Churchill, Gentleman, Greeting: We, reposing especial Trust and Confidence in your Loyalty, Courage and Good Conduct, do by these Presents Constitute and Appoint you to be an Officer in Our Land Forces from the twentieth day of February 1895. You are therefore carefully and diligently to discharge your Duty as such in the Rank of 2nd Lt or in such higher Rank as We may from time to time hereafter be pleased to promote or appoint you to of which a notification will be made in the London Gazette, and you are at all time to exercise and will discipline in Arms, both the inferior Officers and Men serving under you and use your best endeavours to keep them in good Order and Discipline. And We do hereby Command them to Obey you as their superior Officer, and you to observe and to follow such Orders and Directions as from time to time you shall receive from Us or any your superior Officer, according to the Rules and Discipline of War in pursuance of the Trust hereby reposed in you.

Given at Our Court at Saint James's the twelfth day of February, 1895 the fifty-eighth Year of Our Reign.

Winston Leonard Spencer Churchill, Gentleman

2nd Lieutenant
Land Forces   By Her Majesty's Command.
                                              H. Campbell Bannerman[28]

To get an idea of Churchill's place in the scheme of things at the beginning of his military career one must look to his first appearance in *The*

Official Army List, which noted Churchill's place in the seniority list of officers in the British army. Ahead of him in rank and seniority were six field
marshals, seventeen generals, forty-two lieutenant generals, 103 major
generals, 728 colonels, 655 Lt colonels, 1,357 majors, 3,407 captains,
3,882 lieutenants and 1,502 second lieutenants. Only eighty-four second
lieutenants were listed as junior to Churchill and the most junior of all,
Ernest St George Hughes, was commissioned only a month later than
Churchill.[29] Positioned on the bottom one per cent in seniority of all the
officers of the British army would perhaps have reminded the new subaltern of his class standing at Harrow. In any event, with the passage of time
he would work himself up the list in the regiment; and it was his intention
that his reputation grow without regard to the calendar. No doubt he had
in mind his late father's admonition: 'The Army is the finest profession in
the world if you work at it and the worst if you loaf at it.'[30]

One of Churchill's pressing concerns upon joining the regiment was
financial for no cavalry officer could live on his pay alone. Considerable
private means were absolutely necessary not only to keep up appearances
but to meet minimum requirements. It was variously estimated that a
private income of £300–£700 per year was necessary for an officer of a
cavalry regiment of the line.[31] This was far more than the cost of either
Harrow or Sandhurst. Lack of money was a constant worry for Churchill
and his mother and was the topic of most of their letters and a frequent
cause of friction between them.

The pay of a new second lieutenant was only six shillings and eight
pence per day which worked out to £120 per year.[32] Yet an incoming
officer had a huge burden of both initial and on-going expenses. He had
to pay for his own uniforms, civilian clothing, cases, swords, saddlery,
spurs and other equipment, hunting and polo outfits and equipment,
clothes for a personal servant, the furniture and decoration for his quarters, and various subscriptions for the regiment, the officers' mess and
special events. To these were added mess bills for food and drink, the cost
of two horses called chargers and whatever polo ponies he required. Even
after his Aunt Lily, second wife of his Uncle George, the Eighth Duke of
Marlborough, bought one charger for him at the cost of £200, Churchill
calculated the initial cost of equipping himself to join the 4th Hussars was
£653.11.0. In a letter to Lady Randolph he outlined the costs:

Charger	£120.0.0
Tailor	165.0.0
Boots	35.0.0

Sword etc	20.0.0
Saddlery	50.0.0
Spurs	12.0.0
Hunting [?] breeches	30.0.0
Horse furniture (to be bought second-hand mostly – a great economy)	20.0.0
	£452.
	Original Outfit.
Brought forward	. 452.0.0
Subscriptions and sundries (accounted for) due to me	69.0.0 (Paid)
Additional subs not yet due	
a) 1 days pay to squadron	15.0.0
b) sub to new kettle drums	7.10.0
'The Polo Loan'	100.0.0
Furnishing room – (furniture should be included in outfit)	10.0.0
(had it been bought it would have been £50)	
Grand Total	£653.11.0

That is to the best of my belief a tolerable estimate of the cost of joining (including the Polo loan/gift). I would point out that had not my personal charms induced the Duchess Lily to give me a charger it would have been 100 or 120 more.[33]

It was certainly a great deal of money. In fact, the initial outfit cost more than the total pay he would receive during his five years in the army. To supplement his pay Lady Randolph agreed to provide him with an annual allowance of £300 paid quarterly, rather less income than his colleagues. Churchill had no reserves and late payment of his allowance was the cause of pleading letters to his mother and trouble meeting his expenses. To make up the difference he followed the time-honoured practice of going into debt. He had to borrow the £100 to buy polo ponies and simply left other bills unpaid. Sometimes he paid his monthly mess bill late, which was frowned upon. Certain of his tailor's bills went unpaid for years on end.[34] He always seemed to have money problems and was never free of debt the entire time he was in the army.

The amount of equipment necessary and the number and variety of uniforms required was remarkable. First came the distinctive full dress uniform worn on formal and ceremonial occasions. This started with a black sable fur hat called a busby, with a yellow cloth flap – the so-called busby bag – covering the top and hanging down the right side of the hat. This was secured by a gilt corded chain chin-strap lined with black morocco leather and backed with velvet. The busby was topped by a fifteen-inch-high plume of red ostrich feathers. The full dress tunic was made of dark blue cloth with edging of gold chain gimp. The collar was edged with gold lace. The tunic had fancy loops and knots of gold lace on the front and back and on the sleeves above the cuffs. There were plaited gold braid shoulder cords in the place of epaulettes. The breeches, sometimes called pantaloons, were tight fitting trousers worn inside the boots and were made of the same blue cloth and featured two three-quarter-inch-wide stripes of gold lace down each side seam. The levee style or Hessian boots were black leather and knee length with a 'v' cut at the front under the knee, edged in gold gimp lace with an oval boss in front. These were worn with brass spurs.

In addition to the clothing of the full dress uniform was the equipment worn with it. A cavalry pattern sword was carried in a steel scabbard suspended from a black leather sword belt worn on the waist and braced by gold lace sword slings. Attached to the belt was a sabretache, or dispatch pouch, suspended by its own red leather slings. An ornamental sword knot of gold and crimson completed the belt. The sabretache was of crimson cloth and morocco leather edged by the authorised pattern of regiment gold lace (for the lace would vary from regiment to regiment) and featured an elaborate embroidery of the regimental device at the centre flanked by the 4th Hussars battle honours in fine embroidery. Finally, there was a gold lace shoulder belt worn over the left shoulder and under the right arm on the back of which was a pouch in black leather with a silver flap and gilt metal ornaments. It was, all in all, a strikingly fine and colourful outfit.

Churchill had also to fit himself out with the service dress uniforms which were worn on a daily basis and sometimes referred to as 'undress' to distinguish them from the full dress uniform. There was a variety of service dress uniforms. The headgear could be either the forage cap or a field cap. The forage cap was a round pillbox hat of blue cloth edged in the regimental gold lace and surmounted by gold lace pattern and a gold pearl button. It was worn with a chin strap at a jaunty angle on the right side of the head. Indeed, it was sometimes said that you could spot a cavalry man when he was off duty because of the little triangle of forehead that was not sunburned like the rest of his face.[35] The field cap was a folding, envelope-shaped hat of yellow cloth with dark blue side flaps and the regimental badge worn forward on the left side, and with two regimental pattern buttons at the front. It was worn with a chin-strap when the flaps were up. When worn down, the flaps were buttoned under the chin.

The service dress jacket might be a stable jacket, a patrol jacket or a frock depending on the duties and orders of the day. All were single breasted. The stable jacket was waist length, made of dark blue cloth with side seams and the sleeves edged with gold wire cord. Tracing cord was placed on the collar, cuffs, pockets and back seams in distinctive loops. The jacket front was edged with gold lace and closed with seven pairs of tracing cord loops on either side of each button. The stable jacket was worn with dress boots and breeches. The patrol jacket was cut to a length just over the hips; it was of blue cloth edged with black astrakhan and with cuffs and collar also of astrakhan. The tracing cords and braid were of black mohair with seven pairs of flaps of braid at the front. When worn, the right flaps were buttoned down and the left flaps left open. The patrol jacket was worn with trousers (then called over-alls), over black Wellington boots. The frock was a twenty-eight-inch-length uniform jacket in blue serge with five small regimental pattern buttons down the front and shoulder straps covered with chain mail epaulettes called shoulder chains on which rank badges were worn. It featured four outside pockets not unlike service uniforms of today. The frock was worn with trousers, rather than dress breeches, over Wellington boots. The Wellingtons were square-cut black leather boots worn at mid-calf.

In addition to the dress and undress uniforms was a third type of outfit called mess dress. The mess jacket was the equivalent of the civilian dinner jacket and was worn on formal, indoor occasions such as dinners and balls. It featured an open fronted mess jacket of blue cloth with olivets and laces of regimental patterns. The mess jacket was worn with a waistcoat and breeches and other articles as in full dress.

Finally, in addition to the uniforms themselves were two types of cloaks for cold or wet weather. The cape was used as a raincoat over uniforms and was of blue cloth with a scarlet lining cut long enough to reach the knuckles of the wearer. It was without ornament except for four small buttons at the front. The frock coat was a knee-length overcoat for cold weather use, the cavalry equivalent of the familiar infantry greatcoat. It was of dark blue cloth with black mohair tracing cords, and braid and front button flaps similar to the patrol jacket.

Obviously, there was quite a lot of clothing and equipment to purchase at the outset. Churchill bought items second-hand when he could to minimise the costs. When overseas, there was additional clothing to obtain but the uniform requirements were very much simplified as the dress for most duty was a khaki tunic and trousers worn with a 'Sam Browne' belt and scabbard in brown leather. With this uniform went a forage cap, a field cap or a cork sun helmet covered with khaki cloth.[36]

Churchill's arrival at the 4th Hussars on Monday, 18 February 1895 was without ceremony or drama. Being a family friend of Colonel Brabazon and having been recruited for the regiment by him, Churchill rather expected the CO to greet him, show him around and make all the necessary introductions. In that way it would be seen by all and sundry that he was one of the colonel's favourites. But Colonel Brabazon did not come to meet him personally as Churchill expected and he had to introduce himself to the other officers which he found 'awkward'. To make matters worse, his quarters were not ready for him and he had to make use of Captain de Moleyns's rooms in the interim. None the less, he was made welcome by his fellow officers, a number of whom he had met on visits to the mess as a guest while still a gentleman cadet at Sandhurst. He was pleased to learn there were a number of Old Harrovians among them and no doubt reassured to find that his colleagues' public school and family backgrounds were not unlike his own. In fact there were five 4th Hussars officers who were Old Harrovians.[37] The officer class of the British army was, in fact, very cohesive socially.

The newly arrived officer was attractive in appearance and no doubt cut a fine figure in his tailored uniforms. His appearance at about this time was noted by an acquaintance, journalist Richard Harding Davis:

He was just of age, but appeared much younger.

He was below medium height, a slight delicate looking boy; although as a matter of fact extremely strong, with blue eyes, many freckles and hair which theatened to be a decided red ... His manner of speaking was nervous, eager, explosive.

He had then and still has [in 1906] a most embarrassing habit of asking many questions; embarrassing, sometimes, because the questions are so frank, and sometimes because they lay bare the wide expanse of one's own ignorance.[38]

It is likely that Churchill felt he was in a place where he belonged. On 19 February, the day after his arrival, he wrote to his mother with an optimistic outlook: 'The work, though hard and severe is not at present uninteresting, and I trust that the novelty and the many compensating attractions of a military existence will prevent it from becoming so – at any rate for the next four or five years.'[39] Here is an indication at the very outset of his military years that Churchill never intended to make the army a career. As he had stated while still at Harrow, he was destined for great things – at least in his own mind. One senses in Churchill that during his military years every step he took was to further his own fortunes with a definite eye toward his future prospects in politics.

At Aldershot the 4th Hussars were quartered at the Warburg barracks, part of the East Cavalry barracks located at the corner of Wellington Avenue and Barrack Road with its main gate facing the high street. The area of the four-storey cavalry barracks was referred to as the Wellington Lines. The officers' quarters were part of what was known as the regimental mess. Each officer had his own private room or rooms, the amount of space allotted increasing with seniority. These rooms were usually furnished very simply and Churchill planned to purchase his furnishings second-hand. The common area or mess-rooms were much more comfortably furnished and elaborately decorated. The reading or living room was provided with comfortable furniture and adorned with mementos and trophies of the regiment's many campaigns and world travels.

The present-day officers' mess of the Queen's Royal Hussars viewed at Catterick in Yorkshire in 1996 was perhaps representative of how the common rooms of the 4th Hussars' mess would have appeared in earlier years. There are portraits of previous colonels and famous actions including an oil painting of Sergeant Parkes at Balaclava. There are on display sporting trophies and fine silver presentation cups and sculptures. There are framed groups of military medals mounted above bookcases of tomes on military history. Here and there are placed on proud display a relic from an earlier era – a sabretache from a distant campaign, a pair of pig-sticking spears from India, a fading guidon, a silver trumpet with banderol and sling presented to the 4th Hussars to commemorate the proclamation of Queen Victoria as Empress of India on 1 January 1877. Also displayed is a fine grouping of twenty-one caricatures of the officers then serving in the regiment, including Lt Churchill with his forage cap worn at a jaunty angle on the right side of his head and Colonel Brabazon with his moustache fairly billowing as if swept up and back by the wind.

In the mess at Aldershot were also an ante-room, a billiard room, a card room and of course the dining room. The dining room was the home of the regiment's silver plate. The centrepiece of the officers' mess was a sculpture in silver and bronze about two feet tall depicting the murder of the royalist Lord Francis Villiers in 1648 at the hands of the Roundheads during the English Civil War. It was bought by the officers of the regiment in the 1870s at the bazaar at Meerut, India and was, as legend had it, recovered loot from the Indian military.[40]

The dining room was the venue of the evening meals which Churchill had described as like a state banquet. The officers' servants waited on the table at dinner and it was not unusual to have the regimental band serenade the assembly on guest night. The unmarried officers were required to take their evening meal together in the mess and wore formal mess dress. It was an elegant arrangement and for the officer of the Victorian army the mess was more than a residence and a dining facility; it was an exclusive gentlemen's club.

The mess management was handled by an officers' committee with a mess secretary in administrative charge assisted by a sergeant and enlisted men assigned as waiters. Each officer was required to pay an initial mess fee of a month's pay upon joining the regiment and a monthly subscription thereafter into the mess fund. Additional special subscriptions were collected from time to time for special events or presentation gifts. Colonel Brabazon paid close attention to the mess and insisted on high standards. On one occasion, when not satisfied with the quality of the beverages, Churchill heard the colonel enquire of the mess president, 'And what chemist do you get this champagne fwom?'[41]

The 4th Hussars was organised into four squadrons designated A, B, C, and D, plus a headquarters, or staff, section. General A. Low, CB was the colonel of the regiment, an honorary role much like that of the patron of a charitable society with no command authority. Serving under Lt Colonel Brabazon, the actual Commanding Officer, were staff officers Major W. A. Ramsay, Major F. C. Pearson, and Major C. W. Peters. The adjutant, or administrative assistant to Brabazon, was Captain the Honourable F. R. W. Evenleigh-de Moleyns. The riding master, in charge of mounts and instruction in equitation, was Lt Kempthorne. The Quartermaster, in charge of supply, was Lt A. W. Cochrane. The riding master's and quartermaster's ranks were, in fact, honorary only. They held no commissions. The commanders of the four squadrons were Captain Edgar M. La Fone for A Squadron, Captain Frederic D. Baillie for B Squadron, Captain Ronald Kincaid-Smith for C Squadron and Captain Lewis E. Starkey for D Squadron.[42]

Lt Churchill was assigned to C Squadron where the other officers in order of seniority were Captain Daniel P. Sunderland, Lt Arthur L.

Trevor-Boothe and Lt Albert Savory. The squadron had a total of 169 men including twelve sergeants, one lance sergeant, eight corporals, seven lance corporals, 132 privates, two trumpeters and two boys. As a second lieutenant, Churchill would have been the commanding officer of one of four troops of C squadron. Churchill's arrival was noted by Lance Corporal S. Hallaway: 'When Mr. Churchill joined I was in charge of the 3rd Troop of 'C' Squadron, and as Captain Kincaid-Smith and Mr Churchill walked over the squadron parade ground towards my stable I thought how odd he looked, his hair and his gold lace forage cap the same colour. Captain Kincaid-Smith introduced me to him. I had to tell him all I knew about my troops, men and horses and stable management. He kept me very busy asking questions.'[43]

It was the practice in the 1890s cavalry for a new officer to undergo initial recruit training with the other ranks for about six months and Lt Churchill was to be no exception. He began training on 19 February, the very day after his arrival and the same day his commission appeared in *The London Gazette*. The army lost no time putting him to work.

The riding school in a cavalry regiment was as rigorous a training scheme as any in the British army of the day. It was not merely good form to learn to care for and to ride horses, it was on active service a matter of life and death. Sometimes referred to in the army as the 'chamber of 'orrors', Churchill found the riding school a challenge even after private lessons and the course at Sandhurst: 'I was fairly well fitted for the riding-school by the two long courses through which I had already gone; but I must proclaim that the 4th Hussars exceeded in severity anything I had previously experienced in military equitation.'[44]

The training in horsemanship, or cavalry drill, was governed by the *Regulations For The Instruction and Movements of Cavalry*, the riding master's bible. This pocket-sized handbook of nearly 500 pages covered all the basic skills required of a cavalryman on and off his horse. The table of contents of the 1885 edition outlines the course of instruction for recruits and indicated the amount of work they faced in the riding school:

INSTRUCTION OF THE RECRUIT
1. Preliminary Observations
2. Leading the Horse
3. Mounting and Dismounting
4. Extension and Balancing Motions
5. Seat While the Horse is in Motion
6. Dressing
7. Walking and Trotting In the School or Manège

8. Riding in Saddles Without Stirrups
9. Saddling
10. Bridling
11. Fitting the stirrup
12. Mounting and Dismounting Without Stirrups
13. Aids In Turnings and Paces
14. Single Ride[45]

In addition to the basic techniques of handling a horse, the recruits were trained in the methods of fighting on horseback or on foot with sabre, carbine and pistol. The cavalry drill began with the individual trooper and progressed to group movements for the troop, squadron and regiment which were simple in concept but complex and difficult in execution. As Churchill later wrote:

I must explain for the benefit of the ignorant reader that cavalry manoeuvre in column and fight in line, and that cavalry drill resolves itself into swift and flexible changes from one formation to the other. Thus by wheeling or moving in échelon a front can always be presented by a squadron almost at any moment in any direction. The same principles apply to the movements of larger bodies of horsemen; and regiments, brigades and even divisions of cavalry could be made to present a front an incredibly short time as the preliminary to that greatest of all cavalry events – the Charge.'[46]

There is no more succinct explanation than this in all the literature on the subject.

Memoirs of cavalrymen of the late nineteenth century often comment on the sense of pride and accomplishment, and even physical pleasure, in the movements of cavalry. There was something about the unity of man and horse that linked each hussar to the traditions and glories of all who had gone before him. On the parade ground and training fields at Aldershot a cavalryman in full dress uniform could vividly sense the dash and pomp of the cavalry and its unquestioned superiority to the other branches of the service.

As Churchill wrote in his memoirs:

There is a thrill and charm of its own in the glittering jingle of a cavalry squadron manoeuvring at the trot; and this deepens into joyous excitement when the same evolutions are performed at a gallop. The stir of the horses, the clank of their equipment, the thrill of motion, the tossing plumes, the sense of incorporation in a living machine, the suave dignity of the uniform all combine to make cavalry drill a fine thing in itself.[47]

Although the riding school was difficult and the parade ground drill was boring, Churchill never forgot it and never tired of talking about it in later years. During the Second World War, Churchill as Prime Minister travelled to Quebec in 1943 to meet President Roosevelt. On the return voyage aboard HMS *Renown* it was the practice for Churchill and his colleagues and aides to walk on the deck for exercise and fresh air. It is reported that after dinner, he would lead his dining companions to the quarterdeck where he would supervise them in carrying out Cavalry Drill for their mutual amusement.[48] But by then, of course, the horse cavalry was already a thing of the past because the machine gun, the motor vehicle and the aeroplane had made the horse obsolete as a weapon of war. In fact the cavalry drill of 1895 was already obsolescent. Although the 21st Lancers found a use for it in the Sudan in 1898, it had no practical use in the Boer War which began but a year later.

Although Churchill rode extensively, the riding school was a real challenge for him and, no doubt, extremely difficult for the enlisted recruits with no experience at all with horses. As Francis Maitland, an officer of the 19th Hussars later recalled, 'These days in the Riding School are a mixture of great joy and equally great dismay. NCOs are famous for their bitter sarcasm, all NCOs throughout the Army, but none can equal a cavalry rough-rider.'[49] The 4th Hussars' riding master was no exception, especially in the spring of 1895. As Churchill later wrote:

> The Regimental Riding Master, nicknamed 'Jocko', who specialised in being a terrible tyrant, happened during these weeks to be in an xceedingly touchy temper. One of the senior Subalterns had inserted in the *Aldershot Times* as an advertisement: 'Major —, Professor of Equitation, East Cavalry Barracks. Hunting taught in 12 lessons and steeple-chasing in 18.' This had drawn upon him a flood of ridicule which perhaps led him to suppose that every smile that ever flitted across the face of one of his riding-school class was due to some inward satisfaction at his expense.[50]

Although he was a good rider, Churchill faced the same difficulties as everyone else and during his initial training phase he was always conscious of the opinions of others, especially the troopers:

> At the head of the file in the riding-school, or on the right of the squad on the Square, [I] had to try to set an example to the men. This was a task not always possible to discharge with conspicuous success. Mounting and dismounting from a barebacked horse at the trot or canter; jumping a high bar without stirrups or even saddle, sometimes with one's hands clasped behind one's back; jogging at a fast trot with nothing but the horse's hide between your knees,

brought their inevitable share of mishaps. Many a time did I pick myself up shaken and sore from the riding-school tan and don again my little gold braided pork-pie cap, fastened on the chin by a boot-lace strap, with what appearance of dignity I could command, while twenty recruits grinned furtively but delighted to see their Officer suffering the same misfortunes which it was their lot so frequently to undergo.[51]

The riding school and the parade ground drill were not just necessary training in martial skills but were a rite of initiation of the cavalry regiment for all newcomers. They were part of the process of bonding officers and men to their professional duties and to one another.

Recruit training also included familiarisation and training with weapons, a soldier's tools of the trade. The cavalry of the late 1890s was equipped with the Mark I Lee-Metford carbine which was introduced in 1894. Manufactured by the Royal Small Arms Factory at Enfield Lock, Middlesex, it was a .303 calibre, breech-loading weapon with a bolt action and a six cartridge magazine. Its sights were adjustable for distances up to 2,000 yards which gave it a considerable effective range of fire. Its maximum range was 3,500 yards. The wooden stock of the rifle was hollow and housed cleaning equipment and a flask of gun oil. Unlike its infantry equivalent, it was not adapted to carry a bayonet. The carbine was 39.88 inches in length and weighed 7.43 pounds unloaded. This weapon was superseded in 1896 by the Lee-Enfield carbine, an improved version differing from the Lee-Metford by the type of rifling of the barrel made necessary by the introduction of the new smokeless powder cartridge. It was very similar to the Lee-Metford in all other respects.[52] The entire series of Lee-Enfield rifles and carbines were very accurate, very sturdy and reliable in all conditions. With periodic improvements and modifications, the Lee-Enfield served as the standard rifle of the British army until 1957.

The introduction of the smokeless powder cartridge in the British army in the 1890s was revolutionary in its way. No longer would the smoke of black powder rounds give away the position of the rifleman and no longer would the clouds of smoke from many weapons fired in concert obscure the targets at which they sought to aim. The new Lee-Enfield ball cartridge used in the cavalry carbine had a 'brass central fire case, and is charged with 30 grains of cordite, a smokeless compound of nitrocellulose and vaseline. The bullet is made of hardened lead, encased in copper nickel, and weighs 215 grams. The whole cartridge weighs 415 grams.'[53] The round when fired from the Lee-Enfield carbine had a velocity of 1,940 feet per second. In other words, it could travel a mile in less than three seconds, faster than the speed of sound. Its maximum range was about 3,500 yards or almost two miles. It was estimated that within its effective range, the bullet from this weapon could not be stopped by less than nine inches of brick wall, fourteen inches of sun-dried bricks, twenty-seven inches of oak or forty-eight inches of mounded clay.[54] Clearly it was no good hiding behind the bushes when facing the Lee-Enfield.

While trained in the use of carbines, cavalry officers carried revolvers. Churchill was armed with an 1892 model Webley-Wilkinson revolver which he purchased privately. It still survives and is now on display at the Cabinet War Rooms, Imperial War Museum in London. The Webley is a .455 calibre, six-shot, double action revolver with a four-inch barrel. It has a top-breaking, hinged frame design which means it is unhinged at the top for extracting expended cartridges and reloading. It was a sturdy, simple weapon and with variations it was the standard side-arm in the British army until the Webley Mark IV revolver was replaced in 1947 as obsolete.[55]

Although firearms were the primary weapons of the British cavalry, the officer of Hussars was also equipped with a more traditional weapon, the sabre. During his service with the 4th Hussars Churchill used two models of edged weapon, the light cavalry sword and the heavy cavalry sword. The former was in common use when Churchill was commissioned and it is the one he posed with for a series of studio photograph portraits in his full dress uniform upon his commissioning. The light cavalry pattern sword, or sabre, has a slightly curved steel blade thirty-five and one-half inches long and one and one-quarter inches wide, 'suitable for both cutting and thrusting'.[56] It weighs about two pounds. The sword grip is of wood covered in fish skin and bound with silver wire. The hand-grip was protected by a steel three-bar hilt. The scabbard was of steel, weighing about one pound three ounces with two rings for attachment to a sword belt. In June 1896, light cavalry officers, including hussars, were directed by army order to adopt the heavy cavalry pattern sword. It was similar to the light cavalry sword but was slightly heavier at two pounds, two ounces with a blade thirty-five and one-quarter inches long and one and one-eighth inch wide. The grip protection was a scroll bar made of steel. When photographed on horseback in India in 1897, Churchill was carrying the scroll-hilt, heavy cavalry pattern sword.[57] The cavalry swords of both patterns were much heavier than the épee Churchill fenced with at Harrow. Although fighting drill with the sword was a required part of his training, Churchill was never to use a sword in combat, relying instead on firearms.

Even as much of his attention and energy was given over to his training, Churchill was in his early period in the regiment very much concerned with how he would be judged by his fellow officers, every one of them his senior. There was a precedent in the 4th Hussars of some officers bullying others and even forcing out someone they found not to have the right stuff because they were not tough enough, were poor horsemen or had insufficient financial means. In 1894, a cabal of junior officers led by Lts Savory and Barnes forced out Lt George C. Hodge by a combination of physical bullying and a boycott. Hodge not only quit the regiment but resigned his commission and left the army. It is unlikely that Churchill would have been unaware of this episode which occurred only a year before his own arrival. Such bullying and ostracism could befall anyone who did not meet the subjective social standards of the mess by a failing of character or financial resources. And, to make matters worse, it appears that such practices were condoned by the senior officers who left the junior officers to sort such things out among themselves. A new officer was faced with the dilemma of either going along with the bullying and rudeness or becoming a victim of such treatment himself.

Churchill was determined to make a good impression and knew it would be up to him to succeed or fail on his own merits notwithstanding his well-known family name and the evident sponsorship of Colonel Brabazon. His chosen method of creating a good reputation for himself in the regiment was to apply his energies to doing well at his soldierly tasks, particularly riding. In the cavalry, even more than at Sandhurst, this was the key to social acceptance. In this Churchill was fortunate as he was a fine horseman and a hard worker.

The first day at the riding school left Churchill much the worse for wear after his two month layoff since Sandhurst. He wrote to Lady Randolph on 20 February: 'The riding school is fearfully severe and I suffer terribly from stiffness – but what with hot baths and *massage* I hope soon to be better. At present I can hardly walk.'[58] He stuck to the regimen, however, and by the 24th he was able to report that his condition was much improved and that he was moved up to a higher class in the riding school and expected to be released in only three months instead of the standard twelve. By the 22nd, less than a week after joining the regiment, he 'went out with the regiment ... to a route march – which was very fine. No one has ever been allowed out before until they have been 3 or 4 months in the riding school – so I established a precedent.'[59] On 2 March he wrote again to his mother, this time with growing confidence that he was finding acceptance among his fellow officers.

> Things have been going exceedingly well with me. I am making friends and many acquaintances. Everybody is very agreeable and I am beginning to find out exactly how I stand. This is the more satisfactory – as Col Brab has only just come down – so that I have found my footholds for myself.[60]

In fact, even with all the demands of training and squadron and regimental duties, the programme was not by any means overwhelming. He wrote to his brother Jack an outline of his schedule:

> The following is the daily routine: – as I have arranged it
>
> 7.30   Called
> 7.45   Breakfast in bed
> Papers, Letters, etc
> 8.45   Riding School – 2 hours
> 10.45 Hot Bath and massager
> 11.30 Carbine exercises – privately with a Sergeant to catch up a higher class
> 12 noon 'Stables'
> Lasts 1 hour. I have charge of 1 squadron 30 men and have to see the horses groomed – watered-fed & the men's rooms clean, etc.
> 1 o'clock
> Lunch is ready. It does not matter being late.
> 2.15   Drill.
> 1 hours nominally – but as I can't walk I get off at present after a half an hour – which is mostly spent in drilling the men myself. After which for the present – hot baths – medical rubber – Elliman's and doctor – until Mess at 8 – Bezique – 3d points. Bed.[61]

Stable duty was a central function of the regiment as it concerned the care and feeding of the horses and had to be carried out 365 days a year with no exceptions and no holidays. Horses unlike machines are never idle. The standard routine was for the horses to be groomed three times each day, in the morning between 6.30 and 7.30 a.m. in the winter months and between 6.00 and 7.00 a.m. in the summer, at noon after the morning drill and riding school was completed, and again in the evening between 5.00 and 6.00 p.m. According to regulations the horses were watered at least four times a day and fed with oats thrice daily with the morning and midday ration three pounds and the evening feeding of four pounds. The stables were cleared of bedding straw as part of the morning duty and the horses stood on bare floors during the day. A mixture of shaken-out old straw and new straw was spread out for the horses during the evening duty. The officers on duty for the day supervised all the stable duty. The noontime stable duty was witnessed by all officers not assigned to other duties.[62]

In addition to the care of the animals, there was constant work required to keep the stables and the horse furniture clean and in good repair. It was a matter of both duty and pride that all be kept in order. As Francis H. Maitland, an officer of the 19th Hussars, recalled in his memoirs: 'When every piece of headgear, saddlery, leather, steel, and every buckle, is polished, there is a real joy in the final result. To go into the stables, to stand at one end and glance down the long line of saddles meticulously placed on saddle-pegs, offers keen and unadulterated pleasure.'[63] Although not all officers or soldiers would agree, views such as Maitland's held by senior officers would certainly keep young officers and troopers busy at their tasks.

Like all other lieutenants in the regiment, Churchill took his turn on duty when in garrison under supervision of a field officer or captain serving that twenty-four-hour period as field officer of the day. When on such duty it was a lieutenant's job to inspect rations and forage before they were issued, be present at the relief of the guard details and to visit the barracks sentries periodically during the day and the night. He supervised the morning and evening duty in the stables. He was required during the duty tour to visit the other ranks' mess hall during meals and to receive any complaints. He was also obliged to make a report to the field officer of the day accounting for the presence or absence of the men, including any prisoners in cells, and further to present a report on any unusual events during his watch.[64] It was not arduous duty nor did one serve it daily. In fact Churchill often found the time in the leisurely routine of garrison life at Aldershot to spend weekends away from the barracks visiting London, Brighton, Harrow or any of a number of country houses from early March 1895, and after. He was even able to visit his mother in Paris for Easter. He had friends from Sandhurst visit for the weekend from time to time, extending to them the opportunity to visit the real army that Colonel Brabazon had given Churchill when he was a gentleman cadet.

When he was at Aldershot, however, the main preoccupation from dawn to dusk was horses. In the cavalry not only work was centred on horses, but also play. In early March 1895, Churchill was already learning to ride the steeplechase, a race run across country over a course with artificial ditches, walls and ledges for jumping. He was an active participant in the races, using borrowed horses until he could get his own. On 12 March he wrote to his mother: 'I have had the misfortune to smash myself up, while trying a horse on the steeplechase course. The animal refused and swerved – I tried to cram him in – and he took the wings. Very nearly did I break my leg – but as it is I am only bruised and very stiff. I shall be about again in two or three days. In the mean time everybody is very kind – so kind indeed that I am sure I have made a very good impression - (why should I not?)'[65] Lady Randolph considered steeplechasing far too dangerous a sport for her son, thinking it idiotic and that it could prove fatal. Churchill regarded this as 'rather an extreme view' and in reply to her concerns stated his intention to continue racing. 'Everybody here rides one or other of their chargers in the different military races which are constantly held ... In fact I rather think you are rather expected to do something that way – ride in the Regimental races at least.'[66] Other officers must have thought Churchill a good rider as Lt Savory invited him to ride one of his own charges in the Subaltern's Challenge Cup race, part of the Cavalry Brigade's annual Aldershot Races, on 20 March. This was a steeplechase over a course of two miles and five furlongs with regulation fences. There were five entries, all ridden by 4th Hussars subalterns. As he wrote his brother Jack after the race, it went well:

> I rode on Thursday in my first steeple chase-at the Aldershot races. One of our fellows had two horses running the Subalterns cup and could get no one to ride the second. So I said I would and did. It was very exciting and there is no doubt about it being dangerous. I had never jumped a regulation fence before and they are pretty big things as you know. Everybody in the regiment was awfully pleased at my riding more especially as I came in third. They thought it very sporting. I thought so too. It has done me a lot of good here and I think I may say I am popular with everybody. I rode under the name of Spencer as of course it was all put in the papers. No one will know however as I adopted a nom de guerre.[67]

While Churchill's performance as a rider was respectable, the behaviour of at least one of his fellow officers in organising the race was not. The race results published in the *Racing Calendar* the following day listed the order of the finish as follows:

Mr A. D. Francis' Surefoot	1	
Mr A. Savory's Lady Margaret	2	
Mr A. Savory's Traveller	3 (Mr Spencer)	
Mr R. W. R. Barnes' Tartina	–	

Mr H. Watkins' Dolly-do-Little   –
Mr A. Savory declared to win with Lady Margaret.
Won by six lengths; Dolly-do-Little fell.[68]

It appears that after the race it was discovered that Lt Francis's Sure-foot did not actually run the race but rather a 'ringer' was substituted for it without the identity of Francis's actual mount being placed on the race card. This was a matter of some importance as the odds on Surefoot were 6 to 1 against and the odds on Lady Margaret were 5 to 4 on. The odds for the race were based on the real Surefoot's reputation and the fact that Lady Margaret had won a regimental race the day before and was clearly the favourite. With a purse of £28 at stake the reason for the irregularity is readily apparent. This was not merely a prank but obvious fraud in violation of the National Hunt Rules. A year later the scandal was made public in the *Racing Calendar* of 20 February 1896:

> The attention of the Stewards of the National Hunt Committee having been called to certain irregularities in respect of the 4th Hussars Subalterns' Challenge Cup, run at the Cavalry Brigade Meeting at Aldershot, 1895 ... The race has been declared null and void, and all the horses which took part in the same are perpetually disqualified for all races under National Hunt Rules.[69]

It is not known whether Churchill was aware of the irregularity or whether his best friends in the regiment, Savory and Barnes, were participants. Nor is it recorded whether the young officers received sanctions from the army. It was certainly a black mark against them and the regiment. Churchill later stated in a letter to Lady Randolph that the National Hunt Committee sent the War Office 'a letter expressly vindicating us from any charge of dishonestly or dishonourable behaviour'.[70] Still, it was an awful public embarrassment from which Churchill was not protected by the use of a pseudonym.

Churchill's interest in equestrian sports was not limited to the steeplechase but extended to a form of racing known as point-to-point, a cross-county race not unlike a run over hunting country interspersed with obstacles for jumping. He wrote to Lady Randolph about one such race in which he rode on 23 April 1895:

> It was nothing like a steeple chase – being only a hunting run – and not a fast one – but it was a ripping line – 49 fences. Out of 13 starters only 5 got round – I was 4th being beautifully mounted. No one was hurt in the least – though more than half took tosses. It was not the least dangerous and did me a lot of good in the regiment. All the subalterns rode ... I am getting on very well here and all is very satisfactory. When I see how some fellows who are disliked are

treated I feel very thankful I have been so fortunate as to make my own friends and generally find my footing. Altogether, my dearest Mamma, I am having a really good time and enjoying life immensely.[71]

It is likely in writing this letter that Churchill had in mind the treatment of Lt Alan George Cameron Bruce who had passed out of Sandhurst with Churchill and received his commission on 6 March 1895. When it became known in the spring of 1895 that Bruce intended to join the 4th Hussars, a group of subalterns in the regiment, including Churchill, tried to keep him out. It is not clear why they formed a strongly unfavourable opinion of Bruce or who was the leader of those opposing his joining the regiment. It is known he was in the September 1893 intake at Sandhurst with Churchill, and it is not unlikely that it was either Churchill's dislike of Bruce or Churchill's report of the unfavourable opinion of others that led to the opposition to Bruce. Before joining, Bruce was invited by Lt Barnes to dine at the Nimrod Club in London where Churchill was a member. In attendance were Lts Savory, Francis, Walker and Churchill. At the dinner Bruce was frankly informed that he was not welcome in the 4th Hussars. He was told that his income of £500 per annum was inadequate to meet the standards of the regiment. If Churchill joined in this assertion it was certainly hypocritical and cynical for him to do so as his own income was considerably less. Perhaps he was only going along with the others as he was the junior of the officers in the group opposing Bruce and the newest to the regiment. And it is known that Churchill had nothing to do with the bullying and mistreatment of Lt George C. Hodge which forced that officer to resign the previous year.

Churchill seems to have entered the regiment at a time when bullying and boycotting unpopular officers was an accepted practice among his colleagues and one condoned by the commanding officer. In the event, Bruce did join the regiment in April 1895, and was thereafter boycotted by certain of his colleagues. He had a difficult year which included a reprimand from his squadron leader for using abusive language to the troops of his squadron and a further allegation of swearing at a non-commissioned officer of another cavalry regiment during an inter-regimental shooting competition at Bisley. Finally, he was accused of improper conduct in visiting the sergeants' mess on Boxing Day and was asked by the colonel to resign. He did so in January 1896, leaving both the 4th Hussars and the army. Such harassment, including the co-operation of the commanding officer, when viewed from a civilian perspective, seems very discreditable. When the Bruce matter became public knowledge in early 1896 it caused a scandal that very nearly ruined Churchill's career.[72]

It was during this busy spring season of 1895 that Churchill discovered polo, about which he declared, 'It is the finest game in the world and I should almost be content to give up any ambition to play it well and often.'[73] From mid-April 1895, when the season began, Churchill practised at polo as often as he could. This required the expenditure of additional funds. In addition to keeping two chargers, a cavalry officer was expected to have his own string of polo ponies. With his own and his mother's funds exhausted, in May he borrowed £100 from Messrs Cox & Co. to buy the ponies. It is not recorded how many ponies he purchased at that time or of what quality they were but with only £100 to spend – less than half the cost of his best charger – they must have been a bargain. With his own ponies he was able to devote much energy and attention to polo. On 24 July he wrote to Lady Randolph: 'Polo forms my principal amusement and I really think I am improving very fast. I have already been put in the subaltern's team and we have lots of very amusing matches.'[74]

As the summer of 1895 progressed, Churchill was busy, his days filled with sports, social visits and military duties. He was comfortable in his work and also with his reputation in the regiment. He was becoming more and more independent. He wrote to Lady Randolph on 6 July:

> At present I regard the regiment entirely as my headquarters – and if I go up to London for a couple of days – I always look forward to coming back to my friends and ponies here. I am getting on extraordinarily well and when I see how short a time those who don't get on, stay, I feel that it is very fortunate that I do. I have a great many friends and I know my ground, I don't think anybody realises who does not know – how important a day in one's life is the day one first joins a regiment. If you aren't liked you have to go and that means going through life with a very unpleasant stigma.[75]

In the space of four months, Churchill had found his place in the society of real men and had done so on the basis of his own efforts.

The rhythms of army life took over with each day much like the next. There were the routines of stable duty, the supervision of the troops in drill and musketry instruction and the annual cycles of training and inspections. The annual inspection of the Inspector General of the Army, Major General Combe, was made on 25 June and the annual inspection of the Inspector General of Cavalry, Major General Luck, was held on 15 August.[76] By early August, the regiment was spending increasing amounts of time in the field. 'We have field days all day and every day,' he wrote

Lady Randolph on 3 August: 'Very often ten hours in the saddle at a time – without anything to eat or drink the whole time – and after that I invariably play polo for a couple of hours. However I must say I thrive on the treatment.'[77]

Yet, fully as his time was employed, something was missing for Churchill. It may have been the product of boredom or just a reaction to the repetition and routine of military life at Aldershot. Quite possibly it was his first inkling that the army was simply not big enough to hold his interest or challenge his mind. After reading about a political speech by his cousin Charles ('Sunny'), the Ninth Duke of Marlborough, his thoughts turned to his own hopes for a career in politics. He wrote to Lady Randolph from Aldershot on 16 August 1895:

> It is a fine game to play – the game of politics – and is well worth waiting for a good hand – before really plunging. At any rate – four years of healthy and pleasant existence – combined with both responsibility and discipline – can do no harm to me – but rather good. The more I see of soldiering – the more I like it – but the more I feel convinced it is not my métier.[78]

It was clear after only six months' service in the army that Churchill's heart was not in it. The army would only be a brief stop-over on the road to a career in politics. Toward the end of August he realised that the military life was having a depressing effect on him. He accurately diagnosed both the cause and effect in a letter to his mother on 24 August:

> I find I am getting into a state of mental stagnation when even letter writing becomes an effort and when any reading but that of monthly magazines is impossible. This is of course quite in accordance with the spirit of the army. It is indeed the result of mental forces called into being by discipline and routine. It is a state of mind into which all or nearly all who soldier – fall. From this 'slough of Despond' I try to raise myself by reading and re-reading Papa's speeches many of which I almost know by heart – but I really cannot find the energy to read any other serious work.[79]

Within a week of that letter he had begun to form the remedy for his mental stagnation. He decided, after much thought, to extend his own intellectual horizons with a course of self-education by reading, calling it,

> the sort of mental medicine I need ... You see all my life – I have had a purely technical education. Harrow, Sandhurst, James's were all devoted to studies of which the highest aim was to pass some approaching Examinations. As a result my mind has never received that polish which for instance Oxford or

Cambridge gives. At these places one studies questions and sciences with a rather higher object than mere practical utility. One receives in fact a liberal education.[80]

With this in mind he began his reading with Henry Fawcett's *Manual of Political Economy* and set his sights on *The Decline and Fall of the Roman Empire* by Edward Gibbon and Lecky's *European Morals*. His resolution to improve his mind and his prospects was firm. He was to pursue what has been called his 'private university' for the balance of his army years wherever he was stationed. This dogged effort to improve himself set him aside from many of his fellow officers whose ambitions were not focused beyond an army career.

On 9 September 1895, after completion of the cavalry divisional drills at Aldershot, the 4th Hussars left the cavalry brigade there and marched to Hounslow barracks ten miles west of London. Part of the regiment under the command of Major Kincaid-Smith had its outquarters at Hampton Court, and the other part was outquartered at Kensington under the command of Captain J. W. Underwood. The regiment would remain headquartered at Hounslow until its posting to India the following year.[81]

Hounslow Heath had been a traditional place for drilling troops at least since the seventeenth century. King James II held inspections and reviews of troops there and Oliver Cromwell is said to have used it as a site for gathering his forces. Permanent cavalry barracks were built there beginning in 1783 and, even after the heath decreased in size following the Enclosures Act of 1812 and the expansion of urban London, it remained a key military facility into the early twentieth century. It generally served as a cavalry station providing a reserve for the Household Brigade and also as a transit barracks for regiments headed abroad.[82] The cavalry barracks remain to this day on Beavers Lane just a few blocks from the Hounslow West station of the London Underground. It was within easy commuting distance of his mother's home at 35a Cumberland Place.

The regimental pace at Hounslow was even less time-consuming than it had been at Aldershot. With the exception of an inspection of the regiment by the Commander of the Home District, Major General Lord Methuen, on 20 September 1895, all was routine. Much time was given over to social functions and it appeared the autumn would pass uneventfully as the annual training cycle was at an end and the period of several months of winter leave for officers was fast approaching.

4

The Cuban Insurrection

During the autumn of 1895 Churchill was faced with the imminent need to decide what to do and where to go on his annual leave – a period that possibly could be even more idle than garrison duty at Hounslow. By the end of September he was notified he would be required to take his leave between 24 October and 8 January. Facing 'a solid block of two and a half months' uninterrupted repose,' Churchill later wrote, 'I searched the world for some scene of adventure or excitement.'[1]

In the days of rather relaxed garrison life in England in the late 1890s, Colonel Brabazon divided the regiment's year into a summer session of seven months' duration for training and manoeuvres and a five-month winter season during which officers could take extended periods of leave. Many spent the winter months hunting in the English countryside, a pleasant but expensive pursuit. In fact, hunting was encouraged for cavalry officers and was an excellent supplement to formal training. Riding to foxhounds or harriers provided good practice in horsemanship, managing a horse at a gallop across open country and learning to use the terrain to advantage.[2]

Churchill did not have funds for the hunting season because of his limited income and the fact he had exhausted his reserves equipping himself for the service and buying polo ponies. These circumstances, combined with his irrepressible nature, led him to an idea for travel that could provide both adventure and professional advancement – he would go to the Spanish colony of Cuba in the Caribbean Sea where imperial troops were engaged in an expanding campaign to crush a rebel insurgency. The plan was, he thought, 'so excellent I cannot cease commending myself for it'.[3] Here was a way to find excitement abroad at relatively little expense and at the same time witness warfare about which Lt Churchill was both personally and professionally most curious:

From very early youth I had brooded about soldiers and war, and often I had imagined in dreams and day-dreams the sensations attendant upon being for the first time under fire. It seemed to my youthful mind that it must be a thrilling and immense experience to hear the whistle of bullets all around and to play at hazard from moment to moment with death and wounds. Moreover, now that I had assumed professional obligations in the matter, I thought it might be as well to have a private rehearsal, a secluded trial trip, in order to make sure the ordeal was one not unsuited to my temperament.[4]

Such a trip would also give him an opportunity for active service and, perhaps, even a chance to distinguish himself. In the mid-1890s very few of the junior officers of the British army had seen war service. When Churchill joined the 4th Hussars, only five of the twenty-five officers had seen active service. Colonel Brabazon was not only the senior officer but also the most experienced in campaigning. He had served in the Ashanti War (1874), the Second Afghan War (1878–80), the Egyptian Expedition (1884) and the Sudan Expedition (1884–5). Major Peters and Captain Kincaid-Smith had served in the Sudan Expedition and Captain Starkey had been with the Egyptian Expedition (1885–7).[5]

None of the eleven subalterns had been in combat. They envied the more senior officers for their campaign medals, their experience and the stories and tales told in the mess. Most officers of the time sought active service, often taking leave from their regimental duties to do so. As Churchill wrote in *My Early Life*:

It was the swift road to promotion and advancement in every army. It was the glittering gateway to distinction ... Prowess at polo, in the hunting-field, or between the flags might count for something. But the young soldier who had been 'on active service' and 'under fire' had aura about him to which the Generals he served under, the troopers he led, and the girls he courted, accorded a unanimous, sincere, and spontaneous recognition.'[6]

In those distant Victorian days, and from the perspective of the British officer, war was a very different business from what we think of now with the benefit of hindsight and the collective memory of the horrors of two world wars, the Holocaust and the Cold War. The British army's campaigns of the nineteenth century between the Crimean War and the Boer War were many, but mostly on a small scale and of relatively brief duration. Nearly all were fought against less well-armed native armies or bands. 'This kind of war was full of fascinating thrills. It was not like the Great War. Nobody expected to get killed.' The chance of being killed 'was only a sporting element in a splendid game', Churchill wrote.[7] It was a time when the concept of glory in battle was accepted and it was a plausible ambition to set out to become a war hero.[8] Churchill first shared his idea for a venture to Cuba with a fellow officer from the 4th Hussars, Lt

Reginald W. R. Barnes, who agreed to go along. Churchill described Barnes as 'a good friend of mine ... who is one of the senior subalterns and acting adjutant of the regiment & very steady'.[9] Barnes had been commissioned on 10 May 1893, and was fourth in seniority among the lieutenants in the regiment.[10]

Barnes and Churchill discussed their proposal in the mess and received the support of their fellow officers, including Colonel Brabazon. Their plan to go as observers to an active war zone 'was considered as good or almost as good as a season's serious hunting, without which no subaltern or captain was considered to be living a respectable life.'[11] Churchill's next steps indicated how well connected he was both socially and politically. Starting with the Cuban adventure and ever afterwards, Churchill methodically and unhesitatingly exploited his and his family's considerable contacts in the government to seek advantage for his own plans and ambitions. Whether on duty or on leave, he constantly moved in the aristocratic circles of society, meeting and socialising with government ministers, senior army officers, diplomats and powerful politicians. These contacts were available to him by virtue of his family's prestige and also by the skills and connections of his mother. Such doors were not open to many junior army officers even though the army was home to many sons of the aristocracy in the late nineteenth century. Personal influence and the use of social and professional contacts was simply the method of getting things done. It was especially important to someone like Churchill who was just beginning a career and had not yet had the opportunity to display his talents and abilities. To his credit, he always sought the influence and assistance of family and friends to get into battle and never to avoid it.

After he obtained his commanding officer's permission to use leave time to go to Cuba, Churchill wrote to an old friend of Lord Randolph, Sir Henry Drummond Wolff, then serving as British Ambassador to Spain. From Wolff he requested help in obtaining the permission of the Spanish government for himself and Lt Barnes to go to Cuba. Wolff did his work well and by 8 October 1895, he was able to obtain a letter from the Duke of Tetuan, the Spanish Foreign Minister, introducing the two British officers to Marshal Arsenio Martínez de Campos, the Captain-General of the Spanish army who was then in command of Spanish forces in Cuba. Martínez de Campos was a former prime minister and minister of war, a very important person indeed. A letter to him could work wonders. Wolff also obtained a letter of introduction for Churchill and Barnes from General Azcarraga of the Ministry of War.[12] The letters were the Spanish consent and stamp of approval to the subalterns' venture and they owed much to Ambassador Wolff. He also obtained a letter for Churchill from Sir Donald MacKenzie Wallace, head of the foreign department of *The Times*, giving him an introduction to Mr Akers, their correspondent in Cuba.[13] This could be very useful, as journalists are often good sources of information abroad. It is their job to be in the know. It was not the first time Wolff had lent his assistance to Churchill. He had, after all, provided the transport section for Winston's toy-soldier army years before.

Next Churchill went to see Field Marshal Lord Wolseley, the Commander-in-Chief of the British army who, perhaps luckily for Churchill, had succeeded the Duke of Cambridge in that office in 1895. Wolseley was very friendly and his support of the expedition to Cuba all but guaranteed that Churchill and Barnes would receive the permission of the War Office to go. The field marshal did not stop with arrangements for Cuba, for as Churchill wrote in a letter to his mother on 19 October: 'Wolseley also said that if I worked at the military profession he would help me in every way he could & that I was always to come and ask when I wanted anything.'[14] Such a statement reflects that Churchill truly had access and influence unlike other second lieutenants; this is not how the army usually works. Perhaps the field marshal felt some kinship with the young Churchill. In 1894 he had written a two-volume biography of John Churchill, First Duke of Marlborough, the lieutenant's illustrious ancestor.

At Wolseley's suggestion, Churchill next contacted General E. F. Chapman, Director of Military Intelligence for the British army. Chapman provided maps and background information on the situation in Cuba. In exchange, 'We are also requested to collect information and statistics on various points & particularly as to the effect of the new bullet – its penetration and striking power. This invests our mission with almost an official character & cannot fail to help me in the future.'[15] He had not only got official permission to go to Cuba but also an official purpose for the trip. In addition to returning with information useful to the British army, Churchill had plans for souvenirs of his own. 'I shall bring back a great many Havana cigars – some of which can be 'laid down' in the cellars at 35 Great Cumberland Place.'[16] Contrary to popular belief, Churchill did not discover tobacco for the first time in Cuba. He had smoked cigarettes on occasion at least from the age of seventeen and enjoyed cigars on his visit to New York City en route to Cuba in 1895.

One permission Churchill neglected to request was that of Lady Randolph. He wrote to her from Hounslow on 4 October, only after the plan was well in the works. She responded: 'You know I am always delighted if you can do anything which interests & amuses you – even if it be a sacrifice to me ... Considering that I provide the funds I think instead of saying "I have decided to go" it may have been nicer & perhaps wiser – to have begun by consulting me. But I suppose experience of life will in time teach you that tact is a very essential ingredient in all things.'[17] Nevertheless, she too had been won over and offered to buy his steamer ticket as a birthday present. She also put him in touch with friends and family in her native New York who could look after the young officers there, the first stop on their voyage to the Caribbean.

A final step before departing was for Churchill to contact the *Daily Graphic*, a London newspaper, to secure employment as a special correspondent. In those days it was not unusual for newspapers and magazines to accept articles from abroad for publication. In fact, Churchill's father had sent a number of letters from South Africa to the *Daily Graphic* which were printed in 1891. This was to be Churchill's first writing for pay and the agreed price was five guineas for each letter from the war zone in Cuba. This was the true beginning of Churchill's career as a journalist, an important foundation stone for his later career as a politician, for not only did the arrangement to write newspaper articles from Cuba help to defray the expenses of the expedition, it served to place his name before the public. From Cuba to India to the Sudan and on to South Africa, his exploits as a soldier were made known by his efforts as a war correspondent.

Lieutenants Churchill and Barnes left from Liverpool on 2 November 1895, on the Cunard Line's Royal Mail Steamship *Etruria*.[18] It was Churchill's first Atlantic crossing and unfortunately it was a stormy, rough passage. The accommodation was comfortable enough but there was little to do on board, the deck being too wet for sitting outside, and he found the passage and his fellow passengers rather boring. 'I do not contemplate ever taking a sea voyage for pleasure & I shall always look upon journeys by sea as necessary evils – which have to be undergone in the carrying out of any definite plan.'[19]

The RMS *Etruria* docked in New York at midday on 9 November. It was Churchill's first visit to the United States and he got the red-carpet treatment, American-style, from his host Bourke Cockran, a close friend of his American relatives. Churchill wrote to his Brooklyn-born mother: 'What an extraordinary people the Americans are! Their hospitality is a revelation to me and they make you feel at home and at ease in a way that I have never before experienced.'[20] Cockran, a member of Congress and noted Tammany

Hall orator, had the young officers stay at his home at 763 Fifth Avenue in Manhattan and arranged such a schedule of activities and social invitations that the stay in New York was extended from three days to nine. Their calendar was busy with dinners, evenings on the town and visits to the Brooklyn Bridge, a horse show, a criminal trial in court, and even the fire department. On the 10th they dined with the Cornelius Vanderbilts. Churchill's cousin, Charles Spencer Churchill, known as Sunny, who had become the Ninth Duke of Marlborough in 1892, was married to Consuelo Vanderbilt in New York only a week earlier and they were there as well. On Monday, 11 November, Churchill and Barnes were given a tug-boat ride in New York harbour, made a tour of the forts and barracks of Atlantic Military District headquarters and inspected the US navy cruiser *New York*. Churchill noted, 'I was much struck by the sailors: their intelligence, their good looks and civility and their generally businesslike appearance. These interested me more than [the] ship itself, for while any nation can build a battleship – it is the monopoly of the Anglo-Saxon race to breed good seamen.'[21] The following day they were given a guided tour of 'the American Sandhurst', the United States Military Academy at West Point, located on the Hudson river north of New York City. Churchill judged that it did not compare favourably to its British counterpart. He wrote to his brother on 15 November:

I am sure you will be horrified by some of the Regulations of the Military Academy. The cadets enter from 19–22 & stay 4 years. This means that they are most of them 24 years of age. They are not allowed to smoke or have any money in their possession nor are they given any leave except 2 months after the 1st two years. In fact they have far less liberty than any private school boys in our country. I think such a state of things is positively disgraceful and young men of 24 or 25 who would resign their personal liberty to such an extent can never make good citizens or fine soldiers. A child who rebels against that sort of control should be whipped – so should a man who does not rebel.[22]

Although he would not trade places with a West Point cadet, Churchill had no complaints about the welcome he received there, recalling years later: 'I was not twenty at the time of the Cuban War, and only a Second Lieutenant, but I was taken to an inspection at West Point and treated as if I had been a General.'[23]

Churchill's first impressions of the United States were generally favourable and perceptive. He wrote to his brother:

This is a very great country my dear Jack. Not pretty or romantic but great and utilitarian. There seems to be no such thing as reverence or tradition. Every-thing is eminently practical and things are judged from the matter of fact standpoint ... Picture to yourself the American people as a great lusty youth who treads on all your sensibilities perpetrates every possible horror of ill manners – whom neither age [nor] just tradition inspire with reverence – but who moves about his affairs with a good hearted freshness which may well be the envy of older nations of the earth.'[24]

Churchill was greatly impressed by Bourke Cockran and they developed a friendship that lasted some twenty years. Writing in 1932, Churchill said of him: 'I must record the strong impression which this remarkable man made upon my un-tutored mind. I have never seen his like, or in some respects his equal ... It was not my fortune to hear any of his orations, but his conversation, in point, in pith, in rotundity, in antithesis, and in comprehension, exceeded anything I have ever heard.'[25] In later years Churchill told the American politician Adlai Stevenson that he patterned his own public-speaking style on that of Cockran: 'It was an American statesman who inspired me when I was 19 & taught me how to use every note of the human voice like an organ.'[26]

Churchill admired Cockran not only for his oratory and the friendship shown toward his new acquaintance but also for his hospitality. Certainly Cockran had taken good care of the English visitors in New York. He also made the arrangements for their journey to Florida with a private stateroom on the train. Their whirlwind visit over, Churchill and Barnes left New York on Sunday morning, 17 November. They passed through Philadelphia, Washington and Savannah and arrived in Tampa, Florida in the evening of the 18th. The next day they embarked on the steamer *Olivette* for the passage to Havana where they arrived on the morning of 20 November 1895.

As the ship sailed into Havana harbour under the shadow of the El Morro fortress, Churchill sensed that ahead was an adventure right out of *Treasure Island* or *The Boy's Own Paper*. He was moving into unfamiliar territory and toward uncharted realms of experience. 'Here was a place where real things were going on. Here was a scene of vital action. Here was a place where anything might happen. Here was a place where something certainly would happen. Here I might leave my bones.'[27]

Cuba, then fighting for its independence, had been under Spanish control with only a temporary interruption since Christopher Columbus claimed it for King Ferdinand and Queen Isabella in 1492.[28] Referred to by the Spanish as 'The Pearl of the Antilles', it was a large island of some 44,000 square miles, larger than Scotland and Wales combined. It was a tropical island with a rainy season from April to October which brought a slow-down in most activities. The main export was sugar refined from cane and the United States was its primary customer. The United States had long been interested in acquiring Cuba for itself and events there were closely followed by the government in Washington and by the American press, where opinion was strongly against Spain.

There had been a series of unsuccessful uprisings in the early nineteenth century culminating in 'La Guerra Grande' (1868–78). That failed rebellion was ended by the Treaty of Zanjón which left Cuban sovereignty in Spanish hands in exchange for the promise of political and agrarian reforms. After Zanjón, many of the rebel leaders left the country. José Marti went into exile in the United States while Máxmo Gómez and the most influential black insurgent leader, Antoneo Maceo, went to Santo Domingo. For years the exiles plotted a return to Cuba and a renewal of the rebellion. Their umbrella organisation, the Cuban Revolutionary Party or PRC, issued a manifesto in March 1895, which was a call to arms not only to win independence from Spain but also for a social revolution among the Cubans themselves, for land reform, racial equality and a redistribution of wealth and power.[29] By the end of March, Maceo had returned to Cuba at Baracoa on the north-east coast and by 11 April, Gómez and Marti arrived at Playitas near the eastern tip of the island. Military operations were soon commenced. The insurgent tactics were to attack crops and industry, and to harass the Spanish troops and loyalist militia. The strategy was to so exhaust Spain economically that it would abandon the island. The fighting soon settled into classic guerrilla warfare with the rebels in control of the countryside and the army in control of the cities and towns. The rebels, estimated to have a peak strength of from 25,000 to 40,000, were organised into small units, very dependent on the good will and intelligence lent to them by the populace. They utilised hit-and-run tactics, avoiding set piece battles when possible, focusing their attacks on lines of communication and economic targets.[30]

In early 1895, the Spanish government had approximately 20,000 troops in Cuba supported by thousands of loyalist Cuban militiamen. Its response to the latest insurrection was to dispatch 30,000 reinforcements under the command of Marshal Martínez de Campos, the veteran general who had been the victor in the earlier ten years war. Unfortunately, his tactics, based on his earlier experience, were defensive and reactive in nature. They proved to be completely unsuitable to the new realities. His goal was to isolate the insurgency in the eastern Oriente province where it was strongest, to institute political reforms, and to seek a compromise settlement by negotiation much as he had done in 1878. With his head-quarters first set up in Santiago de Cuba on the south coast he ordered reinforcement of a vast *troche* or path, running fifty miles from north to south, cleared of vegetation and supported by a railway and a series of outposts and blockhouses.

The *trochas*, one in Santa Clara province and another in the west between Mariel and Mayana, were formidable obstacles up to two hundred yards wide, comprising lines of downed trees and brush, barbed-wire entanglements, land mines, searchlights and sentry towers. They were the precursors of the static lines of the Western Front in the First World War. Intended to pen in the rebels at the ends of the island, they served instead to tie down thousands of Spanish troops needed to man them. The insurgents continued to move through and around the *trochas* and to operate in every province.[31]

By the summer of 1895, the eastern third of the island was in revolt and 10,000 Spanish soldiers were sent to try to subdue the troubles. The rebels were expanding their area of control and also organising politically, declaring Cuban independence on 15 July 1895. To make matters worse for Marshal Campos, Madrid failed to support his proposed reforms and instructed him instead to pursue a military solution. This was not surprising since the reforms promised in the 1878 peace treaty had never been implemented. At the same time, the insurgents stated their refusal even to negotiate with the Spaniards.

By the time Churchill and Barnes arrived on the scene in November 1895, Spanish reinforcements had more than doubled the size of their army in the field but Spain was nonetheless steadily losing control of the situation. By autumn, Gómez's and Maceo's forces were already operating west of the *trocha* in Camagüey province and Campos had moved his headquarters over 200 miles west to the safety of Santa Clara in the province of that name. The war at that point was one of hide-and-seek, with much manoeuvring but little fighting.

Arriving at Havana that November morning, Churchill and Barnes made prompt use of their letters of introduction from the government in Madrid. 'The letters I have got are a free pass everywhere – and they allowed us to bring our pistols through the Customs as soon as we showed them these letters – in spite of the law being very strict on that point.'[32] In Havana they saw no indication that the war had reached the capital and made it their first order of business to sample the local delicacies – oranges and cigars. They registered at the Gran Hotel Inglaterra, a 'convenient' four-storey hotel with a balustraded roof and a private balcony for each room on the front façade facing the palm trees of the Parque Central across the street. It is still in service at time of writing, the flag of an independent Cuba displayed above the entrance and a red-and-turquoise electric sign on its second storey announcing it as the Hotel Inglaterra. Then they met British Consul-General Alexander Gollan who accompanied them to the offices of the Spanish military authorities. There they reported in and again presented their letters. Although their visit was strictly unofficial, they were well received, the Spanish apparently viewing their mission as a gesture by Great Britain in support of Spain in Cuba. This assured that they would receive every consideration during their stay.

As it happened, Marshal Campos was not in Havana that day but some 150 miles to the east, inspecting troops in Santa Clara. A cable was sent to Campos informing him the British officers had arrived and plans were made for them to meet him the next day. Churchill was anxious to get to the war zone to see some fighting. He also wanted to get out of Havana because so little reliable information was available there. He did not find the official line trustworthy and wrote in a letter to his mother: 'Inaccuracy – exaggeration – and gratuitous falsehood are the main characteristics of the information received through Spanish sources.'[33] Nor did he trust local Cuban sources who were more kindly disposed to the rebels as, 'It was explained to me that while the Spanish authorities are masters of the art of suppressing the truth, the Cubans are adept at inventing falsehood. By this arrangement conflicting statements and inaccuracy are alike assured.'[34] As always, he wanted to see for himself and to form his own judgments. With a soldier's training and the correspondent's brief he was well suited to the task.

On the evening of 20 November in Havana he witnessed a unit of volunteer Cuban militia returning from garrison duty in the eastern provinces. They appeared tired and filthy and did not march to British standards but he found them well armed. The militiamen, numbering some 25,000, were Cubans fighting on the side of the Spanish government. Their simple, practical white cotton outfits and broad-brimmed straw hats were the same uniforms worn by the Spanish forces. These men were returning from the combat zone and Churchill and Barnes wasted little time in setting out in that direction themselves.

On the morning of Thursday, 21 November, the lieutenants boarded a train with the intention of meeting Marshal Campos at his headquarters. The journey through Havana and Matanzas provinces was relatively uneventful but the further they ventured the more evidence of the insurrection was apparent. Starting at Colon in the middle of Matanzas province all the railroad stations were fortified against attack. Every bridge was defended by a blockhouse as bridges and trains were favourite insurgent targets in their drive to cut communications and isolate the Spanish forces. As the train moved eastward into Santa Clara province, a pilot engine and an armoured carriage filled with troops were added to the train. This was Churchill's first experience with an armoured train; it would not be his last.

At Santa Domingo, they were advised that the line to their destination, Santa Clara, had been cut. The last train to leave before theirs had been derailed at a sabotaged culvert a few miles from the town. Fifteen soldiers were injured but their commander, General of Division Suarez Valdez, survived and continued on foot with his remaining troops. Barnes and Churchill continued by train on an alternate route via Cruces, finally arriving late in the day at Marshal Campos's headquarters in Santa Clara.

They were warmly welcomed by the marshal who issued additional letters and passes to them and placed at their disposal an English-speaking staff officer with the not unusual name in Latin America of Juan O'Donnell. He was none other than the son of the Duke of Tetuan, the Spanish Foreign Minister whose letter of introduction to the marshal they had just presented. This was a fortunate arrangement for now the lieutenants had someone of their own rank to question and learn from. It was O'Donnell's advice that the best way to see some fighting was to join a mobile column of troops out in the countryside. General Valdez's column was the nearest but it was already twenty miles from Santa Clara, half-way to its destination, the town of Sancti Spiritus off to the south-east. Churchill and Barnes, realising the column of infantry was only a day's march ahead of them, proposed to ride out on horseback to catch up. But the Cuban countryside was not the plains of Berkshire. 'Our young Spaniard shook his head: "You would not get 5 miles." "Where, then, are the enemy?" we asked. "They are everywhere and nowhere," he replied. "Fifty horsemen can go where they please – two cannot go anywhere." '[35] It was decided that a more prudent route would be by train to Cienfuegos on the south coast, then by boat to the town of Tuna, then again by train to Sancti Spiritus in the interior. The indirect approach was an indication that the insurgents controlled much of the countryside of central Santa Clara province, even by day. The railway line from the coast of Tuna to Sancti Spiritus was considered secure as it was dotted with blockhouses and patrolled by armoured trains. On 22 November they set out on their journey and reached Tuna without incident, only to find they had missed the daily train to Sancti Spiritus. Disappointment abated when the news came in at midday that the train they had failed to catch had been halted when the rebels dynamited a bridge and closed the line. The train was fired upon and attacked with a dynamite bomb and had to return to Tuna for the night. It was a stroke of luck for them to have missed the train - a rare case of unpunctuality rewarded for Churchill.

Churchill's first letter for the *Daily Graphic* was written on 22 November and date-lined Cienfuegos. In it he reported his first impressions from Havana and Santa Clara and a review of the insurgents' strategy and goals, the latter based on his discussions with the Spanish staff officers.[36] He realised that the economic warfare being waged by Gómez's rebels was wreaking havoc:

> The insurrection shows no signs of abating, and the insurgents gain adherents continually. There is no doubt that they possess the sympathy of the entire population, and hence have constant and accurate intelligence. On the other hand Spain is equally determined to crush them, and even now is pouring in fresh troops by the thousand. How it will end it is impossible to say, but whoever wins, and whatever may be the results, the suffering and misery of the entire community is certain.[37]

The destruction of the sugar-cane crop was threatened by the rebels and this he knew was the key to the island's domestic economy and its export profits. The threat highlighted the rebels' strength in Cuba by which they hoped to 'obtain recognition as belligerents from the United States – and by plunging the country into indescribable woe to procure the intervention of some European Power.'[38] In this Churchill correctly discerned the rebels' policy which proved to be successful. The United States recognised the rebels in March 1896. In the event, therefore, it was not the intervention of a European power that defeated Spain in Cuba but the intervention of the United States – its first step on the way to becoming not only a regional power but a world power.

After an overnight stay in Tuna, Churchill and Barnes took the train over the repaired line to Sancti Spiritus arriving on Saturday, 23 November. It had taken them three days to reach their destination. The Tuna to Sancti Spiritus line was heavily fortified and, although only thirty miles in length, had a blockhouse or small fort almost every mile. Twelve hundred soldiers were assigned to guard the line and the trains were sheathed in boiler-plate armour and filled with soldiers and militiamen. Even so, as the previous day's events gave witness, it was not a secure line. Only a week earlier the rebels had assaulted and taken one of the forts on the line, captured the fifty Spanish defenders and taken their weapons. There were unmistakable signs that the tide was turning against Spain.

They found Sancti Spiritus to be an isolated small town suffering from smallpox and yellow fever epidemics. It was then virtually besieged, with an estimated fifteen or twenty thousand rebels in the vicinity with outposts within several hundred yards of the town. Not long after Churchill's arrival, General Suarez's column marched in and the English officers had a chance to see his troops. They were dressed in dirty white cotton uniforms and straw hats and carrying knapsacks, crossed bandoliers of ammunition and German Mauser rifles. The column consisted of about 2,400 infantrymen divided into four battalions, two cavalry squadrons with a total of 300 mounted troops, and an artillery battery carried on mules.[39] Barnes and Churchill reported to General Suarez who was expecting them and made them welcome:

> He explained, through an interpreter, what an honour it was for him to have two distinguished representatives of a great and friendly Power attached to his column, and how greatly he valued the moral support which this gesture of Great Britain implied. We said, back through the interpreter, that it was awfully kind of him, and that we were sure it would be awfully jolly. The interpreter worked this up into something quite good, and the General looked much pleased.[40]

They were provided with horses and orderlies and invited to join the column and to be billeted with the staff officers. Once again the letters of introduction had proved their worth and the Englishmen had benefited from the Spanish wish to read more into their presence than the facts merited. They were shown to their quarters and given necessary and practical advice on sentries and passwords in the operational area:

> It was explained to me that when challenged by any sentry or outpost it was necessary to answer very sharply. If, by a process of deduction which Sherlock Holmes himself might envy, you arrive at the conclusion the outpost is Spanish, you answer 'Spain'; if, on the other hand, you think it is a rebel post, you reply 'Free Cuba'; but if you make a mistake it is likely to be very awkward.[41]

Writing his second letter for the *Daily Graphic* from Sancti Spiritus, Churchill again reported his impression of the widespread popular support for the insurgency. 'The more I see of Cuba the more I feel sure that the demand for independence is natural and unanimous. The insurgent forces contain the best blood in the island, and can by no possible perversion of the truth be classified as *banditti*. In fact, it is a war, not a rebellion.'[42] Knowing the rebels had broad popular support, knowing their intelligence about loyalist troop movements was accurate and detailed, and knowing it was not possible to tell rebel from peasant by appearance alone, he went to his bunk that night confident tomorrow he would be out in the countryside with the Spanish column and might see action for the first time in the company of what might well be the losing side of the conflict.

The next morning, 24 November, the column formed up and moved out at dawn. This was Churchill's and Barnes's first taste of active duty and Churchill's mind raced with the possibilities. As he wrote in his memoirs years later, the impressions of that morning were still vivid:

> Behold next morning a distinct sensation in the life of a young officer! It is still dark, but the sky is paling ... We are on our horses, in uniform; our revolvers are loaded. In the dusk and halflight, long files of armed and laden men are shuffling off towards the enemy. He may be very near; perhaps he is waiting for us a mile away. We cannot tell; we know nothing of the qualities either of our friends or foes. We have nothing to do with their quarrels. Except in personal self-defence we can take no part in their combats. But we feel it is a great moment in our lives – in fact, one of the best we have ever experienced. We think that something will happen; we hope devoutly that something will happen; yet at the same time we do not want to be hurt or killed. What is it then that we do want? It is that lure of youth – adventure, and adventure for adventure's sake. You might call it tomfoolery. To travel thousands of miles with money one could ill afford, and get up at four o'clock in the morning in the hope of getting into a scrape in the company of perfect strangers, is certainly hardly a rational proceeding. Yet we knew there were very few subalterns in the British Army who would not have given a month's pay to sit in our saddles.[43]

The events of the day did not match his anticipation, however, as there was no hostile contact. The only adversaries were the terrain and the vegetation.

The first mission of the column was to escort a supply convoy to the village of Iguara, two days march to the north-east from Sancti Spiritus. Like other towns in Santa Clara province it was surrounded by insurgent forces and military convoys were the only means of communication and resupply. The hilly ground over which the column traveled was difficult with waterways and ravines to cross, swampy areas to circumvent and vast wooded areas all about. It was, in short, excellent ambush country. There was no proper road but rather a narrow wandering track, and the column at times stretched out over two miles. The cavalry attempted its traditional role of reconnaissance and flank security but were frustrated by natural obstacles and often funnelled by the terrain back toward the track.

In his third letter for the *Daily Graphic*, Churchill expressed his admiration for the Spanish foot soldiers who 'marched splendidly'. Carrying all their gear plus weapons and 150 rounds of ammunition each, they still maintained a steady pace of about three miles per hour all day long. 'I was much struck by these infantry. They are by no means the undisciplined boys which I was led to believe they were, but grown men, bearded for the most part, and averaging about twenty-five years of age. Notwithstanding the hot sun and the fact that every man got drenched in fording a river almost as soon as the column started, I saw very few fall out during the day.'[44]

On the first day's march Churchill witnessed the somewhat leisurely Spanish style of campaigning. At about nine o'clock in the morning, after marching eight or so miles, the entire column halted. The horses were unsaddled and rested. The troops brewed coffee and cooked a hot breakfast. The headquarters orderlies set a picnic table for the staff with stew and coffee topped off by rum cocktails prepared by General Valdez's aide-de-camp. Then came a truly surprising development – bed rolls were spread out, hammocks were hung and the column had a four-hour nap in the shade. This was Churchill's introduction to the Spanish custom of the siesta. By three o'clock in the afternoon the column, rested and refreshed, renewed its march and covered an additional ten miles at a steady pace before bivouacking for the night along the trail. Churchill was much taken with the siesta, which he adopted for his own, concluding, 'For every purpose of business or pleasure, mental or physical, we ought to break our days and marches into two.'[45] He later found that in London he could extend his productive working day by two hours if he slept for an hour in the afternoon.

The second day of the march, 25 November, was uneventful and in the evening the column reached Iguara with the needed supplies. It was a small village of no particular significance with only a few houses and barns. The column camped there for the night.

On Tuesday, 26 November, only a week after leaving Tampa and a mere two weeks after his VIP tour at West Point, Lt Churchill spent a long day in the saddle as the column marched twenty-six miles from Iguara to Arroyo, which was located to the north close by the boundary between

Santa Clara and Camagüey provinces. They were moving deeper into rebel territory and signs of the insurrection were ever more in evidence – burned-out buildings and traces of abandoned rebel camps. On that day they had their first contact with the insurgents. The column's point riders came upon small groups of rebel skirmishers who fired a few rounds and melted away. Mounted rebel scouts were now seen from time to time observing the column from a distance. 'The troops managed to shoot a couple of the fellows before they could get away ... and a chance bullet killed an infantry soldier, but so far we have met with nothing that could be called resistance.'[46] It was the rebels who would decide when and where to mount a battle.

Arroyo, a village of some twenty fortified houses, was an important Spanish outpost. It had a two hundred-man garrison which occupied the houses and a series of observation posts around the town. The military operated a heliograph there, a device for sending Morse code messages by flashing the sun's rays from a mirror. By means of a series of heliograph towers, messages could be sent to headquarters at Santa Clara almost at the speed of a telegraph but without the vulnerability of telegraph wires. There was rebel activity near Arroyo the day before Churchill's arrival and the garrison claimed to have inflicted over twenty enemy casualties from the skirmish. On the evening of the 26th, he was invited by Lieutenant-Colonel Benzo, the chief of staff, to inspect the defensive perimeter and the heliograph station. Because the distance was greater than anticipated, or perhaps because they started out too late, they were outside the perimeter as darkness fell and, 'We had a very exciting ride back – a mile and a half through woods infested by the rebels. They did not, however, for some unexplained reason, fire at us. This was very lucky, as our escort consisted only of half a dozen men of the Guarda Civil (loyalist Cuban soldiers), and was much too small to have done any good. Night in Cuba comes on with startling rapidity, and one has to be very careful not to be caught by it.'[47] His baptism of fire would have to wait.

The column remained at Arroyo for three days. Churchill and Barnes, communicating in 'execrable French', had plenty of time to get acquainted with their Spanish counterparts and to gauge their opinions of the conflict, both from the military and the political perspectives:

> The Chief of the staff, Lieut-Col. Benzo, for instance, on one occasion referred to the war 'which we are fighting to preserve the integrity of our country'. I was struck by this. I had not, no doubt owing to my restricted education, quite realised that these other nations had the same sort of feeling about their posses-

sion as we in England had always been brought up to have about ours. They felt about Cuba, it seemed, just as we felt about Ireland. This impressed me much. I thought it rather cheek that these foreigners should have just the same views and use the same sort of language about their country and their colonies as if they were British. However, I accepted the fact and put it in my mental larder. Hitherto I had (secretly) sympathised with the rebels, or at least with the rebellion; but now I began to see how unhappy the Spanish were at the idea of having their beautiful 'Pearl of the Antilles' torn away from them, and I began to feel sorry for them.[48]

He concluded his third *Daily Graphic* letter, which was dated 27 November, his second day at Arroyo, with his views on the likely outcome of the conflict. 'The Spanish officers anticipate a speedy end to the war, and hope to crush the rebellion before the spring. I confess I do not see how this can be done. As long as the insurgents choose to adhere to the tactics they have adopted – and there is every reason to believe that they will do so – they can neither be caught nor defeated.'[49] This was a very clear insight into the heart of the matter of guerrilla warfare. With a popu- larly supported rebel army and both the terrain and climate against them the conventional Spanish army was doomed to fail. The many Spanish columns, 'wandering round and round this endless jungle', were a drain on Spanish financial resources and political will. The army was 'a dumb-bell held at arm's length' for the government across the ocean 5,000 miles away in Madrid. 'Here were the Spanish out-guerrilla-ed in their turn. They moved like Napoleon's convoys in the Peninsula, league after league, day after day, through a world of implacable hostility, slashed here and there by fierce onslaught.'[50]

While in Arroyo, intelligence was received that Máximo Gómez with a force of 4,000 rebels was encamped about six miles to the east and prepara- tions were made to seek him out and tempt him to battle. The column had by now divided with two infantry battalions and one cavalry squadron escorting a supply convoy to a village north-west of Arroyo. The remaining force, for what must be termed a search-and-destroy mission, was about 1,700 men including two infantry battalions, two squadrons of cavalry and the mule battery. Barnes and Churchill went with the column chasing Gómez. It set out from Arroyo on Saturday, 30 November, Churchill's twenty-first birthday 'and on that day for the first time I heard shots fired in anger, and heard bullets strike flesh or whistle through the air'.[51] The Spanish column would remain under fire, on and off, for the next three days.

The column left Arroyo in the misty half light at five o'clock in the morning under the personal command of General Suarez Valdez. After a two-mile march to the south in the direction of Iguara which was intended to mislead the rebels as to its intentions, the force marched east in search of contact with the enemy. Churchill's fourth letter for the *Daily Graphic* dated 4 December stated that although they could hear firing in the vicinity of the distant supply convoy that was travelling separately from Suarez Valdez's force, the column marched all day through grass fields and woodlands without a single rebel challenge, indeed, without sighting the enemy at all.[52] In *My Early Life*, written thirty-five years later, Churchill tells a different and more dramatic story. According to the later account, not long after the column left the village, the rear element was fired on. Even though this was over 200 yards from Churchill's position, it startled him. 'As however no bullets seemed to come near me, I was easily reassured. I felt like the optimist "who did not mind what happened, so long as it did not happen to him." '[53] The column continued its march on a trail so narrow that the troops hacked at the vegetation with their machetes to clear the way. At the halt for breakfast, hostile rifle fire was again directed at the troops from the jungle. This time the firing was quite close and the soldiers charged the source but found no one. It was just a hit-and-run harassment raid by the rebels who vanished and left only expended cartridges to mark their position. Meanwhile, Churchill gave his attention to a chestnut horse which had been right behind him and had started when the shots rang out. It had been shot in the side and was mortally wounded. 'As I watched these proceedings I could not help reflecting the bullet which had struck the chestnut had certainly passed within a foot of my head. So at any rate I had been 'under fire'. That was something. Nevertheless, I began to take a more thoughtful view of our enterprise than I had hitherto done.'[54]

By three o'clock they had discovered what was presumed to be an abandoned rebel campsite and followed the trail that led away from it. At five in the afternoon they reached the village of Lagitas which had, according to the villagers, only recently been abandoned by Gómez. Rather than continue the pursuit late in the day and risk being caught in the jungle in the dark, the column elected to remain the night in Lagitas. The general's staff appropriated the small building which had been Gómez's headquarters with the intention of making it their own. Just as the troops were dismounting, a group of two dozen rebels was spotted a quarter of a mile away. They vanished into the woods before shots could be exchanged and none was captured or killed. Clearly now the column was close to the rebels' sanctuary. That night four companies of infantry were deployed as pickets and guards to defend against any enemy assault of the bivouac area. Whether because of the care given to the defences or because the rebels never intended an attack, none came that night.

The next day, Sunday, 1 December, the column moved out at 5.15 a.m. They were only about half a mile from Lagitas when they received hostile rifle from 200 yards off to their left which lasted about ten minutes. The vegetation from which the firing came was so dense that the ambushers could not be seen and so there was no return fire from the column and no pursuit. As the column progressed during the day the vegetation became denser, giving even more advantage to the guerrillas. The cavalry was unable to scout the flanks as the column was restricted by the terrain and vegetation to the trail through the jungle. The infantry was now placed on point at the head of the column. At 11.00 a.m. a halt for lunch was made in a large clearing and the column was again fired upon from their perimeter. Snipers fired at the staff officers and a guide's horse was shot. Finding the position too exposed, General Suarez ordered the march to the stopping place for the night, a one-hut village called Las Grullas located on the bend of a river which bordered it on three sides. There the bivouac was set up and sentries placed.

Churchill and Barnes found the river inviting after a hot day in the saddle and with some staff officers went in for a swim. As they were drying off and dressing they were interrupted by a shot fired over their heads from the opposite bank. The shot was followed by another, then another and it was suddenly clear that the camp was under attack. Quickly the sentries returned fire. One of the Spanish officers collected the fifty or so men who were near by setting up the tents and organised a firing line along the river bank. Their volley fire prevented the rebels from crossing the river. Churchill and Barnes reported to the general's command post: 'When we arrived there was a regular skirmish going on half a mile away, and the bullets were falling over the camp. The rebels, who use Remingtons, fired independently, and the deep note of their pieces contrasted strangely with the shrill rattle of the magazine rifles [German-made Mausers] of the Spaniards.'[55] The firefight was over in thirty minutes. The rebels retreated but again the column did not pursue them. Churchill did not report whether there were casualties.

That night at about eleven o'clock, the rebels returned and opened fire again, shooting into the camp from the deep darkness outside the perimeter. Their volleys killed and wounded a number of Spanish soldiers including an orderly standing just outside the hut where Churchill had been sleeping. One bullet went through the hut itself. 'I should have been glad to get out of my hammock and lie on the ground. However, as no one else made a move, I thought it more becoming to stay where I was. I fortified myself by dwelling on the fact that the Spanish officer whose hammock was slung between me and the enemy fire was a man of substantial physique; indeed one might almost have called him fat. I have never been prejudiced against fat men. At any rate I did not grudge this one his meals. Gradually I dropped asleep.'[56] The rebels' night firing was probably merely for purposes of harassing the Spaniards and did not amount to an attempt to overrun the camp; but it does demonstrate the tactical differences of the opposing armies. The government troops halted and set up a static defensive position each evening. The rebels operated at night, making use of the darkness for cover and taking advantage of the Spaniards' regular routine to move men and material without fear of interference. The night belonged to the insurgents. Although the rebel fire was only maintained for about an hour that night, it served to keep the Spaniards isolated and their sleep interrupted.

The column moved out in the early morning of 2 December, once again in pursuit of the rebels. By now the Spaniards were deep in rebel-controlled territory. The rebels were certainly aware of the column's presence and strength as they had been shadowing it for days. Almost as soon as the column started its march it came under fire from rebel snipers to the front who were given cover by the terrain, the thick vegetation and the early morning mist. Casualties were taken and the column was forced to halt. The Spanish infantry at the head of the column, under command of General Navarro, located the snipers and silenced them with return rifle fire and the march was resumed. 'From six till eight o'clock we marched continually opposed and constantly under fire. The enemy falling back on its camp took advantage of every position, and though not very many men were hit all the bullets traversed the entire length of the column, making the march very lively for everybody.'[57]

By around eight o'clock in the morning the lead elements of the column had moved from broken ground into an open area. They came upon a ride – a track suitable for horses, which was about a mile long and flanked by wide fields of waist-high grass. The field itself was surrounded by thick forest. At the end of the ride and facing it was a low ridge at the edge of the forest which had a rail fence on its crest. The rebels' position was visible there. General Suarez and his staff sized up the situation through their field glasses and gave orders for an immediate attack. At long last, it appeared, the rebels would stand and fight. They held a good tactical position, whatever their numbers were, but the Spanish troops moved directly toward them.

The Spanish infantry deployed with two companies of the first battalion moving to the left flank and two companies advancing on the right. On the edges of the fields they extended and moved forward. The cavalry advanced up the right side of the field with the artillery moving up the centre to set up a battery firing position. The second battalion of infantry advanced in a column behind the cavalry. General Valdez, his staff and the two British observers advanced right up the centre of the ride at a distance of only fifty yards behind the Spanish firing line. They rode forward 'solemnly', as Churchill later reported it, for about three hundred yards before rebels opened fire. Churchill could see the puffs of smoke from the rebel rifles. They fired two volleys and then commenced rapid independent firing from all along their line. The Spanish infantry returned fire and advanced steadily with the small arms fire becoming heavy in both directions. To be on horseback in such an exchange of fire was to be very exposed and Churchill took in the scene with cool detachment. This was, after all, exactly what he had come all the way to Cuba to see:

> There was a sound in the air sometimes like a sigh, sometimes like a whistle, and at others like the buzz of an offended hornet. General Valdez and his staff rode their horses to within 500 yards of the enemy's firing line. Here we halted, and the infantry fire fight raged for about ten minutes evenly. The general, in his white uniform and gold lace, mounted on a grey horse, was a mark for every sharpshooter, and consequently the number of casualties on the Staff was all out of proportion to those of the rest of the force.'[58]

Churchill and Barnes were very impressed by the general's bravery and remained with the staff throughout the battle. 'The Spaniards were on their mettle; and we had to do our best to keep up appearances. It seemed very dangerous indeed, and I was astonished to see how few people were hit amid all this clatter. In our group of about twenty, only three or four horses and men were wounded, and not one killed.'[59] The rebels, it seemed, had a habit of firing too high. Soon the Spanish fire and advance told and the rebels ceased firing and abandoned their position to the Spanish infantry. They melted away into the dense forest but the column's soldiers did not pursue. Then, abruptly, it was all over and the field was quiet. So ended what was later called the battle of La Reforma.[60]

Churchill and Barnes had finally experienced their baptism of fire. The battle had been of the old-fashioned kind with troops advancing in a line across open ground on foot with their officers accompanying them on horseback. It had been dangerous but Churchill had proved himself to be physically courageous and cool under fire. It must have been very gratifying for him to know in his heart that in the event, the ordeal was not 'one unsuited to his temperament'. La Reforma was the last action he would see in Cuba. Following the battle, the column quit the area and marched south-east under a hot sun. They arrived at the garrison town of La Jicotea at about four in the afternoon, marking the end of their mission. It was a more substantial village than they had seen in several days and they were glad for it. The officers were hosted for a dinner banquet at the home of a prominent loyalist citizen. They enjoyed a lavish meal, the relative comfort of the town, and the freedom from rebel sniping in the night. The column's infantry battalions set up camp in the town and that evening, Churchill wrote:

> I went out to take a last look at them. The only street of the village presented a wonderful sight, Round a score of fires were grouped fourteen or fifteen hundred cotton-clad figures, some cleaning their rifles, others cooking their dinners, but all chattering and singing merrily. These men had marched that day about 21 miles over the worst possible ground, carrying their kit and ammunition, and had in addition been fired at for the best part of four hours. They are fine infantry.[61]

Much as he admired the troops and their steadiness and stamina, his experience with the column left him with serious misgivings about the likelihood of an eventual Spanish victory over the insurgent forces. The actions of the Spanish column and its generals after the battle of Reforma, if representative of the behaviour of their army generally, were strong indications of its eventual failure and defeat. In his critical review of the battle in letter V to the *Daily Graphic*, he wrote:

> The Government troops had taken a week's hard marching to find the enemy, and, having found them, had attacked them promptly and driven them from their position. The natural course was to have kept in touch at all costs, and to have bucketed them until they were forced to either disperse or fight. No pursuit was, however, attempted. Honour was satisfied, and the column adjourned to breakfast ... It seems a strange and unaccountable thing that a force after making such vigorous marches, showing such energy in finding the enemy, and displaying such steadiness in attacking them, should deliberately sacrifice all that these efforts had gained. Such tactics make the war inter-

minable. Here you have a General of Division and two thousand of the best troops in the island out for over ten days in search of the enemy, overcoming all sorts of difficulties, undergoing all kinds of hardships, and then being quite contented with killing thirty or forty rebels and taking a low grass hill which was destitute of the slightest importance. At this rate of progress it would take the Emperor William, with the German Army, twenty years to crush the revolt.[62]

In his analysis of the military situation Churchill was correct. The Spanish lacked both the tactics and the will to seek out and destroy the rebel insurgency. They had neither the generalship nor the technology to prevail against an enemy with broad popular support, in a terrain that was ideal for hit-and-run guerrilla tactics but not for the movement and employment of traditional cavalry and infantry units.

After Churchill's departure, Spanish fortunes continued to decline. Rebel activity spread ever farther west and by Christmas 1895, Marshal Campos and his headquarters returned to Havana in near defeat. By the end of the month he was relieved of command and replaced by General Valeriano Weyler, a hard-nosed commander sent to pursue Madrid's policy of seeking a military solution. By January 1896, the rebels had bypassed Havana and initiated military activity in every province on the island. The opposing sides settled into a strategic stalemate. Spanish troop strength reached a peak of 200,000 but they never regained control of the island and suffered grievously from the climate, from disease and from combat losses. It is estimated that they lost 100,000 men to fatal diseases alone in the period 1895–8.[63]

The insurgents were nearing a military victory with most of the countryside and town after town coming under their control. The Spanish army was isolated, ineffective and exhausted, but still not defeated. Then, on 25 February 1898, the American battleship USS *Maine* blew up and sank in Havana harbour with the loss of 266 lives. This was an electrifying event and led to an American declaration of war against Spain. And for Spanish rule in Cuba, that was that. There followed the one-hundred day Spanish-American War in which US forces decisively defeated the Spanish army so long opposed by the rebels. Spain was divested of Cuba, Guam, Puerto Rico and the Philippine Islands in the bargain. There followed an American military occupation of Cuba and, eventually, Cuban independence in 1902.

On Tuesday, 3 December, Churchill and Barnes left La Jicotea with General Suarez Valdez who had placed the column under the command of General Navarro. Valdez's party proceeded on horseback fifteen miles east to the town of Ciego d'Avilar which was on the railway line. After lunch they went by train to the south coast of Cuba about eighteen miles distant. And thence by a government gunboat west to Tunas in Santa Clara province. 'At Tunas we said good-bye to [General Suarez Valdez] and his staff with profound regret, for their courtesy, their kindness, and their hospitality had made a short visit a very pleasant one.'[64] By 5 December Churchill and Barnes were back at the Gran Hotel Inglaterra in Havana.

Lt Churchill wrote to his mother on 6 December: 'I can't tell what pleasure it gives me to be able to write to you and tell you that we have got back safely. There were moments during the last week when I realised how rash we had been in risking our lives – merely in search of adventure. However it all turned up trumps and here we are.'[65] He reported to her his experiences of active service including viewpoints and details he had not sent to the *Daily Graphic*. He commented on his continual good luck in Cuba – luck in missing trains that were later attacked by the rebels, luck in avoiding illness from the pestilences in Sancti Spiritus, luck in not being shot when bullets passed so close to him. 'So you see my dear Mamma – there is a sweet little cherub.'[66]

He also wrote to Lady Randolph some news of which he was particularly proud. 'The General [Suarez Valdez] has recommended us for the Red Cross – a Spanish Decoration given to Officers – and coming in the train yesterday, by chance I found Marshal Campos and his staff, who told me it would be sent to us in due course.'[67] This was Churchilll's first military award; it would not be his last.

The proper name of the award is the Cross of the Order of Military Merit, First Class, Red Ribbon (Cruz de la Orden del Merito Militar, con distintivo rojo, de Primera Clase). The order was created by royal decree of Queen Isabella II in 1864 to recompense extraordinary service and is awarded in two divisions, one for war service and one for general (non-combat) service. The decree creating the order provides that the first class of the order, which is the lowest ranking, be awarded to qualified junior officers in the ranks of captain, lieutenant or cadet. The badge of the order's first class for war service is a cross of gold and red enamel suspended from a red ribbon with a central white stripe. The obverse of the cross has a round medallion in the centre displaying the royal coat of arms. The reverse bears the script letters 'MM' for 'Merito Militar' in gold. It is a very handsome decoration.

The official notification of the award to Churchill and Barnes, for he was similarly decorated, was dated 6 December 1895, in Havana. It stated:

> To the Lieutenants of the British Army, Winston Spencer Churchill and Reginald Barnes. I have been notified by His Excellency the Commander General of the 5th Military District of the distinguished comportment observed by you in the military action held on the 2nd of this month in Guayos against the joint forces of Maximo Gomez and Maceo. I have granted you, pursuant to the faculties conferred to me by His Majesty's Government, the Red Cross of the Order of Military Merit, First Class. Of which I notify you for your knowledge and satisfaction.[68]

The award, made in the theatre of operations, was ratified by the minister of war, Mr Azcarraga, on 25 January, on behalf of the Queen Regent and the government of Spain. Churchill was thrilled with the medal and sought official permission to wear it as is required for any British subject receiving a foreign decoration. 'We applied to wear our Spanish Decorations (Barnes and I) but they regretfully refused. Still I want to have a miniature made to wear at Balls etc. When not in uniform.'[69]

Although they did not know it at the time, Churchill and Barnes would later receive a second award from Spain. A Cuban Campaign Medal (Medalla de la Campaña de Cuba) was created by royal decree in 1899 to commemorate military service by Spanish land, sea and auxiliary forces in Cuba between 1895 and 1898. The campaign medal, suspended from a silk ribbon of alternating purple and red stripes shows the profile faces of King Alfonso XIII and the Regent Queen on the obverse with the words, 'Campaña de Cuba, 1895–1898.' The reverse features the initials of the king surrounded by the words, 'Al Ejercito De Operaciones' (To the Army of Operations). This medal was awarded for participation in either the Cuban insurrection or the Spanish-American War. Churchill and Barnes were deemed eligible for this award based on their participation in the Spanish column in November and December 1895, and the award to them of the Order of Military Merit. As the medal was not created until after their departure and the end of the conflict, they did not have it to wear for many years.

The Spanish Archivo General Militar in Segovia is the repository of the original documents concerning the awards to the two English observers. The records do not indicate when or how they received their campaign medals. The answer is found in Churchill's 1937 book, *Great Contemporaries*, which included a profile of the Spanish King Alfonso XIII. In that essay Churchill notes that in the spring of 1914 he had a luncheon with the king on a visit to Spain during Churchill's service as First Lord of The Admiralty. 'His deep regard for England was evident in everything he said. Although nearly twenty years had passed since I had accompanied the Spanish forces in Cuba, he presented me with the war medal for that campaign before I left Madrid.'[70] Barnes also received the Cuban Campaign Medal at some stage; probably Churchill obtained it for him in 1914. Barnes's decorations and medals are now displayed in the officers' mess of the Queen's Royal Hussars. Churchill's medals, the two from Cuba included, are now on display at the Cabinet War Rooms, part of the Imperial War Museum in London, where they are on loan from Winston S. Churchill, the grandson of Sir Winston.[71]

Word of the decorations spread quickly to the United States and to Great Britain. The *New York Herald* of 9 December, 1895, announced:

> Madrid – December 8 – A despatch to the Imparcial from Havana says that the military decoration of the Red Cross has been accorded to Lieutenants Churchill and Barnes, of the British Army, for the gallantry displayed by them during the recent engagement between the government forces and the main body of rebels.[72]

There then followed a controversy in the Cuban press which reverberated to the United States and Great Britain where the papers tended to be sympathetic to the rebels. According to a letter from Havana on 10 December from Churchill's acquaintance M. Shaw Bowers: 'After your departure the local newspapers all had notices and every mother's son of them knighted you.' At the same time, Bowers reported:

> The Cuban propaganda machine promptly started the story that you had cut your visit short on account of a row with Suarez Valdez. They gave out that your sympathies went over to the rebels – that you wished to leave the Spanish army and join Gomez, that Valdez would not allow you to do so, and, in consequence, you returned to England. When it was known that you had received the Roja Cruz, and that in your interviews the rebels received no aid or comfort, great was the wrath of the laborantes.[73]

In fact, Churchill had behaved entirely correctly in Cuba and had no disputes with his hosts. On the contrary, he made every effort to avoid criticism of the Spanish leadership in his newspaper columns written while on the island. In a subsequent letter to Lady Randolph on 7 January 1897, he wrote: 'I reproach myself somewhat for having written a little uncandidly and for having perhaps done injustice to the insurgents. I rather tried to make out, and in some measure succeeded in making out, a case for Spain. It was politic and did not expose me to the charge of being ungrateful to my hosts, but I am not quite clear whether I was right.'[74]

Nevertheless, there was criticism from the press on both sides of the Atlantic about Churchill's tour of duty with the Spanish army. The *Newcastle Leader* wrote, 'Sensible people will wonder what motive could possibly impel a British officer to mix himself up in a dispute with the merits of which he had absolutely nothing to do. Mr Churchill was supposed to have gone to the West Indies for a holiday, he having obtained leave of absence from his regimental duties at the beginning of October for that purpose. Spending a holiday in fighting other people's battles is rather an extraordinary proceeding even for a Churchill.'[75] *The New York Times* was strongly critical of Churchill, publishing an article with a date-line of London, 7 December which said: 'No one understands here whether young Winston Churchill is with the Spaniards or with the rebels in Cuba, but in either case it is not seen how he can escape a wigging from the Army authorities here. His friends would not regard it as a misfortune if it meant his leaving the Army, they have high hopes that he will do remarkable things in politics.'[76] Their correspondent was apparently unaware that Churchill had been careful to obtain all the necessary permissions from the army before he sailed for Cuba in the first place. *The New York Times* went even further in the 15 December edition in an article datelined Havana, 11 December, which claimed that Churchill and Barnes, 'came to Cuba with the desire of visiting the camps of the rebels. To conceal their intentions, their services were offered to the Spanish commander and accepted.'[77] The article also claimed the Englishmen had attempted to ride through the Spanish lines to meet the rebels only to be arrested by General Valdez's troops and expelled from the island. This was completely untrue. The only contact Churchill had with the rebels was in combat at the business end of their rifles. Churchill was so indignant about *The New York Times* article that he refused to be interviewed by their reporters when he stopped in New York on his return journey to England.

Arriving back at Tampa, Florida, on 10 December, Churchill was interviewed by the press and was forced to defend himself against assertions that he had actually fought against the rebels stating, 'I have not even fired my revolver. I am a member of General Valdez's staff by courtesy only, and am decorated with the Red Cross only by courtesy.'[78] This allegation of his taking an active part in the fighting, apparently beginning with a false report from the Cuban press, had a protracted life and died a lingering death. The controversy was renewed in 1949 during the foreign aid debates in the United States Congress when Senator Langer claimed that Churchill had fought against American forces in Cuba in 1898. This was clearly untrue on all counts but Churchill felt compelled to telegraph a denial to Senator Connelly, chairman of the Senate Foreign Relations Committee.[79]

From Tampa, Churchill and Barnes returned to New York City by train, arriving in the evening of Wednesday, 11 December 1895. After staying again at the apartment of Bourke Cockran, they took passage on the *Etruria* for the return trip to England on Saturday, 14 December.[80] Although Churchill reached the Cunard pier only five minutes before its scheduled departure, he stood for an interview with waiting reporters from the *New York World* and *New York Herald*. He denied that his trip to Cuba was for the purpose of aiding the Spanish cause and when queried about the alleged political significance of his presence in Cuba, he exclaimed 'Rot!' with an expression that showed how tired the question made him feel.[81] As to the future outlook for the war in Cuba, Churchill gave a balanced appraisal of the military situation:

> I think that the winter campaign now under way in Cuba is one of peculiar importance. If Campos succeeds in clearing the insurgents out of Matanzas and Santa Clara [provinces] before spring he will, in my judgment, break the back of the revolution ... Should the rebels succeed in holding Matanzas and Santa Clara they will be in a position to make a much more protacted and effective struggle ... The Spanish are energetic and brave, but the nature of the country is against them, and furthermore, there is too little combination in the movements of their various columns ... This winter's campaign means much if not everything. If the insurgents hold out until the Spring rains they may win. At any rate, they will be in a position to dictate terms for the peace which everyone in Cuba now longs for.[82]

Churchill's political analysis of the conflict in Cuba continued in his fifth letter for the *Daily Graphic* and in three articles which appeared in *The Saturday Review* in 1896. He was very critical of the Spanish policy of punitive levels of taxation that kept Cuba dependent on Spain and retarded diversified economic development. And he found the corruption of the government at all levels so widespread that 'a national and justifiable revolt is the only possible result of such a system'.[83] While he was admittedly sympathetic to the need for revolution, he was also sharply critical of the rebels and their leadership. He found them to be ungentlemanly, undisciplined, even cowardly. 'The only tactics they pursue are those of incendiaries and brigands – burning canefields, shooting from behind hedges, firing into sleeping camps, destroying property, wrecking trains, and throwing dynamite. These are perfectly legitimate in war, no doubt, but they are not acts on which States are founded.'[84]

His first article in *The Saturday Review* of 15 February 1896 repeated his doubts that the rebel leaders were capable of creating or sustaining a stable government free from racial hatred and division, continuing violence and eventual financial ruin. He thought a compromise end to the war was possible only if Spain adopted a humane reform policy, made more effective use of its military forces, and most importantly, kept the United States from intervening on the side of the rebels. Such a policy could allow Spain to keep her colony which Churchill thought was preferable to an independent Cuba, 'another irresponsible firebrand republic of the South American type. That is not an inviting prospect for the outside world, nor does independence offer much to the islanders themselves. All impartial residents in the island agree that, though the Spanish administration is bad, a Cuban government would be worse – equally corrupt, more capricious, and far less stable.'[85] Most of all, Churchill feared a race war in a liberated Cuba between the black Cubans under Antonio Maceo, who comprised forty per cent of the active rebel fighters, and the lighter-skinned Cubans who he expected to resist Maceo's rightful claim to a large share of power in a national government.[86] This concern foreshadowed by more than fifty years Churchill's fears of sectarian violence between Hindus and Muslims if India were granted independence from the British Empire.

On his return to England and, presumably, after further reflection on the issues, Churchill's view began to favour an end to Spanish sovereignty over Cuba. In a letter to Bourke Cockran on 29 February 1896, he concluded that the best outcome of the conflict might after all be for the United States to intervene on the island: 'It would be the best and most expedient course for both the island and the world in general. But I hold it a monstrous thing if you are going to merely procure the establishment of another South American Republic – which however degraded and irresponsible is to be backed in its action by the American People – without their maintaining any sort of control over its behaviour.'[87] For Churchill, outright annexation of Cuba was preferable to independence. The former, he thought, would not give rise to European intervention but the latter would be subject to justifiable protest. He judged that an American take-over by force would be difficult for the United States but in the best interests of Cuba and the world.[88]

By the time his last article on Cuba was published in *The Saturday Review* of 29 April 1896, the United States had recognised the rebels and formalised its diplomatic position in opposition to continued Spanish rule of Cuba. It was clear to Churchill that the tide was running out for Spain militarily, financially and politically. 'It were rash to forecast the sequel,' Churchill wrote, 'but the eyes of Europe will be turned to that Great Power of the Western Hemisphere on whom the responsibility will then fall. Guided by the determination to be just, and actuated by the desire to be generous, the American people may bring the Cuban question to a solution – equitable to the insurgents, honourable to Spain, and glorious to themselves.'[89]

Churchill's adventure in the Caribbean was in fact an important testing ground for him in several ways. His energy, imagination and practical abilities were put to good use originating the plan, obtaining the necessary permissions, and financing and organising the venture. He secured the approval and assistance of everyone whom he asked to aid him and he did all that he set out to do. His skills as a newspaper correspondent were put to the test and he passed with high marks. He was a fine writer of prose and proved to be an accurate and insightful observer and reporter of events. Importantly, he realised that he was capable of writing for pay and earning more than would a subaltern of cavalry in so short a time.

Although his views and sympathies of the imperial political aspects of the Cuban insurrection changed considerably after his return to England, Churchill showed a good understanding of the military aspects of the guerrilla campaign on both the tactical and strategic levels. The results of his first test as a soldier must have been most gratifying. He had proved to be steady under fire and sturdy enough to endure the rigours of active service in the field. He received good reports on his conduct in action and was awarded his first decoration, a fact that would make him the envy of the other junior officers in the 4th Hussars. He had his 'private rehearsal' in Cuba and as a result knew for certain he was well suited to the demands of the profession of arms.

Docking at Liverpool on 21 December 1895, Churchill was back home in London in time for Christmas.[90] He soon returned to the 4th Hussars at Hounslow with twenty-five guineas from the *Daily Graphic* and stories to tell. One of his most interesting observations had been made to the dockside interviewers in New York – the fact that for all the gunfire in battle that he witnessed, the casualties were relatively few. 'It has always been said, you know, that it takes 200 bullets to kill a soldier, but as applied to the Cuban war 200,000 shots would be closer to the mark,' he told the *New York Herald* reporter.[91] Perhaps he was commenting on his own luck, perhaps on rebel marksmanship. It could have been a genuine insight gained from experience that would guide his conduct in combat on other continents in later years. Nevertheless, one of the souvenirs Churchill carried home from Cuba was a rebel bullet that had killed a Spanish soldier who had been quite close to him in a skirmish there.

5

The Frontier War

As the year 1896 arrived, the 4th Hussars remained at Hounslow cavalry barracks with the prospect of their transfer to India in the autumn overshadowing their garrison routine. It was a period of relative ease and liberal leave for officers with much time given over to social events. As Churchill later recalled: 'I now passed a most agreeable six months; in fact they formed the only idle spell I ever had.'[1] In 1896 he lived with his mother at 35a Great Cumberland Place near Marble Arch. He commuted to Hounslow on the underground railway, a journey of approximately an hour, emerging above ground west of Baron's Court, with a further ten-minute walk to the post. From the front gate of the cavalry station it was only a short walk on Barracks Road to the heath itself where there was plenty of open ground for horseback riding. Churchill only went to Hounslow two or three times a week in the spring and summer of 1896 and, with the exception of polo matches at Hurlingham and Ranelagh with his fellow officers, he wrote: 'I gave myself over to the amusements of the London Season.'[2] Blessed with the entrée of his family connections he spent many weekends visiting the country houses of relatives and family friends, meeting and mixing with important figures in the government, the military and society. That January at Tring, the home of Lord Rothschild, he met the Home Secretary, Herbert Asquith, who would later be Prime Minister and Arthur Balfour, leader of the House of Commons, himself a future Prime Minister. On another occasion he attended a dinner party hosted by Mrs Adair in London where he met Joseph Chamberlain, the Colonial Secretary, Sir Francis Jeune, president of the Probate Division and judge advocate general, and Field-Marshal Viscount Garnet Wolseley, Commander-in-Chief of the British army.[3]

Churchill spent some weekends at Deepdene, the country house of Lord William Beresford, the second husband of his aunt Lilian who was the widow of the Eighth Duke of Marlborough, Winston's late uncle. Beresford was a retired army officer from the 9th Lancers, a veteran of several campaigns, and holder of the Victoria Cross which he won at Ulundi in the Zulu War of 1879. He was well connected in military circles and familiar with India where he had served as military secretary to the

Viceroy. It was at a Deepdene weekend in 1896 that Churchill met General Sir Bindon Blood, a senior commander in India. As Churchill recorded: 'If future trouble broke out on the Indian Frontier, he was sure to have a high command. He thus held the key to future delights. I made good friends with him. One morning on the sunny lawns of Deepdene I extracted from the general a promise that if ever he commanded another expedition on the Indian Frontier, he would let me come with him.'[4] Churchill was never shy about advancing his own career and that season he made many contacts that would be useful to him in the army and in politics. To his credit, though, he always used his family name and connections 'as a springboard, not as a sofa', and always to get into battle and never to avoid it.[5] In developing relationships with the influential people he met, key Churchill traits can be seen at work — his remarkable physical and mental energy, his strong power of concentration and as one biographer later described it, a cold process of calculation about his own future.[6] His social interactions that year certainly paid dividends later.

Against this exciting social backdrop the routine life of the 4th Hussars followed its normal course. Horses and stables had to be seen to, drill and training conducted, equipment and barracks maintained and daily guards posted. A series of inspections was conducted including the annual inspection by the Inspector General of Cavalry, Major General Luck, on 24 March 1896; the annual inspection of the regiment at Hounslow barracks by the general officer commanding the Home District, Major General Lord Methuen, on 14 April and the annual inspection of the troops of the Home District by Field Marshal Viscount Wolseley in which the regiment participated at Wimbledon Common on 24 April. Following the Inspector General of Cavalry's annual mounted inspection of the 4th Hussars at Hounslow Heath on the morning of 29 April, Major General Luck remarked: 'Colonel Brabazon, you ought to be proud to command such a smart and well drilled regiment for in the whole of my military experience I never inspected a smarter, cleaner, and well drilled corps as I have done this day. In fact it is the smartest Cavalry Regiment in the British service.'[7]

On 12 May, Colonel Brabazon relinquished command of the Fourth Hussars to Lieutenant Colonel William A. Ramsey who had been gazetted to the regiment as a second lieutenant in September 1869 and had served with it the entire twenty-seven years since. In his remarks Brabazon thanked the troops and officers 'for the zeal and intelligence they have shown', and said he felt 'certain that they will in the years to come maintain the magnificent reputation they now enjoy and remind[ed] them that this is to be obtained only by the esprit-de-corps, discipline, affection and cohesion of all ranks which alone can make a first class regiment'.[8] His affection for the 4th was reciprocated, for in the evening after his final parade, 'some of the men went to the officers' mess and called for him. When he went out they invited him to get into a brake, manned the shafts and ran around the barrack square, while the rest of the regiment cheered him with the greatest enthusiasm. It was a triumphant ending to a notable period of command.'[9]

One bright spot of the year for Churchill came on 20 May 1896 when he was promoted to lieutenant and entitled to wear the badge of his new rank, a second four-pointed star, or 'pip', on his shoulder chains.[10] He had passed the necessary examinations in regimental duties and drill regulations and had been declared fit and deserving by his commanding officer. Promotion for army officers was often slow, was handled strictly within the regiment and therefore was dependent on the creation of a vacancy by the transfer, resignation, promotion, retirement or death of another officer. Churchill had risen in seniority as well as rank since he joined the regiment and when he departed for India there were one lieutenant and four second lieutenants junior to him. By the time Churchill left the 4th Hussars in the spring of 1899 he was seventh of ten lieutenants in seniority with three lieutenants and five second lieutenants junior to him.[11]

All during the late spring and summer preparations continued for the move to India in September. Between 14 May and 20 August the majority of the troop horses was transferred to other regiments then stationed at Aldershot and on 28 May the officers' chargers were sold at auction by Messrs Tattersalls in London. In May the new recruits and A and C Squadrons completed their musketry course at Pirbright with B and D Squadrons following in June. By 1 September the regimental depot, that portion of the unit that would not go to India, was moved to quarters at St John's Wood barracks and Hampton Court. Under command of Captain Joseph W. Underwood and Lt William E. Long, the depot would later transfer to Thorncliffe with a total of 230 non-commissioned officers and men and sixty-three horses.[12] The depot was the regiment's reserve squadron and in peacetime would remain behind with administrative, recruitment and training duties.

Churchill gave much thought to the regiment's approaching departure for the east. The truth is that he did not want to go to India and tried hard to avoid being sent so far away from friends, family, familiar places and a hoped-for career in politics. The standard overseas tour of duty for a cavalry regiment was nine years with only infrequent home leave.[13] Churchill was bored with garrison life in England, and India, which was then at peace, promised to be even worse. He looked far and wide for a more attractive posting, one better suited to his personal goals and taste for adventure. In June he contacted *The Daily Chronicle* with a proposal to go to Crete as a special correspondent to cover the fighting between Turks and Greeks but they declined to retain him. In August he noted that the 9th Lancers were being sent to South Africa later in the month and were expected to proceed to Rhodesia to suppress an uprising in Matabeleland. He applied to the colonel of the 9th Lancers to be attached to the regiment and had Lord Beresford send a wire in support of the application. He had his mother write to the commander-in-chief for assistance in going to South Africa but was advised that even if the Lancers accepted him it was most unlikely he would receive leave from his own regiment. Churchill's letter to Lady Randolph on 4 August 1896 reflects his sense of urgency: 'My dear Mamma you cannot think how I would like to sail in a few days to scenes of adventure and excitement – to places where I could gain experience and derive advantage – rather than to the tedious land of India where I shall be equally out of the pleasures of peace and the chances of war. The future is to me utterly unattractive. I look upon going to India with this unfortunate regiment – (which I now feel so attached to that I cannot leave it for another) – as useless and unprofitable exile.'[14] As it happened, the 9th Lancers did not go to Rhodesia after all because the uprising ended a few days before their scheduled departure.

Churchill was also closely following the news from Egypt where on 12 March 1896, an Anglo-Egyptian force under Sir Horatio Kitchener, Sirdar of the Egyptian army, had commenced a campaign to recapture the Sudan from control of the Dervish empire. By 5 April Churchill was corresponding with his mother about the possibility of participating in the expedition and seeking her assistance. By June he was in contact with people whose influence might make his plans work. Captain Philip Greene wrote to a friendly MP indicating Churchill's expressed interest in joining the Sudan campaign, 'as a galopper to Kitchener'.[15] Winston begged his mother to exert her influence on his behalf to go to South Africa or the Sudan (or both), writing to her on 4 August:

> When I speculate upon what might be and consider that I am letting the golden opportunity go by I feel that I am guilty of an indolent folly that I shall regret all my life. A few months in South Africa would earn me the S.A. Medal and

in all possibility the [British South Africa] company's Star. Thence hot foot to Egypt – to return with two more decorations in a year or two and beat my sword into an iron despatch box. Both are within the bounds of possibility and yet here I am out of both. I cannot believe that with all the influential friends you possess and all those who would do something for me for my father's sake – that I could not be allowed to go – were those influences are properly exerted.

It is no use preaching the gospel of patience to me. Others as young are making the running now and what chance have I ever of catching up. I put it down here – definitely on paper – that you really ought to leave no stone unturned to help me at such a period.

You can't realise how furiously intolerable this life is to me when so much is going on a month away from here.[16]

Lady Randolph wrote to both Lord Wolseley and to Lord Lansdowne, the Secretary of State for War, on her son's behalf but received no encouragement from either quarter. By the end of August it was clear that Churchill definitely would be going to India. One of his last letters before sailing was to his grandmother Frances the dowager Duchess of Marlborough in which he wrote: 'We are going to Bangalore – a station in the Madras Presidency and one which is usually considered an agreeable place to soldier in ... I fear I shall not be back in England for at least three years as it is very hard to get leave – long enough to allow a voyage home except at the end of that period.'[17]

The 4th Hussars' move began on 9 September 1896, when, according to the regimental diary, 'Major L. E. Starkey, Capt. C. L. Graham, Lt. A. Savory, Lt. and Qr. M. W. A. Cochrane and 120 W.O. [warrant officers], NCOs [non-commissioned officers] & men accompanied by the Married Women & children proceeded by the 9.45 a.m. train from Hounslow Whitton Station to Southampton to embark on board the Hired Transport Britannia.'[18] The next day Lt Colonel Ramsay and the balance of the regiment took the same train to Southampton following a final inspection by Colonel Sir M. E. Colvile, colonel commanding the Home District. When they sailed from the Government Docks at Southampton at 10 a.m. on 11 September 1896, the regimental diary recorded the 4th Hussars' strength as twenty-two officers, two warrant officers, 448 NCOs and other ranks, twenty-eight married women and forty-five children.[19]

The Britannia was owned and operated by the Peninsular and Oriental Steamship Navigation Company, the oldest British line east of Suez. It ran regular routes from Brindisi on the heel of the boot of Italy to Port Said in Egypt – a route often referred to as the Imperial Highway – in addition to chartering troop transports to India. The Britannia was a coal-fired steamship of 6,525 tons carrying two masts with sails forward of the twin smokestacks and two aft of them.[20] It was a large ship and comfortable for the officers in their cabins if not for the 1,200 men below decks. Experienced passengers on the P & O Line booked rooms on the port side on the way to India and on the starboard side on the return voyage to England to avert the effects of the strong southerly sun. Thus was born one of the enduring acronyms of the age, 'POSH', for port out, starboard home, denoting relative comfort in travel and in life.

As one P & O passenger, journalist G. W. Steevens, wrote: 'P and O steamers are not fast and one feels it would be flippancy to ask them to be.'[21] It was a rather leisurely voyage in a temperate season over calm seas. In a ship-board letter to his mother he reported: 'The ship is comfortable – the food good and the weather delicious ... I have been able to thoroughly enjoy the voyage.'[22] As the ship passed through the Straits of Gibraltar into the Mediterranean, past Malta and Alexandria, he passed the time playing chess and piquet, attending concerts and, as seafaring passengers always will, watching the water. Churchill recorded: 'We pass many ships and my telescope is in great demand and constant use. It is a very powerful glass and will be very valuable to India.'[23] In addition to socialising and pastime pursuits, the officers of the 4th Hussars put the voyage to good use planning for sport in India. They organised a regimental polo club to be supported by subscriptions with a view toward a concentrated effort to win the Inter-Regimental Cup, the all-India polo championship.[24]

Britannia reached Port Said, the northern terminus of the Suez Canal, on 20 September where it was re-supplied with coal brought aboard from lighters in baskets carried by native labourers. The passage of the Suez Canal and the Red Sea, interrupted only by a brief stop at Suez where three transfers from the 14th Hussars were taken on board, took three days. Passing Aden and transiting the Arabian Sea, the *Britannia* ended its 6,100 mile, twenty-two day voyage from the south of England to the west coast of India when it dropped anchor off the Sassoon Dock on the east side of Bombay Island on 2 October 1896. It had been an untroubled and safe passage. The medical officer noted that the health of the troops had been very good, the only casualty on the voyage being a three-month-old child who died of undisclosed causes.[25]

Having finally arrived at what Colonel Brabazon once referred to as 'India, that famous appanage of the Bwitish Cwown', Churchill could hardly wait to go ashore to this exotic place that in his eyes 'might well have been a different planet'.[26] As the arrangements were made for disembarking the 4th Hussars and their five hundred tons of baggage and equip-ment, Churchill and a few fellow officers were given permission to go ashore for a look around. They hired a small boat to take them in, with fateful consequences:

> We came alongside of a great stone wall with dripping steps and iron rings for hand-holds. The boat rose and fell four or five feet with the surges. I put out my hand and grasped at a ring; but before I could get my feet on the steps the boat swung away, giving my right shoulder a sharp and peculiar wrench ... Although my shoulder did not actually go out, I had sustained an injury which was to last me for life ...[27]

Ever after he was subject to having his right shoulder dislocate without warning at awkward moments. It affected his ability to play polo – he was required to strap his upper arm to his torso — and also, as will be seen, his choice of personal weapons on active service. As he wrote in *My Early Life*: 'This accident was a serious piece of bad luck. However, you can never tell whether bad luck may not after all turn out to be good luck. Perhaps if in the charge at Omdurman I had been able to use a sword, instead of having to adopt a modern weapon like a Mauser pistol, my story might not have got so far as the telling.'[28]

The regiment disembarked on the day of their arrival and boarded two trains, which left Bombay at 8.30 p.m. and 9.30 p.m. respectively, for the British army rest camp at Poona where they arrived on the morning of 3 October. Their three days at Poona were put to good use for the benefit of the regimental polo club:

> The Bycullah stables at Bombay form the main emporium through which Arab horses and ponies are imported to India. The Poona Light Horse, a native regiment strongly officered by British, had, in virtue of its permanent station, an obvious advantage in the purchase of Arabian ponies. On our way through Poona we had tried their ponies, and had entered into deeply important nego-tiations with them. Finally it was decided that the regimental polo club should purchase the entire polo stud of twenty-five ponies possessed by the Poona Light Horse; so that these ponies should form the nucleus around which we could gather the means of future victory in the Inter-Regimental Tourna-ment.[29]

At Poona, Churchill, in the company of Colonel Ramsay and three other officers, also dined with the British governor of Bombay, Lord Sand-hurst, who later extended to Churchill an open invitation to visit. No time was lost, it appears, in getting to know the people who mattered, an ingrained Churchillian habit. It was perhaps on this first visit to Poona that he and his colleagues visited the stables of the Aga Khan to inspect his horses. Although he did not meet Churchill in person, his cousin Sham-suddin did and in his memoirs the Aga Khan recorded: 'When he later told me of their visit he said that among the officers none had a keener, more discriminating eye, none was a better judge of a horse, than a young subaltern by the name of Winston Spencer Churchill. My cousin described him as perhaps a little over twenty, eager, irrepressible, and already an enthusiastic, courageous, and promising polo player.'[30]

On the afternoon of 6 October the regiment entrained for Wadi where they rested during the day before leaving by train at 4.30 p.m. on the 7th for the rest camp at Guntakal where they arrived at 9.00 p.m. After a further day passing the midday heat under canvas, they boarded trains for their final destination of Bangalore where they arrived at the Agram barracks on 8 October 1896. They replaced the 19th (Princess of Wales's Own) Hussars who were moving to the British station at Secunderabad and took over the 529 troop horses of that regiment. The regimental diary noted the 4th Hussars' strength on 9 October as twenty-two officers, two warrant officers, two attached NCOs and 449 men. They would be augmented by fifty transfers from the 21st Hussars (later the 21st Lancers) on 15 October.[31]

The 4th Hussars were taking their place in the long line of British army regiments to serve in India, a huge country in terms of both area and population. India in 1895 comprised all of what are now the nations of India, Pakistan, Bangladesh, Sri Lanka and Myanmar, an area of 1,807,112 square miles, almost fifteen times the land mass of the United Kingdom and Ireland. The distances were enormous by European standards and it was not unusual for regimental polo clubs to travel hundreds or even a thousand miles in India for a tournament. The distance from the port of Bombay to Bangalore was about 750 miles, farther than the distance from Land's End to John O'Groats. The population of India was 287,361,056 in 1891 and it was governed by a surprisingly small number of British civil servants and British soldiers. The civil service of India numbered only 1,300 officers as late as 1913.[32]

British ships had been trading in India since the early 1600s, and the East India Company, with a royal charter granting it exclusive trading rights in India, acquired a territorial empire there in the eighteenth century and functioned as a surrogate government for Britain into the nineteenth century with its own army of European and native troops. The British

Empire was built on commerce and, as was often the case, it was necessary from time to time to raise or send troops to protect and ensure the continuity of this trade. British regular troops had served in India continuously since the arrival of the 39th Foot in 1754 and they were accustomed to fighting side by side with native regiments. After the Indian sepoy mutiny in 1857–8 the governance of the company's territories was transferred to the crown and Queen Victoria added 'Empress of India' to her title. A British viceroy was appointed to head the civil administration and the company's military forces were transferred to Crown control as well, with both the British-officered native cavalry regiments and infantry battalions of the Indian army and the soldiers of the British army in India under a British commander-in-chief.

In 1893, a year close in time to Churchill's service in India and one for which statistics are available, there were approximately 147,000 native troops in the Indian army organised into 133 infantry battalions and forty regiments of cavalry. There were two mountain batteries of artillery but most artillery and engineer support was provided by the British army. Each infantry battalion had eight British officers and between 832 and 912 native troops called sepoys. Each cavalry regiment comprised eight British officers and approximately 625 troopers (*sowars*) divided into four squadrons.[33] The British army of 1899 had an approximate strength of 10,718 officers and 253,675 other ranks excluding militia, yeomanry, volunteers and reserves. These were distributed among 157 infantry battalions, thirty-one cavalry regiments, 134 horse, field or mountain batteries of artillery and various engineer, specialty or administrative units. At a given time, fifty-two infantry battalions and nine cavalry regiments were stationed in India, more than anywhere else except in the United Kingdom. Of the 73,162 British army soldiers in India in 1899, 5,616 were in the cavalry including 261 officers, eighteen warrant officers, 486 sergeants, eighty-one drummers and trumpeters and 4,770 corporals and privates.[34]

The 4th Hussars' new home, Bangalore, was comprised of two distinct communities, one British and one Indian. The original town of Bangalore was founded in the sixteenth century and its walled fort was built in the late seventeenth and early eighteenth centuries. By 1895, the city had a population of well over 100,000 and was the capital of Mysore state, the third largest in India. Construction of the first British army barracks began in 1807 with British troops transferring there for garrison duty in 1809 from Srirangapatna because Bangalore's elevation of 3,113 feet above sea level provided a relatively cool and healthy climate. The nineteenth century was a period of steady growth for Bangalore as both a centre of civil administration and as one of the largest British military installations in southern India. Commercial and residential districts grew to serve the expanding population. The city was connected by rail to the major cities including Bombay on the west coast and Madras on the east and was in direct communication with London by telegraph. Mail arrived for the British troops weekly after a passage of eighteen or nineteen days from Great Britain.

The British military and civil station in Bangalore, known as cantonment (pronounced *cantoonment*) was a thirteen-and-a-half-square-mile enclave under direct control of the imperial government and separated physically and culturally from the city. That the cantonment was intended and designed to segregate the British and Indian populations was partly due to European racial attitudes and partly the product of British security concerns following the mutiny. Even the British and Indian military lines were separate. The Europeans seldom ventured into the town and the Indians did not have leave to enter the cantonment unless employed or invited there.[35]

The cantonment was an island in a sea of Indians; it was as if a small corner of England had been transported to the southern Indian plateau. Its centrepiece was a mile-and-a-half-long parade ground running east to west, a broad open space lined with shade trees and bordered by broad avenues with names such as South Parade, Infantry Road and Brigade Road, all built for the convenient movement of troops. On the far west end of the parade ground was Cubban Park, named after Sir Mark Cubban, a former British Commissioner, and within the park was the residency, home of the chief civil officer. Holy Trinity Church, the garrison's Protestant house of worship, was located at the east end of the parade ground. Built in 1848–51 in the English renaissance style, its columned portico and imposing spire faced west toward the parade ground. It could seat 700 and was said to be one of the largest Christian churches in the south of India. North of the parade ground were the infantry lines and farther north the Saddar Bazaar, the Europeans' shopping district, and beyond that the cantonment railway station which was separate from the city station. The cavalry lines, home of the cavalry barracks, the stables and the cavalry officers' mess, were located just south-east of Trinity Church and adjacent to the mounted parade, the open area used for cavalry drill and the riding school. The British buildings, both military and civil were mostly built in the classical or Graeco-Roman style featuring prominent columns, high ceilings and deep shady porches. They stood bright in the sun, white or pastel-coloured, and immaculate.[36] The area south of the parade ground was one of wide shaded streets lined with fine residences, gardens and parks which gave to Bangalore its lasting image as a garden city. The cantonment had much open space including five polo grounds and a steeplechase course; a horse-racing oval was located just outside the boundary.

Together with the regimental mess and the polo ground, the centre of social life for the officers of the 4th Hussars was the club. Churchill became a member of the Bangalore United Services Club located on Residency Road about two miles from the cavalry lines. The club was another enclave of old England, patterned on the London gentlemen's club where members could relax in comfortable, familiar surroundings with their own race, gender and class for drinks, cards, books, dinners and social events. Founded in 1868, the club did not vote to admit Indian officers to membership until 1915. Civilian and female memberships came even later.[37]

South of the parade ground, along the wide avenues in the area of the cavalry mess, residential neighbourhoods developed over time featuring the bungalow style of home. In Churchill's time these were mostly built in the classical style featuring wide porches, called verandahs, with sun screens, and Ionic columns supporting tiled and balustraded roofs. Inside, large central drawing rooms and dining rooms were flanked with bedrooms and small private rooms. Most bungalows were set inside a walled compound with an arched or colonnaded front gate, a gravel driveway, trees and gardens featuring both flower beds and potted plants. The servants' quarters and kitchens were in separate buildings behind the bungalow. In this way the British and the Indian residences in each compound were insulated each from the other, mirroring on a miniature scale the separation of the cantonment and the town.[38]

Although the men of the 4th Hussars lived in barracks in the cavalry lines the officers were paid a housing allowance and had to arrange for their own quarters. As Churchill later wrote:

We three, Reginald Barnes, Hugo Baring and I, pooling all our resources, took a palatial bungalow, all pink and white, with heavy tiled roof and deep verandahs sustained by white plaster columns, wreathed in purple bougainvillea. It stood in a compound of perhaps two acres. We took over from the late occupant about a hundred and fifty standard roses ... We built a large tiled barn with mud walls containing stabling for thirty horses and ponies.[39]

Churchill had three private rooms in the bungalow in which he placed his writing table, cigarette box, books and family photographs and which he planned to decorate with sporting pictures and *Vanity Fair* caricatures.[40] The exact location of Churchill's particular bungalow has been the subject of much speculation. Narayan O. Jog, in his 1944 book *Churchill's Blind Spot: India*, places it at No. 46 Trinity Road. This structure, renumbered No. 47 when the street was renamed Mahatma Gandhi Road after independence in 1947, survived until the 1980s when it was razed for the development of blocks of flats.[41] Churchill found life in his new quarters quite comfortable as well it would be with plenty of servants to keep the house and grounds, care for the horses and see to all his domestic needs.

The three officers each had a personal butler to whom they turned over their monthly housing allowances and who supervised the other servants and ran the house and stables. They also employed a first dressing-boy (valet), a second dressing-boy, two gardeners, three *bhistis* (water carriers), four *dhobies* (laundry men), a watchman, and a *syce* (groom) for each horse.[42] Judging from the size of the stables they had built, there was no shortage of horses around. Traditionally each officer kept two chargers and Churchill was on one occasion photographed in India with four *syces* and five polo ponies, and on another, seated in a carriage pulled by four horses. They went almost everywhere on horseback and had 'hacks' for routine travel in the cantonment.

The master-servant system suited the aristocratic Churchill well. As he later recalled in *My Early Life*:

> If you liked to be waited on and relieved of home worries, India thirty years ago was perfection. All you had to do was to hand over all your uniform and clothes to the dressing boy, your ponies to the syce, and your money to the butler, and you need never trouble any more. Your Cabinet was complete; each of these ministers entered upon his department with knowledge, experience and fidelity. They would devote their lives to their task. For a humble wage, justice, and a few kind words, there was nothing they would not do. Their world became bounded by the commonplace articles of your wardrobe and other small possessions. No toil was too hard, no hours were too long, no dangers too great for their unruffled calm or their unfailing care. Princes could live no better than we.[43]

In fact, the only Indians that Churchill saw up close on a regular basis were the servants. Other exceptions were the Indian troops he fought with and the mountain tribesman he fought against on the North-West Frontier in 1897. He appears to have taken no interest in Indian history or culture and never studied native languages. As he explained in a letter to his mother: 'I shall not learn Hindustani. It is quite unnecessary. All natives here speak English perfectly and I cannot see any good wasting my time acquiring a dialect I shall never use.'[44] Although he showed little interest in the people of India, his letters and other writings never refer to those on the same side as the British forces with disrespect and are almost completely devoid of racial epithets or common slang. Churchill had great respect for courage in soldiers regardless of their race or which side of the battle line they were on. When a proposal was made to open eligibility for the Victoria Cross to native troops, he was all for it, writing: 'It would seem that the value of such a decoration must be enhanced by making it open to all British subjects. The keener the competition, the greater the honour of success. In sport, in courage, and in the sight of heaven, all men meet on equal terms.' Nonetheless, like others of his race and class, in matters other than military bravery and sport Churchill never questioned the superiority of the British way of life over that of the subject peoples of the empire. Indeed, he viewed it as essential to the very existence of British power in India to believe that 'intrinsic merit is the only title of a dominant race to its possessions'.[45] He believed that the British were the dominant race in India because they were superior to the indigenous peoples. While he praised the courage and martial skill of the tribesmen of the North-West Frontier of India who resisted British rule and British arms, Churchill often referred to them as savages and barbarians.

With their daily domestic needs seen to by others, the cavalry officers could devote themselves to military duties and personal pursuits. The daily schedule varied little. Churchill arose at 5.00 a.m., before dawn, and had a small breakfast at home. Then he rode over to the cavalry lines where the regiment paraded at 6.00 a.m. for ninety minutes of cavalry drill and manoeuvring. Next it was back to the bungalow for a bath followed by a full breakfast and the reading of newspapers. Stable duty (supervision of troops and horses) and orderly room (administrative meetings and paper-work) ran from 9.00 a.m. or so until 10.30 or 10.45. After the brief round of morning activities, there were no further duties required of junior officers until the late afternoon. The mid-day and afternoon hours, the hottest of the day, were usually spent at home or in the mess. The officers' main non-military interest was polo which was played at 4.00 or 5.00 p.m. for several hours every day with time set aside for another bath and rest, followed by dinner at the mess at 8.15 or 8.30, followed by drinks, smoking and cards until 10.30 or 11.00. As Churchill later recalled: 'Such was the "long, long Indian Day" as I knew it for three years; and not such a bad day either.'[46]

Once in India, Churchill found that peacetime duty overseas was no more exciting or challenging than it had been in England. As he later wrote in an article for *The Saturday Evening Post*:

> The life of the regular soldier is and must be largely a life of routine. The regular army is largely the army of sentry go. The battalions in England are little more than feeders for the garrisons in India, the coaling stations and the colonies. All this vast area called the British Empire has to be watched and protected, and the army, which many regard only as a fighting medium, is spread about the world on guard and picket, performing on a grand scale through long years of peace the prosaic and monotonous duties of the village police.[47]

The daily schedule, which varied little, and the annual scheme of training, military exercises and polo tournaments which was much the same year after year, allowed officers much time to pursue their own interests and to travel. Churchill, ever curious and vigorous, left the cantonment on duty, on detached service or on leave whenever he could. When he finally departed from India in 1899, he had spent as much time away from his station at Bangalore as on it. Although he had hardly enjoyed his stay in India, he had made the best of the situation and profited much more than many of his contemporaries. He seems to have taken to heart a remark his father had once made to him that, 'The Army is the finest profession in the world if you work at it and the worst if you loaf at it.'[48]

Churchill gave proper attention to his military duties which were not too taxing and his abundant energy and natural intelligence allowed him to master them. As Sergeant Hallaway, Churchill's troop sergeant in the 4th Hussars, later recalled: 'But the great thing about him was the way he worked. He was busier then half the others put together. I never saw him without pencils sticking out all over him. And once when I went to his bungalow, I could scarcely get in what with books and papers foolscap all over the place.'[49] Whether supervising his men's training courses, inspecting them at stables and commanding them in drill and on exercises, Churchill seems to have been popular with the troopers. As Hallaway put it: 'Mr Churchill was a real live one. Not stuffy like some of the other officers, if you know what I mean. Easy going, and always ready for a joke. He hated to see chaps punished. The officers used to inspect the stables every day but we never knew when they were coming. But Mr Churchill would whisper to me "Eleven-thirty, sergeant-major."'[50]

Churchill got along well with the officers of the regiment, among whom he made close friends. In the army as in the public schools, success at sports was a sure route to recognition and even popularity, and Churchill's abilities as a horseman and polo player assured his acceptance. Yet he was undeniably arrogant and impatient. He could seldom hold his tongue and was not eager to accept a place low in the social pecking order. Those who knew him least often liked him least and first impressions of him were not always positive.

One such negative impression was recorded in the memoirs of General Sir Hubert Gough who encountered Churchill at the gunner's mess in Peshawar, India, in 1898. Among the many officers congregated there, Gough recalled:

> I often saw a fresh-faced, fair-haired subaltern of the 4th Hussars who talked a great deal. It was Winston Churchill. He had just returned from the fighting north of Peshawar, where he was acting as correspondent for the Morning Post. He used to take his stand in front of the fire, and from that position of advantage he would lecture all and sundry on the conduct of operations with complete confidence – it seemed to me that he was practising making speeches. No one can deny, however, that he is an outstanding example of the truth of the proverb, 'practice makes perfect!' Brought up in the 16th Lancers, I did not at all approve of this somewhat bumptious attitude. Such style would never have been tolerated in our mess, but in the Gunners' mess at Peshawar neither the many generals who gathered there nor anyone else attempted to check him. I used to wonder how the generals stood it, but even then I was dimly aware that they were rather afraid of him and his pen.[51]

Churchill was outspoken on matters great and small and was known to pay attention to detail. He was a frequent contributor to the 4th Hussars' complaint book which was maintained in the officers' mess. On 24 October 1897, Churchill made the following entry: 'Suggested that the mess should be duly carpeted in accordance with common practice of all regiments and indeed of civilised beings generally. Good carpets can easily be got cheaply. Rs 500 would do the whole thing impressively.' Joined by Lt Barnes, he followed up in November: 'Suggested that the mess should be carpeted. Why has no notice been taken of former complaint. Present state of discomfort is intolerable.' He pushed the issue into the next year writing on 30 January 1898: 'In the opinion of WSC the general comfort and furnishing of the Mess being much below the standard of all other cavalry and most Infantry regiments in the army – suggested – that fresh furniture be purchased and that the carpets be [illegible] – that the hideous wallpaper be altered and that the mess generally be rendered more suitable to the dignity of the regiment.' This last entry was followed by a series of editorial comments by his colleagues including 'How?' 'Where?' 'Price?' and notably, 'For "the dignity of the Regiment", read "WSC".' The suggestion book is full of Churchill's comments on topics ranging from 'dirty, filthy, beastly tank water' to unclean tablecloths, inferior cigarettes and even suggestions on food preparation. A splendid entry, well worth repeating, provides one really practical suggestion: '9th Jan 1898. Eggs on toast. To prevent the toast getting all sodden – the eggs should first be put on a piece of stale dry toast. This absorbs the moisture. Then transfer to a fresh piece of hot toast and serve. If this method is adopted it will save the numerous complaints of the neglect of eggs on toast. W. S. Churchill.'[52]

In his letters home Churchill also lodged complaints, but these were of a more serious nature. Shortly before his twenty-second birthday, isolated and chafing at his isolation in India, he dreamed of a career in politics. In a letter to his mother of 4 November 1896, he wrote:

> I see there is a contested vacancy in East Bradford. Had I been in England I might have contested it and should have won – almost to a certainty ... Perhaps it is just as well – that I am condemned to wait – though I will not disguise from you that life out here is stupid dull and uninteresting. I shall not stay out here long my dearest mamma. It is a poor life to lead and even its best pleasures are far below those obtainable in England. I meet none but soldiers and other people equally ignorant of the country and hear nothing talked but 'shop' and 'racing'.[53]

His military duties left him a good deal of time to pursue his own interests. He collected butterflies by the score, tended rose bushes by the dozens of varieties, rode in and watched horse races, went on hunting expeditions and of course, played chukka after chukka of polo.

The 4th Hussars polo team was soon in action, departing on 30 October 1896 for Hyderabad where they competed for the Golconda Cup. They not only defeated the team from the Golconda Brigade of the Indian army who were expected to win but all their other opponents as well. 'We won the polo tournament after three hard matches – thus securing a magnificent silver cup worth Rs 1000. This performance is a record: – no English Regiment having ever won a first class tournament within a month of their arrival in India. The Indian papers express surprise and admiration.'[54] Their investment in the ponies from Poona had paid a handsome dividend and their skill on the field had passed an important test.

Yet for all the time and energy he expended on sports and other pastimes, the remarkable thing about Churchill's stay in India was his seriousness of purpose and the energy with which he pursued his higher ambition of a career in politics while so young and so far away from home. This he did in two ways: first, by seeking out every opportunity for active service as a vehicle for obtaining a reputation and public recognition, and, second, by pursuing an intense course of self-education which has often been referred to as his private university. It was sometime in late 1896 that Churchill said simply: 'The desire for learning came upon me.'[55] When other officers whiled away their afternoons or slept through the heart of midday, Churchill read, studied and wrote, seeking to prepare himself for a life in politics and to set himself apart from those 'who have no ideas beyond soldiering'.[56] His reading matter was sent by parcel from his mother in England and the list was impressive. He started with Gibbon's *Decline and Fall of the Roman Empire* (eight volumes), Macaulay's *History of England* (eight volumes) and Macaulay's *Essays* (four volumes), often spending four or five hours a day reading widely in history, philosophy, economics and ethics. Most interestingly, he had his mother send him all the volumes of the *Annual Register* from 1870 on. He studied these yearly compendia of parliamentary debates intensely, writing to his mother: 'The method I pursue with the Annual Register is [not] to read the debate until I have recorded my own opinion on paper of the subject – having regard only to general principles. After reading I reconsider and finally write. I hope by a persevering continuance of this practice to build up a scaffolding of logical and consistent views which will perhaps tend to the creation of a logical and consistent mind.'[57]

He gave much thought to his own political philosophy, setting out a platform on the issues of the day in a long letter to his mother on 6 April 1897, which concluded: 'I am a Liberal in all but name. My views excite the pious horror of the Mess. Were it not for home rule – to which I will never consent – I would enter parliament as a Liberal. As it is – Tory Democracy [his father's political construct] will have to be the standard under which I shall range myself.'[58] He also maintained correspondence with the American congressman Bourke Cockran whom Churchill admired and of whose public speaking skills he was so envious. 'There is', Churchill wrote, 'no gift so rare or so precious as the gift of oratory – so difficult to define or impossible to acquire.'[59] His regular correspondence with Lady Randolph and brother Jack was full of news of India, gossip from home and disputes about money matters but it is most remarkable for its ongoing exchanges about British politics and public policy. As he consciously and methodically sought to develop the skills needed for a life in the political arena, he was also busy with efforts both to excel in the tasks at hand and to find an opportunity to make a name for himself, 'seeking the bubble reputation even in the cannon's mouth'.[60]

During his first two years in India, Egypt and Kitchener's campaign to reconquer the Sudan were constantly in Churchill's thoughts. It is clear that his mind was often elsewhere and his letters to his mother made frequent reference to his desire to see active service in Egypt and the Sudan. By mid-December 1896, within two months of his arrival in India he had already made formal application to the adjutant general in Simla for special service in Egypt and was planning to send an application directly to Cairo for temporary appointment to the Egyptian army.[61] Writing to his mother on 23 December 1896, he said: 'I revolve Egypt continually on my mind. There are many pros and cons – but I feel bound to take it if I can get it ... two years in Egypt my dearest Mamma – with a campaign thrown in – would I think qualify me to be allowed to beat my sword into a paper cutter and my sabretache into an election address.'[62] He knew a number of officers who had served in earlier campaigns in Egypt and conversations with them in the officers' mess doubtless served to whet his appetite for active service. In the 4th Hussars, Major Cecil W. Peters and Captain Ronald Kincaid-Smith had both served in the Nile campaign of 1884–5, including the battle of Abu Klea, and Captain Lewis Starkey had served in the Egyptian War of 1882 and was present at the battle of Tel-el-Kebir; all had received two campaign medals. Another Churchill contemporary in India, Lt Viscount Fincastle of the 16th Lancers, though only four years senior to Churchill, had earned campaign medals in Egypt in 1896 and Churchill learned a good deal about that campaign from him. After meeting Fincastle, he wrote to Lady Randolph: 'I hope Egypt will come off. I tried on Fincastle's fez: I look splendid.'[63]

By 25 February 1897, Churchill received an official reply to his application to serve in Egypt – a refusal. An earlier letter sent by his mother directly to Kitchener, whom she knew socially, did no better. The Sirdar advised Lady Randolph that there were no vacancies for officers but that her son's name would be put on a waiting list. This was a refusal, albeit a polite one, to assist Churchill in any way. With his initial applications unsuccessful, Churchill once again turned his attention to regimental duties.

The dry season in India runs from December to May and it was then that the 4th Hussars had their busiest training schedule. On 15 January 1897, 275 officers and men of the regiment commanded by Major

Kincaid-Smith marched fifteen miles to Rajankunte for a fifteen-day camp of exercise.[64] The manoeuvres at Kundana camp were much more challenging than exercises in Great Britain, due in no small part to the rugged terrain and climate. In a letter home Churchill referred to the camp as an 'arid place – bare as a plate and hot as an oven'.[65]

The field uniforms worn by the 4th Hussars in India were the product of decades of British experience in such inhospitable climes and Churchill referred to the 'cool and comfortable khaki kit'.[66] The service dress was the standard field uniform of khaki drill or serge cloth adopted for overseas service. Dress regulations for officers of the army provided, 'It will be fitted loosely to admit warm clothing being worn underneath if necessary, in cold weather or on active service.'[67] The uniform frock, or jacket, featured a stand-and-fall collar, patch pockets, five small brass buttons down the front and chain-mail epaulettes, or shoulder chains, to deflect sword cuts from an enemy. A padded, cloth spine protector could be buttoned on the back to shield its wearer from the sun. Campaign ribbons were worn above the left chest pocket. Officers' rank insignia were worn on the shoulder chains, those for other ranks on the sleeves. The uniform trousers were of khaki drill of the infantry style, or brown cord riding breeches or Bedford breeches with soft leather on the inside of the trouser legs. The other ranks wore leather lace-up boots wrapped above the ankle in khaki-coloured woolen puttees. Officers had the option of wearing various types of boots; Churchill wore leather boots and Stowasser gaiters wrapping his legs in leather from the ankles to just below the knees. All the hussars wore detachable steel spurs. The uniform was topped off with a cork sun helmet covered in khaki cloth of either the colonial pattern with a short front brim or the popular 'pith hat' style featuring a three-and-a-half-inch-wide brim all the way around. The pith helmet was supplemented on active service or field duty by a long, quilted covering called a helmet curtain which extended the shade provided to the wearer. A leather Sam Browne style belt was worn over the frock with an attached strap extending from the right shoulder to the left waist to help support the regulation-pattern heavy cavalry sword worn there. Officers' pistols were holstered on the right side. For service in India Churchill was armed with a .455 inch model 1892 Webley-Wilkinson revolver that he purchased from Wilkinson in London.[68]

The troops were housed in tents and drilled and manoeuvred for long hours on horseback during the height of the midday sun. Churchill voiced no complaints about the duty in his letters home although the conditions were difficult, the camp moved frequently as part of the war games, and he suffered severely from sunburn on more than one occasion. The work was all the more interesting because the regimental adjutant, his friend Lt Barnes, was on leave and Churchill was filling in for him. As adjutant he served as the operations officer and chief staff officer to the unit commander with responsibility for record keeping, personnel and military discipline issues, preparation of the duty rosters and distribution of the commander's orders of the day.[69] This was a signal honour for a junior lieutenant, an indication not only of Churchill's ability but the recognition of it by his superiors. He wrote to Lady Randolph on 28 January 1897 from Kundana camp:

> I have had for the first time in my military experience – responsibility & have discharged it, not altogether without success. The regiment has had to adopt itself to the new conditions of a strange country, has had to find out many things which it would have been easy for others to explain; has been exposed to the carping criticism of those Anglo-Indian soldiers who look upon soldiering in England as farcical and in spite of all the difficulties its reputation for smartness has been unimpaired.[70]

Two weeks after their return to Bangalore the regiment, 240 strong, was in the field again on an exercise, called a 'long reconnaissance' of five days' duration which included chart and compass practice.[71] Churchill wrote his mother a proud letter from camp about his additional duties in the multi-regiment exercise: 'I am doing "Brigade Major" a most important duty and one which in England could never have been obtained in under 14 or 15 years of service. I am still doing adjutant so that soldiering prospects are very prosperous. I am becoming my dear Mamma a very 'correct officer.' Full of zeal etc.'[72] He was, in fact, keenly interested in his work and energetic in fulfilling his duties. He reported to his mother in the same letter that Colonel Ramsay had provided a letter of recommendation to accompany his application for service in the Sudan in which he stated Churchill 'was a good rider, 'a very smart cavalry officer' and knew my work in the field thoroughly'.[73] His subordinates also commented on his zeal, though from a different perspective. Sergeant Hallaway recalled:

> After a field day Mr Churchill would arrive at stables with rolls of foolscap and lots of lead pencils of all colours, and tackle me on the movements we had done at the exercise. We were nearly always short of stable men, and there were a lot of spare horses to be attended to, so it was quite a hindrance to me. If I was not paying much attention to Mr Churchill's drawings of the manoeuvres he would roll the paper up and say, 'All right, you are bad-tempered today!' I was not bad-tempered really, but I was a busy man, and I had not time for tactics.[74]

Aside from field problems and encampments, all was routine. On March 6–8 1897, the 4th Hussars underwent their annual inspection by Brigadier General D. J .S. McLeod, the general officer commanding the Bangalore district, after which the annual training scheme plodded along on its usual course. That spring Churchill was well pleased with his prospects as a cavalry officer and planned to stay in the army for two more years unless a seat became available for him in Parliament – the goal that was always on his mind. On 2 April Churchill had another of his many narrow escapes from a fate that would have cut short his political career before it even began, this time on the musketry range. As he reported home in a letter to his mother a few days later:

> We live in a world of strange experiences. In Cuba it was my fortune to be under fire without being wounded. At Bangalore I have been wounded without being under fire. Four days ago I was in charge of the markers in the rifle butts and was sitting on the seat provided thinking myself perfectly safe – when a bullet struck the iron edge of the Target – flew into splinters & rebounded all over me. One entered my left hand near the thumb and penetrated an inch and a half. Several other struck in my khaki coat and many whistled all around. It is to the mercy of God - as some would say - or to the workings of chance or the doctrine of averages – as others prefer, that I was not hit in the eye – in this case I should have been blinded infallibly ... Knowing, as you do, my keen aversion to physical pain or even discomfort I am sure you will sympathise with me.[75]

In spite of this injury and his occasional polo and riding mishaps, Churchill maintained good health in India even though some of his fellow officers were stricken with malaria or enteric fever.

As the spring of 1897 passed by in Bangalore and the weather got hotter, Churchill grew restless and bored. Writing home in April of his plan to return to England for three months of accumulated privilege leave that summer, he stated: 'Poked away in a garrison town which resembles a 3rd rate watering place, out of season and without the sea, with lots of routine work and a hot and trying sun – without society or good sport – half of my friends on leave and the other half ill – my life here would be intolerable were it not for the consolations of literature ... I have lived the life of a recluse here ... I must take a holiday.'[76] Over the strong objections of Lady Randolph who was concerned about the expense of travel and the possible harm to Winston's reputation if he left his duty station after so brief a period overseas, Churchill left Bombay on the P & O's SS *Caledonia* on 8 May, bound for Brindisi. On board he met Colonel Ian

Hamilton of the Gordon Highlanders who was also serving in India. Their acquaintance became a close friendship that lasted for decades. Churchill had hoped to stop over in Turkey to gather material for a book about the conflict there or to work as a correspondent, but the war between Greece and Turkey had ended by the time he reached Port Said in Egypt. Instead, he spent two weeks touring in Italy, his appreciation of Rome enhanced by his study of Gibbon, and then travelled homeward through Switzerland and France.

By 10 June 1897, Churchill was back in London at Great Cumberland Place, looking forward to the London season, and on hand for the big parade for Queen Victoria's Diamond Jubilee which was celebrated on 22 June. He also planned to devote some of his leave to politics and was soon in touch with Fitzroy Stewart, secretary of the Conservative Party central office with the result that he gave the first political speech of his career to the Primrose League in Bath on 26 July 1897. The speech was covered by *The Morning Post* and the *Bath Daily Chronicle,* the latter reporting Churchill's closing remarks as follows:

> There were not wanting those who said that in this Jubilee year our Empire had reached the height of its glory and power, and that now we should begin to decline, as Babylon, Carthage, and Rome and declined. Do not believe these croakers (said Mr Churchill), but give the lie to their dismal croaking by showing by our actions that the vigour and vitality of our race is unimpaired and that our determination is to uphold the Empire that we have inherited from our fathers as Englishmen (cheers), that our flag shall fly high upon the sea, our voice be heard in the councils of Europe, our Sovereign supported by the love of her subjects, then shall we continue to pursue that course marked out for us by the love of her subjects, then shall we continue to pursue that course marked out for us by an all-wise hand and carry out our mission of bearing peace, civilisation and good government to the uttermost ends of the earth (loud cheers) ...[77]

It was an auspicious beginning to a political career that would span six decades. Churchill enjoyed the experience greatly and found speech writing, like combat, not wholly unsuitable to his temperament.

On 26 July 1897, while Churchill was still on leave in England thousands of miles away, a major uprising of Muslim tribesmen began on the North-West Frontier of India along the border with Afghanistan. He noted from newspaper accounts that the Malakand Field Force would be created under the command of General Sir Bindon Blood to quell the rebellion. Churchill promptly sent a telegraph to Blood with a request to serve with the force and a reminder of the promise he had extracted from the general the year before at Deepdene. Without awaiting a reply, Churchill cut short his leave and on 29 July took the train for Brindisi where he boarded the mail ship SS *Rome* and sailed for India. He was anxious to receive a summons from General Blood but arriving off Aden on 8 August, there was no reply telegram nor was there any message for him when he arrived in Bombay or even upon his return to Bangalore on 17 August. Churchill was disgusted and speculated that someone at headquarters had 'put a spoke in my wheel.'[78] Back at the regiment he devoted his spare time to the amusement of writing a novel, which he provisionally entitled *Affairs of State*, a political romance set in a mythical Mediterranean country of Laurania. He wrote to his mother about the project on 24 August: 'I think you will be suprised when you get the MS. It is far and away the best thing that I have ever done ... I am quite enthusiastic about it. All my philosophy is put in the mouth of the hero ... It is full of adventure.'[79] He finished five of the book's twenty-two chapters before he got the news he so eagerly awaited.

Finally, sometime after 24 August, he received a letter from Bindon Blood dated 22 August 1897 from Mingaora camp in the Upper Swat river valley at the North-West Frontier advising Churchill that all his staff positions were presently filled but that 'I should advise your coming to me as a press correspondent, and when you are here I shall put you on the strength on the 1st opportunity ... if you were here I think I could, and certainly would if I could, do a little jobbery on your account.'[80] This was the chance Churchill was waiting for and with adjutant Reggie Barnes's help and Colonel Ramsay's indulgence he obtained a six-week leave from the 4th Hussars and by the evening of 28 August, with a manservant, his kit and two horses, he was on the train for the 2,027-mile journey to Nowshera, the railhead for the Malakand Field Force. Although he left Bangalore before being accredited to any newspaper, by the time he reached the frontier he had received commissions as a war correspondent from both an English newspaper, the *Daily Telegraph*, and an Indian daily, the *Allahabad Pioneer*, the same paper with which Rudyard Kipling had begun his journalistic career. On the six-day rail journey, made a day longer by a stop in Rawalpindi, he found time to write to his mother on 29 August:

Dearest Mamma before this letter reaches you I shall probably have had several experiences, some of which will contain the element of danger. I view every possibility with composure. It might not have been worth my while, who am really no soldier to risk so many fair chances on a war which can only help me directly in a profession I mean to discard. But I have considered everything and I feel that the fact of having seen service with British troops while still a young man must give me more weight politically – must add to my claims to be listened to and may perhaps improve my prospects of gaining popularity with the country. Besides this – I think I am of an adventurous disposition and shall enjoy myself not so much in spite of as because of the risks I run. At any rate I have decided – and having taken a hand I shall do my best to play a good game.[81]

His hoped-for career in politics was always the focus of his ambitions and to see action and possibly win distinction was his unabashed goal as a soldier. 'It is a chance,' he wrote to his brother on 31 August, 'perhaps a good chance of seeing active service and securing a medal.'[82]

On 3 September, Churchill detrained at Nowshera and seven hours in the 'really amazing heat' and fifty miles later arrived via pony cart at the Malakand Pass. Within two hours he was at the Malakand fort and reported to the headquarters staff office, finally at the North-West Frontier.

The Himalayan mountain range, which extends some 1,600 miles from east to west, formed a great natural barrier between India and the great power of imperial Russia. The western part of the range is called the Hindu Kush and to the south of it was the seat of war for the Malakand Field Force, an area perhaps 100 miles wide from west to east and 400 miles long from south-west to north-west, a rugged chain of mountains and valleys that form the border between India and Afghanistan. As Churchill described it: 'Standing on some lofty pass or commanding point in Dir, Swat or Bajaur, range after range is seen as the long surges of an Atlantic swell, and in the distance some glittering snow peak suggests a white-crested roller higher than the rest.'[83] On a more immediate level, Churchill noted: 'The ground is broken and confused as can be imagined. On every side steep and often precipitous hills, covered with boulders and stunted trees, rise in confused irregularity.'[84] It was a vast area of steep slopes, spurs, knolls, re-entrants and dry watercourses, called *nullahs*, but also the scene of broad, fertile river valleys. It was cold at night and very hot in the daytime. It was an area where wheeled vehicles could not operate and supplies had to be carried by man, mules or camels in this, an age before cars, trucks, armoured vehicles or aircraft. Here the terrain dictated both tactics and strategy; there were thousands of hiding places and every elevation seemed to be overlooked by one higher. Such mountain terrain always favoured the tribesmen defending it, not the army columns entering it. As Churchill later wrote in an article for *The United Services Magazine*:

If the savage tribesmen of the hills descend into the plains, a few squadrons and battalions can chase them back into their fastnesses in panic and disorder. All this is changed when the soldiers enter the hills. Great and expensive forces with all the development of scientific war, are harried and worried without rest or mercy by an impalpable cloud of active and well armed skirmishers. To enter the mountains to attack an Afridi [tribesman] is to jump into the water to catch a fish.[85]

Yet that was exactly what the field forces had always done and the latest one was poised to do again. The North-West Frontier was the scene of a subalterns' war where the courage and skills of individuals and of small units counted for everything and the global might of the Royal Navy mattered not at all.

The British and Indian armies were very active throughout the nineteenth century in and around India, including wars or battles in neighbouring Afghanistan, Burma, Nepal and Ceylon. They were nowhere more active than on the North-West Frontier which was the scene of continuous fighting between the British and the local tribes for over a century. These campaigns are commemorated in no fewer than eighteen campaign medals, some issued for single battles or campaigns and others issued for longer periods which had bars or clasps added to the medal ribbon to recognise service in certain campaigns or expeditions. The India General Service Medal (1854–95) had twenty-four bars including 'North-West Frontier' awarded for any of sixteen campaigns there in the period from 1849 to 1868. The India Medal (1895–1902) had seven bars, all for campaigns on the North-West Frontier. The fighting continued well into the twentieth century and the India General Service Medal (1908–35) had twelve bars beginning with 'NW Frontier 1908' and ending with 'NW Frontier 1935'. The last special campaign medal for active service in the British army in India was the India General Service Medal (1936–9) which had two bars, both for campaigns on the North-West Frontier.[86] There had been seven field forces or expeditions on the North-West Frontier in the 1890s before the Malakand Field Force was organised in the summer of 1897 involving a variety of tribes but all were similar in their purposes.[87]

The British army in India was the enforcer of the so-called Forward Policy of expanding British control to the Durand Line, the newly defined border between India and Afghanistan which had been established by treaty in 1893. The Forward Policy was part of the 'Great Game' of keeping the Amir of Afghanistan on the west side of the passes into India and containing the expansionist tendencies of Tsarist Russia and so providing for the protection of India from foreign encroachment. It was a self-interested policy of expanding British military control and so allowing for the expansion of British political power and economic interests. In the area of the frontier it meant keeping the warring tribes in their places in two senses – geographically by restricting them to their mountain villages and politically by responding to every incursion, every attack with military force to demonstrate British authority. The imperial policy was one deterring other tribes and subject peoples from challenging British rule and not only on the North-West Frontier. As Churchill recognized: 'Perhaps it might be well to remember, that the great drama of frontier war is played before a vast, silent but attentive audience, who fill a theatre that reaches from Peshawar to Colombo, and from Kurrâchee to Rangoon.'[88] In truth the audience was world-wide as the British Empire had possessions on every continent and on the islands of every ocean. From the tribes' perspective the conflict was simple. As Churchill later wrote: 'Having seen the forts and roads being made in their territory [by the British], they rightly thought their liberties were threatened by annexation.'[89] And so they were.

When Churchill arrived at Malakand camp on 2 September 1897, General Blood was not there but away leading a flying column to the Upper Swat river valley to deal with the Bunerwal tribe. While awaiting the general's return, Churchill was made a member of the staff mess and got acquainted with his new colleagues and their traditions. According to *My Early Life*, it was during this hiatus that Churchill acquired a taste for whisky, which he had never enjoyed before:

I now found myself in heat which, though I stood it personally fairly well, was terrific, for five whole days with absolutely nothing to drink, apart from tea, except either tepid water or tepid water with lime-juice or tepid water with whisky. Faced with these alternatives I 'grasped the larger hope' ... By the end of these five days I had completely overcome my repugnance to the taste of whisky. Nor was this a momentary acquirement. On the contrary the ground I gained in those days I have firmly entrenched, and held throughout my whole life ... to this day, although I have always practised true temperance, I have never shrunk when occasion warranted it from the main basic standing refreshment of the white officer in the East.[90]

Churchill also took advantage of his wait for General Blood to familiarise himself with the progress of the campaign to date and the strength and composition of the opposing forces.

ve: The Royal Military College Sandhurst, 1895. *By kind permission of the Royal Military*
'emy, Sandhurst.

w: Company E, The Royal Military College Sandhurst, 1894. Churchill is in the fourth row,
from the right. *By kind permission of the Royal Military Academy, Sandhurst.*

row: H. C. Luckhardt, E. G. Drummond, J. M. Bruce, A. J. Allardyce, H. E. Pryce,
. Maclean, G. H. Sawyer, P. S. Allan, C. B. Woodham, E. H. Waring, E. G. Sexton, F. N. Parsons.
h row: R. W. Longfield, O. H. Newmarch, C. H. Lennox, J. T. Ferris, H. C. Stockwell, F. Swabey,
. Hennell, G. J. Wolseley, W. L. Churchill, R. H. Morant, S. J. Carey.
l row: A. D. Strong, G. H. Anderson, H. A. Watson, C. S. Stocks, C. E. Hollins,
Carpenter, V. E. Muspratt, I. G. Hogg, W. S. Leslie, J. H. Jebb, G. S. Palmer, D. M. Cameron,
. Yorke.
d row: Staff-Sergt Girling, I. W. Watson, J. H. Davidson, H. Shipley, L. R. Vaughan,
Grover, A. C. Durnford, H. N. Corbett, F. T. Hill, O. St J. Skeen, F. P. Braithwaite, E. C. Wallace,
Wheatley, A. Armstrong, T. A. Forbes.
row: J. J. Buckley, C. O. Blewitt, H. F. Bundock, F. C. Shirt, C. H. Villiers-Stuart, W. E. Tyndall
er-Officer), Major O. J. H. Ball, V. H. Awdry, W. S. Blackett, C. S. Rome, C. Saunders,
Cooke.

Above: Churchill (left) as a Sandhurst cadet. *Author's collection.*
Opposite Page: Churchill's commission as second lieutenant, 12 February 1895, signed by Que
Victoria. *Churchill Papers CHAR 1/13 held at the Churchill Archive Centre, Cambridge.*

Victoria

by the Grace of God of the United Kingdom of Great Britain and Ireland, Queen, Defender of the Faith, Empress of India; To Our Trusty and well beloved Winston Leonard Spencer Churchill, Gentleman, Greeting.

We, reposing especial Trust and Confidence in your Loyalty, Courage, and good Conduct, do by these Presents Constitute and Appoint you to be an Officer in Our Land Forces from the twentieth day of February 1895. You are therefore carefully and diligently to discharge your Duty as such in the Rank of 2nd Lieutenant or in such higher Rank as We may from time to time hereafter be pleased to promote or appoint you to, of which a notification will be made in the London Gazette, and you are at all times to exercise and well discipline in Arms both the inferior Officers and Men serving under you and use your best endeavours to keep them in good Order and Discipline. And We do hereby Command them to Obey you as their superior Officer, and you to observe and follow such Orders and Directions as from time to time you shall receive from Us, or any your superior Officer, according to the Rules and Discipline of War, in pursuance of the Trust hereby reposed in you.

Given at Our Court at Saint James's, the twentieth day of February 1895 in the Fifty-eighth Year of Our Reign.

By Her Majesty's Command.

H. Campbell-Bannerman

Winston Leonard Spencer Churchill, Gentleman.
2nd Lieutenant
Land Forces.

Left: Lieutenant Winston L. Churchill, 4th (Queen's Own) Hussars, 1895; full dress uniform. *Author's collection.*
Right: The Battle of La Reforma, Cuba, 1895. Taken from a sketch by Churchill which appears in the lower left. From the Daily Graphic, 21 December 1895. *Author's collection.*

Right: Churchill at Bangalore, India, 1898. *Author's collection.*

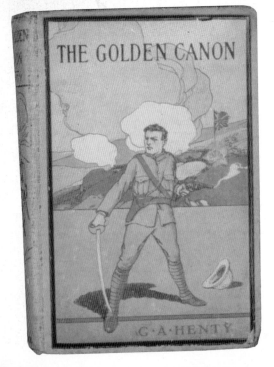

Left: *The Golden Canon* by G. A. Henty (1899). Churchill enjoyed the boisterous novels of Henty when he was a boy. This book cover closely resembles Churchill. *Author's photograph.*

ove: Churchill's telescope and case
d in India. Collection of the Queen's
al Hussars: *Author's photograph.*
posite page, top: Churchill's
galow on South Parade, Bangalore,
a. *Photograph by David Barnard.*
posite page, bottom: The action at
hi-Tangi, on the North-West
ntier of India on 16 September
7, in which Churchill took part with
35th Sikhs. *Illustrated London News.*
ht: Lt Churchill in field uniform,
hed to the 21st Lancers, the Sudan,
8. *Author's collection.*

Above: The charge of the 21st Lancers at Omdurman, the Sudan, 2 September 1898. *From a painting by Caton Woodville. Author's collection.*

Below: The regimental-pattern cavalry swords in use during Churchill's service with the British army. Top: Light Pattern, bottom: Heavy Pattern. *Photograph by Dr Cyril Mazansky.*

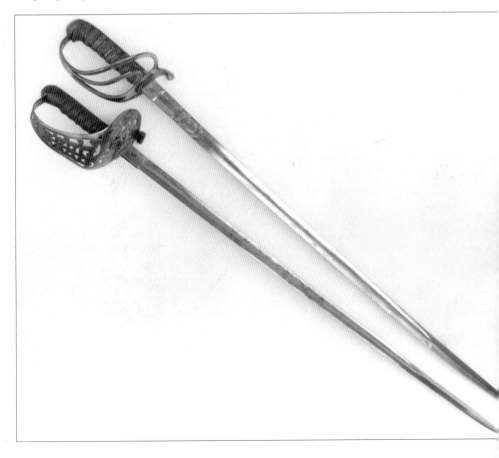

The order of battle of the local tribes is not capable of precise description but Churchill estimated there were 12,000 active fighters confronting the Malakand Field Force.[91] These were from many different tribes under a variety of local warlords and khans, sometimes hostile and sometimes conciliatory depending on a series of ever-shifting alliances, the scenes of action and the periodic truces won by fighting, negotiation or bribery. The tribes were united by two common bonds, however, their Muslim faith and their opposition to British control; these two were inextricably intertwined. They viewed the British as infidels whom their mullahs urged them to destroy or drive from the valleys thus preserving their traditional tribal way of life. Churchill viewed the matter as a fundamental conflict between civilisation and militant Mohammedanism which he believed to be complete opposites. He had no respect for the religious culture of the tribes, referring to them as an 'ignorant, warlike, population of mad dogs fit only to be treated as such'.[92] At the same time, he admired the military characteristics of the tribesmen that made them such a formidable foe. Writing in his second letter to the *Daily Telegraph* from Khar on 6 September, he said: 'The Swatis, Bunerwals, Mohmands, and other frontier tribes with whom the Malakand Field Force is at present engaged are brave and warlike. Their courage has been abundantly displayed in the present campaign.'[93] In *The Story of The Malakand Field Force*, written after his return to Bangalore, his portrait of the tribesmen was more colourfully drawn: 'To the ferocity of the Zulu are added the craft of the Redskin and the marksmanship of the Boer ... The world is presented with that grim spectacle, the strength of civilisation without its mercy.'[94]

As Churchill rightly observed, warfare was an age-old way of life for these mountain people whose culture of violence was incompatible with the British sense of gentlemanly fair play in the conduct of war. For Churchill it was simply a contest between civilisation and social progress represented by the British Empire and the onslaught of barbarism represented by the border tribes. Uncivilised though they might be, however, the tribesmen were challenging opponents armed with modern breech-loading rifles, fighting on their home ground and as certain of the righteousness of their cause as Churchill and his fellow soldiers were of theirs.

The Malakand Field Force assembled to deal with the Pathan uprising was substantial with 6,800 infantry troops, 700 cavalry troopers and twenty-four field guns. A mix of British and Indian units, the force was originally organised as follows:

1st Brigade.
Commanding Colonel W. H. Meiklejohn, CB, CMG, with the local rank of
Brigadier-General.
1st Border Royal West Kent Regiment.
24th Punjab Infantry.
31st Punjab Infantry.
45th (Rattray's) Sikhs.
Sections A and B of No. 1 British Field Hospital.
No. 38 Native Field Hospital.
Sections A and B of No. 50 Native Field Hospital.

2nd Brigade.
Commanding Brigadier-General P. D. Jeffreys, CB.
1st Border East Kent Regiment (the Buffs).
35th Sikhs.
38th Dogras.
Guides Infantry.
Sections C and D of No. 1 British Field Hospital.
No. 37 Native Field Hospital.
Sections C and D of No. 50 Native Field Hospital.

Divisional Troops.
4 Squadrons 11th Bengal Lancers.
1   ”   10th
2   ”   Guides Cavalry.
22nd Punjab Infantry.
2 companies 21st Punjab Infantry.
10th Field Battery.
6 Guns No. 1 British Mountain Battery.
6   ”   No. 7   ”   ”   ”
6   ”   No. 8 Bengal   ”   ”
No. 5 Company Madras Sappers and Miners.
No. 3   ”   Bombay   ”   ”   ”
Section B of No. 13 British Field Hospital.
Sections A and B of No. 35 Native Field Hospital

Line of Communications.
No. 34 Native Field Hospital.
Section B of No. 1 Native Field Hospital. 95

A third brigade under Brigadier-General Wodehouse was placed at
Rustam as a reserve for later employment. The Field Force commander,
General Sir Bindon Blood, had been commissioned in the Royal Engineers
in 1860 and had seen a good deal of active service, participating in the
Jowacki Afridi expedition in India in 1877–8, the Zulu War in 1879, the
Afghan war in 1880, and the war in Egypt in 1882 where he fought in the

battle of Tel-el-Kebir with the Highland Brigade. He had been continuously in India since 1885 in positions of importance. Churchill thought the world of him and in *The Story of the Malakand Field Force* which he dedicated to the general, he wrote: 'I shall content myself with saying that the general is one of that type of soldiers, and administrators, which the responsibilities and dangers of empire produce, a type which has not been perhaps possessed by any nation except the British, since the days when the senate of the Roman people sent their proconsuls to all parts of the world.'[96]

The Pathan uprising began on 26 July 1897, when the tribal forces launched a surprise attack on the British garrison at Malakand at night and soon after laid siege to the garrison at Chakdara eight miles away. These were two key positions as the fort at Malakand protected the Malakand Pass and the fort at Chakdara guarded a key bridge over the Swat river which was essential for communications with the British railhead at Nowshera. Both were necessary to keep open the road to Chitral, 100 miles to the north, which was the most remote British garrison on the frontier. The daily fighting over the next week resulted in 174 casualties among the Anglo-Indian forces including three British officers killed and ten wounded. Relief forces moved immediately toward Malakand from Nowshera and the Governor-General created the Malakand Field Force on 30 July 1897, to secure and reinforce the British positions then under attack and to conduct any necessary operations against the rebellious tribes.

The attacks on the forts at Malakand and Chakdara were successfully repelled and by early August the tribes of the Lower Swat river valley had ceased fighting. After General Blood's arrival to take command in mid-August, the force moved to the Upper Swat to subdue the tribes there. Some fierce but small-scale fighting ensued and on 17 August Colonel Robert Adams, Lt Alexander Fincastle and Lt Hector MacLean won the Victoria Cross for the rescue under fire of a wounded soldier during a cavalry pursuit.[97] By the time Churchill arrived on the scene the worst danger to the British garrisons had passed and the Malakand Field Force was preparing to conduct a punitive expedition in the valleys of the Bajour district to the north-west of Malakand, reasserting British political and military control of the frontier and exacting a toll for the tribes' violent uprising.

The layout of the camp at Malakand was typical of Anglo-Indian bivouacs used on active service. The infantry and artillery were formed in a large defensive square with the cavalry squadrons, pack animals, supplies and tents inside it. A defensive trench line was dug around the perimeter which provided some shelter from incoming sniper fire. The trench was manned at all times by one section from each company of infantry fully dressed and ready, and sentries were placed at twenty-five yard-intervals to warn of enemy movement. The tents were formed in orderly rows with the precision the military mind requires and presented a sight pleasing to Churchill's eye. As he described it:

> To view the scene by moonlight is alone an experience which would repay much travelling. The fires have sunk to red, glowing specks. The bayonets glisten in a regular line of blue-white points. The silence of weariness is broken by the incessant and uneasy shuffling of the horses. All the valley is plunged in gloom and the mountains rise high and black around. Far up their sides, the twinkling watch-fires of the tribesmen can be seen. Overhead is the starry sky, bathed in the pale radiance of the moon. It is a spectacle that may inspire the philosopher no less than the artist.[98]

A few days after Churchill's arrival, General Blood was back at head-quarters. As he recorded in his memoir, *Four Score Years and Ten*: 'When I returned from the Upper Swat at the end of August, I had found my young friend (in his early twenties then), Lieutenant Winston Churchill, of the 4th Queen's Own Hussars, who joined me as an extra ADC – and a right good one he was!'[99] Churchill was attached to Blood's headquarters from the first part of September and would travel all over the area of operations with a freedom of movement denied to most officers who were tied to their infantry companies or cavalry squadrons. On 5 September, before the force moved out from the Malakand camp to confront the tribes, Churchill wrote a thoughtful letter to Lady Randolph:

> I am at present correspondent of the Pioneer ... At the first opportunity I am to be put on the strength of this force – which will give me a medal if I come through.
> As to the fighting – we march tomorrow, and before a week is out, there will be a battle – probably the biggest yet fought on the frontier this year ... I have faith in my star – that is that I am intended to do something in this world. If I am mistaken – what does it matter?
> At any rate you will understand that I am bound for many reasons to risk something ... In any case – I meant to play this game out and if I lose it is obvious that I never could have won any other.[100]

The Field Force moved out from the Malakand camp north-east to Chakdara on 5 September, over the Catgalla Pass to Sarai on 6 September and on to the Kotai camp on the Panjkora river on the 7th. Each day's march was much the same, the troops standing to at 5.00 a.m., the march beginning before the dawn and, after a stop for breakfast, reaching the next bivouac by midday, having covered anywhere from eight to fourteen miles before the worst heat of the day.[101] The Panjkora river bridge was the gateway to the Bajour district where the next round of fighting was expected to take place. The bridge is now gone but the stone abutments remain, a ruin of the Royal Engineers' former glory. On 8 September the force moved to camp at Ghosam where it remained for three days while the political officer, Major Deane, parleyed with the local chieftans and the cavalry squadrons patrolled out in every direction. Although the political agents were the essential diplomatic arm of the Indian government in Calcutta, they were viewed askance by the young British officers who were eager for combat.[102] None the less, always on the look-out for adventure and a good story for the newspapers, Churchill accompanied two squadrons of the 11th Bengal Lancers who escorted Deane on a visit to Barwa in the upper Jandol valley on 10 September, an area only ten or so miles from the border with Afghanistan. Also in the group were Major Beatson, Major Delamain and Lt Waterfield of the 11th Bengal Lancers, Lt Fincastle of the 16th Lancers and Major Edmund Hobday of the Royal Artillery whose drawing of the parties' luncheon with the local khan appeared in his book, *Sketches on Service During the Indian Frontier Campaigns of 1897.*[103] Churchill recorded that it was a pleasant meal of pears, apples, chupattis and dishes of rice served as they sat on a carpet-covered charpoys (bedsteads) in the shade of beautiful chenar trees. Still, guards were posted and all security measures taken.

On 11 September, Churchill accompanied a patrol to the Utman Khel area south of the camp and observed their reconnaissance and map-making efforts. On the 12th, the 3rd Brigade which had come up on Blood's orders, and headquarters staff, Churchill included, marched the twelve miles to Shamshuk and the 2nd Brigade marched seven miles to Jar and set up camp there. That night Churchill witnessed sniping into the camp at night for the first time since he joined the force; it must have reminded him of nights in Cuba.

On 13 September, Blood sent out patrols including two squadrons of the 11th Bengal Lancers which made an incursion to the north up the Mohmand valley. There they set fire to a village and as they withdrew from the valley came under fire from tribesmen on the hillsides. It was a minor skirmish resulting in no casualties but it heralded more serious fighting to come. Churchill was present in camp to observe the Lancers' return and recorded it in his history of the campaign with one of the most memorable comments he ever made on the subject of active service: 'They were vastly pleased with themselves. Nothing in life is so exhilarating as to be shot at without result.'[104]

The next day, the 3rd Brigade, with Blood's headquarters and Churchill, moved seven miles west to Nowagai and the 2nd Brigade marched from Jar to Markhanai eleven miles south near the Rambat Pass. During the night the 2nd Brigade was attacked and suffered sixteen casualties including three British officers killed, and the loss of ninety-eight horses and pack mules.[105] The next day, 14 September, Blood ordered Brigadier-General Jeffreys to take the 2nd Brigade back to the Mohmand valley to conduct punitive operations in retaliation for the attack and by the night of the 15th the brigade set up camp on open ground near Inayat Kila two or three miles from the entrance to the valley. As General Blood later wrote in his memoirs: 'As soon as I heard of General Jeffrey's mishap, I sent for Churchill and suggested his joining the General in order to see a little fighting. He was all for it, so I sent him over at once and he saw more fighting than I expected, and very hard fighting too!'[106]

Churchill accepted the offer and with an escort of Bengal Lancers on the 15th rode the ten miles to the 2nd Brigade's position where sniping into the camp began after dinner and continued until 2.00 a.m. Churchill lay awake late into the night contemplating the stars, 'those impartial stars which shine as calmly on Piccadilly Circus as they do on Inayat Kila'.[107] The next day would bring Churchill his first combat in India and one of the most dangerous days of his life.

The Mohmand valley was a fan-shaped cul-de-sac with a mile-wide opening at its southern end and was perhaps ten miles in length from south to north and about six miles wide at its broadest point. The Watelai river drained through the centre of the valley and terraced fields rose from its floor with more than two dozen villages dotting the terrain from the banks of the river up on to the steep hillsides that formed the perimeter of the valley. The area was only a few miles from the Afghan border.

The 2nd Brigade's mission on entering the Mohmand valley on 16 September was, in Churchill's word, to 'chastise' the tribes in retaliation for their attack on Markhanai by burning crops, destroying reservoirs and blowing up fortified buildings in the villages. The entire brigade took part, divided into three columns with the goal of covering as much of the valley as possible in a single day. With various infantry companies left to guard the camp and others not taking part, the attacks were made by a force of only 1,000 men. Churchill attached himself to the centre column commanded by Lieutenant Colonel Thomas Goldney of the 35th Sikhs which included twelve companies of infantry, six each from the East Kent Regiment (The Buffs) and the 35th Sikh Regiment of Bengal Infantry, a cavalry squadron from the 11th Bengal Lancers, four artillery pieces from the No. 8 Mountain Battery and a half-company of sappers.[108] The objective of Goldney's column was to destroy two villages at the far north end of the valley, Badelai and Shahi-Tangi.

The column set out at 6.00 a.m. and Churchill, boldly riding a conspicuous grey charger much as General Valdez has done in the battle of La Reforma in Cuba, went forward with the Bengal Lancers who led the way. During the advance the villages in the valley seemed deserted and the troops were not fired upon. The Lancers reached the end of the valley at about 7.30 a.m. and opened a dismounted fire with their carbines against tribesmen seen on a conical hill who returned their fire. By the time this preliminary skirmish ended an hour later, the infantry had arrived. It was determined the Sikhs would move on Shahi-Tangi and the Buffs would move on Badelai to their right. Of the six companies of Sikhs, one and a half companies (seventy-five men) were detailed to take the conical hill between the two villages and four and a half companies (225 men) advanced farther. Of these, a half-company was left with the aid station and two companies remained at the foot of the hills in reserve. The last two companies, five officers and eighty-five men, were all that remained to advance up the long spur terminated by Shahi-Tangi.

Churchill dismounted and advanced on foot with the two leading Sikh companies for the final mile-long climb up to the village. That it was hard going was evidenced by the fact it took them two and a half hours to cover that last distance reaching the village at 11.00 a.m. They met no resistance on the way up except for some sniping and after a look around set fire to whatever would burn and were ordered to withdraw about fifteen minutes later. The spur they began to descend consisted of three distinct but connected knolls, each at a lower elevation than the last. Just as the withdrawal began from the village to the first knoll the scene changed dramatically. As Churchill recorded:

Suddenly the mountain-side sprang to life. Swords flashed from behind rocks, bright flags waved here and there. A dozen widely-scattered white smoke-puffs broke from the rugged face in front of us. Loud explosions resounded close at hand. From high up on the crag, one thousand, two thousand, three thousand feet above us, white or blue figures appeared, dropping down the mountainside from ledge to ledge like monkeys down the branches of a tall tree. A shrill crying rose from many points. Yi! Yi! Yi! Bang! Bang! Bang! The whole hillside began to be spotted with smoke, and tiny figures descended every moment nearer to us.[109]

So began what Lt Fincastle described as 'that most difficult of all tasks, the retirement downhill in the presence of a brave and fanatical foe'.[110] A retreat in the irregular warfare of the frontier was hazardous for a number of reasons. The very fact of such a retreat emboldens the enemy to press its attack. The retreating force must bring along its dead and wounded because the tribesmen are known to give no quarter to the injured and to mutilate the bodies of the dead. Every soldier who is carrying a casualty is removed from the ranks of those firing on the enemy, so that the effectiveness of the rearguard is weakened. And in the case of Shahi-Tangi, the narrowness of the spur down which the retreat was made reduced the size of the front that could be presented to the enemy. Finally, it is important for the rearguards to be in proximity to the main retreating body so that the latter can provide adequate covering fire when the rearguard itself pulls back.[111]

The retreat of the 35th Sikhs on 16 September was necessary because the two lead companies were, according to the after-action report prepared by the Intelligence Branch, 'rather far from their supports'.[112] The captain ordering the retreat told Churchill they were 'rather in the air here' which Churchill said was a 'sound observation'.[113] In short, the force at the tip of the column's spear was too small for safety and the two companies of Sikhs held in reserve and the Buffs were too far away to assist in holding the village or fighting off the attack. The fact is that the detachment Churchill accompanied to Shahi-Tangi was routed, forced out of the village and driven a mile down the spur, fighting desperately all the way.

A half-company of twenty-five men served as the rearguard covering the withdrawal from the village and then from the first knoll, both of which were evacuated without casualties. On the second knoll the situation worsened dramatically. Churchill, another British officer and eight sepoys serving as the rearguard were ordered back to the third knoll. At this moment Churchill, who was in the prone position from which he had been firing a borrowed rifle, and the sepoy who had been handing him ammunition, paused to pick up some extra cartridges from the ground before getting to their feet. Of the eight others who rose up immediately, five were shot down by a rapid volley, two killed and three wounded, including the other officer. As they pulled the wounded back with them they were unable to keep on firing and had no rearguard or covering fire to protect them. The adjutant of the 35th Sikhs, Lt Victor Hughes came up with a few sepoys to assist but was himself shot. Tribesmen were firing on them from only thirty yards away and bullets were flying all around. The men carrying Lt Hughes dropped him and Churchill saw him hacked to death by a Pathan swordsman. Churchill drove the man off with shots from his revolver and then, finding he was all alone, joined the retreat, the last man to do so. The further they descended down the spur the more concentrated the retreating Sikh companies became and the more effective their defensive volleys of rifle fire. They were able to bring eight wounded back with them but left Lt Hughes and twelve dead or wounded behind. At the foot of the spur, now joined by the reserve companies, the tide turned:

> Then somebody sounded the charge. The men halted. Bayonets were fixed. It was a supreme moment. The officers ran forwards and waved their swords. Everyone began to shout. Then the forward movement began slowly at first, but gaining momentum rapidly. As the enemy fled back to their hills many dropped under the fire of the Sikhs.[114]

The 35th Sikhs were soon joined by the Buffs who had come over from the right to support them. Together and under the supporting fire of the mountain battery, they marched right back up the spur, completely destroyed all the buildings in Shahi-Tangi, recovered the bodies of their dead and by 4.30 p.m. were back on the valley to begin their return march. They were joined by another company of 35th Sikhs which had been attacked near the village of Chingai on the right of the main action and suffered fifteen killed and twelve wounded. They reached camp at Inayat Kila about 8.30 p.m. having been harassed by snipers for most of the eight-mile march which ended in the dark, deluged by a thunderstorm.

Churchill had certainly been in the thick of the fighting all day and handled himself very creditably. He wrote a letter to his mother from Inayat Kila on 19 September about his role in the battle:

> When the retirement began I remained till the last and here I was perhaps very near my end ... I was close to both officers when they were hit almost simultaneously and fired my revolver at a man at 30 yards who tried to cut up poor Hughes's body ... A subaltern – Bethune by name and I carried a wounded Sepoy for some distance and might, perhaps, had there been any gallery, have received some notice. My pants are still stained with the man's blood. We also remained till the enemy came to within 40 yards firing our revolvers ... It was

a horrible business. For there was no help for the man who went down. I felt no excitement and very little fear. All the excitement went out when things became really deadly. Later on I used a rifle which a wounded man had dropped and fired 40 rounds with some effect at close quarters. I cannot be certain, but I think I hit 4 men. At any rate they fell.

Altogther I was shot at from 7.30 [a.m.] till 8 [p.m.] on this day and now begin to consider myself a veteran. Sir Bindon has made me his orderly officer, so that I shall get a medal and perhaps a couple of clasps.

16th was the biggest thing in India since Afghan war. There will be more tomorrow, but I think the worst is over. When I think what the Empire might have lost I am relieved.[115]

Churchill had acted bravely in rescuing a wounded man under intense fire during the retreat yet received no decoration for it. Before the fight at Shahi-Tangi four Victoria Crosses had been earned in the uprising on the North-West Frontier in 1897. All of them – Lt Costello on 26 July, Lt Colonel Adams, Lt Fincastle and Lt McClean on 17 August – had been won for the rescue of wounded men under fire. Why were not Churchill and Lt Bethune recognised? Churchill's explanation is most probably the correct one. There was no gallery to observe the feat, no senior officer or regimental commander to make a recommendation for an award. By way of contrast, on the night of 16 September, Colonel Jeffreys, the 2nd Brigade commander, together with parts of two companies of infantry and the mountain battery, were cut off during their return to camp and surrounded at the village of Bilot where they fought an all-night battle to survive before being relieved at dawn by a column from Inayat Kila. That action, involving perhaps ten British officers and ninety British and Indian soldiers under direct command of Brigadier Jeffreys, resulted in the award of three Victoria Crosses, two Distinguished Service Orders, and four Distinguished Conduct Medals in addition to a number of Indian Orders of Merit.[116]

Another likely reason for the lack of a decoration is that Churchill's conduct, when reported to his superiors, was simply not thought to qualify for a decoration. It did not go unnoticed altogether for in the dispatch of Major General Sir Bindon Blood on the action of the 16th September which contained Brigadier General Jeffrey's report of the action it was noted: 'He [General Jeffreys] has praised the courage and resolution of Lieutenant W. L. S. Churchill, 4th Hussars, the correspondent of the *Pioneer* newspaper with the force who made himself useful at a critical moment.'[117] This coveted mention in dispatches greatly pleased Churchill. When he learned of it later that autumn he wrote to his mother: 'I cannot

tell you with what feelings of hope and satisfaction I receive your information that I have been mentioned in despatches by Sir Bindon Blood. If that
is the case – and I daresay it may be – I shall feel compensated for any thing.
I am more ambitious for a reputation for personal courage than anything
else in the world. A young man should worship a young man's ideals.'[118]

For his service on the North-West Frontier as an aide-de-camp of
General Blood and later as an attached officer with the 31st Punjabis
Churchill would also receive his first campaign medal, the India Medal
1895. It was his first British medal and all his life it was worn in the place
of honour, the right of the line of all his medals. The medal was authorised
by the Army Order of April 1896 to recognise active service on the North-
West Frontier, initially for the defence of Chitral in 1895, and later
extended through 1902 with a total of seven clasps.[119] Lt Churchill was
awarded the India Medal pursuant to Army Order No. 77 of 1 June 1898.
The record of the award to Churchill notes his entitlement to one clasp
only, 'Punjab Frontier 1897–1898,' and also confirms his Mention in
Dispatches.[120] He was not qualified for the clasp 'Malakand 1897"
because it covered operational service for the period of 26 July to 2 August
1897 only and this was before his arrival on the frontier. He did not win
entitlement to the clasp 'Tirah 1897–8" because he joined the Tirah Expeditionary Force in March 1898, too late to see operational service.
Churchill received the first issue of the India Medal with the profile of
Queen Victoria on the obverse wearing both crown and veil surrounded by
the words VICTORIA REGINA ET IMPERATRIX. The reverse of the
medal depicts a British soldier on the left side supporting a rifle with his
right hand and a flag standard with his left, next to an Indian soldier on
the right side whose left hand rests upon the hilt of a sword and right hand
supports the same standard. Along the left side of the reverse is the word
INDIA and on the right the numerals 1895. The medal ribbon is crimson
with two vertical stripes of dark green. The India Medal was issued with
the recipient's name and regiment inscribed on the rim. Churchill's medal
is engraved in script, 'Lieutt W. L. S. Churchill, 4th Q. O. Hussars'.[121]

The action of 16 September was very costly to the 2nd Brigade which
suffered the highest casualty rate for an Anglo-Indian force in years. Two
British officers were killed, five seriously wounded and two slightly
wounded including Brigadier-General Jeffreys. Two British soldiers were
killed and nine wounded. Thirty-four Indian soldiers were killed and
ninety-five wounded. Of the 149 casualties, the 35th Sikhs suffered most
with Lt Hughes killed, Lts Gunning and Cassells wounded severely,

twenty-two sepoys killed and forty-five wounded. Enemy losses were estimated at 200.[122] It was a large loss for the objective achieved – the destruction of a single village. Churchill found the services for the dead
conducted the next day to be thought-provoking. As he wrote in his
history of the campaign:

> Looking at these shapeless forms, coffined in a regulation blanket, the price of
> race, the pomp of empire, the glory of war appeared as the faint insubstantial
> fabric of a dream; and I could not help realising with Burke: 'What shadows we
> are and what shadows we pursue.'[123]

After the action of 16 September General Blood ordered the 2nd
Brigade to remain in the Mohmand valley to complete its punitive
mission which it did with a vengeance. Over the next two weeks the 2nd
Brigade moved methodically through the valley, burning crops, levelling
houses, destroying wells and reservoirs and blowing up fortifications. The
brigade would move out as early as 5.30 a.m. and, with the combined
power of artillery, cavalry and infantry, take and destroy a village and
return to camp at Inayat Kila by nightfall. One by one the villages were
attacked, captured and destroyed – Damadola on 18 September, Zagai on
the 20th, Dag on the 22nd, Tangi on the 23rd. Churchill participated in a
number of these actions accompanying either the Buffs or the Guides
Cavalry and returning each day to Inayat Kila where he drafted seven of
his fifteen letters for the *Daily Telegraph* and talked about the day's actions
in the mess. Captain Ernest Maconchy, of the East Yorkshire Regiment
but then serving with the Indian army, recalled in his memoirs that after
the 35th Sikhs had suffered their heavy losses on 16 September that
Churchill gave him a detailed description of the action.[124] Lt Donald A.
D. McVean, of the Manchester Regiment and later the commander of the
famous 45th (Rattray's Sikhs) Regiment of Bengal Infantry, recorded in
his diary for 25 September 1897: 'Churchill, son of Late Randolph
Churchill who is with Blood arrived from front and shares my tent for the
night on his way down as his leave is finished'[125] McVean ever after told
others of his impression that Churchill was quite fearless in going about
in the considerable action seen by the Malakand Field Force and that the
only thing Churchill was frightened of was getting wounded in the mouth
so that he could not talk.[126]

As the campaign in the Mohmand valley neared its completion the
action intensified and on 29 September the 2nd Brigade destroyed a dozen
villages in the centre of the valley and blew up more than thirty forts

belonging to the tribes. The last major action took place on the 30th at the villages of Agrah and Gat on the west side of the valley eight or nine miles from the base camp. Once again, Lieutenant Churchill was an active participant.

The attack was mounted by the reconstituted 2nd Brigade under the command of Brigadier-General Jeffreys and consisting of the Royal West Kent Regiment with 380 rifles, the 31st (Punjab) Regiment of Bengal Infantry with 385 rifles, the 38th (Dogra) Regiment of Bengal Infantry with 342 rifles, the Corps of Guides Infantry with 364 rifles, the No. 7 Mountain Battery and the Corps of Guides Cavalry with 163 sabres. Churchill was attached to the 31st Punjabis.[127] He later made the switch from British cavalry to Indian infantry as a replacement because so many officers had been killed and wounded in the campaign. General Blood's memoirs note that the colonel of the 31st requested Churchill and that 'he was most useful for several weeks, though he only knew a few words of the language. The [sepoys] took to him at once, recognising immediately that his heart was in the right place.'[128] In his own memoir, *My Early Life*, Churchill wrote that of all the military units he served with in Asia, Africa and Europe, 'this Punjaub Infantry business' was the oddest experience. Although trained in infantry drill and tactics generally, the language barrier was a problem:

I had to proceed almost entirely by signals, gestures and dumbcrambo. To these I added three words, 'Maro' (kill), 'Chalo' (get on), and Tally Ho! which speaks for itself. However, in one way or another we got through without mishap three or four skirmishes ... I must have done it all by moral influence.

Although I could not enter very fully into their thoughts and feelings, I developed a regard for the Punjaubis. There was no doubt they liked to have a white officer among them when fighting, and they watched him carefully to see how things were going. If you grinned, they grinned. So I grinned industriously.[129]

The village of Agrah was located in a broad re-entrant flanked by rocky ridges or spurs leading down from the peaks behind the village which marked the Durand Line, the border with Afghanistan. The village and the surrounding hillsides were defended by thousands of tribesmen and as the Anglo-Indian forces mounted their attack through terraced fields and a dry river-bed from the south-east at about 8.45 a.m., the firing soon began. As the Guides' cavalry took up a blocking position in the fields on the far left, the Guides infantry took the ridge-line on the near-left, or south-west, of the village by frontal assault. The Royal West Kents moved directly on Agrah in the centre supported by the guns of the mountain battery. The 31st Punjabis scaled the spur on the right, east of the village and then joined the Royal West Kents in assaulting the enemy position above Agrah which was taken but not held for long.

During the fighting on the hillside above the villages of Agrah and Gat, Second Lieutenant Williams Browne-Clayton was shot and killed. Churchill witnessed the episode and the first futile attempt to bring his body back. He mentioned the episode matter-of-factly in *The Story of the Malakand Field Force* but left out the awful details and his own reaction to what he had seen. These were revealed in a heartfelt letter to Lady Randolph months later on 16 May 1898:

> I vy rarely detect genuine emotion in myself. I must rank as a rare instance the fact that I cried when I met the Royal West Kents on the 30th Sept and saw the men really unsteady under fire and tired of the game, and that poor young officer Browne-Clayton, literally cut in pieces on a stretcher – through his men not having stood by him.[130]

It soon became clear that the 2nd Brigade was greatly outnumbered and the tribesmen were turning both flanks inward with their rifle fire, which Churchill found 'accurate and intense'. After the village was set alight, a retreat was ordered under cover of shrapnel shells fired by the mountain battery's guns. The 31st Punjabis were exposed to severe and dropping rifle fire from a rocky ridge on their right and, as Churchill later wrote: 'The fighting soon became close.'[131] As the tribesmen moved to within a hundred yards, Colonel James O'Bryen, the commander of the 31st was shot and killed. Under a steady enemy fire, an orderly withdrawal was made and once the brigade reached the plain, the tribesmen, deterred by the presence of cavalry, did not pursue. Among the British soldiers in the attack two officers and two men were killed, six officers and twenty men wounded. Among the Indian soldiers, seven were killed and twenty-three wounded.[132] In a letter to his mother on 2 October Churchill described the attack and withdrawal from Agrah as 'another severe action' and stated:

> I was under fire for five hours – but did not get into the hottest corners. Our loss was 60 killed and wounded – out of the poor 1,200 we can muster. Compare these figures with action like Firket in Egypt – [10,000 engaged and fifty casualties] wh are cracked up as great battles and wh are commemorated by clasps and medals etc. etc. Here out of one brigade we have lost in a fort-night 245 killed and wounded and nearly 25 officers ... This has been the hardest fighting on the frontier for forty years.

The danger and difficulty of attacking these fierce hill men is extreme. They can get up the hills twice as fast as we can – and shoot wonderfully well with Martini Henry Rifles. It is war without quarter.
If I get through alright – and I have faith in my luck – I shall try and come home next year for a couple of months.[133]

The attack at Agrah, the last in which Churchill participated on the North-West Frontier, was a typical action for the field force — a march from camp, an attack made, a village laid waste, casualties inflicted and casualties sustained. The forward policy was furthered; the policy of retaliation and deterrence was maintained. Churchill's own conclusion in *My Early Life* is an accurate summary: 'Whether it was worth it, I cannot tell. At any rate, at the end of a fortnight the valley was a desert, and honour was satisfied.'[134]

After Agrah, both the campaign and Churchill's extended leave from the 4th Hussars began to wind down. Churchill spent the first week of October at Camp Inayat Kila seeing to his regimental duties and penning letters for the newspapers. He had favourably impressed Sir Bindon Blood who wrote the following to Colonel John Brabazon on 4 October:

My dear Brabazon,
Young Winston Churchill will have told you that I have been looking after him and putting him in the way of seeing some real tough fighting. He is now pro tem an officer of native Infantry – of the 31st P. I. I have put him in as he was the only spare officer within reach, and he is working away equal to two ordinary subalterns. He has been mentioned in despatches already, and if he gets a chance will have the VC or a DSO – and here such chances have sometimes gone begging.[135]

Churchill would certainly have remained on the frontier if permitted to do so but it was not to be. An Indian army replacement officer arrived to take his place with the 31st Punjabis. The scene of fighting with the tribes was shifting from Bajaur to the Tirah region west of Peshawar where the Afridi tribesmen had risen and the Tirah Expeditionary Force under General Sir William Lockhart was being organised to subdue them. Churchill's efforts to join the new force failed. Detached from the Malakand Field Force, without sufficient influence to get a place with the new expeditionary force, and with his colonel requiring his return to Bangalore, Churchill began the long journey back whence he had come five weeks earlier.

Churchill left Inayat Kila on 9 October with a convoy escorted by the Royal West Kents and, after an overnight stay at Jar punctuated by sniping into the camp at night, crossed the Panjkora River on the 11th and rode to the rail terminus at Nowshera where he arrived on the 12th and would remain until he boarded the train on 17 October. From Nowshera he wrote a letter to Lady Randolph on 12 October to let her know his active service was at an end for the time being:

> Since last I wrote I have seen two [or] three sharp skirmishes and have now been 10 complete times under fire. Quite a foundation for a political life ... I intend or rather am seriously contemplating writing 'The Story of the M.F.F.' I know the ground, the men, and the facts. It is a fine idea ... I have earned my medal and clasp fully. Blood says not one in a hundred have seen as much fighting as I have – and mind you – not from the staff or a distance but from the last company of the rearguard every time. A splendid episode.[136]

While in Nowshera Churchill also wrote his final two letters for the *Daily Telegraph*, the first a summary of the military lessons he learned on the campaign, the second his overview of the politics of the frontier policy. The military considerations are all of a practical nature, and most are as true today as they were in the nineteenth century. Logistics are the key to successful military operations. Adequate provision must be made for supplies, pack animals, depots, rest camps, and communications to tie an expeditionary force to its base. Camps must be entrenched for protection from sniping and for adequate defence from attack. Infantry must be detailed to protect an artillery battery on all sides. It is necessary in hill fighting to secure the flanks of an attacking force by securing the high ground around an objective before assaulting it. It is necessary, indeed 'a sacred duty,' to bring out all the wounded in a retreat. Much attention must be given to providing adequate cover fire for withdrawals and rearguard actions. Good fire discipline of infantry is essential and the use of ek-dum or dum-dum bullets is recommended. Officers and other ranks should be dressed the same to reduce drawing attention to officers as targets. Heliographs are of great value signalling in the hills. Artillery must be co-ordinated and its fire concentrated to protect the infantry. Cavalry is of great value in protecting the flanks and covering the retreat of infantry. And, very importantly, it is wise policy to send as many serving officers as possible from British regiments to Indian regiments on the frontier, there to receive practical experience and training in war fighting.[137]

As to the frontier question in general, Churchill's final letter is insightful, sound in its conclusions and diplomatically written. He rightly pointed out that the settlement which brought a truce to the Bajaur region was not a permanent one. The tribes had been chastised but not conquered. They were still hostile and were increasingly well armed. Their religious fanaticism was not altered and their true independence had not been taken from them. Churchill saw no commercial benefit of British possession of the frontier area and a growing cost in lives and money to control it militarily. But, given the imperial goals of containing the Russians and the Afghans, he saw no alternative to pursuing the existing policies.[138] In a subsequent letter to his mother he was more direct, writing:

> At any rate now we are started we can't go back and must go on. Financially it is ruinous. Morally it is wicked. Militarily it is an open question, and politically it is a blunder. But we can't pull up now. Annexation is the word the B.P. [British Public] will have ultimately to swallow, and the sooner they do it, the sooner things will begin to mend.[139]

Indeed, there were years of intermittent fighting ahead on the North-West Frontier, continuing right up to the Second World War. In the long run the forward policy did succeed in preventing foreign encroachment if not in suppressing the mountain tribes. As part of Pakistan since 1947, the region is now administered as a series of provincially administered tribal areas within the North-West Frontier province. The Muslim tribesmen still maintain their isolated independence and the area is off-limits to westerners and not considered safe to travel through.[140]

By 21 October Churchill was back in Bangalore where he noted: 'My brother officers when I returned to them were extremely civil; but I found a very general opinion that I had had enough leave and should now do a steady spell of routine duty.'[141] Writing to his mother from Bangalore he reviewed his recent experiences:

> The period has been the most glorious and delightful that my life has yet contained. But the possibility was always in view that it might be abruptly terminated. I saw a great many people killed or wounded and heard many bullets strike all around or whistle by – so many that if I had counted them you would not perhaps believe me ... My luck throughout was extraordinarily good, Everything worked out just as in Cuba – mechanically ... I am immensely satisfied. And now having had a fine experience and being entitled to a medal ... I am back at Bangalore to polo and my friends with a new stimulus to life.[142]

The 4th Hussars pursued its usual schedule of inspections, training and field exercises that autumn. On 23 October Lt General Sir Mansfield Clarke, commander of the troops in Madras, conducted the annual inspection of the regiment mounted in review order on the general parade ground followed by an inspection of the horse lines and barracks on 8 November. Following the latter, he remarked to Lt Colonel Ramsay: 'The state of the horses [is] creditable to all concerned, and it is apparent that much trouble has been taken to get the saddlery into proper order.' It was hardly a glowing report but was none the less satisfactory.[143] Churchill found the regimental routine rather tame in comparison to his recent experiences on the frontier. He resumed his role with the regimental polo club and went to Hyderabad for a tournament in December where he played well and scored most of the team's goals.

The real focus of his attention remained the furtherance of his own career interests by pursuing more opportunities for active service and looking ahead to the political scene in England. When he received the first copies of the *Daily Telegraph* containing his frontier letters he was not pleased to see that they had appeared without his by-line. He wrote to Lady Randolph on 25 October: 'I will not conceal my disappointment at their not being signed. I had written them with the design, a design which took form as the correspondence advanced, of bringing my personality before the electorate. I had hoped that some political advantage might have accrued.'[144] In the same letter he renewed his efforts to enlist his mother's help in getting him permission to join the ongoing campaign in the Sudan:

> I must now go to Egypt and you should endeavour to stimulate the Prince into writing to Kitchener on the subject ... Indeed my life here is not big enough to hold me. I want to be up and doing and cannot bear inaction or routine. Polo has lost half its charm and no longer satisfies me. I become more in need of serious occupation every day. I shall soldier for two years more, but they must be two busy years.[145]

One serious occupation Churchill settled upon was writing his first book, *The Story of the Malakand Field Force, An Episode of Frontier War*. By 10 November he had decided temporarily to shelve the manuscript of his novel, then in its eleventh chapter, and to devote his energies to his history book which he figured would benefit him both politically and financially.

In a sustained burst of activity, writing from three to eight hours a day during the midday heat when others napped or played cards, he was able to complete the manuscript in less than two months. He was in a hurry to get into print before Lord Fincastle, who was writing a history of the campaign of his own. He posted the manuscript to Lady Randolph on 31 December 1897, and left it to her to select a publisher and arrange a contract. Because he did not want to waste time having the proofs sent to him in India to review, he asked his mother to request her brother-in-law Moreton Frewen to correct and revise the proof sheets for him. Finishing the book proved to Churchill that he had strong powers of application and concentration; having it published could help to make his public reputation and serve as another foundation stone for a political career. He wrote of his hopes in a letter to his mother before the book was published:

> The publication of the book will be certainly the most noteworthy act of my life. Up to date (of course). By its reception I shall measure the chance of my possible success in the world ... If it goes down then all may be well.
>
> In politics a man, I take it gets on not so much by what he does, as by what he is. It is not so much a question of brains as of character and originality.[146]

So intent was Churchill on standing for Parliament that he contemplated transferring to a regiment in England or to the Intelligence Branch in London where he could be closer to the centre of political activity and readily at hand should a constituency become available to him. This would allow him to serve in the army and in Parliament at the same time.

Churchill's immediate goal, however, was a return to active service either on the frontier or in Egypt. Writing to his mother of his continuing efforts to join the Tirah Expeditionary Force, he tried to calm her fears about his return to combat:

> Bullets – to a philosopher my dear Mamma – are not worth considering. Besides I am so conceited I do not believe the Gods would create so potent a being as myself for so prosaic an ending.
>
> I do not expect you will view with much satisfaction the efforts I am making to get to Tirah. But I do not feel justified in neglecting any opportunity of adding to my experience. 'Fame' sneered at, melodramatised, degraded is still the finest thing on earth. Nelson's life should be a lesson to the youth of England.
>
> I shall devote my life to the preservation of this great Empire and to trying to maintain the progress of the English people. Nor shall anyone be able to say that vulgar consideration of personal safety ever influenced me.[147]

In January 1898 Churchill obtained ten days of Christmas leave and went to Calcutta, the seat of the Indian government, to lobby for a place on the Tirah Expeditionary Force, planning to 'tap the stream of patronage at its source'.[148] There he stayed with the viceroy, Lord Elgin, spoke to the commander-in-chief, General Sir George White, and bent every ear he could, but all to no avail. The adjutant-general, who was in charge of all appointments to the expeditionary force, refused to grant him an interview and Churchill returned to Bangalore empty-handed.

All through the last months of 1897 and the first months of 1898 Churchill carried on a vigorous correspondence with Lady Randolph and others trying to secure a place with Kitchener's force in the Sudan. He watched the progress of the Sudan expedition with growing impatience and wrote to Lady Randolph on 31 December 1897: 'You must make a tremendous effort to get me to Egypt ... I shall run Tirah as a second string but the other is a better business – as Egypt is a more fashionable theatre of war. This is most important. It would mean another medal – perhaps two – and I have applied to wear my Cuban decoration so that with a little luck I might return quite ornamented. Now do stir up all your influence.'[149] On 10 January 1898, his first letter to her of the new year had the same theme: 'Oh how I wish I could work you up over Egypt! I know you could do it with all your influence – and all the people you know. It is a pushing age and we must shove with the best. After Tirah and Egypt – then I think I shall turn from war to peace and politics. If – that is – I get through all right.'[150]

Lady Randolph wrote directly to Kitchener trying to get her son a place with the Egyptian army. He replied in February to advise he would note Churchill's name for later employment in the Sudan but made no promises.[151] Churchill's former commander in the 4th Hussars, Colonel Brabazon, contacted the War Office in London to try to get him attached to the 21st Lancers, a British cavalry regiment then stationed in Egypt and expected soon to join the Sudan expedition. Nothing seemed to be working to get him to Egypt so Churchill again took the initiative.

On 17 February 1898, Churchill and the 4th Hussars polo team began a term of leave to participate in the annual inter-regimental polo tournament in Meerut, 1,400 miles to the north. Meerut was only twenty-four hours by train from Peshawar, the headquarters of the Tirah Expeditionary Force, which was expected to begin its spring campaign in early March. Churchill's plan was to take the three days' leave allotted for returning to Bangalore after the tournament and go to Peshawar instead to lobby in person for attachment to the force. He knew the only positions not controlled from Calcutta were those on the personal staff of General Lockhart which were made by the general himself. After the tournament, in which the 4th Hussars came in second place after losing to the club from the Durham Light Infantry, Churchill boarded the train for Peshawar. He ran a real risk to his career in doing so because if he failed to secure a place on Lockhart's staff he could never get back to Bangalore before his leave expired and would surely face disciplinary action.

Once again, Churchill had good luck. His friend Colonel Ian Hamilton had been appointed to the command of a brigade of the Tirah Expeditionary Force and had done some lobbying on Churchill's behalf with an influential member of Lockhart's staff, Captain Aylmer Haldane, a fellow Gordon Highlander. Hamilton had encouraged Churchill to go to Peshawar, writing to him about Haldane: 'He has much influence ... If he were well disposed towards you, everything could be arranged. I have tried to prepare the ground ... If you came up here, you might with your push and persuasiveness pull it off.'[152] Churchill arrived at the expeditionary force headquarters on 5 March and duly met Haldane who, after discussing Churchill's fervent wish to join the force with him for half an hour, went in to see Lockhart and emerged with the general's decision to allow Churchill to take the place of another orderly officer who was leaving. As Churchill recorded in his memoir:

'Sir William has decided,' [Haldane] said when he returned, 'to appoint you an extra orderly officer on his personal staff. You will take up your duties at once. We are communicating with the Government of India and your regiment.'

So forthwith my situation changed in a moment from disfavour and irregularity to commanding advantage, Red tabs sprouted on the lapels of my coat. The Adjutant-General published my appointment in the Gazette. Horses and servants were dispatched by the regiment from far-off Bangalore and I became the close personal attendant of the Captain of the Host. To the interest and pleasure of hearing the daily conversation of this charming and distinguished man, who knew every inch of the frontier and had fought in every war upon it for forty years, was added the opportunity of visiting every part of his army, sure always of finding smiling faces.[153]

By the time Churchill began his service with the Tirah Expeditionary Force, settlement discussions were well under way between the Afridi chiefs and the British command, and the major military operations were already over. In letters home Churchill wrote: 'Of course I hope for a fight, but I do not delude myself. Both sides are sick of it.' and, 'Meanwhile, I have nothing to do of any kind whatsoever – for until we take the field an orderly officer is a gilded superfluity.'[154] In fact, Churchill stayed very busy getting to know the general and his staff and travelling all over the area of operations as an observer or accompanying General Lockhart for inspections of the expeditionary force's five brigades – 30,000 troops – or for parleys with tribal leaders. He journeyed all over the Bara and Bazar river valleys visiting the Khyber Pass, Lundi Kotal, Ali Masjid, and Barkai as far as Gala Hindoo, the farthest outpost of the force, seeing much of the frontier between Peshawar and the border with Afghanistan. Although some skirmishing was still going on, Churchill did not record that he was ever under fire in Tirah and never commanded troops there. But, he realised, 'The chief value lies elsewhere. I now know all the generals who are likely to have commands in the next few years. Sir William Lockhart will always give me an appointment with any Field Force and I now have a great many friends in high places – as far as soldiering is concerned.'[155] And although he did not see combat on his second period of service on the frontier, it would entitle him to three months' paid leave which he hoped to put to good use later to get to Egypt.

One of those who befriended Churchill in India was Captain Haldane who left a vivid portrait of the young Churchill based on his brief acquaintance in Tirah:

> I cannot recall exactly how long he remained with us at a time when the activities of the Tirah Field Force had practically come to an end. The period, however was quite long enough to allow one to form an opinion of the young cavalry officer who was widely regarded in the Army as super-precocious, indeed by some as insufferably bumptious and realise that neither of these epithets was applicable to him. On the contrary, my distinct recollection of him at this time was that he was modest and paid attention to what was said, not attempting to monopolise the conversation or thrust his opinions – and clear-cut opinions they were on many subjects – on his listeners. He enjoyed giving vent to his views on matters military and other, but there was nothing that could be called aggressive or self-assertive which could have aroused antagonism among the most sensitive of those with whom he was talking. He struck me at almost first sight as cut out on a vastly different pattern from any officer of his years I had so far met; and though I cannot pretend that I foresaw the height of fame to which he would one day rise, still less that it would fall to him later on to be the saviour of his country, I might almost say the civilised world, I had a feeling that such prodigy would go far and was not 'born to blush unseen and waste its sweetness on the desert air'.
>
> We were in each other's company during a good part of each day, as the work at this time was not heavy, and I was able to go about with him whenever the spirit moved me. Many a mile did we cover on foot and otherwise, while I listed to the story of his experiences in Cuba two years earlier, when he was attached to the Spanish Forces, and in return told him a few of my own.

Amongst other things I gathered that he had no intention of making the Army his profession, but proposed to follow in the footsteps of his father, for whom he seemed to have much admiration, mingled with awe rather than affection. He was fond of quoting his speeches in the House of Commons.[156]

While on Lockhart's staff, Churchill took the opportunity to bolster his position with the military authorities in India by writing a long letter to *The Times* in defence of the Tirah Expeditionary Force and its leadership which had come under criticism in the British press. It was both a defence and a critique of the critics and ended:

> The peculiar difficulty which attends mountain warfare is that there are no general actions on a great scale, no brilliant successes, no important surrenders, no chance for coups de theatre. It is just a rough hard job, which must be carried through. The war is one of small incidents. The victory must be looked for in the results. And after all – what are those results. The troops have marched where they were ordered. They have taken every position – accomplished every task. The business has been finished and yet while the army receives the humble submission of the most ferocious savages in Asia, we are assailed by the taunts and reproaches of our countrymen at home.[157]

Churchill very much enjoyed being at the centre of action and being taken seriously by senior officers in staff discussions. As he recorded in *My Early Life*, he 'was treated as if I were quite a grown up. Indeed I think that I was now favorably situated for the opening of the Spring Campaign, and I began to have hopes of getting my teeth into serious affairs. The commander-in-chief seemed well pleased with me and I was altogether "in the swim'. Unhappily for me at least my good fortune had come too late.'[158] By April the political negotiations had finally resulted in a peace treaty and the expeditionary force was disbanded. Churchill left the frontier on 4 April 1898 and, with stop-overs at Rawalpindi, Mian Mir, Meerut and Agra, arrived in Bombay on 13 April, and then returned to Bangalore.

Back in Bangalore his attention and his correspondence were focused on the publication of his book on the Malakand Field Force and with his future plans. The book was published in London in mid-March 1898. By 21 March he had received a set of proof sheets in the post and by 31 March had a final copy of the book in his hands. He was mortified at what he read and wired Longman's in a futile effort to stop publication until necessary corrections could be made. He wrote to Lady Randolph: 'The book – well – I have seen a final copy. It is useless bewailing – but it is awful. Six or seven absolutely unpardonable errors, twenty or thirty minor ones. And a great number of emendations which have made my blood boil.'[159] Entrusting the proof reading to Moreton Frewen in an effort to get his history of the campaign into print before Fincastle's turned out to be a poor choice. By all accounts, Frewen made a terrible mess of his task, with many errors of spelling, punctuation and word choice. None the less, the book was well received. The review in *The Athenaeum* stated: '*The Story of the Malakand Field Force* (Longmans) needs only a little correction of each page to make its second edition a military classic.'[160] *The Times* called the book 'an extremely interesting and well-written account' and noted, 'The author shows a keen insight into frontier questions and his outspoken comments frequently go straight to the mark.'[161] Churchill received favourable letters from influential people in and out of the service including Lord Roberts, the commander-in-chief of the British army, George Curzon, who would become Viceroy of India in 1899, and the Prince of Wales, who wrote:

> I cannot resist writing a few lines to congratulate you on the success of your book! I have read it with the greatest possible interest and I think the descriptions and the language are generally excellent. Everybody is reading it, and I only hear it spoken of with praise. Having now seen active service you will wish to see more, and have as great a chance I am sure of winning the V.C. as Fincastle had; and I hope you will not follow the example of the latter, who I regret to say intends leaving the army in order to go into Parliament.
>
> You have plenty of time before you, and should certainly stick to the Army before adding M.P. to your name.[162]

Churchill was well pleased with the reception of the book and, overcoming his disappointment with the flaws of the first edition, sent the publisher corrected proof sheets for a possible second edition on 22 April. He also completed three magazine articles which he sent to his mother for publication and by the end of May had completed his novel and sent the manuscript to Lady Randolph with the following:

> It is a wild and daring book tilting recklessly here and there and written with no purpose whatever, but to amuse. This I believe it will do. I have faith in my pen. I believe the thoughts I can put on paper will interest & be popular with the public. The reception accorded to my first book, in spite of its gross and damning errors proves to me that my literary talents do not exist in my imagination alone.[163]

He looked ahead to the possibility of a literary career to supplement his pay and allowance with plans to write a biography of Garibaldi, a book of short stories, and 'a short and dramatic History of The American Civil War'.[164] In May he received a letter from the London publishing house James Nisbet & Co asking him to write a biography of his father and another on his great ancestor, the First Duke of Marlborough.[165] All of this, however, came second to his ongoing plans to participate in Kitchener's expedition in the Sudan.

By late spring, Churchill still had not received an appointment to the Egyptian army under Kitchener, any orders attaching him to a British regiment, or an appointment to a staff position that would allow him to participate in the Sudan campaign which he was monitoring with growing impatience and which was expected to reach its climactic phase in early autumn. As he later wrote, 'I was deeply anxious to share in this.'[166] Continuing his letter-writing campaign, he wrote his mother on 22 May:

> I am determined to go to Egypt and if I cannot get employment or at least a sufficient leave, I will not remain in the army. There are other and better things ahead. But the additional campaign will be valuable as an educational experience – agreeable from the point of view as an adventure – and profitable as far as finance goes as I shall write a book about it.[167]

He originally planned to use his three-month leave from the Tirah expedition to go directly to Egypt, travel up the Nile to the headquarters and present his application for attachment in person much as he had done in Peshawar. This was a risky proposition with much expense of time and money involved and no promise of success. In the end, the call of home and his considered belief that further lobbying could best be pursued in London combined to make up Churchill's mind. He began his home leave sailing from Bombay on SS *Oriental* on 18 June and arriving home on 2 July, having decided with characteristic bravado, 'to proceed without delay to the centre of the Empire and argue the matter out in London'.[168]

6

The War on the Nile

The Anglo-Egyptian campaign to reconquer the Sudan in which
Churchill took part was a long time in the making and he had
followed newspaper accounts of events in Egypt and the Sudan for years.
When the Mahdist army of Sudanese Muslims conquered Khartoum in
January 1885 and killed Britain's pro-consul, General Charles Gordon,
Churchill was ten years old, a schoolboy in Brighton. He read the newspapers even then including accounts of the relief expedition which had
been sent to rescue Gordon. After the battle of Abu Klea on 17 January
1885, Churchill wrote to his father: 'Is it not bad about poor Col.
Burnaby?' referring to the death in that action of Colonel Fred Burnaby,
commanding officer of the Royal Horse Guards.[1] Eleven years later the
Mahdi's successor, the Khalifa, and his Dervish followers still controlled
the Sudan but much had changed in Great Britain, in Egypt, and in the
life of Winston Churchill. In London, a Conservative government under
the leadership of Lord Salisbury concluded it was necessary to reassert
British control over the Upper Nile area of the Sudan to discourage
French expansion from West Africa into the region and also to wrest it
finally from Dervish control. National interest was involved as it was
perceived that control of the Sudan would enhance the security of British-
controlled Egypt, itself essential to the protection of the Suez Canal, the
imperial lifeline to India. At the same time, a long-simmering popular
desire to avenge the death of Gordon and so erase the memory of the
failed relief campaign of 1884–5 served to support the new government's
policy. Public opinion had been much influenced by the publication of
books such as Milner's *England in Egypt* with its strong imperial tone, and
by accounts of European prisoners who had escaped from the Sudan
detailing the cruel conditions of the Khalifa's rule, notably *Ten Years'
Captivity in the Mahdi's Camp* by Father Ohrwalder and *Fire and Sword in
the Sudan* by Rudolph Slatin.[2] Popular support and the determination of
the new government made it possible for a new expedition to be sent and
supported with necessary forces and funds. By 1896, the reforms and
financial controls put in place by Sir Evelyn Baring, the British agent and
consul-general in Cairo, who was the de facto ruler of Egypt from 1883 to

1907, enabled the Egyptian government to rebuild its army and to bear a larger part of financing the new campaign.

From 1883 the reorganisation of the Egyptian army was conducted by a cadre of British army officers and NCOs under the leadership of Sir Evelyn Wood and, after 1885, by Sir Francis Grenfell. Among the original twenty-six officers was Horatio Herbert Kitchener of the Royal Engineers. Commissioned from the Royal Military Academy at Woolwich in 1871, he had been posted in 1874 to Cyprus and then to Palestine where he learned Arabic. When the British army and navy went to Egypt in 1882 to seize control of the country, Captain Kitchener took medical leave from his posting and secured a position with the British force. He stayed on and rose rapidly in rank and authority. Promoted major in October 1884, he served as an intelligence officer with the desert column of the Gordon Relief Expedition. In 1886 he was appointed governor of Suakin, a port district on the Red Sea coast. In January 1888 he led a scratch force of Egyptian troops in a successful attack against a Dervish stronghold threatening Suakin and suffered serious wounds in the process. In September 1888 he was appointed adjutant-general of the Egyptian army. He participated with distinction in the battle of Toski in August 1889, again in command of Egyptian troops. In 1892, Baring, now Lord Cromer, appointed the forty-two-year-old Kitchener to be Commander-in-Chief, or Sirdar, of the Egyptian army with the local rank of major general, even though his rank on the British army rolls was then only colonel. Although successful, Kitchener was not well liked. His rapid promotion over more senior officers was the cause of much resentment and his imperious, rude manner was not at all admired. But he was intelligent and hard-working, methodical and capable. As it turned out, an engineer officer was just who was needed to organise and lead a successful campaign. He understood the primary importance of the transportation, communications and logistics necessary to overcome the vast distances, harsh desert conditions and the Dervish army. Having participated in the Gordon Relief Expedition he had gained valuable experience. He knew the Nile, the terrain and the climate and, importantly, he had the ability to learn from the mistakes of those who had gone before him. In the four years after his appointment, Kitchener continued to increase the size and improve the capabilities of the Egyptian army with a view toward their eventual employment in a new expedition against the Dervishes in the Sudan.

When Lord Cromer gave Kitchener the order to begin the campaign to reconquer the Sudan on 12 March 1896, Winston Churchill was a second lieutenant with only twelve months' seniority serving with the 4th Hussars at Hounslow in west London. Churchill was occupied not only with his military duties but with a series of scandals surrounding allegations of hazing and irregularities at horse racing by officers of the regiment. On the very day of Cromer's order Churchill had won a slander suit he had filed against A. C. Bruce-Pryce, father of one of the young officers who had left the 4th Hussars under pressure.[3] The Nile valley was very far away in every sense and Churchill would not reach it until twenty-nine months later and then only by a most indirect route. Yet such was the deliberate, almost plodding, nature of the preliminary stages of the Sudan campaign that he would be present for the decisive final battle at Omdurman two and a half years later. Churchill followed the progress of the campaign from afar in the press.

Kitchener's campaign to retake the northernmost Sudanese province of Dongola, including the battle of Firket on 7 June 1896, the gunboat bombardment of Hafir on 19 September and the capture of the town of Dongola on 23 September, were all over before Churchill and the 4th Hussars reached India. Churchill was still stationed at Bangalore or on home leave while the Anglo-Egyptian force pushed a military railway from Wadi Halfa on the Egypt–Sudan border south to Abu Hamed and on to Berber between January and August 1897. While the Atbara campaign proceeded up the Nile farther into the Sudan between February and April 1898, Churchill remained in India. All this time he was well aware of Kitchener's march into the Sudan, eager to join in it, mentioning it in almost every one of his letters home, and pulling every lever of influence within his or Lady Randolph's reach. Colonel Brabazon contacted the War Office in London, lobbying to have him attached to the 21st Lancers, a British cavalry regiment then stationed in Egypt and expected soon to join the Sudan expedition. Lady Jeune, a family friend of the Churchills, prevailed upon Sir Evelyn Wood, the adjutant-general of the British army, to wire Kitchener saying that both he and the Prince of Wales thought Churchill should be allowed to join the campaign. Wood wired to Kitchener: 'I strongly recommend Churchill as good value for you and army.'[4] Kitchener was not swayed and nothing seemed to be working.

One may ask why there was such resistance to Churchill by Kitchener and his staff, a question that perplexed him a good deal at the time. He was widely perceived as a self-advertiser and medal hunter by senior officers.[5] He was outspoken, ambitious and egocentric and did not know his place. It was well known he wrote for the newspapers and had published a book about his military experiences in India. Churchill was well aware of the controversy. As he later wrote, 'The hybrid combination of a subaltern officer and widely-followed war correspondent was not unnaturally obnoxious to the military mind.'[6] Churchill was, in fact, a serious critic of each of the several campaigns he saw. The British army was a small professional army, not unlike a village where everyone knew of everyone else's doings. It was understandable for commanding officers to be reluctant to employ a junior officer with a pen in his hand, connections in the London press, and a future in politics in mind. In one of the last telegrams to Kitchener on Churchill's behalf, Lady Jeune addressed this concern directly, writing: 'Hope you will take Churchill. Guarantee he won't write.'[7]

There was another argument for not wanting Churchill, perhaps Kitchener's main reason, and that was his view that Churchill, rather than letting the army make use of him was making use of the army for his own purposes. Frank Rhodes, a correspondent for *The Times* on the campaign, spoke with Kitchener about Churchill and later reported the conversation to Winston who passed it on to Lady Randolph in a letter of 26 August 1898: 'Kitchener said he had known I was not going to stay in the army – was only making a convenience of it; that he had disapproved on my coming in place of others whose professions were at stake.'[8]

As Churchill's lobbying campaign proceeded in the spring of 1898, Kitchener's military campaign continued its inexorable movement towards Omdurman, gaining additional troops and momentum. On 8 April, while Churchill was still in India, the battle of Atbara had been fought and won by the Anglo-Egyptian forces in the Sudan, setting the stage for the final advance to Khartoum. It was the biggest battle of the campaign to date and it was a subject of interest which Churchill compared to his own combat experience.

After reading the news of the Anglo-Egyptian victory over the Dervishes at Atbara, Churchill wrote to his brother Jack on 9 May:

I do not at all agree with you that the Atbara is the end of the Soudan campaign. Much more severe fighting will ensue – especially at Omdurman. It seems good fighting – short and sharp. But I don't expect it is any more exciting & less dangerous than the Frontier. At Atbara – 16,000 men – lost 500 killed & wounded (60 killed). On 16th September in Mahmund Valley 1,000 men - lost 150 – (of whom 50 killed) or four times as heavy a proportion. Also the Egyptian fight lasted 28 minutes. I was under fire exactly 13 hours on the 16th. However I look forward with much interest to see both kinds.'[9]

By mid-June 1898, the military railway reached Fort Atbara and by early July Kitchener's force would move south to Wadi Hamed and concentrate there sixty miles from the Dervish capital of Omdurman. Churchill clearly sensed that time was running out for him and returning to London to lobby in person made good sense. In any event, it was his last chance to win a place in the Sudan campaign.

While in London Churchill had an exceptional stroke of good luck. It happened that Lord Salisbury, the Prime Minister, had read *The Story of the Malakand Field Force* with interest and wanted to meet the author to discuss it.[10] During the second week of July Salisbury's Private Secretary extended an invitation to Churchill to visit, which the young officer accepted without hesitation. During their meeting Salisbury received Churchill warmly, expressed his admiration for the book and, as Churchill later wrote, 'dismissed me in the following terms, "I hope you will allow me to say how much you remind me of your father, with whom such important days of my political life were lived. If there is anything at any time that I can do that would be of assistance to you, pray do not fail to let me know." '[11] Churchill grasped the opportunity to enlist the Prime Minister in his efforts to get to Egypt in a military capacity and made the request of the PM's Private Secretary within a matter of days. Here certainly was some political influence the Sirdar would have to reckon with.

Salisbury's request to include Churchill in the campaign, communicated via Lord Cromer, was promptly dispatched but received a negative reply from Kitchener. Just as final failure seemed likely, another bit of good fortune came Churchill's way. His family friend, Lady Jeune, was a close friend of Sir Evelyn Wood, who told her at a dinner party of his displeasure with Kitchener's control over selection of officers for the expeditionary force, exercising a veto over War Office recommendations not only for the Egyptian army but also of the British units participating in the campaign. While the Sirdar could rightfully control personnel matters in the Egyptian army which he commanded, Wood felt it was strictly the business of the War Office to staff the British army units. When Lady Jeune, at Churchill's suggestion, told Wood that Salisbury's personal recommendation of Churchill had been snubbed, Sir Evelyn apparently stood up for his authority over Kitchener.[12] Two days later Churchill received the following wire from the War Office:

> You have been attached as a supernumerary Lieutenant to the 21st Lancers for the Soudan Campaign. You are to report at once at the Abassiyeh Barracks, Cairo, to the Regimental Headquarters. It is understood that you will proceed at your own expense and that in the event of your being killed or wounded in the impending operations, or for any other reason, no charge of any kind will fall on British Army funds.[13]

Churchill received this welcome news by Saturday, 23 July and sent a letter of thanks to Lord Salisbury indicating that he would set out early the next week for the seat of war. Churchill hurriedly made arrangements with the *Morning Post* to send a series of letters about the campaign for publication at £10 per article. Churchill wired the authorities in India for permission to extend his leave to take part in the campaign but left England before he received a reply. It was the same method of going without permission and hoping not to be recalled later that Kitchener himself had used to go out to Egypt for the first time in 1882. It worked equally well for both of them. No recall telegram ever reached Churchill and by the time he was on the move up the Nile, he wrote, 'I think I may now conclude with certainty that silence has given consent.'[14]

Departing London in the last week of July 1898, he travelled to Marseilles and boarded the Messageries Maritime Paquebot *Sindh* for the Mediterranean crossing. He arrived in Cairo in the evening of Tuesday, 2 August and reported immediately to the 21st Lancers barracks on the city's outskirts. Two years of hoping and scheming had finally paid off and he was back in his element – on active service with a cavalry regiment, in what he referred to as 'the real world of honest effort and common sense'.[15]

The regiment to which Lt Churchill was attached was the only British cavalry regiment to participate in the Sudan campaign. Churchill believed that a place with the 21st Lancers had been made available when one of their officers, Lt Chapman, died of disease in Egypt on 12 July 1898. The regimental diary indicates that a second 21st Lancers officer, Lt Martin, also died in Egypt, on 19 July.[16] Churchill was not the only one to be seconded to the 21st. Lt F. W. Wornald and his servant Private J. Cope from the 7th Hussars and Lt T. Conolly of the Scots Greys came to join Churchill in A Squadron. Lts J. C. Brinton of the 2nd Life Guards and R. S. Grenfell of the 12th Lancers were seconded to B Squadron. Lts J. Vaughan of the 7th Hussars and Lt the Hon. R. Molyneux of the Royal Horse Guards were assigned to C Squadron. They were also joined by a civilian, Hubert Howard, correspondent of *The Times*.[17] Several hundred British officers had applied for service in the Sudan and as Churchill later wrote, this was not surprising as, 'The British officer serving in India has always looked with longing eyes toward the land of the Nile as a happy hunting ground for decorations and distinction.'[18]

The 21st Lancers had a long though not a distinguished history.[19] Originally raised in 1759 by the Marquis of Granby as the 21st Light

Dragoons, it was disbanded and recalled to service several times before being finally disbanded in 1820. The more modern history of the regiment had its origins in India following the Indian mutiny of 1857–8. In the latter year, the 3rd Bengal Light Cavalry, which had been organised earlier by the Honourable East India Company became the 3rd Bengal European Light Cavalry as Indian troopers were replaced by British recruits. In 1858 the British Crown took over governance of India from the East India Company and by 1861 the regiment became part of Her Majesty's Forces designated as the 21st Light Dragoons. They were renamed the 21st Hussars the same year with changes in uniforms but not in duties. There then followed thirty-seven years of garrison service in India, England and Ireland with no active service at all. By the time the regiment arrived in Egypt it was suggested by rival regiments that because of its unique lack of combat experience among British cavalry regiments the 21st should adopt the motto, 'Thou shall not kill'. Indeed, the regiment had no battle honours before the Sudan campaign.[20]

In September 1896, the same month Kitchener and the Egyptian army completed the reconquest of Dongola province in northern Sudan, the 21st Hussars were transferred from India for a two-year tour of duty in Egypt. Upon arrival, they took up residence at the Abbassiyeh barracks three miles outside of Cairo. Pursuant to army orders on 1 April 1897, the regiment was redesignated as the 21st Lancers and was so known when Churchill arrived to join them. The regiment had received official notification on 22 June 1898, that they would go up to take part in the campaign. Their commander, Lt Colonel Rowland Hill Martin, anticipated the orders and the 21st Lancers had been conducting strenuous route marches and desert exercises since January 1897, testing men, animals and equipment for service in the Sudan.[21] At the time of its departure from Cairo the strength of the regiment was thirty officers, one warrant officer, 453 NCOs and men and 450 troop horses.[22]

There were four phases in the 1896–8 Sudan campaign leading up to the climactic battle at Omdurman, each an essential foundation for those that followed. The first phase was the rebuilding of the Egyptian army by Kitchener and his predecessors between 1883 and 1896. This was essential for two reasons. First, the bulk of the troops for the campaign would be drawn from the Egyptian army. Second, after the presumably successful campaign and defeat of the Dervish army, the Egyptian troops would be responsible both for occupying and policing the Sudan after the British troops departed. By the time the force moved into the Sudan to begin the campaign, the Egyptian army had grown substantially in size and capability. The army of approximately 18,000 men and 140 British officers was organised into nineteen battalions of infantry, ten squadrons of cavalry, four field batteries, one horse battery of artillery and a Camel Corps – cavalry on dromedaries rather than horses.

Each infantry battalion was divided into six companies of 100–120 men armed with the old Martini Henry .450 calibre single-loader rifle. It fired a heavy bullet with great stopping power and was accurate to 800 yards. Thirteen of the battalions included Egyptian troops, six (the 9th–14th) had black Sudanese troops. All the infantry battalions had British officers for the campaign; the 5th–8th battalions also had Egyptian officers. Every infantry battalion had a British NCO as an instructor. The ten squadrons of cavalry each comprised approximately one hundred troopers – all Egyptian. Seven of the squadron leaders were British officers, three Egyptian. The cavalry troopers were armed with lances, Martini carbines and sabres. The two artillery batteries were equipped with Maxim-Nordenfeldt nine-pounder guns and the one horse artillery battery had twelve-pounder Krupps and nine-pounder Maxim-Nordenfeldt guns. All the artillery officers were British, all the gunners Egyptian. The Camel Corps, which was also led by British officers, consisted of 800 men, half Egyptian and half Sudanese, divided into eight companies. The corps served as mobile infantry and were armed with the Martini rifle and bayonet. The uniform for the Egyptian army was a brown jersey, khaki-coloured trousers, dark blue puttees and a fez, or tarbush, for headgear.[23]

The use of British officers to command native troops proved to be an excellent combination of talents. The Sudanese soldier, Churchill wrote, 'displayed two tremendous military virtues. To the faithful loyalty of a dog he added the heart of a lion. He loved his officer and feared nothing in the world. With the introduction of this element the Egyptian army became a formidable military machine.'[24] The skirmishes between the Egyptian army and the Dervishes in the 1880s and 1890s built the army into an experienced and confident force. Organised into four brigades for the Sudan campaign, it would fight side by side with the British battalions and share their hardships and victories alike.

The second phase of the campaign was the invasion and capture of Dongola, the northernmost province of the Sudan on the southern border of Egypt. This phase began on 12 March 1896 and was successfully completed six months later after an advance of more than 450 miles. The column advanced slowly up the Nile actively patrolling and setting up a series of fortified positions to protect their line of communication along the river. From the start of the campaign at Wadi Halfa on the Egypt–Sudan border there was little opposition to the advance. The first battle took place about eighty-five miles south at Firket on 7 June 1896. It was also the first action to merit a clasp on the Khedive's Sudan Medal.[25] There a Dervish force of some 3,000 men in an encampment were overwhelmed by the 9,000-strong column in a dawn assault supported by Maxim guns, an early machine gun. In an intense two-hour and twenty-minute firefight the Dervishes lost 800 killed, 500 wounded and 600 captured at a cost to the Egyptian brigades of one British officer wounded, twenty native troops killed and eighty-three wounded.[26]

After Firket there was a considerable delay before the next advance as the force awaited the arrival of reinforcements and the first gunboats which would be used as mobile artillery. In the following months, the column was augmented by the arrival of additional Egyptian battalions and the first British infantry, the 1st battalion of the North Staffordshire Regiment. By 5 September, all sixteen Egyptian battalions had arrived and the column's strength rose to 16,000 men, thirty-six guns and eight war vessels.[27] From September onward the gunboats on the river kept pace with the troops on shore, providing artillery support and also towing supply barges upriver.

The next action was the battle of Hafir but to call it a battle is an exaggeration. As Churchill later wrote: 'Of all the instances of cheaply bought glory which the military history of recent years affords, Hafir is the most remarkable.'[28] At Hafir, a further 100 miles upriver from Firket, a Dervish force of approximately 5,600 men with six cannon established an entrenched position of about a half mile in length on the west bank of the Nile. Kitchener could not leave a force of this size in place behind his line of advance and an attack was planned with heavy reliance placed on the gunboats and artillery fire. At 6.30 a.m. on 19 September, the Egyptian horse battery opened fire. The gunboat flotilla moved up opposite Hafir and exchanged fire with the Dervish battery joined by Maxim guns and the rifle fire of two companies of the South Staffords on the boats. After a three-hour exchange of fire in which three gunboats were damaged and most of the Dervish guns were put out of action, the gunboats moved upriver out of range and towards Dongola. There followed a day-long stand-off with only intermittent firing and no infantry attack. During the night, the Dervishes simply abandoned the position and retreated to the south, leaving more than

200 dead behind. The flotilla lost only one man killed and a few wounded on each boat.[29]

The next objective, the village of Dongola, a further twenty-two miles upriver, was abandoned by the Dervishes in face of the growing column's advance and the menacing approach of the gunboats on the river. The capture of Dongola on 23 September 1896 completed the capture of the province and concluded active operations for the year. The Sirdar's force now had the means by rail and water to move men and supplies far into the Sudan without interference. They halted on the Nile at Dongola and pursued no further offensive operations until 1897.

The intervening months were put to good use by Kitchener for the third phase of the campaign, the construction of the Sudan Military Railway, the lynchpin of the entire enterprise. The importance of the railway cannot be overstated. As Churchill later wrote in *The River War*, his history of the campaign: 'In savage warfare in a flat country the power of modern machinery is such that flesh and blood can scarcely prevail, and the chances of battle are reduced to a minimum. Fighting the Dervish was primarily a matter of transport. The Khalifa was conquered on the railway.'[30] A railway was essential because of the scale of material necessary for the campaign and because the Nile is simply not passable at all places or in all seasons and so is not a reliable transportation route. The river is blocked by several impassable cataracts including the second, third, fourth and fifth, all of which block the river between Wadi Halfa and Berber, the point of farthest advance in 1897. A railway was needed to link the navigable stretches of the Nile and would provide a method of moving infantry troops, cavalry, artillery and stores forward regardless of the season and with little hindrance from the desert climate.

Construction of the railway was a monumental task requiring the importation of every tool used, every rail and sleeper, every plate and every worker needed to assemble them. There was no water, food or wood along the route; these all had to be brought in. With Kitchener selecting the route and the entire operation managed by a handful of subalterns of Royal Engineers, the line progressed steadily in difficult conditions, eventually employing 2,000 plate layers, a 1,500-man railway battalion, over twenty engines and more than 200 trucks. Work began at Wadi Halfa on 1 January 1897; when completed the line would stretch almost 400 miles to Atbara on the other side of the inhospitable Nubian Desert. Step by step construction progressed with supply depots, water storage points, workshops, and a telegraph line built alongside. Kitchener followed the progress of railway construction closely with his usual attention to detail. As Churchill wrote: 'He knew the exact position of every soldier, coolie, camel or donkey at his disposal.'[31] No doubt the same was true for trains, ordnance and supplies of every description.

When the rail line neared the half-way point to Abu Hamed towards the end of July, Kitchener sent a brigade of 3,600 men under General Archibald Hunter to force the Dervishes from that village. This flying column reached Abu Hamed in a forced march covering 133 miles of a sandy, stony route in eight days.[32] The Dervishes were assaulted by Hunter's Sudanese infantry battalions supported by artillery and Maxim gunfire, and victory was achieved on 7 August 1896. Of the 400 Dervish defenders, 250 were killed and fifty made prisoner. Two British officers were killed and the native troops suffered twenty-one killed and sixty-one wounded.[33]

The railway arrived at Abu Hamed by 31 October and continued to follow the advance of the leading elements of the column. After the skirmish at Abu Hamed, the Dervishes abandoned the strategic village of Berber which was occupied on 31 August 1896. The column then paused to consolidate and await the railway and the reinforcements and stores it would bring. A base camp was established at the confluence of the Nile and Atbara rivers south of Berber.

By 2 January 1898 the 1st Battalion Royal Warwickshire Regiment, the 1st Battalion Cameron Highlanders, the 1st Battalion Seaforth Highlanders and the 1st Battalion of the Lincolnshire Regiment arrived to form a British brigade under General William F. Gatacre at the Atbara encampment. In late March a 10,000-strong Dervish force moved into a blocking position at Nakheila on the Atbara about twelve miles to the south. There they constructed an intricate fortified position of barricades and entrenchments surrounded by an enclosure (*zariba*) of interlocking thorn branches. Kitchener realised that the Dervishes had to be dislodged if he were to proceed to Khartoum and planned accordingly. There followed the battle of the Atbara on 8 April, the biggest conflict in the campaign until Omdurman. The Anglo-British force night-marched to the Dervish camp and took up their positions. A preliminary artillery barrage opened up at 6.15 a.m. preceding the general advance which began at 7.40 a.m. 'The plan of attack for the army was simple,' Churchill wrote, 'The long deployed line was to advance steadily against the entrenchments, subduing by its continual fire that of the enemy.'[34] It was, in fact, an old-fashioned frontal assault in broad daylight, just like Hafir and Firket, and of exactly the same kind the Dervishes would later use against the British at Omdurman. The attack was led by the kilted Camerons, shouting 'Remember Gordon'. The battle raged fiercely for thirty-five minutes and was won only by intense hand-to-hand fighting. In the brief battle the Anglo-Egyptian force of approximately 13,000 men lost twenty-four killed (three officers) and 101 wounded (ten officers) in the British battalions and fifty-six killed and 371 wounded in the Egyptian and Sudanese battalions including five British officers and two British NCOs serving with them.[35] Of the Dervish force, estimated to be 12,000 strong, at least 3,000 were killed in and around the *zariba*, the balance fled into the desert and were not seriously pursued.[36] One Dervish leader, Emir Mahmud, was captured. Another, Osman Digna, escaped and with his surviving followers retreated toward Omdurman and would not offer battle again until the Anglo-Egyptian army arrived at the outskirts of their capital four months later.

Even though the battle of the Atbara resulted in a swift and complete victory, Churchill was critical of British tactics which in his view were flawed and resulted in unnecessary casualties. In his opinion the artillery barrage before the assault should have been longer than ninety minutes and the attack should also have been preceded by intensive rifle fire from fixed positions. Both steps, he concluded, could have reduced Anglo-Egyptian casualties. As he later wrote in a passage illustrative of his 'subaltern's advice to generals' style:

> Civilised troops should take full advantage of their weapons; and the spectacle of the assaulting columns advancing on the entrenchments after an insufficient artillery preparation, and disdaining to open fire till they were within a range when their rifles were on an equality with those of the Dervishes, however magnificent it may be, suggests the hog-hunter who dismounted from his horse, flung away his spear, then dealt the boar a tremendous kick in the throat, and eventually made an end of him with his hands.[37]

It is one of the great failures of the Khalifa's generalship that he never attacked the military railway or the supply depots on which the invading army depended. By mid-July 1898 the railway finally reached Atbara, making possible the consolidation of overwhelming manpower and weaponry for the final advance and assuring resupply of the food, water, ammunition and support services necessary for success. The victory at Atbara and the completion of the Sudan Military Railway marked the end of the third phase of the campaign. As Churchill later wrote: 'On the day that the first troop train steamed into the fortified camp at the confluence of the Nile and the Atbara rivers the doom of the Dervishes was sealed ... Though the battle was not yet fought, the victory was won. The Khalifa, his capital, and his army were now within the Sirdar's reach.'[38]

After the battle the Anglo-Egyptian force returned to the Fort Atbara encampment and went into summer quarters. Again they delayed to await the arrival of additional troops and supplies and, importantly, for the Nile to rise. The river was navigable by all the boats in the flotilla from Atbara to Khartoum in the season of high water. With the river in flood stage and with the completion of reinforcement and resupply, the flotilla and the land force would be able to proceed upriver in tandem for the fourth phase, the final advance to Omdurman. This phase, from early August to early September, 1898 was the one in which Lt Churchill participated and earned his campaign medals. By the time Churchill arrived in Egypt, Kitchener's forces had already overcome the elements, bent the terrain to its will, solved the problems of supply and communications, made the Nile their ally, and cleared the Dervish forces from their path. It remained only to close with and defeat the Dervish army and occupy Omdurman to bring the Sudan back under Anglo-Egyptian control. A fifth and final phase of the campaign in which Churchill did not participate was to take place after the battle of Omdurman and involved the tracking down and capture of the Khalifa and mopping-up operations against small, scattered units of the Dervish army which fled Omdurman, a process that took about a year.

The 21st Lancers proceeded from Cairo up the Nile in three squadrons designated A, B and C. First to depart was B Squadron which left on 31 July 1898, with the remainder of the unit seeing them off at the railway station and the band playing 'Auld Lang Syne'. According to Churchill's autobiography, *My Early Life*, he had been detailed to command a troop in B Squadron but due to his late arrival this place was given to Lt Robert Grenfell who was seconded from the 12th Lancers. 'Fancy how lucky I am, here I have got the troop that was Winston's, and we are to be the first to start,' Grenfell wrote to his family.[39] As shall be seen, it was a fateful event for both men. Churchill was assigned to A Squadron under command of Major Harry Finn which would leave for the Sudan on 3 August, the very day after Churchill's arrival in Egypt. C Squadron would follow on 6 August. On the morning of the 3rd, the 21st Lancers paraded at their barracks west of Cairo in what Churchill described as 'Christmas tree order' with full equipment and mounts. The service dress of the

Lancers was the standard khaki field uniform adopted by the British army for overseas service, just like that worn by Churchill in India. His uniform displayed the crimson-and-green India Medal ribbon even though he had not yet received the medal itself. The service dress uniform was topped off with standard issue Wolseley-style cork helmet covered in khaki. For the Sudan campaign the Lancers were issued a quilted cotton sun shade to extend the brim of the helmet all around, and a quilted cloth 'spine pad' worn on their backs to protect the brain and spine from the rays of the sun.[40] The badge of the 21st Lancers featured crossed lances with streaming pennants, surmounted by a royal crown, with the roman numerals XXI superimposed on the lances.[41]

As Lancers, the non-commissioned officers and other ranks were armed with a nine-foot-long bamboo lance with a steel tip and decorated by a red-and-white pennant. They were also armed with the 1896 model Lee-Enfield carbine of .303 calibre. This was a bolt action weapon with a five-round magazine firing a hollow-nosed, smokeless cordite bullet. These were high velocity rounds which expanded on striking a body causing a large, often deadly, exit wound. Those armed with carbines wore a leather bandolier over the left shoulder which held fifty rounds of ammunition. The standard-issue weapons for officers were the Webley revolver and the regulation-pattern heavy cavalry sword. Churchill and Major Crole-Wyndam, the 21st Lancers' second-in-command, carried a non-regulation Mauser semi-automatic pistol in a holster worn butt forward with a lanyard around the neck connected to the pistol to save dropping it. The Mauser was a 7.63 mm weapon with a ten-round magazine. It was an effective weapon for close combat that Churchill thought highly of, dubbing it a 'ripper', and he would take the same weapon to South Africa the following year. To their clothing and weapons were added the equipment slung over their shoulders, water bottles and a haversack for personal items, and attached on and around the saddle were a brown leather carbine boot placed behind the rider's right leg, a canvas bucket for watering the horse, a bag of horse-feed, and a rolled-up waterproof cloak.[42]

The soldiers' equipment for the campaign was generally excellent; after all the British army had much experience of campaigning in hostile climates. There were, however, two notable exceptions – boots and bullets. The British infantry brigade participating in the earlier phases of the campaign found that their leather boots were not up to the abrasion of desert rock and sand. This was something of a scandal, the source of much

complaint by the British infantry and bitter commentary by the correspondents. George W. Steevens of the *Daily Mail* wrote:

> We have been campaigning in the Sudan off and on, for over fourteen years;
> we might have discovered the little peculiarities of its climate by now. The
> Egyptian army uses a riveted boot; the boots our British boys were expected to
> march in had not even a toe cap. So that when the three battalions and battery
> arrived in Berber hundreds of men were all but barefoot: the soles peeled off,
> and instead of a solid double sole, revealed a layer of shoddy packing sand-
> wiched between two thin slices of leather.[43]

Churchill also wrote about the sub-standard footgear, stating: 'The
simplicity of the War Office and the knavery of the contractors had
combined to produce the most expensive and the least durable boot in the
Soudan.'[44] This piece of equipment was a problem more for the infantry
than for the cavalry which had the advantage of being mounted much of
the time.

The problem with the rifle ammunition was even more inexcusable and
was never really resolved during the campaign. It, too, had a greater
impact on the infantry than the cavalry. The British infantry battalions
were armed with the Lee-Medford .303 magazine rifle. The Lee-Medford
bullets (Mark II) were nickel-plated and considered to have insufficient
killing power for close-in fighting:

> General Gatacre considered it desirable to have them altered to meet that
> requirement; and ... a million rounds of ammunition were converted into
> improvised Dum-Dum bullets by filing off the tips so as to expose the heavy
> core within the outer case. These missiles were afterwards used at the Atbara,
> and the results were found satisfactory as far as killing power was concerned.
> Two serious disadvantages must be recorded. The roughly cut bullets
> destroyed much of the accuracy of flight. The fact that their filed tips were
> uneven caused them to jam when used in the magazine of the rifle.[45]

As the 21st Lancers were armed with the Lee-Enfield carbine, the
ammunition problem did not affect their marksmanship. Because
Churchill was to use his Mauser pistol rather than a rifle, it affected him
not at all. The Egyptian forces, using the older, single loader Martini-
Henry rifles, were similarly not inconvenienced.

Having already travelled from Bangalore to Bombay, from Bombay to
London and thence to Cairo, a distance of nearly 10,000 miles, Churchill
still had a long way to go to reach the seat of war. As he later recalled:

'The movement of the regiment 1,400 miles into the heart of Africa was effectuated with the swiftness, smoothness and punctuality which in those days characterised all Kitchener's arrangements.'[46] The journey to the railhead at Atbara by steamer and train took eleven days; before the Sudan Military Railway was built and cut 300 miles off the journey it had taken four months.

The regiment proceeded southward up the Nile in several stages. The first stage took them by train from Cairo to Khizam, just north of Luxor, on the Nile. The men rode in railway carriages, the horses in open cargo trucks. The loading of men, equipment, animals, saddlery, forage, food, filtered water and other necessary equipment was hard work and the journey itself, about 375 miles in twenty-four hours was 'very hot and dusty, and attended with considerable difficulty in watering the horses en route'.[47] George W. Steevens had taken the trip earlier in the year at a slightly more rapid pace and called it 'the filthiest seventeen hours in Egypt', writing: 'We choked ourselves to sleep; in the morning we choked no longer, the lungs have reconciled themselves to breathe powdered Egypt.'[48]

At Khizam, the regiment transferred to water craft for the second stage of the journey to Assouan (present-day Aswan). The men were carried in the stern paddle-wheel steamers provided by Thomas Cook & Sons, a British travel company, and the horses and equipment were transported in towed barges. The journey to Assouan was leisurely; against a six-knot current the steamers averaged only four miles per hour. The journey of approximately 200 miles passed quite pleasantly for Churchill. During the passage he had time to write three long letters to his mother. He felt welcome in the 21st Lancers as two former Harrow classmates, Lt Henry Johnstone of the 7th Hussars and Lt Thomas Conolly of the Royal Scots Greys were also attached. In addition, his squadron commander, Major Finn, knew Churchill from India where Finn had been a staff officer at Bangalore. After the pressures and rush of his stay in London and quick departure for Egypt he described his new situation.

It is a vy strange transformation [of] scene that the last 8 days have worked. When I think of the London streets – dinners, balls, etc and then look at the Khaki soldiers – the great lumbering barges full of horses – the muddy river and behind and beyond the palm trees and sails of the Dahabiahs. And the change in my own mind is even more complete. The ideals and speculations of politics are gone. I no longer contemplate harangues. The anticipations of Parliament – of speeches – of political life generally have faded before more vivid possibilities and prospects and my thoughts are more concerned with swords – lances – pistols – & soft-nosed bullets – than with Bills – Acts & bye elections.[49]

In a 10 August letter to Lady Randolph he reflected on the fighting ahead in the Sudan, writing: 'Life is very cheap my dearest Mamma ... I am not careless of the possible results for I want as you know to live and accomplish much but I do not fear them nor do I complain.' He added with characteristic humour: 'Besides these fortifying, philosophic reflections I have a keen aboriginal desire to kill several of those odious dervishes and drive the rest of the pestiferous breed to Orcus and I anticipate enjoying the exercise very much.'[50] But his mind was not only on the campaign. He told his mother he expected to be back in London by November and looked forward to giving speeches at political meetings in Bradford and Birmingham. Without any command duties on the steamer, Churchill also found time to write two letters for publication which he forwarded to his mother for delivery to the *Morning Post* in London. He would eventually write fifteen articles for the newspaper, all devised with what he referred to as the 'Addisonian Conceit' that they were private letters to a friend finding their way into print by accident.[51] In fact, the identity of the author was known to many before the editors of the *Morning Post* included Churchill's by-line at the conclusion of the last letter printed. As Hubert Howard, a correspondent for *The Times*, noted in his diary at Atbara camp on 15 August: 'Winston arrived yesterday ... I hear he has been writing what he calls 'descriptive articles' all the way up for the *Morning Post*; he does not want this known but it will be, naturally.'[52] Churchill's letters were very good – colourful and detailed. They would serve as the 'foundations and scaffold' for the book he intended to write about the campaign.

A Squadron arrived at Assouan on Friday, 12 August 1898 and disembarked to walk around the first cataract of the Nile to exercise the horses. They marched the six miles to Shellal where vast amounts of military supplies were stored awaiting transport upriver. Churchill had time at Assouan to view the ancient Egyptian ruins. He later wrote: 'Among the dark rocks of the river gorge the broken pillars and walls of the Temple of Philae were outlined against the sunset sky. The past looked down on the present, and, offended by its exuberant vitality, seemed grimly to repeat the last taunt that age can fling at youth: you will be as I am one of these days.'[53] At Shellal the squadron boarded stern-wheel steamers for the third stage of the journey to Wadi Halfa about 220 miles upriver. The officers sat during the day and slept during the night under awnings on the top deck with nothing to look at but the occasional timeless village and rows of date palms nourished by the river. Churchill also noted:

> There is one other sign of life, and it is a sign of a busy life that belongs to a civilised age. Along the bank of the river runs the telegraph wire. Looking at the slender poles and white insulators – for the wire itself is invisible against the background of rock – it is impossible not to experience a glow of confidence in the power of science, which can thus link the most desolate regions of the earth with its greatest city and keep the modern pioneer ever within hail of home.[54]

The squadron reached Wadi Halfa, just over the border in Sudan, two days later on 14 August. There they transferred to the Sudan Military Railway for the 400-mile, thirty-six hour transit of the Nubian Desert. Churchill later described the desert in vivid detail in *The River War*:

> It is scarcely within the power of words to describe the savage desolation of the region into which the line ... plunged. A smooth ocean of bright-coloured sand spread far and wide to the distant horizons. The tropical sun beat down with senseless perserverance upon the level surface until it could scarcely be touched with a naked hand, and the filmy air glittered and shimmered as over a furnace. Here and there huge masses of crumbling rock rose from the plain, like islands of cinders in a sea of flame.[55]

Travelling via Abu Hamed, Darmali and Berber, the train reached Atbara at noon on 15 August.

At Atbara A Squadron was reunited with B Squadron and the headquarters staff of the 21st Lancers which had arrived on the 12th. C Squadron would follow, being delivered upriver at Wad Hamed by boat. Upon his arrival, Churchill commenced his regimental duties. As recorded in a letter by his fellow lieutenant Robert Smyth: 'Winston Churchill is only 23 and frightfully keen. Started by telling me he was more interested in men than in horses, so I asked him to look after the rations, etc. and said I would do the horses. He asked to see the men and spoke to them (very well too) and had a great success; in fact, they liked him.'[56] A and B Squadrons would march to Wad Hamed, the point of concentration for the entire Anglo-Egyptian army.

After a visit by the Sirdar and General Gatacre, commander of the British Division of the force, the Lancers, their mounts and equipment were ferried from the east to the west bank of the Nile at first light on 16

August. After the river crossing, the two squadrons, accompanied by two Maxim guns, moved out to the south escorting 1,400 mules, donkeys and camels, which would serve as transport for the British division and as remounts for the Egyptian cavalry. So began a difficult nine-day march to Wad Hamed. There had been heavy rain on the night of 15 August with the result that many of the *khors*, dry watercourses running to the Nile, were flooded and impassable.[57] Long detours into the desert were required to avoid them, adding many miles to the march. The column averaged thirty miles a day to reach Wad Hamed. Because of the additional distance and the fact it was too dark at night to pass through broken ground in unfamiliar territory, the two squadrons had to march in the heat of the day, which Churchill had noted in a letter from Atbara as 116° F. Man and beast suffered. Four or five horses a day had to be destroyed and one Lancer, Private Bishop, died of exhaustion; others went down with heat-stroke; all suffered from thirst and the unforgiving glare of the sun. The column on the march was strung out over three miles with the Lancers reconnoitring ahead and halting to wait for the slower animals to catch up. 'Two squadrons of Lancers rode in front whilst the rest of the troopers were supposed to protect the flanks and act as 'whippers-on' to the column ... After a few days of such marching as we had, straggling became the normal condition of affairs except so far as the leading squadrons of Lancers were concerned. The last three days of the journey, in fact, became a sort of "go-as-you-please" tramp.'[58] The nightly bivouacs were uncomfortable, the air still hot at night and the troopers were bothered by swarms of flies and, according to Churchill, 'every variety of biting, crawling, stinging insect'.[59] But the Nile supported them, enabling supplies to be brought up and the sick to be removed to aid.

On occasion during the march, men were separated from the main body and became lost in the desert. One of these was Churchill. He had stayed behind at Atbara fort on the 15th in charge of a detail of men moving stores. He found time to visit General Gatacre's headquarters and mingle with friends. He also met Colonel Wingate, the chief of intelligence for the Egyptian army, who complimented Churchill on *The Story of the Malakand Field Force*. Churchill was ferried across the Nile on the evening of the 16th and was planning to ride on alone and catch up with the Lancers at their first camp fifteen miles ahead. Tardy in his departure, he set out at dusk and was soon enveloped by a silent moonless darkness. He endeavoured to steer by the stars but clouds came in to mask his celestial sign-posts. After three hours he was hopelessly lost, alone with an exhausted horse, without food, forage or adequate water. Wisely, he halted to wait for dawn. Then at 3.30 a.m. the clouds broke up and steering by the 'glorious constellation of Orion' he made his way back to the Nile which was a two-hour ride away. He located the Lancers' encampment only to find they had already moved on. He did not catch up to the squadron until the evening of the 17th after obtaining food and directions from local villagers. From their route of march along the Nile, the Lancers watched the procession of steamers ferrying the second British brigade of infantry and the necessary stores forward and no doubt envied the comfort of those on the boats.

Although the march was arduous and conditions difficult, Churchill was at home while campaigning. Writing to Lady Randolph on 19 August, he reported: 'I am well – never better. The 21st feed like pigs – we get nothing to eat but bully-beef, biscuits and warm beer. But my philosophic temperament enables me to enjoy life immensely. I am very happy and contented and eagerly look forward to the approaching actions.'[60] In another letter on the march he wrote: 'Who knows – I like this sort of life – there is very little trouble or worry but that of the moment – and my philosophy works best in such scenes as these.'[61]

The column reached Metemma on 21 August where they bivouacked for the night. This was a thought-provoking place as it was the point of farthest advance of the desert column of the Gordon relief expedition in 1885. The entrenchments and the graves of the column's dead were still there. Churchill wrote:

It was with a strange emotion that we looked at the scene at the end of that historic march, and reflected on the mournful news [of Gordon's death and the fall of Khartoum] the steamers brought back from Khartoum to those who had dared and done so much. With the ground before me I could imagine the Desert Column – weak, exhausted, encumbered with wounded, yet spurred by a maddening thirst – toiling painfully toward the river; or, when they had learned they were too late, marching off disconsolately across the plain towards the north. We were the first British soldiers to camp on the ground since then.[62]

Indeed, the 21st Lancers were going where no other British cavalry had ever gone before. They continued their gruelling march south arriving at Wad Hamed at noon on Tuesday, 23 August. The encampment was sixty miles from Khartoum and covered the west bank of the Nile for two miles, its western perimeter ringed by a *zariba* of thorn bushes. Here Kitchener's entire army, 22,000 men, concentrated for the final drive to the Dervish capital at Omdurman. It was a formidable force.

The British Division, commanded by Major General Gatacre, comprised two brigades of infantry. The 1st Brigade, under command of Brigader General Andrew G. Wauchope, consisted of the 1st Battalion, Royal Warwickshire Regiment (Lt Col Morey Q. Jones), the 1st Battalion, Lincolnshire Regiment (Lt Col Frank R. Lowth); the 1st Battalion, Cameron Highlanders (Col G. L. C. Money); and the 1st battalion, Seaforth Highlanders (Col Robert H. Murray). Also included were a detachment of Royal Engineers and a detachment from 16th company, Eastern Division Royal Artillery with six Maxim guns. The Second Brigade, under command of Col Neville G. Lyttleton, consisted of the 1st Battalion, Northumberland Fusiliers (Lt Col Charles G. C. Money); the 1st Battalion, Grenadier Guards (Col Villiers Hatton); the 2nd Battalion, Lancashire Fusiliers (Lt Col Cuthbert G. Collingwood); and the 2nd Battalion, Rifle Brigade (Col Francis Howard). Also included in the Second Brigade were a detachment of Royal Engineers and a detachment of Royal Irish Fusiliers with four Maxim guns. The Egyptian Division was commanded by Major-General Archibald Hunter and was comprised of four brigades of infantry each consisting of four battalions made up of either Egyptian or Sudanese troops, most commanded by British officers. The 1st Brigade, Col Hector MacDonald commanding, consisted of the 2nd Egyptian (Major Francis J. Pink), and IXth (Major W. F. Walter), Xth (Maj. F. J. Nason) and XIth (Major H. W. Jackson) Sudanese battalions. The 2nd Brigade, Col J. G. Maxwell commanding, consisted of the 8th Egyptian (Kiloussi Bey), XIIth (Lt Col C. V. F. Townshend), XIIIth (Lt Col Horace Smith-Dorrien) and XIVth (Major H. P. Shekleton) Sudanese battalions. The 3rd Brigade, Col D. F. Lewis commanding, consisted of the 3rd (Major J. Sillem), 4th (Major W. S. Sparkes), 7th (Fathy Bey), and 15th (Major T. E. Hickman) Egyptian battalions. The 4th Brigade under command of Lt Col John Collinson, consisted of the 1st (Cpt. W. R. B. Doran), 5th (Burham Bey), 17th (Cpt. Vesley T. Bunbery) and 18th (Cpt. H. G. K. Matchett) Egyptian battalions. Attached to the Egyptian Division were the mounted forces: four squadrons of the 21st Lancers commanded by Col Rowland H. Martin, nine squadrons of Egyptian cavalry commanded by Col R. G. Broadwood and the eight company Camel Corps commanded by Major R. J. Tudway.

The artillery was commanded by Lt Col Long and consisted of the 32nd Field Battery, Royal Artillery, with eight guns; the 37th Field Battery, Royal Artillery, with six five-inch howitzers; and five batteries from the Egyptian army. The Egyptian units were the horse battery and the No. 1,

No. 2, No. 3 and No. 4 Field Batteries each with six guns and two maxims, and a horse battery with six Krupp guns.

The flotilla, under command of Commander Colin R. Keppel, Royal Navy, included ten gunboats and five steam transports. The three 1898 class screw-driven gun boats, *Sultan*, *Melik* and *Sheikh*, each carried two Nordenfeldt guns, one quick-firing twelve-pounder, one howitzer and four Maxims. The three 1896 class stern-wheel gunboats, *Fateh*, *Naser* and *Zafir*, each carried one quick-firing twelve-pounder, two six-pounder guns and four Maxims. The four 'Old Class' armoured stern-wheel gunboats each carried two Maxim-Nordenfeldt guns and one twelve-pounder gun. These were *Tamai*, *Hafir*, *Metemma* and *Abu Klea*, all named for battles of the Gordon Relief Expedition. Churchill recorded: 'The total strength of the Expeditionary Force amounted to 8,200 British and 17,600 Egyptian [and Sudanese] soldiers with 44 guns and 20 Maxims on land, with 36 guns and 24 Maxims on the river, and with 2,469 horses, 896 mules, 3,524 camels and 229 donkeys, besides followers and private animals.'[63] This was the force that would march up the west bank of the Nile to Omdurman. An irregular Arab force of 2,500 troops would advance along the east bank under command of Major Edward J. M. Stuart-Wortley of the 60th Rifles, guarding the column's eastern flank.

The 21st Lancers were reorganised at Wad Hamed for the advance to Omdurman and the fighting expected ahead, C Squadron having arrived by boat on 26 August. One troop was taken from A, B and C Squadrons to form a fourth which was designated D Squadron and placed under the command of Captain Frank H. Eadon. Then each of the four squadrons was reorganised into four troops from its remaining numbers. The result was sixteen troops of approximately twenty-five men each under command of a captain or a lieutenant. Terry Brighton, the assistant curator of The Queen's Royal Lancers Regimental Museum at Belvoir Castle, has perhaps the best statement of the total strength of the regiment. After excluding thirty-nine men who left Cairo with the regiment but did not charge, thirty-six who were sent downriver sick and three who died before the battle, he calculates that the total participating in the charge on 2 September 1898 was 447 including thirty-four officers, 412 men and one civilian, Hubert Howard correspondent of *The Times*.[64] During a three-day halt at Wad Hamed, the men had their final opportunity to write letters, repair equipment, rest horses and contemplate their fate before the final advance. The scene in camp was one of intense activity as the battalions made their preparations, but at the same time peaceful with no enemy troops in sight during the day and no sniping into the lines during the hours of darkness. Churchill spent a good deal of his time at Wadi Hamed writing. Fellow correspondent Hubert Howard was busy with his own letters and expressed admiration for Churchill's abilities, writing on the 24th, 'There is Winston who sits down and in a couple of hours turns out a letter, neat and ready, 100 times better than mine.'[65]

Churchill managed to complete his fifth and sixth letters for the *Morning Post* at Wadi Hamed writing in his grandest style of the coming battle, 'No terms but flight or death are offered. The quarrel is à l'outrance. The red light of retribution plays on the bayonets and lances, and civilisation, elsewhere, sympathetic, merciful, tolerant, ready to discuss or to argue, eager to avoid violence, to submit to law, to effect a compromise, here advances with an inexorable sternness, and rejecting all other courses offers only the arbitrament of the sword.'[66] Writing privately to his mother what he thought would be his last letter before the battle, Churchill was characteristically calm and detached:

> Within the next ten days there will be a general action – perhaps a vy severe one. I may be killed. I do not think so. But if I am you must avail yourself of the consolations of philosophy and reflect on the utter insignificance of all human beings. I want to come back and shall hope all will be well. But I can assure you I do not flinch – though I do not accept the Christian or any other form of religious belief. We shall see what will happen and in that spirit I would leave the subject. Nothing – not even the certain knowledge of approaching destruction would make me turn back now – even if I could with honour.
>
> But I shall come back afterwards the wiser and the stronger for my gamble. And then we will think of other and wider spheres of action. I have plenty of faith – in what I do not know – that I shall not be hurt.[67]

Churchill did have faith – in his own destiny – and the optimistic, invincible attitude typical of the young Victorian-era officer in the British army. In his 1930 memoir, *My Early Life*, Churchill added a touch of humour to his recollection of the period before the battle:

> This kind of war was full of fascinating thrills. It was not like the Great War. Nobody expected to be killed. Here and there in every regiment or battalion, half a dozen, a score, at the worst thirty or forty, would pay the forfeit; but to the great mass of those who took part in the little wars of Britain in those vanished light-hearted days, this was only a sporting element in a splendid game.[68]

Early in the morning of 25 August, the first battalions of infantry marched south out of camp to continue the advance. They were followed in late afternoon, after the worst heat of the day had passed, by the balance of the British foot soldiers. The Egyptian cavalry squadrons performed their usual duties patrolling several miles ahead and providing flank protection. Their destination was a bivouac on the west bank of the Nile across from Royan Islands some twenty miles ahead. This was to be the final point of concentration where the entire force would assemble and thereafter proceed in a co-ordinated advance. The two-day march was uneventful and free from enemy harassment, although on the 26th Captain Douglas Haig, a 7th Hussar serving with the Egyptian cavalry, and his patrol encountered and exchanged fire with a group of hostile Baggara horsemen about ten miles ahead of the main body.[69]

On Saturday, 27 August the 21st Lancers began its final series of marches toward Omdurman which was about sixty miles away, a matter of five days' easy marching. They moved from Wadi Hamed to the Royan encampment which was on the river a few miles south of the heights of Shabluka. This massive rock formation, some 700 feet high, was left undefended by the Dervishes. Flanking the Nile on the west for six or seven miles, it was a natural defensive position paralleled on the east bank by a series of smaller rocky hills. Between the two elevations was the sixth cataract of the Nile through which the gunboats and supply barges passed laboriously.

The Dervishes could have slowed the advance from Shabluka, perhaps could have sunk some boats and slowed or damaged the rest, but it was not to be, another indication of the Khalifa's determination to force a single winner-take-all confrontation closer to Omdurman. Churchill was of the opinion that they would have suffered serious losses defending the Shabluka Heights which could have been flanked, surrounded and eliminated, and that the Dervishes were right to abandon it.[70] In any event, the Khalifa's tactics allowed the column and its flotilla to proceed unimpeded towards his capital and defending army. Facing no armed opposition on the march, the Lancers had only to contend with the oppressive heat, the glare of the sun, the blowing sand and the dust raised by so large a group of horsemen. After riding in the parched desert all day they took great pleasure in their return to the river at dusk. As Churchill wrote: 'How delicious it was in the evenings when, the infantry having reached and ordered their bivouac, the cavalry screen was withdrawn, and we filed down in gold and purple twilight to drink and drink and drink again from the swift abundant Nile.'[71] The nightly bivouacs were always on the river-side to facilitate resupply, watering the animals and proper defensive precautions.

On 28 August the entire column moved out from Royan on an eight-mile march to a new encampment at Wadi el Abid, referred to by some as Um Terif. The daily marches now were of relatively short distance and completed in the earlier hours of the day to avoid the worst heat of the sun. The column moved in reconnoitring formation, a convoy on land. The left flank was the Nile itself guarded by the flotilla and its formidable array of maxims and guns. The 21st Lancers rode up front, patrolling as far as ten miles ahead, closest to the river. The Camel Corps rode ahead as well off to the right of the Lancers. They were followed by the infantry marching in squares and by the baggage train. The Egyptian cavalry patrolled ahead into the desert south-west of the column providing a screen on the right flank of the main body in a wide arc. George W. Steevens of the *Daily Mail*, the man who had described the Lancers as looking like Christmas trees because of all the equipment they carried, observed and described the impressive movement of the cavalry:

> But though each man carried a bazaar, the impression of clumsiness lasted only a moment. When they moved, they rode forward solidly yet briskly – weighty and light at the same time, each man carrying all he wanted as behoves men going to live in an enemy's country. The sight was a better lecture in cavalry then many text-books. It is not the weapons that make the cavalryman you saw, but the mobility; not the gallop, but the long, long walk; not the lance he charges with, but the horse that carries him far and fast to see his enemy in front and screen his friends behind.[72]

The route to Wadi el Abid was generally flat with vast numbers of thorny mimosa bushes along the river through which the Lancers, ever wary of ambush, searched for hiding Dervishes, finding none. Since Churchill's arrival, the climate and the weather had proved to be greater obstacles to overcome than the enemy. The days were hot and dusty, the nights cool and often punctuated by rain, an uncomfortable situation for men sleeping on the ground with little shelter.

On 29 August, the column enjoyed a rest day at Wadi el Abid. Rest day is, of course, a relative term. As the infantry remained in their camp along the river-bank, the Egyptian cavalry sent out patrols to gather information and to serve as the early warning line for the column while the 21st Lancers remained as a reserve. Colonel Martin and his officers were eager to be employed and upset at not being sent out on reconnaissance. The colonel went to see the Sirdar who promised that they would be employed later.

Reveille was at 4.00 a.m. on 30 August and the column got an early start on its ten mile march from Wadi el Abid to its next encampment at Tamaniat. The force now moved in fighting formation with combat precautions in effect. The Lancers provided the cavalry screen to the left front, the Egyptian cavalry to the right front and right flank. The infantry marched in two lines of three brigades each ready to deploy into attack or defensive positions from whatever direction the enemy might come. The Camel Corps rode to the right of the infantry, the baggage animals to the rear. At about 8.00 a.m. the troop led by Lt Churchill on advanced patrol made contact with the enemy for the first time. About 100 yards ahead he saw a Dervish in the traditional white cloak, or *jibba*, armed with barbed spears, advance toward his men. He called a warning and galloped ahead. He saw one Lancer thrust his lance at the Dervish but miss. At this moment Churchill reports: 'I had meanwhile arrived, and now invited him to lay down his arms. This he did, making friendly gestures.'[73]

Having captured the first prisoner of the campaign for his new regiment, Churchill proudly sent him under guard to Wingate's intelligence staff in the rear. Churchill bragged about the capture to Mr Howard over lunch but his moment of glory was fleeting. As George W. Steevens later described it, the capture, 'the first fruits of victory – produced a great and gratifying sensation. Unluckily, Colonel Wingate, riding up with the staff, recognised this desperado as one of his excellent and most trustworthy spies, who was just returning with valuable information from Omdurman. The incident, as they say in diplomatic reports, then closed.'[74] Churchill was told of the identity of his willing captive when the patrol returned to camp at dusk. Not only would he receive no commendation for the capture, he faced a bit of teasing about it from his colleagues in the press. In *The River War*, he proved to be a good sport about the episode, writing with characteristic self-deprecating humour: 'Mr Lionel James, Reuter's correspondent, even proposed to telegraph some account of this noteworthy capture. But I prevailed on him not to do so, having a detestation of publicity.'[75]

During the afternoon of the 30th, the 21st Lancers occupied Merreh Hill, south-east of the Tamaniat bivouac. From this elevation Major Finn's A Squadron, Churchill included, observed the first skirmish between British soldiers and the Dervishes since Atbara. Two troops under Lieutenants Conolly and Smyth had been sent out to patrol a mile or so beyond the hill and were approached by a body of several dozen enemy horsemen. Although they exchanged fire, the skirmish had no importance and did not develop into a larger confrontation. It buoyed the Lancers' spirits. As Churchill wrote:

> The sun no longer seemed hot or the hours long. After all, there they were. We had not toiled upon a fruitless errand. The fatigues of the march, the heat, the insects, the discomforts – all were forgotten. We were 'in touch'; and that is a glorious thing to be, since it makes all the features of life wear a bright and vivid flush of excitement, which the pleasures of the chase, of art, of intellect, or love can never exceed and rarely equal.[76]

The march of 30 August was typical. The infantry marched from early morning to mid-day behind the protective screen of the cavalry. A defensive *zariba* was built by the infantry during the afternoon and the cavalry withdrew into it at dusk. As usual, the infantry provided the guard details for the bivouac and the night at Tamaniat passed without incident or excitement.

On Wednesday, 31 August, the army awoke in the dark and at first light the cavalry was once again sent out in its reconnoitring and patrolling role with the infantry following in battle array. During a watering stop at the foot of Merreh Hill, Churchill climbed to the top, there to view the panorama of the entire Anglo-Egyptian expeditionary force, 'the grand army of the Nile', advancing in formation toward its next encampment at Wadi Suetne, which was referred to by some as Sururat. He could also see Dervish patrols in the distance to the south. This day B Squadron provided the advance patrols and the other squadrons marched behind in line ready to manoeuvre into attack formation. Lts Pirie and Montmorency rode ahead on reconnaissance and saw some Dervish horsemen in the bush and gave pursuit which resulted in an exchange of fire and a narrow escape by the young officers. Lt Smyth thought they were 'very plucky', but Churchill was critical, calling them 'reckless and foolish'. Writing later, he said: 'Had they taken such liberties with any enemy but the Dervishes ... they would have been killed. The Afridis [on the North-West Frontier of India] would have fired only two shots. It is this reckless, happy-go-lucky spirit that costs the country the lives of many brave officers as the years pass. It is to be expected that young men will dare whenever they get an opportunity, particularly till they have been shot at a good deal.'[77] The contact, though dangerous, was brief and isolated, and Colonel Martin elected not to pursue the enemy horsemen without orders to do so.

On the evening of the 31st, Churchill dined in the mess of some British officers serving with a Sudanese battalion of the Egyptian army. He brought with him the current scepticism of the British cavalry as to whether the Dervishes would ever appear in force to stand and, finally, to fight. His hosts, who had been campaigning in Egypt and the Sudan for years, were certain the Dervishes would offer battle before the column reached Omdurman, which was now less than twenty miles away. Churchill was convinced the battle was not far off and, after conversing with Slatin Pasha of Wingate's staff about the possibility that the Dervishes might even attack their camp that night, Churchill 'lay down to sleep with a feeling of keen expectancy'.[78] There was no attack that night but rather the crash of violent thunderstorms that started at 9.00 p.m. and went on all night, robbing the officers and men of their rest and drenching the entire encampment.

It was a real failure of the Khalifa's generalship that no attack was made at Wadi Suetne during the night of 31 August–1 September. He was close to his base of operations, the column far from its own. The darkness could have masked the Dervish movements and the storm its sounds. He was familiar with the terrain and avenues of approach. He knew from observation that the British and Egyptian cavalry patrols were recalled at dusk. The darkness could remove some of the advantage of superior British arms. In the opinion of the *Daily Telegraph* correspondent, Bennet Burleigh, a veteran of the earlier Gordon Relief Expedition, 'It was one of the real surprises of the campaign that the Mahdists never really harassed us, or ventured to rush our lines under cover of night or in the fog of a dust storm ... In such a conflict the Sirdar's losses could have been great.'[79]

It was still raining steadily at reveille on Thursday morning, 1 September. This day the route of march would take the army the eight miles from Wadi Suetne to Egeiga, a tiny village six to eight miles from Omdurman. The march began at 5.45 a.m. with the 21st Lancers moving out in their screen as much as eight miles in front and the Camel Corps and Egyptian cavalry squadrons in their wide protective screen on the right. After riding only a mile the Lancers noticed a strange sight – a flock of a hundred or so vultures appeared on the scene and circled overhead, an omen of impending death, perhaps of the clash of arms the men expected soon to begin.

As the Lancers advanced, the naval flotilla moved up opposite Omdurman and at 5.30 a.m. fired its first guns against the Dervish forts that stood between the river and the immense walls of the city. This went on all day to the delight of the land forces who were observing from a considerable distance. By nightfall all the Dervish guns had been silenced, the forts battered and the Mahdi's tomb bombarded, its landmark dome pierced by naval gunfire.

By 8.00 a.m. the Lancers had reached the Kerreri Hills, the largest elevation between the previous night's bivouac and Omdurman, and found that the hills had been left undefended. Colonel Martin and Lt Clerk, the signals officer, climbed to the top to survey the scene ahead. They signalled to the squadrons below, 'Khartoum in sight', and as the regimental journey recorded: 'More than thirteen years had passed since an Englishmen could have said that with truth.'[80]

The Lancers then moved around the right shoulder of the Kerreri Hills and through their field glasses could see from a distance of eight miles the fork in the river marking the confluence of the Blue Nile and the White Nile. Between the branches of the river lay Tuti Island and beyond it the city of Khartoum, site of the ruins of the governor's palace where General Gordon had been slain in 1885. To their right, on the west bank of the White Nile, was the Dervish capital of Omdurman, a vast accumulation of mud-brick buildings, its skyline dominated by the dome of the Mahdi's tomb. Here they were, at long last, within reach of their goal. From the Kerreri Hills Churchill and his colleagues could clearly see what would become the battlefield the next day. It was bordered on the east by the Nile, on the west some five miles distant by a series of high hills. To the north were the Kerreri Hills and three miles to the south was a high solitary hill, Jebel Surgham, later referred to by various participants in the battle as Signal Hill or Heliograph Hill. The terrain formed what Churchill rightly described as 'this spacious amphitheatre'; it was a natural stage of huge proportions, an outdoor coliseum worthy of the clash of arms to come.[81] The ground between Jebel Surgham and the Kerreri Hills was of hard ochre sand, nearly flat with no vegetation and few folds of ground offering cover. From Jebel Surgham, 'a long ridge running from it [westward] concealed the ground beyond, for the rest there was a wide, rolling, sandy plain of great extent, and patched with course starveling grass'.[82]

By 9.00 a.m. the advance patrol began to report sightings of possible Dervish movements on the horizon to the south. This was exciting news to Churchill and members of A Squadron which was in a support role this day. By 10.30, all four squadrons of the 21st Lancers, the Camel Corps and several squadrons of Egyptian cavalry had moved into place and halted on the ridge, the last obstacle between them and the city. News came back from the patrol that the enemy was in sight. As the regimental sergeant major rode back to report he was asked how many Dervishes they were facing and he replied, 'A good army. Quite a good army.'[83] This was no understatement. Confronting the Lancers at a distance of three or four miles to the right front, or west, was arrayed the entire Dervish army shoulder to shoulder, several men deep in an unbroken line four miles long. The strength of the Dervish army has been variously estimated. Bennet Burleigh, an eyewitness, reckoned 30,000–32,000 Dervishes.[84] In his seventh letter to the *Morning Post* Churchill wrote: 'It was, perhaps, the impression of a lifetime, nor do I expect ever again to see such an awe inspiring and formidable sight. We estimated their number at not less than forty thousand men and it is now certain [as of 5 September 1898] fifty thousand would have been nearer the truth.'[85] At the time of writing *The River War* later in the year, and with the benefit of access to official records, Churchill wrote that the Khalifa had amassed an army exceeding 60,000 men in the environs of Omdurman of which an estimated 56,000 were in the line on 1 September and 52,000 would take part in the battle the next day.[86] The Dervish army was organised into five groups, or divisions of unequal numbers, most identified by a distinctive banner. The Dark Green Flag Division under Uthman al-Din had 28,378 men, 2,925 horsemen, 12,872 rifles and three artillery pieces. The Black Flag Division commanded by Yaqub totalled 14,128 men, 1,588 horsemen, 1,053 rifles, and two artillery pieces. The Bright Green Flag Division led by Khalifa Ali Wad Ullu included 5,398 men and 794 horsemen. Osman Digna commanded a division with no flag numbering 3,371 men, 187 horsemen and 365 rifles. There were numerous smaller units attached to the larger divisions but for all the Dervish units the vast majority of the men were foot soldiers armed with swords and spears rather than firearms.[87]

During the mid-morning Dervish horsemen and advance patrols of the 21st Lancers scouted ahead, taking each other's measure and occasionally exchanging shots. At about 11.00 a.m. the whole mass of the Dervish army began to move forward compelling the Lancers to retire, leaving a few patrols out as skirmishers. From the outpost line Colonel Martin called for a subaltern with a fresh horse and Major Finn sent Churchill forward. Martin wanted Churchill to serve as galloper with a message for Kitchener, the very role Churchill had imagined for himself two years before. 'Good morning,' Martin said. 'The enemy has just begun to advance. They are coming on pretty fast. I want you to see the situation for yourself, and then go back as quickly as you can without knocking up your horse, and report personally to the Sirdar. You will find him marching with the infantry.'[88] Here was a mission of real importance for a mere seven miles separated the two armies and they were not in sight of each other because of the terrain. The climactic battle was in the offing and it was Churchill who would bring this intelligence in person to the commanding general.

Trotting and cantering across the sand in the midday heat Churchill took care not to exhaust his mount and found the Sirdar and his staff at the centre of the massed Anglo-Egyptian infantry about forty minutes later. Churchill rode up next to Kitchener, saluted and made his report. The Sirdar said, 'You say the Dervish army is advancing. How long do you think I have got?' Churchill replied, 'You have got at least an hour – probably an hour and a half, sir, even if they come on at their present rate.'[89] With this the general rode on and Churchill fell back among the staff officers. He was reintroduced to Sir Reginald Wingate, Director of Intelligence of the Egyptian army and invited to lunch. As the infantry battalions halted, moved into defensive positions and rapidly began construction of yet another *zariba* of thorn bushes, the intelligence staff sat down to a lunch of bully-beef, mixed pickles and cool drinks all set out on a white oilcloth-covered table assembled of wooden boxes. Churchill enjoyed the meal and the company, writing, 'Everyone was in the highest spirits and the best of tempers. It was like a race luncheon before the Derby.'[90] The young lieutenant asked Wingate whether there would be a battle and was assured there would be and on that very site within a couple of hours. He later recalled, 'It really was a good moment to live, and I, a poor subaltern who had thought himself under a ban, applied my knife and fork with determination amid the infectious gaiety of all these military magnates.'[91] Churchill's mind raced with the possibilities of the battle to come as he finished his meal and rode back to his regiment.

Just before 2.00 in the afternoon the Dervish army inexplicably halted and, firing a resounding *feu-de-joie*, moved no further. During the afternoon Dervish and English patrols moved between the lines, probing, exchanging fire and reporting back but it appeared that the Mahdists would not offer battle that day. They lay down for the night in formation three miles from the Sirdar's camp. As dusk arrived the Lancers were withdrawn inside the *zariba* along the river-bank. The defensive position facing west with its back to the Nile was in the shape of an irregular half circle extending perhaps two miles along the shore and 800 yards inland. In front of the British section of the perimeter was a dense thorn-bush *zariba* three to four feet high. The Egyptian and Sudanese infantry perimeter had no *zariba* but was edged by a series of shallow trenches. Within the *zariba* was the entire force Kitchener had brought south. The perimeter was manned on the left side by the British infantry battalions, and on the middle and right by the Egyptian and Sudanese infantry battalions. Interspersed with these units were the Maxim guns and artillery batteries. To the rear were the baggage column, the field hospitals, supply dumps and reserves. The boats of the flotilla rode at anchor near by, their guns pointed inland and, after dark, their searchlights sweeping the ground in front of the *zariba* through the night.

Within the defensive perimeter the troops lay down to sleep in attack formation – clothed, armed and equipped for battle. Sentries and patrols remained on guard all night, posted at regular intervals but it is unlikely that many slept soundly. There was not only the probability of a huge battle the next day to contemplate but also the very real possibility of a night attack by the enemy. This was certainly on Churchill's mind. Lt Ronald Meiklejohn of the Royal Warwickshire Regiment recorded in his diary on the evening of 1 September: 'Then Winston Churchill, who was attached to the 21st, strolled up and we had a long talk. He was far less argumentative and self-assertive then usual. He said the enemy had a huge force, and if they attacked during the night, he thought it would be 'touch and go' about the result. A massed attack through the Gyppies or Sudanese would probably break through, with highly unpleasant results.'[92] It was a realistic concern. The darkness was broken only to a distance of 1,000 yards by the searchlights and the full moon allowed visibility to only about 400 yards. The British were well aware that these same Dervish spearmen had been formidable foes in the past, had broken British infantry squares at the battles of Tamai (1884) and Abu Klea (1885), had taken Khartoum and beheaded Gordon. Yet for all the danger of attack and serious losses, Churchill was confident the Dervishes would not prevail, even in a night attack.

During the evening, Churchill and another officer exchanged banter with officers of the flotilla who jokingly offered them refuge on the boats if a battle in the night did not go well. The conversation ended on a pleasant note when a Royal Navy officer, Lt Beatty, tossed Churchill a bottle of champagne with which he happily returned to the mess for dinner.[93] Churchill went to sleep that night comparing in his mind the British chances in the battle ahead to those of the smaller British column which was annihilated at Isandlwana in the Zulu War of 1879. 'Fortified by such reflections, I slept ... And hardly four miles away another army –

twice as numerous, equally confident, equally brave – was waiting impatiently for the morning and the final settlement of the long quarrel.'94 As it happened, there was no attack during the night. The Khalifa forfeited the advantage that darkness might have offered in favour of a mass frontal attack to take place in broad daylight next morning. General Sir Archibald Hunter, who commanded the Egyptian Division in the battle, commented on the Khalifa's failure to mount a night attack, writing in October 1898: 'So long as the enemy came on in daylight I had no fear, but my conviction till I die will be that if he had attacked us in the dark before dawn, with the same bravery he attacked us next day by day-light, we should have been pierced, divided, broken and rolled into the river.'[95]

Friday, 2 September 1898 began early for the Anglo-Egyptian force as the soldiers stood to arms at 3.30 a.m. in the semi-darkness of the full moon. Reveille was called at 4.00 a.m. Inside the *zariba* weapons and equipment were checked and rechecked and the experienced men ate a hearty breakfast to fortify them for a long day ahead. Although everyone expected a big battle, its exact nature, place and timing were, of course, unknown. The fortified *zariba*, although in the open, was an excellent defensive position offering broad fields of fire for the defenders and the flotilla. As Captain Neville Cameron of the 1st Battalion, Cameron Highlanders recalled, 'It was an ideal position from our point of view, but perfect madness on their part to dream of attacking us there, for it was almost quite flat and open ground with an infinitesimally small amount of cover even for men lying down.'[96] Churchill assumed the Dervish army would withdraw to Omdurman during the night, writing: 'I rejected the idea that they would advance across the open ground to attack the *zariba* by daylight, as it seemed absurd.'[97] It has since been considered another signal failure of the Khalifa's generalship that he fought the battle in the open rather than in the town. A fight inside the city would have neutralised the Sirdar's advantage in firepower. Omdurman, from which Kitchener needed to oust the Dervishes to win, had it been fought precinct by precinct, street by street and house by house, would have consumed much time and effort for the Sirdar's force and caused potentially devastating casualties.

The Khalifa, however, did have a battle plan. The advantage in the battle could be his if he struck first and that is what he intended to do. His plan was to attack in two phases, each phase comprised of two assaults from different directions in a kind of pincer movement. The first phase of the plan contemplated that a force of 4,000, later labelled as the White

Flag Army, would attack the *zariba* from the south after sweeping out from behind Jebel Surgham on the right. At the same time, a force of 8,000 would move around from the left of Jebel Surgham and attack the Sirdar's force from the west. While these attacks took place the Green Flag Army and associated units totalling about 14,000 would move from south to north out of sight and range of the *zariba* and take up positions north and west of the Kerreri Hills. Osman Digna's force would occupy the Khor Abu Sunt for a 1,000 or so yards south of the *zariba*, to act as a blocking force between the invaders and Omdurman. The Khalifa himself with the Black Flag Army of 12,000–13,000, would lie in wait as a reserve west of Jebel Surgham also out of sight of the zeriba. The Khalifa's goal was to cause significant damage to the defenders, breaching the *zariba* if possible, and so setting the scene for the Black Flag Army to join the fray and complete the victory. If the first phase attack failed to reach its objective the Khalifa planned to withdraw the remnants of the assault forces and by so doing lure Kitchener's troops out of the *zariba* into open ground in pursuit.

The second phase of the plan would take effect if the British and Egyptian Army troops moved out of their defensive position and marched south on Omdurman. In that event, the Black Flag Army would attack from the west on what would be Kitchener's right flank and simultaneously the Green Flag Army would attack from the Kerreri Hills at the north end of the battlefield on what would be Kitchener's rear. Once the opposing forces were intermingled in close combat, the gunboats would be rendered useless for fear of hitting their own men and the British-Egyptian superiority in numbers of rifles would melt away in a hand-to-hand mêlée in which the Dervishes would have the advantage of numbers. 'The plan was, as it were, an ambush on a huge scale.'[98] The success of the plan would depend on many factors, but it was flexible and thought through. Its fatal flaw was an inadequate appreciation of the sheer volume of fire the Anglo-Egyptian force could concentrate on the attackers. Such a firestorm was outside the Khalifa's experience and, perhaps, beyond his imagination.

As soon as there was enough light to see, Colonel Martin sent out two officers' patrols under Lts Churchill and Smyth to determine whether the Jebel Surgham ridge was occupied by the enemy and to find the precise location of the Dervish army. The Egyptian cavalry and Camel Corps were sent into the Kerreri Hills on a similar reconnaissance. Riding out with six men and a corporal, Churchill went up the slope of Jebel Surgham between its peak and the river and surveyed the scene ahead, not knowing what awaited him. He later wrote: 'There is nothing like the dawn. The quarter of an hour before the curtain is lifted upon an unknowable situation is an intense experience of war ... For cool, tense excitement I commend such moments.'[99] As dawn broke and Churchill had enough light to use his field glasses, he quickly established that the massive Dervish army was still to his front where he had last seen it the day before. He sent back the first of two written messages at 6.00 a.m. 'Dervish army, strength unchanged, occupied last nights position with their left well extended. Their patrols have reported the advance and loud cheering is going on. There is no *zeriba*. Nothing hostile between the line drawn from Heliograph Hill to Mahdi's tomb, and river. Nothing is within three miles from the camp.'[100] He marked the message xxx for 'with all dispatch'. Not long afterwards, the Dervish army began to move to the attack and Churchill sent back a second message at 6.20 a.m. reporting the Dervish advance and advising that a portion of it would pass south of Jebel Surgham toward the left side of the *zariba*.[101] Churchill was fascinated by the scene, the roar of the Dervish battle cries, the glitter of their thousands of weapons in the morning sunlight, the vast numbers of white-cloaked soldiers, the many colourful battle flags, and the rapid advance of the organised enemy units on foot and horseback. 'We see for ourselves what the Crusaders saw,' he wrote. 'Here we are scarcely 400 yards away from the great masses ... The enemy come on like the sea ... This is no place for Christians.'[102] Churchill's patrol remained on the ridge as observers until ordered back inside the *zariba* by Major Finn.

By 6.40 a.m. the Dervish units attacking the left and centre sections of the Sirdar's perimeter came into view and the first phase of the battle began in earnest. A Dervish force of 4,000–6,000, referred to as the White Flags, swept south and east of the slopes of Jebel Surgham to attack the *zariba* from the south. The frontal assault from the west was made by 8,000 men led by Amir Osman Azark over 3,000 yards of open ground. The British artillery fire began at 6.45 a.m. when the 32nd Field Battery opened up at a range of 2,800 yards. They were soon joined by the flotilla's gunboats and the other batteries. Churchill's patrol saw the effect of the artillery on the White Flag unit from his position near Jebel Surgham. 'We were so close, as we sat spellbound on our horses, that we almost shared their perils. I saw the full blast of death strike this human wall. Down went their standards by dozens and their men by hundreds. Wide gaps and shapeless heaps appeared in their array. One saw them jumbling and tumbling under the shrapnel bursts; but none turned back.'[103] At 1,700 yards the Maxim guns opened their rapid fire; the infantry battalions commenced their rifle fire in disciplined volleys at 1,500 to 2,000 yards. It was an unequal combat as the weapons of a modern army with its massed firepower brought to a halt a medieval army with its antiquated weapons and frontal assault tactics. All told, the Dervishes were rushing into a hail of fire of sixty cannon, twenty machine guns and 20,000 rifles.[104] George W. Steevens reported on the first phase of the battle from his vantage point inside the *zariba*:

> They came very fast, and they came very straight; and then presently they came no farther.
> No white troops would have faced that torrent of death for five minutes, but [the enemy] came on. The torrent swept into them and hurled them down in whole companies.
> It was the last day of Mahdism and the greatest. They could never get near, and they refused to hold back. By now the ground before us was all white with dead men's drapery. Rifles grew red-hot; the soldiers seized them by slings and dragged them back to the reserve to change for cool ones. It was not a battle, but an execution.[105]

The attack on the left and centre of the *zariba* never got closer than 700 yards to the defensive perimeter and was repulsed by 8.00 a.m. The British and Egyptian battalions, however, did not emerge unscathed. The hundreds of Dervish rifles firing from both the heights of Jebel Surgham and from the ranks of the attackers found their marks even at long range. The British troops were forced to stand up to fire over the *zariba* and were exposed to fire. The Egyptian and Sudanese infantry, on the other hand, fired from the prone position or from their trenches. The defenders lost several score killed and wounded while the enemy losses were in the several thousands. Their remnants retreated to the west to reform their ranks.

As the main attack of the first phase of the battle was in progress, the Dark Green Flag Unit led by Osman Sheik el Din with 15,000 men and a bright green flag of 5,000 men under Khalifa Ali Wad Helu moved north, according to plan, across open ground beyond the range of the battle and into positions in the Kerreri Hills, and forced the Egyptian cavalry and the Camel Corps from positions there. They were prevented from advancing to attack the right flank of the *zariba* only by the intense and deadly gunfire from the flotilla and the land batteries. Instead, they remained in and behind the Kerreri Hills. Throughout the first phase of the battle the largest Dervish force, the 12,000–14,000 men of the Black Flag, remained in reserve with the Khalifa out of sight west of Jebel Surgham.

The first phase of the attack was predestined to fail. The Khalifa made no attempt to use the little available cover of the ground or darkness to mask the attacks. He failed to concentrate his available rifle and cannon fire to force a breach in the *zariba*'s defensive line and failed to concentrate his available cavalry to this purpose. Instead, his riflemen and cavalry were scattered among the many spearmen and had no significant impact. Finally and most importantly, the Dervish commander had inadequate intelligence about the massive amount and excellent accuracy of the firepower his soldiers would face. Had he known, he might not have attempted the daylight frontal assault that was made and which ended in such rapid, decisive defeat.

After the initial Dervish attack failed, it was Kitchener's turn to take the initiative. His general plan was to march his entire force out of the *zariba* in a large-scale left wheel from his position facing west to a new line facing south and so advance to Omdurman some six miles away. As a preliminary to this movement he ordered the 21st Lancers to advance toward the Dervish capital by a route between Jebel Surgham and the Nile. They rode out of the *zariba* and arrived on the ridge east of the hill by 8.15 a.m. At 8.30 a.m. the Sirdar's orders were delivered to Colonel Martin requiring him to, 'Annoy them as far as possible on their flank and head them off if possible from Omdurman.'[106] Advancing at a walk in a column of troops with Churchill in command of the next to the last troop, the regiment came upon a line of Dervish foot soldiers to their right at a distance of 300 yards in a blocking position across the road to Omdurman. Lieutenant Pirie's patrol had estimated this force at 1,000 but upon closer view only a few hundred could be seen. Churchill thought there were about 150. It was not known to Colonel Martin that behind the Dervishes visible to him were 2,600 others under Osman Digna concealed in a deep ravine, the Khor Abu Sunt. Most of these were spearmen but the thirty or so riflemen among them brought the fire of their Remingtons to bear on the column and both men and horses were hit. At that, Martin gave up all thought of flanking the Dervish line and positioning the regiment between the city and the enemy force. Rather than leave his men exposed to hostile fire while crossing the Dervish front, he ordered the trumpeter to sound the command, 'right wheel into line'. In response, all sixteen troops turned as one to the right and formed a line over 400 yards long, the 440 troopers riding flank to flank. The usual, progressive orders of 'canter,' 'gallop' and 'charge' were never called because as soon as the regiment moved into line the charge began at once as if every officer and trooper *knew* this was the moment for the long-awaited charge. Colonel Martin rode in front followed close behind by Major Crole-Wyndham, and then the four squadron commanders in front of their squadrons with the C Squadron on the far left, D Squadron to its right, B Squadron next and A Squadron on the far right. Of the four troops of A Squadron in the charge, Churchill was the second from the right in the squadron and also from the end of the entire line.[107] It only took the lancers thirty or so seconds to cover the 250 to 300 yards to the Dervish line. After the first 100 yards, Major Finn ordered 'right shoulders' and A Squadron curved inward to their left 'like the horns of the moon'. At 50 to 100 yards out, the Lancers could suddenly see they were riding into a trap on 'deceitful ground' as it was then apparent that behind the line of Dervish riflemen was a *khor*, four to six feet deep and twenty or more feet across, that was jammed with Dervishes, twelve deep in some places, armed, ready to receive them and unmoving.[108]

There was no time to change direction or the plan as the meeting was but seconds away. The collision of the charging Lancers and the awaiting Dervishes was a tremendous impact, knocking many of the defenders off their feet and a number of their attackers off their mounts. There followed a desperate two-minute mêlée as the Lancers and their horses which had leapt into the *khor* thrust, slashed, shot, fought and struggled to get across and out the other side. The *khor* was deepest, widest and most densely packed with Dervishes toward the centre where D and B Squadrons entered and shallower and not so crowded on the ends through which C Squadron passed on the left and A Squadron on the right. It was a deadly fight with the Lancers greatly outnumbered and those who were unhorsed set upon from all sides. The intense hand-to-hand fighting in the *khor* was unlike that of any other part of the entire battle of Omdurman. Here artillery and Maxim guns meant nothing. As Churchill wrote: 'It was the kind of fighting they thoroughly understood. Moreover, the fight was with equal weapons, for the British too fought with sword and lance as in days of old.'[109] Churchill, however, fought with his Mauser automatic pistol because his old shoulder injury made it impossible to fight with a sword. It was a choice of weapons that saved his life.[110]

There were many acts of individual bravery among the lancers, three of whom were later recognised by the award of the Victoria Cross. Private Thomas Byrne of B Squadron was hit in the right arm by a bullet and dropped his lance before he even reach the *khor*. He drew his sword and continued the charge and was one of the last Lancers to enter the fray. Rather than continuing through the *khor*, he stopped and went to the aid of Lt Molyneaux who had been wounded and unhorsed. Byrne charged four Dervishes who were closing in to finish off the officer and suffered a second serious wound when a spear struck him in the chest. His brave actions alone allowed Molyneaux to escape. After rejoining his squadron west of the *khor*, Byrne refused to fall out for medical attention until he fainted from loss of blood.[111] Lt Raymond de Montmorency of B Squadron had ridden clear of the danger when he saw Lt Grenfell lying on the ground in the *khor* surrounded by Dervishes. He rode back into the *khor* to go to Grenfell's rescue, moved the enemy back and dismounted only to find Grenfell was already dead. He attempted to put Grenfell's body across the saddle of his own horse but it bolted, leaving De Montmorency with the body, alone and surrounded.[112] Only through the efforts of B Squadron's Captain Philip Kenna did de Montmorency survive. Kenna had performed another act of gallantry only moments before when Major Crole-Wyndham was unhorsed as they both rode into the *khor*. Seeing this, Kenna pulled the major up behind him on his own horse and rode out to safety. Then, having cleared the *khor*, Kenna saw Lt de Montmorency who was trying to recover Grenfell's body. With the help of Corporal S. W. Swarbrick, Kenna retrieved De Montmorency's horse, allowing all three to escape to rejoin the regiment.[113]

For saving comrades who had been unhorsed in or near the *khor*, seven Lancers were later awarded the Distinguished Conduct Medal. These were Sergeant W. Chalmers, Lance-Corporal M. D. Penn and Private F. Pedder all of A Squadron, Corporal F. W. Swarbrick, Private W. Brown and Private W. Bushell of B Squadron and Private B. H. Ayton of C Squadron.[114]

Churchill's troop rode through the *khor* where it was not so densely packed with Dervishes; he estimated the enemy to be four deep where he entered. As he approached the *khor* he rode between two Dervishes who both fired, missing him but hitting a Lancer immediately behind him. His horse leapt into the six-foot-deep *khor* but Churchill kept his seat and his wits. He pushed through the crowd of Dervishes out of the other side of the *khor*, but not out of danger. Still assailed by the enemy, he shot one Dervish who was raising his sword to disable Churchill's horse and another swordsmen only an arm's length away. Luckily, Churchill and his mount emerged unscathed. As he later wrote:

In one respect a cavalry charge is very like ordinary life. So long as you are all right, firmly in your saddle, your horse in hand, and well armed, lots of enemies will give you a wide berth. But as soon as you have lost a stirrup, have a rein cut, have dropped your weapon, are wounded, or your horse is wounded, then is the moment when from all quarters enemies rush upon you. Such was the fate of not a few of my comrades in the troops immediately on my left.[115]

Finding himself alone outside of the *khor* and being fired upon, Churchill rode out to rejoin the regiment which was reforming 200 yards to the west. As A Squadron got organised, a Dervish leapt up in their midst and Churchill shot him dead with the last round in his Mauser's clip. As he counted his men he found three or four missing and noted six Lancers and nine or ten horses had been wounded. He fully expected that they would be ordered to charge again and got the men ready to do so.

As Churchill later wrote to his mother and to his friend Ian Hamilton, he was ready to charge back again or even twice more, 'pour la gloire'. He thought 'Another fifty or sixty casualties would have made our performance historic – and made us proud of our race and our blood', and admitted, 'My soul becomes very high in such moments.'[116] Churchill asked his sergeant if he had enjoyed the first charge. The sergeant replied, 'Well, I don't exactly say I enjoyed it, sir; but I think I'll get more used to it next time.'[117] But by now Colonel Martin had become aware of the serious casualties the 21st had suffered in both men and horses as more wounded emerged from the action. The colonel wisely did not order a second charge but moved the regiment to the south-east flank of the Dervish force where at a distance of 300 yards two squadrons dismounted and drove the Dervishes out of the *khor* and into the desert with carbine fire. Twenty minutes after the charge began it was all over with the 21st Lancers back at the *khor* to bury their dead, aid the wounded and have breakfast.

In combat in his third war, Churchill comported himself very capably, showing his characteristic dash and indifference to danger. Trumpeter A. Norris of A Squadron later recalled: 'Mr Churchill was in command of my troop and I must say that he was a daring and resourceful soldier ... I saw him firing away for all he was worth.'[118] The regimental magazine of the 21st Lancers, *The Vedette*, referred to Churchill as 'a very cool-headed young officer' in its issue about the campaign.[119] In his eighth letter for the *Morning Post*, written in Khartoum four days after the battle, Churchill belittled the danger to himself and claimed no heroics on his part:

One impression only I will record. I remember no sound. The whole event seemed to pass in absolute silence. The yells of the enemy, the shouts of the soldiers, the firing of many shots, the clashing of sword and spear were unnoticed by the senses, unregistered by the brain. Others say the same. Perhaps it is possible for the whole of a man's faculties to be concentrated in eye, bridle-hand, and trigger-finger, and withdrawn from other parts of the body.[120]

One episode involving Churchill was never written of by him. According to Bennett Burleigh of the *Daily Telegraph*, after Churchill and Lt Thomas Conolly cleared the *khor* they turned about and rescued two non-commissioned officers who were trapped underneath fallen horses west of the *khor*. The officers rode out, dismounted and brought back the men before the Dervishes could get to them.[121] Whether Churchill and Conolly should have received a commendation is debatable; no doubt many selfless and gallant acts went unreported. In the end, Churchill received only the two campaign medals for his participation in the campaign and the charge. As he told his private secretary, Anthony Montague Browne, many years later: 'I have many medals for adventure, but none for bravery.'[122]

The casualties to the regiment were severe, the worst in proportion to numbers of any British unit in the campaign. C Squadron on the left of the line during the charge had only two casualties, with Lt Molyneaux and one trooper wounded. D Squadron, second from the left, had twenty-three casualties including Lt Nesham and eleven Lancers wounded, eleven Lancers killed. B Squadron, second from the right, suffered the worst with Lt Grenfell killed, Lt J. Brinton wounded, nine men killed and twenty-three wounded. Churchill's A Squadron on the far right had Lt O. Brinton wounded, one man killed and six men wounded. In addition, an estimated 119 horses had been killed or wounded.[123] But for all their gallantry and all their losses the charge of the 21st Lancers was but a sideshow and had no effect on the battle.

Many were critical of the charge, not least of whom was Kitchener himself. Captain Douglas Haig, serving with the Egyptian cavalry, wrote that the 21st 'was keen to do something and meant to charge something before the show was over. They got their charge but at what cost? I trust for the sake of the British Cav. that more tactical knowledge exists in the higher ranks of the average regiment than we have seen displayed in this one.'[124] Some contemporary accounts were enthusiastic, including that of Lt Smyth of A Squadron who wrote, 'As far as cavalry goes it is the biggest thing since Balaclava and I am very proud of belonging to the 21st

Lancers. Wise or unwise, it was a brave deed nobly done, and as Colonel Martin said, he was so proud and pleased that it had happened, as it proved that cavalry still existed and that we did not come here to play at mounted infantry.'[125] In fact, it was the enfilading carbine fire of the dismounted Lancers after the charge that drove the Dervishes from the *khor* and back toward their main body, where, crossing the front of the advancing British Division, they were decimated by artillery fire. A judicious summary of the action was provided by George W. Steevens in a post-war lecture at Aldershot in which he declared: 'The charge of the 21st Lancers was costly, and the losses they incurred detracted from their utility and the subsequent pursuit [of the fleeing Khalifa]. On the other hand it must not be forgotten that such heroic actions often do more for the morale of an army and of a nation than less brilliant operations more correctly conducted.'[126] The Lancers had found their glory and most survived to tell the tale of what has been called the last great charge of the British cavalry. It was, even in 1898, a most dangerous method of attack by an outmoded arm. It could have been an even worse disaster had the Dervishes been better armed. In later years when asked by his Private Secretary about his thoughts on the famous charge, Churchill replied, 'Oh yes, it was most exhilarating. But I did reflect: "Supposing there were a spoil-sport in a hole, with a machine gun?" '[127]

At the same time the 21st Lancers were in action at Khor Abu Sunt, the second phase of the main battle was in progress. At 8.30 a.m. Kitchener's army began its advance on Omdurman leaving the *zariba* and moving in a wide arc stretching from the Nile east of Jebel Surgham to the middle of the Kerreri Plain. It was the Sirdar's plan to push to Dervish army to the west into the desert and away from its base in Omdurman. The brigades moved out in the same order from left to right in which they had been positioned in the defensive perimeter overnight – Lyttleton's 2nd Brigade and Wauchope's 1st Brigade of the British Division, then Maxwell's 2nd Brigade, Lewis's 3rd Brigade and McDonald's 1st Brigade of the Egyptian Division on the far right. Each unit brought along its maxim guns and artillery pieces. The Camel Corps and Collinson's brigade remained in the rear as reserves and Broadwood's Egyptian cavalry was miles to the north of the Kerreri Hills, forced there by the Green Flag attack and effectively out of action. By 9.40 a.m. the British division was on the Jebel Surgham's slopes and the Egyptian brigades were picking their way through the corpse-strewn battlefield north of the ridgeline. The units on the extreme right had the greatest distance to cover and were spread out, McDonald almost a mile from Lewis. At this moment the Black Flag Army, 12,000–14,000 strong, moved from its position behind Jebel Surgham and attacked in force. Although the first phase of the battle is the one most often referred to by historians as emblematic of the entire battle of Omdurman, it was the second phase that was the critical engagement and the key to victory.

As the Black Flag Army swept west around Jebel Surgham and crested the ridge, McDonald formed his brigade, together with its eighteen guns and eight Maxim guns, into a line 1,500 yards long to await their assault. Within fifteen minutes the battle was engaged. McDonald's 2nd Egyptian Battalion stood firm and fired away. His 9th, 10th and 11th battalions, comprised of black Sudanese troops, 'as cool as any Scotsman, stood and aimed likewise'.[128] While this was going on, Lewis's brigade was also engaged and Kitchener moved Wauchope's brigade up between Lewis and McDonald to extend and strengthen the line. Meanwhile, the balance of the British Division reached the crest of Jebel Surgham and its artillery and Maxim fire was brought to bear on the mass of Dervishes. By 10.00 a.m. the Dervish attack began to falter, again defeated by the superior firepower and fine discipline of the Sirdar's forces.

At 10.10 a.m., the approximately 14,000-strong Green Flag Army swept down from their positions in and behind the Kerreri Hills from the north on to the plain in a strong attack on McDonald's right flank, indeed, the right flank of Kitchener's entire army. This was the pivotal moment in the battle. If McDonald folded up then Lewis's brigade was at risk and the reserve brigade and Camel Corps would be in real danger. If Kitchener had to move 2nd British (Lyttleton) Brigade and 2nd Egyptian (Maxwell) Brigade from the far left of the line to meet the Green Flag assault it would leave the way open for the Khalifa and the remaining Black Flag soldiers to return to Omdurman and defend it in force. McDonald handled the crisis with calm. As G. W. Steevens recorded: '"Cool as on parade", is an old phrase; McDonald Bey was very much cooler. Beneath the strong, square-hewn face you could tell that the brain was working as if packed in ice ... He saw everything; he knew what to do; he knew how to do it; he did it.'[129] Following his orders with speed, discipline and courage, McDonald's four battalions changed their front from south to west then to the north to meet the new attack. Wauchope sent a battalion of the Lincolns to extend McDonald's right and their accurate rifle fire joined in to slow and then defeat the Green Flag Army. Like the Black Flag, its superior numbers had been beaten by the superior firepower of cannon, Maxim guns and thousands of rifles held by well-trained troops. And because the two second-phase attacks were not simultaneous, the Dervish pincer plan failed. The delay between the Black and Green Flag attacks allowed McDonald just enough time to change front and protect the flank from being over-whelmed. In broad daylight the attacks of the Khalifa's forces were doomed to fail even though they fought with unquestioned bravery and determination and their leading elements got within a few yards of McDonald's lines. By 11.00 a.m. the second phase of the battle was over and the Egyptian cavalry arrived at last, forcing the Dervish survivors from the field. For the next hour or so the Sirdar's force moved to the west, pushing the enemy ever farther from the Nile and the city, killing many wounded Dervishes along the way but nevertheless taking many hundreds of prisoners.

At noon, Kitchener announced that the Dervishes had received 'a good dusting' and deployed his brigades to resume the advance south to Omdurman.[130] Between 12.30 and 3.00 p.m. the various units reached the flooded Khor Shambat three miles north of the city; there and along the Nile they rested, watered horses and took their lunch. At 4.00 p.m. the Sirdar, accompanied by the infantry battalions of Maxwell's brigade and the 32nd Field Battery, Royal Artillery, resumed the advance. As Kitchener proceeded into the city at the head of the victorious army, three local officials met him on the road and surrendered the city with a presentation of the keys to government buildings. The Khalifa and his bodyguards were nowhere to be found, having fled into the desert south-west of the town after the battle. The march into the city was met with only sporadic, light resistance as throngs of people crowded the streets to see the arrival of the infidel army. The Sirdar set up a headquarters in the square surrounding the Mahdi's tomb guarded by the XIIIth Sudanese Battalion of infantry and four guns. The tomb and the Khalifa's house were occupied, the arsenal seized and the gates to the prison opened by troops of Maxwell's brigade. Hubert Howard, *The Times* correspondent who had ridden with the 21st Lancers in the charge earlier in the day, was killed by an errant British artillery shell in the town before the cease-fire was completed.[131] The Sudanese troops of the Egyptian army occupied the city and the British troops were for the most part kept in the outskirts. It was just as well, for as journalist G. W. Steevens reported, in the town, 'Everything was wretched. And foul ... the stench of the place was in your nostrils, in your throat, in your stomach. You could not eat; you dared not drink.'[132]

The mounted forces, the 21st Lancers included, were posted around the edges of the city where they served as a blocking force and took the surrender of additional hundreds of prisoners. Several squadrons of Egyptian cavalry accompanied by gunboats were sent south in pursuit of the fleeing Khalifa, an unsuccessful mission from which they would not return until the next day. By 10.00 p.m. the 21st Lancers were called in from their outpost and bivouacked with the 2nd British Brigade north of the city near Khor Shambat. Churchill saw to the picketing of the troop's horses and a meal for his men and then, as an enquiring reporter would, went to headquarters to check what was going on. He saw Colonel Wingate up late drafting by lantern light the telegram that would send news of the victory to Cairo and London.[133] That evening Churchill drafted his own telegram to his mother that did not get sent until the next day. It read simply, 'All right – WINSTON.'[134] Before he slept Churchill reflected on this long day – the dangers he had faced, the deaths of his friends Grenfell and Howard, the losses and awful wounds in the regiment. He wrote privately to Lady Randolph: 'These things – and at the time they were reported as worse – made me anxious and worried during the night and I speculated on the shoddiness of war. You cannot gild it. The raw comes through.'[135]

The casualties for the battle of Omdurman were enormous but fell mostly on the Dervishes. The figures are much in dispute as various estimates were made and recorded. In *The River War*, Churchill lists total casualties for the British Division at 175 – three officers and twenty-five men killed and eleven officers and 136 men wounded. Of this total, seventy-one were from the 21st Lancers, 104 from the eight infantry battalions and service detachments. Many of the infantry casualties were attributed to the fact the British soldiers had to stand up to fire over the *zariba* and so were more exposed than the Egyptian troops. The Egyptian army suffered 301 casualties including two officers and eighteen men killed, eight officers and 273 men wounded.[136] The total casualties for the Anglo-Egyptian force were less than they had suffered at the battle of Atbara in April 1898. But, it must be remembered, at the Atbara it was the British and Egyptians rather that the Dervishes making a frontal attack in broad daylight.

The Dervish casualties were far greater. In *The River War*, Churchill estimated 9,700 had been killed, 10,000–16,000 wounded and 5,000 taken prisoner.[137] Lt Hamilton Hodgson of the Lincolnshire Regiment reported in a contemporary letter that two days after the battle 10,700 Dervish bodies were counted within three miles of the *zariba*.[138] A more recent account makes reference to Colonel Wingate's official dispatch from March 1899 that gives the total of Dervishes killed as 10,800 and the total wounded as 16,000.[139] The only Sudanese account available gives estimates of 2,800–2,900 Dervishes killed and 4,200–4,500 wounded in the first phase attack, 1,600 killed and 1,850 wounded in the Black Flag attack and 4,000 killed and 2,000–2,400 wounded in the Green Flag attack.[140] If one accepts Wingate's official report and Churchill's estimate of 5,000 prisoners, Dervish casualties of 31,800 seems the appropriate total – a horrible butcher's bill for a single day's combat. Of interest is Churchill's report of the ammunition expended by the Sirdar's force to cause such carnage. The British Division fired 172,000 rounds of rifle ammunition, the Egyptian Division 272,000 rounds. The artillery fired 3,500 case or shrapnel shells and the combined British and Egyptian Maxim guns fired 67,000 rounds.[141] It was an enormous and, as it proved, decisive concentration of firepower.

For all practical purposes the military victory over Mahdism was won that day on the battlefield at Omdurman. As most of the British troops would soon leave the Sudan, it was left to the Egyptian army to complete the fifth and final stage of the campaign, to hunt down the scattered Dervish forces that had fled after the battle and to take control of the rest of the country. A number of columns were sent out along the Blue Nile and the White Nile, often accompanied by gunboats and supply barges. A series of successful actions were fought in the area of Gedaref from September to December 1898, as the Egyptians forced the Dervishes west and set up a series of garrisons to take control of south-eastern Sudan. An Egyptian attack on Rosaires Island on the Blue Nile on 26 December forced the Dervishes under Amir Ahmed Fedil into the desert of Kordofan west of the White Nile. On 24 November 1899, after a further year of campaigning, a column under Colonel Reginald Wingate located the combined forces of Fedil and the Khalifa in the area of Gedid, some 400 miles south of Khartoum in south-western Sudan. This, the final effective Dervish fighting formation, was brought to battle and destroyed with both Fedil and the Khalifa killed and more than a thousand Dervishes killed and 3,150 taken prisoner. This was the true end of the military campaign to reconquer the Sudan.[142]

While the British forces were departing and the Egyptian forces began the final campaign in pursuit of the Khalifa, important military – diplomatic events took place to resolve unfinished imperial business concerning French encroachment on British interests in southern Sudan. The British government learned that in 1896 a French military mission commanded by Major Jean-Baptiste Marchand had marched from West Africa into the interior. Kitchener learned that by July 1898, Marchand had established himself at Fashoda some 400 miles south of Omdurman on the White Nile. There, with the support of eight French officers and NCOs and 120 native troops from Niger to back him, he claimed Sudan for France.

Having defeated the Dervishes, the Sirdar left for Fashoda to deal with the French on 8 September accompanied by five gunboats, two battalions of Sudanese infantry, two companies of Cameron Highlanders, an artillery battery and four Maxim guns. He arrived at Fashoda on 19 September and met Marchand. After an exchange of pleasantries and in complete disregard of the claims of France, he then hoisted the Egyptian and British flags and established a garrison consisting of the XIth Sudanese battalion, two guns and two Maxims under command of Colonel Jackson. Later the same day a second outpost was established sixty-two miles farther south at Sobat manned by half of the XIIIth Sudanese battalion with two guns. In addition, two gunboats were left to support the garrisons and patrol the river. With this show of force, Great Britain's point was made – the watershed of the Nile was British and France would have to withdraw her forces and her claims. Kitchener was back in Omdurman by 24 September. Marchand returned to France for instructions in October and by mid-December 1898, the French at Fashoda struck their colours and departed. The diplomatic confrontation which held the possibility of much greater crisis thus ended without a shot being fired. An Anglo-French treaty was signed in London on 21 March 1899, leaving Britain and Egypt in complete control of the Sudan. Diplomatically, as well as militarily, the Anglo-Egyptian victory was then complete.[143]

On the morning of 3 September the 21st Lancers were ordered south of Omdurman at 8.00 a.m. as observers. They received additional prisoners all day as Dervishes straggled in from the desert. The Lancers gave quarter to enemy wounded although this was not the practice in all units. Churchill later wrote: 'I must personally record that there was a very general impression that the fewer the prisoners, the greater would be the satisfaction of the commander.'[144] It was characteristic of Churchill to be magnanimous to a defeated enemy and he reported with great pride in his ninth *Morning Post* letter from Omdurman: 'I rejoice for the honour of the British cavalry when I reflect that they held their heads very high, and that the regiment that

suffered by far the greatest loss also took the greatest number of prisoners.'[145] Churchill was very critical of Kitchener's attitude in victory after
the Sirdar ordered the Mahdi's tomb to be razed and his body disinterred,
decapitated and thrown into the Nile. The young subaltern found these
actions abhorrent and condemned them in *The River War* as 'vandalism and
folly'.[146] He wrote as well to Ian Hamilton on 16 September 1898: 'I am in
great disfavour with the authorities here. Kitchener was furious with Sir E.
Wood for sending me out and expressed himself freely. My remarks on the
treatment of the wounded – again disgraceful – were repeated to him and
generally things have been a little unpleasant. He is a great general but he
has yet to be accused of being a gentlemen.'[147]

The main event of 4 September was the memorial service for General
Charles Gordon held at the ruins of the former governor's palace across
the Nile in Khartoum. Every available officer, Churchill not included, and
representatives of each battalion were present. The crescent flag of the
Khedive and a conspicuously larger Union Flag were raised over the ruins
and the national anthems were played by regimental bands, guns fired a
salute and cheers were given for the Queen and the Khedive. There
followed a Christian memorial service for Gordon led by army chaplains
and concluding with a bagpipe dirge and the playing of 'Abide With Me'.

On 4–5 September the regimental duties of cleaning up after the battle,
inspecting, and selecting horses to be transferred to the Egyptian cavalry
still allowed officers and men to see the sights in and around the town.
Churchill visited the Mahdi's tomb and the Khalifa's house and on the 5th
rode over the battlefield with Lt John George Murray, the Marquis of
Tullibardine, son and heir of the Duke of Atholl, then serving in the Royal
Horse Guards. They rode out from Omdurman across the ground of the
Lancers' charge where he stopped at the Khor Abu Sunt and estimated it
to be twenty-five feet wide and four feet deep. From there they rode up
Jebel Surgham to survey the scene where thousands of Dervish bodies lay
under a scorching sun in patterns that told the story of the battle, of each
charge, and where it had been stopped. The stench was horrible and the
scene ugly. Churchill compared in his mind the military funeral services
attending the British dead with what he saw: 'But there was nothing dulce
et decorum about the Dervish dead. Nothing of the dignity of uncon-
querable manhood. All was filthy corruption. Yet these were as brave men
as ever walked the earth.'[148]

On the afternoon of 6 September 1898, the 21st Lancers, re-formed
back into three squadrons, began their march back to Atbara. This was

their fate as the only British calvary regiment on the campaign. The infantry would return to Egypt in sailing barges. Kitchener saw the 21st off in person with the following remarks:

> Colonel Martin, officers and men of the 21st Lancers, I am very proud to have had you under my command: the fine charge you made the other day will long go down to history in the Annals of your Regiment and be looked upon with pride by the whole of the British cavalry. I will not keep you any longer, but I hope you will have a pleasant march down to the Atbara.[149]

The regiment gave the Sirdar three cheers, then rode in a column of troops across the scene of its charge, across the battlefield in front of the *zariba* along the Nile, headed northward at last. They reached Fort Atbara on the 19th, then proceeded north by a combination of trains and boats. A Squadron and half of B Squadron arrived back at Abassiyeh Barracks outside Cairo on the morning of 26 September as the Egyptian cavalry band played them in with 'Soldiers of the Queen'. C Squadron and the second half of B Squadron returned by the morning of the 29th, and so for the Lancers the campaign was at an end.

The Sirdar's dispatch of 30 September mentioned twenty of the Lancers. In addition to those mentioned for gallantry in the field, the three Victoria Cross and seven Distinguished Conduct Medal recipients noted above, the following were mentioned 'for good services,' Col R. H. Martin (commander), Major W. G. Crole-Wyndham (second in command), Major H. Finn (commanding A Squadron), Major J. Fowle (commanding B Squadron), Captain F. H. Eadon (commanding D Squadron), Lt C. J. Clerk (signals officer), Lt A. M. Pirie (Adjutant), Lt R. N. Smyth (A Squadron), Lt A. H. Taylor (C Squadron), and 2nd Lt C. S. Nesham (D Squadron).[150]

In November the Queen sent the regiment a letter with additional honours:

> Balmoral Castle
> 4th November, 1898
>
> The Queen Empress has much pleasure in approving that the 21st Lancers should assume the title of 'Empress of India's' Regiment, and have French grey facings; their bravery deserves recognitions.[151]

This directive allowed the regiment to add Queen Victoria's cypher to its badge and thereafter to be known as the '21st (Empress of India's)

Lancers'. The reference to facings restored to the regiment uniform colours consistent with its Indian army antecedents.

In the *London Gazette* of 15 November 1898 the Victoria Crosses and Distinguished Conduct Medals were officially announced together with additional honours. Colonel Martin and Lt Colonel Wyndham were appointed companions of the most Honourable Order of the Bath and Lt A. M. Pirie was appointed to be a companion of the Distinguished Service Order. Two brevets, promotions to a higher, honorary rank, were also announced – Major Finn to be a Lt Colonel and Captain Eadon to be a Major.[152] In addition to the awards for individual heroism or meritorious service, two campaign medals were authorised and awarded to all the officers and men who took part in the campaign to retake the Sudan.

Great Britain issued the Queen's Sudan Medal in March 1899. The medal was issued in silver for British troops and bronze for native troops. The obverse features a half-length figure of the Queen and the reverse shows a winged victory holding a laurel in her left hand and a palm branch in her right. Behind the victory are the British and Egyptian flags and below her the inscription 'SUDAN'. The ribbon from which the medal is suspended features lines of yellow, red and black, symbolising the desert, the British forces and the Sudan. The government of Egypt issued the Khedive's Sudan Medal in 1897 in silver and bronze with clasps to commemorate participation in particular battles. The clasp 'Khartoum' was issued for the battle of Omdurman. The obverse bears the Arabic inscription for 'Abbas Hilmi The Second', the Khedive, and the Arabic date 1314 (AD 1897). The reverse displays a trophy of flags, banners and weapons with the Arabic inscription, 'The Reconquest of The Sudan 1314'. The ribbon is of yellow with a central stripe of blue which symbolise the desert and the Nile.[153] The 21st Lancers paraded at Abdin Square, Cairo, 19 October 1898 to receive the Khedive's Sudan medals from Kitchener himself.

Churchill did not leave Omdurman with the 21st Lancers but was kept back for 'transport work'. He put his personal time to good use sending an additional six letters to the *Morning Post* between 5 and 12 September. When his duties were completed at Omdurman he began his return to Cairo by boat, sharing a sailing barge, or *gyassa*, with the Grenadier Guards, the same regiment he would later train with in France in 1915. It was a leisurely journey to Atbara following the wind and current past the scenes of earlier battles and bivouacs, covering a distance in five days that had taken seventeen days going the other direction on land in August. He arrived at Atbara by 16 September and sent his fourteenth newspaper letter from there. The details of his return are little known but he took the similar series of railway trains and boats that had earlier brought him south. He reached Wadi Halfa on the Sudan Military Railway by the 17th, Shellal near Aswan a day later and from there proceeded to Cairo by train. On the trip north he travelled with Lt Richard Molyneaux of the Royal Horse Guards, who had ridden in the charge and suffered a serious sword cut wound on his right forearm. Accompanying him on a hospital visit Churchill was drafted by the surgeon into giving a skin graft to assist in Molyneaux's recovery. As Churchill reported the episode in *My Early Life*, he was confronted by the doctor:

> He was a great raw-boned Irishman ... There was no escape, and as I rolled up my sleeve he added genially, 'Ye've heard of a man being flayed aloive? Well, this is what it feels loike.' He then proceeded to cut a piece of skin and some flesh about the size of a shilling from the inside of my forearm. My sensations as he sawed the razor to and fro fully justified his description of the ordeal ... This precious fragment was then grafted on to my friend's wound. It remains there to this day and did him lasting good in many ways. I for my part keep the scar as a souvenir.[154]

It was the only blood Churchill shed in the Sudan campaign. He recalled the episode on 22 January 1945 when he received a letter from Molyneaux, who referred to the skin-graft, writing: 'I never mention and always conceal it for fear people might think was bucking.' Churchill wrote in reply: 'Thank you so much dear Dick. I often think of those old days, and I should like to feel that you showed the bit of pelt. I have frequently shown the gap [on his right forearm] from which it was taken.'[155] From Egypt Churchill returned, not to duty in India, but to England where he arrived by the end of September. After a period of leave, he left for India 1 December 1898, and was back in Bangalore three weeks later after an absence from his regiment of six months.

As Churchill aptly put it, 'Nothing like the battle of Omdurman will ever be seen again. It was the last link in the long chain of those spectacular conflicts whose vivid and majestic splendour has done so much to invest war with glamour.'[156] It was, perhaps, the last easy victory ever won by the British army. By a combination of careful training and planning, superb transportation and logistics, and concentrated, accurate artillery, machine gun and rifle fire the Sirdar's army had defeated a force three times its number with negligible loss to itself. The Dervish army was destroyed and with it the Mahdist hold on the Sudan. With the capital captured and the

Khalifa forced out, the misery to the people caused by his oppressive rule began at last to be alleviated. With the occupation of the Sudan by the Egyptian army, the country was restored to British control and the military threat to Egypt and the Suez Canal was removed. With Kitchener's venture to Fashoda, the threat of French intrusion against British interests in the upper reaches of the Nile was thwarted. And, importantly, British national self-respect had been regained. As Churchill wrote in his tenth letter for the *Morning Post* a week after the battle:

> And now the British People may, through their Ministers and agreeably with the wishes of the Sovereign, tell some stone mason to bring his hammer and chisel and cut on the pedestal of Gordon's statue in Trafalgar Square the significant, the sinister, yet the not unsatisfactory word, 'Avenged'.[157]

Little remains of the British presence in Khartoum. The Governor's palace was rebuilt as were the Mahdi's tomb and the Khalifa's residence. A single 1898 gunboat, believed to be the *Melik,* survives on dry land in Khartoum under the auspices of the Blue Nile Sailing Club. The battlefield itself is off-limits to tourists as a military airfield was built in the vicinity. A radar station now sits atop Jebel Surgham from which one can look down toward the Khor Abu Sunt and see the Lancer's Memorial. It is a simple stone obelisk surrounded by an iron fence erected in 1899 on the field where the lancers charged and is inscribed, 'In memory of the officers, N.C.O.s and men of the 21st Lancers who fell here.'[158]

Churchill's service in the Sudan was another important stepping stone toward his sought-after career in politics. He had once again tested his courage and was not found wanting. His articles for the *Morning Post* had brought him name recognition in England among people who counted and the general public. His articles and the success of his books convinced him that he could earn a living outside the army. He was able to look ahead to standing for Parliament because once again his luck had been with him. He was quite aware of this especially after a charge at Omdurman which he called '... the most dangerous 2 minutes I shall live to see'.[159] As he wrote to Lady Randolph: 'You know my luck in these things. I was about the only officer whose clothes, saddlery, or horse were uninjured.'[160] He was in fact lucky – to get attached to the 21st Lancers upon the death of Lts Martin and Chapman, to have Lt Grenfell take his place in B Squadron, to find his way safely back to the Nile after being lost and alone in the desert, to survive the heat, the charge itself and the fatal enteric fever that cost the lives of so many colleagues.[161]

He and others who participated in the campaign never forgot their experience. The 21st Lancers and its successor regiments ever afterwards celebrated 2 September, 'Khartoum Day', as their anniversary day. Fifty years after the charge, Churchill sent the following letter:

Chartwell Westerham Kent

I send my very best wishes to my old comrades of the 21st Lancers on the 50th Anniversary of our charge on Omdurman. I wish I could be with you.

/s/ Winston S. Churchill
September 2, 1948[162]

7

The South African War:
Capetown to Pretoria

When the British Division dispersed following the battle of Omdurman, Churchill did not return directly to the 4th Hussars in India but went instead to England for several weeks of leave. Staying with Lady Randolph at Great Cumberland Place in October and November 1898, he considered his position and his future. He had known all along that he would not remain in the army but rather would seek a career in politics. His military service had already been a most rewarding adventure. In less than three years he had seen active service in Cuba, India and the Sudan. His book on the Malakand Field Force was well received and his Sudan letters for the *Morning Post* had a large readership. He found that writing for publication was profitable as well as pleasurable and that his earnings as a journalist compared quite favourably to a subaltern's pay even when supplemented by the annual allowance provided by his mother. He knew his expenditures had exceeded his income every year since Sandhurst and that his widowed mother was no longer able to support him. Considering his financial predicament he realised that his professional writing since his trip to Cuba 'had already brought in about five times as much as the Queen had paid me for three years of assiduous and sometimes dangerous work ... I therefore resolved with many regrets to quit her service betimes.'[1] He set out his goals for the coming year of 1899 as returning to India with hopes of winning the inter-regimental polo tournament, resigning from the army, becoming financially independent, finishing his next book, to be entitled *The River War*, and seeking an opportunity to stand for election to Parliament.

During his home leave Churchill was well received in Conservative Party circles in part because of his father's name but also because of his participation in the Sudan campaign and the publicity he had received from his letters to the *Morning Post*. He met and was much impressed by Lord Hugh Cecil, Lord Percy and other young Tory MPs and envied their university education, their wealth and social position and, most of all, their safe constituencies in Parliament. No doubt wanting to be more like them, he made enquiries about going to Oxford University upon his return from India. He later recorded: 'However, it appeared that this was impossible. I must pass examinations not only in Latin, but even in Greek. I could not contemplate toiling at Greek irregular verbs after having commanded British regular troops; so after much pondering I had to my keen regret to put the plan aside.'[2]

In October Churchill went to the Conservative Party Central Office in London where he was welcomed by party officials who promised to help him find a constituency and encouraged him to start giving political speeches to become better known to the party and to the public. He spoke at the Conservative Association meetings at Rotherhithe on 24 October and at Southsea on 31 October. Churchill was delighted to be speaking at political meetings and overcame his initial apprehension by careful preparation of his texts and hours of practising delivering them before he ascended the platform. He was gratified by the warm reception given by the audiences and was surprised and a bit self-conscious at the flowery introductions he received. It was a world away from the regiment, as he recalled in *My Early Life:*

> At Sandhurst and in the army compliments are few and far between, and flattery of subalterns does not exist. If you won the Victoria Cross or the Grand National Steeplechase or the Army Heavyweight Boxing Championship, you would only expect to receive from your friends warnings against having your head turned by your good luck. In politics it was apparently quite different. Here the butter was laid on with a trowel.[3]

The experience of speech-making was a positive one for Churchill, for which he proved very well suited.

Having made useful political contacts in England and made up his mind about the future, Churchill left London on Friday, 1 December 1898, to return to India for the last time. Taking the train to Italy and sailing on SS *Osiris* from Brindisi to Aden and SS *Shannon* from Aden to Bombay, Churchill was back with his regiment by 22 December. Ever the student of politics, he wrote to Lady Randolph from the ship off Aden requesting that she send him the *Annual Register*, which included parliamentary debates for 1884, 1885 and 1886.[4]

As soon as he was back in India he wrote to Captain Aylmer Haldane enquiring after his campaign medal for service on the North-West Frontier:

> I am leaving the army in April. I have come back merely for the Polo Tournaments. I naturally want to wear my medals while I have a uniform to wear them on. They have already sent me the Egyptian one. I cannot think why the Frontier one has not arrived. Do try and get mine for me as soon as possible ...

I come in either as attd to the 31st P.I. in Malakand Field Force or on Sir William's staff. The latter of course would be the best place to figure in. Will you try and get the medal sent me – there is only the general clasp – so that there should be no great difficulty.[5]

Back in Bangalore, Churchill maintained an active correspondence with his mother about politics in England and about his writing projects, including a new corrected edition of *The Story of the Malakand Field Force*, some proposed magazine articles and his work in progress in the Sudan campaign. Although he thought it would be 'absolutely judicious' and 'not a bit venomous' he wrote to Lady Randolph on 29 December 1898, 'The book grows rather in bitterness about K [Kitchener]. I feel that in spite of my intention it will be evident no friend has written it. I expect they had just about had enough of him when he went back to his Soudan. A vulgar common man – without much of the non-brutal elements in his composition.'[6] His criticisms of the Sirdar in *The River War* would come back to haunt Churchill later in South Africa when Kitchener was once again his superior officer. Already Kitchener's displeasure with Churchill was apparent as Churchill received word in January that Captain James Watson, Kitchener's aide-de-camp, had been denied permission to supply documents to Churchill for his book.[7]

With the all-India tournament fast approaching, much of Churchill's energy and that of his 4th Hussar team-mates was devoted to polo. They went to Madras for a week of practice and on to Jodhpore on 2 February for two weeks of preparation with Sir Pertab Singh, the regent of the Maharajah of Jodhpore, and a polo expert. It was at Jodhpore, that Churchill suffered 'an abominable piece of ill luck'.[8] On 8 February he fell down a flight of stairs, spraining his ankle and dislocating his right shoulder just a week before the tournament was to begin. Churchill offered to sit out in favour of a substitute but the team decided to have him play in the tourney and, with his right elbow strapped to his side to protect his shoulder, he did so with excellent results.

The inter-regimental tournament determined the polo championship of the British army in India which was the goal on which the 4th Hussars had set their sights before they even arrived there in 1896. The tournament was held in late February in Meerut, 1,400 miles from Bangalore about the same distance that Cairo is from Khartoum. The 4th Hussars handily defeated the team of the 5th Dragoon Guards in the first round by a score of sixteen to two and then won a close match over the 9th Lancers in the second round two goals to one, setting the stage for a final with the 4th Dragoon Guards which was to be played on 24 February. There was more than the usual competitiveness between the finalists because, as the regimental history states:

> At that time a coolness existed between the two regiments, caused by the flippancy of a 4th Hussar. An officer of the 4th Dragoon Guards had telegraphed to a Captain of the 4th Hussars, 'Please state your lowest terms for an exchange into the 4th Dragoon Guards.' The Hussar Captain had replied, '£10,000, a Peerage and a free kit.' The 4th Dragoon Guards had not been amused.[9]

It was a hard-fought match but the 4th Hussars team was up to the task. They came from behind to win the final, four goals to three, with Churchill scoring three of the Hussars' goals.[10] The victory was commemorated with a large, three-handled silver championship trophy that is still displayed in the officers' mess of the Queen's Royal Hussars, the successor regiment to the 4th Hussars, together with a group portrait of the team. It is inscribed as follows:

Indian Polo Association Inter-regimental Challenge Cup

1899
Won By
4th Hussars
1. Lieut. Winston S. Churchill
2. Lieut. A. Savory
3. Major R. Hoare
4. Lieut. R. W. R. Barnes

After the final match there was a festive dinner in Meerut hosted by the 5th Dragoon Guards and their commander, Lt Colonel Robert Baden-Powell, who later found fame as the hero of the siege of Mafeking in the Anglo-Boer War and as founder of the Boy Scouts movement. Baden-Powell later recalled events following the dinner at which much alcohol had been consumed:

> The health of the winning team was drunk collectively and individually with all honours, and each member of it in turn tendered his thanks to the assembled company. Then the winning team proposed the health of the losers, and they naturally returned their thanks in a similar way, and proceeded to propose the toast of the runners-up, and so it went on during the greater part of the evening

until every team in the place had had its health proposed, and speeches had been made without number, all harping on the one topic of polo.

When all was over and a sigh of relief was going round, there suddenly sprang to his feet one of the members of the 4th Hussars' team, who said: 'Now, gentlemen, you would probably like to hear me address you on the subject of polo!' It was Mr Winston Churchill. Naturally there were cries of 'No, we don't! Sit down!' and so on, but disregarding all their objections, with a genial smile he proceeded to discourse on the subject, and before long all opposition dropped as his honied words flowed upon their ears, and in a short time he was hard at it expounding the beauties and the possibilities of this wonderful game. He proceeded to show how it was not merely the finest game in the world but the most noble and soul-inspiring contest in the whole universe, and having made his point he wound up with a peroration which brought us all cheering to our feet. When the cheering and applause had died down one in authority arose and gave voice to the feelings of all when he said: 'Well, that is enough of Winston for this evening,' and the orator was taken in hand by some lusty subalterns and placed underneath an overturned sofa upon which two of the heaviest were then seated, with orders not to allow him out for the rest of the evening. But very soon afterwards he appeared emerging from beneath the angle of the arm of the sofa, explaining: 'It is no use sitting upon me, for I'm india-rubber', and he popped up serenely and took his place once more in the world and the amusement that was going on around him. I have often remembered the incident on occasions since then when in politics or elsewhere he has given proof of his statement.[11]

Winning the polo championship was one of the happiest experiences of Churchill's military years and one never to be repeated. The 4th Hussars team did not play together again. The next year Albert Savory was killed in action, and Reginald Barnes was seriously wounded in South Africa.

Because Churchill had already sent in his resignation in January, there was little for him to do upon his return to Bangalore except to wrap up his affairs, a task in which he was less than thorough. When he departed from India he left an unpaid bill at the club to the amount of thirteen rupees. His was one of seventeen such officer's bills, and by no means the largest, which were written off as 'irrecovered sums' at the club's sub-committee meeting on 1 June 1899. The meeting minutes were preserved, placed in a frame and are today prominently displayed in the bar at the Bangalore Club, the modern-day successor to the United Services Club.[12] His focus was now on his Sudan book and on politics at home. In February he had received a letter from Robert Ascroft, MP for Oldham, who invited him to stand for the second Oldham seat in the general election that he expected to be called in the autumn. Churchill was 'much flattered' by the invitation and promised to meet with party officials immediately upon his return to England.[13] He recalled his leaving India and his regiment in *My Early Life*,

'The regiment were very nice to me when eventually I departed for home, and paid me the rare compliment of drinking my health the last time I dined with them. What happy years I had with them and what staunch friends one made! It was a grand school for anyone. Discipline and comradeship were the lessons it taught; and perhaps after all these are just as valuable as the lore of the universities.'[14]

Churchill sailed from India in mid-March 1899, never again to return. On the ship crossing the Arabian Sea he made friends with George W. Steevens of the *Daily Mail,* whom he thought 'the most brilliant man in journalism I have ever met', and who offered Churchill advice on his writing.[15] Their admiration was apparently mutual and Steevens wrote a glowing article for his newspaper about the young officer. It is one of the earliest biographical sketches of Churchill and a very insightful one. In it Steevens refers to Churchill as 'the youngest man in Europe':

> In years he is a boy; in temperament he is also a boy; but in intention, in deliberate plan, purpose, adaptation of means to ends he is already a man.
>
> From his father he derives the hereditary aptitude for affairs ... From his American strain he adds to this a keenness, a shrewdness, a half-cynical, personal ambition, a natural aptitude for advertisement and, happily, a sense of humour.
>
> He is ambitious and he is calculating; yet he is not cold – and that saves him. He was born a demagogue, and he happens to know it.
>
> The master strain of his character is rhetoritician. At dinner he talks and talks, and you can hardly tell when he leaves off quoting his one idol, Macaulay, and begins his other, Winston Churchill.
>
> At present he calls himself a Tory Democrat. Tory – the opinions – might change; democrat – the methods – never. He has the twentieth century in his marrow.
>
> What he will become, who shall say? At the rate he goes there will hardly be room for him in Parliament at thirty or in England at forty.[16]

Churchill stopped in Cairo for two weeks on his way back to England staying at the Savoy Hotel across from the El Ezbekeya gardens and conducting interviews and research for *The River War*. He met with many key personalities including Lt Edouard Girouard, the Royal Engineers officer who built the Sudan military railway; Rudolf Slatin, author of *Fire and Sword in the Sudan*; and Sir Reginald Wingate, head of intelligence for the Egyptian army. Lord Cromer, the British agent, granted him three interviews and took the time to review some early chapters of Churchill's manuscript providing some useful suggestions. While in Cairo Churchill also had dinner at the mess of the 21st Lancers, an opportunity for further information-gathering and fact-checking. He departed Egypt to return to England on the P&O via Marseilles and by mid-April was back in London. He was soon a civilian again, his resignation from the army taking effect on 3 May 1899.[17] Although his years in India were viewed by Churchill at the time as a period of useless exile, his military service was in fact a valuable training period and a springboard for him as a journalist, author and politician. It was time well spent.

Back in England, Churchill busied himself with political meetings and society dinners with a view toward a general election later in the year. Then, on 19 June, Robert Ascroft, the member for Oldham who had invited Churchill to stand with him for election, died quite unexpectedly and a by-election was called. Churchill accepted the invitation of the local Conservative Party committee to stand as a candidate even though it was widely predicted that the two Oldham seats would surely be lost to the Liberal opposition. 'But in those days any political fight in any circumstances seemed to me better than no fight at all,' Churchill later recorded. 'I therefore unfurled my standard and advanced into battle.'[18] In the event, when the votes were counted on 7 July Churchill was defeated in his first election bid. As reported by the *Manchester Guardian*: 'As for Mr Churchill, he looked upon the process of counting [ballots] with amusement. A smile lighted up on his features, and the result of the election did not disturb him. He might have been defeated, but he was conscious that in his fight he had not been disgraced.'[19] Indeed, the first-time candidate had acquitted himself well on the speaking platform and at the polls. He received a number of very encouraging consolation messages from such personages as Prime Minister Lord Salisbury, Arthur Balfour, and Lord Cromer and knew he would try again.

After the election Churchill focused his energies on completing *The River War* which was eventually published in two volumes by Longmans, Green and Company in London on 6 November and in New York on 9 December 1899. Grateful for the help of others in getting to the Sudan and ever the ambitious politician, Churchill dedicated the book to Lord Salisbury and forwarded advance copies to him, to Sir Evelyn Wood, to Lord Wolseley and to Arthur Balfour with his compliments.

Having seen his book about the war in North Africa to a successful conclusion, Churchill's attention, and that of the nation, was increasingly drawn to the possibility of war breaking out in South Africa. By 18 September he had written to Lady Randolph that he thought war was certain and that he had contacted the *Morning Post* seeking employment as their correspondent should negotiations between the British representatives in Cape Colony and President Paul Kruger of the South African Republic of Transvaal fail. Churchill got the job as the *Morning Post*'s war correspondent on favourable terms, underscoring the fact that his decision to leave the army to better his financial position had been the correct one. The newspaper agreed to pay him £1,000 for four months' work and £200 per month thereafter, to pay all his expenses and for him to retain the copyright of his work so that it could be used in later books.[20]

By early October Churchill's characteristically thorough preparations for departure were coming together. He made arrangements for a letter of introduction from the Colonial Secretary, Joseph Chamberlain, to the British High Commissioner in Cape Colony, Lord Milner, and other letters from Alfred Beit, a wealthy South African businessman and close friend of Cecil Rhodes, to introduce him to various British and Boer men of influence. He had his Ross telescope and Voigtlander field glasses repaired and adjusted and purchased a new compass. He packed the Mauser pistol he had used in the Sudan and, from Randolph Payne & Sons of St James's Street, ordered thirty-six bottles of vintage wines and port, six bottles of French vermouth, eighteen bottles of ten-year-old Scotch whisky, and twelve bottles of Rose's Cordial Lime Juice to be delivered to his ship to see him through the coming campaign.[21]

On 14 October 1899, accompanied by his valet, Thomas Walden, Churchill boarded the Castle Line's RMS *Dunottar Castle* at Southampton to begin his long journey to the seat of war in South Africa. Also on board was Sir Redvers Buller, who had been awarded the VC during the Zulu War, and now was being sent to take command of the British forces there together with his staff. They were the latest in a long succession of British soldiers who had gone to campaign in southern Africa; they would be followed by almost half a million British imperial troops before the war was over.

The 6,000-mile sea voyage to Cape Town took more than two weeks during which time all on board, including General Buller, were in the dark as to what was happening in South Africa. During the trip Churchill had the opportunity to meet and converse with Buller and his officers and wrote to Lady Randolph from the ship: 'Evidently the General expects that nothing of importance will happen until he gets there. But I rather think that events will have taken the bit between their teeth ... Fourteen days is a long time in war, especially at the beginning.'[22] None the less,

Churchill was sanguine about a British victory and expected to be home by March 1900, 'after a successful campaign'.[23] His optimism was no doubt based on his own prior experiences. After the First World War, and tempered by his experiences in the South African War and on the Western Front, he would voice a more measured view of war. As he was to write in *My Early Life:*

> Let us learn our lessons. Never, never, never believe any war will be smooth and easy, or that anyone who embarks on that strange voyage can measure the tides and hurricanes he will encounter. The Statesman who yields to war fever must realise that once the signal is given, he is no longer the master of policy but the slave of unforeseeable and uncontrollable events. Antiquated War Offices, weak, incompetent or arrogant Commanders, untrustworthy allies, hostile neutrals, malignant Fortune, ugly surprises, awful miscalculations – all take their seats at the Council Board on the morrow of a declaration of war. Always remember, however sure you are that you can easily win, that there would not be a war if the other man did not think he also had a chance.[24]

Indeed, events did not await Buller's arrival and would not await the arrival of his corps of reinforcements. While the general was still at sea the Boers took the initiative and began their offensive.

The European presence in the south of Africa had begun in the seventeenth century with the arrival of Dutch settlers at Cape Town who were followed later by French Huguenot and German immigrants. Their descendants developed over time their own language, Afrikaans, and their own national identity, calling themselves 'Boers' from the Dutch word for farmers. The British presence began when the Royal Navy captured the strategic port of Cape Town from the Dutch in 1806 during the Napoleonic Wars and by 1814 the Cape was permanently ceded to the British Empire. In the early years, the Boer and British settlers fought the indigenous black Africans to establish and expand their territorial holdings on the southern tip of the continent. Over time, differences developed between the two white communities and in the 1830s the Boers began a mass migration to the north and north-east, seeking freedom from British control. There they established two independent republics, the Orange Free State and the Transvaal. Eventually, most of the Cape Boer population migrated to the new areas but a significant number remained behind, enough to cause concern of a Boer uprising in the British colonies when war began between the two white communities in 1899.

In the decades that followed, the British gradually expanded their territory and by 1843 had annexed Natal to the south-east of the Boer republics, effectively blocking the Orange Free State from the sea. In 1867 diamonds were discovered in Griqualand to the west of the Orange Free State and in 1871 it was annexed by Great Britain. In 1877, facing bankruptcy and native uprisings beyond its power to control, the Transvaal agreed to a voluntary annexation by the British Empire. This was to be, however, only temporary. It ended with a Boer declaration of independence in 1880 and a brief armed conflict between Britons and Boers, often referred to as the First Anglo-Boer War, in which Boer forces defeated British troops at Laing's Nek and again at Majuba Hill in February 1881. Thereafter the Gladstone government sought a truce and the Transvaal regained its autonomy. Nevertheless, Boer independence was challenged in the last two decades of the nineteenth century by constant British expansion of its own territory. The British established a protectorate in Bechuanaland (present-day Botswana) in 1885 and thus blocked any possible Boer expansion to the west or north-west while the activities of Cecil Rhodes's British South Africa Company in Matabeleland (a region of present-day Zimbabwe) blocked Boer expansion to the north. In 1887 Great Britain annexed Zululand (part of present-day KwaZulu Natal), the last area of contested land between Transvaal and the Indian Ocean, thus denying the Boers a seaport of their own.

In 1887 huge gold deposits were discovered at Witwatersrand near Johannesburg in the Transvaal which transformed the poor, agricultural country into a literal and figurative gold mine. The discovery of gold spurred an increased migration of foreigners, called 'uitlanders' by the Boers, of mostly British and British colonial stock into the Transvaal. There followed continual tension between Boers and uitlanders over issues of suffrage and taxation, but in fact over political and economic control of the Transvaal and its mineral wealth. The uitlanders served as surrogates for British imperial claims in the Boer republics. The war that eventually broke out in 1899 may be seen in retrospect as a civil war between the two white populations in South Africa for dominance over the other, and over the whole region with Great Britain squarely on the side of the Cape Colonists.[25]

In 1890 Cecil Rhodes, an arch-imperialist with significant ownership interests in the gold and diamond mines, became Prime Minister of the British Cape Colony giving further impetus to British imperial designs. In December 1895, he covertly sponsored the Jameson Raid, a small-scale invasion of the Transvaal by a mercenary force in an amateurish and failed attempt to spark an uitlander uprising in Johannesburg. The hope was that such an uprising would invoke an intervention by London to separate the warring factions and facilitate a British-controlled federation of the Boer republics with Cape Colony and Natal. The raid was a prompt and complete failure and served mainly to feed Boer fears of British perfidy. After the Jameson Raid the Transvaal and the Orange Free State formed an alliance and began to arm themselves in earnest against future British incursions procuring the finest arms and ammunition in large quantities from German and French manufacturers. Although Rhodes's role in the raid was exposed and he was removed from political office, a new British High Commissioner in Cape Town, Sir Alfred Milner, arrived in 1897 and pursued the goal of a British-Boer Federation dominated by Great Britain. The competing interests of the Boers and the British-backed uitlanders led to a crisis by mid-1899 and preparations for war began even as negotiations continued. The Cabinet in London decided to reinforce the British garrisons in South Africa with troops from India and to dispatch an army corps under General Sir Redvers Buller from England which was expected to arrive in November or December. The British government viewed this as a purely defensive precaution; the Boers saw it as a threat to their very independence. Meanwhile, the Boer leaders made contingency plans to invade the British colonies with the goal of seizing the ports of Cape Town in Cape Colony and Durban in Natal to prevent British rein-forcements from landing. The negotiations ended with a Boer ultimatum on 9 October 1899 that Great Britain withdraw all of its military forces from the borders of Transvaal, remove all the troop reinforcements the British had brought in the previous summer and to agree not to land the army corps being assembled in England. The ultimatum was rejected out of hand and on 11 October the two Boer republics found themselves at war with the mighty British Empire.[26] The Boers viewed the coming conflict as their second war for independence. For the British, it was the latest in a series of imperial wars not unlike those fought earlier in India, Burma, Zululand, Egypt and the Sudan. It was their first major conflict against a 'European' enemy since the Crimean War but the British under-estimated the Boers' military capabilities.

In Churchill's view, the issue was nothing less than Britain's predomi-nance in South Africa and in the world. In a letter to Bourke Cockran he wrote: 'But as you probably know, our existence as an Imperial power is staked on the issue and I do not believe that the nation will shrink from any sacrifice however great, however prolonged, to remove the causes of unrest in South Africa.'[27] Historians usually refer to the conflict as the second

Anglo-Boer War or, simply, as the Boer War. It was not only Britain's longest colonial war but also the costliest both in terms of men and of money. Unlike the other tribes the British had done battle with, the Boers were equally well-armed, were highly mobile, and employed effective tactics refusing, unlike the Dervishes, to attempt a frontal assault in broad daylight preferring instead the use of cover and the indirect approach.

The theatre of war included both semi-autonomous British colonies, Natal and Cape Colony, and the two Boer republics, Transvaal and Orange Free State, an area of approximately 455,000 square miles. Much of the action took place on the high veldt of the Boer republics, a vast plateau extending over national boundaries. The veldt was intersected by a series of non-navigable rivers and streams that presented a series of obstacles rather than routes of advance for the British. The whole area of operations was knitted together by a series of railway lines that were of great strategic value for the movement of men and the material of war. The terrain often favoured the Boer defenders. As the American war correspondent Richard Harding Davis described it:

> No map, nor photograph, nor written description can give an idea of the country which lay between Buller and his goal. It is an eruption of high hills, linked together at every point without order or sequence ... They stand alone or shoulder to shoulder, or at right angles, or at a tangent, or join hands across a valley. They never appear the same; some run to a sharp point, some stretch out forming a table-land, others are gigantic ant hills, others perfect and accurately modelled ramparts. In a ride of half a mile, every hill completely loses its original aspect and character. They hide each other, or disguise each other. Each can be enfiladed by the other, and not one gives the secret of its strategic value until its crest has been carried by the bayonet.[28]

It was terrain where infantry, artillery and supplies laboured to move and horsemen had every advantage. As in the hill country of the North-West Frontier of India, the vast might of the Royal Navy was of no consequence except to bring troops, horses and munitions from overseas.

The Boer forces were comprised of citizen soldiers, as all males between the ages of sixteen and sixty were subject to military service. They were organised into commandos of 300 to 3,000 men based on the electoral sub-divisions or districts of the two Boer republics. Unlike conventional armies, they wore no common uniform and elected their officers. Although they were amateur soldiers, they were excellent horsemen and marksmen, among the best mounted infantry in the world. The only permanent, professional Boer contingents were the state police and the artillery. The state police (or so-called Zarps) numbered about 1,500. The artillery totaled some 1,200 and were often commanded by foreign military officers and equipped with modern Krupp and Creusot cannon and 37mm Maxim-Vickers guns, the famous 'pom-poms'. Estimates of the Boer forces in October 1899 vary from 38,000 to 48,000.[29] At the outset of the war, British forces in South Africa numbered 27,000 including approximately 8,500 raised in Cape Colony and Natal. Buller's corps of reinforcements was expected to number 42,000 but was not scheduled to arrive until December 1899. Only at the very beginning of the war did the Boer forces outnumber those of the Empire. The Boers had a very limited window of opportunity in which to act decisively.

For purposes of overview, the South African War may be divided into four phases: the Boer offensive in October and November 1899; the first British offensive in December 1899; the second British offensive from February to September 1900; and an overlapping period of Boer guerrilla warfare from March 1900 to May 1902.[30] Although Churchill arrived in South Africa at the end of October 1899, his participation in military operations was focused on the third phase in what was mostly conventional warfare. The first phase began while Churchill was still at sea between Southampton and Cape Town and his participation in it would be brief.

The Boer offensive into Cape Colony and Natal began on 12 October 1899, the day after war was declared and two days before Churchill sailed. By the time Buller arrived, much had already happened. Between 14 and 16 October, Boer forces entered the northern part of Cape Colony where the towns of Mafeking and Kimberley, both on the Western Railway Line, were cut off and surrounded. At Mafeking, 1,200 British troops under the command of Colonel Robert Baden-Powell were besieged by a force of 6,000 Boers. At Kimberley, 4,800 British troops were trapped by 7,500 Boers and taken out of action. Other Boer columns, 14,000 strong, entered northern Natal through Laing's Nek along the route of the Natal Railway Line and headed toward Ladysmith, an important railroad junction town and British supply depot, 110 miles to the south. At Talana Hill near Dundee in northern Natal the British defeated a Boer force on 20 October but suffered almost 500 casualties including their commander, Major General W. Penn Symons, who was killed. On 21 October at Elandslaagte to the north-east of Ladysmith, the British again stopped an advancing Boer column in a sharp battle during which Churchill's friends, Lt Reginald Barnes and Captain Aylmer Haldane, were both wounded, Barnes seriously.

Despite these local successes, the British forces did not have the numbers or the leadership to advance into the Transvaal or to expel the Boers from Natal. By 30 October the Boer columns from the two republics had met, and with a combined force of more than 23,000 moved on Ladysmith into which the British commander, General George White, had withdrawn the British forces from Dundee and Elandslaagte. White planned a three-pronged attack on the Boer force to the north and east of Ladysmith. The battles at Lombard's Kop, Nicholson's Nek and Long Hill on 30 October failed to dislodge or defeat the Boers and, having lost 1,000 men captured and many killed and wounded, the remaining British forces, numbering about 13,500, withdrew into Ladysmith where they were duly surrounded and besieged. Thus, by the end of October, although the British had successfully and for the moment blunted the Boer invasion of Natal, they had over half their forces bottled up in Mafeking, Kimberley and Ladysmith incapable of anything but local defensive operations.

The Boers, while achieving tactical successes against the British, had tied up perhaps half of their own men in the sieges and left themselves with insufficient mobile forces to pursue their larger strategic aim of winning the war, or at least a favourable truce, before British reinforcements could arrive. In a sense the final outcome of the war was decided in this first month of fighting because the Boers really had no reserves while the British could and would reinforce their initial garrisons twenty times over and resupply them by sea without interference from the Boers who were land-locked and without allies. Such was the situation at the time of Churchill's arrival on the scene. The few thousand British troops not surrounded and besieged were spread thinly in a wide defensive arc trying to anticipate the next moves of a highly mobile Boer force twice their number who were threatening to advance on Durban. Another complication was the worry that further Boer successes might lead to an uprising of the considerable Boer population in Cape Colony which could pose a serious threat to British control of Cape Town. It appeared the outcome of the war could go either way and that much tough fighting lay ahead.

The *Dunottar Castle* dropped anchor off Cape Town at 10.00 p.m. on Tuesday, 30 October 1899, marking the beginning of Churchill's participation in his fourth war in as many years. He faced the conflict with his usual optimism, excitement and good humour. On ship he had declined an inoculation against enteric fever, remarking in his first letter to the *Morning Post*: 'But if they will invent a system of inoculation against bullet wounds I will hasten to submit myself.'[31] Rather than dwell on the dangers

inherent in being a war correspondent, in a conflict that Churchill estimated would be 'a fierce and bloody struggle ... in which at least ten or
twelve thousand lives will be sacrificed', he wrote in a letter to his mother
soon after arrival what was now for him a core belief: 'I shall believe I am
to be preserved for future things.'[32]

During the voyage from England Churchill made friends with J. B.
Atkins, the correspondent for the *Manchester Guardian* who, like
Churchill, would write a book about the war.[33] They spent a good deal of
time talking together on the voyage and in South Africa. Of their encoun-
ters on the ship Atkins later recorded his impressions of young Churchill:

> I had not been many hours on board before I became aware of a most unusual
> young man. He was slim, slightly reddish-haired, pale, lively, frequently
> plunging along the deck 'with neck out-thrust', as Browning fancied Napoleon;
> sometimes sitting in meditation, folding and unfolding his hands, not nervously
> but as though he were helping himself to untie mental knots.
>
> He coveted a political career above all. It was obvious that he was in love
> with words. He would hesitate sometimes before he chose one or would change
> one for a better ...
>
> But when the prospects of a career like that of his father, Lord Randolph,
> excited him, then such a gleam shot from him that he was almost transfigured.
> I had not before encountered this sort of ambition, unabashed, frankly egotis-
> tical, communicating its excitement, and extorting sympathy.
>
> He stood alone and confident, and his natural power to be himself had
> yielded to no man.[34]

Churchill exuded a remarkable self-confidence about his own ability
and his future and talked not only about politics and writing but also about
military subjects which he believed he could master. As Atkins recalled,
'Winston also liked to talk of strategy and tactics. His belief was that both
were "just a matter of common sense. Put all the elements of a problem
before a civilian of first-rate ability and enough imagination," he said, "and
he would reach the right solution, and any soldier could afterwards put his
solution into military terms."'[35] There was a heartfelt reason for
Churchill's ambition to act boldly to make a name for himself and for his
impatience about getting into politics at a young age. As he confided to
Atkins: 'The worse of it is that I am not a good life. My father died too
young. I must try to accomplish whatever I can by the time I am forty.'[36]
This revelation does much to explain Churchill's unabashed ambition and
his reputation for being pushy and egotistical.

Going ashore on the morning of 31 October, Churchill visited the
Mount Nelson Hotel and set out to learn all he could about the war situ-

ation, meeting the army officers at the hotel as well as Milner, and also reading all the newspapers he could get his hands on.[37] With Atkins he formed a plan to steal a march on the other correspondents on the ship and to be first to reach the scene of the fighting in Natal. They determined that they could gain four days on the *Dunottar Castle* by taking a train to the port of East London and then a steamship to Durban where they could take another train north toward Ladysmith. They left Cape Town on the evening of 31 October and travelled the 700 miles to East London via DeAar Junction and Stormberg near the Orange Free State border on the last train to get through before the line was cut by the Boers. The sea journey on the little steamer *Umzimbuva* left Churchill prostrate with seasickness but brought them safely to Durban at midnight on 4 November. At Durban Churchill visited his old friend Lt Reginald Barnes on the hospital ship *Sumatra*. Barnes had been shot in the right thigh and would be a long time recovering. He impressed upon Churchill that the Boers were a formidable adversary, 'skilful ... with horse and rifle', and predicted a drawn-out conflict.[38]

The morning after their arrival in Durban Atkins and Churchill took an overnight train to Pietermaritzburg and another train next day took them the further seventy-six miles to Estcourt, the railway town that was then the most forward position of the British army in Natal still in touch with the coast. It was very thinly garrisoned with a battalion of Royal Dublin Fusiliers, a battalion from the Border Regiment, one squadron of Imperial Light Horse, 300 volunteers from the Natal Carbineers and the Durban Light Infantry, two or three nine-pounder artillery pieces and an armoured train – about 2,000 men all told.[39] The balance of the British forces in Natal were already besieged forty miles to the north in Ladysmith by the time Churchill arrived. At Estcourt he found two acquaintances, Leo Amery, an old Harrovian then serving as *The Times* correspondent and Captain Aylmer Haldane of the Gordon Highlanders who had been so helpful to Churchill in Tirah two years earlier. Haldane had been wounded in the foot at Elandslaagte and was then in temporary command of a company of the Royal Dublin Fusiliers. Also present at Estcourt was Bennet Burleigh of the *Daily Telegraph* who, like Churchill, had been at Omdurman.[40]

Estcourt was in a precarious position with no other British garrison between it and Durban; and until Buller's force arrived there would be no reinforcements to hold the line much less to take the counter-offensive. Each day cavalry patrols were sent out ten or fifteen miles to ascertain the location and movements of the enemy. On 9 November Churchill rode out with one hundred men from the Natal Carbineers and Natal Mounted Police toward Colenso on a reconnaissance, and they were able to hear the artillery firing in the distance around Ladysmith. Most days the armoured train, locally nicknamed 'Wilson's death trap', was sent out to reconnoitre on the only line it could take, the Natal Railway track toward Ladysmith. Churchill rode on the train on 8 November to within a half mile of Colenso. With the troops he entered the town on foot to find it empty and both the railway line and the telegraph wires cut. He described the train as 'a locomotive disguised as a knight errant' and 'a very puny specimen' with little armament.[41] None the less, the train made its trip without incident and returned safely to Estcourt by dusk.

The armoured train was a poor choice of vehicle for the task of reconnaissance as it was noisy, could only follow the path of the tracks and marked its entirely predictable progress with a towering plume of black smoke from the locomotive. As Churchill later wrote: 'Nothing looks more formidable and impressive than an armoured train; but nothing is in fact more vulnerable and helpless. It is only necessary to blow up a bridge or culvert to leave the monster stranded far from home and help, at the mercy of the enemy.'[42] Even so, when Haldane invited Churchill to accompany him on a second trip in the train, according to Churchill: 'Out of comradeship, and because I thought it was my duty to gather as much information as I could for the *Morning Post*, also because I was eager for trouble, I accepted the invitation without demur.'[43] It was a fateful decision.

On the morning of 15 November, 1899, Churchill arose before dawn and invited his tent-mate, Atkins, to join him on the armoured train but he declined. Atkins had ventured out on the train previously and judged it not only a waste of time, but likely to place him in danger of being captured and thus unable to report on the war for his newspaper. He told Churchill: 'He would either see too little or too much.'[44] According to Atkins, Churchill replied: 'That is perfectly true. I can see no fault in your reasoning. But I have a feeling, a sort of intuition, that if I go something will come of it. It's illogical, I know.'[45] So Churchill went to join Haldane and pursue his fate while Atkins and Burleigh remained abed in Estcourt.

On the morning of the 15th mounted patrols were sent west and northwest of the town but these were not co-ordinated with the armoured train which would depart without flank security or advance scouts, as would have been prudent. The train was made up of an engine and tender with five trucks. In the front was an ordinary flat truck on which was mounted a nine-pounder gun. Next came an armoured truck with sheet metal armour on its sides and loopholes cut into it to allow the occupants to return fire without exposing themselves to harm. The armour was sufficient to stop rifle bullets but not artillery rounds. Behind these were the locomotive and its tender operated by the driver, Charles Wagner, and the fireman, Alexander James Stewart. Next were two additional armoured trucks, and last in line was another ordinary flat truck carrying extra rails and equipment for repairs to the line.[46]

On the train were four sailors and Lt Alexander from HMS *Tartar* to man the gun on the forward open truck. Haldane, Churchill and three sections of the Royal Dublin Fusiliers rode in the first armoured truck in front of the engine, and one section of Fusiliers, a company of the Durban Light Infantry and a small civilian breakdown gang occupied the two armoured trucks behind the engine. In addition, the train carried a telegraphist, R. T. McArthur, whose task it was to send back reports from stations along the line. Accounts of exactly how many men were on the armoured train are varied. Churchill wrote in his *Morning Post* letter that there were 120 men; Haldane's official report does not give a total number but lists only that there were two companies of infantry plus the sailors and civilians. Bennet Burleigh, who turned up later that day, reported 131 in total: Churchill, the telegraphist, seventy-two non-commissioned officers and men of the Royal Dublin Fusiliers under Haldane and Frankland, forty-five non-commissioned officers and men of the Durban Light Infantry under the command of Captain James S. Wylie, and nine railwaymen comprising the driver, fireman and seven plate-layers.[47]

It was chilly and a drizzling rain was falling when the train pulled out of Estcourt at between 5.10 and 5.30 a.m. and a mist hung over the countryside, limiting visibility. The train proceeded north to Frere where it arrived at 6.20 a.m. and then on to Chieveley, a station about sixteen miles from Estcourt, arriving at 7.10 a.m. This proved to be a station too far as there were Boer columns in the area of the town and, as it proved, between Chieveley and Frere, making it impossible for the train to return south without interference. It was not known to Haldane until he arrived at Chieveley that the Boers had been in the town the previous night. In his 1948 memoir, Haldane admitted it was bad judgment on his part to have gone so far north, declaring:

> I do not wish to lay blame on anyone but myself, but had I been alone and not had my impetuous young friend Churchill with me, who in many things was prompted by Danton's motto, de l'audace, et encore de l'audace et toujours de l'audace, I might have thought twice before throwing myself into the lion's jaws

by going almost to the Tugela. But I was carried away by his ardour and departed from an attitude of prudence, which in the circumstances was desirable considering that we were confronting a force which was in process of invading British territory. I therefore telegraphed to Colonel Long what I had just seen and intimated that the train was about to return to Frere.[48]

Haldane stated nothing like this in his contemporary report. In any event, the responsibility for the decision was his. Churchill wrote at the time it was Haldane's decision to go as far as Chieveley and this would not necessarily be seen as unduly risky as the armoured train had ventured even farther north during the previous week, to within a half mile of Colenso, unhindered. In any event, the train waited only a few minutes in Chieveley before heading south. About a mile and three-quarters north of Frere, Boers were seen on a hilltop ahead and about 600 yards away. The train soon came under shellfire and picked up its speed to forty miles per hour to hasten to safety. It had just come around a curve in the line and passed over a stone bridge above a small stream when it suddenly hit an obstacle placed on the line, with a terrific crash. The train was partly derailed and brought to a sudden stop about a half-mile from Frere. At the moment of impact it had been backing up, so the order of the trucks was the reverse of that on the journey out. The first vehicle to hit the obstruction was the flat truck with building materials which flipped completely end over end and landed clear of the tracks. The two following trucks full of soldiers were knocked off the tracks, the first coming to rest on its side, the other remaining upright but derailed, and blocking the line between the engine and Frere, the only path of escape. As Arthur Conan Doyle described the situation in his history of the war: 'A railway accident is a nervous thing, and so is an ambuscade, but the combination of the two must be appalling. Yet their were brave hearts which rose to the occasion.'[49]

Many men were wounded and a few killed in the derailment and the train soon came under intense fire from Boer rifles, three Creusot cannon and a rapid-firing Maxim gun. Haldane and Churchill were in the armoured truck now behind the engine and were knocked down by the train's sudden halt. As Haldane later recorded, Churchill responded quickly to the crisis:

For a few seconds I was so dazed by the suddenness of the crash that the power of collecting my thoughts to decide what had best be done deserted me, but Churchill, quick witted and cool, was speedily on his feet. He volunteered to see what the situation was, and soon he returned with the suggestion that if I could keep in check the fire from the Boer guns and rifles, which had opened from the surrounding hills, he thought he might manage to get the line cleared. As my association with him had only been military, I naturally regarded him from that point of view. I knew him well enough to realise that he was not the man to stand quietly by and look on in a critical situation, and it flashed across my mind that he could not be better employed than in a semi-military sense such as he suggested ... I therefore gladly accepted Churchill's offer and directed him to undertake what he proposed. His self-selected task, into which he threw all his energy, was carried out with pluck and perseverance, and his example inspired the platelayers, the driver of the locomotive, and others to work under the fire which the Boers were directing on the train.[50]

Churchill ran to the front of the train to find the light infantrymen seeking shelter from the heavy incoming fire behind the derailed trucks. It was his first experience of being on the receiving end of shrapnel shellfire. The Cuban rebels, the Pathans in India and the Dervishes in the Sudan had all lacked artillery. A shell burst right above the engine as Churchill passed by and a piece of shrapnel hit the engine driver in the face, forcing him to jump out and get behind the trucks. Realising that Wagner's help was essential, Churchill went to him to bolster his courage. He told the driver that no man in battle was ever hit twice in one day and that if he stayed at his post he would get a medal for distinguished gallantry in action. To his credit, Wagner got back in the engine and thereafter followed Churchill's directions. Surveying the scene, Churchill found the line itself was intact and that the engine, the tender and two trucks were still on the rails. He concluded that if the two derailed trucks could be moved off the tracks, the rest of the train could escape and the troops with it. He ran back to Haldane, got approval for his plan and returned to the engine to get the job done. In the end he was only partly successful.

For the next hour and more, Churchill directed the train driver and volunteers from the Durban Light Infantry in uncoupling the first armoured truck which was completely off the rails and on its side, from the second which was upright but half on and half off the rails. With tremendous effort the second truck was pushed and pulled off the tracks, only to fall back toward them so that a few inches of its bulk blocked forward progress of the train. At great risk Churchill directed the driver to back up the train and then steam forward at full-tilt to batter past the obstructing truck. Just before the engine hit the derailed truck a shell-burst severed the coupling which attached the trailing armoured truck and the gun truck from the engine so that they were left fifty yards to the rear of the engine and tender which alone got past the derailed truck which still blocked the line. Strenuous efforts to push the two trucks up to the engine failed.

All this time Churchill was in the open and exposed to enemy fire as he directed the work of the railway men and troops to free the train, encouraging and humouring them with such remarks as, 'Keep cool, men,' and 'This will be interesting for my paper.'[51] The fire from the Boers' Creusot fifteen-pounder guns, their Maxim gun and rifles was continuous. Haldane estimated that ninety rounds of shrapnel shell were fired during the fight, more than one per minute. There were many casualties including Captain Wiley, who received a bullet wound in the thigh, but Churchill was not hit. As he later recalled:

> The heat and excitement of the work were such as to absorb me completely. I remember thinking that it was like working in front of an iron target at a rifle range at which men were continually firing. We struggled for seventy minutes among these clanging, rending iron boxes amid the repeated explosion of shells and the ceaseless hammering of the bullets.[52]

Finally, realising that only the engine and the tender could escape, Haldane directed Churchill to load the wounded on them and ordered the troops to withdraw on foot toward Frere, using the train as a shield as there was no other cover. The remaining armoured truck and flat truck from which the naval gun had been dismounted by enemy shellfire were left behind. Churchill was on the engine directing the driver while Haldane was on the ground. With the engine on a downgrade approaching the Blau Krantz river bridge close to Frere, it gathered speed and soon left the foot soldiers behind by some 300 yards. Churchill told Wagner to proceed with the wounded and then himself dismounted to go back to find Haldane and assist in the withdrawal of the troops.[53] As Atkins, who interviewed eyewitnesses, later reported, Churchill 'said he was going back to the scene to assist the wounded and stand by the men. The last seen of him was as he trudged alone away down into the area of battle, where the shot and shell were still screaming, splintering rock and ploughing the ground. A few of the luckier fugitives passed him on the way, but failed to turn him back from his purpose.'[54]

Churchill had gone about 200 yards back down the line when he was confronted by two Boers some 100 yards to his front, aiming their rifles in his direction. As he turned and began to run after the engine, both Boers fired, one bullet passing close on Churchill's right, the other to his left. He moved to the side of the cutting but its banks provided no cover and he started to scramble up to escape. Again the Boers fired and their bullets narrowly missed him. As he reached the top of the embankment and sought cover in a shallow depression, 'The earth sprang up beside me, and something touched my hand ...'[55] He had been hit by a bullet splinter – it was a minor wound, the only one Churchill would ever receive in combat. As he quickly looked around catching his breath, a Boer horseman galloped up, rifle in hand, stopped forty yards away and yelled at him to stop and surrender. Churchill instinctively reached for his Mauser pistol, only to realise he had left it on the engine while trying to clear the train wreckage from the line. He was now quite unarmed and in the sights of the Boer horseman who was levelling his rifle at him. He had, in fact, no choice but to surrender. As he later wrote: 'Death stood before me, grim sullen Death without his light-hearted companion, Chance. So I held up my hand, and like Mr Jorrocks's foxes, cried "Capivy".'[56] Churchill's Mauser had come to the rescue the previous year at Omdurman when he had shot a path through the Dervishes as he made his way out of the *khor* near Jebel Surgham. Now it saved his life again by being left behind. Had he drawn the pistol at the rail cutting he would almost certainly have been shot down where he stood.

By the time Churchill surrendered, Haldane, Lt Frankland and most of the other troops had been taken prisoner. Haldane was furious because the surrender of his remaining men was the result of the unauthorised raising of white handkerchiefs by two troopers in disobedience to his orders. In any event, the deed was done and by 8.50 a.m. the action was over – a total rout of the British soldiers by the better-armed Boers who far outnumbered them. As the prisoners were collected, rain began to pour down, adding to the prisoners' gloom and discomfort.

British casualties were heavy, as Haldane's official report stated. Four men were killed at the site of the ambush and two others later died of their wounds. Thirteen wounded British soldiers were in Boer hospitals and sixteen in British hospitals. Fifty-three, including Churchill, Haldane and Lt Thomas Frankland were taken prisoner – seven of them being slightly wounded. The Boers, by contrast, had two killed, four wounded and none taken prisoner. If Churchill's number of 120 men on the train is correct, that would leave only twenty-six who got away including those who escaped on the engine and tender. This would be a casualty rate of thirty-five per cent and an even higher seventy-eight per cent if those taken prisoner were counted as battle casualties. On 17 June 1900, after both had escaped from the prisoner-of-war camp, Churchill wrote to Haldane:

I find the casualties in the train episode were much heavier than was expected: 21 wounded escaped on the engine: 23 fell into the hands of the Boers of whom 18 were sent into Ladysmith & 5 to Pretoria total 44. 5 D.F. [Dublin Fusiliers] & 3 D.L.I. [Durban Light Infantry] & 2 platelayers were killed 7 slightly wounded, grand total 61 out of 130. No one can dispute such figures.[57]

Churchill gave no source for his later figures but, if correct, the casualty rate for the action would be forty-seven per cent including killed, wounded and prisoners. Churchill at the time considered it a complete disaster and blamed himself for going on the train in the first place and then for returning when his escape on the engine was assured.

Churchill's bravery in the armoured train fight did not go unnoticed. Back in Estcourt Captain Wylie spoke to the *Natal Witness* which reported him as describing 'Mr Winston Churchill's conduct in the most enthusiastic terms as that of as brave a man as could be found'.[58] A 16 November 1899 letter from Inspector Campbell of the Natal Government Railways to the general manager of railways, sent on behalf of the railway workers who witnessed the action, stated: 'The railway men ... ask me to convey to you their admiration of the coolness and pluck displayed by Mr Winston Churchill ... who accompanied the train and to whose efforts, backed up by driver Wagner, is due the fact that the armoured engine and tender were brought successfully out ... and was able to bring the wounded in here. The whole of our men are loud in their praises of Mr. Churchill...'[59] In a letter to Lady Randolph dated 18 December 1899, a Miss Lizzie B. Wells quoted a letter she had received from her brother, a private in the Durban Light Infantry who had taken part in the armoured train ambush and who, incidentally, was wounded twice in the same day:

> Churchill is a splendid fellow. He walked about in it all as if nothing was going on, & called for volunteers to give him a hand to get the truck out of the road. His presence and way of going on were as much good as 50 men would have been. After the engine got clear he came about a ½ mile on it and then coolly got off & walked back to help the others.[60]

The armoured train fight and Churchill's part in it were headline news in South Africa and in England. *Black & White* magazine reported in its 23 December 1899 issue, 'It is rumoured that both Mr Churchill and the engine driver will be recommended for the Victoria Cross which they appear to richly deserve.'[61] Captain Haldane's report of the action was written in Pretoria on 30 November and forwarded to the chief of staff of the Natal Field Force. His dispatch referred to Churchill's 'indomitable perseverance' and 'valuable services' and noted: 'Owing to the urgency of the circumstances, I formally placed him on duty.' In further acknowledgement of Churchill's role, he stated: 'I would point out that while engaged in the work of saving the engine, for which he was mainly responsible, he was frequently exposed to the full fire of the enemy. I cannot speak too highly of his gallant conduct.'[62] This was strong praise indeed and by all accounts well deserved. Still, Churchill never received a decoration or other official recognition for his actions in the armoured train incident and the question naturally arises why this was so. First, it must be recognised that the clash never would have occurred if ordinary caution had been exercised by the commander at Estcourt, and that it was in the end a disastrous and utter defeat. Decorations are more often given for successful battles than for defeats. Eleven Victoria Crosses were given for the heroic defence of Rorke's Drift by some hundred British troops in the Zulu War in January 1879. That same day a British and native encampment had been massacred at Isandlwana with 1,300 killed by the Zulu *impis* in a fierce battle with only three Victoria Crosses awarded, two posthumously for trying to save the colours. Second, Churchill's non-military status at the time must be considered. The only decorations available to officers for heroism under fire in 1899 were the Victoria Cross and the Distinguished Service Order, and these were considered to be reserved for serving officers. The Victoria Cross has only been awarded to civilians five times: to three members of the Bengal Civil Service and to one merchant marine officer under a royal warrant of 1858 making eligible certain 'non-military persons' who volunteered for service during the Indian Mutiny and also to a Protestant chaplain serving with Bengal Ecclesiastical Department and attached to the field army during the Second Afghan War in 1879 under a special clarifying royal warrant issued in 1881.[63] The Distinguished Service Order was created in 1886 and restricted to commissioned military officers.

Despite Haldane's statement that he had placed Churchill on duty, Churchill held no commission at the time even though he had previously taken steps to obtain one. Before he left England for Africa he had drafted a letter to Lord Chesham, the honorary colonel of the Royal Bucks Hussars, requesting that he forward Churchill's application for a commission to the Adjutant General of the army stating, 'It is of some importance to me to have the status of any officer before the war begins.'[64] The letter was never sent, perhaps because Churchill thought he could find a better appointment when he was on the scene in South Africa. On 31 October 1899 he telegraphed Lady Randolph Churchill to forward his application for a yeomanry commission to the Lancashire Hussars.[65] In a letter to Sir Evelyn Wood from Estcourt on 10 November Churchill remarked: 'I hope that I am now a Lancashire Hussar.'[66] In any event, the application was not acted upon, perhaps because Churchill was known to be in a prisoner-of-war camp and unable to serve. He would not obtain a commission until January 1900. How painful to Churchill it must have been to have done what he did without a commission in hand. His reason for wanting one in the first place was undoubtedly to make him eligible for a campaign medal and a possible decoration. It is ironic that by the time he had done the acts worthy of an official reward he was in no position to argue the point as he was vigorously negotiating with his captors to be released on the grounds that he was a non-combatant at the time of the ambush.

Might Churchill have received some recognition even as a civilian? His actions under fire saved many lives – those of all the men who escaped on the engine and tender – when many a Victoria Cross has been awarded for rescuing a single man under fire. Indisputably there had been 'a gallery' for Churchill's actions with both Captain Haldane and Captain Wylie recognising his bravery. In fact, there was a suitable civilian award available, the Albert Medal, which had been created in two classes in 1866 for gallantry in saving life at the risk of one's own. The award could be given to soldiers, sailors or civilians and was indeed the highest gallantry award for civilians.[67] But no Albert Medal recommendations were forthcoming. It was not until May 1910 that Churchill himself, then Home Secretary, submitted driver Charles Wagner for the Albert Medal, First Class and fireman Alexander James Stewart for the Albert Medal, Second Class. His recommendation to King George V stated in part:

> The danger was exceptional. The heavy fire of shells & bullets inflicted many casualties, & more than ¼ of all in the train were killed or wounded. The shells repeatedly struck the engine & at any moment might have exploded the boiler. The driver a civilian, under no military code, was wounded severely in the scalp by a shell-splinter almost immediately. Although in great pain he did not fail during the whole of this affair to manage his engine skilfully, & by clearing the line saved from death & wounds a proportion at least of the 50 or 60 persons who effected their escape upon the engine & its tender.[68]

Churchill's recommendation was approved and the awards to the trainmen were announced in the *London Gazette* on 14 June 1910.[69] The recommendation Churchill made for Stewart and Wagner could easily have served as the basis of his own Albert Medal but Churchill had no patron to advance his cause. Captains Wylie and Haldane were junior officers and, relatively speaking, without influence. Moreover, Wylie was preoccupied after the action recovering from wounds, and Haldane was to remain a prisoner in Pretoria far from the centres of military influence until his escape in March 1900.

Finally, it must be noted that by the time Churchill had made his escape from the Boers in December 1899 and obtained a commission the following month, the Chief-of-Staff for the British army in South Africa was none other than Major General Lord Kitchener, his old nemesis from the Sudan, with his known antipathy for journalists generally and stated dislike for Churchill in particular. For this variety of reasons it appears no recommendation was made for an award for Churchill's actions on 15 November.

Two years later, after his return from the war and following his election to Parliament, Churchill wrote a private letter to Joseph Chamberlain 'on a small personal matter'. In it he made reference to the testimonials to his conduct in the armoured train fight from the Durban Light Infantrymen and Natal Railway crew which had been sent to the Colonial Office and also to Haldane's report. He stated:

> It has occurred to me that if the papers sent by the Natal people to the Colonial Office were forwarded to the War Office, they would look vy imposing taken in conjunction with this Haldane's dispatch, and I might get some sort of military mention or decoration. As it is I suspect the authorities think the whole thing purely a piece of journalistic humbug: which it is not. Of course in common with all the other members of Parliament I care nothing for the glittering baubles of honour for my own sake: but I have like others – as you know – to 'think of my constituents' – and perhaps I ought also to consider the feelings of my possible wife.[70]

This remarkable bit of lobbying apparently met with no success; whether it failed with Chamberlain or the War Office is unknown.

The scene of the armoured train incident is remarkably intact today, more than a century later. The old railway line is no longer in place; the metals and sleepers were moved a few dozen yards to the east and straightened slightly to accommodate the faster electric trains of the present day. But the dry stream-bed and stone bridge abutment remain and the area of the old rails is still open, its rocky soil marked with tyre tracks. The ground is largely free of vegetation and cover and the hills where the Boers sited their guns (in perfect range for a gunner) 750 yards to the north are clearly seen. To the west of the present line is a memorial tablet of stone surrounded by white gravel inside a silver-painted iron fence enclosure which reads:

> THIS MARKS THE PLACE
> WHERE THE ARMOURED TRAIN
> WAS WRECKED
> AND
> THE RT. HON. WINSTON CHURCHILL
> CAPTURED BY BOER FORCES
> NOV. 15TH, 1899

It was placed there by the South Africa Monuments Council. To the east on the other side of the tracks is a more poignant memorial, the graves of four British soldiers killed in the ambush who still lie there. One grave is made of whitewashed cement and local stones with a simple headstone bearing a royal crown and the following inscription:

> V.R.
> 1899
> HERE LIES A BRAVE BRITISH SOLDIER
> 'KNOWN UNTO GOD.'

Next to it is a second grave, also of white cement, which is a bit more elaborate than the first. The headstone reads:

> HERE
> LIE
> THE REMAINS
> OF THOSE KILLED
> IN THE
> ARMOURED TRAIN
> ON NOV. 15TH 1899.

The grave is covered by a cement slab featuring a white Christian cross and the following words formed by spent cartridge cases pushed into the mortar:

> ERECTED
> BY THE
> GORDON REGT.
> IN
> MEMORY
> OF OUR
> COMRADES
> WHO FELL
> ON
> NOV.

The numerals are missing, lost to time and souvenir hunters. At the base of the grave is a third tablet with an additional cross on which is inscribed:

TO THE
MEMORY
OF
PTE. J. BIRNEY
PTE. J. McGUIRE: R.D.FS
PTE. M. BALFE

These three privates were from the Royal Dublin Fusiliers. The Gordons who placed the monument are the Gordon Highlanders, a Scottish regiment of the British army, the regiment of Captain Aylmer Haldane. Had it not been for good luck, both Haldane and Churchill might have come to rest there as well. Instead, it was their lot to be made prisoners-of-war by the Boers.

Churchill was led along the railway under guard and soon rejoined Haldane, Frankland and the other captured soldiers who were then marched in the rain to a Boer encampment north of the battlefield. When he protested that he was a press correspondent and asked to see the officer in charge to request that he be released, Churchill's press credentials were confiscated and he was separated from the others. Here was a further moment of real peril for him. As he stood alone in the rain he grew increasingly anxious because he was aware that a civilian who had actively participated in a battle could be subjected to a drumhead court martial and shot for it. After waiting fifteen minutes he was told to rejoin the others, the Boers having decided neither to execute him nor release him. As a Boer officer explained to him: 'We are not going to let you go, old chappie, although you are a correspondent. We don't catch the son of a lord every day.'[71]

The captives were, in fact, treated humanely by the Boers and Churchill came in a sense to admire them, finding them tough and inflexible but civil. He engaged the guards in debate as they marched to the north on the causes of the war and each side asserted the righteousness of its own point of view. In these exchanges Churchill discovered the root cause of British and Boer differences. He wrote in a 30 November 1899 letter to the *Morning Post* of the following exchange:

Boer: No, no old chappie, we don't want your flag; we want to be left alone. We are free, you are not free.

WSC: How do you mean 'not free'?

Boer: Well, is it right that a dirty Kaffir should walk on the pavement – without a pass too? That's what they do in your British Colonies. Brother! Equal! Ugh! Free! Not a bit. We know how to treat Kaffirs.

Probing at random I had touched a very sensitive nerve. We had got down from underneath the political and reached the social. What is the true and original root of Dutch aversion to British rule? ... It is the abiding fear and hatred of the movement that seeks to place the native on a level with the white man. British government is associated in the Boer farmer's mind with violent social revolution. Black is to be proclaimed the same as white. The servant is to be raised against the master; the Kaffir is to be declared the brother of the European, to be constituted his legal equal, to be armed with political rights. The dominant race is to be deprived of their superiority; nor is a tigress robbed of her cubs more furious than is the Boer at this prospect.[72]

For all their disagreements Churchill found no cause for complaint about his treatment. A mounted Boer gave Churchill a cap to wear in the rain-storm, an Irish Fusiliers side-cap that he guessed had been taken as a souvenir in the earlier fighting near Ladysmith.[73]

Over a two-day period the prisoners hiked to Elandslaagte where they would board a train for a twenty-four-hour journey to Pretoria in the Transvaal. At the railway station a Boer doctor cleaned and rebound Churchill's wounded hand, an important kindness in the days before antibiotic drugs, as the wound had become infected. Arriving at Pretoria on 18 November, Churchill, the officer prisoners and Sergeant-Major Brockie of the Imperial Light Horse who was masquerading as an officer to get better treatment, were separated from the other ranks and marched to the Staats Model School which would be their place of detention.

The one-storey, red-brick building with a metal roof still stands in central Pretoria on the north-east corner of VanderWalt and Skinner streets where it serves as the education library for the Gauteng Department of Education. It was declared a monument in 1962 and bears a bronze plaque concerning the school's history with mention of Churchill's imprisonment and later escape.[74] Its appearance is much as it was a century ago with long verandahs along the front and back sides. In 1899, there was a rear compound, 120 yards square, that was surrounded on two sides by chest-high iron railings and on two sides by iron palings that were six and a half feet tall. Within it were the prisoners' exercise area, the servants' tents, the latrines, and the tents of the state police who guarded the prisoners and stood at intervals as sentries. Inside, twelve of the sixteen rooms aligned on either side of a long central hallway served as dormitories for the sixty or so officer prisoners; one served as a gymnasium and one as a dining room. Although the officers were kept under armed guard, they had many privileges including the right to have visitors, to send and receive mail, to obtain current newspapers and to purchase items for personal use. Churchill bought a new dark tweed suit upon arrival to replace the outfit he was wearing when captured.

Churchill absolutely hated being a prisoner-of-war, having lost not only his freedom but also his employment as a correspondent and his chance to further distinguish himself in action. He entitled the chapter in *My Early Life* about this period 'In Durance Vile' and complained of life in detention. 'The days are very long. Hours crawl like paralytic centipedes. Nothing amuses you. Reading is difficult; writing impossible. Life is one long boredom from dawn to slumber... you feel a sense of constant humiliation.'[75] The men passed the time conversing, pacing, smoking, playing chess and cards, and game after game of rounders. Frankland made a large map of Natal on the plaster wall of one of the dormitory rooms and they plotted the war news they received on it. Churchill kept up a correspondence with the outside, including four letters to the *Morning Post* and a letter to Bourke Cockran on his birthday in which he wrote, 'Nov. 30th 1899 (I am 25 today – it is terrible to think how little time remains!)'[76]

Churchill spent most of his time and energy in captivity seeking released. On 18 November, the very day of his arrival, he wrote to F. Louis de Souza, the Under-Secretary of State for War in the Commandant-General's office, asking to be set free, arguing that he was indeed a correspondent with proper credentials, that his identity was verified, and that he was unarmed in the armoured train fight. The last point was open to interpretation, of course, as Churchill had been armed at the outset of the skirmish, removing his Mauser and holster later to help load the wounded on the train, and thus was unarmed at the time of his capture. He had not fired a shot but he did have ammunition in his pockets which he took care discreetly to discard. The Boer Commandant-General of the Transvaal, Petrus J. Joubert, had read the Natal newspapers with their glowing accounts of Churchill's role in saving part of the armoured train and telegraphed the Transvaal government on 19 November his recommendation that Churchill not be released 'during the war'. An impatient Churchill wrote to De Souza again on 21 November repeating his arguments and adding that the *Morning Post* would pay the costs of his repatriation and that since he had been treated so kindly by the Boers he could be expected to write newspaper accounts that would reflect favourably on them after his release. Receiving no response, Churchill wrote a third letter to De Souza on 26 November amplifying his pleas for release, noting that international press opinion would be focused on the issue and even offering to give his parole that he would either serve only as a non-combatant or even leave South Africa until the end of the war if so required by the Boer authorities. The Transvaal officials did not budge from their position and their internal messages made it clear that they did not plan to release Churchill. On 8 December Churchill wrote again to De Souza asking that his request for release be forwarded to the Commandant-General for review. But by 9 December, he had come to the conclusion that he would not be released as a non-combatant or included in an exchange of officers with the British. He therefore resolved to escape.[77]

Churchill had thought of escape since the moment of his capture. Between Frere and Pretoria they were too closely guarded to find an opportunity. In Pretoria he concocted a grandiose scheme for the British officers held at the Staats Model School to overwhelm the guards, break out of the compound, free the 2,000 British soldiers being held at the Pretoria racecourse, take control of the town, capturing President Kruger in the process, and then, holding out like the brave souls in Mafeking and Ladysmith, perhaps forcing a negotiated end to the war. The plan did not win approval of the senior British officers, however, and was quietly dropped. A more modest scheme had been worked up by Haldane and Brockie who, being fluent in both Taal, the local dialect of Dutch, and the Kaffir language, was a valuable partner in such an enterprise. The plan was simple enough – to climb over the back wall of the compound in the dark of night when the guards were looking the other way and to hop on an eastbound train from Pretoria to Delagoa Bay in Portuguese East Africa (present-day Mozambique) about 300 miles away.[78]

On 9 December Churchill asked Haldane to be included in their escape plan. Brockie was strongly opposed to this and Haldane was concerned because Churchill was a real subject of interest in the camp and his absence would be quickly noticed. Churchill promised Haldane that he would share in a 'blaze of triumph' in the press, no doubt to be authored by himself, if they made their way back to Durban, but this did not sway him. Rather, Haldane agreed to include Churchill, later writing: 'He had, however, done gallant work at the armoured train mishap, for which he has always had my unstinting praise. Like me, he was eating his heart out at our incarceration, and I was loth to seem ungenerous, as would be the case if I went without him.'[79]

The trio planned to make their escape from the east side of the compound farthest from the school in the dimly lit area of a row of latrines near the iron paling which provided them with both an innocent reason for approaching the edge of the enclosure and some cover as they went over the fence. Aside from this, they would have to depend entirely on the combination of darkness and good luck in picking a moment when the guards were not looking, for a quick vault over the fence. The guards were posted every fifty yards inside the compound perimeter, one pair only fifteen yards from the latrines, and all were well armed. To be caught in the attempt was to risk being shot. The first attempt to escape on 11 December was aborted because the guards were too alert, and success depended entirely on moving from the latrine enclosure and over the fence when they were looking the other way. The next evening, 12 December, the second attempt was made and a controversy was born.

The plan was for Churchill and Haldane to go over in quick succession, followed soon after by Brockie. Haldane assumed that because Churchill was relatively short in comparison to the fence, was not too fit from lack of regular exercise and had a shoulder subject to dislocation, Haldane would need to give him a leg up to help him get quickly and quietly over the wall. On this night Haldane and Churchill approached the latrine as planned but, failing to find a moment when the guards' attention was diverted, walked back across the yard. Brockie, who had been watching, accused them of cowardice, headed for the latrine himself, but could not find an auspicious moment either. As Brockie was walking back to the school, Churchill returned to the latrine but the words they exchanged are lost to history. There was evidently a misunderstanding because while Haldane and Brockie went in to dinner, Churchill found his moment and at about 7.15 p.m. went over the fence, dropped into the back garden of the villa next door and hid there in some bushes awaiting the others. When Haldane learned that Churchill had got out he returned to the latrine area but a guard saw him trying to climb over the fence and he was ordered back down at gunpoint. Brockie apparently never got his own chance. After about an hour of waiting alone, Churchill heard a voice inside the fence in the dark whisper, 'They cannot get out. The sentry suspects. It's all up. Can you get back in again?'[80] Then Haldane came close to the fence and offered to toss Churchill his compass. Churchill declined for fear of the noise it might make. It was impossible for him to climb back over the fence without help – and certainly without being noticed – nor could the others get over to join him. So after ninety minutes of waiting he whispered back that he would go on alone.

It has been suggested from time to time that Churchill's escape was unnecessary, that he violated his parole by escaping, and that he acted dishonourably in leaving without Haldane and Brockie. The first assertion is easily dismissed. Although Commandant-General Joubert sent a message to De Souza on 12 December withdrawing his objection to Churchill's release, no such action was taken before Churchill's escape. Captured Transvaal government documents obtained by Haldane later in the war, including a 10 December telegram from Joubert to the acting Commandant-General in Pretoria convinced him that the Boers had no intention of releasing Churchill.[81] In any event, Churchill was not privy to the Boer communications and had himself concluded he would not be released. It has also been suggested that Churchill violated his parole by escaping and later taking an active part in the war but this allegation is also without merit. Although Churchill had given his word that he would leave Africa in exchange for his release in letters to De Souza on both 26 November and 8 December, the offer was never accepted. As no parole was granted, there could be no violation.

The more difficult question is whether Churchill acted honourably in leaving without Haldane and Brockie.[82] To say Haldane was unhappy with Churchill at the time is to put it mildly. He wrote in his private diary years later:

> I must admit that I was surprised and disgusted to find myself in the lurch, for Churchill had walked off with my carefully thought-out plan or what he knew of it, and had simply taken the bread out of my mouth. Brockie, I need hardly say, was furious, and the escaped correspondent of the Morning Post came in for a full dose of approbrious epithets of which Brockie had a liberal command. It requires no effort of memory at this distance of time to recall his sneering allusions to 'Your trusted friend – a nice kind of gentleman!' and so on who contrary to his advice I had allowed to join in our plot. Nor was he alone in his abuse of the escaped war correspondent, for many, indeed most, of our fellow-prisoners, some of whom had pressed me to let them share in the enterprise and who now began to realise the far greater difficulties of evasion in the future, joined in the chorus of vituperation that arose and continued for some days.[83]

Haldane was understandably disappointed that he did not get out with Churchill for he too longed to escape and return to his duties. Further, once it was learned by the Boers that Churchill had escaped by climbing over the fence, additional precautions were taken and no one was ever able to get out that way again. Haldane was unable to escape until 16 March 1900 when he, Brockie and Lt Frederick Le Mesurier of the Royal Dublin Fusiliers, who had hidden under the floor of the Staats Model School for over two weeks awaiting transfer of the prisoners to another facility, simply walked away unnoticed. They too pursued the original railway escape plan and, with the eventual assistance of some of the same people who helped Churchill, made their way to Portuguese East Africa on a goods train.

Haldane certainly could have resented his further three months' imprisonment and held it against Churchill. Moreover, Churchill's own accounts of his escape either down-played or omitted Haldane's role. In the early interviews and newspaper columns it is understandable that Churchill would not want to draw attention to Haldane, who was still a prisoner, any more than he would wish to publish the role of the civilians who aided his escape. But even later accounts by Churchill in articles in the *Strand Magazine* in December 1923 and January 1924, and in *My Early Life*, published in 1930, Churchill took credit for the escape plan without mention that it was Haldane's creation. Haldane's own final opinion was that Churchill had 'given him the slip' by leaving alone because he had acted on the spur of the moment when he saw his chance to go over the wall. This Haldane could understand and forgive. But Churchill's later, and less than full, accounts of the events of his escape caused Haldane to record in his diary in 1935:

> Had Churchill only possessed the moral courage to admit that, in the excitement of the moment, he saw a chance of escape and could not resist the temptation to take advantage of it, not realising that it would compromise the escape of his companions, all would have been well. A frank admission of that nature, made early after his escape, would have gone far to disarm much criticism as might have followed. I myself would have been the first publicly to do anything in my power to silence the tongues of any who might rail at him or taunt him with 'not having played the game'. Indeed it will be remembered how I have stated that any resentment which I felt regarding his action on the 12th December had quickly passed away, and since those days I have never borne the least animosity towards him for what occurred. But it was not to be, and the false step, once taken, made the difficulty of retraction, if ever contemplated, a thousand times more difficult, until, as time went on, it became impossible; for what would have been overlooked in the spontaneous admission of an impetuous youth of twenty-five, would have been condemned in the maturer man.[84]

Yet it must also be remembered that Haldane was very discreet in his public statements. He refused to give testimony against Churchill in a 1912 libel lawsuit against *Blackwood's Magazine* that Churchill brought concerning statements that he had violated his parole and acted dishonourably toward his comrades.[85] Haldane's final word on the subject is found in his 1948 memoir, *A Soldier's Saga*, in which, while referring to Churchill's escape as a 'moonlight flitting', he wrote that although he did not acquiesce in Churchill's version of events it was 'at this point best to draw a veil over subsequent events'.[86]

Churchill, in his own memorandum to himself on the subject written in 1912, states:

> My conscience is absolutely clear on the subject; I acted with perfect comradeship and honour the whole way through ... there was no more agreement, or bargain, or stipulation, as to who should go first, or how we should go, than there is among a dozen people in the hunting field who are waiting to take their turn at an awkward gap. When I had got over, I waited for an hour and a half at imminent risk of recapture for the others to come, and the fact that they were not able to come seemed to me and seemed to them to deprive me of all reasonable chance of escape.[87]

The fact of the matter is that Churchill and the others did plan to escape together, though not all to go over the fence at the same time. Churchill wanted the benefit of Brockie's facility with local languages. He knew his chance of reaching the coast was better with them than without them. Someone had to go over the fence first and although it turned out to be Churchill it could have been anyone. Initially Churchill and Haldane together tried and failed, while Brockie waited on the school verandah. Then Brockie made an unsuccessful attempt as Haldane and Churchill waited and watched. Eventually it was Churchill who grasped his moment and got over. Finally, Haldane made his escape bid, only to be caught. It was not Churchill's success that prevented Haldane and Brockie from trying again, it was Haldane's failure. Churchill was not necessarily braver or more assertive than the others, but he had the Churchill luck on this occasion and they did not. And that made all the difference.

Lying in the shrubbery near the fence, Churchill found himself alone but free, at least for the time being. He had the clothes he was wearing including a civilian slouch hat borrowed from fellow prisoner-of-war Adrian Hofmeyer, £75, and four slabs of chocolate and some biscuits in his pockets. He was in the centre of the Boer capital with almost 300 miles of enemy territory between him and the border with Portuguese East Africa at Komatipoort. He did not speak Dutch or any of the native dialects. He had no horse, no firearms, no knife, no contacts outside the compound, no maps, no compass, little food and no water bottle. Without Haldane, and especially Brockie, his chances of reaching the coast were much diminished. It was by then after 8 p.m., the moon had risen and by mid-morning the next day he would surely be missed. But he had pluck, a strong will to be free and the outlines of Haldane's plan in his head. When it was obvious that he would have to proceed alone he stood up, walked out of the garden and out into Skinner Street and thence south for about a half-mile where he came upon the railway line which he hoped would be his escape route to Portuguese East Africa. After walking along the tracks for two hours he found an appropriate spot and jumped aboard a goods train in the dark knowing he was moving rapidly away from Pretoria but not sure of his direction of travel. Before dawn he left the train at a point about sixty miles from Pretoria and found a hiding place in a clump of trees on the side of a ravine from where he could observe the railway. The sunrise brought good news for as Churchill later wrote: 'Presently the dawn began to break, and the sky to the east grew yellow and red, slashed across with heavy black clouds. I saw with relief that the railway ran steadily towards the sunrise, I had taken the right line, after all.'[88]

Churchill spent a long, hot and thirsty day in his hideout surveying the rail traffic and being himself watched by a perching vulture 'who manifested an extravagant interest in my condition, and made hideous and ominous gurglings from time to time'.[89] After much prayerful waiting, he resolved to make his way back to the railway after dark and hop another eastbound goods train, repeating the process of riding by night and hiding by day and thus making his way to the border. That night he moved to a suitable place on the line to catch a train but after several hours of waiting and no train passing, he grew impatient and started to walk east along the tracks in the bright moonlight. Making frequent detours to avoid guarded bridges and stations, he was soon wet and exhausted as well as hungry. Taking stock of his difficult position, he realised he could not go on alone and resolved to seek help from natives. Believing he saw the campfires of a Kaffir kraal in the distance and trusting the occupants would aid him, he set out across country. In the early hours of the morning he reached his destination only to find it was not a native kraal at all but a coal mine. At that point Churchill was too exhausted to go on or to formulate a new plan. He approached the first building and knocked on the door to ask for help. It was the home of John Howard, the manager of the Transvaal and Delagoa Bay Collieries near Witbank, a British-born but naturalised citizen of the Transvaal, who exclaimed, 'Thank God you have come here! It is the only house for twenty miles where you would not have been handed over. But we are all British here, and we will see you through.'[90] And so they did. Mr Howard fed Churchill and before dawn took him deep down into the coal mine. Providing him with bedding, candles, food, whisky and cigars, he hid him there out of reach of Boer patrols and police for the next three days while his guest waited and passed the time reading Robert Louis Stevenson's *Kidnapped.*

Indeed, there was an active search under way for Churchill, whose absence had been discovered at a 9.30 a.m. roll call on the morning of 13 December. In his bed the guards found a dummy placed there by Haldane, and Churchill's final letter to Louis de Souza dated 11 December 1899 which, in addition to expressing his appreciation for the kindnesses extended to him in captivity, announced: 'I do not concede that your Government was justified in holding me, a press correspondent and a non-combatant, and I have consequently resolved to escape.'[91] Soon an arrest warrant was issued for Churchill, a copy of which was later obtained in English translation by William Kennedy-Laurie Dickson, an English film-maker employed by British Biograph Company, from the Bloemfontein Chief of Police on 27 May 1900. Dickson noted that the document he received was 'translated from the Dutch into English by a Dutchman'. It read:

Description of a deserted prisoner of war named Winston Spencer Churchill, escaped out of the State Model School, Pretoria, on the 12th December, 1899.

Englishman, 25 years old, about 5 feet 8 inches high – indifferent built – walks a little with a bend forward – pale appearance – red brownish hair – small moustache hardly perceptible – talks through the nose, cannot pronounce the letter S properly, and does not know one word of Dutch. When last seen had a brown suit of clothes.
The portrait that was taken about 18 months ago can be seen at the police-station, Bloemfontein.

The undersigned requests any one finding him, to arrest him and report to the Commissioner of Police O.V.S.
(Signed)

J. A. E. Markus.[92]

This matches the description contained in a letter from the deputy superintendent of police in Pretoria to the Chief of Intelligence which was circulated with Churchill's picture in the Transvaal.[93]

Searches were conducted and some arrests were made in Pretoria but Churchill had got clean away. John Howard conspired with several others to help him escape, including the mine captain, Joe McKenna; the mine engineer, Dan Dewsnap; a miner named John McHenry; James Gillespie, a local physician; Charles Burnham, a merchant and two women who brought food for Churchill, Ada Blunden and Ellen David. They hid Churchill in the mine and later in a colliery building from the night of 14 December until 2.00 a.m. on 19 December when they secreted him in a goods train among bales of wool that Burnham was having shipped to Lourenço Marques at Delagoa Bay. Burnham accompanied the train to see Churchill safely through to the coast. Provided with food, bottles of tea and a pistol, he remained in his hiding place for the forty-eight-hour railway journey. The train pulled into Lourenço Marques on the afternoon of 21 December and, with the help of Burnham, Churchill arrived at the British consulate at 4.00 p.m. Once identified, he was taken in, given a bath, fresh clothing, a meal and the newspapers. That evening, accompanied by armed British sympathisers, Churchill boarded the mail packet SS *Induna* and at 10.00 p.m. sailed for Durban, the port where his adventures in Natal had begun only five weeks earlier. He had spent fifteen days as a correspondent, twenty-seven days as a prisoner and nine days as an escapee. Burnham telegraphed Howard, 'Goods arrived safely.'

Churchill never forgot the men and women who had helped him escape. He later sent each of the eight a gold pocket watch with an inscription on the following lines: 'To Joe McKenna from Winston S. Churchill in recognition of timely help afforded him in his escape from Pretoria during the South African War, December 13, 1899.'[94] After Churchill returned to England he sent Howard's pistol back to him with an engraved brandy flask that was kept by the Howard family for more than a century.[95]

The press and the newspaper-reading public in England and South Africa had followed Churchill's escape with avid interest. In the eleven days between his disappearance from Pretoria and his arrival in Durban there had been much speculation, and misinformation too, published as to his whereabouts, with news and conjecture moving at the speed of the telegraph. By the time he reached Durban, Churchill was an international celebrity and as he termed it, 'a popular hero. I was received as if I had won a great victory.'[96] He arrived at Durban harbour just after 4.00 p.m. on

Saturday, 23 December 1899, and was greeted by an enthusiastic crowd of thousands of well wishers. He was carried on their shoulders from the ship to the main wharf where he was prevailed upon to give an impromptu speech. Then he was taken in a rickshaw in a procession led by a pair of Union Flags the two miles to the town hall in Fairwell Square where he mounted a jaunting-car and was asked to speak again. After the cheering crowd had sung 'Soldiers of the Queen' and 'Rule Britannia', Churchill addressed them:

> I need not say how deeply grateful I am for the great kindness you have shown in your welcome to me. This is not the time for a long speech. We have got outside the region of words; we have got to the region of action. We are now in the region of war, and in this war we have not yet arrived at the half-way house. (Hear, hear.) But with the determination of a great Empire surrounded by Colonies of unprecedented loyalty we shall carry our policy to a successful conclusion, and under the old Union Jack there will be an era of peace, purity, liberty, equality and good Government in South Africa. (Cheers.) I thank you once again for your great kindness. I am sure I feel within myself a personal measure of that gratitude which every Englishman who loves his country must feel towards the loyal and devoted Colonists of Natal. (Tremendous Cheers.)[97]

A plaque was later placed on the building to commemorate the speech. Although the old town hall now serves as a post office, the plaque remains to this day commemorating the man and the event.[98] Churchill was next taken to the town commandant's office where he received a number of telegrams of congratulation, was received by prominent local citizens and held a press conference. He gave an account of his escape, one which had him wandering about in the bush for five days before he boarded his train to freedom but omitting all reference to the assistance he received at Witbank.

At the local railway station he boarded the 5.40 p.m. train for Pieter-maritzburg where he would spend the night as the guest of the Governor of Natal, Sir Walter Hely-Hutchinson. The next day, Christmas Eve, he returned to Frere and the area where his greatest adventure had begun on 15 November.

Churchill's role in the armoured train fight, his capture and escape made him an instant international celebrity as the telegraph and the Reuters news service spread his story far and wide. As he summarised the situation in *My Early Life*: 'Youth seeks adventure. Journalism requires Advertisement. Certainly I had found both. I became for the time quite famous.'[99] And so he had. He was the subject of numerous magazine and newspaper articles in Britain and the United States with titles such as 'The Bravery of Winston Churchill' in the March 1900 issue of *Current Literature*. He entered popular culture on cigarette cards, including one that depicted him hopping on a freight train to escape the Boers, and as the subject of a humorous dance-hall tune which included the lyric, 'You've heard of Brimstone Chapel, So of course I needn't say, He's the latest and the greatest Correspondent of the day.'[100]

Certainly the events of November and December 1899 were a turning point in Churchill's life. What had appeared to be his worst nightmare when captured by the Boers proved to be the key to his success as a writer and as a politician. His bravery under fire in the armoured train fight was widely publicised, as was his pluck in escaping from the Boers. And no one wrote or spoke about it more than Churchill himself. He realised his great good fortune in surviving his South African adventures and receiving such public attention. He had found the 'blaze of triumph' he promised Haldane and did nothing to dampen the flames of fame it offered. When his first twenty-seven newspaper articles were published in book form on 15 May 1900 as *London to Ladysmith via Pretoria*, the cover illustration depicted the armoured train. He dedicated the book to 'The staff of the Natal Government Railway whose careful and courageous discharge of their every-day duties amid the perils of war has made them honourably conspicuous even among their fellow colonists.'

Not only was Churchill's adventure a great human interest story but it came at a time when it was virtually the only good news for Britain from South Africa, hot on the heels of 'Black Week' which had seen a trio of serious military reverses. On 10 December Lt General William Gatacre's forces were beaten in a battle at Stormberg in Cape Colony. On 11 December Lt General Lord Metheun's advance toward the relief of Kimberley was stalled at Magersfontein with over 900 casualties. On 15 December General Buller's attempt to recapture Colenso in Natal was repulsed with almost a thousand casualties including Lt Freddie Roberts, the son of Field Marshal Lord Roberts, the next Commander-in-Chief of British forces in South Africa, who won a posthumous Victoria Cross trying to save British guns from capture.[101] When Churchill returned to Natal in December 1899 the war was at a stalemate and British fortunes were at an unexpectedly low ebb.

8

The South African War: Ladysmith to Diamond Hill

The 'Black Week' battles that took place in South Africa in mid-December 1899 were part of the second phase of the war, the first British offensive. This phase comprised three northward thrusts, one in the west from Cape Town through Cape Colony with the goal of relieving Kimberley and Mafeking and moving into the Orange Free State from the west, one from Port Elizabeth and East London on the central coast of Cape Colony aimed at the southern border of the Orange Free State, and one in the east through Natal with the goal of relieving Ladysmith. Although Kimberley and Mafeking were located on the Western Railway and Ladysmith was near an important junction on the Natal Railway, their importance was more political than strategic. British honour required that the sieges of those embattled towns be lifted and the soldiers and civilians be rescued. Churchill believed the 'true line of advance' to defeat the Boer republics was through the Orange Free State from the south, but he also knew that the main fighting in the immediate future would be focused on the relief of Ladysmith in Natal. He therefore resolved to stay there.[1] Lifting the siege of Ladysmith would be a big morale booster for Britain and its army, and it was hoped that the thousands of troops trapped there could participate in further offensive operations when freed. The setbacks of 'Black Week' had effectively stalled the first British offensive by the time Churchill escaped and made his way back to Durban.

The day after the battle of Colenso, Field Marshal Lord Roberts was appointed to replace Buller as Commander-in-Chief of the British and imperial forces in South Africa with General Lord Kitchener of Khartoum as his chief of staff. Roberts would take personal command of the army in the west and, with reinforcements from overseas, would renew the drive toward Kimberley with the aim of attacking through the Orange Free State from the west to capture its capital, Bloemfontein. General Buller was relegated to command of the Natal Field Force, the eastern wing of the army, which was then centred around Frere and Chieveley in Natal. There the field force rested, resupplied and regrouped in anticipation of the commencement of the third phase of the war, the second British offensive, in February, 1900. The arrival of reinforcements in Natal more than made up for the losses suffered at Colenso. The Natal Field Force, numbering some 19,000 infantry, 3,000 cavalry and sixty artillery pieces included the following:

Commander-in-Chief: SIR REDVERS BULLER

CLERY'S DIVISION	WARREN'S DIVISION
consisting of	consisting of
Hildyard's Brigade,	Lyttelton's Brigade,
Hart's Brigade,	Woodgate's Brigade,
1 squad. 13th Hussars,	1 squad. 15th Hussars,
3 batteries,	3 batteries,
R. E.	R. E.

CORPS TROOPS
Coke's Brigade (3 battalions),
1 field battery RA,
1 howitzer battery RA,
2x4.7 naval guns and Naval Brigade,
8 long-range naval 12-pounder guns,
1 squadron 13th Hussars,
RE, &c.

CAVALRY (DUNDONALD)
1st Royal Dragoons.
14th Hussars.
4 squadrons South African Light Horse.
1 squadron Imperial Light Horse.
Bethune's Mounted Infantry.
Thorneycroft's Mounted Infantry.
1 squadron Natal Carabineers.
1 squadron Natal Police.
1 company KRR Mounted Infantry.
6 machine guns.[2]

As mentioned, when Churchill arrived back in Durban on 23 December 1899, he stayed only a few hours before taking a train north. By Christmas eve he was back in Frere and reunited with his fellow journalists who were following the activities of Buller's army.

The next day he went to headquarters to see Sir Redvers Buller. He found the general mentally and physically tired and doubted whether he was up to the tasks his duty required.[3] Although he did not hold a high opinion of Buller, the general was impressed with Churchill's exploits. The day after meeting Churchill, Buller wrote in a letter to Lady Londonderry, 'Winston Churchill turned up here yesterday escaped from Pretoria. He is really a fine fellow and I must say I admire him greatly. I wish he was leading irregular troops instead of writing for a rotten paper. We are very short of good men, as he appears to be, out here.'[4] At the end of their meeting on Christmas day, Buller asked if there was anything he could do for the young man. It was an offer not unlike that extended to him by Sir Bindon Blood at Deepdene four years previously and Churchill accepted it without hesitation, saying he would like to be given a commission in one of the regiments of cavalry raised in South Africa and serving with the British forces.

Because Churchill was still under contract to the *Morning Post*, this raised the ticklish issue of whether under current regulations a serving officer could also work as a war correspondent. A War Office policy was instituted following the Sudan campaign barring the dual role, based in no small part on Churchill's own critical writing on the Nile expedition. After some hesitation Buller agreed to make an exception and told Churchill, 'All right. You can have a commission in Bungo's [Major Julian Byng's South African Light Horse] regiment. You will have to do as much as you can for both jobs. But ... you will get no pay for ours.'[5] This arrangement was readily accepted by Churchill who wanted to be a soldier and knew that a lieutenant's pay was a mere fraction of the remuneration from his newspaper. He was well pleased with himself and wrote to his mother on 6 January: 'Sir Redvers Buller has given me a lieutenancy in the S. A. Light Horse without requiring me to abandon my status of correspondent so that I am evidently in very high favour. I thought perhaps this might have been done to qualify me for some reward they may care to give me.'[6] Although no reward came his way, being on the army rolls would qualify Churchill for the campaign medal for the South African War.

Churchill's new regimental commander was Major Julian H. G. Byng, late of the 10th Hussars, who held the local rank of lieutenant colonel. He was an old acquaintance and had accompanied Churchill on his first visits to the 4th Hussars at Aldershot when Winston was still a Sandhurst cadet and later had served as a judge in some of his riding competitions. Byng took Churchill into the regiment as a supernumerary lieutenant and the young officer served as an assistant adjutant and did not lead a troop. Byng later provided Churchill with a certificate stating, 'I certify that Lieut. Winston Spencer Churchill served as Lieutenant in the "South African Light Horse" from 2d January 1900 to 23d March 1900, & was present at all actions & engagements in which the Regiment took part.'[7] Byng let Churchill move about at will when the regiment was not engaged which allowed him to continue reporting for the *Morning Post*. Thereafter, Churchill recorded, he 'lived day to day in perfect happiness'.[8] He liked the idea of active service so much that he obtained a commission in the regiment for his brother Jack, who sailed from England on 5 January, 1900 to join him. His cousin, Charles, the Ninth Duke of Marlborough, then an officer in a yeomanry regiment in England, accepted a position on Roberts's staff and left for South Africa two days later.

The South African Light Horse was a regiment of irregular cavalry trained to move on horseback and to fight on foot with rifles rather than the traditional cavalry sabres or lances. Raised in Cape Colony in November 1899, the regiment had a mixed membership of South African colonists, uitlanders from the Boer republics, and various other horsemen from around the world including English gentlemen, regular officers on leave from their regiments in the British army and even a Confederate veteran from the American Civil War.[9] The unit comprised approximately 700 men organised into six squadrons and a horse-drawn battery of Colt machine guns. At the time of Churchill's arrival the four squadrons in Natal were part of Lord Dundonald's cavalry brigade, the order of battle of which is noted above. The troopers were, to Churchill's experienced eye, 'first-rate fighting men'.[10]

The uniform of the regiment was based on the standard British army field uniform of khaki cloth that Churchill had worn on active service in India and the Sudan. The uniform frock, or jacket, had brass buttons featuring a miniature of the regimental insignia and was buttoned up at the collar. The shoulder chains of the British cavalry were not worn and officers displayed their badges of rank on their epaulettes. All ranks carried brass shoulder titles, 'S.A.L.H.' on their epaulettes and other ranks wore cloth badges of rank on their sleeves, their chevrons either gold on blue or black on red, depending on the squadron. Cavalry-style khaki breeches were worn with the lower leg covered in leather or cloth leggings and spurs on the boots. The wide-brimmed slouch hat with a *pagri* of khaki had the left side of the brim pinned up to the crown Australian-style. Many officers, Churchill included, wore a Sam Browne belt or a lanyard around their neck to support a holstered pistol but swords were not carried. Non-commissioned officers and other ranks were armed with rifles, the brown leather cartridge belts being draped from the left shoulder to the right waist. There were two forms of regimental badges, both made of brass. The first was a Maltese cross with the letters SALH on the arms and the date 1899 in the centre. This badge was worn by Churchill in the photographs taken in South Africa and was used to pin up his hat brim. The second badge had the same Maltese cross plus a feather plume above its top arm and a brass ribbon below on which was inscribed the regimental motto in Zulu, 'USIBA ENJALOH NGAPAMBELE' ('Feathers to the Front'). Adorning the hat on the left side were the long black tail feathers of the sakabulu bird (long-tailed swallow), which gave the whole outfit a rather jaunty appearance. The feathers were a key feature of the regimental identity and the South African Light Horsemen were sometimes referred to as the 'Sakabulas' or, later, as the 'Cocky-Ollie Birds'.[11]

In his dual role as correspondent and soldier Churchill dressed in a somewhat personalised variation of the regimental uniform. His khaki jacket was worn open at the collar with a white shirt and dark bow-tie. The jacket also had four chest pockets rather than the usual two. He wore no collar insignia but did wear the two stars of a first lieutenant on his epaulettes. Above the pockets on the left side of the jacket he wore three ribbons for the India Medal, the Queen's Sudan Medal and the Spanish Order of Military Merit. On occasion he was photographed in South Africa with a binoculars case strapped over his shoulder and a cartridge belt around his waist, and even wearing a civilian pin-striped suit while on campaign with Colonel Byng.[12] However attired, as a personal friend of the colonel and as an experienced campaigner, Churchill fitted in well with the regiment as the new offensive began. In January and February 1900 Buller's army made repeated attempts to force the Tugela river and advance to Ladysmith, and Churchill either participated in or observed from close quarters all the battles during that time. If his regiment was not engaged, he was often in harm's way reporting for the *Morning Post*.

The area of operations in Natal was actually rather small, about 600 square miles. Ladysmith was some sixteen miles north of the British base camp at Chieveley. The far western edge of the Boer line near Acton Homes was twenty-eight miles from the far eastern end near Monte Cristo ridge. The initial stages of the renewed British offensive in Natal were focused on crossing the Tugela river which ran its winding course from west to east just north of Colenso and six to twelve miles south of Ladysmith. The first attempt to cross in force had been defeated in December 1899 at the battle of Colenso. Buller decided next to attempt a crossing in an area about sixteen miles west of Colenso in a manoeuvre designed to turn the right flank of the Boer position which was ranged along a series of ridges north of the Tugela. The ridge-line has a most forebidding appearance from the hills south of the river which is eighty-five yards across and swift-flowing in that area. The river and ridges were a formidable natural defensive position. Churchill thought it would be wiser to try to go around rather than attack the Boer position which he described as a 'natural trap' and a 'mighty rampart' defended by twelve to fifteen thousand 'of the best riflemen in the world armed with beautiful magazine rifles, supplied with an inexhaustible supply of ammunition supported by fifteen or twenty excellent quick-firing guns all artfully entrenched and concealed'.[13]

The army began its advance on the morning of 11 January 1900, with Dundonald's cavalry brigade and Warren's division moving west from Chieveley camp. It was a laborious movement with thousands of infantry, dozens of guns and a baggage train over ten miles long. Dundonald's cavalry was ordered to conduct a reconnaissance in force and seize a bridge over the Little Tugela river at Springfield. This they did by early afternoon, having met no resistance. Encouraged by his progress and the enthusiasm of his junior officers, Dundonald decided to exceed his specific orders and press on toward the Tugela leaving 300 troopers and two guns to guard the bridge at Springfield. By 6.00 p.m. Dundonald had reached and secured the heights south of the Tugela river and, with 700 troopers and four guns, set up positions overlooking Potgeiter's Drift.[14] He needed to communicate his position to General Cleary at Chieveley camp and Lt Churchill volunteered to make the eighteen-mile ride to deliver the dispatch. In his memoir, *My Army Life*, Dundonald recorded: 'I thought his offer was a gallant one, as neither he nor I knew what parties of Boers might be lurking in the neighbourhood.'[15] The next morning troopers of the South African Light Horse seized the ferry at Potgeiter's Drift and secured it to the south bank of the river. The cavalrymen then spent five days holding the heights, including Spearman's Hill and Mount Alice, which would later be Buller's headquarters, and patrolling south of the Tugela while awaiting the arrival of the infantry, the guns and the baggage train.

The movements of the main army were remarkably slow due in part to rain and muddy conditions. The advance to the Tugela Heights did not begin until almost a month after the battle of Colenso. Then it took five days to move the army the eighteen miles from Chieveley to be in position to move across the Tugela on 16 January. Buller was cautious in all his army's movements, because he was wary of being cut off from the Natal Railway and encircled, and also because his large army moved only at the pace of the infantry and the wagons. When the attack across the Tugela did take place it would come as no surprise to the Boers who had been observing the British for weeks and improving their entrenchments and siting their guns.

Buller's second attempt to force the Tugela river was planned as a two-pronged infantry attack backed by artillery, with the right prong crossing at Potgeiter's Drift and the left prong crossing six miles to the west in the area of Trichardt's Drift, the former intended as a demonstration and the latter as the main attack. The crossing began at Potgeiter's on 16 January with the first infantry moving across on the ferry and the rest crossing over two pontoon bridges built by the Royal Engineers. The troops of Lyttleton's brigade, Coke's brigade and Bethune's Mounted Infantry took part in this advance, a total of seven battalions of infantry, 300 horse and twenty-two guns with Major General Neville Lyttleton in command. The advance on the left under Lt General Sir Charles Warren began its crossing at Trichardt's Drift on the 17th with the men of Hart's, Hilyard's and Woodgate's brigades and the cavalry brigade under Lord Dundonald, a total of twelve battalions of infantry, thirty-six guns, and 1,600 horse.

A thousand men of Dundonald's cavalry brigade, Churchill among them, crossed the river at Trichardt's Drift on 17 January with orders to protect Warren's left flank and to locate the right end of the Boer lines. The brigade comprised one squadron of Imperial Light Horse, the 60th Rifles Mounted Infantry, one squadron of Natal Carbineers, four squadrons of South African Light Horse, Thorneycroft's Mounted Infantry, the 13th Lancers and the 1st Royal Dragoons.[16] By early afternoon on the 17th they had established a five-mile line north of the Tugela and were patrolling and probing the Boer positions. On the 18th a sharp firefight broke out on the far western end of the line near Venter's Spruit (stream) at Acton Homes about ten miles west of Potgeiter's Drift with the British getting the better of it and forcing the Boers into retreat. Churchill and a squadron from the S.A.L.H. were there for the end of the skirmish which resulted in ten Boers killed, eight badly wounded and two dozen taken prisoner at the cost of two British killed and two wounded. Churchill wrote of the results of the action in a letter to the *Morning Post*: 'I have often seen dead men, killed in war – thousands at Omdurman – scores elsewhere, black and white, but the Boer dead aroused the most painful emotions.'[17] Lying on the ground was a dead field cornet holding a letter from his wife in his lifeless hand. Next to him was a teenaged Boer shot dead, and not far away the two dead British soldiers 'with their heads smashed like eggshells'. Churchill's continuing education in war brought sadness rather than exultation. He wrote: 'Ah, horrible war, amazing medley of the glorious and the squalid, if modern men of light and leading saw your face closer, simple folk would see it hardly ever.'[18]

Meanwhile, the British forces that crossed at Trichardt's and Potgeiter's Drifts assembled north of the Tugela with Lyttleton's attack beginning on the 18th and Warren's on the 20th. The infantry attacks did not fare well and they and the thousands of artillery shells fired in their support failed to dislodge the Boers from their positions on the heights. Between the 18th and the 22nd, the British took hundreds of casualties with little advance. The plan of frontal assault against a well-armed, entrenched enemy was doomed to fail but the British generals had not learned this lesson. On the left flank the cavalry brigade had found the right end of the Boer line on the 18th but their request for reinforcements and guns was denied and they were recalled by Warren to guard his supply train. Here was a major tactical error by Warren, for beyond the ridge-line held by the Boers was relatively open country and in Churchill's view from Acton Homes it was only 'two easy marches into Ladysmith'.[19] Again on the 20th, the cavalry, including Churchill and the South African Light Horse, was sent out to demonstrate on the left flank. They succeeded in taking Bastion Hill to keep this high ground out of Boer hands as Warren's attack continued. Churchill took part in the action at Bastion Hill in which Major Charles Childe was killed and four troopers were wounded.

Although Buller may have viewed the present attacks as a flanking movement in the sense that the main assault was far west of the Boer centre near Colenso, it was still a frontal offensive on a portion of the Boer's extended line. A flanking attack in the tactical sense of reinforcing and exploiting Dundonald's flanking movement might well have succeeded in the relief of Ladysmith much sooner and at much less cost in lives. Rather than flanking the Boer line, Buller continued to hammer at their fortified ridge-line. And the plodding nature of Warren's advance allowed the Boers to shift troops to reinforce the line in front of him at Trichardt's Drift. By 23 January it was clear that the British attack had stalled and Warren convinced Buller his next move should be to seize Spion Kop (Spy Hill), the highest point of the Boer defensive line at an elevation of 1,470 feet above the river, which was located between the two prongs of the British attack. The plan was for Warren's troops to seize Spion Kop in a night attack on 23 January, to build and hold an entrenched position, and to move up artillery the second night so as to bring the Boer positions to both the east and west under enfilading fire and render them untenable.

The attack began at one o'clock in the morning of 24 January up a long spur on the south-west corner of Spion Kop. The 1,700-man attacking force included troops from the Lancaster Fusiliers, the Royal Lancaster Regiment, Thorneycroft's Mounted Infantry, and two companies of the South Lancashires under command of Major General E. R. P. Woodgate. Advancing in mist and darkness they took the summit at bayonet point by 3 a.m. and occupied it. They immediately set about preparing their positions on the summit but all was not well. The British had no proper maps of Spion Kop or, importantly, the area around it. Nor did their reconnaissance reveal the nature of the summit of Spion Kop. It was not, in fact, a single hill but the highest point on an extended ridge-line with several spurs and adjacent hills of similar height. The summit was like a plateau, relatively flat and in Churchill's description 'about as large as Trafalgar Square'.[20] Into this space were crowded the almost 2,000 men of the British force. To make matters worse, the boulder-strewn summit of the kop was laced with veins of dolomite rock just below the surface, and the rust-red, rocky soil could only be excavated to a depth of six inches. So the soldiers piled up rocks in front of them. As a result the combination sangar and trench in front of the main position only offered eighteen inches of cover, barely enough for a man to lie flat behind it. As the morning mist of 24 January began to lift, the British realised their position was too far back from the edge of the plateau to prevent Boer riflemen from scaling the steep north slope, which quickly brought the British troops under close-range rifle fire. The British also came under fire from Boer artillery and pom-pom guns located on a series of kops and knolls to their front and flanks. Bennet Burleigh of the *Daily Telegraph* described it as 'one continuous roar' from very early morning until dusk as the British were 'rained upon from three sides, [by] a hellish tornado, of bullet and shell, that pierced and shattered our soldiers by scores'.[21]

The battle of Spion Kop was a disaster for the British, characterised by poor communications, poor gunnery and poor generalship. By mid-morning General Woodgate was mortally wounded and out of action. There was much confusion about who was then in command on the summit. Neither General Buller, who watched the battle through a telescope from Mount Alice four and a half miles away, nor General Warren on Three Tree Hill three miles away, was aware of the terrible difficulties on Spion Kop. Colonel Thorneycroft and other officers on the summit requested reinforcements but their messages were delayed and they received no information or orders from either general. Thorneycroft in particular was so fully engaged in the close-quarter battle that he was effectively isolated and unable to keep his superiors informed. General Buller, in overall command, neglected to order other attacks in co-ordination with that on Spion Kop and so not only failed to relieve the pressure on the troops there but also failed to exploit the opportunity created to flank or force the Boer lines. Neither Buller nor Warren seemed to have grasped the importance of sending troops to attack the Boer gun positions that were bombarding Spion Kop with such great accuracy. The only successful attack, by the 60th Rifles on Twin Peaks, one of the Boer positions overlooking Spion Kop, was negated when Buller recalled them after dark. Similarly, Warren took no steps to widen the battle or aid Thorneycroft except to send reinforcements which had little effect. Most of the fresh troops could not engage the enemy because the summit was actually too small to hold them and, more importantly, because the Boer fire was too severe. No attempt was made to move the reinforcements around Spion Kop to attack the Boer rear.

A decisive factor in the outcome of the battle was that all through the daylight hours and into the night the Boer artillery was effective and the British guns were not. The Boer Creusot and Krupp cannon and Maxim pom-pom guns situated on Green Hill to the north-west, Conical Hill to the north and Aloe Knoll and Twin Peaks to the east from distances of two miles or less were zeroed in on the summit. The British gunners at Three Tree Hill to the west and Naval Gun Hill to the south-east could not see their targets and never succeeded in silencing or slowing the Boer barrage which Churchill estimated was landing seven rounds per minute on the summit by late afternoon.[22] The British guns that were supposed to be placed on Spion Kop – this was the purpose of the operation after all – never reached it. The naval guns proved too heavy to manhandle to the top and if they had been emplaced there it is likely that the Boer rifle fire would be too heavy to allow them to be served anyway.

As the South African Light Horse were not engaged at Spion Kop, Churchill was free to observe the battle in his role as war correspondent. He began the day near Buller's headquarters on Mount Alice and could see the Boer bombardment of Spion Kop in progress. After lunch he and Captain Ronald George Brooke of the 7th Hussars rode over to Warren's headquarters at Three Tree Hill and by four o'clock rode to Spion Kop, 'to see what the situation was'. They left their horses at the ambulance park on the south-west base of the mountain and climbed up toward the top on foot. They were shocked by what they saw. As Churchill wrote in his letter of 25 January to the *Morning Post*:

> Streams of wounded met us and obstructed the path. Men were staggering along alone, or supported by comrades, or crawling on hands and knees, or carried on stretchers. Corpses lay here and there. Many of the wounds were of a horrible nature. The splinters and fragments of the shell had torn and mutilated in the most ghastly manner. I passed about two hundred while I was climbing up. There was, moreover, a small but steady leakage of unwounded men of all corps. Some of these cursed and swore. Others were utterly exhausted and fell on the hillside in stupor. Others again seemed drunk, though they had had no liquor. Scores were sleeping heavily. Fighting was still proceeding, and stray bullets struck all over the ground, while the Maxim shell guns [pom-poms] scourged the flanks of the hill and the sheltering infantry at regular intervals of a minute ...
>
> The dead and injured, smashed and broken by the shells, littered the summit till it was a bloody, reeking shambles.[23]

They proceeded to the summit for a further investigation but as Churchill wrote, 'We crawled forward a short way on to the plateau, but the fire was much too hot for mere sight-seeing.'[24] They decided at once to report their observations to General Warren and arrived at his headquarters at dusk. Churchill's description of the situation was the best and latest intelligence Warren had received as he had been out of touch with Thorneycroft for many hours. Churchill sat in on Warren's staff meeting and was sent to take a written message to Thorneycroft that overnight the general would send up naval guns, sappers and working parties and so try to see the original plan through. Churchill was directed to ascertain the colonel's views and report back to Warren. He climbed back up Spion Kop in the dark, found Colonel Thorneycroft on the summit and presented the message. But it was already too late. An exhausted Thorneycroft told Churchill he had ordered a general retirement from Spion Kop an hour earlier. When Churchill said, 'Had I not better go and tell Sir Charles Warren before you retire from the hill? I am sure he meant you to hold on,' the colonel replied, 'No, I have made up my mind. Better six good battalions safely off the hill to-night than a bloody mop-up in the morning.'[25] Nothing would change Thorneycroft's mind. On the way down the south slope an officer of the Royal Engineers brought the colonel another message from General Warren advising him that the officer was bringing up sappers to reinforce the position on the summit and fresh infantry to replace casualties, but Thorneycroft stood by his decision and ordered the reinforcements to march back down. Captain Gough of the cavalry brigade staff was sent up to Thorneycroft, after news of the retreat reached Warren, with the message that the withdrawal was to be halted and the hill reoccupied. He too found it was not to be so as the withdrawal was all but complete. On his way back Gough overheard a wounded Scottish soldier remark, 'What the hell are we leaving the bloody hill for?'[26] It was a good question without a satisfactory answer.

All day and into the dark the British and Boers on the summit had fought each other to a standstill with neither side able to dislodge the other from the plateau by force. Unknown to the British, the Boers had largely abandoned Spion Kop during the night of 24–25 January at the same time as the British retirement was in progress. One of the Boer participants in the battle, a teenage burgher named Deneys Reitz, recorded in his memoir of the war: 'We fully believed that the morning would see them streaming through the breach to the relief of Ladysmith, and the rolling up of all our Tugela line.'[27] At dawn on the 25th the Boers realised the British were gone, reoccupied the summit and claimed victory. For the British it was a costly engagement for no gain. They suffered an estimated 1,740 casualties including 383 killed and 303 missing (some of these blown to bits) or taken prisoner. Among the British dead were Lt H. S. McCorquodale, a Harrow classmate of Churchill, who had only joined Thorneycroft's Mounted Infantry the day before the battle, and Lt Vere H. A. Awdry, Lancashire Fusiliers, a contemporary from Churchill's Sandhurst intake.[28] The estimated Boer casualties were 160 killed and 140 wounded.[29]

It is interesting in retrospect to note several participants in the battle of Spion Kop. In addition to young Lt Churchill, who was destined to be Prime Minister of England, was Louis Botha, the general in command of the Boer forces in the battle, who became Prime Minister of the Transvaal in 1907. When the Union of South Africa became independent in 1910, he became its prime minister in which role he visited London for the Imperial Conference, when Churchill, as Under Secretary of State for the Colonies, was a participant. Indeed, it was widely rumoured that Churchill had proposed marriage to Botha's daughter. Botha also served as the commanding general of the South African forces for the invasion of German South West Africa in 1915. By 1918 he attended the Versailles Peace Conference as a member of the British delegation of which Churchill was also a member.[30] Deneys Reitz, the young burgher who had fought on top of Spion Kop, later took part in the German South West Africa campaign with General Smuts. By early 1918 he was in command of the 1st Battalion of the Royals Scots Fusiliers, the 6th Battalion of which was commanded by Churchill in 1916. Reitz was employed in the South African High Commission in London where he died in October 1944 during Churchill's wartime premiership.[31] Also on Spion Kop during the battle and 'within the firing line' was M. K. Gandhi, a Middle Temple lawyer then living in South Africa who served as a stretcher-bearer marching 'from twenty to twenty-five miles a day' carrying British casualties to field hospital. He and Churchill would later be spokesmen for opposite points of view concerning Indian independence in the 1930s and Gandhi would be the subject of one of Churchill's most regrettable remarks, yet also the object of his encouragement in subsequent years.[32]

There was plenty of blame to go around for the débâcle. In *My Early Life*, Churchill wrote: 'Colonel Thorneycroft erred gravely in retiring against his orders from the position he had so nobly held by the sacrifices of his troops', and called the withdrawal a 'military crime'.[33] Buller blamed Warren for his failure to exercise proper command and control of the battle and promptly removed him. Sir Redvers then took personal command, ordered a general withdrawal and by the early morning of 27 January the entire British force had crossed back over the Tugela river to camp south of Spearman's Hill and Mount Alice where they had set off sixteen days and 1,800 casualties earlier. The South African Light Horse suffered sixty casualties in this period.[34]

Churchill's role in the battle of Spion Kop was a minor one although he seemed to be everywhere. He served in the two roles to which he was by then accustomed – correspondent and galloper for senior officers. Because his own regiment was not engaged, he was free to move from place to place as an observer. As a responsible serving officer he was duty bound to report his observations of Spion Kop to General Warren, which is just what he did. Warren and his staff made the decision on what was to be done next and wrote the message for Churchill to take to Thorneycroft. What they decided was based not merely on Churchill's observations and recommendations; rather, it was to proceed with the original battle plan of fortifying the summit and bringing up artillery. It was not his own recommendation to hold out that Churchill carried to Thorneycroft but Warren's orders. Thorneycroft did not decide to retire from the summit in contravention of Churchill's advice but in violation of his own orders. Indeed, Churchill did not even reach Thorneycroft until an hour after the latter's decision had been made.[35] None the less, Churchill had once again shown his characteristic initiative and courage; and he certainly faced danger along the way. As he reported in a 28 January 1900, letter to Pamela Plowden: 'I have had five very dangerous days – continually under shell & rifle fire and once the feather in my hat was cut through by a bullet. But – in the end I came serenely through.'[36]

The battlefield of Spion Kop is well preserved today as part of the Spioenkop Dam Nature Reserve in KwaZulu-Natal. The summits of Spion Kop, Aloe Knoll, Twin Peaks, Conical Hill and Green Hill are all clearly visible and have not been built upon. In 1900 Spion Kop was covered all over by green veldt grass; today its boulder strewn summit is covered with tambuki grass, spotted with aloe plants and little more. The main British trench line that provided such meagre shelter to the Lancashire regiments and Thorneycroft's Mounted Infantry has been preserved and now serves as a war grave. There are stone memorials to the fallen on both the British and the Boer sides, regimental monuments of stone and individual gravesites scattered here and there, some marked with simple tablets such as 'Here lies a brave British soldier known unto God.' It is a peaceful hill now, empty and quiet, the opposite of its atmosphere in January 1900.

After the battle of Spion Kop Churchill took a few days' leave to go down to Government House in Pietermaritzburg to see his brother Jack who was coming out to take up his subaltern's commission in the South African Light Horse, and his mother who was arriving on the SS *Maine*, an American hospital ship for which she had helped raise £41,597 as chairman of the American Ladies' Hospital Ship Fund. The ship, a private venture, was 'lent to the British government for use in the Transvaal War' by Bernard N. Baker, President of the Atlantic Transport Company and was fitted out as a hospital ship by Messrs Fletcher, Son & Fearnall, Ltd., of London in 1899.[37] It sailed from Britain on 23 December 1899 and, after stopping in Cape Town, was anchored in Durban harbour. It served as a floating hospital and on 17 March 1900, it left on its return voyage to England as a transport carrying several hundred wounded troops home.

Following the withdrawal from Spion Kop, the Natal army remained in camp for a week south of Spearman's Hill resting, recuperating and receiving 2,400 infantry replacements plus two squadrons of the 14th Hussars and additional guns. As the mounted forces were augmented, they were divided into two brigades. The 1st Cavalry Brigade under Lt Colonel John F. Burn-Murdoch consisted of the regular army cavalry units – the Royal Dragoons, the 13th Hussars, the 14th Hussars and 'A' Battery of

Royal Horse Artillery from India. The 2nd Cavalry Brigade, under Lord Dundonald, consisted of the irregular cavalry units – the South African Light Horse (300 men), Thorneycroft's Mounted Infantry (300 men), a composite regiment including elements of the Imperial Light Horse and the Natal Carbineers (270 men) and a Colt gun company of four machine guns. Lord Dundonald named Captain Hubert Gough to command the composite regiment calling him 'a most capable officer'.[38]

Buller's next plan to force the Tugela river was but a variation of the previous attempts. Unsuccessful in his attacks on the centre and the right end of the Boer line facing Potgeiter's Drift, he now planned to assault what he perceived to be the left end of the position. The plan was for a strong demonstration against the Boer line at Brakfontein north of the drift starting on 5 February followed by a multi-brigade attack on the Vaal Krantz Ridge two miles to the east. If the infantry managed to take the positions and bring guns upon the ridge and into action, their success would then be exploited by the 1st Cavalry Brigade which would charge into Ladysmith. The 2nd Cavalry Brigade's role was to guard the right and rear of the advancing infantry. They moved down toward the Tugela below the summit of Spearman's Hill where they spent the night without their baggage which was left in camp so as not to impede their advance next morning. Except for some shelling by the Boer guns, it was an uneventful night for the South African Light Horse but it was cold and damp by the river. As Churchill recorded in *My Early Life*: 'Colonel Byng and I shared a blanket. When he turned over I was in the cold. When I turned over I pulled the blanket off him and he objected. He was the Colonel. It was not a good arrangement. I was glad when morning came.'[39]

In the event, the attack at Vaal Krantz did not succeed and the cavalry was not employed. Once again the Boer rifles and cannon were effective in halting the British advance; and the British guns, though greater in number, were unable to silence them. Again the British attempt to take and hold the ridges failed, hundreds of casualties were suffered, and on 7 February Buller ordered a withdrawal south of the river. It was the third repulse in a month and the fourth overall if the battle of Colenso is counted. With the SALH providing flank security between the river and the infantry columns, the entire army then moved back to its camps along the Natal railway at Frere and Chieveley from where it had started a month before, arriving on 11 February.

Having failed to force the Tugela in the Boer centre along the railway at Colenso in December and on the Boer right in the area around Potgeiter's

Drift in January and February, it now occurred to General Buller to try the Boer left to the east of the railway. He would find the true left flank of the Boer defences after all and the South African Light Horse would have a role to play in the battles ahead. The area east of Colenso features a series of hills and ridges. Five miles to the south-east is Hussar Hill. North-east at a distance of two miles and four miles lie Hlangwane Hill and Green Hill, along which were placed the Boer entrenchments. In an arc from the north-east to the east at a distance of five and a half miles are Monte Cristo ridge and, connected by a nek (neck, or saddle), is Cingolo, a hill which was the true right flank of the Boer position south of the Tugela River.

On 12 February 1900 Buller ordered a reconnaissance of Hussar Hill five miles east of the railway by Dundonald's cavalry brigade. Both Lts Churchill took part with the South African Light Horse, this being the first action for Winston's brother Jack. The hill was south of the enemy lines and the Boer patrols were pushed back so that Buller and his staff could come up to survey the scene to the north and west. Hussar Hill was the highest ground opposite Hlangwani, Monte Cristo and Cingolo and thus was the best place for observation. At about one in the afternoon and after the staff had departed, the cavalry were ordered to withdraw and return to their camp at Stuart's Farm. They left the hill without incident but came under fire from it when riding out. Churchill described what happened next in *My Early Life*:

> I was by now a fairly experienced young officer and I could often feel danger impending from this quarter or from that, as you might feel a light breeze on your cheek or neck. When one rode for instance within rifle shot of some hill or watercourse about which we did not know enough, I used to feel a draughty sensation. On this occasion as I looked back over my shoulder from time to time at Hussar Hill or surveyed the large brown masses of our rearmost squadrons riding so placidly home across the rolling veldt, I remarked to my companion, 'We are still much too near those fellows.' The words were hardly out of my mouth when a shot rang out, followed by the rattle of magazine fire from two or three hundred Mauser rifles. A hail of bullets whistled among our squadrons, emptying a few saddles and bringing down a few horses. Instinctively our whole cavalcade spread out into open order and scampered over the crest now nearly two hundred yards away. Here we leapt off our horses, which were hurried into cover, threw ourselves on the grass, and returned the fire with an answering roar and rattle.[40]

At a range of about 2,000 yards the light horsemen returned fire with rifles and their Colt machine guns and a hot exchange ensued. As Churchill was passing along the line on foot he saw his brother Jack lying on the ground, having at that very moment been shot through the calf by a Boer bullet. As Churchill wrote in his 15 February letter to the *Morning Post*:

> It was his baptism of fire, and I have since wondered at the strange caprice which strikes down one man in his first skirmish and protects another time after time. But I suppose all pitchers will get broken in the end.[41]

His less elegant statement at the time was reported as, 'Jack, you silly ass. You've only been here five minutes and you've got yourself shot.'[42] The younger Lieutenant Churchill was only one of eight casualties sustained in the retirement from Hussar Hill. He was evacuated from the front for medical treatment and was out of action for a month, part of which was spent as a patient on the *Maine* under his mother's supervision. By the time he returned to the regiment, the garrison at Ladysmith had already been relieved.

Buller's final drive toward Ladysmith began on 14 February 1900, with a successful attack on Hussar Hill led by the South African Light Horse. Artillery was promptly moved into position on the summit. The plan was to turn the Boer right flank, the end of their defensive line east of Colenso. If the British could seize Hlangwane Hill to the northeast of and overlooking Colenso it would render the Boer position indefensible and so open the way, at long last, to Ladysmith. To Churchill's mind this was the plan that should have been pursued in the first place.[43]

On 15–16 February more artillery was moved up and entrenched and the infantry and supply train moved from Chieveley in preparation for the general attack which began two hours before dawn on the 17th when sixty-six artillery pieces opened their barrage on the Boer positions. As the infantry began their attack on the Cingolo ridge-line from the west, the 2nd Cavalry Brigade moved ten miles to the east in an effort to locate and assault the Boers' far left flank. They rode through rough country and climbed up the eastern side of Cingolo through vegetation so dense they had to dismount and ascend on foot. This time they had found the true left flank of the Boer line along the Tugela river which was lightly defended and without defensive artillery or machine gun emplacements. By 11.00 a.m. the first two squadrons had reached the summit and by the end of the day the cavalry squadrons, in co-ordination with the British infantry attacking up the hill from the west, had cleared Cingolo of the enemy and had forced the Boer line north and back on to the Monte Cristo ridge-line. At 8.00 a.m. on the 18th the infantry, well supported by artillery, resumed its attack on Monte Cristo and by noon they had cleared the entire ridge of Boers at bayonet point at a cost of 100 casualties. In the meantime, the bulk of Dundonald's cavalry brigade had moved into a blocking position north and east of Monte Cristo ridge. Finding the position west of the ridge-line on Green Hill flanked and enfiladed, and with the British cavalry moving to their rear, the Boers began to retreat and Green Hill between Cingolo and Hlangwane Hill was taken the same day with little loss to the British. This two-day action was a dramatic success. From Monte Cristo ridge Churchill could see Ladysmith only eight miles away. As he wrote in his 19 February letter to the *Morning Post*: 'The victory of Monte Cristo revolutionised the situation in Natal. It has laid open a practicable road to Ladysmith.'[44]

On 19–20 February the British continued to roll up the Boers' Colenso position from its eastern flank. The taking of Hlangwane Hill and consolidation of the British positions on the ridges east of Colenso and the placement of heavy guns there rendered Colenso untenable and it was taken without resistance. By nightfall on the 20th the entire area south of the Tugela was in British hands and the Boer main defensive line was shifted three miles north of the river to a series of hills south of Pieters.

Now, at the moment when the combination of frontal attack, effective artillery support and rapid flanking cavalry movements was bringing rapid success at relatively little cost in casualties and, indeed, promised to continue to roll-up and capture the Boers' hilltop positions from the east, a most curious, and in retrospect, indefensible decision was taken by General Buller. He decided to move the main attack from his right along Monte Cristo ridge to his left along the Natal Railway line through and against a difficult series of gorges, hills and spurs. He gave up the advantages of high ground and manoeuvre for an intense and bloody engagement that would last a week. He apparently made the decision in the belief that the Boers were in full retreat and would abandon Pieters as they had Colenso.[45] His miscalculation would cost his army dearly as once again he was sending them in a frontal attack against a well-entrenched enemy. 'The purblind viciousness of these manoeuvres was apparent to many,' Churchill later wrote.[46] As the battle began he interviewed a staff officer who opined, 'I don't like the situation; there are more of them than we expected. We have come down off our high ground. We have taken all the big guns off the big hills. We are getting ourselves cramped up among these kopjes in the valley of the Tugela. It will be like being in the Coliseum and shot at by every row of seats.'[47]

On 21 February the infantry began its advance across the Tugela toward the Boer positions. Due to the relatively close quarters of the area through which the advance was to be made, this would be an infantry-only battle. The cavalry were left to wait upon the success of the foot soldiers and the South African Light Horse were camped on the nek between Cingolo and Monte Cristo. The battle raged all day on the 22nd with the British taking a series of low kopjes between the Tugela and the Boer lines and the Boers counter-attacking at dusk as Churchill observed the action from Hlangwane Hill through his telescope. The fighting went on through the night of 22–23 February and the cavalry crossed the river to join them in the morning, being held in reserve at Fort Wylie just north of Colenso. The town of Pieters, the last obstacle between the British and Ladysmith, was protected on the south by a line of entrenchments and positions extending four miles west and a mile and a half east of the railway. The line was anchored on three hills – Inniskilling Hill which was three-quarters of a mile west of the railway, Railway Hill, which was a quarter-mile west of the line, and Barton's Hill, a mile to the east. The infantry would attack these from west to east, or left to right. As the attack on Inniskilling Hill began at 4.00 p.m. on the 23rd Churchill rode up alone to observe proceedings with General Neville Lyttelton from a vantage point about a mile behind the battle line. As the infantry of the Irish Brigade made its way on to open ground to assault the hill, Churchill reported:

> Then at once above the average fusillade and cannonade rose the extraordinary rattling roll of Mauser musketry in great volume. If the reader wishes to know exactly what this is like he must drum the fingers of both his hands on a wooden table, one after the other as quickly and as hard as he can.[48]

The fighting went on all evening into the darkness but the British were unable to dislodge the Boers from the hill. Of the 1,200 assaulting troops Churchill recorded that two colonels, three majors, twenty other officers and 600 men had fallen.[49]

Churchill returned to his regiment's bivouac for the night and at dawn on the morning of the 24th rode ahead with Captain Brooke to observe the scene. Just as they reached the place from which Churchill had watched the fighting the previous evening, a shrapnel shell burst in the air directly above them with a loud crash and sprayed shell fragments all around them. Although Churchill and Brooke and their mounts were unscathed, eight men were killed or wounded by the single shell. Two more shells arrived within a couple of minutes, wounding eleven others. Later in the day he wrote in a letter to Pamela Plowden, 'I am safe – preserved by my strange luck, or the favour of Heaven – which you will – perhaps because I am to be of use ... I was vy nearly killed two hours ago by a shrapnel. But though I was in the full burst of it God preserved me ... I wonder whether we shall get through and whether I shall live to see the end ... The war is vy bitter but I trust we shall not show ourselves less determined than the enemy. My nerves were never better and I think I care less for bullets every day.'[50] By the end of the day Buller realised that the attack was a failure and withdrew the big guns back to Hlangwane Hill and Monte Cristo ridge. The wagons were withdrawn on the 25th and by the 26th many of the troops were pulled back from the area of the railway south of the Pieters position and redeployed for a renewed attack from the east where they had been a week earlier. Certain infantry brigades were left to occupy the low kopjes between the Tugela and Inniskilling Hill to be available to co-ordinate with the next attack. It had taken Buller three days to get them back out with little gain to show for it.

On 26 February the two sides exchanged artillery fire and the British prepared for the next attack which would begin on the 27th – Majuba Day. The cavalry had little to do for the past week except for patrolling and waiting. As was customary, the officers exchanged visits. As Lord Dundonald recorded in his memoirs, on the evening of 26 February:

> I walked over to see Colonel Byng at the bivouac of the S. A. L. H., and in the course of conversation he laughed and said: 'I must tell you what Winston said this evening.' Colonel Byng went on: 'Winston said he wanted to get the D. S. O., as it would look so nice on the robes of the Chancellor of the Exchequer.' He added: 'I told him he must first get into Parliament, if he could get any constituency to have him!'[51]

In fact, Churchill's mind had not been solely occupied with military matters. As early as 14 January 1900, he had been contacted by the Conservative Party agent for the Southport division and offered their nomination as a candidate for Parliament. Although he cabled back that he would be unable to decide from Natal he had the possibility in mind all that spring. By 1 May he had also received an offer to stand for election again for Oldham and would accept it.[52] At the same time he was participating in his regiment's actions, corresponding with Conservative Party agents and writing his column for the *Morning Post*, he was also considering offers for a post-war lecture tour in Great Britain and the United States, arranging for his newspaper articles to be published in book form, negotiating through his literary agent, A. P. Watt, to sell articles to American magazines, and even contemplating writing a play about South Africa. As it turned out, he achieved all he set out to do, except that the play was never written.

The South African Light Horse had moved their camp from the Cingolo–Monte Cristo nek on 26 February to a position between the ridge and the Tugela river gorge on the north end of the Hlangwane plateau. It was an excellent vantage point from which to watch the coming battle. As Churchill remarked, 'It was like a stage scene viewed from the dress circle.'[53] The co-ordinated attack began on the morning of the 27th with a large volume of artillery, machine-gun and rifle fire directed against what was later named Barton's Hill from Monte Cristo ridge to the east and Hlangwane Hill to the south. The attack by Barton's brigade of infantry began at 10.00 a.m. and by noon the hill, which subsequently bore his name, was taken. The Boers put up little opposition due in no small part to the deadly hostile fire raining down on them from Monte Cristo ridge, only a mile and a quarter away. Soon after, Kitchener's brigade of infantry commenced its attack on Railway Hill from the south, aided by the British artillery and now rifle fire from Barton's Hill. The attack on Inniskilling Hill was resumed by Hart's brigade and the Lancashire Brigade, supported by every British gun that could be brought to bear. Facing enfilading fire and co-ordinated assaults on their front and flank, the Boer commandos abandoned their trenches and withdrew to the north. In a single day the Natal army had captured all the key hills of the Pieters position – which task had earlier frustrated them for an entire week. The last natural barrier and entrenched Boer positions between the British on the Tugela and the British in Ladysmith had fallen.

Observing that the artillery was now firing north of the three hills and hearing the cheers of the infantry all along the British line, the cavalry brigade was ordered to mount up and moved toward the pontoon bridge over the Tugela, fully expecting to pursue the fleeing Boers. But Buller met them at the bridge and forbade them to cross for fear they would lose too many horses and men to the enemy artillery that was covering the Boer retreat. The cavalry then returned to its bivouac. That evening Churchill was sent as a galloper from Dundonald to warn the naval battery sited on Monte Cristo to be prepared for a counter-attack on Barton's brigade during the night. From the ridge he was able to observe the flashes of Boer cannon and pom-poms in the distance before he returned to his regiment. He recorded his thoughts that evening for the *Morning Post*:

We got neither food nor blankets that night, and slept in our waterproofs on the ground; but we had at last that which was better than feast or couch, for which we had hungered and longed through many weeks, which had been thrice forbidden us, and which was all the more splendid since it had been so long delayed – Victory.[54]

On the morning of 28 February the cavalry crossed the Tugela to put out patrols toward Pieters and Churchill went to Inniskilling Hill to inspect the abandoned Boer trenches. He found them knee-deep in expended cartridges and also came across boxes of dum-dum bullets of a type sufficient to kill big game. The Natal army's pursuit of the Boers was cautious and deliberate, even though the area north of Pieters was fairly open, because of delaying rifle and artillery fire from the Boers. The British expected every kopje and every spruit to be defended as had often been the case in the past. Dundonald's brigade led the way with Captain Hubert Gough in command of the advance guard of one squadron from the Imperial Light Horse and one from the Natal Carbineers. Although everyone was eager to be the first to arrive and lift the siege, progress was remarkably slow. It took several hours to pass through the Pieters position and for Dundonald to order the advance.

Captain Gough, whose brother Johnnie of the Rifle Brigade was among the soldiers besieged in Ladysmith, found the delays inexplicable and recorded in his memoir: 'There were no signs of "dash" and rapidity in Dundonald's movements, no indication that we were in hot pursuit of a defeated enemy.'[55] The afternoon passed in overcoming the Boer rearguard but Gough advanced steadily with little loss. There is considerable discrepancy among the memoir writers as to the events of the late afternoon and early evening of 28 February. Dundonald recorded that he was exchanging messages with Gough and sometime after 3.00 p.m. had sent the following to him: 'Push on toward Ladysmith, I am supporting.'[56] Then, coming up to a large hill with difficult approaches between his brigade and the town, realising that darkness was fast approaching, and not knowing the numbers or location of the Boers, Dundonald ordered a halt. He decided that he and the staff would ride up to join Gough but that Colonel Thorneycroft would take the brigade to Nelthorpe to bivouac for the night. He reported that he then made a mad gallop of six miles into Ladysmith accompanied by his staff – Major Birdwood, Lieutenants Clowes and Churchill and some orderlies – and reached Ladysmith 'some few minutes' after Gough in time to be greeted by General Sir George White and his staff, with whom he and Churchill dined at 7.00 p.m.[57]

Churchill was with Dundonald when the order to halt was given and when the general received Gough's message that the way was clear to Ladysmith. He reported in the 9 March dispatch to the *Morning Post* that he joined Dundonald in the gallop into Ladysmith which they reached within an hour. He added that as they reached the picket line a sentry challenged, 'Halt, who goes there?' and that his party replied, 'The Ladysmith Relief Column'. Then, having caught up with Gough, he watched as the Natal Carbineers and Imperial Light Horse, formed up side-by-side in a column of twos and with Gough at their head, marched into town in an orderly fashion to be greeted by General White. Churchill dined that evening with Generals Sir George White, Sir Ian Hamilton, and Sir Archibald Hunter, noting, 'Never before had I sat in such brave company nor stood so close to a great event.'[58] No mention was made in his dispatch of Dundonald or Gough being invited to dinner. In *My Early Life* Churchill tells the story in a more abbreviated form but wrongly recalls that he made the ride into Ladysmith with two squadrons of South African Light Horse, who in fact were bivouacked six miles away at the time. [59] Major Birdwood recorded in his memoirs that it was he, Dundonald, Churchill and Clowes who 'joined in a great gallop, never to be forgotten: a mad gallop right into Ladysmith'. He recalled greeting General White at his headquarters just as it was getting dark.[60]

Gough's memoir states the Dundonald was not in close touch with him during the day of the 28th and that except for Gough's two squadrons of advance scouts the 2nd Cavalry Brigade advanced no more than three and a half miles that day before they made camp at Nelthorpe six miles from Ladysmith. Dundonald and his staff never came forward during the afternoon and Gough only mentions one message from the general, 'to retire at once'. Gough's advance toward Ladysmith was not much impeded either by Boer firing or the terrain and he doubted the very existence of the steep hill reported by Dundonald, so Gough disregarded Dundonald's order to retire and made his way to the Intombi hospital three miles southeast of the town by 5.30 in the afternoon, and formed up his troopers for an orderly ride into the town at a walk. At this time he also sent a message back to Dundonald that he was inside the Ladysmith perimeter and was proceeding at once into town. When Gough's columns entered the town they were greeted by General Sir George White and a dozen generals and staff officers. According to Gough, White's only words at this historic moment were, 'Hello, Hubert, how are you?' As they proceeded to White's headquarters at Budleigh House, crowds of townspeople surrounded them and urged the general to make a speech. He made brief remarks which,

Gough recalled, ended with the phrase, 'Thank God, we kept the old Flag flying.' Gough wrote that about 8.00 p.m.:

We had begun dinner when the door suddenly opened and Dundonald and Winston Churchill burst in, considerably heated and somewhat excited after their long gallop of about six miles – for Dundonald must have been in or near Nelthorpe when my message reached him, telling him that I was already inside the Ladysmith defences, and was going straight into town. He and Churchill at once decided they must come in too; and leaving his brigade without any orders, Dundonald started, accompanied by Churchill, to gallop after me in the hope of being present at my meeting with Sir George White. It must have taken them a good hour to get into Ladysmith, galloping on indifferent ponies over what was, at times, pretty rough going, and a good deal of scrub and almost in the dark.[61]

Given the time it would take for Gough's messenger to ride from Intombi to Dundonald's position, for Dundonald to decide to ride on, and then actually to gallop into Ladysmith, it is unlikely that he and Churchill rode into town with Gough or can properly claim to have done so. Certainly a correspondent of Churchill's calibre would have reported Sir George White's remarks for his paper if he had been there to hear them. In any event, Churchill was present on the day that Ladysmith was relieved from its 118-day siege and arrived there in time for dessert.

On 1 March Dundonald rode back to advise General Buller of the situation and Churchill returned to the 2nd Brigade bivouac with Gough's squadrons. The Boers were in full retreat to the north except for their usual rearguards, and the way into Ladysmith from the south was open for a general advance by the Natal army. Buller's orders for the day on 1 March were:

The Force will move in the direction of Ladysmith; 1st Cavalry Brigade (Burn-Murdoch) covering the right front and right flank of the advance; the 2nd Cavalry Brigade (Dundonald) the left front and left flank. Each Brigade will detach a squadron as rear-guard to the whole Force.[62]

Pursuant to this order the South African Light Horse did not participate in General Buller's formal entry into Ladysmith on 3 March when the infantry brigades paraded through the town, having taken two days to march less then ten miles. The regiment was out patrolling west and north along the slopes of the Drakensberg Mountains which separate Natal from the Orange Free State.

Churchill remained in Ladysmith and his letter of 10 March to the *Morning Post*, his last from Natal, describes the victory parade in great detail together with his inspection of the town and the British lines. His happiness to know that his friend, Ian Hamilton, had survived was offset by the news that his comrade and fellow-correspondent, George W. Steevens, had died of enteric fever during the siege.[63] Before he departed, Churchill was allowed an extended interview with Sir George White. The general defended his actions that had led to the siege of Ladysmith and the encirclement of almost all of the British troops present in Natal at the outset of the war. It was necessary to defend the town, he said, because it controlled an important junction of the Natal railway and because it was a major supply depot with huge stores of munitions that he could not allow to be captured by the Boers. And, once surrounded, he had no choice but to defend Ladysmith. Although the Boers had succeeded in isolating White's army, the siege of Ladysmith had turned out to be a strategic failure. With so many men tied up in the siege, they lacked the numbers to capture the capital of Natal, Pietermaritzburg, to raid widely in Natal, or to prevent the debarkation of Buller's relief corps at Durban. Although White was generous in granting the interview, he had mixed feelings about Churchill, as illustrated by an anecdote related by Captain Douglas Gilfillan of the Imperial Light Horse who was with Sir George and a group of officers in Ladysmith soon after the relief:

> A young officer came up to the group: with a good deal of sang-froid and not much ceremony he made his way through the group until he faced the general, and in a very audible voice at once engaged him in a short conversation, then went off. An older officer said to Sir George 'Who on earth is that?' He answered 'That's Randolph Churchill's son Winston: I don't like the fellow, but he'll be Prime Minister of England one day.'[64]

The siege of Ladysmith and Buller's campaign to lift it were costly. The series of actions to relieve Ladysmith cost 300 officers and 5,000 men killed or wounded out of a force of 23,000 British soldiers, a loss of about twenty percent. The losses in the two weeks fighting in the second half of February were about ten percent of those engaged including two generals, six colonels in command of regiments, 105 lower-ranking officers and 1,511 other ranks. Among the regiments in Dundonald's 2nd Cavalry Brigade, Churchill reported that the South African Light Horse, Thorney-croft's Mounted Infantry and the single squadron of Imperial Light Horse all lost just under a quarter of their numbers.[65] A marble tablet at All Saints Church, which still stands in Ladysmith, lists the names of the war dead including the men of the South African Light Horse under the badge of the regiment.[66]

There is no doubt that Buller's Natal army was tired by the end of February and that the troops liberated in Ladysmith were much weakened by malnutrition, inaction and illness. Yet what Buller did next was viewed by many serving officers as a serious mistake. He did nothing. He failed to pursue the Boer forces which then withdrew to the Drakensberg Mountains that separated Natal from the Orange Free State. Instead, he set up a series of encampments for his troops and was content to send patrols to the areas west, north and east of Ladysmith for the next two months. His army did not take the offensive to clear the rest of Natal of the Boers or when finally ordered to do so, move into the Boer republics to link up with General Lord Roberts until May. By that time Churchill would be long gone. As he later wrote of the situation in Natal after the relief of Ladysmith: 'All this might be war, but it was not journalism.'[67] He realized that the main events in Natal were at an end and that the real scene of action, and the most newsworthy events for his newspaper, had shifted to Lord Roberts's campaign then in progress in the Orange Free State.

Churchill spent most of March in Natal, dividing his time between Ladysmith and Durban. He visited Lady Randolph and Jack Churchill on the *Maine* in Durban harbour and wrote the last five letters that would soon be published as *From London to Ladysmith via Pretoria* from Durban between 4 and 10 March. He was back in Ladysmith on 21–22 March and wrote letters to his mother and to Pamela Plowden from there. During this time Churchill also wrote a letter to the editor of the *Natal Witness* which was printed in the 29 March 1900 edition and which drew a good deal of attention to Churchill, much of it unfavourable.[68] The letter, clearly intended for publication, was an appeal to the people of Natal to show magnanimity to the defeated enemy, a theme to which Churchill would often return in later years. In the letter he declared that the spirit of revenge was both 'morally wicked' and 'practically foolish'. The goal of British policy was simple – victory. The road to 'an honourable and lasting peace' was the defeat of the Boer armies and the annexation of the Transvaal and the Orange Free State by Britain. But, Churchill wrote, it was also important 'to make it easy for the enemy to accept defeat' by allowing Boers to surrender and return to their homes and farms without punishment except for reasonable reparations and restrictions on their civil rights. To do the opposite, to imprison them or try them for treason, would be to prolong the war and make more difficult the post-war goal of peaceful British and Dutch communities living together in South Africa under British rule. He warned, 'Beware of driving men to desperation. Even a cornered rat is dangerous. We desire a speedy peace and the last thing in the world we want is that this war should enter upon a guerrilla phase.'[69]

On 29 March Churchill took leave of the South African Light Horse, still retaining his commission.[70] He took the train from Ladysmith, through Colenso and Chieveley, past the scene of the armoured train fight, through Pietermaritzburg to Durban where he boarded the *Guelph* for East London in Cape Colony. From there he took a train to Stormberg where he was told that Roberts would not begin the next phase of his offensive for two weeks. Rather than sit and wait, Churchill soon departed for Cape Town which was forty-eight hours and 700 miles away to the south-west. In Cape Town he interviewed Sir Alfred Milner and other political figures, rode to the hounds with the Duke of Westminster for sport and enjoyed the comforts of the Mount Nelson Hotel which he made his base of operations. It was surely a luxury, after three months on campaign in the veldt; it was the newest and one of the best of the city's hotels.[71] Here also he fought a brief struggle to have his *Morning Post* application approved so that he could be accredited to Lord Roberts's army.

Lord Frederick Sleigh Roberts had been awarded the VC during the Indian Mutiny and was now Commander-in-Chief of all British forces in South Africa. He had been offended by Churchill's nineteenth letter published in the *Morning Post* in which he had strongly criticised an army chaplain for a weak sermon to the troops after Spion Kop and the Army Chaplain Corps for not sending their best men to the war zone.[72] Roberts, a man of deep religious faith, had read the article and not forgotten it. In addition, the appearance at that time of the plea for magnanimity letter in the *Natal Witness* certainly came to the attention of Roberts and his staff, one more example of the self-assured and outspoken Lt Churchill never being shy at publicising his thoughts far beyond his superiors. Finally, Roberts's Chief-of-Staff was General Lord Kitchener, the man whom Churchill had strongly criticised in *The River War*, which had been published only six months earlier on 6 November 1899. Fortunately for Churchill, he had two influential friends on Roberts's staff – General Ian Hamilton and General Sir William Nicholson who had formerly been on General Lockhart's staff on the Tirah Field Force in India. Both were old friends of Roberts and their lobbying on Churchill's behalf, together with that of the Colonial Secretary, Joseph Chamberlain, won Churchill his accreditation. On 11 April Roberts's staff wired Churchill, 'My dear Churchill, Lord Roberts desires me to say that he is willing to permit you to accompany this force as a correspondent –

for your father's sake.[73] Roberts had been a 'great friend' of Lord Randolph who, as Secretary of State for India in 1885, had assisted him in getting appointed to command the Indian army.[74] Churchill soon headed for the front by train, arriving at Mounted Infantry headquarters at Bethany in the Orange Free State by 13 April and at the capital of Bloemfontein by the 16th.

Lord Roberts had arrived in Cape Town from England on 10 January. Since 'Black Week' the British forces had gone no farther than the Modder river along the Western Railway and Colesberg on the Central Railway. While Buller was battling difficult terrain and the bulk of the Boer forces in northern Natal, Roberts gathered a substantial force and carefully planned for his new offensive from Cape Colony into the Orange Free State which would begin in the early morning hours of 11 February. The concept of the offensive might be seen as a massive flanking attack not only in the strategic sense that it would operate in the western part of the Orange Free State in conjunction with Buller's approach toward its eastern border but also in the tactical sense; rather than advance straight up the Central Railway from Colesberg toward Bloemfontein or on the Western Railway toward Kimberley through Magersfontein, he would move east from Modder river station away from the railway and directly across open country to the Orange Free State's capital, completely avoiding the Boers' prepared defensive positions. The Boers never expected the British army to leave the lines of advance along the railways because of the enormous amount of material that Roberts would need to sustain his army.

Lord Roberts's force numbered approximately 37,000 men including 18,000 infantry and 7,795 cavalry accompanied by a huge number of mule and oxen-drawn wagons to carry all the food, water, fodder, ammunition and equipment necessary to support them.[75] As the main columns moved east along the Modder river, the cavalry division under Major General John French liberated Kimberley in a daring cavalry attack on 15 February. Between 17 and 27 February Roberts's troops caught up with the main Boer force in the Western Orange Free State under Piet Cronje and after several days of attacks and bombardment of its laager forced it to surrender at Paardeberg on the 27th. In the series of actions around Paardeberg the Boers lost 117 killed and 2,700 men from the Transvaal and 1,400 from the Orange Free State taken prisoner. The British losses were 300 killed and 1,000 wounded, but these were far smaller in percentage than those of the Boers which were equivalent to ten per cent of their entire army. In the days following Cronje's surrender, the Boers retreated, abandoning their prepared positions fifteen miles to the east at

Poplar Grove, fought a one-day delaying action near Driefontein, and finally evacuated their commandos from the capital of Orange Free State which Roberts entered and occupied on 13 March 1900. On arrival he sent a telegram to Queen Victoria: 'The British flag now flies over the Presidency vacated last evening by Mr Steyn, late President of the Orange Free State.'[76] President Steyn and his Cabinet moved to Kroonstad, one hundred miles to the north-east on the Central Railway.

Between 13 March and the start of the next phase of the offensive on 3 May, Roberts's forces in and around Bloemfontein received reinforcements and resupply, and rested both men and horses. At the same time, they fought a series of skirmishes with the highly mobile and daring Boer commandos. Several of these forays were offensive in nature intended to capture or to destroy the Boer forces or at least drive them out of the Free State and into the Transvaal to the north and so protect the British lines of communication and supply. Other actions were defensive as Boer columns under Christiaan de Wet began to employ hit-and-run tactics to disrupt British supply lines and to harass its flanks. Although this, the third phase of the war, the British second offensive, would not end until September 1900, the fourth phase, an overlapping period of guerrilla warfare, began in March 1900 and would not end until the final peace agreement was signed over two years later. Such was the situation when Churchill arrived at Bloemfontein on 16 April.

Churchill soon learned that his cousin, Sunny, the Ninth Duke of Marlborough and a captain in the Imperial Yeomanry, was attached to Lord Roberts's staff as assistant military secretary and that his former commander in the 4th Hussars, General John Brabazon, was then in command of a brigade of Imperial Yeomanry, mounted infantry volunteers recently arrived from England. He resolved to join Brabazon who was part of the five-brigade force trying to clear the Boers from what Churchill described as 'the whole of the right-hand bottom corner of the Free State'. [77] He left Bloemfontein on 17 April and, travelling by train and wagon via Edenburg and Reddersburg, caught up with the British column on the night of the 19th eleven miles west of Dewetsdorp and joined Brabazon's brigade the next day. From this time until his departure from South Africa Churchill was often under fire since it was his duty as a war correspondent to follow the sound of the guns. As he wrote in *My Early Life*:

Equipped by the *Morning Post* on a munificent scale with whatever good horses and transport were necessary, I moved rapidly this way and that from column to column, wherever there was a chance of fighting. Riding sometimes quite alone across wide stretches of doubtful country, I would arrive at the rear guard of a British column actually lapped about by the enemy in the enormous plains, stay with them three or four days if the General was well disposed, and then dart back across a landscape charged with silent menace to keep up a continuous stream of letters and telegrams to my newspaper.[78]

Indeed, it was an intense, even dangerous experience. Writing to his Aunt Leonie a month later, he said: 'I have had so many adventures that I shall be glad of a little peace and security. I have been under fire now in forty separate affairs, in this country alone.'[79]

On 22 April 1900, Churchill attached himself to Montmorency's Scouts, then commanded by Angus McNeill (who had provided sketches to illustrate *The River War*), who were on the move to locate the left flank of the Boer position before Dewetsdorp.[80] At one point they raced toward a kopje only to find the Boers had got there first. No sooner had McNeill ordered a withdrawal at the gallop than Boer bullets started flying about. Churchill's horse was frightened by the gunfire and bolted when he tried to mount, leaving him on foot, out in the open in easy range of the enemy Mausers, a mile or more from cover and some 200 yards from most of the other men. As he wrote in his account of the event for the *Morning Post*: 'I turned, and for the second time in this war, ran for my life on foot from the Boer marksmen, and I thought to myself, "Here at last I take it." '[81] Then, fortuitously and quite unexpectedly, a single scout rode up from Churchill's left, stopped, offered him a stirrup and, with Churchill behind him on the saddle, galloped to the safety of another kopje. Churchill later recorded their words during the wild ride under fire:

'Don't be frightened,' said my rescuer; 'they won't hit you.' Then, as I did not reply, 'My poor horse, oh, my poor – horse; shot with an explosive bullet. The devils! But their hour will come. Oh, my poor horse!'
I said, 'Never mind, you've saved my life.'
'Ah,' he rejoined, 'but it's the horse I'm thinking about.' That was the whole of our conversation.[82]

It was a great escape: Churchill later wrote to his mother, 'I do not think I have ever been so near destruction.'[83]

The scout who saved Churchill's life was Trooper Clement Roberts of Montmorency's Scouts. He was thought by some to be worthy of the Victoria Cross for the rescue but instead received a mention in Lord Roberts's dispatch of 2 April 1901, and the Distinguished Conduct Medal.[84] The latter was the other ranks' equivalent of the Distinguished Service Order for officers, only one level below the Victoria Cross, and was awarded for 'distinguished conduct in the field'. The *London Gazette* notice makes reference to the recipients' 'gallant conduct during the operations in South Africa'.[85] Trooper Roberts was of the opinion he should have received the Victoria Cross and in 1906 corresponded with Churchill about it. He also had a local Justice of the Peace, R. J. Orpen, write to the British High Commissioner's Office in Johannesburg with a request to 'put him in the way to get the Victoria Cross – which is in itself a recommendation through life, and would help his family'.[86] Although it is not known whether Churchill contacted the War Office on his behalf, he did send a personal, handwritten letter to Clement Roberts on 10 December 1903, which stated in part:

I need not say that I have myself very great admiration for the coolness and courage with which you assisted me at Dewetsdorp. I have always felt that unless you had taken me up on your saddle, I should myself certainly have been killed or captured, and I spoke myself very strongly to General Rundle on your behalf.

I was very glad to see you had received the Distinguished Service Medal – a decoration of very great distinction and honour ...

I fear it would be quite impossible to get the Authorities to reconsider their decision about the Victoria Cross, so many men have done brave actions in the war and especially when so many of the mounted branches have picked up dismounted comrades, that the Authorities have found it difficult to discriminate among them. Unless the General in the field sends up a recommendation for the Victoria Cross, it is not possible for the War Office to award it; and at this distance of time, I do not think that Sir Leslie Rundle is likely to alter it. I do not see what grounds he would show for his change of mind.

The Victoria Cross is a decoration often very capriciously awarded and there is a great deal of chance in its distribution, but the Distinguished Service Medal is much prized and respected in the Army and you will no doubt find it a satisfactory memento of what was beyond all question, a very faithful and self-sacrificing action on your part.

Let me, at this distance of time once again thank you for the service you rendered me.

Yours very truly,
Winston S. Churchill[87]

By the first week in May 1900, Lord Roberts's force was finally ready to resume its march toward Pretoria, the capital of the Transvaal. He had under his command over 38,000 men, a third of them cavalry or mounted infantry, and more than one hundred guns. The army was divided into three columns and would advance north right up the route of the Central Railway. The centre column, commanded by Roberts, included the 7th Infantry Division under Lt Charles Tucker, the 11th Infantry Division under Lt General Reginald Pole-Carew, and a 4,000-man mounted infantry brigade under Major General E. T. H. Hutton. Lt General John French commanded a cavalry division of 4,500 men organised into three brigades which served as the left column. On the right of Roberts and the railway was Lt General Ian Hamilton's Mounted Infantry Division of approximately 16,000 men, 4,000 of them mounted and organised as follows:

Divisional Staff (Lieutenant General Ian Hamilton)
Divisional Troops – Rimington's Guides

2nd Mounted Infantry Brigade (Brigadier General R. Ridley)
2nd Mounted Infantry Corps (Lieutenant Colonel de Lisle)
6th M. I. Battalion
New South Wales Mounted Rifles
West Australians

5th Mounted Infantry Corps (Lieutenant Colonel Dawson)
5th M. I. Battalion
Roberts's Horse
Marshall's Horse
Ceylon M. I.

6th Mounted Infantry Corps (Lieutenant Colonel Legge)
2nd M. I. Battalion
Kitchener's Horse
Lovat's Scouts

7th Mounted Infantry Corps (Lieutenant Colonel Bainbridge)
7th M. I. Battalion
Burmah M. I.
P. Battery (Major Mercer, R. H. A.)
Ammunition Column
Bearer Company and Field Hospital

2nd Cavalry Brigade (Brigadier General Broadwood)
Household Cavalry
10th Lancers
12th Lancers
Q Battery, R. H. A.
Bearer Company and Field Hospital
Ammunition Column

19th Brigade (Major General Smith-Dorrien)
2nd Duke of Cornwall L. I.

Shropshire L. I.
Gordon Highlanders
Royal Canadians
74th Battery
Bearer Company and Field Hospital

21st Brigade (Major General Bruce-Hamilton)
1st Royal Sussex
1st Derbyshire Regiment
1st Cameron Highlanders
City Imperial Volunteers
76th Battery
Bearer Company and Field Hospital

Divisional Artillery (Lieutenant Colonel Waldron, R. H. A.)
81st Battery
82nd Battery
1 section of 5 inch guns
Ammunition Column

All told, Hamilton's column had thirty-six field guns, two five-inch guns, twenty-three machine guns and six pom-poms.[88] It was – and acted as if it were – almost an independent force.

Roberts's army was opposed by approximately 15,000 Boers with those from the Orange Free State under General Christiaan de Wet and those from Transvaal under Generals Louis Botha and Jacobus de la Rey. The Boers were no match for Roberts's force which employed the combination of rapid flanking movements by mounted troops and co-ordinated infantry attacks supported by effective artillery fire. The British advance was inexorable. In contrast to, the route of Roberts's army presented little in the way of natural obstacles and was suitable for cavalry movements. Roberts also faced fewer Boers than did Buller who had been opposed by approximately 25,000 of the enemy in Natal.

Churchill attached himself to Hamilton's column for the advance to Pretoria, often travelling with his cousin Sunny, the Duke of Marlborough, who had been appointed as an aide-de-camp to Hamilton. Churchill enjoyed his time with Ian Hamilton's force. He referred to it in *My Early Life* as 'a jolly march' and recalled: 'My wagon had a raised floor of deal boards beneath which reposed two feet of the best tinned provisions and alcoholic stimulants which London could supply. We had every comfort, and all day long I scampered about the moving cavalry screens searching in the carelessness of youth for every scrap of adventure, experience or copy.'[89] He and Marlborough shared not only the comforts of Churchill's larder but also the dangers of the campaign. In a letter to his mother near the end of the campaign he wrote: 'Sunny ... and I have listened to a good many bullets and shells together.'[90] One souvenir that survives from the South African War is a piece of shrapnel that Churchill kept on a window ledge in the study at his home, Chartwell in Kent. It was a gift from his cousin with a little plaque inscribed, 'This fragment of a 30 lb shrapnel shell fell between us and might have separated us for ever but is now a token of union.'[91]

Roberts's columns moved on a broad front, often as much as fifty or sixty miles wide, slowed as much by their own supply column and the exhausted horses of their mounted forces as by the harassing fire and rearguard actions of the Boers. Aside from a set-piece battle against 6,000 Boers when forcing the Sand river which cost about 250 casualties, the British faced little serious opposition. Roberts reached Kroonstadt on 12 May and occupied it without a fight. Then one after another Boer town was captured after brief battle or none at all – Thabanchu, Windburg, Ventersburg, Lindley, Heilbron. On 17 May Mafeking, on the far northern frontier of Cape Colony, was relieved, the last of the besieged towns to be liberated. This was accomplished by a flying column led by Lt Colonel Brian Mahon advancing up the Western Railway from Cape Colony in conjunction with a Rhodesian force under Lt Colonel Herbert Plumber coming down from Bechuanaland. Also in mid-May General Buller resumed his offensive in Natal, moving up the Natal Railway to approach the Transvaal from the south-east. The tide seemed to be receding for the Boer republics.

On 24 May Roberts ordered Hamilton to move from the right flank to the left which was accomplished with a crossing of the Vaal River on the 26th. By the 28th Roberts's army was formed up to a few miles from Johannesburg with French's and Hamilton's divisions on the south-west near Doornkop and Roberts to the south having captured the railway line between Germiston and Vereeniging. The Boers held a strong position on the south edge of the city on the main Rand ridge and the kopjes to the south of it. The action before Johannesburg was fought on 29 May 1900, with French's cavalry division moving west to seek the Boers' right flank and all of Hamilton's infantry attacking the kopjes in mid-afternoon with artillery support. Led by the kilted Gordon Highlanders, the British took the kopjes, which resulted in a general retreat of the Boer forces west of Johannesburg to the north towards Pretoria. In this action Churchill had another narrow escape as he and General Smith-Dorien were confronted at close quarters by Boer riflemen and made a hasty retreat as rifle bullets whizzed past them, one grazing a horse.[92]

On 30 May Hamilton's force took Florida on the Portchefstroom railway eight miles west of Johannesburg, with no resistance. There he stopped to gather provisions and await orders for the final assault on the city from Lord Roberts who was twelve miles south of Johannesburg. Although only twenty miles from Roberts's headquarters, Hamilton was out of touch with the commanding general and the city lay between them. He had already sent messengers to Roberts but their route going back south and then north again would take a considerable time to cover. On the evening of 30 May Hamilton's need to get dispatches to Roberts and Churchill's desire to send his reports to the *Morning Post* by the telegraph available at Roberts's headquarters came to a common resolution. Among the numerous civilians leaving the city and passing through the British lines was a Frenchman, M. Lautre, who offered to conduct Churchill on bicycles through Johannesburg to Roberts's lines south of the city. Churchill accepted, changed into civilian clothes, and with Hamilton's dispatches and his own in his pockets set out that afternoon. It was an enterprise not without risk for there were Boer soldiers in the city in unknown numbers. As Churchill wrote in his memoir, 'According to all the laws of war my situation, if arrested, would have been disagreeable. I was an officer holding a commission in the South African Light Horse, disguised in plain clothes and secretly within the enemy's lines. No court-martial that ever sat in Europe would have had much difficulty in disposing of such a case. On all these matters I was quite well informed.'[93] The pair made it through the city, conversing in French when Boers passed by them on the streets, and reached Roberts's headquarters by 10.30 p.m. Churchill was ushered in to see Lord Roberts and after delivering Hamilton's dispatches gave an account of Hamilton's action the previous day and reported his own observations that the Boers were clearing out of Johannesburg. Roberts gave him a friendly reception, his eyes twinkling when Churchill told the general how he had got there.[94]

Their close proximity to the city on the west and the south and the strength of Roberts's army caused the civil authorities to confer with the British. Their offer to surrender the city and its gold mines intact in exchange for a twenty-four hour truce was accepted by Roberts on 30 May. The surrender allowed the British to capture Johannesburg without further fighting but it also enabled the Boers to withdraw without interference, taking with them all their artillery, their ammunition reserves and wagons, and all the available gold from the Rand mines. The Boer army escaped without loss, hurried but intact. Although the truce made sense at the time as a way to avoid further casualties and the ruin of the gold mines, Roberts's decision to grant the truce has since been criticised as a serious strategic misjudgment that might have prolonged the war. After a two-day halt for rest and replenishment during which the Boers continued to retreat the twenty-five miles north to Pretoria and beyond, Roberts renewed his advance on 3 June. Again the army moved in three columns with French's cavalry division on the left, Hamilton's mounted infantry division in the centre and the main army under Roberts on the right. They met little opposition on 3 June and next day the cavalry made broad flanking movements on both flanks while the artillery bombarded the Boer forts on the city outskirts. The Boer artillery did not respond because it already had been removed. The Johannesburg truce had also given a twenty-four hour breathing space for Pretoria and again the Boer forces escaped with all their guns, munitions and equipment.

By 5.30 p.m. on 4 June, the fighting was over. Orders were given to renew the advance at dawn but before midnight the civil authorities contacted Lord Roberts and surrendered the city. On the morning of 5 June, Roberts sent an advance guard under General Pole-Carew to go to the city centre and arrange for a victory parade to be staged that afternoon. Churchill and Marlborough followed close on the heels of the advance guard and entered Pretoria early that morning with plans of their own. Knowing that the British officer prisoners in Pretoria had been moved from the Staats Model School earlier in the year, they learned the location of the new prisoner-of-war compound and soon arrived there at the gallop. There followed a wild scene. As Churchill gave out a cheer Marlborough called on the camp commandant to surrender. The sentries dropped their weapons and the British prisoners took control of the camp. 'The Transvaal emblem was torn down, and, amid wild cheers, the first British flag was hoisted over Pretoria. Time 8.47 [a.m.], June 5.'[95] Just short of six months after his own escape, Churchill had won a final victory over his captors. The two cousins, with ho help from Roberts's army, had liberated 168 British prisoners and taken the commandant, four corporals and forty-eight guards captive. As recorded in the diary of Augustus Goodacre, a newly liberated Royal Engineer: 'It was roarable and splendid.'[96]

At 2.00 p.m. Lord Roberts and his staff entered Pretoria and rode to the central square where he watched the Union Flag raised over the Parliament House. He basked in his victory as his army marched past in review for three hours. It was a victory in the nineteenth-century European sense, as he had routed the enemy armies and captured both enemy capitals. He had not won the victory the British needed, however, as the Boer governments had not surrendered and their armies were still in the field. A force of 7,000 Boers with twenty-five guns had moved into positions astride the Delagoa Bay Railway fifteen miles east of Pretoria at Diamond Hill. This force presented a real threat to British possession of Pretoria and in the days after entering the city Roberts decided it had to be removed. To the task he assigned the 11th Division of 6,000 infantry and twenty guns under Pole-Carew, French's cavalry division now numbering 2,000 and Hamilton's force with 3,000 infantry, 1,000 cavalry, 2,000 mounted infantry and thirty guns.

The British moved to the attack on the morning of 11 June 1900, on a front sixteen miles wide, with the goal of removing the Boers from their strongpoint and if possible capturing their guns. French was directed to turn the Boer flank on the north and to sweep around to cut off the Boer line of retreat to the east. Hamilton sent Broadwood's cavalry brigade to the south to flank the Boer right and planned himself to direct an infantry assault on the enemy centre up the high, steep hills of the Diamond Hill ridge line. The battle began at 8.00 a.m. with the Boer positions on the ridge-line that ran north to south and the British attacking from the west. French reached the Boer right flank and was soon engaged. The cavalry on the Boer left could not flank the position and so attacked it frontally. In the middle, Hamilton began with artillery shelling and followed with an infantry attack in an attempt to pierce the Boer centre. Churchill was stationed on the left of the firing line of the Corps of Gillies in the centre of the battle. By the end of the day the British forces had taken the first lower ridge but the Boers held the main ridge.

Early on the morning of 12 June the battle resumed with heavy exchanges of rifle and artillery fire with the Boers on the summit and the British facing them and the steep, grassy slope of the higher ridge. In *Ian Hamilton's March*, Churchill described the battle but modestly left out his own important role in it. For this we must rely on General Hamilton's 1944 memoir, *Listening for the Drums*, in which he recorded:

> During the South African War Winston gave the embattled hosts at Diamond Hill an exhibition of conspicuous gallantry (the phrase often used in recommendations for the VC) for which he has never received full credit. Here is the story: My Column, including Broadwood's Cavalry and a lot of guns, lay

opposite and below a grassy mountain, bare of rocks or trees, not unlike our own South Downs where they meet the sea. The crest line was held by the Boer left. The key to the battlefield lay on the summit but nobody knew it until Winston, who had been attached to my Column by the High Command, somehow managed to give me the slip and to climb this mountain, most of it being dead ground to the Boers lining the crestline as they had to keep their heads down owing to our heavy gun-fire. He climbed this mountain as our Scouts were trained to climb on the Indian Frontier and ensconced himself in a niche not much more than a pistol shot directly below the Boer Commandos – no mean feat of arms in broad daylight and one showing a fine trust in the accuracy of our own guns. Had even half a dozen of the Burghers run twenty yards over the brow they could have knocked him off his perch with a volley of stones. Thus it was that from his lofty perch Winston had the nerve to signal me, if I remember right, with his handkerchief on a stick, that if I could only manage to gallop up at the head of my Mounted Infantry we ought to be able to rush the summit.[97]

Hamilton did follow the route Churchill had shown him up the ridge with sufficient men to turn the left flank of the Boers on the summit. By mid-afternoon the British had moved artillery on top of the ridge, suppressed the enfilading fire of the Boers from an adjacent hill and forced the enemy to retreat. During the night of 12–13 June the Boers abandoned their remaining positions and marched away to the east. At the cost of 200 casualties the British had won an important victory. The capture of Diamond Hill, which was then garrisoned by the British, removed any Boer threat to recapture Pretoria and ensured it would remain in the possession of Roberts's army.

Hamilton thought very highly of Churchill's conduct at Diamond Hill and wrote in his memoir:

> Persistent efforts were made by me to get some mention made or notice taken of Winston's initiative and daring and of how he had grasped the whole lay-out of the battlefield; but he had two big dislikes against him, – those of Bobs and K. And he had only been a Press Correspondent – they declared – so nothing happened. As it was under me at Gudda Kalai that he had enjoyed a brief but very strenuous course of study in the art of using ground to the best advantage either for attack or defence, this made me furious with impotent rage.[98]

Although the records of recommendations for decorations from 1900 do not survive, Hamilton's use of the phrase 'conspicuous gallantry' and reference to the Victoria Cross strongly suggest his recommendation was for that top award. In Lord Dundonald's memoir, *My Army Life*, Churchill's commander in Natal, after relating the anecdote about

Churchill wanting a Distinguished Service Order to wear on his Chancellor of the Exchequer robes, recorded: 'As a matter of fact I did, when the war was over recommend Lieutenant Winston Churchill for a reward, but he got nothing. This may have arisen from the system of limiting the number of decorations awarded to any one regiment; I do not know.'[99] Another officer impressed with Churchill's soldierly qualities was Captain Percy Scott, Royal Navy, of HMS *Terrible*, a gunnery expert who devised the gun carriages that allowed naval guns to operate on land in support of British troops. Before leaving for his next position in China, he wrote to Churchill from Durban on 24 March 1900: 'I hope I get to congratulate you on receiving some high honour for your gallantry in the Armoured Train it will be a cruel shame if the pluck you showed and the example you set to those who wavered is not recognised in a very substantial manner.' He added: 'I feel certain that I shall someday shake hands with you as Prime Minister of England, you possess the two necessary qualities genius and plod, combined I believe nothing can keep them back.'[100]

Churchill received no decoration, military or civilian, and no mention in dispatches for his actions in the South African War. He did receive the Queen's South Africa Medal with six clasps, representing his participation in specific theatres and battles in a military capacity. The medal was created by Army Order in 1900 to recognise operational service of British and colonial troops in the war in the period beginning 11 October 1899, and eventually extended to May 1902. Approximately 177,000 of the medals were struck and twenty-six clasps were authorised. The maximum number awarded to one medal in the army was nine, in the Royal Navy eight.[101] Lieutenant W. L. S. Churchill was included on the Roll of Individuals entitled to the medal under the Army Order of 1 April 1901, granting the medal to members of the South African Light Horse. The record also confirms his entitlement to the six clasps – Cape Colony, Tugela Heights, Orange Free State, Relief of Ladysmith, Johannesburg and Diamond Hill. The medal roll was certified 15 July 1901, and the award was issued to Churchill on 27 July 1901.[102] The medal itself was struck in silver for British troops with the profile of Queen Victoria in veil and crown on the obverse with the inscription, VICTORIA REGINA ET IMPERATRIX. The reverse features the figure of Britannia carrying the Union Flag in her left hand and extending a laurel wreath with her right. The medal is suspended from a straight suspension bar from a ribbon with a wide central band of orange with flanking bands of dark blue and a narrow band of red on each edge. The clasps are worn on the ribbon.

Churchill's medal is inscribed on the lower edge, 'Lieut. W. L. S. Churchill, S. A. LT. HORSE.'[103]

After Diamond Hill, Churchill resolved to return to England where 'Politics, Pamela [Plowden], finances and books all need my attention.'[104] He knew the major conventional war operations were at an end and he had no interest as a correspondent in covering a 'shapeless and indefinite' guerrilla war with the prospect of a general election in England beckoning him homeward. He departed from Johannesburg by train for Cape Town on 20 June and soon had his last adventure in South Africa. In the early morning near Kopjes Station [now Koppies Station] 100 miles south of Johannesburg the troop train stopped suddenly. He got off the train to see what was going on just as a Boer shell exploded quite close by and, seeing the bridge ahead aflame, he realised at once the train was being ambushed. Along with his experiences in the armoured train this was indeed a remarkable book-end to his South African adventure. As he recorded the events in *My Early Life*:

> No one was in command. The soldiers began to get out of the carriage in confusion ... I saw no officers. My memories of the armoured train made me extremely sensitive about our line of retreat. I had no wishes to repeat the experiences of November 15; I therefore ran along the railway line to the engine, climbed into the cab, and ordered the engine driver to blow his whistle to make the men re-entrain, and steam back instantly to Kopjes Station. He obeyed. While I was standing on the foot-plate to make sure the soldiers had got back into the train, I saw, less than a hundred yards away ... a cluster of dark figures. These were the last Boers I was to see as enemies. I fitted the wooden stock to the Mauser pistol and fired six or seven times at them. They scattered without firing back.[105]

Again, Churchill had shown coolness under fire and resolution in action. Again, as he would say, he had thrown double sixes. After some delay, he was back on his way to Cape Town. There he finished his correspondence and had a third interview with Sir Alfred Milner at Government House. In Cape Town he learned that *London to Ladysmith via Pretoria*, published 15 May 1900, had already sold 11,000 copies. This was indeed good news for Churchill, and not just because it had earned £720 in royalties.[106] He had finally arrived as a popular public figure in England by virtue of his exploits and his reporting. He had started in Cuba in 1895 to prove himself to himself. When he left South Africa on 7 July 1900, he had gained an enviable reputation for courage and resourcefulness for all to see. It truly paved his path to Parliament.

The war in South Africa did not end that summer or even that year. Although Roberts's army pursued the Boers northwards to the Brandwater Basin and at the end of July forced the surrender of a Boer Commando there under Martin Prinsloo and by the end of September captured the Delagoa Bay Railway up to the border with Portuguese East Africa, the fourth phase of the war, the guerrilla war, had begun in earnest. Led by capable and resourceful men whose names would become very well known – de Wet, Herzog, Kritzinger, Botha, de la Rey, Viljoen and Smuts – the Boers were to reorganise in the autumn of 1900 and their commandos would move and fight through the Transvaal, Orange Free State and even Cape Colony for the next year and a half. Although Roberts believed he had won the war by the time he handed command over to Kitchener in November and sailed for home, it would take Kitchener's methodical campaign to defeat the Boers. It required a widespread network of 10,000 block-houses and 5,000 miles of barbed wire, a policy of burning Boer farms and placing civilians in concentration camps, and an orderly campaign of mobile pursuing columns to bring the Boers ultimately to the bargaining table. The final Peace of Vereeniging was signed on 30 May1902, ending the conflict.

The war cost the United Kingdom £220,000,000. The Empire had employed almost 450,000 troops in the conflict, including regulars, reserves, imperial yeomanry volunteers, men enlisted in South Africa, and colonial troops from Canada, Australia and New Zealand. The cost in casualties was the highest the British Empire had suffered in any conflict to date. The *Official History* stated that the British and imperial forces sustained 52,156 casualties including 7,582 killed in action or died of wounds and 13,139 who died of disease. It recorded that the Boer forces had a total of 87,365 engaged during the course of the conflict although *The Times* history mentioned 65,000. By the end of the war 25,000 Boer prisoners-of-war were in camps abroad. It is estimated that 4,000–7,000 Boers were killed in action and that 18,000–20,000 civilians and Boer ex-combatants died of disease in the camps. In addition, an estimated 7,000–12,000 natives died of disease in the camps.[107] The peace settlement purchased with all this blood and treasure placed the former Boer republic under British control but promised them eventual self-rule, which they achieved in 1910. The franchise for blacks and other minorities was postponed until after the grant of self-government and it was not until almost the end of the twentieth century that the minority Boer, later Afrikaaner, hold on the government was ended.

9

Between Wars

Winston Churchill sailed from Cape Town on 7 July 1900, on the *Dunottar Castle*, for England and home. He was once again a civilian, having relinquished his army commission before leaving Africa. He arrived in Southampton on 20 July and by 25 July had already appeared in Oldham where he was adopted as a prospective candidate for a seat in Parliament by the local Conservative Party committee in anticipation of a general election in the autumn. Churchill was by then a celebrity and was warmly welcomed wherever he went. The former lieutenant visited General Garnet Wolseley, the Commander-in-Chief of the British army, General Evelyn Wood, the Adjutant General, and went to Parliament at the invitation of George Wyndham, the Conservative MP for Dover, then in the government as Under-Secretary of State for War. After the visit Churchill wrote to his brother Jack, who was still in South Africa: 'Mr. Wyndham told me yesterday that a dispatch had been received dealing with the armoured train incident in which I was very favourably spoken of, but I do not expect I shall get anything out of it, not at any rate the one thing that I want. I have, however, had a very good puff.'[1] The 'one thing' was certainly a military decoration.

He renewed contacts with senior politicians such as Joseph Chamberlain and Lord Rosebery, a former Prime Minister, and was much in demand as a speaker, almost always talking about the war or matters relating to the army. Parliament was dissolved on 17 September 1900, with polling to begin on 1 October for what the critics called the 'khaki election', because the Unionist government under Lord Salisbury intended to take advantage of recent successes in the war in South Africa to keep or increase its majority. As Churchill later wrote in *My Early Life*: 'I fought on the platform that the war was just and necessary, that the Liberals had been wrong to oppose it, and had in many ways hampered its conduct; that it must be fought to an indisputable conclusion, and that thereafter there should be a generous settlement.'[2] This policy clearly foreshadows the moral of Churchill's proposed inscription for a French war memorial after the First World War: 'In war: resolution. In defeat: defiance. In victory: magnanimity. In peace: good will.'

stcourt armoured Train.
mpt to run the gauntlet.

Southernbank
2/R.D.F. /99.

The Sketch

: The armoured train fight, November 1899, Natal, South Africa. Sketch by Lt Thomas H. C.
and, Royal Dublin Fusiliers. *Courtesy of Winston Churchill Memorial and Library, Fulton,*
ri.

: The armoured train fight – memorial near Frere, Natal. It reads, 'This marks the place
the armoured train was wrecked and the Rt. Hon. Winston Churchill captured by Boer forces,
5th 1899'. Note the displacement of the new rail line some distance away. *Author's collection.*

e: The State's Model
l, Pretoria, where
hill was held as a
er of war in 1899, and
which he escaped alone.
r's collection.
site page: Lt W. L. S.
hill, South African Light
, 1900. Author's collection.
: Trooper Clement
ts, Montmorency's
s, who won the DCM
Churchill's life under
the South African War in
Photograph courtesy of
Maud.

ite Page, top: Churchill, South African Light Horse, Natal, South Africa, 1900. *Photograph y of the Director, National Army Museum, London.*

site page, bottom: Major Winston S. Churchill, Officer Commanding the Henley Squadron, 's Own Oxfordshire Hussars. *Photo courtesy of the Oxfordshire Yeomanry Trust.*

: The Churchill family in the Queen's Own Oxfordshire Hussars, left to right: the 9th Duke lborough, Viscount Churchill, Winston S. Churchill, John S. Churchill. *Photo courtesy of the 'shire Yeomanry Trust.*

Above: General Sir Ian Hamilton inspecting the horse lines with officers of the Queen's Own Oxfordshire Hussars, including Major Winston S. Churchill. *Photograph courtesy of the Director, NationalArmy Museum, London.*
Below: Churchill's First World War poilu helmet. Collection of the National Trust, Chartwell: *Author's photograph.*

Colonel Winston Churchill, Officer Commanding the 6th Battalion, Royal Scots Fusiliers, the *tern Front, 1916. From the collection of Major General Edmund Hakewill Smith, Courtesy of Sir Martin Gilbert.*

Above: The decorations and medals awarded to Churchill for service as an officer in the British Army, 1895–1924. Top row, left to right: The Order of Military Merit (Spain), The Cuban Campaign Medal (Spain), The India Medal, The Queen's Sudan Medal, The Khedive's Sudan Medal. Bottom row, left to right: The Queen's South Africa Medal, The 1914–1915 Star, The British War Medal, The Victory Medal, The Territorial Decoration. *Author's photograph.*

Left: Churchill's regimental badges, top row, left to right: [...] Military College, [...] (Queen's Own) Hussars, 21st Lancers [...] Bottom row, left to right: South African Light Horse, Royal Scots Fusiliers, Queen's Own Oxfordshire Hussars. *Author's photograph.*

The war in South Africa was the central issue in the campaign. It was not only something Churchill knew a good deal about but also the reason the public knew a good deal about him. His army years were the foundation for his political years. Churchill's early and continuing interest in politics was attributable to the fact that his father, Lord Randolph Churchill, had been an MP and a member of the Cabinet, and moved in high political circles throughout the early years of Winston Churchill's life. It was the son's goal from a young age to enter politics at the father's side and so to earn the love and respect which, sadly, he never seemed to gain. After Lord Randolph's death, Churchill never wavered in his pursuit of a career in politics, partly from respect for his father, partly from personal ambition.

On polling day, 1 October 1900, Churchill won a seat in Parliament as a member for Oldham coming second in a four-seat constituency, defeating a young Liberal high-flier, Walter Runciman, by 222 votes out of more than 30,000 votes cast.[3] Letters and telegrams of congratulation flowed in from the public and from leading figures in the government alike. The Prime Minister, Lord Salisbury, wrote: 'I can well understand your African performances, of various kinds, should have had a persuasive effect on the minds of the electors of Oldham.'[4] Indeed the fame and reputation Churchill had made for himself in the armoured train episode was the key to his success in the election, as Churchill noted in *My Early Life*. Churchill's colleague both at Harrow and as a war correspondent in Natal, L. S. Amery, had declined to travel on the train early in the morning that November day in 1899. He recalled in a foreword to a book in 1955:

> Once many years after, when Winston and I were discussing the merits and demerits of early rising I reminded him of our experience on that day as proving that the early worm was apt to get caught by the bird. His rejoinder was prompt: 'If I had not been early, I should not have been caught. But if I had not been caught, I could not have escaped, and my imprisonment and escape provided me with materials for lectures and a book which brought me in enough money to get into Parliament in 1900 – ten years before you!'[5]

By mid-autumn 1900 Churchill had seen action in Cuba, on the North-West Frontier in India, in the Sudan, and in South Africa. He had earned an order and four medals and had been mentioned in dispatches. He had written five books and become a respected and well-paid journalist. He had won his coveted seat in Parliament and had scheduled lecture tours in the United Kingdom and North America that would earn him thousands of pounds in just a few months. In *My Early Life*, Churchill wrote: 'Twenty to Twenty-five! Those are the years.'[6] Indeed, they were for him. Churchill turned twenty-six on 30 November 1900. He had arrived at the place he had long sought and had no regrets about leaving behind a military career. On 16 January 1901, in a letter to George Cornwallis-West, an army officer (and his mother's fiancé, shortly to be her husband) who was considering leaving the army himself, Churchill wrote:

> Unless you are absolutely resolved to be Commander in Chief or upon the other hand are quite convinced that 'orderly officer' is the limit of your capacity the army is a miserable waste of time. It is not a source of income, but rather a channel of expenditure; the drudgery is tedious, the waste of time & energy awful, and the rewards barren – unless you count killing life pleasantly a reward.[7]

Even after leaving the army for this second time Churchill maintained a strong interest in military matters. His lecture tour focused on the South African War which was also the subject of his maiden speech in Parliament on 18 February1901. He continued to speak in public to Conservative Association meetings and on the floor of the House of Commons about the war in South Africa and army reform. He gave a notable address about his impressions of the war at the Royal United Services Institution in London on 27 April 1901, to an audience of military men. His remarks were preserved for history in the Institution's Journal for July 1901. In the speech, he summarised the lessons he had learned as a soldier and as a correspondent in the South African War. For such a young man, even after five years in the army, he made many valuable comments. He recommended greater co-ordination between the artillery and the infantry during attacks and improved, more rapid communication between the Royal Artillery commander and his batteries – what today would be called command and control. He called for more realistic cavalry training, not the shock tactics of the nineteenth-century charge or the conventional drill of the parade ground, but the practical work of the twentieth century – scouting, screening, skirmishing, range-finding and target-spotting for the artillery, and dismounted attacks with firearms rather than sabres and lances. To be successful they needed to think of themselves as rifle-armed cavalrymen. He also advocated better organisation and training for the Yeomanry cavalry, which could easily become among the best volunteer soldiers in the world – mounted, mobile and well armed, advocating better use of the Yeomanry, as the volunteer force reflected the 'national genius' of the British people.

Increased communication within and between the branches of the army, the significance of speed and mobility, and the reliance on the firepower of artillery and cavalry in co-ordination with each other were key issues and would remain so in the wars to come. The speech to the Royal United Services Institution showed not only that Churchill was a flexible and open-minded thinker about military matters, but also that he studied them seriously. He also published other, less serious, articles with military themes such as 'Officers and Gentlemen' in the *Saturday Evening Post* on 29 December 1900, 'British Cavalry' in the *Anglo-Saxon Review* of March 1901, and 'Are We a Military Nation?' in the *Daily Mail* of 17 June 1901.[8] Such popular articles would be a feature of Churchill's political life for the next four decades, earning him income and keeping his name in the public eye.

Churchill was aware of the ongoing military service of his brother Jack and his cousin Charles, Ninth Duke of Marlborough, both of whom held commissions in the Queen's Own Oxfordshire Hussars, a cavalry regiment of the Yeomanry, a reserve element of the British army. Jack Churchill had followed his elder brother's footsteps into the army class and the volunteer rifle corps at Harrow. He wanted to enter the regular army, which Winston assumed he would do. But Lady Randolph had other ideas and wrote to Churchill while he was still serving in India: 'You talk glibly of Jack going into the Army – but you know he wld never pass the medical examination with his eye — & besides how could I give him an adequate allowance? Everyone thinks my plan for him the best.'[9] Her plan was for the younger son to go to Germany for a year to study German and book-keeping and then turn to the City for a career in business. At the very time he was being directed away from a career in the regular army in January 1898, Jack had joined the Oxfordshire Hussars. As has been seen, both he and the Duke of Marlborough had volunteered for service in South Africa and saw active service there with at least fifty other members of the regiment including Lord Valentia, its commanding officer.[10]

While serving in India in the spring of 1898 Churchill had written to Jack with advice on how to become a good officer and troop leader. At that time he wrote:

I am afraid I have no vy great opinion of the Yeomanry as a fighting force. They are splendid material but they are not trained. Their officers are many of them very ignorant and the horses are mostly unbroken. The great metier would be reconnaissance, and it is to this that they should be trained. Individually they are of course much superior in intelligence and other qualities to the soldier of the line. This is their chance as reconnaissance is entirely a matter of individual talents.'[11]

During the Boer War Churchill had many opportunities to see the Yeomanry and other volunteers in action; indeed Clement Roberts was one of the latter, and Churchill revised his opinion considerably. Dundonald's cavalry brigade in Natal had more volunteer units raised in South Africa than regular cavalry regiments of the British army. Churchill was greatly impressed with them.[12] By late autumn 1901 he decided to join the Yeomanry himself. His name first appeared on the rolls of the Queen's Own Oxfordshire Hussars among the staff appointments on 19 November 1901, as a captain and as second-in-command of the Woodstock Squadron under the Duke of Marlborough. His brother Jack is listed in the same squadron.[13] Churchill's official appointment was announced in *The London Gazette* on 3 January 1902:

IMPERIAL YEOMANRY
Oxfordshire (Queen's Own Oxfordshire Hussars)
Winston Leonard Spencer Churchill, Esq.,

late Lieutenant, South African Light

Horse, to be Captain. Dated 4th January, 1902.[14]

With this announcement Churchill ended a period of seventeen months out of uniform, the longest such period from September 1893 until his death in January 1965. He also achieved his highest rank to date, as a captain, in recognition of his prior service in the regular army.

Great Britain's system of military reserves developed gradually over the centuries with militias existing in one form or another at least since the reign of King James I (1603–25). As an island nation, the United Kingdom's security had been primarily provided by the surrounding seas and the predominance of the Royal Navy; no large standing army was thought necessary. But as Britain's imperial reach and responsibilities expanded in the eighteenth and nineteenth centuries, and the threat of foreign invasion by revolutionary and, later, Napoleonic France grew, the need for auxiliary forces to supplement the regular army in times of crisis likewise increased. Without a policy of conscription for the military, another method was needed and it became Crown policy to expand and formalise the reserves. Over time, these reserve forces would also be used on occasion to assist the civil authority in preserving or restoring domestic order, as the country had no national police force for that purpose.

The oldest of the reserve forces was the Militia which assumed many forms over the centuries arising from feudal arrangements for defence of the nation. It became by 1852 a volunteer organization, mostly of ex-servicemen whose purpose was to support the regular army during wartime with either garrison or active service. The officers of the Militia were often of the land-owning class and the other ranks from the labouring classes. During the period from 1891 to 1899 the average effective strength of the total Militia was 113,554 officers and men. During the South African War many militiamen volunteered for active service and 1,691 officers and 43,875 other ranks from the Militia served in South Africa.[15]

The Volunteers were the second type of reserves in the British system and traced their history back to the founding of the Honourable Artillery Company in the sixteenth century. Voluntary units of infantry, artillery, medical men and engineers were originally raised locally, sometimes by the Lord Lieutenants of counties, sometimes by schools, like the Harrow School Volunteer Rifle Corps. Under the Regulation of Forces Act of 1871, the Crown took over administration of these forces. Although no Volunteer organisation served in the South African War as a unit, many individuals from the Volunteer forces served in other regiments.[16]

The third form of British reserves was the Yeomanry, locally raised cavalry units made up of volunteers, with the landed gentry often providing the officers, and farmers and farm workers serving in the lower ranks. Volunteer cavalry units had existed since the English Civil War (1642–51). A statute formally creating a Volunteer Cavalry was promulgated in 1794. The first Yeomanry battle honour, 'Fishguard', was won in February 1797 with the defeat of a small French invasion force at Fishguard in Pembrokeshire by the local yeomanry. During the eighteenth and nineteenth centuries the troops of yeomanry were most often small in number and were semi-autonomous. By 1871 the various Yeomanry units were placed under Crown control. By 1899 there were thirty-eight Yeomanry cavalry regiments in Great Britain with a total establishment of 11,891 plus a permanent staff of 167 seconded from the regular army. By the end of the nineteenth century the Yeomanry regiments were brigaded, sharing a single adjutant and often taking their training together. The yeomen provided their own horses and were paid seven shillings per day during training. Recruits attended twelve drills and a musketry course for their initial training and attended six to eleven squadron drills each year. This was in addition to their annual training period with the entire regiment which was called 'permanent duty' and lasted eight days.[17] By 1901, renamed the 'Imperial Yeomanry', the Yeomanry regiments were generally organised with a headquarters section, a machine-gun section and four cavalry squadrons of four troops each. The authorised full war-time establishment of officers and men varied over time between 596 and 449 officers and men. Although yeomanry regiments did not serve as units in the South African War, more than 35,000 yeoman volunteered for service and saw action.[18]

As part of the reforms undertaken in 1908 by Secretary of State for War Richard Haldane, the auxiliary forces were again reorganised with the Yeomanry and the Volunteers combined to become the Territorial Force and the Militia becoming the Special Reserve. The Territorial Force was designated as Britain's second line of defence behind the regular army. It had many men in its ranks who had completed some years of their enlistment but still owed a period of service to the Crown. The Territorial Force was organised into fourteen infantry divisions and fourteen cavalry brigades with horse artillery. The intended purpose of the Territorial Force was home defence but in the First World War some territorial units saw active service and many thousands of individuals from the Force volunteered individually for duty in the war. In its final change of name, the Territorial Force was redesignated as the Territorial Army in 1920, and is so known today. Its principal award was the Territorial Decoration (TD).

Churchill's Yeomanry regiment, the Queen's Own Oxfordshire Hussars, had its origin in 1798 with the formation of the first troop at Watlington by the Earl of Macclesfield followed within the year by three more troops of about fifty men each, one at Wooton, the second drawn from Bloxham and Banbury, and the third from Bullingdon, Dorchester and Thame. In 1803 and in response to the threat of a French invasion, three additional troops were formed at Woodstock, Oxford and at Ploughly and Bicester. The chief duty of the Yeomanry in the eighteenth century was to support the civil authority in providing or restoring order in cases of domestic unrest and rioting. Various of the Oxfordshire troops performed this duty at Otmoor in 1830, 1831 and 1832 and at Chipping Norton in 1845. The Oxfordshire yeomen also provided escorts and guards of honour for royal visitors to Oxford. In 1835 the wife of King William IV, Queen Adelaide, visited the university city; her carriage was accompanied by mounted Oxfordshire yeomen under command of Lord Churchill, the brother of the Fifth Duke of Marlborough, to and from the city and on her visit to Blenheim Palace. Following the Queen's visit she expressed her appreciation by approving the designation 'The Queen's Own' for Lord Churchill's 1st Regiment of Oxfordshire Yeomanry Cavalry.[19] During the nineteenth century the Oxfordshire Yeomanry was both popular and prestigious with many connections to the aristocracy and especially to the Spencer-Churchill family. The first Woodstock troop was raised by Lord Francis Spencer, who was later created the first Lord Churchill. He was in command of the regiment during Queen Adelaide's visit. The Sixth Duke of Marlborough was commandant for ten years beginning in 1847 and his heirs served in the regiment for decades. Winston Churchill's cousin, the Ninth Duke, began service as a cornet (an old form of subaltern) and was in command of the regiment from 1910 to 1914.

Although the regiment saw a period of low recruitment and reduced activity in the 1870s, the 1880s brought a revival of interest and the decades surrounding the turn of the century marked the high point in the regiment's prestige. In 1881 the regimental name was changed from The Queen's Own Regiment of Oxfordshire Yeomanry Cavalry to The Queen's Own Oxfordshire Hussars. It was nicknamed the 'Agricultural Cavalry' by some, due to the fact its membership was drawn mostly from the farming sector of the county. It was sometimes referred to by army regulars in the First World War as 'Queer Objects On Horseback', a good-natured play on the acronym QOOH.[20] The addition of a number of former regular army officers who served as commanding officers for various periods increased the professionalism of the regiment. Important among these were Lieutenant Colonel Edmund Ruck-Keene of the 2nd Dragoon Guards (1878–85), Lt Colonels John Baskerville (1885–92) and Albert Brassey (1892–94) of the 14th Hussars, and Lt Colonel Viscount Valentia of the 10th Hussars (1894–1904). Both Valentia and the Ninth Duke of Marlborough were close friends of the Prince of Wales who became colonel-in-chief of the regiment in 1896 and continued to serve in that capacity when he became King Edward VII upon the death of his mother Queen Victoria. This was a high honour for the regiment which had acquired a reputation for good horsemanship and smartness on parade. The prince inspected the regiment at Blenheim in 1896 during its permanent duty training and the Oxfordshire Hussars served as his honour guard when he visited Oxford in 1897 to dedicate a new town hall. That year he posed for a picture with the officers of the regiment at Blenheim wearing their full dress uniform.

The full dress uniform of the Queen's Own Oxfordshire Hussars was colourful and ornate. Based on the standard Hussar uniform similar to that of the 4th Hussars, it featured a navy blue tunic with elaborate silver braid on the chest, sleeves and collar and mantua purple facings. The trousers were mantua purple with a single silver stripe on each leg and silver braid on the front above the knee. The black fur busby hat was ornamented with a purple busby bag with silver trim, a silver boss and a silver chinstrap. The busby plume was made of short purple vulture feathers at the base and fifteen-inch-long white ostrich feathers at the top. The highly polished Hessian-style boots had silver edging on the top with a purple boss and pink heels. The uniform had a grand appearance and made a fine show for levées, balls and parades. The shabraque, or saddle cloth, and the sabretache, or dispatch case, were dark blue and edged with silver lace and red piping with the regimental insignia prominently displayed. The Duke of Marlborough's own shabraque included an embroidered Order of the Garter insignia as well.[21]

The service dress uniform was dark blue serge with cavalry shoulder chains in place of epaulettes. Field caps were blue on the bottom flaps with a mantua purple crown and silver piping and buttons. The officer's brimmed service hat was of mantua purple cloth with a black leather brim and silver buttons and the regimental insignia in white metal on the front peak. Many contemporary photographs show Churchill and other QOOH officers in this hat with a dark lower band and a white crown. These show the white corduroy dust covers that many officers wore on their purple hats to keep them clean when outdoors as cavalry manoeuvres do kick up a good deal of dust. After the South African War the blue serge service uniform was supplemented with the standard khaki uniform of the regular army with officers' rank insignia worn on the sleeve. Churchill was photographed during his yeomanry service in each of the uniforms described. The cap badge of the regiment was made of white metal, brass or bronze and featured the cypher of Queen Adelaide, 'AR,' with a Georgian-style crown above it and a scroll below reading 'Queen's Own / Oxfordshire / Hussars.'

In December 1899 the yeomen of Oxford responded to a War Office request for volunteers to go to South Africa, with more men stepping forward than Colonel Valentia sought. The 40th Company of the 10th Battalion and the 59th Company of the 15th Battalion, Imperial Yeomanry, were made up largely of men recruited from Oxfordshire, many yeomen among them. Lord Valentia became Assistant Adjutant of the Imperial Yeomanry and the Duke of Marlborough served on Roberts's and later Hamilton's staff. Captains Leonard Noble and Cecil W. Boyle and Lts Eustace Fiennes, John Churchill, Ferdinand St John and Brian Molloy served as cavalry officers and Lt H. C. Jagger as a veterinary officer. Oxford yeomen participated in the action at Dreifontein, near Boshof, on 5 April 1900, and Captain Boyle, commanding officer of the Banbury Troop of the QOOH was killed in action, the first British Yeomanry officer to die in combat.[22]

By the time Churchill received his commission as a captain in the Oxfordshire Hussars, the Yeomanry was beginning to become a more serious enterprise because of the recognised need of the government to mobilise large numbers of trained horsemen within a short time for war service in support of the regular army. One result of the South African War was that the experience of the men who fought in South Africa and then returned to duty in the Yeomanry would serve to improve the professionalism of the reserve cavalry. The annual permanent duty training was increased to fourteen days. Greater emphasis was placed on weekend drills and training, especially in musketry. Recruiting was stepped up and the regiment grew from the 150 to 200 men who could be expected to parade for training in the mid-1890s so that it reached and remained at close to its full establishment. In 1901 the regiment was reorganised into four squadrons which were located at Henley, Oxford, Banbury and Woodstock. An account written in 1910 places the strength of the regiment at that time as twenty-two officers and 396 other ranks.[23] A period photograph of the Henley squadron of the QOOH shows Churchill with seventy-eight officers and men.

The first listing of Winston Churchill on the rolls of the Queen's Own Oxfordshire Hussars placed him in the Woodstock squadron which was commanded by the Duke of Marlborough, a major, and included his brother Jack who held a lieutenant's commission. A 1901 group photograph of twelve officers of the regiment shows all but two in standard khaki service undress uniforms with peaked service caps. The commanding officer, Colonel the Viscount Valentia, and Winston Churchill wear the broad-brimmed hats from their South African service pinned up on the left side. Churchill wears an open-collared khaki jacket with a most un-military civilian shirt and tie. Later photographs, after his captain's commission, show him in correct regimental uniform. The Woodstock squadron was a natural choice for Churchill with its close ties to Marlborough and to Blenheim Palace. The village of Woodstock is just outside the gates of the Blenheim grounds. Yet when Churchill attended his first drill with the regiment on 4 January 1902, it was at Henley, which was conveniently closer than Woodstock to Churchill's home at 105 Mount Street in the Mayfair district of London.

In addition to attending drills at Henley, Churchill took part in the annual permanent duty during most years before the First World War. These yearly military exercises were not only for purposes of training but also served as regimental reunions where all four squadrons would be together. They were commonly held in the parks of great country houses where officers and men lived under canvas and the officers enjoyed the hospitality of the house. Contemporary photographs of an early twentieth-century permanent duty at Blenheim show the conical military tents pitched at the foot of the First Duke of Marlborough's victory column, and the regiment in full dress in parade formation in the courtyard of the palace or attending Church Parade in a grassy field. Permanent duty, usually held in May or June, also provided an occasion for social gatherings, picnics and balls that were popular with the soldiers' families. The public was invited to attend certain events and there were often big crowds present to watch the march past on the last day of the encampment. Consuelo Vanderbilt, who as the wife of the Ninth Duke of Marlborough was his duchess, wrote in her autobiography that the permanent duty days the yeomanry held at Blenheim 'under canvas were a gay time with dinners and dances and sports. I remember an exciting paper chase which I won on a bay mare, thundering over the stone bridge up to the house in a dead heat with the adjutant.'[24] The permanent duty weeks also featured inspections of the men and horses by visiting generals. Churchill's old friend Sir Ian Hamilton performed this duty one year and the hero of Mafeking, Lieutenant General Robert Baden-Powell, did so in another year during Churchill's Yeomanry service.

Churchill attended his first permanent duty encampment with the Queen's Own Oxfordshire Hussars in May 1902 at Fawley Park, Henley. A contemporary newspaper cutting in the Henley album of the regiment's activities noted that Fawley Park was placed at the disposal of the regiment by Lieutenant Colonel MacKenzie. The ground was well suited for the encampment with a good water supply for men and horses and a field large enough for the regiment to drill 'at the trot or gallop'. The article reported:

> The regiment is stronger probably this year than ever it has been before, and there were about 360 officers and men turned in ... Owing no doubt to the re-organised condition of the Yeomanry, which makes it much more economical and brings it within the reach of everyone with an ambition to become an efficient mounted member of the volunteer forces, there is, this year, a larger number of recruits than ever before, about two-thirds of the whole. This naturally makes the work of the officers and NCOs much more arduous; but no

effort is being spared by them, and with the help of the older members the recruits are quickly 'knocking into shape' and before the end of the training the regiment should be a smart one. There is a good number of men bearing the South African stripes, and a majority of the officers have also been to the front.[25]

The newspaper article provides one of the few contemporary accounts of the schedule for a permanent duty camp and listed the following as the daily routine: Reveille, 5.30 a.m.; stables, 6.00; breakfast, 7.30; parade, 8.45; drills for the day; forage, 4.00 p.m.; watering order and roll call, 5.00 p.m.; dismiss, 6.30; tea, 6.30; guards mounted, 7.00; first post, 11.15; canteens close, 11.00; last post, 11.45; and lights out, 11.30. Such was the typical training scheme for permanent duty, the culmination of the year's drills and its most public display.

Churchill enjoyed the permanent duty camps not only for the military training but also because he enjoyed the camaraderie of his fellow officers. In addition to seeing and socialising with his brother Jack and his cousins the Duke of Marlborough and Viscount Churchill, he particularly enjoyed the friendship of his good friend and fellow officer F. E. Smith, later the first Earl of Birkenhead, a Member of Parliament and barrister of great reputation. Smith was well known for his witty repartee in court and in conversation, and treated inspecting generals at summer encampments in a way a regular army officer never would. On one occasion when asked by the inspecting officer what was the standard ration of oats for a horse, Smith replied, 'I don't know, but there is a man over there', pointing to the regimental sergeant major, 'who could tell you what you want to know.' When pressed as to what he knew about the amount of an oats ration, Smith replied, 'About as much as would fill an ordinary sized top hat.'[26]

Captain Churchill attended the permanent duty at Blenheim from 25 May to 11 June in 1903. He invited his future wife, Clementine Hozier, to a house party in honour of the King of Portugal who was a guest during the permanent duty at Blenheim in 1903. At the same year's encampment Churchill incurred some fines in the officers' mess for infractions that are lost to history. He had an exchange of letters with his commanding officer, Lord Valentia, arguing that the fines levied by the officers' mess were excessive and were not authorised by the King's Regulations and then suggested that the general in command of the corps to which the QOOH belonged should be called upon to review the matter. Valentia reminded the junior officer that he was in the Yeomanry and that the vote of the mess was sufficient authority for the fines. He urged Churchill to pay and commented, 'What a Barrack Lawyer you are.' [27] It is not recorded whether a compromise was reached or whether Churchill paid his fines, but he did remain an officer in good standing. From 1902 until 1911 the records show that he missed only one permanent duty, the training at South Park, Oxford in 1904 from which he obtained an excused absence 'on grounds of political business and state affairs'.[28]

On 28 April 1905, Churchill assumed command of the Henley squadron, replacing Major the Honourable E. Twistleton-Wykeham-Fiennes.[29] On 25 May 1905, Churchill was promoted to the rank of major at the age of thirty and was then entitled to wear the badge of his new rank, an imperial crown. The entry in *The London Gazette* for his promotion stated:

War Office
30th May, 1905

IMPERIAL YEOMANRY
Oxfordshire (Queen's Own Oxfordshire Hussars)
The undermentioned Officers to be Majors:
Captain W. L. S. Churchill. Dated 25th May, 1905[30]

After taking command, Churchill played an active role in the regiment which continued until just before the First World War. He issued detailed squadron orders each November for the training programme to be followed from November to the following April and additional orders each spring concerning the squadron's preparation for and move to the site of the year's permanent duty camp.[31] He attended the permanent duty exercises as squadron commander 6–20 June 1905, at Woodstock, and 28 May to 14 June 14 1906, again at Woodstock. The training orders issued in November 1906 by Major W. L. Spencer Churchill, MP, over the signature of Captain Alwyn Foster, for the coming drills was typical of such annual orders. They provided the dates and times of drills for members of the Henley squadron for the coming six months at four locations – Thame at the Spread Eagle Hotel, Henley-on-Thames at the town hall, Watlington at the local lecture hall, and Whitchurch, Coombe Park. The Henley-on-Thames drills, as an example, would include instructions for NCOs and scouts from 6.00 to 7.00 p.m. and squad and recruits' drills from 7.00 to 8.00 p.m. The uniform for drills was drill order, dismounted, that is service undress uniforms without horses. The orders also included the notice, 'Members are particularly requested to do their utmost to obtain Recruits for the Squadron, which is very much below establishment.'[32]

Service in the Oxfordshire Hussars was a pleasant pastime for Churchill who remained a major for the balance of his service with the regiment. It was not the primary focus of his energies and attention, however; these were reserved for politics in which he rose rapidly. He was never out of Parliament from his first election until after the First World War and served in a series of posts of increasing importance and responsibility. He was named Under Secretary of State for the Colonies on 9 December 1905, and became a Privy Counsellor in 1907. He attained Cabinet rank as President of the Board of Trade on 24 April 1908, and served in that capacity until he was named Home Secretary on 10 February 1911.

As an MP and as a Cabinet Minister Churchill maintained his continuing interest in military matters. In contrast to his later campaign for British rearmament in the 1930s, he published a book of his speeches in 1903 concerning the proposals of Secretary of State St John Brodrick, for permanently enlarging the regular army.[33] In the book, *Mr Brodrick's Army*, Churchill urged that primary reliance for defence should be placed on the Royal Navy and argued that expansion of the army on the lines proposed would take public monies needed elsewhere and would not effectively prepare Great Britain for a general war on the European continent. Such a war would require conscription and an even more rapid and far-reaching expansion of the army because, he prophesied, 'The wars of peoples will be more terrible than the wars of kings.'[34] Churchill's grasp of what military policy would have to be for a general European war was much like his view in the 1930s. His opinions were remarkably consistent and his interest in military policy was continuous.

In 1906 Churchill was invited as an observer to the annual manoeuvres of the German army in Silesia. The German military attaché in London, Count von der Schulenberg, made all the arrangements down to advising him what uniforms to bring – levée dress for the grand review and a state dinner and undress field service uniform with sword for the manoeuvres. Churchill followed this advice and wore the blue serge uniform of the Queen's Own Oxfordshire Hussars rather than court dress or a diplomatic uniform. As the guest of Kaiser Wilhelm II, he was met at the railway station at Breslau, the capital of Silesia, and was housed with other official guests at a hotel in the city and taken to and from the manoeuvres each day by special train. In the field he spent ten to twelve hours each day on horseback and this, combined with a busy social schedule of nightly banquets and imperial tattoos, left him exhausted. The scale of the German army and the manoeuvres was impressive, with more than 50,000 troops taking part in the march past of the grand review, of which Churchill later wrote:

> The Infantry, regiment by regiment, in line of Battalion quarter columns, reminded one more of great Atlantic rollers than human formations. Clouds of cavalry, avalanches of field guns and – at that time a novelty – squadrons of motor-cars (private and military) completed the array. For five hours the immense defilade continued. Yet this was only a twentieth of the armed strength of the regular German Army before mobilisation; and the same martial display could have been produced simultaneously in every province of the Empire. I thought of our tiny British Army, in which the parade of a single division and a brigade of Cavalry at Aldershot was a notable event. I watched from time to time the thoughtful, somber visage of the French Military Attaché, who sat on his horse beside me absorbed in reflections which it would not have been difficult to plumb. The very atmosphere was pervaded by a sense of inexhaustible and exuberant manhood and deadly panoply. The glories of this world and force abounding could not present a more formidable, and even stupefying, manifestation.[35]

Yet no matter how massive the scale and martial splendour of the military parades, Churchill noted that the German troops, particularly the infantry, tended to move in large, dense formations, and were vulnerable to artillery and gunfire. As he wrote after the manoeuvres to Lord Elgin, the Secretary of State for the Colonies: 'I do not think they have appreciated the terrible power of the weapons they hold & modern fire conditions, and have in that & in minor respects much to learn from our army.'[36] He had from his experiences in South Africa and even more so from his observations at Omdurman a realistic knowledge and understanding of the devastating power of artillery, machine guns and massed, co-ordinated rifle fire. He considered that the German tactics displayed in Silesia were not realistic in light of the capabilities of modern weapons. Nonetheless, as he concluded in his letter to Elgin, for the German army 'Numbers, quality, discipline & organisation are four good roads to victory.'[37] On his return to England he stated his conclusion about the German manoeuvres succinctly to his Aunt Leonie: 'I can only thank God there is a sea between England and that army!'[38]

In addition to attending his regiment's permanent duty the next year from 25 May to 11 June 1907, at Thame Park, Churchill found time to attend the manoeuvres of the French army that September in the company of his friend F. E. Smith, also an officer in the QOOH. Afterwards,

Churchill sent Lord Elgin a recommendation for the organisation of artillery batteries of the new South African army based on his observations of the French four-gun battery system.[39] He also forwarded a memorandum on the French exercises to General Ian Hamilton, who thought it good enough to send on to the War Office.[40]

In 1908 Churchill attended permanent duty camp with the Oxfordshire Hussars held at Wytham from 25 May to 11 June and in 1909 participated in the permanent duty at Streatly from 24 May to 7 June. Although still a middle-grade officer in 1909, Churchill maintained his characteristically independent and critical frame of mind. He wrote to his wife Clementine from Camp Goring on 30 May 1909, to complain about the way the troops were handled by their officers. He was of the opinion he could do better:

> I daresay you read in the papers about the Field Day ... There were lots of soldiers & pseudo soldiers galloping about, & the 8 regiments of yeomanry made a brave show. But the field day was not in my judgment well carried out... These military men vy often fail altogether to see the simple truths underlying the relationships of all armed forces & how the levers of power can be used upon them.
>
> Do you know I would greatly like to have some practice in handling large forces. I have much confidence in my judgment on things, when I see clearly, but on nothing do I seem to feel the truth more than in tactical combinations. It is a vain and foolish thing to say – but you will not laugh at it. I am sure I have the root of the matter in me – but never I fear in this state of existence will it have a chance of flowering – in bright red blossom.[41]

He had confidence in his military judgment but despaired of a chance to exercise it on the scale of his dreams. When the time came, it would be as a Cabinet official rather than as an army officer that Churchill would have high command in wartime.

In 1909 Churchill once again attended the manoeuvres of the German army as the guest of the Emperor, this time near Würzburg in Bavaria. Much had changed in the years since his last visit. Churchill himself was a member of the Cabinet rather than an Under Secretary. The European political scene was shifting with a British-German naval race in progress and British and French interests moving closer together. The Emperor, who had been friendly and accessible to Churchill in 1906, was much less so in 1909 and did not engage in any discussion of military matters as he had on the previous visit. Churchill was still impressed by the size, the discipline and the capabilities of the German army and observed what he called 'a great change' in its military tactics. The scale of the mock battle-field was much larger than before. The artillery was not lined up in long rows as if on the parade ground but dispersed to take advantage of what-ever cover the terrain provided. The infantry moved in more spread-out formations to make them less vulnerable, as the British had learned to do in the South African War. The cavalry were relegated to the flanks of the battlefield rather than charging gun emplacements in the tens of squadrons with the Emperor in the lead. The use of cavalry as a subordi-nate arm for reconnaissance and in reserve to exploit gaps in the enemy line was the more modern, more practical conception. Churchill also noted an increase in the numbers of machine guns employed by the Germans, an omen of things to come. He found, in short, that the German army had made 'an enormous advance upon 1906'.[42]

As a soldier, Churchill was impressed by what he saw in Würzburg. As a man and a maturing politician it gave him second thoughts. He wrote to Clementine Churchill from Germany on 15 September 1909:

> This army is a terrible engine. It marches sometimes 35 miles in a day. It is in number as the sands of the sea – & with all the modern conveniences. With us there are so many shades. Here it is all black & white (the Prussian colours) ... Much as war attracts me & fascinates my mind with its tremen-dous situations – I feel more deeply every year – what vile & wicked folly & barbarism it all is.'[43]

He would not see the German army again until 1915, and then in quite different circumstances.

Returning to England, Churchill pursued his career in government, while remaining in command of the Henley squadron of the Oxfordshire Hussars. From the spring of 1910, with the might of the German manoeu-vres strongly on his mind, he stepped up the training regimen of his squadron. On 1 April 1910, he issued orders for nine drills to be held before that year's permanent duty camp at Ludgershall, on Salisbury Plain from 20 May to 5 June. The 'Orders for Day of Assembly at Permanent Duty, 1910' are illustrative of the orders Major Churchill issued to his squadron each year. The orders provided that the men of the Henley squadron were to join a special train in marching order on 6 May 1910, with the fare for each man and his horse to be defrayed by the govern-ment. Each man was to report fifteen minutes ahead of the train's depar-ture time to one of the four stations where it would stop – Henley, Thame, Cholsey and Goring. The orders covered the arrangements for baggage, horse-boxes, horse-shoeing, and uniforms. The officers and non-commissioned officers were to bring blue serge uniforms and all men were to bring khaki uniforms.[44]

On 3 August 1910, the Henley squadron participated in the annual rifle marksmanship competition with the Bucks Yeomanry at Maidens Grove and won all the significant prizes.[45] In November 1910 Major Churchill issued detailed squadron orders for training and drills for the period from 6 December, 1910, to 28 April, 1911, which were later supplemented by his squadron orders for additional mounted drills to be held between 4 May and 17 May in anticipation of the permanent duty camp to be held at Blenheim from 25 May to 6 June 1911.[46] He enjoyed the exercises that year, writing to Clementine on 2 June: 'The weather is gorgeous and the whole Park in gala glories. I have been out drilling all the morning & my poor face is already a sufferer from the sun. The air however is deliciously cool. We have 3 regiments here, two just outside the ornamental gardens, & a third over by Bladon. I have 104 men in the squadron ...'[47] He wrote again on 5 June to describe the final day's activities at Blenheim, the kind of cavalry spectacular he loved to take part in:

We all marched past this morning – walk, trot & gallop. Jack & I took our squadrons at the real pace and excited the spontaneous plaudits of the crowd. The Berkshires [Berkshire yeomanry cavalry] cd not keep up & grumbled. After the march past I made the General form the whole Brigade into Brigade Mass and gallop 1,200 strong the whole length of the park in one solid square of men & horses. It went awfully well. He was delighted.[48]

After the 1911 permanent duty camp, Major Churchill issued a further order for musketry practice during the summer. The order provided:

The Annual Course of Musketry will be carried out as follows: – INSTRUCTIONAL PRACTICES at Maidens Grove, Bix Bottom, near Nettlebed. June 21st, 28th, 29th; July 12th, 13th, 20th, 26th; August 2nd, 3rd, 17th. Firing will commence at 2 p.m. each day. 'Standard Tests' will take place 19th and 27th July, commencing at 10.30 a.m... . All rifles, complete with pull-throughs, oil bottles and slings to be returned to Stores on conclusion of the course of Musketry. It is notified for information that the Regimental Rifle Meeting will be held during the last week in July at Bicester. All ranks are invited to attend the Range for practice any day that firing is taking place... W. L. SPENCER CHURCHILL, M. P., Commanding Henley Squadron.[49]

Churchill's emphasis on increased training was designed to improve the standards of the yeomen to the level of the regular army and to prepare them to support the regulars if called upon to do so in time of war. As an experienced officer Churchill knew that better training would enhance performance; this would in turn lead to greater unit pride and cohesion – the building blocks for even better performance. Certainly Churchill drove his squadron hard in the years before the First World War, particularly after his visit to Germany in 1909. It was characteristic of him that whenever he was given a task, in government or the military, on the training ground or on active service, he would devote his considerable intellect and inexhaustible energy to its successful completion.

The Henley squadron's hard training paid off and it managed to 'sweep the boards' at the annual regimental rifle meeting in August 1911. A contemporary newspaper article reported:

> Q. O. O. H. Rifle Meeting. The annual Rifle meeting of the Queen's Own Oxfordshire Hussars was held at Bicester on August 9th and 10th, when the Henley Squadron did exceedingly well and even surpassed their brilliant performances of last year. The NCOs and men won all the cups that were to be won and there is no doubt that the MacKenzie Cup, open to officers of the Regiment, would also have been won by the Henley Squadron had it not been that Lieut. Valentine Fleming, MP had to leave the range early to be in his place at the House of Commons ... Lieut. Fleming and the other officers of the squadron as well as Sergt. Major Collier, who have taken such a keen interest in the men's shooting, have every reason to be proud of the Squadron's achievements and are to be congratulated on such conspicuous success.[50]

As a further reward for the efforts of Churchill and his men, the Henley squadron was selected from all of the Yeomanry units in the entire British Territorial Force to participate in the manoeuvres with the regular army cavalry, including the Household Cavalry Brigade, on Salisbury Plain from 14–24 September. This was a considerable honour and testifies to Churchill's strong leadership abilities and his belief that with proper training reserve soldiers could reach a high level of proficiency.

On 25 October 1911, Churchill was appointed First Lord of the Admiralty, the civilian head of the Royal Navy. The Yeomanry major in charge of 104 cavalrymen in the summer of 1911 was overnight in charge of the entire Senior Service. He was one week from his thirty-seventh birthday. Even as his political duties increased, Churchill maintained his commission in the QOOH and was active at least into 1912.[51] On one occasion he took the Henley and Woodstock squadrons to Portsmouth for a tour of the naval installation and the dreadnoughts there, combining his political and reserve officer roles.

As Churchill's governmental activity intensified, he took a less active role in the Queen's Own Oxfordshire Hussars, although he retained his commission. By July 1914 he had relinquished command of the Henley squadron to Major C. R. I. Nicholl. The Banbury squadron was now commanded by Jack Churchill, who had been promoted to major. The Oxford squadron was commanded by Captain J. S. Scott who had seen active service with the Royal Artillery. The Woodstock squadron had been broken up and the men distributed to the remaining three squadrons. Lord Valentia had become Honorary Colonel of the regiment and command had been passed in March 1914 to Lt Colonel Arthur Dugdale, TD, who had spent his entire career in the regiment since he was first commissioned in 1892. The second in command was Major E. E. Twistleton-Wykeham-Fiennes and Captain Guy Bonham-Carter, late of the 19th Hussars, served as adjutant. The Regimental Sergeant Major was J. L. Goldie, formerly of the 3rd Hussars, who had been with the regiment in one capacity or another since 1896.[52]

The summer of 1914 marked the rapid decline of Europe into war following the assassination of Archduke Franz Ferdinand, heir to the throne of the Hapsburg Empire, on 28 June at Sarajevo in Bosnia. There followed mobilisations of the armies of the Central Powers of Germany and Austro-Hungary, and the Triple Entente of Britain, Russia and France, accompanied by diplomatic manoeuvring which failed to avert the crisis which was building its own momentum. Germany declared war against Russia on 1 August 1914, against France on 3 August and then invaded Belgium on 4 August. As Great Britain had guaranteed Belgium's neutrality in an 1839 treaty, it declared war against Germany that same day to honour its commitment. The Queen's Own Oxfordshire Hussars headquarters in Oxford received its orders to mobilise by telegram at 6.00 p.m. on 4 August and over the next six days the troopers assembled at the squadron stations at Henley, Banbury and Oxford and began the process of assembling horses and stores and accepting recruits to come up to full strength. The QOOH had been part of the 2nd South Midland Mounted Brigade under the command of Brigadier General the Earl of Longford, who was later killed at Gallipoli. Following mobilisation, the brigade was placed in the South Midland Mounted Division under the command of Major General E. A. H. Alderson.

The Oxfordshires moved by road and rail to join the brigade at Reading pursuant to orders on 11–12 August. There on the evening of 13 August the officers of the Henley and Banbury squadrons had dinner at the

Caversham Bridge Hotel with General Sir Ian Hamilton, then Commander-in-Chief of the Home Forces, and their own Major Winston Churchill. What a remarkable gathering: the Commander-in-Chief of the entire British army sitting down to dinner in a local hotel with the squadron officers of a part-time Yeomanry regiment within ten days of the outbreak of a major war involving the European powers. It says much for Churchill's interest in the regiment that he should invite General Hamilton to come; it is a tribute to Churchill's friendship with the general and his strong standing in the government that Hamilton should accept the invitation. At the dinner Churchill advised the disbelieving officers that the war would last at least two years and told them that the military strength of German was 'immense'.[53] The brigade moved several times in the next few weeks by rail, filling twelve trains with men, horses and equipment. They ended up at Churn on 30 August and began individual, troop and squadron training. They were told to expect to remain there for several months of regimental training and rumours circulated that they might be sent to Egypt.

In retrospect, it might seem these part-time soldiers, accustomed to galloping across English parkland in full-dress uniforms, were not good material for an all-out European war against the army of Kaiser Wilhelm II. But as the historian of the Oxfordshire Hussars in that conflict, Adrian Keith-Falconer, has written, they were just the right stuff. The officers came from a variety of backgrounds but 'All, however, had spent much of their life in the country, and had been accustomed to horses and hunting from their earliest days ... and even the least gifted among them were endowed with that common sense which, next to courage, is perhaps the most necessary quality in a regimental officer.'[54] Six of the officers had served in the South African War which provided the benefit of experience not available in Oxfordshire. The NCOs included in their number the regimental sergeant major and all three squadron sergeant majors who had also seen active service in South Africa. The other ranks, whatever their upbringing, offered a 'combination of the countryman's shrewd common sense, hardy physique, and knowledge of horseflesh, with the townsman's business ability and quickness of perception'.[55] And, importantly, the officers and men shared the experience of working and training together, and had full confidence in one another.

Although Churchill was fully occupied with his duties as First Lord of the Admiralty at the beginning of the war, he never forgot the Queen's Own Oxfordshire Hussars and communicated directly with his brother

Jack about the possible deployment of the regiment overseas. In mid-September 1914 the War Office, headed by Lord Kitchener, received a request from Field Marshal Joffre for additional British troops to 'co-operate' with French army units in the area of Dunkirk. Kitchener asked the Admiralty to make available the Royal Naval Division – a formation of Royal Navy sailors and Royal Marines organised to fight as infantry on land. Churchill acceded to the request on condition that a regiment of Yeomanry cavalry be sent along as divisional cavalry and recommended the Queen's Own Oxfordshire Hussars for this role. At 1.30 a.m. on 19 September the regiment received orders to be ready to move by train to Southampton to embark for overseas service, scrambled to get ready, requisitioned the sixty-eight horses they were short of from their brigade mates – the Berkshire Yeomanry and the Bucks Yeomanry – and entrained that morning. By 3.30 p.m. the entire regiment was at dockside in Southampton to begin the process of loading the Blue Funnel Line's *Bellerophon* which would take them to France. Major John Churchill received a telegraph from Winston 'to say we were in for a jolly good show, and would be well looked after by the Admiralty which encouraged our already exuberant spirits'.[56] Jack was in touch with the First Lord several times with requests for additional stores and equipment and received assurances that all would be taken care of promptly. The regiment sailed - for the Continent the next day following a roll call at dockside that indicated twenty-four officers, 447 other ranks and 455 horses present for duty. They would receive fifty-five replacement officers during the war.[57] The Oxfordshire Hussars were among the first units of the Territorial Force to reach France and, in early October, 1914 near Cassel, became the first to come under hostile fire.

The regiment remained in Europe from its arrival on 22 September at Dunkirk until after the armistice four years later. They finally returned to England in May 1919 having served all that time with their horses in a cavalry division. They received more battle honours than any other Yeomanry regiment, including those for Messines, 1914; Armentières, 1914; Ypres, 1915; St Julien; Bellewaarde; Arras, 1917; Scarpe, 1917; Cambrai, 1917, 1918; Somme, 1918; St Quentin; Lys; Hazebrouck; Amiens; Bapaume, 1918; Hindenburg Line; Canal Du Nord; Selle; Sambre; and France and Flanders, 1914–18.[58] During the war the Queen's Own Oxfordshire Hussars lost twelve officers and 138 other ranks killed in action or died of wounds or illness, seventeen officers and 238 other ranks wounded in action and nine other ranks taken as prisoners of war, a total of 414 casualties. The number of killed, wounded and taken prisoner is staggering, the equivalent of eight-eight per cent of the regiment's original strength at Southampton.[59]

Many individual honours were earned by the members of the regiment led by Colonel Dugdale who was awarded the Companion of the Order of St Michael and St George in 1915 and the Distinguished Service Order in January 1919. Other officers received a combined total of six DSOs including one with a bar for a second award to Major A. G. C. Villiers, and eleven Military Crosses including one with a bar to Captain A. J. Muirhead. The men of the regiment were awarded three Distinguished Conduct Medals, thirty-three Military Medals and three Meritorious Service Medals. There were also thirty-six mentions in dispatches, some men featuring more than once. Major John Churchill, who left the regiment after a few months to serve in staff positions in Turkey and France, is listed in the regiment's war history as having received the following honours and awards while on staff: Distinguished Service Order (3 June 1918), Chevalier of the *Legion d'Honeur* (from France, 30 March 1916), *Croix de Guerre* (from France, in 1918), Military Order of Avis (from Portugal, in 1919) and mentions in dispatches 15 May 1917 and 20 May 1918.[60] Whether Major Winston Churchill would have been included in this roll of honour had he served throughout the war with the QOOH is a matter of speculation. In fact, he was later to see active duty service in the First World War not with the Oxfordshire Hussars but with the regular army. According to the summary of the particulars of Churchill's military service held by the Ministry of Defence, he remained on the rolls of the QOOH until he took command of the 6th (Service) Battalion of the Royal Scots Fusiliers on 5 January 1916. When he left that regiment on 16 May 1916, he was transferred to the Territorial Force Reserve and was not restored to the QOOH until 7 August 1920.[61]

There is little record of Churchill's level of participation in the activities of the Queen's Own Oxfordshire Hussars after the war. It is clear, however, that he remained on the rolls of the regiment. In 1922 he made application for the Territorial Decoration, which would have been a fitting recognition at the end of his military career. The decoration was at that time awarded for twenty years' meritorious service as an officer in the Territorial Force or its predecessor, the Yeomanry, upon the recommendation of the commanding officer and upon certification of the appropriate authorities as 'having been an efficient and thoroughly capable officer in every way deserving of such decoration'.[62] The award is not a decoration in the usual sense so much as an officer's long-service medal – recognising a career of service and often given as a valediction. The War Office, however, turned down Churchill's application for the decoration, having determined that his total service in the Territorials was a few months short of the required period.

Churchill then sought reinstatement in the Territorial Army so as to be eligible to be considered for the award. What was to be his final stint as a serving officer was announced in *The London Gazette* on 10 April 1923:

War Office,
10th April, 1923.

TERRITORIAL ARMY

Royal Field Artillery
100th (Worcestershire and Oxfordshire Yeomanry) Brigade (T. A.)
Major Rt Hon. W. L. S. Churchill, C. H. (late Lieutenant, South African Light Horse) from Oxfordshire Yeomanry, to be Major, with precedence as in the T. A. – 11th April, 1923[63]

This new brigade was one of the successor units to the Queen's Own Oxfordshire Hussars which had been disbanded as a cavalry regiment on 3 March 1922, and transferred to the Royal Artillery on 18 April of that year. The former Hussars formed No. 399 and No. 400 batteries of the new brigade. The change from cavalry to artillery was not welcomed by many older members of the regiment and even though horses were retained initially these would soon be replaced by motor vehicles. The annual permanent duty camps were no longer held at the parks of the great country houses and the festival atmosphere and sense of community of the pre-war period were never the same. The annual training camps were held at the artillery ranges on the Salisbury Plain and the cavalry sabre and carbine were now replaced by 18-pound field guns and 4.5 inch howitzers. Newly returned to duty, Churchill was not a gunner by inclination or by training. When he attended the summer camp at Okehampton, Dartmoor in 1923 he declined to sleep under canvas and retreated to the local inn. Perhaps, not far from fifty years of age, he felt like many an old soldier that his camping days were behind him. Yet he did not neglect his military duty. He invited the adjutant from a regular army Royal Artillery unit to dinner and to tutor him on the finer points of the art of gunnery with the result that Churchill's battery performed well on the range the following day.[64]

Having completed his necessary years of service, Churchill resigned his commission in the summer of 1924, twenty-two years, seven months and two days after he was commissioned into the Oxfordshire Hussars. The entry in *The London Gazette* read:

War Office,
5th August, 1924.

TERRITORIAL ARMY

Royal Regiment of Artillery
100th (Worcestershire and Oxfordshire Yeomanry) Field Brigade Major Rt. Hon. W.L. S. Churchill, C. H. resigns his commission and retains the rank of Major, with permission to wear the prescribed uniform – 6th August, 1924[65]

So ended Churchill's career as a serving officer which had begun in the reign of Queen Victoria. The next, and final, entry in *The London Gazette* concerning Churchill's service in the Territorials was on 31 October 1924, and announced the award to him of the Territorial Decoration:

War Office,
31st October, 1924.
TERRITORIAL ARMY

The King has been graciously pleased to confer the Territorial Decoration upon the undermentioned Officers under the terms of the Royal Warrant dated 13th October, 1920:
Royal Artillery
100th (Worcestershire and Oxfordshire Yeomanry) Field Brigade Major Rt. Hon. W. L. S. Churchill, C. H. (retired)[66]

The decoration had been created by royal warrant of King Edward VII on 14 August 1908. Several further royal warrants amended terms of the award and Churchill received his award of the decoration under that of 13 October 1920, which he himself had signed as Secretary of State for War. The decoration itself is quite handsome, featuring the royal cypher of King George V and a royal crown in gold surrounded by an oval oak leaf wreath in silver suspended from a dark green ribbon with a central stripe of yellow.

The Territorial Decoration was the only decoration Churchill ever received for service as an officer of the British army. It was awarded not for combat service or for bravery in the far reaches of the British Empire where his life had been at risk so many times, but rather for twenty years of honourable and faithful participation in squadron drills at Henley and permanent duty camps with his fellow Oxfordshiremen at places like Blenheim Park. Such service, however, should not be under-rated. Churchill was in a command position and guided his squadron toward excellence in military skills that were important to their survival and success in the Great War of 1914-18. His Yeomanry service demonstrates his dedication and patience as a long-term crusader. It also reflects his strongly held belief that service in the army reserves was honourable and valuable for men from all walks of life be they farmers or statesmen, and his conviction that the energy and enthusiasm of part-time soldiers under the leadership of capable officers could make them as good as the troops of the regular army. Earlier that year, on 7 January 1924, at the age of forty-nine, Churchill had been appointed Chancellor of the Exchequer, the second most important post in the Cabinet. He had finally acquired the robes of office which Colonel Byng and Lord Dundonald had made light of in South Africa years before. If he did not have the DSO to wear on his robes, he had at least his well-deserved TD.

After his retirement from army life Churchill did not cut his ties completely with the Queen's Own Oxfordshire Hussars. The regiment was converted in 1938 from its artillery role to that of an anti-tank unit and was designated as the 63rd Anti-Tank Regiment in 1939. They took part in the coastal defence of England after Dunkirk in 1940 and were then posted to Northern Ireland, again in a defensive capacity. In September 1941 one of the regiment's batteries was detached for service in the defence of Singapore, and were taken prisoner when the base fell to the Japanese in February 1942. The balance of the 63rd (Oxfordshire Yeomanry) Anti-Tank Regiment remained in Northern Ireland in a static defence role until February 1943 and was then moved back to England where it continued training but was not included in the D-Day landings. Fearing that the regiment would be left out of the show, their commanding officer, Colonel John Thomson, made contact with Churchill through intermediaries requesting a combat assignment. The former Oxfordshire Hussar was by now Prime Minister and Minister of Defence and the regiment's request was granted. As in 1914, Churchill assured an active wartime role for the regiment, members of which served in an amalgamated unit with the 91st (Argyll and Sutherland Highlanders) Anti-Tank Regiment in north-west Europe from October 1944 through the end of the Second World War. After the war, the 63rd Anti-Tank Regiment was reformed as the 387th (Oxfordshire Yeomanry) Field Regiment which in the 1950 reorganisation was amalgamated with its old brigade comrades, the Bucks Yeomanry, to form the 299th (Royal Bucks Yeomanry and Queen's Own Oxfordshire Hussars) Field Regiment, Royal Artillery, Territorial Army. The Berkshire Yeomanry were added to the new regiment in 1956. Each of the three counties was home to an artillery battery and the title, insignia and traditions of the Queen's Own Oxfordshire Hussars were continued by 'Q' Battery in Oxfordshire with troops based in Banbury and Oxford as in days past.

In a further down-sizing of the British military in 1967, the QOOH was again disbanded. It was revived in 1971 when a Royal Signals squadron obtained permission to use the title 5 (QOOH) Squadron. The regiment's name survives today in this form and the squadron is part of the 39th (Skinners) Signal Regiment, Territorial Army with its headquarters at the TA Centre, Banbury where a banner is displayed listing all the battle honours of the Queen's Own Oxfordshire Hussars dating back to the South African War. Also on display are period photographs of the most famous Oxfordshire Hussar of all, Winston Churchill. As a recognition of Churchill's service and long association with the regiment he was designated as its Honorary Colonel in 1953 and sent a letter as Prime Minister to Q Battery on 25 December of that year, wishing the officers and men 'every good wish for the New Year'.[67] He continued as the regiment's Honorary Colonel until his death.

When Churchill died on 24 January 1965, Q Battery was on weekend duty at Banbury. After the news was received, a moment of silence was observed and the men were sent home with advice that they might be called back to duty, perhaps to line part of the funeral route, as they had for the funeral in 1953 of Queen Mary, the previous Honorary Colonel of the regiment. The battery commander, Major Timothy L. May, opened the sealed orders marked 'Operation Hope Not' in the headquarters safe and learned that a detachment of the regiment had been selected, not to guard the route of the funeral but to march in it. A contingent of three officers and twenty-one other ranks was selected and began training under the supervision of a Guards drill sergeant at the drill hall on Marston Road in Oxford and on the nearby streets. In addition to practising the slow march step for the funeral they had to learn to march and to rest with arms reversed, which is not a standard procedure for Yeomanry gunners. Two days before the funeral they were moved to the Regent's Park barracks in London for more drill and a rehearsal march through the streets of London.

In the funeral procession on 30 January the Oxfordshire Hussars marched in a place of honour ahead of Churchill's coffin, the fifth detachment of soldiers from the front of the entire procession and ahead of all the detachments of the Guards regiments. It was a fine recognition for the regiment to participate in the procession, which was itself a fitting farewell from his comrades-in-arms from the Oxfordshire Yeomanry.[68]

10

The Great War

The First World War began for Winston Churchill at 11.00 p.m. on 4 August 1914, when he sent the following message to all the ships and stations of the Royal Navy: 'COMMENCE HOSTILITIES AGAINST GERMANY.'[1] It was Churchill's duty to issue the order as First Lord of the Admiralty in which position he had served as civilian head of the navy since October 1911. Upon his appointment, Churchill remarked to his friend Violet Asquith: 'This is a big thing – the biggest thing that has ever come my way – the chance I should have chosen before all others. I shall pour into it everything I've got.'[2] He took great pleasure in this office, its power and the trappings of power. He applied every bit of his prodigious capacity for hard work and concentration to his new responsibilities. It seemed he had finally reached the destiny for which fate had spared him and one well-suited to the scope of his abilities, a position of great authority in the military sphere.

In the years before the outbreak of the Great War, Churchill pursued progressive policies to increase significantly the capabilities of the Royal Navy. His pre-war tenure at the Admiralty saw the creation of the Naval War Staff at his direction to prepare for the eventuality of war and to co-ordinate planning with his army counterpart, the Imperial General Staff. He participated in the revision of naval war plans to adopt the strategy of a distant blockade of the Continent in the event of war with Germany and supervised the creation of a new class of battleships with fifteen-inch guns, the largest ever made. He directed the conversion of the Royal Navy from coal- to oil-fired ships to provide greater range and speed to the fleet and took the necessary steps to assure the required oil supplies. He worked for and won higher naval budgets from the Parliament. He was instrumental in creating the Royal Naval Air Service in 1914 and in forming the Royal Naval Division, manned by navy reservists trained to fight as infantry on land. He was an early and consistent believer in the value of military aviation and in 1913 and 1914 took flying lessons himself. As First Lord he was also a member of the Imperial Defence Committee and paid much attention to matters of budget, strategy, personnel and technology for both the army and the navy and prepared a series of memoranda on the military aspects of international political problems.

In the years prior to the war Churchill had monitored German naval expansion and pressed the Royal Navy to prepare itself for a possible conflict and to secure the fleets and the nation from surprise attack by Germany. He supervised fleet manoeuvres in 1912 and 1913 and, amid the growing European political crisis in the summer of 1914, ordered the first ever test mobilisation of the entire Royal Navy. When the exercise ended on 23 July, and because of the high state of international tension caused by the Austro-Hungarian Empire's ultimatum to Serbia, Churchill held the first and second fleets at Portland on the south coast of England rather than dispersing them to their usual stations. On 28 July 1914, Austria declared war on Serbia and the war began. At midnight on the 28th Churchill wrote to his wife Clementine from his office at the Admiralty in Whitehall:

> Everything tends towards catastrophe & collapse. I am interested, geared up & happy. Is it not horrible to be built like that? The preparations have a hideous fascination for me. I pray to God to forgive me for such fearful moods of levity. Yet I wd do my best for peace, & nothing wd induce me wrongfully to strike the blow. I cannot feel that we in this island are in any serious degree responsible for the wave of madness wh has swept the mind of Christendom.
> We are putting the whole Navy into fighting trim (bar the Reserve). And all seems quite sound & thorough ... Everything is ready as it has never been before. And we are awake to the tips of our fingers. But war is the Unknown & the Unexpected!
> I feel sure however that if war comes we shall give them a good drubbing.[3]

That same night, without authorisation from the Cabinet, which could not be obtained until the following day, Churchill ordered the combined fleet to steam from Portland through the English Channel to the Royal Navy base at Scapa Flow in the Orkney Islands north of Scotland, there to be held in readiness to meet the German fleet should war be declared. Churchill later described this movement in lyrical prose:

> We may now picture this great Fleet, with its flotillas and cruisers, steaming slowly out of Portland Harbour, squadron by squadron, scores of gigantic castles of steel wending their way across the misty, shining sea, like giants bowed in anxious thought. We may picture them again as darkness fell, eighteen miles of warships running at high speed and in absolute blackness through the narrow Straits, bearing with them into the broad waters of the North the safeguard of considerable affairs ... The King's ships were at sea.[4]

On 1 August Germany declared war against Russia and Churchill ordered the mobilisation of the third fleet comprised of the naval reserves. By the time Britain declared war against Germany on 4 August, the Royal Navy was already mobilised and at its appointed war stations. In the next two weeks the navy implemented its joint plans with the army and transported the British Expeditionary Force, four full divisions of the British army with all its horses, weapons and equipment to France, without loss. All the staff planning and preparations for war undertaken at the Admiralty under Churchill's direction had been put successfully into effect.

After the initial drive of the German army through Belgium and into France was halted at the battle of the Marne (9–15 September), the German goal of winning a quick victory by capturing Paris or destroying the French and British armies in the field was at an end. In September and October 1914 the clashing armies moved west and north in a series of flanking movements that were later known as the 'race to the sea'. Each side sought to turn the flank of the other and to gain a decisive tactical advantage but neither was able to do so. As the German army advanced through once-neutral Belgium, the port of Antwerp on the River Scheldt came under concentrated attack and the Belgian field army was threatened with being surrounded and either captured or annihilated. The British Cabinet, including Lord Kitchener of Khartoum as Secretary of State for War, realised the vital importance of Antwerp to both sides in the conflict. As Churchill later wrote:

> Antwerp was then not only the sole stronghold of the Belgian nation: it was also the true left flank of the Allied front in the west. It guarded the whole line of the Channel ports. It threatened the flanks and even the rear of the German Armies in France. It was the gateway from which the Great Amphibian might emerge at any moment upon their sensitive and even vital communications. No German advance to the sea coast, upon Ostend, upon Dunkirk, upon Calais and Boulogne seemed possible while Antwerp was unconquered.[5]

On 2 October the Belgian government notified London of its intention to withdraw to Ostend with the bulk of its army, in effect surrendering Antwerp and its ring of defensive forts to the German army. On Saturday, 3 October, the British government obtained the agreement of the Belgians to delay the evacuation of Antwerp in exchange for the promise of British troops to be sent to aid them. The Cabinet sent Churchill to Antwerp as its representative to try to convince the Belgian government to hold on and also to report on the situation there. Churchill arrived the same day with a brigade of British Marines, with two brigades of the Royal Naval Division to follow the next day. Additional steps were taken to land two additional divisions of British troops in France to move north into Belgium if Antwerp could hold out. Churchill at once put all his energy to work. General French's representative on the scene, Colonel J. E. B. Seely, arrived a day after Churchill and recorded in his memoirs:

> From the moment I arrived it was apparent that the whole business was in Winston's hands. He dominated the whole place; the King, ministers, soldiers, sailors. So great was his influence that I am convinced that with 20,000 British troops he could have held Antwerp against any onslaught.[6]

Churchill made it his purpose to be everywhere, meeting with the government, conferring with generals, and touring the front lines under artillery and rifle fire. He was outfitted in the uniform of Trinity House of which he had been appointed an Elder Brother in 1913 – a blue jacket with a double row of brass buttons down the front and elaborate embroidered cuffs, topped with a military-style peaked cap with gold braid on the brim. It was an odd outfit to wear when Churchill was acting in his civilian capacity. Contemporary photographs even show him wearing his military ribbons on the uniform above the left chest pocket, just as they would be worn on his Hussar uniform. It can only be described as an attempt at an amateur soldier's uniform that might not have impressed any professional officer, but made the soldiers, almost all of them volunteers, appreciate that he was one of them.

Once on the scene, Churchill was confident that with additional British forces sent to Antwerp, a successful defence could be mounted, and he was sure that there was no one better to lead the effort than himself. On the morning of 5 October he sent the Prime Minister a remarkable, even strange, telegram offering to resign from the Cabinet and remain in Antwerp:

> If it is thought by HM Government that I can be of service here, I am willing to resign my office and undertake command of relieving and defensive forces assigned to Antwerp in conjunction with Belgian Army, provided that I am given necessary military rank and authority, and full powers of a commander of a detached force in the field. I feel it my duty to offer my services, because I am sure this arrangement will afford the best prospects of a victorious result to an enterprise in which I am deeply involved. I should require complete staff proportionate to the force employed, as I have had to use all the officers now here in positions of urgency. I wait your reply. Runciman would do Admiralty well.[7]

As the anticipated relieving troops would include a number of army divisions, to put Churchill in command would have made the Yeomanry major a lieutenant general overnight, an unprecedented move that would not be favourably viewed by the army. To appoint him to such a command would also deprive the Royal Navy of its civilian leadership at a critical stage of the war when it was unknown what moves the German fleet might make in the North Sea. It did not seem a wise request for Churchill to make but it was no doubt sincere. In a 1968 interview with Martin Gilbert, Field Marshal Earl Alexander of Tunis recalled that during the Second World War Churchill said to him: 'I do envy you, you've done what I've always wanted to do – to command great victorious armies in battle. I thought I got very near to it once, in the First World War, when I commanded those forces at Antwerp. I thought it was going to be my great opportunity.'[8]

To say that Churchill's proposal was rejected out of hand by Prime Minister Asquith is to state the case politely. When he read Churchill's telegram to the assembled Cabinet it was met with a 'Homeric laugh'. Churchill was not viewed as heroic but rather as childishly over-enthusiastic. In any event, most of the relieving force never reached Antwerp and the First Lord was called home. The War Office telegraphed Churchill on 5 October that the only action left to take was to arrange for an orderly evacuation of the city. The British and Belgian field army forces conducted a disciplined withdrawal to the south bank of the Scheldt on the night of 6–7 October. The Belgian government and field army escaped, leaving their fortress troops to fight a delaying action to allow their departure. Churchill left Antwerp on 6 October and, crossing the English Channel overnight, reached London the next morning. The German army occupied Antwerp on 10 October. The Royal Naval Division, which Churchill had created in the summer of 1914 and sent to Antwerp, lost seven officers and fifty-three men killed, three officers and 135 men wounded, five officers and 931 men made prisoners-of-war and thirty-seven officers and 1,442 men interned in Holland, where they would remain until the end of the war.[9]

It will never be known what a properly reinforced Antwerp garrison led by Churchill could have achieved. Colonel Seely wrote in his memoir:

It may well be that he was right in his plan and that it would have succeeded: we could probably have held the place for many weeks, and if so, it would have altered the whole course of the war. However, it was decided otherwise.
Looking back on it, I am positive that the expedition was worthwhile, even on so small a scale. From all I learned and from all I saw, I think it very possible

that had Winston not brought his naval men to Antwerp the Belgian Field Army [30,000–40,000 men] would not have escaped. Had Winston been vigorously supported, even this late in the day, the Germans would have been forced to detach such large forces that their advance on Ypres would have been stayed, and might have been prevented altogether.[10]

It may be said with assurance that the prolonged defence of Antwerp directed by Churchill gained an extra five or six days for the Allies, allowing them to reach the Belgian city of Ypres before the Germans could. By reaching this area of Flanders so near the English Channel with time to re-form, the British army was able to meet the German army and halt them in the first battle of Ypres (19 October to 17 November 1914). The race to the sea was virtually complete by the end of October and the failure of the German army to break through at Ypres effectively ended their chances of capturing the Channel ports except for Ostend which came within their lines. British General Tom Bridges, who was sent to meet King Albert during the siege of Antwerp as a representative of General French, the commander of the BEF, recorded a significant judgment on the time won by the Antwerp operation in his 1938 memoir, *Alarms & Excursions*: 'That those few days were priceless I had from the lips of Lord Kitchener who said they saved Dunkirk and Calais for us, and possibly Boulogne.'[11] The critical importance of these Channel ports to the re-supply and reinforcement of the Allied armies cannot be overstated. It was the loss of these same ports in the Second World War in 1940, culminating in the evacuation of the British army and elements of the French army from Dunkirk, that effectively excluded the Allies from operating on the Continent until the D-Day invasion.[12]

Although in retrospect the operations at Antwerp had real value, the public perception at the time was much different. It seemed that the defence of Antwerp was an utter failure, a futile effort led by a Cabinet minister who should have remained at his post at the Admiralty in London. It was an unwise idea for Churchill to offer to give up his seat on the War Council, where he had real influence on the strategy of the biggest war in Great Britain's history to become one of many generals in the field and a politically appointed one at that. In a 1932 essay entitled 'A Second Choice', Churchill admitted his mistake:

> When the Great War broke out and I started with the enormous prestige of having prepared the fleet in spite of so much opposition ... I made the singular mistake of being as much interested in the military as in the naval operations. I ought, for instance, never to have gone to Antwerp, I ought to have remained

in London and endeavoured to force the Cabinet and Lord Kitchener to take more effective action than they did, while I all the time sat in my position of great authority with all the precautions that shield great authority from rough mischance.

Lucky indeed it was for me that my offer [to resign] was not accepted ... I might have lost all esteem I gained by the mobilisation and readiness of the fleet, through getting mixed up in the firing-lines of Antwerp. Those who are charged with the direction of supreme affairs must sit on the mountain tops of control; they must never descend into the valleys of direct physical and personal action.[13]

Churchill did pay a political price. His behaviour raised questions about his stability in the mind of the Prime Minister. Further, there was a negative effect on public opinion about Churchill when the Antwerp mission was portrayed in the press as the 'Antwerp blunder'.

After his return to London, Churchill resumed his role as a member of the inner Cabinet, responsible for all aspects of the conduct of the war. By the end of 1914, the lines of trenches, barbed wire, and machine-gun and artillery positions of the opposing armies on what would become known as the Western Front stretched from the Swiss border to the English Channel. The British Expeditionary Force had suffered staggering losses and the focus of the War Office was on integrating the Territorial Force divisions with the regular army and raising new volunteer divisions from scratch – the so-called Kitchener's Army – to meet troop needs at the front. A general stalemate had been reached that would last at great cost to both sides until 1918.

Churchill was constantly looking for ways for the Allies to take the offensive, to break the stalemate. As he wrote to Asquith in a 29 December 1914 memorandum: 'Are there no other alternatives than sending our armies to chew barbed wire in Flanders?'[14] He was regularly sending memoranda to the Prime Minister, to General French, and to Admiral Fisher, the First Sea Lord. One memorandum to the Prime Minister on 5 January 1915 advocated the development of an armoured caterpillar vehicle that later became the tank. When no action was taken he set up a 'landships' committee at the Admiralty to study the issue and provided Admiralty funding to develop prototypes.[15] He sought alternatives to a slugging match on the ground in France and Flanders, and had the imagination to propose using the Royal Navy to create new fronts by sea, to outflank the entire Western Front. He considered attacks on islands in the North Sea off the coast of Germany to use as observation posts and airfields. He discussed the possibility of naval support for a Russian attack on Germany's Baltic sea-coast and landing a British force in Salonika in the Mediterranean to link up with the Serbian army. He ordered bombing raids on Zeppelin bases and transportation facilities in Germany, creating an altogether new front in the air above enemy territory. His Royal Naval Air Service pilots were active in bombing German military installations from the North Sea coast as far east as Cologne and Düsseldorf. He was clearly open to new ideas and not shy about advocating them.

One of the plans forwarded by Admiral Fisher in January 1915 was a British attack on Turkey, which had concluded an alliance with Germany just before the outbreak of the war the previous summer. The original plan was for a naval attack on the Dardanelles. The amended plan proposed landing troops on the Gallipoli Peninsula which comprised the northern shore of the Dardanelles, the strait that linked the Mediterranean Sea with the Sea of Marmara, which was itself connected by the strait of the Bosphorus and the Black Sea on the southern border of Russia. The Turkish capital Constantinople (present-day Istanbul) was situated on the Bosphorus. Such a landing, when combined with a naval attack on the Dardanelles, could, if successful, achieve two worthwhile goals. First, capturing Constantinople might break Turkey off from its alliance with Germany and force it out of the war. Second, opening the sea route from the Mediterranean to Russia's warm-water ports on the Black Sea could greatly aid the Tsar's forces in their war against Germany and Austria on the Eastern Front and benefit the Allies on the Western Front.

The Dardanelles plan had the approval of Fisher and Kitchener and, once Churchill's initial misgivings were overcome, he became a strong advocate of the scheme as an alternative means of striking at the enemy in an effort to break the stalemate in Europe and bring the war to a successful conclusion. It is beyond the scope of this work to set out in detail the progress and ultimate failure of the Dardanelles campaign of 1915–16, which is properly considered as an event in Churchill's political rather than military career.[16] It was, in fact, the political fall-out from the failed Dardanelles campaign that led to Churchill's last period of active duty as a serving army officer. As First Lord of the Admiralty, Churchill was a focus of dissatisfaction with the campaign both in the government and in the country. Outliving both Kitchener, who died in 1916, and Fisher, who died in 1920, Churchill also had to face the consequences the longest.

The execution of the plan to attack Turkey was effectively outside Churchill's control once it began. The first naval bombardment of the

Turkish forts along the Dardanelles took place on 19 February 1915. The first Allied naval attempt to force the straits commenced on 18 March but failed. A second naval attack on 12 May also failed. On 25 April the first Allied landings were made at Cape Helles on the southern tip of the Gallipoli Peninsula and at a site later named ANZAC Cove thirteen miles north of Cape Hellas on the Aegean. The land attacks failed to dislodge the Turkish army from its positions on the high ground it held above the invasion beaches and the Allied and Turkish lines were soon reduced to static entrenchments like those in Europe but unlike them in that the Turkish army had all the advantages the terrain could offer. It was a new front in the war but it was another blood-stained stalemate.

As one of the primary advocates of the campaign, though not the originator of the idea, and without either the responsibility or the authority to co-ordinate the movement and actions of the naval and ground forces that might have seen the plan through to a successful conclusion, Churchill in later years came in for a large share of blame for its failure, even though his responsibility for the operation ended seven months before the enterprise was abandoned. Fisher resigned as First Sea Lord on 15 May 1915, having become a critic of the plan he had originally tabled. As the political crisis over the Dardanelles grew, Asquith was forced to create a coalition government and, under pressure from its Conservative members, told Churchill he would have to resign from the Admiralty. Hearing this, Mrs Churchill wrote a heartfelt letter of protest to the Prime Minister that was as insightful about her husband's character as it was prescient about his later role in the Second World War:

> Why do you part with Winston? unless you have lost confidence in his work and ability? But I know that cannot be the reason. Is not the reason expediency – 'to restore public confidence'.
>
> If you throw Winston overboard you will be committing an act of weakness and your Coalition Government will not be as formidable a War machine as the present Government.
>
> Winston may in your eyes & in those with whom he has to work have faults but he has the supreme quality which I venture to say very few of your present or future Cabinet possess, the power, the imagination, the deadliness to fight Germany.[17]

Asquith not only disregarded her advice, he later referred to it as 'the letter of a maniac'.[18]

For his part, Churchill still sought to be of service in the war effort. On 21 May 1915, the day of his forced resignation from the Admiralty, he wrote in a private letter to Asquith: 'Count on me absolutely – if I can be of any use [in another Cabinet position]. If not, some employment in the field.'[19] After Churchill's resignation but before he left the Admiralty on 22 May, Lord Kitchener, his old nemesis from the Sudan and South Africa and more recently his Cabinet colleague, came to see him. Churchill later described the scene in *The World Crisis*:

> As he got up to go he turned and said, in the impressive and almost majestic manner which was natural to him, 'Well, there is one thing at any rate they cannot take from you. The Fleet was ready.' After that he was gone.[20]

When the new coalition government was formed, Asquith demoted Churchill to the post of Chancellor of the Duchy of Lancaster, a supernumerary post often given to elder statesmen and which had no departmental staff and no duties relating to management of the war effort. Even though Churchill remained in the Cabinet and retained his seat on the War Council, his real influence on policy was at an end. As the Duke of Marlborough correctly concluded in a 24 May 1915 letter to Churchill: 'I gather that you have been flung a bone on which there is little meat.'[21] Indeed, the Cabinet shake-up was a serious blow to Churchill and his once-bright future in politics. For the next several unhappy months he tried in vain to influence the conduct of the war by participating in Cabinet meetings and meetings of the War Council and by circulating a series of memoranda on national policy and military strategy. He maintained a regular correspondence with General Sir Ian Hamilton who was in command of the imperial troops in Gallipoli and with his brother Jack who was serving on Hamilton's staff. In July it was proposed by the Prime Minister, with Kitchener's approval, that Churchill be sent to the Dardanelles on a fact-finding mission. It was intended that he inspect the Allied positions, confer with the officers in command, both army and navy, and then return to London with recommendations for the conduct of the campaign and for British policy in the Mediterranean theatre of the war.[22] Churchill was planning to leave for Turkey on 19 July and to be gone for three or four weeks. In anticipation of his trip to the Dardanelles, Churchill wrote a letter to Clementine to be opened in the event of his being killed in action, which summed up his philosophical attitude about the dangers ahead:

> Do not grieve for me too much. I am a spirit confident of my rights. Death is only an incident, & not the most important wh happens to us in this state of

being. On the whole, especially since I met you my darling one I have been happy, & you have taught me how noble a woman's heart can be. If there is anywhere else I shall be on the look out for you. Meanwhile look forward, feel free, rejoice in life, cherish the children, guard my memory.
God bless you.
Good bye. W.[23]

At the last minute, objections from Lord Curzon and Andrew Bonar Law scuttled the mission and Asquith withdrew his authorisation for Churchill to go. This was but one further indication of the decline of Churchill's influence on government policy. There would be no repeat of Antwerp and no chance to return to the centre of policy-making in the Cabinet.

It was extremely frustrating for Churchill to be on the sidelines during the greatest challenge to Great Britain during his lifetime. When interviewed by Martin Gilbert for his multi-volume biography, Clementine Churchill related how being fired from the Admiralty affected her husband: 'The Dardanelles haunted him for the rest of his life. He always believed in it. When he left the Admiralty he thought he was finished. He did not believe he would ever be asked back into the government. I thought he would never get over the Dardanelles. I thought he would die of grief.'[24] At the same time that Churchill's political fortunes continued to decline in the summer and autumn of 1915, the campaign in Gallipoli was meeting with little success and the casualties continued to mount. A third landing was made at Suvla Bay a few miles from ANZAC Cove but British offensives at Helles, ANZAC and Suvla all failed to dislodge the Turkish defenders. To add to his personal political predicament and the frustrations of the Gallipoli campaign, Churchill was burdened with personal anxiety over friends and family members serving in the peninsula whose lives were at risk and with the sadness occasioned by the deaths of old friends in action there. His colleague from their prisoner-of-war days at Pretoria, Brevet Major Thomas Frankland of the Royal Dublin Fusiliers, was killed in the initial landings at Suvla Bay on 25 April 1915. On 21 August his Harrow classmate, Sir John Peniston Milbanke, VC, then serving as a lieutenant colonel in the Nottinghamshire Yeomanry, was killed in action at Suvla. Nine days later Brigadier General Paul Aloysius Kenna, VC, formerly of the 21st Lancers and with whom Churchill had charged at Omdurman, was killed in action while in command of the Nottinghamshire and Derbyshire Division at Suvla.

As the autumn of 1915 wore on, opinion in the Cabinet shifted away from pursuing the campaign in Gallipoli and in favour of withdrawing the forces from the peninsula. On 16 October, General Hamilton, Churchill's friend and ally, was ordered to relinquish his command and return to England; he was never to receive another command. He was replaced by Lt General Sir Charles Munro, who completed his assessment of the Gallipoli situation by the end of October and recommended to Kitchener that the troops be evacuated and the campaign abandoned. Kitchener opposed the withdrawal and was dispatched on a fact-finding mission of his own. While Kitchener was in the Mediterranean, a further Cabinet reshuffle was announced by the Prime Minister. The Dardanelles Committee, the successor of the War Council, was to be replaced by a Cabinet War Committee comprising Asquith (Prime Minister), Arthur Balfour (First Lord of the Admiralty), David Lloyd George (Minister of Munitions), Andrew Bonar Law (Secretary of State for the Colonies), and Reginald McKenna (Chancellor of the Exchequer). The absent Lord Kitchener remained in the Cabinet as Secretary of State for War, but was not named to the Committee. Nor was Churchill, who had been a member of both the War Council and the Dardanelles Committee. That same day he submitted his resignation as Chancellor of the Duchy of Lancaster. For the first time since April 1908 he had no position in the Cabinet; for the first time since the beginning of the war he was excluded from the true inner circle of the government.

Although he remained a Member of Parliament, Churchill was left with no effective role to play in the conduct of the war. His strong sense of duty would not allow him to be idle and as his daughter Mary Soames has so aptly noted, 'An honourable door was open to him' and he decided without hesitation to return to the army.[25] Churchill had often thought of this before. In the first month of the war he had written from the Admiralty to Jack Churchill who was already serving in France that, 'As soon as the decisive battle has been fought at sea – I shall try to come out too; if there is any use for me.'[26] When dismissed from the Admiralty on 21 May 1915, he stated in a letter to the Prime Minister that if no other Cabinet position were available for him he would accept 'some employment in the field'.[27] His colleague from the 4th Hussars, Brigadier General Reggie Barnes, who was now in command of a brigade at Andover, wrote to Churchill on 4 June 1915 enquiring whether he would be 'going out to fight'.[28] That same month Lt General Pitcairn Campbell, in charge of Southern Command, offered Churchill the command of the 2/1st Oxfordshire Hussars. But Churchill was determined to remain in the government and continue to try to influence war policy.[29] In August 1915 he corresponded with his friend Sir Archibald Sinclair who was then serving as brigade major for Colonel J. E. B. Seely with the 1st Canadian Cavalry Brigade in France, about returning to the army; but Sinclair thought Churchill should stay in London because at the front, 'You would be wasted, your position would be hopelessly anomalous & difficult... out here a Privy Councillor & an ex-Minister is no better than any other Major ... The Army is a jealous Army!'[30] On 10 September Churchill had requested Asquith's permission to resign from the Cabinet and command an army corps in France, but Kitchener objected and the Prime Minister said no. [31] Yet by mid-November it was clearly time for Churchill to leave the government. In his words, 'I thought it necessary to quit their counsels and betook myself to the Armies.'[32]

As his regiment, the Queen's Own Oxfordshire Hussars, was already in France, he crossed the English Channel on 18 November 1915 to join them, describing himself as the 'escaped scapegoat'. Arriving in France at Boulogne, Churchill was met by the port landing officer who advised that there were orders for Major Churchill to report to General Sir John French, the Commander-in-Chief of the British Expeditionary Force at General Headquarters at St Omer; he did so after first visiting the Oxfordshire Hussars. French had commanded a cavalry division in the South African War and he and Churchill had known each other there. General French had served as Chief of the Imperial General Staff when Churchill was First Lord of the Admiralty, and working together on joint-service war plans, they had become close friends. It is a measure of the general's esteem for Churchill that he sent for him right away. They dined together and discussed the war situation at length, including the fact that Whitehall was pressuring French to relinquish command of the BEF. As French described it, 'I am only riding at single anchor.'[33] Next day French offered Churchill the command of a brigade of infantry, a formation of approximately 5,000 men, which would mean promotion to the rank of brigadier general. Churchill did not demur for, as he later wrote, ' having been trained professionally for about five years as a soldier, and having prior to the Great War seen as much actual fighting as almost any of the Colonels or Generals in the British Army, I had certain credentials which were accepted in military circles. I was not a Regular, but neither was I a civilian volunteer.'[34]

Churchill proposed that before he assume command it would be well for him to spend a period in the line at the battalion level to learn about trench warfare and conditions. Given his choice of divisions with which to train, he selected the Grenadier Guards which he thought 'the best school of all'.[35] Churchill was familiar with this famous regiment of foot. First raised as His Majestie's Regiment of Guards (Wentworth's Regiment) in 1656, it had served under the First Duke of Marlborough in the battles of Blenheim, Ramillies, Oudenarde and Malplaquet in the War of the Spanish Succession (1701–13). It had since participated in most of the major wars and campaigns, including the French Revolutionary Wars (1793–1802), the Peninsular War (1808–14), the battle of Waterloo in 1815, the Crimean War (1854–6), the campaigns in Egypt (1882 and 1885), and the Sudan (1882–4 and 1896–8), including the battle of Omdurman. In the Great War the regiment had already fought in the battles of the Marne, Aisne and Ypres in 1914.[36] Churchill had a high opinion of the regiment and was grateful for the opportunity to serve with them. He later dedicated his four-volume biography *Marlborough, His Life and Times* 'To the Grenadier Guards ... in memory of the courtesies and kindness shown to him by the regiment in the Great War.'[37]

On 20 November 1915, two days after his arrival in France, Churchill was driven to the sector of the front manned by the Grenadier Guards between Merville and Neuve Chapelle in France south of the Belgian border. The diary of the 2nd Battalion, Grenadier Guards for that date recorded:

> The brigade took over line of Trenches opposite PIETRE. All in a very bad state, communications trenches flooded and front line breastworks crumbling and were not bullet-proof. Major Rt Hon Winston Churchill, who has just resigned from Government, arrived to be attached to the Battalion for instruction, and accompanied the Battalion to the Trenches.[38]

From the drop-off point in the reserve lines it was about a three-hour march through an icy drizzle to reach the battalion's front-line positions. On the march the battalion adjutant informed Churchill, 'I am afraid we have had to cut down your kit rather, Major ... We have found a servant for you, who is carrying a spare pair of socks and your shaving gear. We have had to leave the rest behind.'[39] This was a very different type of operation from that to which Churchill had been accustomed as a cavalry officer in previous campaigns. This close to no-man's-land there were no horses, wagons or motor vehicles. Since everything had to be carried, the men travelled light. Churchill arrived with only the equipment he wore: his khaki Oxfordshire Hussars uniform with his major's crown insignia on the cuff flaps, a khaki peaked cap, and a side-arm. Before going to France he had purchased an American-made Colt Model 1911, .45 inch automatic pistol which was standard issue to American officers from before the First World War to the

Vietnam War. He had the pistol engraved 'WINSTON SPENCER CHURCHILL', using it during his service in France and later keeping it in his possession throughout the Second World War.[40] In the course of his front-line service in December 1915, he replaced his service cap with a French blue steel helmet, the casque Adrian, popularly called the *poilu* helmet, which featured a comb-like ridge on the top and an embossed grenadier emblem on the front. This was certainly not standard issue for the British, but Churchill liked wearing it and later sat, wearing the helmet, for an oil portrait by Sir John Lavery.[41] For the remainder of his service on the Western Front he sent a steady series of requests to Clementine Churchill for food parcels to supplement rations, for liquor and cigars, and for non-regulation equipment to help him combat the cold and wet conditions.

The headquarters of the 2nd Battalion was at Ebenezer Farm about 1,000 yards behind the front-line trenches and just north of Neuve Chapelle. It was an area pocked with shellholes, dotted with the ruins of buildings and damaged trees. There were no civilians or livestock, only soldiers positioned in trenches and behind barricades erected against shell and rifle fire. In one of his first letters from France to his wife Churchill described the scene and his feelings about being there and away from politics at home:

> Filth & rubbish everywhere, graves built into the defences & scattered about promiscuously, feet and clothing breaking through the soil, water & muck on all sides; & about this scene in the dazzling moonlight troops of enormous bats creep & glide, to the unceasing accompaniment of rifle & machine guns & the venomous whining & whirring of the bullets wh pass over head. Amid these surroundings, aided by wet & cold & every minor discomfort, I have found happiness & content such as I have not known for many months.[42]

In these conditions Churchill and the Grenadier Guards kept to a rotation of forty-eight hours in the front line, then forty-eight hours in support, for twelve days followed by six days in divisional reserve. During his stay with the Guards Churchill received his education in the construction and maintenance of trenches and bunkers, the sounds and effects of bullets and shells, the prevention of trenchfoot, and all the details of the administration of an infantry battalion. He spent much time in the front-line trenches and accompanied the battalion commander on his twice-daily inspections of their sector, a two- or three-hour hike each time.

During the months of November and December 1915 that Churchill spent with them, the Grenadier Guards were not involved in any battles or major actions but danger was more or less constant with at least a few men killed or wounded almost every day. The front-line trenches and forward battalion headquarters were subject to rifle, machine-gun and artillery fire and even the support trenches were within range of the enemy's artillery. On 25 November Churchill had a narrow escape. That afternoon he was in the sandbagged battalion area when he received a telegram from the XI Corps Commander summoning him to headquarters at Merville and advising him a motor would pick him up on the main road that afternoon. After a three-mile walk across sodden, muddy fields in broad daylight Churchill reached the road at Rouge Croix, only to find no car had arrived. Some time later a staff officer arrived to tell him the meeting had been cancelled and he should return to his unit. Churchill then retraced his steps in the darkness and rain thinking unkind thoughts about the general and the waste of time. Arriving at the battalion area he learned that fifteen minutes after he had left earlier in the day the dugout where he had been sitting before being summoned to meet the corps commander had been hit by a shell which destroyed the structure and killed a mess orderly. If he had not gone on his wild-goose chase, Churchill might have been killed. In the same letter to his wife in which he described the episode, Churchill wrote:

Now see from this how vain it is to worry about things. It is all chance and our wayward footsteps are best planted without too much calculation. One must yield oneself simply & naturally to the mood of the game and trust in God wh is another way of saying the same thing. These are commonplace experiences out here wh do not excite wonder or even interest.[43]

Churchill spent 30 November, his forty-first birthday, under shellfire but had already found that he was no more affected by incoming fire than he had been as a subaltern. As he wrote to his wife about the shelling: 'It has not caused me any sense of anxiety or apprehension, nor does the approach of a shell quicken my pulse, or try my nerves or make me about to bob as do so many. It is satisfactory to find that so many years of luxury have in no way impaired the tone of my system. At this game I hope I shall be as good as any.'[44] He remained with the Grenadier Guards until late December having completed his last rotation in the line on the 15th. He had learned the conditions of trench warfare by living them, if only for a few weeks.

Churchill also enjoyed his days in the divisional reserve and in a letter to Clementine on 27 November described leaving the line and entering the reserve as, 'like getting to a jolly good tavern after a long days hunting, wet & cold & hungry, but not without having had sport'.[45] He made good use of his time. In late December, he and Captain Edward Spiers, a British liaison officer with the French 10th Army, spent an entire day inspecting the French lines, going as far as Vimy Ridge. He also visited other units in France including the Queen's Own Oxfordshire Hussars, and met friends from his early army days, many of whom now held high command positions. He was constantly in conversation about military matters and politics. On 7 December, in a discussion with Captain Spiers, he talked about all manner of strategies for taking the offence against Germany, including putting Royal Navy ships in the Baltic Sea and firing torpedoes from seaplanes, this exactly twenty-six years before the attack on the American fleet at Pearl Harbor by Japanese bombers and torpedo planes.[46]

His mind was active with ideas on breaking the stalemate on the Western Front and in early December he produced a memorandum on the subject entitled, 'Variants of The Offensive', which he circulated at General Headquarters. It is an interesting document in that it shows Churchill's understanding of the use of new technology, particularly the tank, which he advocated should be used in massive surprise attacks to shock the enemy and overcome the obstacles of barbed wire, machine-gun fire and trenches. He was equally willing to reconsider old ideas, such as having infantry advance behind armoured shields and digging siege trenches toward the enemy trenches through no-man's-land between the lines. The paper is also notable for its realisation of and emphasis on the fact that if a war of attrition were wisely waged on the Western Front, the Allies would prevail. As he stated: 'After all, it is the enemy's *army* we are fighting and not the enemy's *position*.'[47] That he wrote the memorandum at all is further evidence that Churchill was a serious student of military matters and not content merely to submerge himself in routine. That he circulated it to the highest levels of command was proof that his old 'subaltern's advice to generals' style had not changed over the years. He never lacked self-confidence.

On 3 December Churchill met General French to discuss his next assignment. Churchill proposed that he should be given command of a battalion of his own but the general insisted he should have a brigade as soon as it could be arranged. On 10 December French told Churchill that he would be named to lead the 56th Brigade of the 19th Division, which was commanded by General Tom Bridges. The brigade consisted of four Lancashire battalions of infantry and was expected to hold part of the line to the right of the Grenadier Guards. Churchill wrote of this welcome news to his wife and asked her to order him a new khaki tunic as a brigadier general. 'Of course there will be criticism & carping,' he wrote. 'But it is no good paying any attention to that. If I had taken a battalion for a few weeks, it must equally have been said "he has used it merely as a stepping stone etc." I am satisfied this is the right thing to do in the circumstances & for the rest my attention will concentrate upon the Germans.'[48]

Churchill continued to do his duty with the Grenadier Guards, serving his regular rotations into the front line while events quite out of his control in London resulted in the withdrawal of the promise of a brigade. French was recalled to England and relieved of command of the British Expeditionary Force to be replaced by General Sir Douglas Haig who was then in command of I Army Corps. French telephoned Churchill on the 15th to break the news that he would be given a battalion to command and Churchill later learned that it was Prime Minister Asquith who had vetoed the general's plan to give Churchill a brigade. Asquith sent a note to French which French shared with Churchill that stated, 'With regard to our conversation about our friend – the appointment might cause some criticism – & should not therefore be made. Perhaps you might give him a battalion.'[49] Having removed Churchill from the Admiralty in May and from the Dardanelles Committee in November, Asquith robbed him of his heart's desire, the command of a large formation in combat. It was an insult to Churchill, who never forgave Asquith for it, and an embarrassment to General French who had already announced the appointment of Churchill to a brigade command, but neither officer could do anything about it. Churchill wrote to his wife of his bitter disappointment and even suggested he might leave the army and return to parliamentary duties in England.

French left as Commander-in-Chief on 18 December and Haig arrived the same day as Commander-in-Chief of the British Expeditionary Force. After discussing Churchill's situation with French, Haig called Churchill in for an interview. As Churchill reported the conversation in a letter to Clementine, Haig was very sympathetic and had received reports from the Grenadier Guards about his 'excellent work' there. He offered Churchill the command of a battalion and held out the possibility of promotion and a brigade later.[50] Churchill accepted, although it was unlikely he would be further promoted in light of the views of the Prime Minister who had just appointed Haig to the post which was the crowning moment in his own career.

It was a mark of Churchill's sense of duty that he agreed to a battalion command even though he had relied on French's promise to make him a general. Colonel Seely saw Churchill soon after he got the bad news and recorded in his memoirs:

> In forty years of close friendship I have never seen him so deeply disappointed and hurt. Indeed, he had every reason. He had served through every rank in the army from a second lieutenant to a lieutenant-colonel commanding a battalion in the field. He had been through Sandhurst, and, either as an observer or a combatant officer, had served in five campaigns with distinction, mentions in dispatches, medals and clasps.
>
> He had come up to the exacting standard of the Guards brigade.
>
> It was an extraordinary instance of the rigid exclusiveness of the old-fashioned military mind. The fact that he could write well should have taught them that he could think well. The fact that he could rise in parliament from a private member to be first Secretary of State and then First Lord of the Admiralty should have taught them that here was a man with a strong constitution and a powerful, alert and clear brain.[51]

Churchill continued to serve with the Guards and focused on his next command even though the unit he would take over had not yet been selected. Although ever aware of politics and especially the politics of the Cabinet, Churchill wrote to Clementine on 20 December, after he had left the Grenadier's trench line for the last time:

> I am simply waiting d'un pied a l'autre for orders. It is odd to pass these days of absolute idleness ... when one looks back to the long years of unceasing labour & hustle through wh I have passed. It does not fret me. In war one takes everything as it comes, & I seem to have quite different standards to measure by. As one's fortunes are reduced, one's spirit must expand to fill the void.
>
> I think of all the things that are being left undone & of my own energies & capacities to do them & drive them along all wasted – without any real pain. I watch & as far as I can – the weak irresolute & incompetent drift of Government policy and turn over what ought to be done in my mind, & then let it all slide away without a wrench.
>
> I shall be profoundly absorbed in the tremendous little tasks wh my new work will give me. I hope to come to these men like a breeze. I hope they will rejoice to be led by me & fall back with real confidence into my hands. I shall give them my vy best.[52]

Churchill was in divisional reserve during the third week of December 1915 and, being between assignments, was allowed to go home to England at Christmas for a few days of leave. By the 28th he was back in France and on the 30th left the Grenadier Guards.

On New Year's Day 1916, Churchill learned that he would be appointed to command the 6th Battalion of the Royal Scots Fusiliers in the IXth (Scottish) Division. That evening he went to divisional headquarters for dinner, met the commanding officer, General William T. Furse, and got reacquainted with the staff officers, most of whom he knew from his earlier service in the army. The Royal Scots Fusiliers was a regiment of infantry originally raised as the Earl of Mar's Regiment in 1678 and after 1751 known as the 21st Foot. Its battalions served in all the wars and major campaigns of the eighteenth and nineteenth centuries including the War of the Spanish Succession (1701–15), the War of the Austrian Succession (1740–8), the Seven Years' War (1756–63), the French Revolutionary Wars, the War of 1812, the Crimean War, the Zulu War (1877–9), the Third Burma War (1885–7), the Tirah campaign in India (1897–8) in which Churchill had taken part, and the South African War (1899–1902), including the campaign for the relief of Ladysmith. It had participated in most of the Great War battles up to that time including Le Cateau, the retreat from Mons, Aisne, La Bassée and Langemarck in 1914 and Gheluvelt, Nonne Bosschen, Neuve Chapelle, Aubers and Festubert in 1915.[53] In September and October 1915 the 6th Battalion took part in the battle of Loos and suffered severe casualties which Churchill noted included three-quarters of the officers and over half of the other ranks. Many new and inexperienced officers and men had been sent as replacements by the time Churchill arrived.

On 4 January Churchill wrote to his wife to send him a one-volume collection of the poetry of Robert Burns so he could 'soothe and cheer ... the spirits' of his Scottish troops by quoting from it. He also requested that she order for him a new uniform as a lieutenant colonel and a new uniform cap. The next day he received his commission as a temporary lieutenant colonel, the highest rank he would achieve in the army, the insignia of which was a royal crown placed above a single four-pointed star, or 'pip,' which was worn on the cuff of the service tunic.[54] The appointment was announced in due course in *The London Gazette*.

War Office,
25th March, 1916
REGULAR FORCES
Infantry, Service Battalions, The Royal Scots Fusiliers

Major the Right Honourable Winston L. S. Churchill (Oxfordshire [Queen's Own Oxfordshire Hussars] Yeomanry, Territorial Force) to be Temporary Lieutenant-Colonel while commanding a Battalion. Dated 5th January, 1916[55]

The uniform of the Royal Scots Fusiliers was the standard khaki service dress uniform that Churchill had already been wearing but the peaked service cap was replaced by the Glengarry cap, similar in shape to a standard field cap but had a band of red-and-white chequered material around the lower edge and two long ribbons trailing from the rear seam. The regimental insignia was in the shape of a burning grenade with the British royal crest embossed on the grenade. The insignia was worn on the left front of the Glengarry cap and on the upper lapels of the service tunic which had an open collar and was worn with a khaki shirt and tie.[56] When in the line Churchill would continue to wear the blue steel *poilu* helmet he had been given in December and wrote to Clementine: 'My steel helmet is the cause of much envy. I look most martial in it – like a Cromwellian. I always intend to wear it under fire – but chiefly for appearance.'[57]

The 6th Battalion which Churchill was to command was one of four battalions comprising the 27th Brigade of the IXth (Scottish) Division, the other three being the 11th and 12th Royal Scots and the 10th Argyll and Sutherland Highlanders. The authorised establishment for the 6th Battalion was 1,050 officers and men but before the battle of Loos it had nine hundred and upon Churchill's arrival it was down to about seven hundred[58]. Only one of the officers was regular army, Lt Edmund Hakewill Smith, who had passed out of Sandhurst in June, 1915 and was nineteen years old. Churchill requested and got his close friend, Captain Sir Archibald Sinclair, attached as second-in-command; he would be responsible for much of the administrative detail and housekeeping paperwork for the battalion. The other officers were very young and Churchill, himself forty-one years old, referred to them as 'quite young boys'.[59] The men in the battalion were mostly Lowland Scots with a few Englishmen mixed in. The battalion was organised into four companies: A company under Captain Foulkes, B company under Captain Andrew Dewar Gibb, C company under Captain Harvey and D company under Captain Ramsey. Lt Hakewill Smith was made the instructor for grenade-throwing and Churchill called him the 'bomb boy'.

The battalion was then in the reserve area near the village of Moolenacker in France about five miles from the Belgian border and ten miles from the front-line trenches. The unit had suffered severely in the battle of Loos and from an extended period in the line at Ypres coping with flooding, thigh-deep mud and miserable winter weather. They were due to return to the line toward the end of the month and Churchill had only three weeks to impose himself on the officers and men and to train them, especially the replacements, for front-line duty.

Lt Colonel Churchill arrived to take command of the battalion on 5 January 1916. He called all the officers together for lunch, to introduce himself, to get to know them and to try to make a strong first impression. As Lt Hakewill Smith reported the event: 'At the end of lunch, he made a brief speech: "Gentlemen, I am now your Commanding Officer. Those who support me I will look after. Those who go against me I will break. Good afternoon gentlemen." Everyone was agreed that we were in for a pretty rotten time.'[60] But after this stern beginning Churchill set out to win over the officers and men with all the force of his personality and by the care he showed for their well-being. The second meeting with the officers was reported by Captain Gibb in his memoir, *With Winston Churchill at the Front*:

> 'War is declared, gentlemen,' observed Winston to an audience now thoroughly aroused to attention, 'on lice'. With these words did the great scion of the house of Marlborough first address his Scottish Captains assembled in council. And with these words was inaugurated such a discourse on *pulex Europaeus*, its origin, growth and nature, its habitat and its importance as a factor in wars ancient and modern, and left one agape with wonder at the erudition and force of its author.
> We certainly were a liceless battalion.[61]

The next three weeks were spent in replacing worn-out equipment, marching, drilling and in weapons training. As Churchill described the grenade training in a letter home, 'In the morning Archie [Sinclair] & I practised bomb-throwing. It is a job to be approached gingerly. You pull out the safety pin, & ... then 5 seconds afterwards there is a real good bang & splinters fly all over the place ... It is perfectly safe so long as you do it right.'[62] As the weeks passed, the battalion got used to its new commander and prepared for its next tour of duty in the front-line trenches. All of Churchill's hard work paid off. As Captain Andrew Gibb later described it:

> From day to day the C. O. introduced particular little innovations which he liked and by the end of ten days he had produced a manifest smartening up on every side ... it is only just to admit he improved us greatly. Meantime he improved on us. All the company commanders were invited to dine in the H. Q. mess and there they learnt a little of the charm and courtesy of the man as distinct from the Colonel. No doubt he sought to win us, but for that he is only to be admired, and his capacity for coaxing and charming the best out of even the most boorish is a gift which I never ceased to wonder at. He materially altered the feelings of the officers towards him by this kindliness ... the

wonderful genius of the man. And so he began a conquest which when he left us was complete – a complete conquest achieved in two or three short months and over men of a race not easily moved or won over.[63]

On 20 January Churchill and Sinclair spent the day inspecting the section of the line the battalion was to take over, near the town of Ploegsteert, and found the trenches and approaches satisfactory. The trenches were well-drained and dry with wooden duck-boards. There was adequate barbed wire to the front. The parapets were in good repair and thick enough to stop bullets. There were sufficient bunkers and traverse trenches to provide reasonable protection from artillery fire. The battalion HQ at Laurence Farm was located in a brick farmhouse about 500 yards from the front-line trenches. He found the orderly room and mess to be clean.[64] The reserve headquarters at Maison 1875 was located about three-quarters of a mile from the front line, still well within the range of German artillery. On 24 January the battalion moved to billets in the village of La Crèche. Two days later they marched into their reserve positions behind the front line and during the night of 26–27 January they took over a 1,000-yard- wide section of the front line trenches in Belgium near the town of Ploegsteert, known to the British as 'Plugstreet'.[65] Of his new responsibilities, Churchill wrote to his wife: 'Rest assured there will be no part of the line from the Alps to the sea better guarded. It will be watched with the vigilance that mobilised the Fleet.'[66] Before entering the front line Churchill gathered all the officers for a final briefing where he gave them his ideas, directions and various hints:

> Don't be careless about yourselves – on the other hand not too careful. Keep a special pair of boots to sleep in and only get them muddy in a real emergency. Use alcohol in moderation but don't have a great parade of bottles in yr dugouts. Live well but do not flaunt it. Laugh a little, & teach your men to laugh – gt good humour under fire – war is a game that is played with a smile. If you can't smile grin. If you can't grin keep out of the way till you can.[67]

At long last, Churchill was no longer a subaltern giving advice to his superiors but a commander giving advice to subalterns; and good advice it was, too.

For the next three months the 6th Royal Scot Fusiliers followed a fairly regular rotation of about six days in the front line and six days in the support trenches. The front line trenches faced no-man's-land which separated them by about eighty yards from the German trenches. Churchill himself was constantly in the trenches sharing the discomforts of the weather and the danger of enemy fire with his men. Captain Gibb noted: 'From the very day of our arrival in the line, it was apparent to all that Winston's motto was going to be "work", in the sense of trench building and trench repairing and improvements.'[68] Churchill paid great attention to the details of the fortifications and trenches and regularly had the parapets checked to make sure they were three feet thick – the thickness necessary to stop bullets. It took two hours to inspect the entire sector and Churchill did so regularly. As Gibb recorded:

> Early and late he was in the line. On average he went round three times a day, which was no mean task in itself, as he had plenty of other work to do. At least one of these visits was after dark, usually about 1 a.m.... . He was always in the closest touch with every piece of work that was going on, and, while at times his demands were a little extravagant, his kindliness and the humour that never failed to flash out made everybody only too keen to get on with the work, whether the ideal he pointed out to them was an unattainable one or not.[69]

In fact, the only two areas in which the other officers tended to disagree with Churchill were the sufficiency of the sandbagged fortifications and discipline of the men. As to the former, it is understandable that the views of the man ordering the digging and sandbagging would differ from those doing the heavy lifting. Churchill always wanted more and better fortifications. With regard to the latter, Churchill was simply too kind-hearted always to enforce the strict regulations against insubordination by private soldiers to the orders of sergeants and corporals. He was, in the view of the other officers and NCOs, too ready to give a second chance to an offender or to consider a mitigating circumstance. In mid-March he received a written reprimand from his brigadier for 'undue leniency' in punishments.[70] Despite this, unit cohesion was maintained and Churchill held the respect of his officers and his men. He was always mindful of the responsibilities of his command, writing on 27 January 1916, 'One has to keep on thinking – so many directly dependant on one being right; & the German army heavy on our front. You know a Colonel's day in the line is almost the greatest personal demand on a man's qualities – vy like being the captain of a vy big ship in submarine infested waters.'[71]

All duties of the battalion commander and his men were carried out under periodic shelling and sniping of varying intensity. Churchill had several more near misses. On 3 February 1916 he and his staff were just finishing lunch at Laurence Farm, the advance battalion headquarters, when an artillery shell came through the roof and burst in the next room, sending splinters and dust flying, shattering the crockery, and covering them all with debris. The adjutant, Lt Jock McDavid, was wounded in the finger. As McDavid later stated: 'Winston had been toying about with his lamp ... when the shell came along. A piece of shrapnel almost split the battery holder in two – it lodged in the metal of the battery holder. It was less than two inches from his right wrist. If it had been any nearer it certainly would have taken off his wrist.'[72] On 12 February, while observing an artillery 'strafe' with the commander of the divisional artillery, General Tudor, Churchill was caught up in the German counter fire. Artillery and trench mortar shells burst all around them in the air and against the parapet, covering them all with dirt and debris. Churchill found it very exciting but also very dangerous. He was impressed with the protection the trenches offered and wrote to Clementine: 'I found my nerves in excellent order ... But after it was over I felt strangely tired; as if I had done a hard day's work at a speech or article.'[73] On 16 February, as he and Sinclair sat down to breakfast, their headquarters was hit again, scattering debris and splinters everywhere. The dining room was pierced by shrapnel, their unoccupied bedroom riddled and the adjacent message centre destroyed. Lt Laurence Kemp, the signals officer, suffered five wounds and one other man was also hit.[74] Churchill took it all with resignation, trusting as ever in his star. In a letter home, he described his adjustment to the daily dangers of the Western Front: 'One lives calmly on the brink of the abyss. But I can understand how tired people get of it if it goes on month after month. All the excitement dies away and there is only a dull resentment.'[75]

On 13 February Churchill wrote: 'I never expected to be so completely involved in the military machine. It almost seems to me as if my life in the gt world [of politics] was a dream, & I have been moving slowly forward in the army all these years from subaltern to Colonel.'[76]

It is interesting to consider what Churchill's life and fate might have been if he had remained in the 4th Hussars in May 1899 rather than resigning and had moved slowly forward all those years. In the spring of 1899 the lieutenant in the 4th (Queen's Own) Hussars next junior to Churchill was Ian G. Hogg who had received his commission on 15 January 1896 and had joined the regiment in February of that year. When Churchill resigned from the army and then went to South Africa in the autumn of 1899, Hogg was seconded for service in the Niger Coast Protectorate in West Africa from 23 September to 31 December 1899. When Churchill joined the South African Light Horse as a supernumerary lieutenant in January 1900, Hogg was beginning a period of service with the West African Frontier Force which lasted until 23 May 1905 and during when he received the Distinguished Service Order. When Hogg was promoted to captain on 3 November 1900, Churchill was out of the army again and celebrating his election to the House of Commons the previous month. Hogg received a brevet promotion to major on 7 July 1904 and so reached that rank six months before Churchill, who was then in the Oxfordshire Yeomanry. Hogg was promoted to lieutenant colonel on 13 May 1913, at which time Churchill was still a major in the reserves but also a member of the Cabinet. On the outbreak of the First World War, Lt Col Hogg was in command of the 4th Hussars, having risen to the top after seventeen years of duty. The 4th Hussars were sent to France on 18 August 1914, within two weeks of the declaration of war and remained on the Continent until March 1919. The regiment entered combat for the first time on 24 August and was part of the cavalry screen for the British retreat from Mons at the end of the month. On 1 September, at Haramont near the Compiègne forest Hogg was severely wounded and captured by the Germans. He died on 2 September 1914 and is buried in the Haramont village cemetery.[77]

The 4th Hussars were in action until the armistice and suffered significant casualties. Seventeen officers were killed in action or died of wounds and twenty-six were wounded. Among the other ranks, 104 were killed in action or died of wounds, twelve died of accidental injuries or illness, 442 were wounded and thirty-three taken as prisoners of war.[78] In the history of the regiment in the First World War, there is a group photograph of the 4th Hussars officers taken at Curragh in June 1914. Of the twenty officers in the photograph, nine were killed in action in the war and five wounded including two who were also taken prisoner and one officer who was wounded twice.[79] It was a toll similar to that paid by many regiments and many communities in the Great War. Whether Churchill's luck would have seen him safely through four years of war with his old regiment is, of course, unknowable, but that the risks would have multiplied with a longer period of active service is certain.

Although he was not required to go on combat patrols in between the lines in no man's land, which he called 'the frontier between right and wrong', Churchill did so on many occasions.[80] He described one such patrol in a letter of 15 February 1916 as going out into the area between the lines, 'prowling about looking at our wire and visiting our listening posts. This is always exciting.'[81] Typically these forays were for purposes of inspection and observation but sometimes they sought intelligence information by the capture of prisoners for interrogation. Patrols in the dark and the mud were extremely dangerous because there was no cover except for shellholes in no-man's-land and if detected by an enemy patrol or a vigilant German sentry, or betrayed by an errant movement when the area was illuminated by a flare shell, there was nowhere to hide. As always, Churchill showed a complete disregard for danger and was unshaken by the sound of gunfire and bursting shells. He realised that this set him apart and noted, 'I do not mind noise as some vy brave people do.' But after a near miss from a German shell on 26 March 1916, he wrote to Clementine:

> I felt – 20 yards more to the left & no more tangles to unravel, no more anxieties to face, no more hatreds & injustices to encounter: the joy of all my foes, relief of that old rogue, a good ending to a chequered life, a final gift – unvalued – to an ungrateful country – an impoverishment of the war-making power of Britain wh no one wd ever know or measure or mourn.[82]

Churchill's fearlessness was remarked on by his junior officers. Lt Hakewill Smith recalled:

> He would often go into no man's land. It was a nerve wracking experience to go with him. He would call out in his loud, gruff voice – far too loud it seemed to us – 'You go that way, I will go this ... Come here, I have found a gap in the German wire. Come over here at once!' He was like a baby elephant out in no man's land at night.
>
> He never fell when a shell went off; he never ducked when a bullet went past with its loud crack. He used to say after watching me duck: 'It's no damn use ducking; the bullet has gone a long way past you by now.'[83]

Captain Gibb recalled Churchill wanting to raid the German trenches, after a number of fusiliers were wounded by enemy fire, to 'get some of his own back'. Going over the top, into no-man's-land, Churchill said, 'Come on, war is declared.' – his way perhaps of playing the game with a smile.[84] Gibb came to believe that Churchill revelled in war and wrote: 'There was no such thing as fear in him.'[85]

Although Churchill's battalion did not engage in any offensives or face any major German attacks during his more than one hundred days in command, there was a steady toll of casualties from raids, shelling and sniping. During his period of command the 6th Royal Scots Fusiliers lost fifteen men killed and 123 wounded, a casualty rate of over twenty per cent.[86] For all the near misses, Churchill's luck held and he was never wounded. It was his good fortune that his front-line service did not take place during the major campaigns of the Western Front. The battles of the Marne, Ypres and Loos were all fought before his arrival. The terrible slaughter of the Somme, Passchendaele and the war-ending breakthrough battles all came after Churchill's return to government service in London.

Although Churchill's energy was mainly focused on his military duties in the winter of 1915–16 he was never completely out of touch with politics in Great Britain. He carried on a regular, almost daily correspondence with his wife which usually included exchanges about government policy and the politics of the Cabinet. He was also in frequent touch with Cabinet members and a regular topic of conversation with both his senior and junior officers was politics and war policy. He often mused about returning to Parliament and to a place in the Cabinet and was confident he would survive. In letters to Clementine he wrote: 'If my destiny has not already been accomplished I shall be guarded surely.' And, 'Don't worry about my safety – the Fates have decided that.'[87] He dwelt at times on the idea of leading the opposition against what he believed was a government war policy of vacillation, drift and inaction. Throughout the early months of 1916 Churchill carried on an internal debate as to whether to leave the army or to remain. During a week when his battalion was in reserve in early March, he went on leave to England. He gave a speech in the House of Commons critical of current Admiralty policies. Although the speech was not well received because it called for the reinstatement of Admiral Fisher as First Sea Lord, the experience served to whet his appetite to go back to London. He revealed his thoughts to Clementine on 13 March 1916 after his return to the front:

> Across the troubled waters one can only steer by compass – not to do anything that is not honourable & manly, & subject to that to use my vital force to the utmost effect to win the war – there is the test I am going to try my decision by.
>
> Dual obligations, both honourable, both weighty have rent me. But I am sure my true war station is in the H of C. There I can help the movements of events.[88]

Churchill's decision to leave the army was a product of events in Flanders as well as England. On 19 March he learned that a brigade command in which he was interested had been given to someone else. The next day he advised Clementine in a letter that he had definitely decided to return to the House of Commons as soon as arrangements could be made; it was then just a matter of timing. At the front in late 1915 he had written to Lord Curzon: 'I do not feel any prick of conscience at being out here. I did not go because I wished to disinterest myself in the great situation or because I feared the burden or the blow: but because I was and am sure that for the time being my usefulness was exhausted & that I cd only recover it by a definite & perhaps a prolonged withdrawal.'[89] But while away on active service Churchill always knew he would return to politics at an appropriate time, whether in power or in the opposition. As he contemplated leaving the army again for his 'true war station' in London, he knew he could do so honourably, acting again without any prick of conscience. He wrote on 22 March:

> I do not think any reason is needed beyond the general reason – wh is the true one – that I think it right to resume political & Parlt. Duties wh are incompatible with holding a military command ... I shall have served for nearly five months at the front, almost always in the front line, certainly without discredit – discharging arduous & difficult duties to the satisfaction of my superiors & to the advantage of my officers and men.'[90]

Through April and into May Churchill planned his return, receiving the advice of some political colleagues to leave the army right away and the advice of others, including Clementine, counselling patience.

The timing of his departure was finally determined by events in the army. Churchill was told by the end of April that the 6th and 7th Battalions of the Royal Scots Fusiliers, both seriously under-strength by that time, would be merged. Further, because the commanding officer of the 7th Battalion was senior to Churchill, that officer would be given command of the new formation. After Churchill and his men came out of the line for the last time on 3 May 1916, he obtained the necessary permissions from his commanders at each level and was granted leave to return to England as soon as he handed over his battalion on 7 May. In a farewell letter to Churchill, IXth Division Commander Lieutenant General Sir Charles Fergusson wrote: 'I am glad that you have come through the experience safely. And there is no doubt that your knowledge of the difficulties and deficiencies out here, obtained first hand, will be of immense use to the service hereafter.'[91]

On his last day as battalion commander, Churchill held a final orderly room meeting with his officers. The adjutant stated that their commander had been 'devilish decent to us' after which Lieutenant Colonel Churchill addressed them. As Captain Gibb later recalled:

He told us, I remember, that he had come to regard the young Scot as a 'formidable fighting animal', and he touched on his other connections with Scotland [his wife and his constituency] in the most appreciative fashion. As he rose to shake hands, the Adjutant spoke up and told him what we were all thinking, and what it had been to serve under him. Certainly he was sincere and I believe every man in the room felt Winston Churchill's leaving us as a real personal loss.[92]

This assessment was echoed by others, for Churchill had performed his duties in command of the battalion very well. Colonel J. E. B. Seely wrote that Churchill 'was fully competent to command a battalion ... The officers and men loved Churchill and would have followed him anywhere ... He was heart and soul in the business, spending all the spare time he could find in thinking out new methods of attack and defence for this novel kind of warfare, and writing memoranda on the subject.'[93] Captain Jock McDavid recollected:

After a very brief period he had accelerated the morale of officers and men to an almost unbelievable degree. It was sheer personality. We laughed at lots of things he did, but there were other things we did not laugh at for we knew they were sound. He had a unique approach which did wonders to us. He let everyone under his command see that he was responsible, from the very moment he arrived, that they understood not only what they were supposed to do, but why they had to do it ...

No detail of our daily life was too small for him to ignore. He overlooked nothing ... Instead of a quick glance at what was being done he would stop and talk with everyone and probe to the bottom of every activity. I have never known an officer take such pains to inspire confidence or to gain confidence; indeed he inspired confidence in gaining it.[94]

Captain Gibb was also totally won over by Churchill and concluded his 1924 memoir of his First World War service with the following:

I am firmly convinced that no more popular officer ever commanded troops. As a soldier he was hard working, persevering, and thorough ... He was out to work hard at tiresome but indespensible detail and make his unit efficient in the very highest possible degree. I say nothing of his tactical and strategic ability – these were not tested in our time, but I cannot conceive that exceptionally creative and fertile brain failing in any sphere of human activity to which it was applied. And moreover, he loved soldiering: it lay very near his heart and I think he could have been a very great soldier.

We came to realise, to realise at first hand, his transcendent ability ... And much more, he became our friend. He is a man who is apparently always to have enemies. He made none in his old regiment, but left behind him there men who will always be his partisans and admirers, and who are proud of having served in the Great War under the leadership of one who is beyond question a great man.[95]

Although Churchill received no decorations or mention in dispatches for his service in France and Belgium, he did receive three service medals from the British government: the 1914-1915 Star, the British War Medal and the Victory Medal. The 1914-1915 Star was awarded to more than two million British and Imperial service members serving in designated theatres of war between August 1914 and 31 December 1915, and Churchill qualified for the award by reason of his attached service with the Grenadier Guards.[96] The British War Medal was awarded to more than six million British and Imperial troops for service in recognised theatres of war during the period from 4 August 4 1914 and 11 November 1918, for mine-clearing work in 1919, and for duty in Russia in 1919 and 1920. Churchill's service with both the Grenadier Guards and Royal Scots Fusiliers qualified him to receive this campaign medal.[97] The Victory Medal was authorised in 1919 to commemorate the Allied victory over the Central Powers in the Great War. Fourteen of the victorious nations issued such a medal and all used the same colourful, watered-silk rainbow ribbon which makes it one of the most beautiful of all campaign medals. The medallion is made of bronze and features a winged figure of victory on the obverse and the inscription, 'THE GREAT WAR FOR CIVILISATION 1914–1919' on the reverse. The medal was awarded to all recipients of the 1914 Star or 1914–1915 Star and to most recipients of the British War Medal. Churchill's was one of 5,725,000 awarded by the United Kingdom.[98]

Churchill left France for England on 7 May and formally relinquished his command of the 6th Royal Scots Fusiliers and the temporary rank of lieutenant colonel on 16 May 1916. *The London Gazette* of 2 June 1916 made the announcement:

War Office
2nd June, 1916

Infantry
Service Battalions
Royal Scots Fusiliers

Major the Rt. Hon. W. L. S. Churchill, Oxfordshire Yeomanry (T. F.) relinquishes the temporary rank of Lieutenant-Colonel on ceasing to command a Battalion – 16th May, 1916.[99]

Upon relinquishing the rank and the command, Churchill was transferred the same date to the Territorial Force Reserve.

His departure from France marked Churchill's last day of active service with the British army. All his future soldiering would be in England as a major in the Queen's Own Oxfordshire Hussars. He had spent more than five months in France and Flanders exclusive of periods of leave, most of it either in the front line or the support trenches within range of German artillery. He spent more time in action in the First World War than he had in Cuba, India and the Sudan combined, and almost as long as he had served in South Africa. Churchill's days under fire on the Western Front exceeded those he had experienced in Natal and the Boer republics, and certainly the conditions of wet winter weather and a soggy, muddy battlefield of Europe were worse.

It is hard to imagine the squalor and destruction of the Western Front today; the town of Ploegsteert has been rebuilt and the farms where Churchill made his battalion headquarters and monitored his 1,000-yard sector have largely returned to farm fields and woods. There is a Commonwealth War Graves Commission cemetery just east of the town in which many Royal Scots Fusiliers are laid to rest. A few hundred yards beyond the white headstones, the flowers, the manicured lawns and the low brick wall of the cemetery one can look out past the cornfields and over ploughed fields to see the area of the positions once held by the 6th Battalion, Royal Scots Fusiliers. There is not much to see now; yet as a reminder of their past presence and their sacrifices there is a white stone bas-relief plaque on the wall of the town hall which depicts the ruined Ploegsteert church, a Christian cross, a sandbagged entrenchment manned by Tommies with their rifles ready, and the badge of the Royal Scots Fusiliers. Above the trench is a figure of the later Churchill, leaning on his cane, smoking a cigar and looking off across no man's land with the men. The simple inscription on the plaque reads, 'WINSTON CHURCHILL, JANVIER–MAI 1916.'[100]

Within two days of his return to England on 7 May 1916, Churchill was back speaking in the House of Commons. In the following months he addressed the issues of the day which all revolved around the prosecution of the war – manpower needs and conscription, finance, the need for more guns and munitions, the air defence against Zeppelin attacks, and the creation of a Cabinet-level Air Ministry. His experiences in the war informed and animated his speeches as he became a strong critic of government policy. In a speech in the Commons on 23 May 1916 he said:

'I say to myself every day, what is going on while we sit here, while we go away to dinner, or home to bed? Nearly 1,000 men – Englishmen, Britishers, men of our own race – are knocked into bundles of bloody rags every twenty-four hours and carried away to hasty graves or field ambulances ...'[101] In a speech on 24 July, he made a plea for a fairer distribution of decorations to the men in the fighting lines:

> It is the privates, non-commissioned officers, and the regimental officers whose case requires the sympathetic attention of the House and the Secretary of State. Honours should go where death and danger go, and these are the men who pay all the penalties in the terrible business that is now proceeding.[102]

While the terrible business was proceeding, Churchill sought a voice in the government but found the political climate decidedly hostile. He was sometimes interrupted in the House with shouts of 'What about the Dardanelles?' What, indeed, had been the outcome? The Gallipoli campaign, over which Kitchener had full authority, had ended in total failure with the evacuations of Suvla and ANZAC on 19–20 December 1915 and of Helles on 8–9 January 1916. Of the 410,000 British and Imperial troops engaged there were 205,000 casualties including 34,000 killed.[103] Asquith appointed a Dardanelles Commission of inquiry and Churchill spent a good deal of his time in the year after his return from Flanders gathering documents and preparing his defence for the commission.

Over time, Churchill's political position improved and his friend David Lloyd George became Prime Minister at the head of a new coalition government, replacing Asquith in December, 1916. On 18 July 1917, Lloyd George brought Churchill back into the Cabinet as Minister of Munitions, a position which he held until after the armistice, which ended the war on 11 November 1918. Characteristically, Churchill poured his energies into his new task and made a significant contribution to the war effort, assuring an adequate supply of guns and ammunition for the big battles that led to an Allied victory on the Western Front.[104] For his civilian contributions to the war effort Churchill was decorated with the Army Distinguished Service Medal by the United States of America. The War Department's General Order of 10 May 1919 announced the award to 'Hon. Winston Churchill, British Minister of Munitions, for exceptionally meritorious and distinguished services. He rendered the allies service of inestimable value ... he was confronted with a task of great magnitude. With ability of a high order, energy, and marked devotion to duty, he handled with great success the trying problems with which he was constantly confronted. In performance of his great task he rendered valuable service to the American Expeditionary Forces.'[105] American General John J. Pershing, Commander of the AEF, went to the War Office in London on 16 July 1919 and personally presented the medal to Churchill.[106]

After Lloyd George was returned to Parliament and retained the premiership in December 1918, he appointed Churchill Secretary of State for War, the position held by Kitchener at the outbreak of the war. Churchill was also made Minister for Air and held the dual appointment as civilian head of the army and air force from 15 January 1919 until he left the War Ministry on 14 February 1921 and the Air Ministry on 1 April 1921. It appeared that Churchill was correct in his decision to leave the army for his true war station in London in 1916 even though he was not returned to the Cabinet for almost two years after his resignation. After his services as Minister for Munitions, War and Air Churchill was appointed Secretary of State for the Colonies on 14 February 1921. On 7 November 1924, a few weeks before his fiftieth birthday, he became Chancellor of the Exchequer, the second highest position in the government matching the peak achievement in his father's career. With his political fortunes recovered, the future held much promise.

In a number of ways, Churchill was never able to leave the terrible business of the Great War behind him. As a military strategist and war planner by both avocation and profession he sought to learn the lessons that both Cabinet service and active service offered. Some of the lessons had to be relearned and his conclusions modified in light of events in the decades ahead, but much of what he acquired was of lasting value. He came to recognise the importance of aerial warfare, both defensive and offensive, and how it created a new dimension to waging war. He learned the significance of armoured warfare and how it could change the dynamics of war on land. He was reminded of what he had already discovered in the Sudan and Natal, that frontal assaults by infantry alone were doomed to fail against modern weapons and were a futile waste of lives. He laid emphasis on the importance of close co-ordination between sea and land forces in amphibious operations, so that the failures of the Dardanelles should not be repeated. He learned the strategic importance of multiple fronts against an enemy, the failure of Gallipoli and the collapse of Russia notwithstanding. Alliances, too, were crucial. Where, after all, would Great Britain have been without the French army, the troops and resources provided by its Commonwealth partners, and, finally, the weight of American manpower and industry? He laid stress upon logistics, particularly the provision of adequate manpower and munitions and the allocation of them to the places where and at the times when they would do the most good. Strong, unified political leadership in the Cabinet was essential to guide the course of a war. He never wavered in his basic approach to war-making, always taking the offensive when possible and, in any event, always to continue fighting stubbornly. He found that he was still possessed of a strong personal constitution, strong enough to survive the battles of politics as well as the dangers of active military service. It was reassuring, too, to realise that his strong belief in his star, that fate would perhaps spare him for bigger things, was not misplaced. He learned the value of keeping an open mind to new strategies and tactics and especially to new technologies. Finally he came to view war not as romantic or as glorious but as merely tragic. The sporting game of the colonial wars on the fringes of empire in the nineteenth century bore no resemblance to the scale, the duration and the mechanised violence of a general European war. He was profoundly moved by the sufferings of the common people and the other ranks and never forgot them.

In January 1916 Churchill had attended a lecture for officers at Haze-brouck, France, given by Colonel Arthur Holland on the topic of the recent battle of Loos which had not only failed to break through the German front but had also caused sixty per cent casualties in the IXth (Scottish) Division. As Churchill wrote to Clementine: 'Afterwards they asked what was the lesson of the lecture. I restrained an impulse to reply 'Don't do it again.' But they will – I have no doubt.'[107] In a sense this was the great lesson of the Great War. Do not let a war like this happen again if it can be honourably avoided. And if such a war should recur, do not wage it the way the First World War was waged, but rather apply the lessons that were there to be learned.

As a historian and writer of history, Churchill never renounced the subject of war. His great labour after the Great War was *The World Crisis*, on which he worked steadily until the sixth and final volume was published in 1931. This was Churchill's highly personal and eloquently written account in which he not only related the history of the conflict and his role in it but made the case in defence of his own decisions and role in the Dardanelles campaign. It is a series of volumes that presents a grand political and strategic overview, and as J. M. Keynes called it, 'a tractate against war'; it also exhibits a genuine sensitivity to the suffering of the peoples involved.[108]

In a very personal sense, the terrible business of the war stayed with Churchill. He was always willing to write an introduction to books by his friends on the subject. Yet he could never forget the cost of the conflict in human terms. Great Britain suffered 880,000 men killed in action in the First World War.[109] His cousin Norman Leslie, the son of Aunt Leonie, was killed at Armentières in 1914. His brother-in-law William Hozier, after service in the Royal Navy, committed suicide in 1918. Among his friends and political colleagues who lost family in the war were former Prime Minister Lord Rosebery, Prime Minister Asquith, the leaders of the Labour and Conservative parties, Lord Lansdowne, the Duke of West-minster, Lord Stamfordham, Lord Crewe and Prince Louis. Among the war dead, too, were close friends of Churchill from Harrow, the 4th Hussars, the 21st Lancers, the Queen's Own Oxfordshire Hussars and the Royal Scots Fusiliers. Churchill frequently paused when he entered the St Stephen's Lobby at the House of Commons and looked at the names of the many Members of Parliament – friends and contemporaries – who had been killed in the war. The scenes he had witnessed and the deaths of so many of his generation haunted Churchill and caused him deep sorrow; the fact he had survived was thought-provoking. While serving as Secretary of State for the Colonies, Churchill wrote out a poem in longhand, on India Office stationery, that set out his private reflections:

A Grave in Flanders

Here in the marshland, past the battered bridge,
One of a hundred grains untimely sown,
Here with his comrades of the hard-won ridge
He rests unknown.

His horoscope had seemed so plainly drawn –
School triumphs, earned apace in work and play;
Friendship at will, then love's delightful dawn
And mellowing day:

Home fostering hope; some service to the State;
Benignant age; then the long tryst to keep
Where in the year the shadows congregate
His father's sleep.

Was here the one thing needed to distil
From life's alembic, through this holier fate,
The man's essential soul, the hero will?
We ask; and wait.[110]

Conclusion

In a 1995 essay, American historian David McCullough wrote: 'Among the most difficult and important concepts to convey in the teaching or writing of history is the simple fact that things never had to turn out as they did. Events past were never on a track. Nothing was foreordained any more then than now.'[1] This is particularly worth remembering concerning Winston Churchill both as a soldier and statesman. It was a very long and winding path from his birth at Blenheim Palace to his arrival as Prime Minister at No. 10 Downing Street in June 1940 at the age of sixty-five. He overcame many obstacles and faced many dangers along the way.

Although Churchill was born into the aristocracy in the peak years of the British Empire, his parents had little money of their own and his mother was widowed when Winston was only twenty. He inherited neither the Marlborough title nor the family estates. He established himself in the ranks of power in Great Britain by virtue of his own talent and drive, the combination of genius and plod. Although his family's social and political connections helped him to get his start, he was a self-made man. His achievements were the result of a tremendously energetic personality harnessed to a prodigious personal ambition.

Churchill was a man of many parts but the military aspect of his life was central to his character and to the person he became. He went into the army because his father thought he was not clever enough to go to university, but once consigned to a military education and employment as a soldier, Churchill worked hard and excelled. He sought out active service whenever and wherever he could and managed in a few short years to see combat on three continents and to make a reputation for himself as a brave and resourceful soldier. As a young officer he pursued the ideals and goals of his class and his era – glory in sport and glory in battle – with real success both on the polo ground and the battlefield. He liked soldiering and found that it simplified life by focusing him on the tasks at hand. He enjoyed the comradeship of the regiment and ever after maintained an identification with old friends and old settings from his army days. His combat experience was important in proving his courage to himself as much as to others. To behave well under fire gave him self-assurance and to survive brushes with death reaffirmed his own life-long belief in his destiny to be spared from harm so that he could achieve great deeds in the defence of Great Britain.[2]

Churchill's courage was often demonstrated during his early years in the army and often remarked upon by others. His fellow soldiers commented at the time not only about his cool leadership under fire but also his absolute fearlessness. In later years the pattern continued as he engaged in front-line service in the First World War that could easily have been avoided. Even as a civilian he faced physical danger without hesitation. As Minister of Munitions in 1918 he visited the Western Front and was under fire; and in the Second World War as Prime Minister and Minister of Defence he visited the armies in North Africa, France and Italy, often venturing close to the front lines. During the Battle of Britain he took what his bodyguard referred to as 'deliberate risks' by refusing to remain in underground shelters during air raids.[3] He wanted very much to accompany the fleet to the Normandy beaches on D-Day and was only prevented from doing so by the personal intervention of King George VI. His physical courage and refusal to flinch in the face of an enemy was a key component of Churchill's make-up as a statesman and war leader. After Churchill's visit to the Eighth Army in Egypt in August 1942, American General Douglas MacArthur remarked to a senior British intelligence officer: 'If disposal of all the Allied decorations were today placed by providence in my hands, my first act would be to award the Victoria Cross to Winston Churchill. No one of those who wear it deserves it more than he. A flight of 10,000 miles through hostile and foreign skies may be the duty of young pilots, but for a statesman burdened with the world's cares, it is an act of inspiring gallantry and valour.'[4]

Another aspect of Churchill's character that developed during his military service was his magnanimity towards defeated enemies, which was itself a reflection of his essential humanity.[5] In his personal correspondence and his published writings during his military service, Churchill would sometimes refer to the enemy fighters as barbarians because of their cruelty or as fanatics because of their messianic religious beliefs, but he consistently admired and complimented their fighting qualities and their remarkable bravery under fire. He criticised his own commanding officers, especially in the Sudan campaign, for their cruelty toward enemy wounded and prisoners. Significantly, he did not give voice to the racial epithets that were commonly used in those days to refer to native peoples.

During his army service in the 1890s Churchill was accused by some of being a 'medal hunter' and a 'self-advertiser' and both charges were true. He was interested in medals because they represented the ideals of service and courage he highly valued. And he was not only interested in getting medals to pin upon his own tunic. He went out of his way to assist others, notably the armoured train driver and fireman in South Africa, in getting the recognition they deserved. He considered military medals 'the poor man's escutcheon' and with a keen eye for medal ribbons could determine a serviceman's campaign history at a glance. Once, between the world wars, he was accompanied to the theatre by his daughter Mary and, noticing the ribbons on the coat of a commissionaire, asked the veteran whether they might have the honour of shaking the hand of a holder of the Victoria Cross. As Prime Minister he would often invite young officers who had been decorated for heroism to come to dinner.[6]

Churchill's 'self-advertisement' took the form of the newspaper articles and books he wrote about the military campaigns in which he took part. His writings, however, did not merely concentrate on his personal role. They contained very courageous criticism of war policy and the conduct of individual campaigns in which he was involved. His career as a journalist began with the series of reports from his trip to Cuba as a military observer in 1895 and continued in a brilliant sequence of articles and books. The writing and analysis, beginning with *The Story of the Malakand Field Force* in 1898, was consistently of a very high quality. *The River War*, *Marlborough His Life and Times*, *The World Crisis* and *The Second World War* were all critically acclaimed and have been reprinted in many editions and abridgments.[7] Excerpts from a number of Churchill's military books were published in anthologies of the finest war writing.[8] His writings about his adventures in South Africa were, as has been seen, instrumental in bolstering his political career by making his name and reputation known to the British public.

With the battle of Omdurman, Churchill's view of war began to change and his heroic view of warfare was replaced by a growing sense of its waste and tragedy. His months in the line during the First World War only served to reaffirm and strengthen that view. Particpation in the lesser wars as a subaltern was a minor influence on Churchill's preparation as a war leader compared to his service in the Great War. After that he had no illusions about the ugly, brutal aspect of war and the awful scale of carnage caused by modern weapons. But his service was valuable in affording him first-hand experience of the conditions and problems of land war in the twentieth century. By the time Churchill completed his last period of service in Flanders in 1916 he had more actual combat experience than any senior British politician, more indeed than many Americans who would be general officers in the Second World War including Marshall, Eisenhower and Patton.

Churchill never intended to make a career of the army and said so early and often. Kitchener was right when he remarked in the Sudan that Churchill was merely making a convenience of the army for his own benefit. He never could have remained because it would have smothered him. It lacked the atmosphere of intellectual curiosity that came naturally to him; the talk was mostly of sport and shop. Moreover, it lacked the grand stage for his ambitions that a political career could provide. The army was simply not big enough to hold him.

Churchill's service in the army left him with a life-long love of uniforms. When he retired from the Territorial Army in 1924 he was given permission to wear the uniform of his old regiment. In addition to this he had to wear from time to time the full dress uniform, including a cocked hat with ostrich plume, of Privy Counsellor to which position he had been appointed in 1907, or the full dress uniform of an Elder Brother of Trinity House. He wore the more restrained double-breasted blue coat and cap of the Royal Yacht Club at his August 1941 summit conference with President Roosevelt in Newfoundland. On 4 April 1939 Churchill was appointed Honorary Air Commodore of No. 615 (County of Surrey) Squadron of the Royal Auxiliary Air Force and thereafter wore an RAF uniform on many occasions, not least at the Tehran Conference with Roosevelt and Stalin in November 1943 and on his third visit to Normandy in August 1944.[9] He was also appointed Honorary Colonel of several army regiments during and after the Second World War and was entitled to wear their uniforms with the appropriate badges of rank and his many rows of medal ribbons. He wore the uniform of Honorary Colonel of the 5th (Cinque Ports) Battalion, the Royal Sussex Regiment at the Rhine crossing in 1945, at the Yalta and Potsdam conferences and at the victory parade in Berlin on 21 July 1945.[10]

Yet for all his military experience and love of the badges of rank and service, one must not underestimate the importance of Churchill's long and varied political career as preparation for his leadership in the Second World War. From the time he entered Parliament in 1900 he maintained a regular interest in military matters. Even during his 'wilderness years' from 1929 to 1939 when he was in political disfavour and excluded from the

Cabinet, he was a one-man shadow government in support of rearmament in face of the growing threat of Nazi Germany. He consistently advocated his view that military strength was the best guarantor of peace and absolutely essential in case of war. By the time war began in September 1939 Churchill had held all the important Cabinet posts except foreign affairs and the premiership. In addition to being Home Secretary, Secretary of State for the Colonies and Chancellor of the Exchequer, he had been Minister of Munitions and, at one time or another, civilian head of the army, the navy and the air force. He had vast administrative and political experience and these, combined with his military interest and background, prepared him as well as anyone could be prepared to serve as Prime Minister during the Second World War, his and Great Britain's finest hour. As Churchill later wrote in the first volume of his history of that conflict, the night after he was appointed Prime Minister on 10 May 1940, he went to bed with 'a profound sense of relief. At last I had authority to give directions over the whole scene. I felt as if I were walking with destiny, and that all my past life had been but a preparation for this hour and this trial.'[11]

Maps

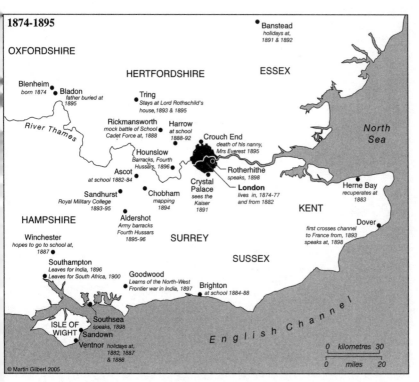

1874-1895

OXFORDSHIRE

HERTFORDSHIRE

ESSEX

Banstead
*holidays at,
1891 & 1892*

Blenheim
born 1874

Bladon
*father buried at
1895*

Tring
*Stays at Lord Rothschild's
house, 1893 & 1895*

Rickmansworth
*mock battle of School
Cadet Force at, 1888*

Harrow
*at school
1888-92*

Crouch End
*death of his nanny,
Mrs Everest 1895*

River Thames

Hounslow
*Barracks, Fourth
Hussars, 1896*

Ascot
at school 1882-84

Rotherhithe
speaks, 1898

Crystal
Palace

London
*lives in, 1874-77
and from 1882*

North
Sea

Sandhurst
*Royal Military College
1893-95*

Chobham
*mapping
1894*

*sees the
Kaiser
1891*

Herne Bay
*recuperates at
1883*

KENT

HAMPSHIRE

Aldershot
*Army barracks
Fourth Hussars
1895-96*

SURREY

Winchester
*hopes to go to school at,
1887*

Dover
*first crosses channel
to France from, 1893
speaks at, 1898*

Southampton
*Leaves for India, 1896
Leaves for South Africa, 1900*

Goodwood
*Learns of the North-West
Frontier war in India, 1897*

SUSSEX

Brighton
at school 1884-88

ISLE OF
WIGHT

Southsea
speaks, 1898

Sandown

Ventnor *holidays at,
1882, 1887
& 1888*

English Channel

0   kilometres 30

0   miles   20

© Martin Gilbert 2005

1. The Home Counties of England, 1874–1895.

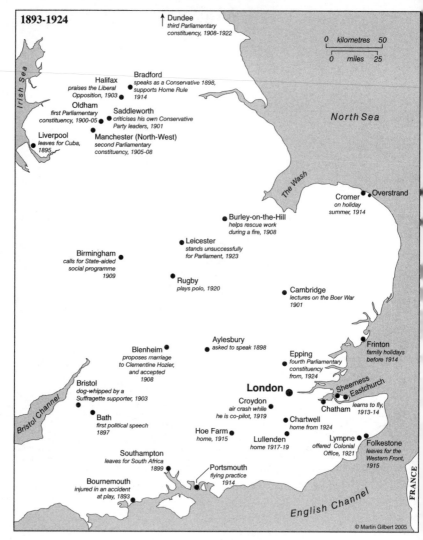

1893-1924

Dundee
*third Parliamentary
constituency, 1908-1922*

0 kilometres 50

0 miles 25

Irish Sea

North Sea

Halifax
*praises the Liberal
Opposition, 1903*

Bradford
*speaks as a Conservative 1898,
supports Home Rule
1914*

Oldham
*first Parliamentary
constituency, 1900-05*

Saddleworth
*criticises his own Conservative
Party leaders, 1901*

Liverpool
*leaves for Cuba,
1895*

Manchester (North-West)
*second Parliamentary
constituency, 1905-08*

The Wash

Cromer
*on holiday
summer, 1914*

Overstrand

Burley-on-the-Hill
*helps rescue work
during a fire, 1908*

Leicester
*stands unsuccessfully
for Parliament, 1923*

Birmingham
*calls for State-aided
social programme
1909*

Rugby
plays polo, 1920

Cambridge
*lectures on the Boer War
1901*

Aylesbury
asked to speak 1898

Blenheim
*proposes marriage
to Clementine Hozier,
and accepted
1908*

Epping
*fourth Parliamentary
constituency
from, 1924*

Frinton
*family holidays
before 1914*

Bristol
*dog-whipped by a
Suffragette supporter, 1903*

London

Sheerness
Eastchurch

Croydon
*air crash while
he is co-pilot, 1919*

Chatham

*learns to fly,
1913-14*

Bristol Channel

Bath
*first political speech
1897*

Chartwell
home from 1924

Hoe Farm
home, 1915

Lullenden
home 1917-19

Lympne
*offered Colonial
Office, 1921*

Folkestone
*leaves for the
Western Front,
1915*

Southampton
*leaves for South Africa
1899*

Portsmouth
*flying practice
1914*

FRANCE

Bournemouth
*injured in an accident
at play, 1893*

English Channel

© Martin Gilbert 2005

2. Southern England, 1893–1924.

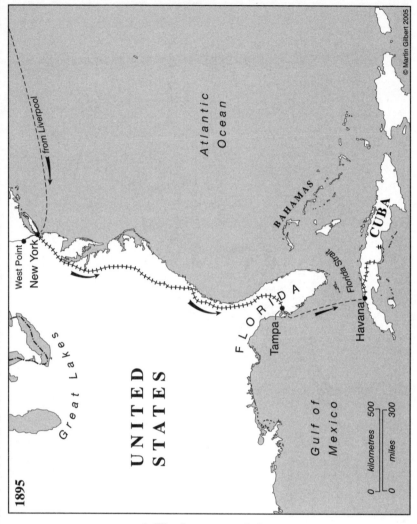

3. The Journey to Cuba.

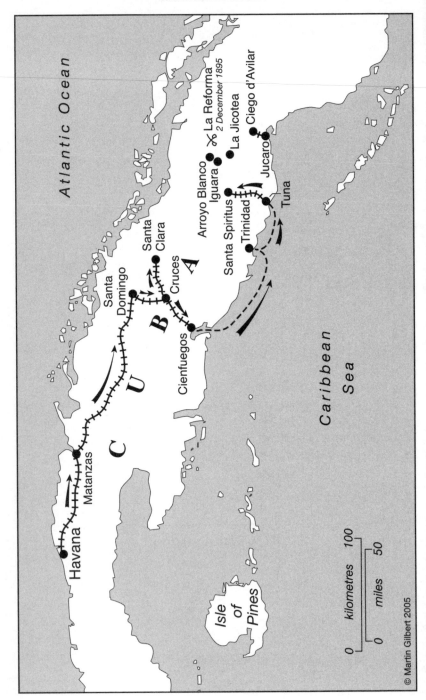

4. Cuba, 1895.

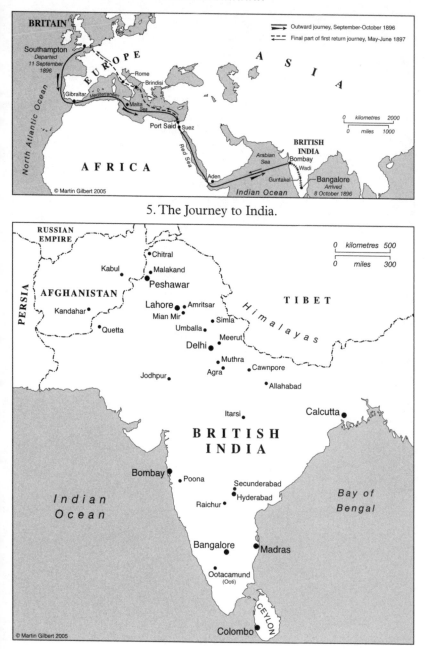

5. The Journey to India.

6. British India, 1896.

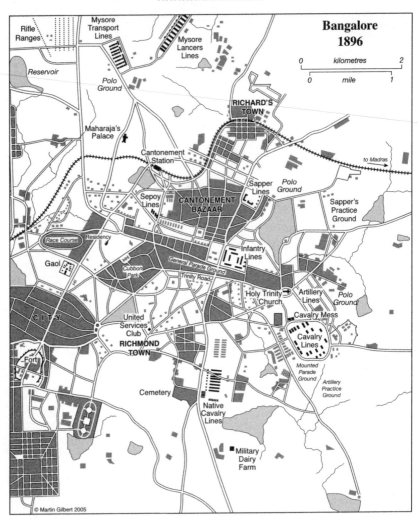

7. Bangalore, 1896.

0. North-West Frontier of India.

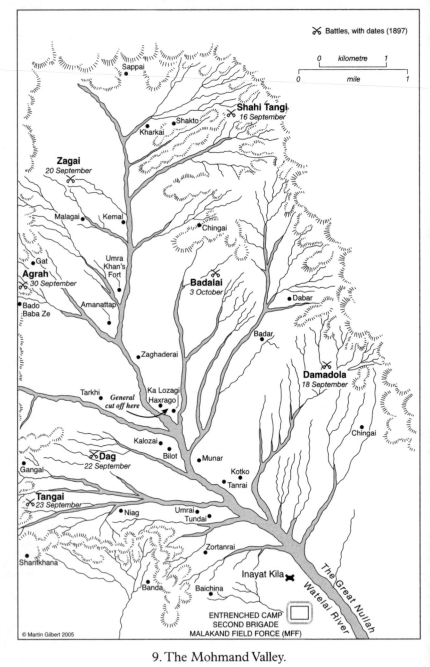

9. The Mohmand Valley.

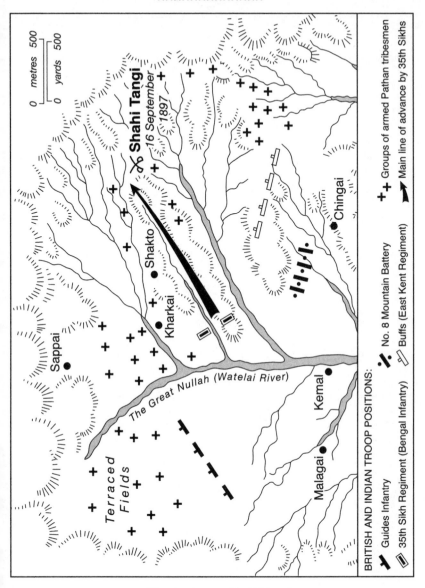

The map key:

BRITISH AND INDIAN TROOP POSITIONS:

No. 8 Mountain Battery

Buffs (East Kent Regiment)

Guides Infantry

35th Sikh Regiment (Bengal Infantry)

Groups of armed Pathan tribesmen

Main line of advance by 35th Sikhs

Map labels: Shahi Tangi, 16 September 1897, Shakto, Kharkai, Sappai, Chingai, Kemal, Malagai, The Great Nullah (Watelai River), Terraced Fields

Scale: metres 500, yards 500

10. The Action at Shahi Tangi.

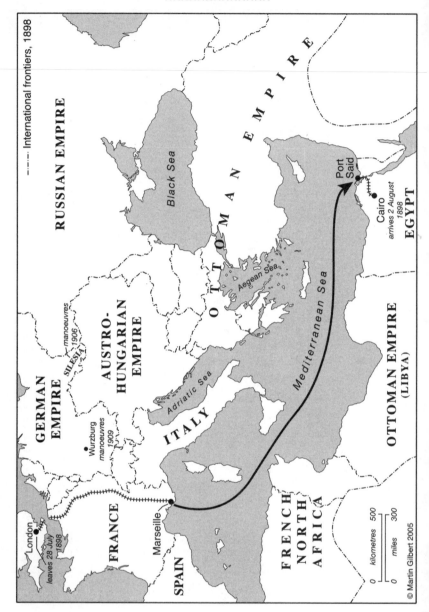

11. The Journey to Cairo.

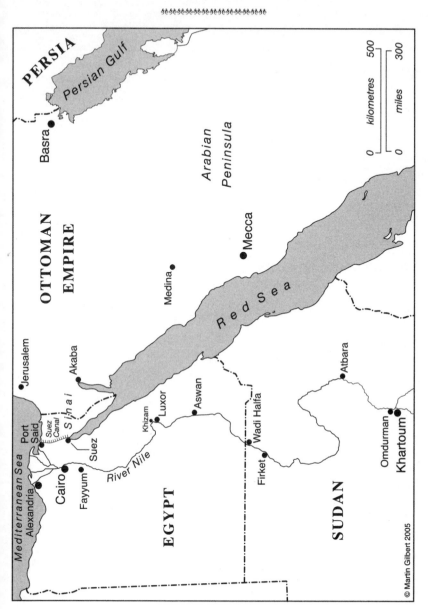

12. Egypt and the Anglo-Egyptian Sudan.

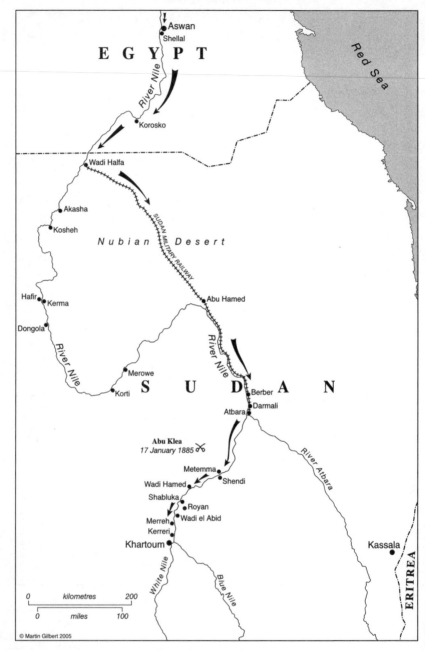

13. From Aswan to Khartoum.

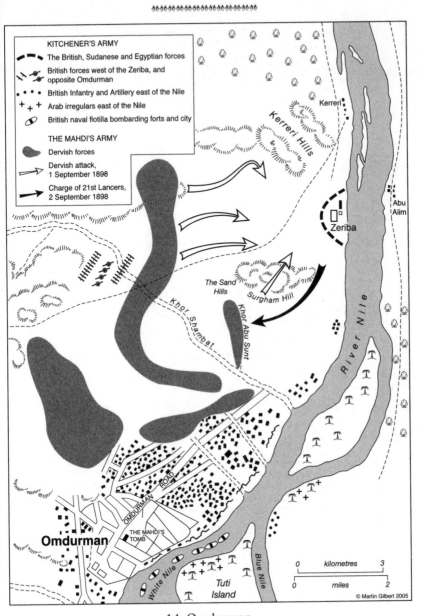

14. Omdurman.

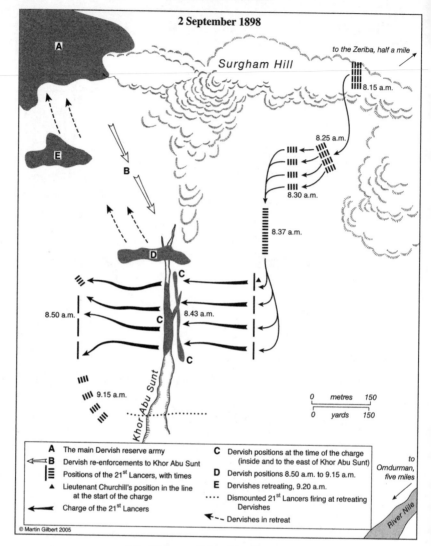

2 September 1898

A The main Dervish reserve army

B Dervish re-enforcements to Khor Abu Sunt

Positions of the 21st Lancers, with times

▲ Lieutenant Churchill's position in the line
   at the start of the charge

Charge of the 21st Lancers

C Dervish positions at the time of the charge
   (inside and to the east of Khor Abu Sunt)

D Dervish positions 8.50 a.m. to 9.15 a.m.

E Dervishes retreating, 9.20 a.m.

···· Dismounted 21st Lancers firing at retreating
   Dervishes

◄-- Dervishes in retreat

© Martin Gilbert 2005

15. Charge of the 21st Lancers.

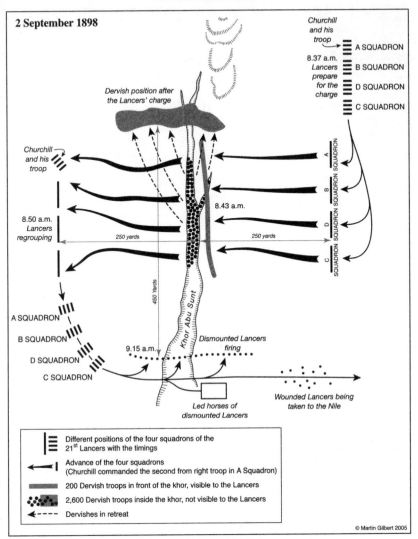

Churchill
and his
troop

A SQUADRON

8.37 a.m.
Lancers
prepare
for the
charge

B SQUADRON

D SQUADRON

C SQUADRON

Dervish position after
the Lancers' charge

Churchill
and his
troop

A SQUADRON

8.50 a.m.
Lancers
regrouping

B SQUADRON

250 yards

8.43 a.m.

D SQUADRON

250 yards

C SQUADRON

450 Yards

Khor Abu Sunt

A SQUADRON

B SQUADRON

9.15 a.m.

Dismounted Lancers
firing

D SQUADRON

C SQUADRON

Led horses of
dismounted Lancers

Wounded Lancers being
taken to the Nile

Different positions of the four squadrons of the
21st Lancers with the timings

Advance of the four squadrons
(Churchill commanded the second from right troop in A Squadron)

200 Dervish troops in front of the khor, visible to the Lancers

2,600 Dervish troops inside the khor, not visible to the Lancers

Dervishes in retreat

© Martin Gilbert 2005

16. Details of the Charge.

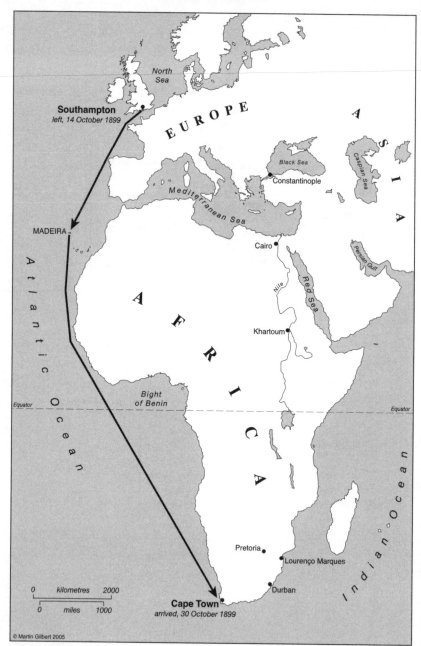

17. The Journey to South Africa.

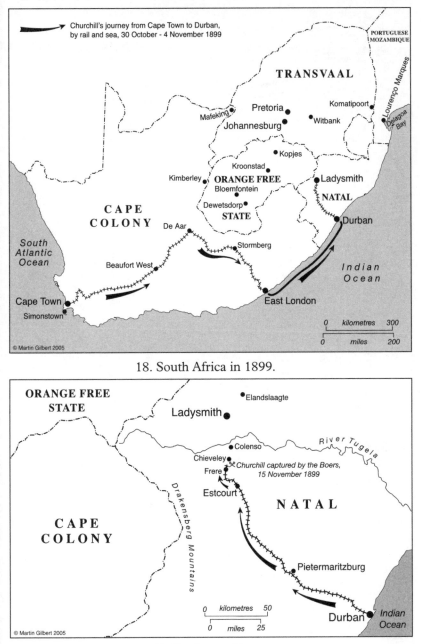

18. South Africa in 1899.

19. Durban to Frere.

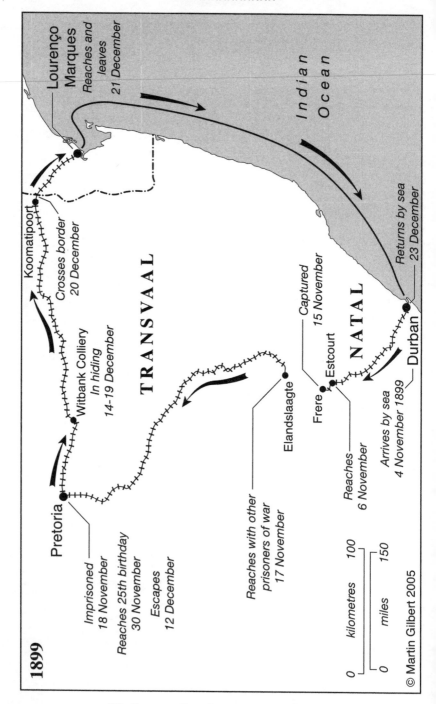

20. Capture, Imprisonment, and Escape.

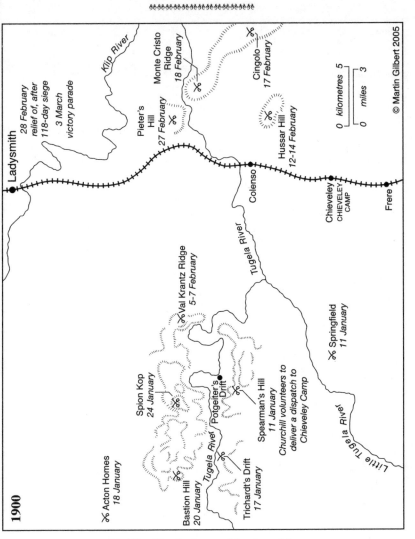

21. The Battle Around Ladysmith.

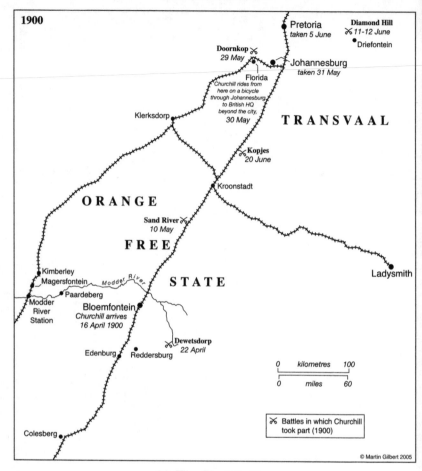

1900

Pretoria
taken 5 June

Diamond Hill
✗ *11-12 June*
• Driefontein

Doornkop ✗
29 May

Johannesburg
taken 31 May

Florida
*Churchill rides from
here on a bicycle
through Johannesburg,
to British HQ
beyond the city,
30 May*

Klerksdorp

T R A N S V A A L

Kopjes
20 June

Kroonstadt

O R A N G E

Sand River ✗
10 May

F R E E

Kimberley
Magersfontein *Modder River*

S T A T E

Ladysmith

Paardeberg
Modder
River
Station

Bloemfontein
*Churchill arrives
16 April 1900*

Dewetsdorp
22 April

Edenburg Reddersburg

0	kilometres	100
0	miles	60

✗ Battles in which Churchill
took part (1900)

Colesberg

© Martin Gilbert 2005

22. The Final Battles.

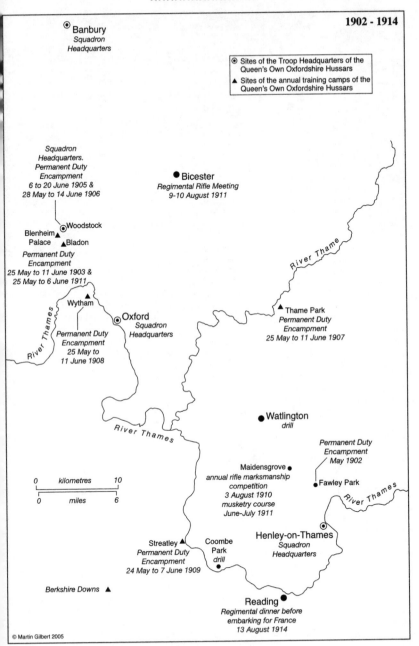

Banbury
*Squadron
Headquarters*

⊙ Sites of the Troop Headquarters of the
Queen's Own Oxfordshire Hussars
▲ Sites of the annual training camps of the
Queen's Own Oxfordshire Hussars

*Squadron
Headquarters.
Permanent Duty
Encampment
6 to 20 June 1905 &
28 May to 14 June 1906*

● Bicester
*Regimental Rifle Meeting
9-10 August 1911*

⊙Woodstock
Blenheim▲
Palace ▲Bladon
*Permanent Duty
Encampment
25 May to 11 June 1903 &
25 May to 6 June 1911*

▲
Wytham

⊙ Oxford
*Squadron
Headquarters*

*Permanent Duty
Encampment
25 May to
11 June 1908*

River Thame

▲ Thame Park
*Permanent Duty
Encampment
25 May to 11 June 1907*

River Thames

● Watlington
drill

River Thames

*Permanent Duty
Encampment
May 1902*

Maidensgrove ●
*annual rifle marksmanship
competition
3 August 1910
musketry course
June-July 1911*

● Fawley Park

River Thames

0   kilometres   10

0   miles   6

Streatley ▲
*Permanent Duty
Encampment
24 May to 7 June 1909*

Coombe
Park
drill
●

Henley-on-Thames ⊙
*Squadron
Headquarters*

Berkshire Downs ▲

Reading ●
*Regimental dinner before
embarking for France
13 August 1914*

© Martin Gilbert 2005

23. The Queen's Own Oxfordshire Hussars, 1902–1914.

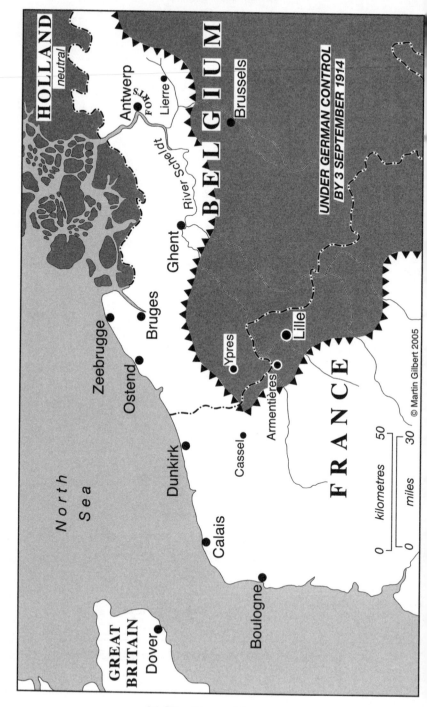

24. The Siege of Antwerp.

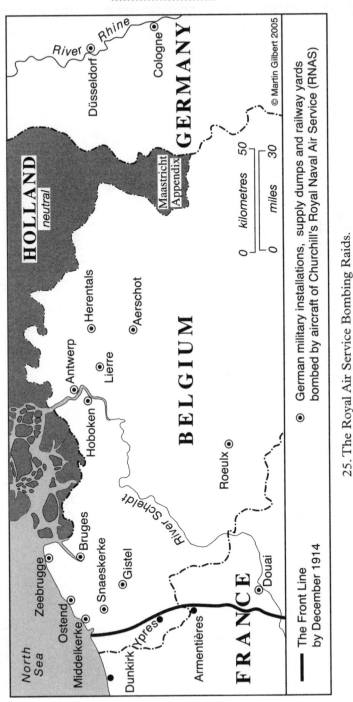

25. The Royal Air Service Bombing Raids.

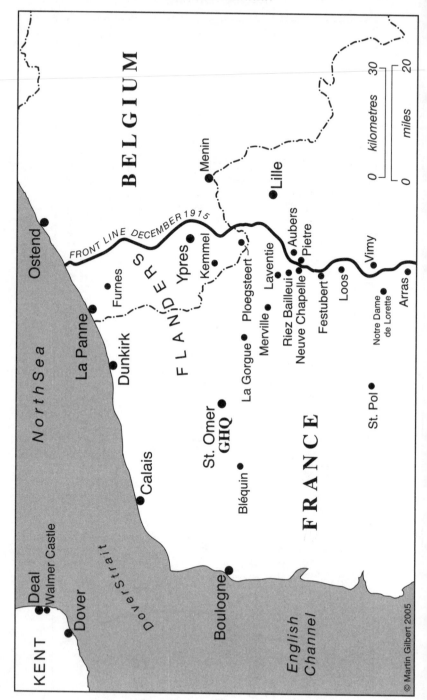

26. The Western Front from La Panne to Arras.

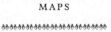

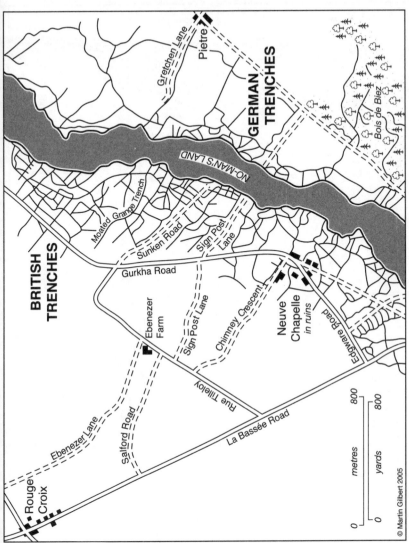

27. With the Grenadier Guards.

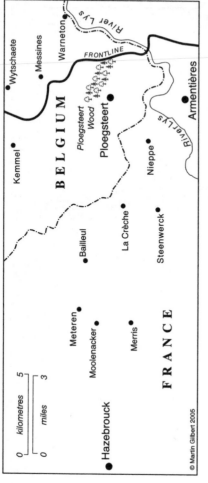

28. The 6th Royal Scots Fusiliers in Reserve.

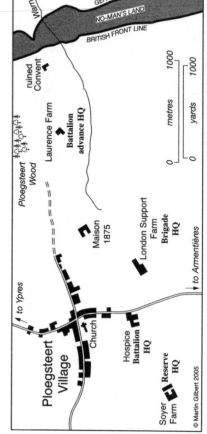

29. Plugstreet Village, Farms, and Headquarters

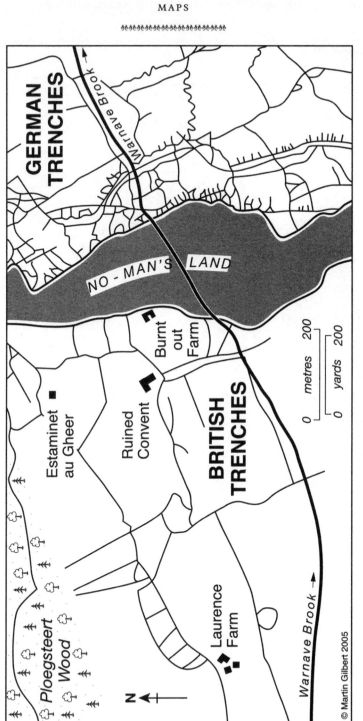

30. Plugstreet, the Trenches.

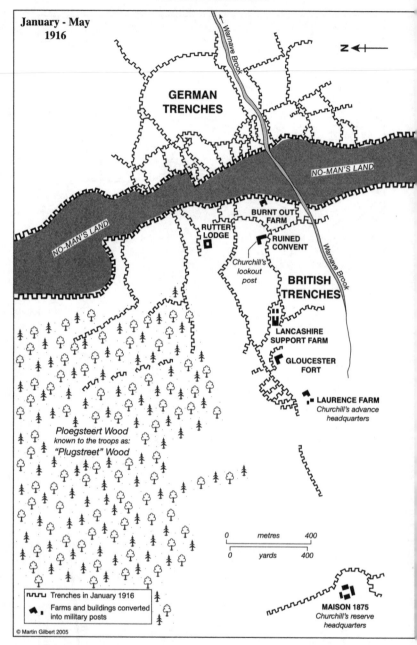

31. Plugstreet, the Front Line.

Appendices

Royal Military College, Sandhurst September 1893 Intake

	Name	Date of Birth	Final Exam	Date of Retirement	Inf/ Cav.	Regiment	Date of Appt.
1.	Airey, Robert Berkeley	21.9.74	2,069	Feb.1895	Inf.	S. Wales Borderers	6.3.95
2.	Allan, Percy Stuart	11.12.74	2,368	Feb.1895	Inf.	Gordon Highlanders	6.3.95
3.	Allan, William Munro	5.9.74	2,333	Feb,1895	Inf.	King's Own Scottish Borderers	6.3.95
4.	Arbuthnot, Archibald Hugh	7.12.74	2,437	Feb.1895	Inf.	Royal Inskilling Fus.	6.3.95
5.	Armstrong, Allan	11.2.75	2,467	Feb.1895	Inf.	Wiltshire Regt	20.2.95
6.	Ashburner, Lionel Forbes[1] (Senior Corporal)	18.9.74	2,339	Feb.1895	—	Unattached List1	16.1.95
7.	Atchison, Charles Ernest[2]	12.5.75	2,765	Feb.1895	Inf.	Shropshire LI	20.2.95
8.	Awdry, Vere Henry Ambrose[3] (Senior Corporal)	3.6.75	2,477	Feb.1895	Inf.	Lancashire Fus.	20.2.95
9.	Battye, Ivan Urmston[1] (Senior Corporal)	5.3.75	2,649	Feb.1895	—	Unattached List	16.1.95
10.	Bennett, Lionel Edmond Anstey	18.4.75	2,182	Feb.1895	Inf.	Oxford LI	6.3.95
11.	Bevan, Frank (Corporal)	4.7.74	2,719	Feb.1895	Inf.	North'd Fusiliers	20.2.95
12.	Birch, Valentine Kingston[1]	4.7.75	2,043	Feb.1895	—	Unattached List	16.1.95
13.	Blackett, William Stewart[4]	23.10.73	2,292	Feb.1895	Inf.	Grenadier Guards	8.5.95
14.	Boevery, Edward Martin Crawley[4]	26.3.73	2,356	Feb.1895	—		
15.	Bramly, Alwyn William Jennings (Senior Corporal)	27.3.75	2,112	Feb.1895	Cav.	2nd Dragoons	6.3.95
16.	Brooke, James Sleeman[5] (Senior Corporal)	3.2.75	None	Feb.1895	Cav.	Resigned Cadetship	31.8.94
17.	Bruce, Alan George Cameron	29.9.74	2,357	Feb.1895	Cav.	8th Hussars	6.3.95
18.	Bruce, Edward Maunsell	29.9.74	2,251	Feb.1895	Cav.	6th Dragoons	6.3.95
19.	Bruce, Jonathan Maxwell[14]	26.6.73	2,178	Feb.1895	—	Unattached List	16.1.95
20.	Buckley, Basil Thorold (Senior Corporal)	28.9.74	2,575	Feb.1895	Inf.	North'd Fusiliers	20.2.95
21.	Buckley, John Joseph[1]	11.2.76	2,345	Feb.1895	—	Unattached List	16.1.95
22.	Bundock, Hugh Frederick (Corporal)	9.1.75	2,320	Feb.1895	Inf.	Essex Regt	6.3.95
23.	Burnett, Stuart	14.3.75	2,637	Feb.1895	Inf.	Rifle Brigade	6.3.95
24.	Carey, Seymour James[6]	5.8.74	2,532	Feb.1895	Inf.	Suffolk Regt	20.2.95
25.	Channer, George Kendall[4]	5.10.73	2,548	Feb.1895	—	Unattached List	16.1.95
26.	Chapman, Edward Henry	25.4.75	2,622	Feb.1895	Inf.	Yorkshire Regt	20.2.95
27.	Chapman, Wilfred Constantine[7] (Senior Corporal)	26.12.74	2,375	Aug.1895	—	On sick lv 2nd term	
28.	Chichester, Claud Oswald	29.1.75	2,420	Feb.1895	Inf.	Oxford LI	6.3.95
29.	Churchill, Winston Leonard Spencer	30.11.74	2,646	Feb.1895	Cav.	4th Hussars	20.2.95
30.	Clarke, Fredrick Lawrence Stanley (Senior Corporal)	30.6.75	2,365	Feb.1895	Inf.	Scottish Rifles	6.3.95
31.	Conway-Gordon, Esme Cosmo William[1]	29.8.75	2,319	Feb.1895	—	Unattached List	16.1.95

ჰჰჰჰჰჰჰჰჰჰჰჰჰჰ

Name	Date of Birth	Final Exam	Date of Retirement	Inf/ Cav.	Regiment	Date of Appt.
32. Cook, Bertram Hewett Hunter	3.7.74	2,304	Feb.1895	Inf.	Rifle Brigade	22.5.95
33. Courtenay, George Edward[8]	25.3.75	2,450	Feb.1895	Inf.	Argyll/Suth'd Highlanders	20.2.95
34. Craig-Brown, Ernest (Corporal, Under Officer)	20.6.71	2,731	Feb.1895	Inf.	West India Regt	20.2.95
35. Davidson, Francis Coventry Dudfield[9]	18.8.74	1,823	Feb.1895	Inf.	Royal Lancaster Regt (hon: Queen's)	6.3.95
36. Davies, John Munsey	22.12.74 6.3.95	2,321	Feb.1895	Inf.	Durham Light Infantry	
37. Davis, George Henville	11.10.74	2,574	Feb. 1895	Inf.	E. Yorkshire Regt	20.2.95
38. de la Condamine, Henry John[4]	5.4.73	2,291	Feb.1895	Inf.	Duke of Cornwall's Light Infantry	30.1.95
39. de Saumarez, Lionel Wilfred	13.7.74	2,203	Feb.1895	Inf.	King's Royal Rifle Corps	12.6.95
40. Deverell, Cyril John	9.11.74	2,250	Feb.1895	Inf.	W. Yorkshire Regt	6.3.95
41. Dickinson, Arthur Thomas Searle	7.3.75	2,614	Feb.1895	Inf.	Somerset Light Infantry	20.2.95
42. du Boulay, Thomas Wm. Houssemayne	26.1.75	2,388	Feb.1895	Inf.	Border Regt	6.3.95
43. Dunn-Pattison, Richard Phillipson[10]	22.12.74	2,894	Feb.1895	Inf.	Argyl & Suth'd Highlanders	20.2.95
44. Du Pre, William Baring	5.4.75	2,638	Feb.1895	Inf.	King's Royal Rifle Corps	12.6.95
45. Elwes, Henry Cecil	25.8.74	2,236	Feb.1895	Inf.	Scots Guards	6.3.95
46. Ewart, Godfrey Douglas Henry	9.8.74	1,942	Feb.1895	Inf.	S. Lancashire Regt (hon. Queen's)	6.3.95
47. Fagan, Bernard Joseph	8.10.74	2,355	Feb.1895	Inf.	Royal Munster Fus.	6.3.95
48. Fox, Michael Francis	26.7.74	2,154	Feb.1895	Inf.	P. of Wales Leinster Regt	6.3.95
49. Gardiner, Richard	31.10.74	2,380	Feb.1895	Inf.	S. Lancashire Regt	6.3.95
50. Geddes, Malcom Henry Burdett[4] [1]	20.2.74	2,139	Feb.1895	—	Unattached List	16.1.95
51. Godbold, George Augustus James	15.8.74	2,482	Feb.1895	Inf.	The Manchester Regt	20.2.95
52. Godwin, Charles Alexander Campbell[1] (Senior Corporal)	28.10.73	2,465	Feb.1895	—	Unattached List	16.1.95
53. Goodfellow, Robert Charles[1] (QIC)	16.5. 75	2,260	Feb.1895	—	Unattached List	16.1.95
54. Graham, Bertram Robert[1] (Corporal, Under Officer)	19.12.74	2,257	Feb.1895	—	Unattached List	16.1.95
55. Graham, Jocelyn Henry Clive	23.12.74	2,355	Feb.1895	Inf.	Coldstream Guards	6.3.95
56. Greenley, Walton Howarth[11] (Senior Corporal, Under Officer)	2.1.75	2,720	Feb.1895	Cav.	12th Lancers	20.2.95
57. Grover, Percival Charles[12]	16.3.75	2,670	Feb.1895	Inf.	Shropshire LI	20.2.95
58. Henderson, Arthur Francis[1]	21.11.74	2,720	Feb.1895	—	Unattached List	16.1.95
59. Hennell, Alfred Montagu	16.8.74	2,598	Feb.1895	Inf.	Hampshire Regt	20.2.95
60. Hesketh, Algernon Ernest[13]	12.11.74	2,480	Feb.1895	Cav.	16th Lancers	20.2.95
61. Hill, Frederick Thomas Cecil[4]	16.7.74	2,154	Feb.1895	Inf.	York & Lanc Regt	6.3.95
62. Hill, Frank William Roland	19.2.75	2,703	Feb.1895	Inf.	Dorset Regt	20.2.95
63. Hincks, Thomas Cowper	31.1.75	2,764	Feb.1895	Inf.	Royal Berkshire Regt	20.2.95
64. Hodgson, Hamilton	6.7.74	2,759	Feb.1895	Inf.	Lincoln Regt	20.2.95
65. Home, Archibald Fraser	14.9.74	2,471	Feb.1895	Cav.	11th Hussars	no date
66. Hope, Richard Berwick (Corporal)	25.10.74	2,682	Feb.1895	Inf.	Royal West Kent Regt	20.2.95
67. Hoskyn, John Cunningham Moore[1]	20.12.75	2,591	Feb.1895	—	Unattached List	16.1.95

Name	Date of Birth	Final Exam	Date of Retirement	Inf/ Cav.	Regiment	Date of Appt.
68. Howard-Vyse, George Aubrey (hon: Queen's)	1.7.74	2,355	Feb.1895	Inf.	Liverpool Regt	6.3.95
69. Hutchinson, William Arthur (hon: Queen's)	14.11.74	2,084	Feb.1895	Inf.	Royal Munster Fus.	6.3.95
70. Isacke, Reginald (Corporal)	3.8.74	2,462	Feb.1895	Inf.	N. Yorks Regt	20.2.95
71. Keyes, Charles Valentine[115]	14.2.76	2,416	Feb.1895	—	Unattached List	16.1.95
72. Kidd, Bertram Graham Balfour[1]	6.12.75	2,635	Feb.1895	—	Unattached List	16.1.95
73. Knocker, Arthur Gerald	17.9.74	2,215	Feb.1895	Inf.	Royal Irish Fus.	6.3.95
74. Lance, Fred'k Fitz Hugh[1]	8.12.75	2,065	Feb.1895	—	Unattached List	16.1.95
75. Lee, Harvey Romer (Corporal, Senior Corporal)	21.7.74	2,456	Feb.1895	Cav.	20th Hussars	20.2.95
76. Lee-Dillon (Hon.) Harry Lee Stanton	25.7.74	2,305	Feb.1895	Inf.	Rifle Brigade	14.4.95
77. Lennox, Claud Henry Maitland[4]	20.10.73	1,764	Feb.1895	—	North'd Fusiliers	6.3.95
78. Lethbridge, William Agar Lander (Senior Corporal)	12.9.74	2,584	Feb.1895	Inf.	Royal Lancaster Regt	6.3.95
79. Lethbridge, Ambrose Jarburgh (Senior Corporal)	2.11.74	2,248	Feb.1895	Inf.	Grenadier Guards	20.2.95
80. Longridge, James Atkinson (Corporal)	5.2.75	2,879	Feb.1895	Inf.	R. West Surrey Regt	20.2.95
81. Luckhardt, Hubert Cecil[1]	3.4.74	1,760	Feb.1895	—	Unattached List	16.1.95
82. McTaggart, Maxwell Fielding	1.11.74	2,543	Feb.1895	Cav.	5th Lancers	20.2.95
83. Macdonald, Clarence Reginald	4.2.76	2,138	Feb.1895	Inf.	Leinster Regt	6.3.95
84. Magniac, Francis Arthur[1]	2.8.75	2,112	Feb.1895	—	Unattached List	14.8.95
85. Marshall, William Muir Knox	17.10.74	2,270	Feb.1895	Inf.	Gordon Highlanders	6.3.95
86. Maxwell, Denis Wellesley	24.3.75	2,544	Feb.1895	Inf.	Highland LI	20.2.95
87. Mercer, Archibald Ariel[16]	24.2.75	2,384	Feb.1895	Inf.	Dorset Regt	6.3.95
88. Milne Home, Thomas Patrick	11.7.74	2,018	Feb.1895	—	—	—
89. Montgomery, Hugh Wyndham	26.4.75	2,525	Feb.1895	Cav.	17th Lancers	20.2.95
90. Morant, Rowland Hay	4.8.74	2,281	Feb.1895	Inf.	Linc. Regt	6.3.95
91. Mourilyan, Hubert Lionel[17] (Corporal)	28.11.75	2,026	Feb.1895	Inf.	N. York Regt	6.3.95
92. North, Roger Edward Napier	1.2.75	2,059	Feb.1895	Inf.	E. Surrey Regt	6.3.95
93. Pakenham, George[1] de la Poer Beresford	4.12.75	2,819	Feb.1895	—	Unattached List	16.1.95
94. Palmer, Gerard Steuart[1]	4.6.75	2,523	Feb.1895	—	Unattached List	16.1.95
95. Pollock, Percy Napier	8.3.75	2,619	Feb.1895	—	—	—
96. Pryce, Henry Edward ap Rhys[1]	30.11.74	2,668	Feb.1895	—	Unattached List	16.1.95
97. Richards, Bernard Ogilvie	20.7.74	2,456	Feb.1895	Inf.	Worcester Regt	20.2.95
98. Rivett-Carnac, John Stirling[1]	25.2.75	2,606	Feb.1895	—	Unattached List	16.1.95
99. Rolland, Edward Lewis	24.7.74	2,262	Feb.1895	Inf.	Highland LI	6.3.95
100. Ronald, John James	19.9.74	2,412	Feb.1895	Inf.	Highlander LI	6.3.95
101. Royston-Pigott, Arthur George	18.12.74	2,563	Feb.1895	Inf.	Northamptonshire Regiment	20.2.95
102. Sands, Charles Edward Walker	13.2.75	2,749	Feb.1895	—	—	—
103. Searight, Hugh Fforde (Corporal)	9.6.75	2,328	Feb.1895	Cav.	Dragoon Gds	6.3.95
104. Shirt, Frederick Christian[18] (Corporal)	24.12.74	2,656	Feb.1895	Inf.	Manchester Regt	20.2.95
105. Simpson, William Hugh[14]	25.6.75	2,595	Feb.1895	—	—	—
106. Skeen, Oliver St. John[1]	2.11.74	2,152	Feb.1895	—	—	—

Name	Date of Birth	Final Exam	Date of Retirement	Inf/ Cav.	Regiment	Date of Appt.
107. Stevenson, Walter Wilton Campbell	21.8.74	2,464	Feb.1895	Inf.	Manchester Regt	20.2.95
108. Stewart, Ian (Senior Corporal)	2.11.74	2,304	Feb.1895	Inf.	Scottish Rifles	6.3.95
109. Stone, Lionel George Tempest	16.11.74	2,389	Feb.1895	Inf.	R. Fusiliers	6.3.95
110. Striedinger, Oscar	26.4.75	2,478	Feb.1895	Inf.	R. Berks Regt	20.2.95
111. Strong, Addington Dawsonne[1]	13.3.75	2,418	Feb.1895	—	Unattached List	16.1.95
112. Strong, Charles Powlett[19]	9.1.75	2,354	Feb.1895	—	Bedford Regt	16.1.95
113. Swabey, Frederick	9.6.72	2,095	Feb.1895	Inf.	West India Regt	6.3.95
114. Swinley, George Dighton Probyn[1]	13.11.74	2,290	Feb.1895	Inf.	Unattached List	16.1.95
*** Sym, Hugh Gordon[20]	3.3.75	—	—	—	—	—
115. Thompson, Bernard Anthony	14.10.75	2,261	Feb.1895	Inf.	W. Yorks Regt	6.3.95
116. Tillard, Arthur George	10.11.74	2,517	Feb.1895	Inf.	The Manchester Regt	20.2.95
117. Toppin, Harry Stanley[21]	27.7.74	2,461	Feb.1895	Inf.	North'd Fusiliers	20.2.95
118. Tyndall, Henry Stuart[1] (Under Officer)	16.7.75	2,383	Feb.1895	—	Unattached List	16.1.95
119. Tyndall, Wm. Ernest Marriott	2.2.75	2,406	Feb.1895	Inf.	W. Riding Regt	6.3.95
120. Villiers-Stuart, Charles[1] Herbert (Senior Corporal)	2.9.74	2,561	Feb.1895	—	Unattached List	16.1.95
121. Wakefield, Henry Gerald Rawdon	10.5.75	2,374	Feb.1895	Inf.	Leinster Regt	6.3.95
122. Wardell, Geoffrey Francis Evan	23.11.74	2,381	Feb. 1895	Inf.	Oxford LI	6.3.95
123. Wheatley, Guy Rutherford Prescott	12.5.75	2,681	Feb.1895	Inf.	Norfolk Regt	20.2.95
124. Wise, Alexander	2.2.75	2,182	Feb.1895	Inf.	Connaught Rangers	6.3.95
125. Wolseley, Garnet John[4]	2.4.73	2,500	Feb.1895	Inf.	Derby Regt	14.4.95
126. Wood-Martin, James Isidore	3.9.74	2,458	Feb.1895	Inf.	Northamptonshire Regt	20.2.95
127. Worsley, Frank Pickford	23.8.74	2,534	Feb.1895	Inf.	West York Regt	20.2.95
128. Wyllie, Frederick Arthur	7.3.75	2,722	Feb.1895	Inf.	Welsh Regt	20.2.95
129. Yatman, Arthur Hamilton	1.7.74	2,402	Feb.1895	Inf.	Som. LI	6.3.95
130. Yorke, Ralph Maximilian	23.10.74	2,438	Feb.1895	Cav.	11th Hussars	6.3.95

1. 'Unattached List' meant to the Indian Army. An officer first had to be commissioned into the British army. Following graduation from Sandhurst, the cadets on the Unattached List were assigned or attached to regiments in India, often following interim assignment to the Indian Staff Corps. The assignments noted in the Indian army List for 1 July 1896, were as follows:

Ashburner, L.F.	Durham Light Infantry
Battye, I.U.	(The Queen's Own) Corps of Guides
Birch, V.K.	9th Regiment of Bombay Infantry
Bruce, J.M.	45th (Rattray's Sikh) Regiment of Bengal Infantry
Buckley, J.J.	Not Listed 1896
Channer, G.K.	12th (The Kelat-i-Ghilzai) Regiment of Bengal Infantry
Conway-Gordon, E.C.W.	3rd Regiment of Bengal Calvary
Geddes, M.H.B.	4th Regiment of Madras Infantry (Pioneers)
Godwin, C.A.C.	25th Regiment Madras Infantry
Goodfellow, R.C.	10th Regiment of Bombay (Light) Infantry
Graham, B.R.	1st Bn, Royal West Surrey Regiment
Henderson, A.F.	24th Regiment of Madras Infantry
Hoskyn, J.C.M. .	20th Regiment Bombay Infantry
Keyes, C.V.	34th (Punjab) Regiment of Bengal Infantry
Kidd, B.G.	23rd Regiment of Bombay Infantry
Lance, F.F.C.	19th Regiment of Bengal Lancers
Luckhardt, H.C.	2nd (Prince of Wales' Own) Regiment of Bombay Infantry (Grenadiers)
Magniac, F.A.	1st Bn, Royal West Surrey Regiment
Pakenham, G. de la P.B.	17th (The Loyal Purbiya) Regiment of Bengal Infantry

Palmer, G.S.	3rd Regiment of Bombay (Light) Infantry
Pryce, H.E.	18th Regiment of Bengal Infantry
Rivett-Carnac, J.S.	19th Bengal Lancers
Simpson, W.H.	33rd Regiment (3rd Burma Bn.) of Madras Infantry
Skeen, O.St.J.	26th Regiment of Madras Infantry
Strong, A.D.	1st Bn, Royal West Surrey Regiment
Swinely, G.D.P.	37th (Dogra) Regiment of Bengal Infantry
Tyndall, H.S.	40th (Pathan) Regiment of Bengal Infantry
Villiers-Stuart, C.H.	21st Regiment of Madras Infantry (Pioneers)

2. Atchison, Charles Ernest, DSO. Killed in action as Major, acting Lt Col, in First World War on 24 August 1917.

3. Awdry, Vere Henry Ambrose. Killed in action as Lt in the Boer War at Spion Kop, 24 January 1900.

4. The cadets referred to by this footnote are those passed out with Churchill in February 1895 but actually began as part of the February 1893 intake and were delayed from completing the course on schedule due to illness, sick leave or missed examinations. They are included in the calculations of Churchill's class standing.

5. Brooke, J. S. appears in the 1896 Army List as an officer in the Militia Artillery, Eastern Division, The Kent Artillery.

6. Carey, Seymour James. Killed in action in the Boer War as Lt near Rensburg, 6 January 1900.

7. Chapman, Wilfred Constantine. Killed in action in First World War.

8. Courtenay, George Edward. Killed in action as Lt in the Boer War near Paardeberg, 18 February 1900.

9. Davidson, Francis Coventry Dudfield. Died on 23 February 1900 of wounds received as a Lt in the Boer War in the operations on the Tugela River.

10. Dunn-Pattison, Richard Phillipson. Commissioned as Pattison. Killed in action as Cpt. in First World War.

11. Greenely, Walton Howarth. This cadet won the Sword of Honour, passing out highest in overall order of merit.

12. Grover, Percival Charles. Died of wounds received in action as Lt in the Boer War at Bloemfontein Waterworks, 31 March 1900.

13. Hesketh, Algernon Ernest. Killed in action as a Lt in the Boer War near Kimberley, 15 February 1900.

14. Hill, Frederick Thomas Cecil. Killed in action as temporary Major in First World War, 7 August 1915.

15. Keyes, Charles Valentine. Killed in action in West Africa, 1901.

16. Mercer, Archibald Ariel. Killed in action as a Major in First World War, 17 November 1915.

17. Mourilyan, Hubert Lionel. Killed in action as a Lt in the Boer War at Pieter's Hill, 27 February 1900.

18. Shirt, Frederick Christian, changed name to Hirst under Horse Guards letter of 19 January 1895.

19. Strong, Charles Powlett, D.S.O. Killed in action as Lt in the Boer War at Graspan near Reitz, 6 June 1901.

20. Sym, Hugh Gordon. Resigned his cadetship owing to ill health, authority Horseguard #7611/6988 dated 14 Dec. 1893. Went to hospital the day he joined. He is not included in the calculation of Churchill's class standing.

21. Toppin, Harry Stanley. Died of wounds as Captain in First World War, 13 September 1914.

Sources: Regimental panels and memorial plaques, The Royal Memorial Chapel, Sandhurst. *The Last Post, Being a Roll of All Officers (Naval, Military Or Colonial) Who Gave Their Lives for Their Queen, King and Country, In The South African War, 1899–1902*, by Mildred G. Dooner. First published 1903, details not available. Republished (Polstead, Suffolk: J. B. Hayward & Son, 1988). Royal Military College, Sandhurst, September 1893 Intake, The Register of Gentlemen Cadets. Vol. 4, 1890 Feb. to 1897 Jan. (WO 151/4) provided courtesy of The National Archives (PRO) and is used with permission. Collected by Douglas S. Russell 20 November 1992 and 25 November 1994. *Officers Died In The Great War, 1914–1919* first published by HMSO in 1919, Republished (Polstead, Suffolk: J. B. Hayward & Son, 1988).

APPENDIX B
THE IVth (QUEEN'S OWN) HUSSARS
BATTLE HONOURS AND SUCCESSOR REGIMENTS

Dettingen	Ghuznee, 1839	Le Cateau	Langemarck, 1914
Talavera	Afghanistan, 1838	Retreat from Mons	Gheluvelt
Albuhera	Alma	Marne, 1914	St. Julien
Salamanca	Balaklava	Aisne, 1914	Bellewaarde
Vittoria	Inkerman	Messines, 1914	Arras, 1917
Toulouse	Sevastopol	Armentieres, 1914	Scarpe, 1917
Peninsula	Mons	Ypres, 1914, 1915	Cambrai, 1917

෪෪෪෪෪෪෪෪෪෪෪෪෪෪෪෪෪෪෪

Somme, 1918	Gazala	Coriano	Santerno Crossing
Amiens	Defence of Alamien	San Clemente	Argenta Gap
Hindenburg Line	Line	Senio Pocket	Italy, 1944–5
Canal du Nord	Ruweisat	Rimini Line	Proasteion
Pursuit to Mons	Alam el Halfa	Conventello-	Corinth Canal
France and Flanders,	El Alamein	Comacchio	Greece, 1941
1914–18	North Africa, 1942	Senio	

Successor Regiments

24 October 1958 – The Fourth (Queen's Own) Hussars was amalgamated with the 8th King's Royal Irish Hussars to form The Queen's Royal Irish Hussars. Elements of the regiment served in Germany, Aden, Malaya, Borneo, UK, Cyprus, Rhodesia, Northern Ireland and in Iraq and Kuwait in the 1991 Gulf War.

September, 1993 – The Queen's Royal Irish Hussars was amalgamated with the Queen's Own Hussars (formerly the 3rd and 7th Hussars) to form The Queen's Royal Hussars, now the senior light cavalry regiment of the British army. The Regiment is presently part of NATO's Rapid Reaction Force and has served in Bosnia with IFOR under NATO command and in Northern Ireland, Germany and UK.

Source: *4th Hussar, The Story of a British Cavalry Regiment* by David Scott Daniell (Aldershot: Gale & Polden, 1959).

APPENDIX C
Churchill's Commission, Promotions and Appointments

1. Second Lieutenant. 20 February 1895.
Regular Army
THE LONDON GAZETTE of Tuesday, 19 February 1895 (p.1001)
War Office,
Pall Mall.
19 February 1895.
4th Hussars
Gentlemen Cadet Winston Leonard Spencer Churchill, from the Royal Military College, to be Second Lieutenant in succession to Lieutenant G.H.B. Gaine, seconded. Dated 20 February, 1895.

2. Lieutenant. 20 May 1896.
Regular Army
THE LONDON GAZETTE of Tuesday, 23 June 1896 (p. 3642)
War Office,
Pall Mall.
23 June 1896
4th Hussars
Second Lieutenant W. L. S. Churchill to be Lieutenant vice R. W. R. Barnes, appointed Adjutant.   Dated 20 May 1896.

3. Resignation from the army. 3 May 1899
THE LONDON GAZETTE of Tuesday, 2 May 1899 (p. 2806)
War Office,
Pall Mall.
2 May, 1899.
4th Hussars
Lieutenant Winston L. S. Churchill resigns his commission. Dated 3 May 1899.

4. Lieutenant, South African Light Horse, Imperial Yeomanry, 2d January to 23rd March, 1900. 'Certificate. 6 August 1900. Paardekop. I certify that Lieut. Winston Spencer Churchill served as Lieutenant in the South African Light Horse from 2d January 1900 to 23rd March 1900, and was present at all actions and engagements in which the Regiment took part. J. Byng. Lieut Colonel Commanding South African Light Horse.' *Winston S. Churchill, Companion Volume I, Part 2, 1896–1900* by Randolph S. Churchill (Boston: Houghton Mifflin Company, 1967) p. 1141.

5. Captain, Imperial Yeomanry, 4 January 1902.
THE LONDON GAZETTE of Friday, 3 January 1902 (p.10)
War Office,
Pall Mall.

APPENDICES

꙳꙳꙳꙳꙳꙳꙳꙳꙳꙳꙳꙳꙳꙳꙳꙳

3rd January, 1902.
IMPERIAL YEOMANRY
Oxfordshire (Queen's Own Oxfordshire Hussars)
Winston Leonard Spencer Churchill, Esq., late Lieutenant, South African Light Horse, to be Captain.
Dated 4 January 1902.

6. Major, Imperial Yeomanry, 25 May 1905.
THE LONDON GAZETTE of Tuesday, 30 May 1905 (p. 3866)
War Office,
30th May, 1905
IMPERIAL YEOMANRY
Oxfordshire (Queen's Own Oxfordshire Hussars)
The undermentioned Officers to be Majors:-
Captain W. L. S. Churchill. Dated 25 May 1905.

7. Embodied for service in the rank of Major, and restored to the Establishment of The Queen's Own Oxfordshire Hussars Yeomanry, Territorial Force. 17 November 1915. Ministry of Defence, Army Personal File.

8. Lieutenant-Colonel (Temporary) Regular Army, 5 January 1916
SUPPLEMENT TO THE LONDON GAZETTE of Friday, 24 March, 1916
Saturday, 25 March, 1916
(Page 3260)
War Office,
25th March, 1916.
REGULAR FORCES
Infantry
Service Battalions
The Royal Scots Fusiliers
Major the Right Honourable Winston L. S. Churchill (Oxfordshire (Queen's Own Oxfordshire Hussars) Yeomanry, Territorial Force) to be Temporary Lieutenant-Colonel while commanding a Battalion.
Dated 5 January 1916.

9. Relinquishment of Temporary Rank of Lieutenant-Colonel, 16 May 1916.
THE LONDON GAZETTE of Friday, 2 June 1916 (Page 5471)
War Office,
2nd June, 1916.
REGULAR FORCES
Infantry
Service Battalions
Royal Scots Fusiliers
Major the Rt. Hon. W.L. S. Churchill, Oxfordshire Yeomanry (T.F.), relinquishes the temporary rank of Lieutenant-Colonel on ceasing to command a Battalion – 16 May 1916.

10. Transferred to Territorial Force Reserve. 16 May 1916. Ministry of Defence, Army Personal File.

11. Transferred from Territorial Force Reserve to The Queen's Own Oxfordshire Hussars Yeomanry (Disembodied Territorial Force) on 7 August 1920, in rank of Major with seniority from 27 May 1905, Ministry of Defence, Army Personal File.

12. Transfer to Royal Field Artillery (Disembodied Territorial Army) 11 April 1923.
THE LONDON GAZETTE of Tuesday, 10 April 1923 (p. 2648)
War Office,
10th April, 1923.
TERRITORIAL ARMY
Royal Field Artillery
100th (Worcestershire and Oxfordshire Yeomanry) Brigade T.A.
Major Rt. Hon. W.L.S. Churchill, C.H. (late Lieutenant, South African Light Horse) from Oxfordshire Yeomanry, to be Major, with precedence as in the T.A. – 11 April 1923.

13. Resignation from Territorial Army. 6 August 1924.
THE LONDON GAZETTE of Tuesday, 5 August 1924 (p. 5891)

War Office,
5th August, 1924.
TERRITORIAL ARMY
Royal Regiment of Artillery
100th (Worcestershire and Oxfordshire Yeomanry) Field Brigade
Major Rt. Hon. W .L. S. Churchill, C.H. resigns his commission and retains the rank of Major, with
permission to wear the prescribed uniform – 6th August 1924.

14. Honorary Air Commodore, 4 April 1939.
No. 615 (County of Surrey) Squadron, Auxiliary Air Force
THE LONDON GAZETTE of Tuesday, 4 April 1939 (p. 2266)
Air Ministry
4th April, 1939
AUXILIARY AIR FORCE
No. 615 (County of Surrey) Squadron
The Right Honourable Winston Leonard Spencer Churchill, C.H., M.P. is appointed Honorary Air
Commodore 4 April 1939

15. Honorary Colonel, 21 October 1939
63rd (Oxfordshire Yeomanry) Anti-Tank Regiment, Royal Artillery
SUPPLEMENT TO THE LONDON GAZETTE of Friday, 20 October 1939
(p. 7103)
Friday, 20 October 1939
War Office,
20th October, 1939
TERRITORIAL ARMY
Royal Artillery
Major Rt. Hon. W. L. S. Churchill, P.C., C.H., T.D., M.P. (retd. T.A.)
to be Honorary Colonel – 21 October 1939

16. Honorary Colonel, 24 January 1940
6th Battalion, Royal Scots Fusiliers
SUPPLEMENT TO THE LONDON GAZETTE of Friday, 19 January 1940
Tuesday, 23 January 1940
War Office,
23rd January, 1940
TERRITORIAL ARMY
Infantry
Royal Scots Fusiliers
Major Rt. Hon. W. L. S. Churchill, P.C., C.H., T.D., M.P. (retd. T.A.) to be Honorary Colonel – 24
January 1940

17. Honorary Colonel, 22 October 1941
4th (Queen's Own) Hussars, Royal Armoured Corps
SECOND SUPPLEMENT TO THE LONDON GAZETTE of Tuesday, 28 October 1941, War Office
(p. 6303)
31 October, 1941.
REGULAR ARMY
Royal Armoured Corps
4th Hussars
Rt. Hon. W. L .S. Churchill, C.H., T. D., LL.D, M.P. (23212), Honorary Colonel, Royal Artillery and
Royal Scots Fusiliers, is appointed Colonel (vice Major-General Sir Reginald Barnes, K.C.B., D.S.O.
(54076) retired pay) – 22 October 1941

18. Honorary Colonel, November 14, 1941
5th (Cinque Ports) Battalion, Royal Sussex Regiment.
SECOND SUPPLEMENT TO THE LONDON GAZETTE of Tuesday, 11 November 1941
Friday, 14th November, 1941 War Office, (p. 6570)
14 November, 1941.
TERRITORIAL ARMY
Infantry
Royal Sussex Regiment

Rt. Hon. W.L.S. Churchill, C.H., T.D., LL.D., M.P. (23213), Colonel, 4th Hussars, Honorary Colonel, Royal Artillery and Royal Scots Fusiliers, to be Honorary Colonel –14 November 1941

19. Honorary Colonel, 20 February, 1942
89th (Cinque Ports), Heavy Anti-Aircraft Regiment, Royal Artillery
SECOND SUPPLEMENT TO THE LONDON GAZETTE of Tuesday, 17 February 1942
Friday, 20 February, 1942
War office,
20 February, 1942.
TERRITORIAL ARMY
Royal Artillery
H.A.A. Regiment
Rt. Hon. W.L.S. Churchill, C.H., T.D., LL.D., M.P. (23213), Colonel, 4th Hussars, Honorary Colonel
Royal Artillery, Royal Scots Fusiliers and Royal Sussex Regiment, to be Honorary Colonel – 20 February 1942

20. Honorary Colonel, 20 February, 1945
Territorial Army, The Essex Regiment
SUPPLEMENT TO THE LONDON GAZETTE of Friday, 16 February, 1945
Tuesday, 20 February 1945
War Office,
20 February, 1945.
TERRITORIAL ARMY
Infantry
Essex Regiment
Rt. Hon. W. L. S. Churchill, C.H., T.D., LL.D., M.P. (23213), Colonel, 4th Queen's Own Hussars, to be Honorary Colonel (vice Brigadier – General J. T. Wigan, C.B., C.M.G., D.S.O., T.D., who has completed the term of his appointment) – 21 January, 1945

21. Honorary Colonel, 29 August 1946
6th (Cinque Ports) Cadet Battalion, The Buffs.
Ministry of Defence, Army Personal File.

22. Colonel, 24 October 1958
The Queen's Royal Irish Hussars upon relinquishment of appointment as Colonel, The 4th (Queen's Own) Hussars.
SUPPLEMENT TO THE LONDON GAZETTE of Tuesday, 21 October 1958.
Friday, 24 October 1958
ROYAL ARMOURED CORPS
QUEEN'S ROYAL IRISH HUSSARS
Regular Army
By virtue of the provisions of the Royal Warrant dated 27th Aug. 1958 (Published in Army Order No. 67 of 1958), all officers of the Land Forces belonging to the 4th Queen's Own Hussars and the 8th King's Royal Irish Hussars will be transferred to the Queen's Royal Irish Hussars with effect from 24 Oct. 1958.
4th HUSSARS
Regular Army
The Rt. Hon. Sir Winston Leonard Spencer Churchill, K.G., O.M., C.H., T.D., LL.D., M.P. (23213), relinquishes the appointment of Colonel, 4th Queen's Own Hussars, 24 October 1958 on amalgamation.

Note: Most of the information for Appendix C was collected from *The London Gazette*; some is from the official biography. With the consent of the Churchill family the author was granted access to Churchill's Army Personal File in 1994. Remarkably, the file had been vetted in 1941 pursuant to the then War Office practice of weeding-out papers deemed to be of no further administrative use. Thus most of Churchill's army record, including annual rating reports, any recommendations for decorations that may have been made and any administrative records, were removed and destroyed. This is a great loss to history. All that remained was a brief summary of Churchill's military career, the period from 1895 to 1958 reduced to a single page. The remaining information was provided by Mr Joseph E. Kelly, Head of Ministry of Defence Archives with correspondence dated 14 November 1994. The information listed in Appendix C is confirmed by the Army Personal File.

APPENDIX D
Churchill's Dates and Places of Service

1. The Royal Military College, Sandhurst. 1 September 1893–15 December 1894.
2. The Fourth (Queen's Own) Hussars at Aldershot. 19 February 1895–9 September 1895.
3. Observer with Spanish forces in Cuba. 20 November 1895–9 December 1895.
4. The Fourth (Queen's Own) Hussars, at Hounslow. 9 September 1895–2 November 1895. 21 December 1895–11 September 1896.
5. The Fourth (Queen's Own) Hussars, Bangalore, India. 2 October 1896–May, 1899.
6. Attached to Malakand Field Force, Northwest Frontier, India. Active service with 31st Punjab Regiment, Bengal Infantry and 35th Sikh Regiment, Bengal Infantry, both Indian Army, September–October 1897.
7. Attached to Tirah Field Force, North-West Frontier, India, March–April 1898.
8. Attached to 21st Lancers, Egypt and Sudan. 2 August 1898–September, 1898.
9. South African Light Horse, Imperial Yeomanry. 2 January 1900–23 March 1900. Further unattached service, March–July 1900.
10. Imperial Yeomanry, Oxfordshire (Queen's Own Oxfordshire Hussars). 4 January 1902–12 November 1915. Includes visits to German Army manoeuvres as an observer in Silesia in September 1906 and Würzburg in September 1909.
11. The Grenadier Guards, 2d Battalion. 20 November 1915–18 December 1915. Ebenezer Farm, near Neuve Chapelle, France, Western Front.
12. The Royal Scots Fusiliers, 6th Battalion. 5 January 1916–16 May 1916. Ploegsteert, Flanders, Belgium, Western Front.
13. Territorial Army, Oxford Yeomanry. 16 May 1916–6 August 1924.

APPENDIX E
Churchill's Medals and Mention in Dispatches
(Listed in the order they were earned)

1. The Order of Military Merit, First Class, Red Ribbon, Spain. Granted 6 December 1895. Ratified 25 January 1896.
2. The Cuban Campaign Medal, Spain. Authorised 1899. Received 1914.
3. The India Medal (clasp, Punjab Frontier 1897–1898), United Kingdom, Authorised 10 December 1898.
4. The Queen's Sudan Medal 1896–1898, United Kingdom. Authorised 27 March 1899.
5. The Khedive's Sudan Medal (clasp, Khartoum), Egypt. Authorised 19 January 1899.
6. The Queen's South Africa Medal (clasps, Diamond Hill, Johannesberg, Relief of Ladysmith, Orange Free State, Tugela Heights, Cape Colony), United Kingdom. Authorised 15 July 1901.
7. The 1914–1915 Star, United Kingdom. Authorised 10 October, 1919.
8. The British War Medal 1914–1918, United Kingdom. Authorised 13 October 1919.
9. The Victory Medal, United Kingdom. Authorised 4 June 1920.
10. The Territorial Decoration, United Kingdom. Authorised 31 October 1924.
   THE LONDON GAZETTE of Friday, 31 October 1924 (p. 7861)
   War Office, 31st October, 1924. TERRITORIAL ARMY. The King has been graciously pleased to confer the Territorial Decoration upon the undermentioned officers under the terms of the Royal Warrant dated 13th October, 1920 –
   Royal Artillery
   100th (Worcestershire and Oxfordshire Yeomanry) Field Brigade
   Major Rt. Hon. W. L. S. Churchill, C.H. (retired)
11. Mention in Dispatches
   THE LONDON GAZETTE of Tuesday 11 January 1898 (p. 151)
   Operations of the Malakand Field Force. The Action of the 16th September. From Sir Bindon Blood's Despatch, Containing The Summary of Brigadier-General Jeffrey's Report of the Action. 29 . . . and finally he has praised the courage and resolution of Lieutenant W. L. S. Churchill, 4th Hussars, the correspondent of the *Pioneer* newspaper with the force, who made himself useful at a critical moment.

Note: Churchill received many more awards during his political career including military medals and knighthood orders; the final total was thirty-seven. These are the subject of *The Orders, Decorations and Medals of Sir Winston Churchill* by Douglas S. Russell (Hopkinton, NH: The International Churchill Society, 1990; Second Edition; (Washington, D.C.: The Churchill Centre, 2004).

APPENDICES

ჭჱჭჱჭჱჭჱჭჱჭჱჭჱჭჱჭჱჭჱ

Appendix F
THE CHURCHILL CENTRE

Headquartered in Washington, D.C. and active internationally, The Churchill Centre was founded in 1968 to inspire leadership, statesmanship, vision, and boldness among democratic and freedom loving peoples through the thoughts, words, works and deeds of Winston Spencer Churchill. Membership numbers over 3,500 with an average age of 48, including the affiliated Churchill Societies of Great Britain, Canada, Australia and Portugal.

The Churchill Centre publishes a quarterly magazine, Finest Hour; a newsletter, the Chartwell Bulletin; and periodic collections of papers and speeches, the Churchill Proceedings. It sponsors international and national conferences and Churchill tours, which have visited Britain, Australia, France, South Africa, Morocco, and Germany. Its expansive website includes classroom components to educate young people on Sir Winston's life and times.

The Churchill Centre has helped bring about republication of over thirty of Winston Churchill's long out-of-print books. In 1992, it launched a campaign for completion of the remaining document volumes to the official biography, three of which have now been published.

More recently, the Centre sponsored academic symposia in America and Britain; seminars where students and scholars discuss Churchill's books; scholarships for Churchill Studies at the Universities of Edinburgh and Dallas; and important reference works. In 1998 it launched the Churchill Lecture Series, in which prominent world figures apply Sir Winston's experience to the world today. In 2005 it received a grant to distribute 5,000 Churchill biographies to high school teachers in North America who use Churchill in their curricula, and began a series of seminars for teachers conducted by college professors. In 2003 the Churchill Centre opened its first official headquarters in Washington, which houses its administrative staff, library, and computer facilities linked to the major Churchill archives. Future programs include video aids for schoolchildren; college and graduate level courses on aspects of Churchill's career; fellowships to assist students; and visiting professorships. The overall aim is to impress Churchill's qualities of leadership firmly on the leaders of the 21st Century.

Membership is available for a subscription of $50 (UK and Canada rates are comparable), with a special low rate of only $10 for students. For more information please contact:

The Churchill Centre
1150 Seventeenth Street, NW, Suite Suite 307
Washington, DC 20036 USA
telephone: (888) WSC-1874-(202) 223-5511
facsimile: (202) 223-4944
website: www.winstonchurchill.org

Notes

CHAPTER ONE: A VICTORIAN CHILDHOOD

1. *Marlborough: His Life and Times*, by Winston S. Churchill (London: George G. Harrap & Co., Ltd., 1933), Vol. 1, p. 3.

2. My thanks to John Forster, Schools Liaison Officer, Administrator's Office at Blenheim Palace for details about the buildings and grounds.

3. *Winston S. Churchill, His Complete Speeches, 1897–1963*. Edited by Robert Rhodes James (New York, Chelsea House Publishers, 1974), Volume VIII, p. 8338.

4. *Winston S. Churchill, Volume I, Youth, 1874-1900* by Randolph S. Churchill (Boston: Houghton Mifflin Company, 1966), p. 106. This first volume of the official Churchill biography will be referred to in footnotes as OBI and the later volumes will be referred to by number, thus: OBII and so on. Each of the eight volumes of the biography has one or more accompanying companion volumes of related documents which will have similar abbreviations in footnotes. *Winston S. Churchill, Companion Volume I, Part 1* by Randolph S. Churchill (Boston: Houghton Mifflin Company, 1967) for example will be referred to as OBI, CV1 and part two as OBI, CV2.

5. *My Early Life – A Roving Commission* by Winston S. Churchill (London: Thorton Butterworth, 1930), pp. 18–19. The US edition is *A Roving Commission, My Early Life* (New York: Charles Scribner's Sons, 1930). Hereafter, this title will be abbreviated in footnotes as MEL.

6. *The River War* by Winston S. Churchill (London: Longmans, Green, and Co., 1899), Vol. 1, p. 37.

7. MEL, p. 26.

8. *Naked Truth* by Clare Sheridan (New York: Harper & Bros., 1928), pp. 4–5.

9. My thanks to Donald P. Grant for details of lead soldiers by Maison Lucotte and C. B. G. Mignot and the collection at Blenheim. Churchill wrote an introduction for Maze's book *A Frenchman in Khaki* (London: William Heinemann Ltd., 1934).

10. MEL, p. 26.

11. *The Reminiscences of Lady Randolph Churchill* by Mrs George Cornwallis-West (New York: The Century Co., 1908), p.78.

12. ibid, p. 124.

13. OBI, CVI, p. 136.

14. *A Roving Commission (Or Through the Black Insurrection of Hayti)*, 1900. For more information about Henty including a bibliography of his works, see *Held Fast for England: G.A. Henty, Imperialist Boys' Writer*, by Guy Arnold (London: Hamish Hamilton, 1980).

15. *Routledge's Every Boy's Annual Illustrated* (London: George Routledge & Sons, 1884). Churchill's own copy, complete with his name written in his own youthful hand in 1883, is in the collection of the Harrow Archives, the gift of Churchill's cousin Shane Leslie.

16. MEL, p. 90.

17. OBI, CV1, p. 103.

18. MEL, p. 20.

19. MEL, p. 27.

20. MEL, p. 27.

21. MEL, pp. 36–7.

22. MEL, p. 27.

23. OBI, pp. 68–72.

24. Other notable Harrovians include Lord Byron of poetic fame; Stanley Baldwin, British Prime Minister from 1923 to January 1924 and November 1924 to 1929; Jawaharlal Nehru, first Prime Minister of independent India; Field Marshal Viscount Alexander; King Hussein of Jordan; and General Sir Peter de la Billière, commander of the British forces in the 1990 Gulf War.

25. The Harrow VCs are Captain William Peel, Royal Navy, Crimean War, 1854; Lieutenant Alexander Roberts Dunn, 11th Hussars, Crimean War, 1854; Lieutenant William James Montgomery Cunninghame, The Rifle Brigade, Crimean War, 1854; Ensign John Worthy Chaplin, 67th Regiment (later the Hampshire Regiment), Taku Forts, China, 1860; Lieutenant Lord Edric Rederick Gifford, 24th Regiment (later the South Wales Borderers), Ashanti War, 1874; Lieutenant Teignmouth Melville, 24th Regiment (later The South Wales Borderers), Zulu War, 1879; Lieutenant Percival Scrope Marling, The King's Royal Rifle Corps, the Sudan 1884; Captain Walter Norris Congreve, The Rifle Brigade, Boer War, 1899; Lieutenant John Peniston Milbanke, 10th Hussars, Boer War, 1900; Captain George Murray Rolland, 1st Bombay Grenadiers, Indian Army, Somaliland, 1903; Major Ernest Wright Alexander, Royal Field Artillery, First World War, 1914; Captain Richard Raymond Willis, The Lancashire Fusiliers, Gallipoli, First World

War, 1915; Captain Garth Neville Walford, Royal Regiment of Artillery, Gallipoli, First World War, 1915; Acting Captain Thomas Riversdale Colyer Fergusson The Northamptonshire Regiment, First World War, 1917; Acting Lieutenant Colonel Viscount John Standish Gort, Grenadier Guards, First World War, 1918; Acting Major George de Cardonnel Elmsall Findlay, Corps of Royal Engineers, First World War, 1918; T/Captain Ian Oswald Liddell, Coldstream Guards, Second World War, 1945.

26. *Winston Churchill and Harrow, Memories of the Prime Minister's Schooldays, 1888–1892.* Collected by E. D. W. Chaplin (Harrow: Harrow School Bookshop, 1941), p. 24.

27. 'Churchill at Harrow' by Sir Gerald Woods Wollaston in *Churchill by His Contemporaries,* Edited by Charles Eade (New York: Simon and Schuster, 1954), p. 7.

28. *Harrow School Songs,* published by the Harrow School Book Shop, 1993 edition (Henley on Thames: The Gresham Press, 1993), pp. 98–9.

29. *The Harrovian,* ii, 1889, p. 188.

30. OBI, p. 117.

31. *The Harrovian,* ii, 1889, pp. 164–5. The doings of the Rifle Corps were regularly reported in the school magazine and all the field days, mock battles and annual inspections may be followed there.

32. J. W. S. Tomlin, 'Harrow in Churchill's Time,' in *Winston Churchill and Harrow, ibid,* pp. 28–9.

33. OBI, p. 117.

34. MEL, p. 33.

35. MEL, p. 33–4.

36. 'The Dream' is the name given by the family to the story which Churchill himself called 'Private Article'. The piece first appeared in the *Sunday Telegraph* on 30 January 1966. It was first published in single volume format by the International Churchill Societies in 1987. It appears in *The Collected Essays of Sir Winston Churchill, Centenary Limited Edition, Volume IV, Churchill at Large* (London: Library of Imperial History, 1976) at p. 504.

37. MEL, p. 34.

38. OBI, CV1, p. 189.

39. OBI, p. 121.

40. Harrow School Bill Books, published by J. C. Wilbee, booksellers to Harrow School. Courtesy of Harrow Archives.

41. OBI, CV1, p. 169. As to Churchill's difficulty with examinations, see Martin Gilbert's account of Churchill's Harrow entrance examinination which refers to 'nervous excitement' and 'a severe attack of sickness', *Churchill, A Life* by Martin Gilbert (New York: Henry Holt & Co., 1991), p. 17.

42. MEL, p. 31.

43. *Winston Churchill and Harrow, ibid,* p. 34.

44. From 'Prizes in The Headmaster's House', an unpublished compilation, courtesy of Harrow School Archive. The poem was later published in *The Harrovian,* 10 December 1940, and also in *Winston Churchill and Harrow, ibid,* pp. 55–7.

45. OBI, CV1, p. 311. Also see *My Political Life, Volume One, England Before The Storm, 1896–1914* by Leopold S. Amery (London: Hutchinson, 1953), p. 40.

46. *Winston Churchill and Harrow, ibid,* p. 22.

47. MEL, p. 31.

48. In French 'Le Marais' would be 'The Swamp'. I am indebted to the Governors, Headmaster and Masters of Harrow School for permission to view the essay which is in the collection of the Archives Room.

49. From a letter from Churchill to Mr Moriarty dated 19 December 1905, and quoted in *Winston Churchill and Harrow, ibid,* p. 16.

50. OBI, CV1, p. 202. Commissioned in 1892, Milbanke won the Victoria Cross in 1900 during the Boer War. He was later killed in action at Suvla Bay, Gallipoli, in the First World War. His was a fate that Churchill might well have shared had he made a career of the army.

51. OBI, CV1, p. 203.

52. OBI, CV1, p. 217.

53. OBI, CV1, p. 248.

54. OBI, CV1, p. 268.

55. OBI, pp. 132–3.

56. OBI, CV1, p. 259.

57. OBI, CV1, p. 269.

58. OBI, CV1, p. 291.

59. OBI, CV1, pp. 291–2.

60. OBI, CV1, p. 297.

61. OBI, CV1, p. 307.

62. OBI, CV1, p. 325.

63. Churchill's medal for the public schools fencing championship survives to this day in the collection at Chartwell, the Churchill home and museum near Westerham in Kent. Probably Churchill's first medal of any kind, it is in the form of a Maltese Cross surmounted by a lion with the obverse featuring a male figure surrounded by a garland wreath.

64. *The Harrovian,* 21 May, 1892, OBI, CV1, 328.

65. *The Harrovian,* Vol. VI, No. 1, 18 February 1893.

66. OBI, p. 172.

67. OBI, CV1, p. 338.

68. MEL, p. 44.

69. OBI, p. 178.

70. MEL, pp. 42–3.

71. *The Last Lion, Winston Spencer Churchill, Visions of Glory, 1874–1932.* by William Manchester (Boston: Little, Brown and Company, 1983), p. 179. An 1885 survey showed seventy-nine per cent of the cadets had studied with crammers. See *Sandhurst,*

The Royal Military College Sandhurst and Its Predecessors by Alan Shepperd (London: Country Life Books, 1980), p. 92.

72. OBI, CV1, p. 372.

73. OBI, CV1, p. 376.

74. OBI, CV1, p. 380.

75. MEL, p. 40.

76. OBI, pp. 185–6.

77. MEL, p. 41.

78. MEL, p. 49.

79. OBI, CV1, pp. 390–1.

80. OBI, CV1, p. 394.

81. OBI, CV1, pp. 190–1.

82. OBI, CV1, p. 397.

83. OBI, CV1, p. 397.

84. OBI, CV 1, p. 400.

85. 'Churchill At Harrow' in *Churchill by His Contemporaries, ibid*, p. 7.

86. *In Search of Churchill* by Martin Gilbert (London: HarperCollins Publishers, 1994), p. 216.

87. *ibid*, p. 215.

88. MEL pp. 52–3.

CHAPTER TWO: THE ROYAL MILITARY COLLEGE SANDHURST

1. MEL, p. 51.

2. *Mr Kipling's Army* by Byron Farwell (New York: W.W. Norton & Company, 1987), p. 47. Horrocks was commander of XXX corps of the British army in the Second World War.

3. MEL, p. 50.

4. OBI, CV1, p. 394, p. 403.

5. OBI, CV1, p. 403.

6. To make matters even more interesting, the schools at Woolwich and Sandhurst were amalgamated in 1947 to form the Royal Military Academy Sandhurst. Three fine histories are *Annals of Sandhurst, A Chronicle of the Royal Miliary College from Its Foundation to the Present Day* by Major A. F. Mockler-Ferryman (London: William Heinemann, 1900), *Sandhurst, The History of The Royal Military Academy, Woolwich, The Royal Military College, Sandhurst, and The Royal Miliary Academy, Sandhurst 1741–1961* by Sir John Smyth (London: Weidenfeld and Nicholson, 1961) and *Sandhurst, The Royal Military Academy Sandhurst and Its Predecessors* by Alan Sheppard (London: Country Life Books, 1980).

7. 'The Royal Military College Sandhurst' by 'A Cornet of Horse,' *Pall Mall Magazine*, December 1896. The unnamed cornet was Lt W. L. S. Churchill. The article is reprinted in OBI, CV1, pp. 548–52. In an accompanying footnote, official biographer Randolph Churchill explains the pseudonym thus: Evidently he had in mind, in selecting his pseudonym, a rank which was held by William Pitt, Earl of Chatham, and which became a matter of notoriety when Walpole, writhing under the attacks of Pitt, was prompted to say:

'We must muzzle this terrible young Cornet of Horse.' Pitt was dismissed from the army. WSC was to take the precaution of resigning his commission before entering Parliament. A simpler explanation exists. A popular G. A. Henty novel was published in 1881 titled, *A Cornet of Horse, A Tale of Marlborough's Wars*. It is equally likely that the twenty-two-year-old author of the *Pall Mall* essay (a descendent of Marlborough and a reader of such adventure stories) had read the Henty book as it is he was aware of Walpole's statement about Pitt.

8. *Fields of Battle, The Wars of North America* by John Keegan (New York: Alfred A. Knopf, 1996), pp. 146-7.

9. 'Other ranks' in the British army are those below the rank of commissioned officers and warrant officers, i.e. sergeants, corporals and privates. The American equivalent is 'enlisted men'.

10. *Annals of Sandhurst, ibid*, pp. 74–86.

11. See Appendix A for details.

12. OBI, CV1, pp. 422, 429.

13. *Sandhurst* (Smyth), *ibid*, p. 27.

14. *Annals of Sandhurst* by Major A. F. Mockler-Ferryman. (London: William Heinemann, 1900), p. 68.

15. OBI, CV1, p. 409.

16. This was also the motto of several hussar regiments of the day and is the motto of the Queen's Royal Hussars, successor regiment to Churchill's regiment, the Fourth (Queen's Own) Hussars.

17. *Annals of Sandhurst, ibid*, pp. 66–7 and 292, and *Sandhurst* (Smyth), *ibid*, pp. 258–9.

18. OBI, CV1, p. 409.

19. OBI, CV1, p. 411. Ball retired in 1904 but was called back to duty as a brigadier general in the First World War.

20. MEL, p. 63.

21. MEL, p. 64.

22. *The Register of the Victoria Cross*, revised edition compiled by Nora Buzzell (Cheltenham: This England Books, 1988), p. 249.

23. MEL, p. 73.

24. See Appendix A which sets out the details of the September 1893 intake at Sandhurst including their examination marks and later service information.

25. MEL, pp. 57–8.

26. *Sandhurst* (Sheppard), *ibid*, p. 95.

27. The curriculum details are based on the Sandhurst Syllabus for 1900 in *Annals of Sandhurst, ibid*, pp. 284–92.

28. MEL, p. 57.

29. *Letters on Cavalry* (second edition) by Prince Kraft ZuHonhenlohe Ingelfingen (London: Edward Stanford, 1893), p. 9.

30. OBI, CV1, p. 480.

31. *The Operations of War Explained and Illustrated* (fourth edition) by Edward Bruce Hamley (Edinburgh and London: William

Blackwood and Sons, 1878).

32. MEL, p. 58.

33. MEL, p. 57.

34. Interview with Lady Mary Soames, 21 November 1996, London.

35. OBI, CV1, p. 411.

36. OBI, CV1, p. 411.

37. OBI, CV1, p. 414.

38. OBI, CV1, p. 421.

39. OBI, CV1, p. 412.

40. OBI, CV1, p. 422.

41. OBI, CV1, p. 416.

42. OBI, CV1, p. 420.

43. OBI, CV1, p. 427.

44. *Royal Military College Sandhurst, The Register of Gentlemen Cadets, Vol. 4, 1890, Feb. to 1897 Jan.*, W.O. 151.

45. OBI, CV1, p. 430.

46. OBI, CV1, p. 433.

47. OBI, CV1, pp. 433–4.

48. OBI, CV1, p. 439.

49. MEL, p. 59.

50. OBI, CV1, p. 445.

51. *Pall Mall Magazine*, ibid, at OBI, CV1, p. 550.

52. *Annals of Sandhurst*, ibid, p. 62.

53. MEL, p. 60.

54. OBI, CV1, pp. 465–6.

55. OBI, CV1, p. 470.

56. OBI, CV1, p. 471.

57. OBI, CV1, p. 475. Julian Hedworth Byng (1862–1935) later served as Churchill's commanding officer in the Boer War and rose to become a general in the First World War. He retired as a field marshal.

58. MEL, p. 75.

59. OBI, CV1, p. 477.

60. OBI, CV1, p. 478.

61. OBI, CV1 p. 499.

62. MEL, p. 63.

63. OBI, CV1, p. 504.

64. OBI, CV1, p. 509.

65. OBI, CV1, p. 515.

66. *Royal Military College Sandhurst, The Register of Gentlemen Cadets*, ibid.

67. OBI, CV1, p. 517.

68. OBI, CV1, p. 518.

69. MEL, pp. 58–9.

70. MEL, p. 65.

71. MEL, p. 71.

72. The speech is variously reported in *Winston Churchill, the Era and the Man* by Virginia Cowles (London: Hamish Hamilton, 1953), p. 40, *The Last Lion, Winston Spencer Churchill, Visions of Glory, 1874–1932* by William Manchester (Boston: Little, Brown and Company, 1983), p. 199, and 'Winston Spencer Churchill' in *Real Soldiers of Fortune* by Richard Harding Davis (New York: Charles Scribner's Sons, 1914), pp. 84–5. As Churchill wrote in *My Early Life* at p. 71, 'No very accurate report of my words has been preserved.'

73. MEL, p. 72.

74. OBI, CV1, pp. 532–3.

75. OBI, CV1, p. 537.

76. OBI, CV1, p. 540.

77. OBI, CV1, p. 542.

78. MEL, p. 76.

79. Royal Military College Sandhurst, Register of Gentlemen Cadets, ibid. There is no apparent explanation of why the 190 marks recorded for riding differs from the 199 marks Churchill claimed in the letter to his father.

80. MEL, p. 73.

81. OBI, p. 233. To make matters even more confusing, and to show how small details may sometimes give rise to errors, Volume One of the official biography lists the marks correctly while Companion Volume One, Part One, gives a different mark for Military Law, 222 instead of the correct figure of 227.

82. *Sandhurst* (Sheppard), ibid, p. 99. The 1900 Standing Orders state, 'A sword will be given at each final examination as a special reward to the most deserving cadet of his term.' *Annals of Sandhurst*, ibid, p. 293.

83. Correspondence from Dr T. A. Heathcote, TD, Curator, Royal Military Academy Sandhurst, 19 January 1995.

84. I must also beg to differ on class standing issues with Martin Gilbert and his conclusions at page 16 of his excellent *In Search of Churchill* (London: HarperCollins, 1994). Having established what I believe to be the correct information as to Churchill's academic ranking at Sandhurst, I cannot but feel great trepidation at contradicting both Sir Winston and Sir Martin.

85. *Pall Mall Magazine*, in OBI, CV1, p. 552.

86. MEL, p. 73.

CHAPTER THREE: THE 4TH (QUEEN'S OWN) HUSSARS

1. MEL, p. 76.

2. MEL, p. 76.

3. *Anglo-American Memories* by George W. Smalley (London: Duckworth & Co., 1912), p. 88.

4. OBI, CV1, p. 553.

5. OBI, CV1, p. 554.

6. For a splendid introduction to the regimental system and the Victorian British Army see *Mr Kipling's Army, All the Queen's Men* by Byron Farwell (New York: W. W. Norton & Company, Inc. 1981).

7. *The Story of Aldershot: A History and Guide to Town and Camp* by Lt Col. Howard N. Cole (Aldershot: Gale & Polden Limited, 1951), p. 109.

8. *4th Hussar, The Story of the 4th Queen's Own Hussars, 1685-1958* by David Scott Daniell (Aldershot: Gale & Polden Ltd., 1959). This is the indispensable source. It includes a foreword by Sir Winston Churchill. The cavalry of

the British army was divided into three classes based on the size and weight of the rider and the horse. Heavy cavalry with men five feet eight inches to five feet eleven inches included five regiments including the 1st and 2nd Life Guards, the Royal Horse Guards, the 1st Royal Dragoons and the 2nd Dragoons. Medium cavalrymen were five feet seven inches to five feet nine inches and included thirteen regiments of Dragoons and Lancers. Dragoons were cavalrymen trained to fight on foot. Lancers were distinguished by the use of a lance as their primary weapon. Light cavalry was comprised of the smallest cavalrymen, five foot six inches to five foot seven inches tall. The light cavalry was made up of thirteen regiments of hussars. Hussars were used for reconnaissance and actions where speed was essential.

9. A complete list of the regiment's battle honours is in Appendix B.

10. 'The Charge of The Light Brigade' by Alfred, Lord Tennyson in *The Norton Anthology of English Literature, Volume 2*, Abrams, M. H., general editor (New York: W. W. Norton & Company, Inc. 1968), pp. 898–9.

11. Daniell, *4th Hussar*, p. 197.

12. The citation appeared in the *London Gazette* on 24 February 1857, 'Samuel Parkes, No. 635, Private, 4th Light Dragoons. In charge of the Light Cavalry Brigade at Balaclava, Trumpet-Major Crawford's horse fell and dismounted him, and he lost his sword; he was attacked by two Cossacks, when Private Samuel Parkes (whose horse had been shot), saved his life by placing himself between them and the Trumpet-Major, and drove them away by his sword. In attempting to follow the Light Cavalry Brigade in the retreat, they were attacked by six Russians, whom Parkes kept at bay, and retired slowly, fighting and defending the Trumpet-Major for some time, until deprived of his sword by a shot.'

13. *The British Army* by a Lieutenant-Colonel in the British Army (J. M. Grierson) (London: Sampson Low, Marston & Company, 1899), pp. 44–8. This is a remarkably complete source book which is bound in the khaki uniform cloth of 'our soldiers in South Africa'.

14. *The Late Victorian Army 1868–1902* by Edward M. Spiers (Manchester and New York: Manchester University Press, 1992), p. 63.

15. *The British Army*, Grierson, pp. 44–6.

16. *The Medal Yearbook 1997*, edited by James Mackay, John W. Mussell and the editorial team of *Medal News* (Honiton, Devon: Token Publishing Limited, 1997). As Prime Minister and Minister of Defence during the Second World War, Churchill was awarded six of the ten medals for the Second World War.

17. An excellent illustrated history is *British Artists and War, The Face of Battle in Paintings and Prints, 1700–1914* by Peter Harrington (London: Greenhill Books, 1993).

18. 'Soldiers of The Queen' by Leslie Stuart (pseudonym of Thomas A. Barret). Lyrics in *Songs and Music of the Redcoats, A History of the War Music of the British Army 1642–1902*. by Lewis Winstock (Harrisburg, PA: Stackpole Books, 1970), pp. 253–5.

19. *Hark Back* by Colonel Wilfred Jelf (London: John Murray, 1935), quoted in *The Story of Aldershot* at p. 109.

20. Daniell, *4th Hussar*, p. 212.

21. *The Official Army List for the Quarter Ending 30th March, 1895* (London: War Office, 29 April, 1895), p. 731. The quarterly Army List includes data on all officers of the British army including their seniority, dates of rank and service records. A 'mention in dispatches' was an official commendation for meritorious duty in the field which did not merit a decoration.

22. MEL, p. 81.

23. MEL, p. 82.

24. *Military Customs* by Major T. J. Edwards (Aldershot: Gale & Polden, Ltd., 1954), p. 166.

25. Daniell, *4th Hussar*, p. 224.

26. 'The Queen's Royal Hussars (The Queen's Own and Royal Irish)', undated pamphlet, courtesy of the regiment.

27. The *London Gazette* of Tuesday, 19 February 1895, entry at page 1001, read 'War Office, Pall Mall, 19th February, 1895. 4th Hussars. Gentleman Cadet Winston Leonard Spencer Churchill, from the Royal Military College, to be Second Lieutenant in succession to Lieutenant G. H. B. Gaine, seconded. Dated 20th February, 1895.' Churchill's *My Early Life* incorrectly states he was gazetted to the regiment in March 1895.

28. OBI, CV1, pp. 557–8. Campbell-Bannerman was Secretary of State for War. As Prime Minister in 1906 his gave Churchill his first ministerial appointment, Under-Secretary of State for the Colonies.

29. *The Official Army List for the Quarter Ending 30th March, 1895* (London: War Office, 29th April, 1895), p. 731.

30. OBI, p. 233.

31. *Social Life in the British Army* by a British Officer (Captain William Elliot Cairnes) (London: John Long, 1901), p. xii. See also Spiers, *The Late Victorian Army*, p. 104.

32. OBI, CV1, p. 559.

33. OBI, CV1, pp. 569–70.

34. OBI, p. 247.

35. *Soldiering On* by General Sir Hubert Gough (London: Arthur Baker, Ltd., 1954), p. 32.

36. *Dress Regulation for Officers of the Army* (London: War Office, 1900), pp. 22 et seq. See also, *Simkin's Soldiers, The British Army in 1890* by Lieutenant Colonel P. S. Walton

(Dorking: The Victorian Military Society, 1981), pp. 61–6, and *British Hussar Regiments 1805–1914* by A. H. Bowling (London: Almark Publishing Co. Ltd, 1972), pp. 39–42, 56, 64, 68–9.

37. The Old Harrow Boys and their dates of attendance were: Cecil W. Peters, 1870–4; Hon. Frederick R. W. Evenleigh-De Moleyns, 1876–9; Joseph W. Underwood, 1879–83; Charles L. Graham, 1881–4; and Edgar M. Lafone, 1881–5.

38. *Real Soldiers of Fortune* by Richard Harding Davis (New York: Charles Scribner's Sons, 1914), p. 81. The book was originally published in 1906. The Churchill chapter was a biographical profile with emphasis on the Boer War. As to Churchill's height, *The Register of Gentleman Cadets at Sandhurst* listed him at five feet six and seven-tenths inches in September 1893.

39. OBI, CV1, p. 555.

40. Daniell, *4th Hussar*, pp. 216–17.

41. MEL, p. 83.

42. 4th (Q.O.) Hussars/Muster Roll/1895. This large (59 x 46.5 cm) lithograph made by Sgt G. Hicks was made available from the collection of and through the courtesy of the Regimental Headquarters, The Queen's Royal Hussars. A copy is on display at the Queen's Royal Irish Hussars Museum at Eastbourne.

43. Daniell, *4th Hussar*, p. 223.

44. MEL, p. 77

45. *Regulations for the Instruction and Movements of Cavalry* (London: HMSO, 1885) pp. IV–XIV. This manual was revised and updated periodically. The 1885 edition is quoted as being illustrative of other editions. The 1896 revision was written by two cavalry officers destined to command the British army in the First World War, John French and Douglas Haig. The last edition was issued in 1898.

46. MEL, p. 78.

47. MEL, p. 78.

48. I am grateful to The Lady Soames, Churchill's daughter, for this anecdote. She accompanied her father to the 1943 Quebec Conference and was one of the participants in the ocean-going cavalry drill. See also *The War and Colonel Warden* by Gerald Pawle (London: George G. Harrap & Co. Ltd., 1963), p. 251.

49. *Hussar of the Line* by Francis Hereward Maitland (London: Hurst & Blackett, Ltd, 1951), p. 26. This fine memoir is 'Proudly dedicated to the Rt. Hon. Winston Churchill, C.H., O.M., the greatest Hussar of them all.'

50. MEL, pp. 77–8.

51. MEL, pp. 77.

52. *Rifles of the World* by John Walter (Northbrook, IL: DBI Books, Inc. 1993), pp. 118–19. See also *Small Arms of the World* (12th revised edition) by Edward Clinton Ezell (New York:

Barnes & Noble, 1983), pp. 305–7.

53. *The British Army*, Grierson, pp. 121–3.

54. *ibid*, p. 123.

55. *Military Pistols and Revolvers* by Ian V. Hogg (Poole, Dorset: Arms and Armour Press, Ltd., 1987), pp. 24–5. See also *Small Arms of the World*, Ezell, p. 291–2. I am greatly indebted to Dean M. Lewis for his guidance and instruction on the history of firearms. He is a straight shooter in every respect.

56. *The British Army*, Grierson, p. 124.

57. For details of the swords see *Swords of the British Army – The Regulation Patterns 1788–1914*, The Revised Edition, by Brian Robson (London: The National Army Museum, 1996), pp. 89, 94, 98. I am much indebted to Dr Cyril Mazansky for sharing his expertise, source materials and photographs of British army swords.

58. OBI, CV1, pp. 555–6.

59. OBI, CV1, pp. 559–60.

60. OBI, CV1, pp. 560.

61. OBI, CV1, pp. 556–7.

62. *The British Army*, Grierson, p. 248.

63. *Hussar of the Line*, Maitland, p. 97.

64. *The British Army*, Grierson, p. 205–6.

65. OBI, CV1, p. 562.

66. OBI, CV1, p. 562–3.

67. OBI, CV1, p. 565.

68. Racing Calendar, 21 March 1895, quoted in OBI, CV1, p. 629.

69. Racing Calendar, 20 February 1896, quoted in OBI, CV1, p. 630.

70. OBI, CV2, p. 701. The letter dated 12 November 1896 was sent from Bangalore, India, after the Challenge Cup scandal was the subject of articles in *Truth* magazine and Churchill was contemplating a libel suit.

71. OBI, CV1, p. 571.

72. OBI, CV1, pp. 631–62.

73. OBI, CV1, p. 575. For an excellent article on Churchill's life-long interest in polo see 'Churchill and Polo, The Hot Pursuit of His Other Hobby' by Barbara F. Langworth in *Finest Hour* No. 72, Third Quarter, 1991, pp. 25–9.

74. OBI, CV1, p. 580.

75. OBI, CV1, p. 579–80.

76. 'Historical Account of the 4th, THE QUEEN'S OWN Historical Papers 1801–1921, 4th Hussars,' p. 155. Unpublished archive document courtesy of Home Headquarters, The Queen's Royal Hussars, London.

77. OBI, CV1, p. 581.

78. OBI, CV1, p. 583.

79. OBI, CV1, p. 584.

80. OBI, CV1, p. 585.

81. 'Historical Account of the 4th', p. 156. Churchill mistakenly states in *My Early Life* that the regiment moved to Hounslow in the spring of 1896.

82. *Old Cavalry Stations* by B. Granville Baker (London: Heath Cranton Limited, 1934), pp. 118–23.

CHAPTER FOUR:
THE CUBAN INSURRECTION

1. MEL, p. 89.
2. This is an insight I owe to Lyn MacDonald and her fine book, *1914* (New York: Atheneum, 1988), p. 157.
3. OBI, CV1, p. 593.
4. MEL, p. 90.
5. *The Official Army List for the Quarter ending 30 March 1895.* War Office, 29 April 1895.
6. MEL, pp. 88–9.
7. MEL, p. 195.
8. This insight I owe to William Pfaff of *The New Yorker*. In his 'Critic At Large' column in the 8 May 1989 issue he rightly points out it was plausible before the First World War to seek military glory but never again after that conflict which altered warfare forever.
9. OBI, CV1, p. 589.
10. Barnes went on to have a fine army career. He served in the Boer War in which he was the adjutant of the Imperial Light Horse from 1899 to 1900, was wounded, mentioned in dispatches and awarded the Distinguished Service Order. He served as a lieutenant colonel in the Imperial Yeomanry 1901–2. In the First World War he was wounded twice, mentioned in dispatches seven times and received the French Croix de Guerre. He retired as Major General Sir Reginald Barnes in 1921, having been made a Knight Commander of the most honourable order of the Bath (KCB). He was made colonel of the 4th (Queen's Own) Hussars in January 1918. He was succeeded in that position by Churchill in October 1941.
11. MEL, p. 90.
12. OBI, CV1, p. 591.
13. OBI, CV1, p. 594.
14. OBI, CV1, p. 592.
15. OBI, CV1, p. 593. In 1892 Mauser introduced a new rifle cartridge, the 7X57, which was the best cartridge of the era with muzzle velocity and penetrating ability superior to its rivals. It also featured smokeless powder, providing a significant tactical advantage for those who used it in combat. An interesting article on the Mauser rifle and cartridge by Paul S. Scarlata appeared in *Military History*, June 1998.
16. OBI, CV1, p. 593.
17. OBI, CV1, p. 590.
18. The *Etruria* was built by John Elder & Co. and had her maiden voyage from Queenstown (Liverpool) to Sandy Hook (New York), on 25 April 1885. Her second westbound voyage set the speed record of six days, five hours, thirty-one minutes, an average speed of 18.87 knots.

In March 1887, it set the then eastbound speed record of six days, four hours, thirty-six minutes, an average speed of 19.45 knots. The Cunard Line ships *Etruria, Umbria, Aurania* and *Servia* combined to provide weekly passenger service between New York and Liverpool. *North Atlantic Seaway*, Volume 1, by N. R. P. Bonsor and J. H. Isherwood (New York: Arco Publishing Company, Inc., 1975), pp. 96–7.
19. OBI, CV1, p. 595.
20. OBI, CV1, p. 597.
21. OBI, CV1, p. 598.
22. OBI, CV1, p. 599.
23. *Churchill, The Struggle for Survival 1940–1965* by Lord Moran (Boston: Houghton Mifflin Company, 1966), p. 576.
24. OBI, CV1, pp. 599–600.
25. *Thoughts and Adventures* by Winston S. Churchill (London: Thornton Butterworth Limited, 1932), p. 52.
26. OBI, p. 272.
27. MEL, p. 91.
28. The one interruption in Spanish rule was in 1762 when the Royal Navy captured Havana and so controlled the island. Cuba was returned to Spain the following year in the Treaty of Paris in exchange for Florida on the North American mainland.
29. In his *Cuba Between Empires 1878–1902* (Pittsburgh: University of Pittsburgh Press, 1983) Professor Louis A. Pérez, Jr., argues persuasively that the Cuban revolution of 1895 was not merely the latest of the nineteenth-century colonial wars of independence in Spanish Central and South America, 'but the precursor of a genre: a guerrilla war of national liberation aspiring to the transformation of society'. p. xix.
30. *The War with Spain in 1898* by David F. Trask (New York: MacMillan Publishing Co., Inc., 1981), pp. 3–6.
31. See 'The Trochas' by Michael Blow in *Military History Quarterly*, Vol. 10, No. 4, Summer 1998.
32. OBI, CV1, p. 601.
33. OBI, CV1, p. 602
34. OBI, CV1, p. 605.
35. MEL, p. 92.
36. Churchill's five articles from Cuba appeared in the *Daily Graphic* under the headline 'The Insurrection in Cuba, Letters from the Front (From Our Own Correspondent).' They were numbered I through V and were printed in the 13, 17, 24 and 27 December 1895, and 13 January 1896, issues respectively. They were signed 'W.S.C.' and included pen-and-ink drawings of 'War Scenes from Cuba . . . From sketches by our Correspondent with the Spanish Army.' The articles are reprinted in OBI, CV1, pp. 604–18, also in *Winston S. Churchill, War Correspondent, 1895–1900*

edited by Fredrick Woods (London: Brassey's, 1992), pp. 3–22 and in *The Collected Essays of Sir Winston Churchill, Volume I, Churchill and War,* General Editor Michael Wolff (London: Library of Imperial History, 1975), pp. 3–16.

37. OBI, CV1, p. 606. From Letter 1, dateline Cienfuegos. Although undated it is probably from 22 November 1895.

38. OBI, CV1, pp. 606–7.

39. OBI, CV1, p. 608. From Letter II, 23 November 1895, dateline Sancti Spiritus.

40. MEL, p. 93.

41. OBI, CV1, p. 608.

42. OBI, CV1, p. 608.

43. MEL, pp. 93–4.

44. OBI, CV1, pp. 609-10. From Letter III, November 27, 1895, dateline Arroyo.

45. MEL, p. 95.

46. OBI, CV1, p. 610.

47. OBI, CV1, p. 610.

48. MEL, p. 96.

49. OBI, CV1, p. 611.

50. MEL, pp. 96-7.

51. MEL, p. 97.

52. OBI, CV1, p. 612.

53. MEL, p. 97.

54. MEL, p. 98.

55. OBI, CV1, p. 613. While Churchill first heard Mausers at the side of the Spanish army, he would later face them in South Africa in the hands of the Boers and in the First World War in the hands of the German army.

56. MEL, p. 99. The story of the portly Spanish officer is not recorded in Churchill's contemporaneous account sent to the *Daily Graphic.*

57. OBI, CV1, p. 614. The events of 30 November–1 December 1895 are the subject of Letter IV, dated 4 December 1895, from Cienfuegos.

58. OBI, CV1, p. 614. The term 'fire fight', it appears, precedes the Vietnam War by decades.

59. MEL, p. 100.

60. This is a rather grand name for the events of 2 December, but as Churchill wrote in the *Daily Graphic*: 'Cuban battles are many of them imaginary, most of them exaggerated, and all of them devoid of importance.' OBI, CV1, p. 617.

61. OBI, CV1, p. 616.

62. OBI, CV1, p. 615. Letter V for the *Daily Graphic* with a dateline of Tampa Bay, Florida, was written after Churchill left Cuba and the hospitality of the Spanish Army. This letter bears the date 14 December 1895 in all the references noted in footnote 36. The date appears to be in error as Churchill was leaving New York on that date, not Tampa.

63. *Cuba Between Empires*, Perez, p.75.

64. OBI, CV1, p. 616. The bracketed language was added by the author.

65. OBI, CV1, p. 603.

66. OBI, CV1, p. 604.

67. OBI, CV1, p. 603.

68. Archivo General Militar, Segovia, Spain, Seccion I, Legajo E-1344. Unpublished archival documents provided courtesy of Major Luis F. Núñez, Military Attaché, Embassy of Spain, Washington, D.C.

69. OBI, CV2, p. 928.

70. *Great Contemporaries* by Winston S. Churchill (London: Thornton Butterworth, Ltd, 1937), p. 212.

71. Barnes's awards are Knight Commander of the Most Noble Order of the Bath; Distinguished Service Order; Queen's South Africa Medal with six clasps; King's South Africa Medal with two clasps; 1914 Star with clasp; British War Medal; Victory Medal with palm; Dehli Durbar Medal; Coronation Medal (1911); Jubilee Medal (1935); Order of Military Merit, First Class (Spain); Cuban Campaign Medal (Spain); and Croix de Guerre with two palms (France). The thirty-seven awards received by Churchill are the subject of *The Orders, Decorations and Medals of Sir Winston Churchill* by Douglas S. Russell (Hopkinton, New Hampshire: The International Churchill Society of the United States, 1990), second edition (Washington, D.C., The Churchill Centre, 2004).

72. OBI, CV1, p. 618.

73. OBI, CV1, p. 618.

74. OBI, p. 269.

75. OBI, p. 266.

76. *The New York Times*, 8 December 1895, p. 1, col. 2.

77. *The New York Times*, 15 December 1895, p. 5, col. 3.

78. OBI, p. 266.

79. *The Times*, 1 April 1949, p .3.

80. *The New York Times*, 14 December 1895, p. 9. 'Passengers Bound for Europe . . . On the Cunard Line Steamship *Etruria* will be Winston Spencer Churchill . . .'

81. *New York World*, 15 December 1895 in OBI, CV1, p. 620.

82. *New York Herald*, 15 December 1895 in OBI, CV1, pp.621–2.

83. OBI, CV1, p. 616.

84. OBI, CV1, p. 617.

85. *The Saturday Review*, 15 February 1896, reprinted in *The Collected Essays of Sir Winston Churchill, Volume I, Churchill and War*, General Editor Michael Wolff (London: Library of Imperial History, 1975), p. 18.

86. *ibid.*

87. OBI, CV1, p. 666.

88. *The Saturday Review*, 29 April 1896, reprinted in *The Collected Essays, supra*, at p. 22.

89. *The Saturday Review*, 29 April 1896, reprinted in *The Collected Essays, supra*, at p. 25.

90. *The Times*, 23 December 1895, p. 6, col. 5.

91. OBI, CV1, p. 622.

CHAPTER FIVE: THE FRONTIER WAR

1. MEL, p. 103. In *My Early Life* Churchill recollected that the regiment moved from Aldershot to Hounslow in the spring of 1896 and so refers to his six-month stay at the latter station. In fact, according to the regimental records the move was made in September 1895. Subtracting the time he was occupied with going to Cuba, he spent nine months in Hounslow.

2. MEL, p. 103. The Hounslow cavalry barracks is still in use as a military post, its parade ground and brownish-yellow brick buildings surrounded by a substantial brick wall topped by iron pickets or barbed wire. The heath is still used by officers to exercise their horses. At the end of Barrack Road across from the north entrance to the heath is a pub named, fittingly enough, The Hussar.

3. OBI, pp. 274–6.

4. MEL, pp. 106–7.

5. OBI, p. 276.

6. *Churchill 1874–1922* by The Earl of Birkenhead (London: Harrap Books, Ltd., 1989), p. 48.

7. 'Historical Account of the 4th', *supra*, pp. 156–7.

8. *Ibid*, pp. 157–8.

9. *4th Hussar*, *supra*, p. 224. A brake is a horse-drawn carriage.

10. The *London Gazette*, 23 June 1896, p. 3642.

11. *The Official Army List for the Quarter Ending 30th March 1899* (London: War Office, 28 April 1899) p. 905.

12. 'Historical Account of the 4th', *supra*, pp. 158–9.

13. Churchill certainly had a reasonable concern about being away from the centre of society and politics for so long a period. When his eventual resignation from the army took effect in May 1899, the 4th Hussars were still in India. When the regiment transferred from India to South Africa in October 1905, Churchill had already been in Parliament for five years and would be serving as Under-Secretary of State for the Colonies by the end of the year. By the time the 4th Hussars returned to duty in England in December 1909, he was already in the Cabinet as President of the Board of Trade.

14. OBI, CV1, p. 676.

15. OBI, CV1, p. 673.

16. OBI, CV1, p. 676. Churchill's reference is to the British South Africa Company's Medal (1890–7) issued to British troops for participation in various campaigns in Mashonaland, Matabeleland and Rhodesia. Although he missed getting this medal, he eventually would serve in both South Africa and the Sudan and receive campaign medals for both.

17. OBI, CV1, p. 678.

18. 'Historical Account of the 4th', *supra*, p. 159. The brackets are supplied by the author.

19. *ibid.*, pp. 160–1. The officers embarked on *Britannia* were Lt Col W. A. Ramsay, Majors R. Kincaid-Smith and L. E. Starkey, Captains F. D. Baillie, R. Hoare, E. M. Lafone, and C. L. Graham, Lts A. L. Trevor-Boothe, A. O. Francis, A. Savory, H. G. Watkin, E. R. Clutterbuck, W. L. S. Churchill, and Hon. H. Baring, Second Lt A. F. C. Williams, A. M. Rotheram, E. O. B. Black-Hawkins, L. E. Dening, Lt and Quartermaster W. A. Cochrane, Lt and Riding Master W. J. Rose and Lt and Acting Paymaster D. G. Hogg. The following officers did not accompany the regiment to India: Major C. Peters who was on leave awaiting retirement. Captain Hon. F. de Moleyns detached and serving as commandant of the British African Police; Captain F. Lee serving as an ADC in Devonport and Captain J. W. Underwood and Lt W. E. Long who remained behind for duty with the regimental depot.

20. Information on the *Britannia* is from *The Story of the P & O* by David and Stephen Howarth (London: Weidenfeld and Nicolson, 1966), p. 110 and *The Ships, Channel Packets and Ocean Liners 1850–1970* by John M. Maber (London: Her Majesty's Stationary Office, n.d.), p. 25.

21. *Egypt in 1898* by George W. Steevens (New York: Dodd, Mead & Company, 1899), p. 11.

22. OBI, CV2, p. 679.

23. *ibid.* Churchill's brass telescope, imprinted 'Ross of London No. 24074' and engraved 'Winston S. Churchill 4th Q.O. HUSSARS', is now in the collection of the Queen's Royal Hussars.

24. MEL, pp. 120–1.

25. 'Historical Account of the 4th', *supra*, p. 161. No doubt Churchill spent time on deck in very hot temperatures of the Red Sea seeking the relief of a breeze. He later wrote a short story, 'Man Overboard', about an English passenger returning from India who fell from the deck of a mail steamer into the Red Sea and avoided drowning only because he was first devoured by a shark. The story appeared in *The Harmsworth Magazine* in January 1899 and was reprinted in *The Collected Essays of Sir Winston Churchill, Volume IV, Churchill at Large* (London: Library of Imperial History, 1976), pp. 3–5.

26. MEL, pp. 115 and 117.

27. MEL, p. 116. In her essay 'Churchill and Polo, The Hot Pursuit of His Other Hobby,' *Finest Hour* No. 72, Third Quarter 1991, pp. 24–9, Barbara Langworth expresses doubt as to whether this incident occurred because Churchill did not mention it in his letters at

the time and because the regiment moved its 500 tons of luggage that same day. She asserts the shoulder dislocation occurred at Jodhpore in 1898 when he fell down a staircase. The author disagrees. In *My Early Life* Churchill did not say that he dislocated his shoulder on arriving at Bombay ('my shoulder didn't actually go out') but rather that he wrenched it, which made it subject to going out of joint unexpectedly thereafter. As to the luggage, the lifting would be done by the men, not the officers. As regards not mentioning it in correspondence, Churchill had much else to preoccupy him in those first busy weeks in India. The shoulder dislocation in Jodhpore in 1898 was written about at the time by Churchill in a letter home and no doubt occurred. It was perhaps made more likely because of this incident in Bombay in 1896.

28. *ibid.* An 1898 photograph of the polo team in India clearly shows Churchill with his right shoulder harness.

29. *ibid.*, pp. 120–1.

30. *The Memoirs of Aga Khan* (London: Cassell & Co., Ltd., 1954), p. 85. The reference to Churchill in these memoirs must be viewed with some scepticism as it places the event in the late summer of 1896 before the 4th Hussars arrived in India, and contains much detail about a very junior officer. It was written almost sixty years after the events. But it is included as it has the ring of truth and does capture the essential character of the young Lt Churchill in India. It is the way the old Aga Khan remembered or at least like to remember Churchill. Khan's memoir had a foreword by W. Somerset Maugham and, on the backside of the dust jacket, an advertisement for a forthcoming book entitled *Winston Spencer Churchill, Servant of Crown and Commonwealth, a Tribute.*

31. 'Historical Account of the 4th', *supra*, pp. 161–2. The details of the regiment's movement from ship to shore and from Bombay to Bangalore are based on this document rather than on *My Early Life* which was written thirty-five years later and is at odds with the contemporary record in some details.

32. *The Oxford Survey of The British Empire, Volume II, Asia*, A. J. Herbertson and O. J. R. Howarth, editors (Oxford: The Clarendon Press, 1914), pp. 261, 463, 469.

33. *The Army Book for the British Empire* by Lt General W. H. Goodenough and Lt Colonel J. C. Dalton (London: Printed for her Majesty's Stationery Office by Harrison and Sons, 1893), pp. 453–6. Among the several excellent studies consulted concerning the Indian army and its relationship to the British were *The Indian Army, The Garrison of British Imperial India, 1822–1922* by T. A. Heathcote (London: David & Charles (Holdings) Ltd.,

1974), *A Matter of Honour* by Philip Mason (New York: Holt, Rinehart and Winston, 1974, *Armies of the Raj from the Mutiny to Independence 1858–1947* by Byron Farwell (New York: W.W. North & Company, 1989), *Bugles and a Tiger* by John Masters (London: Michael Joseph, Ltd., 1956), *The Indian Army*, by Boris Mollo (Poole, Dorset: New Orchard Editions, 1986), and *The Indian Army of the Empress* by Alan Harfield (Tunbridge Wells, Kent: Spellmount, Ltd., 1990).

34. Grierson, *The British Army, supra*, pp. 108–9. Goodenough and Dalton at p. 453 put the number of British troops in India in 1892–3 at 72,997. The nine British army cavalry regiments in India in the autumn of 1897 were the 4th (Royal Irish) Dragoon Guards at Jamrud Column, Punjab; the 5th (Princess Charlotte of Wales's) Dragoon Guards at Meerut, Bengal; the 4th (Queen's Own) Hussars at Bangalore, Madras; the 5th (Royal Irish) Lancers at Muttra, Bengal; the 11th (Price Albert's Own) Hussars at Sialkote, Punjab; the 16th (Queen's) Lancers at Umballa; the 18th Hussars at Lucknow, Bengal; the 19th (Princess of Wales's Own) Hussars at Secunderabad, Madras; and the 20th Hussars at Mhow, Bombay. *The Official Army List For The Quarter Ending 30th September, 1897* (London: War Office, 1897)

35. *The British Soldier, A Social History from 1661 to the Present* by J. M. Brereton (London: The Bodley Head, 1980), p. 84.

36. Two excellent works on British architecture in India are *Stones of Empire, The Buildings of the Raj* by Jan Morris and Simon Winchester (Oxford: Oxford University Press, 1983) and *Splendours of the Raj, British Architecture in India 1660–1947* by Philip Davies (London: John Murray, 1985).

37. 'A Club's World,' by M. Bhaktavatsala, a publication of the Bangalore Club. No date available.

38. Three excellent sources of information on old Bangalore, the cantonment and the architecture of each upon which I have relied are *Bangalore Through the Centuries* by M. Fazlul Hasan (Bangalore: Historical Publications, 1970), *The City Beautiful, A Celebration of the Architectural Heritage and City – Aesthetics of Bangalore* by T. P. Issar (Bangalore: Bangalore Urban Art Commission, 1988), and *Monkeytops: Old Buildings in Bangalore Cantonment* by Elizabeth Staley (Bangalore: Tara Books, 1981).

39. MEL, p. 120.

40. OBI, CV2, pp. 688–9.

41. *Churchill's Blind Spot: India* by Narayan G. Jog (Bombay: New Book Company, 1944), p. 2. See also *The City Beautiful, supra*, at pp. 12–13, 236, and *Monkeytops, supra*, at p. 24.

42. OBI, CV2, p. 688.

43. MEL, p. 117.

44. OBI, CV2, p. 703.

45. *The Story of the Malakand Field Force, An Episode of Frontier War* by Winston L. Spencer Churchill (London: Longmans, Green and Co., 1898), pp. 103 and 297. This is Churchill's first book and the quotations used are from the first English edition, punctuation errors included. Further references to the book in footnotes will be abbreviated as MFF.

46. OBI, CV2, p. 693 and MEL, pp. 121–2.

47. 'Officers and Gentlemen' by Winston S. Churchill, *The Saturday Evening Post*, 29 December 1900 and in modified form in *The Pall Mall Magazine*, January 1901. Reprinted in *The Collected Essays of Sir Winston Churchill, Vol I, Churchill at War* (London: Library of Imperial History, 1976), p. 45.

48. OBI, CV2, p. 720.

49. *Winston Churchill, the Era and the Man* by Virgina Cowles (London: Hamish Hamilton, Ltd., 1953), p. 55. Ms Cowles states that in preparing her book she interviewed Hallaway who was eighty-two years old at the time and living in Wimbledon.

50. *ibid*, p. 55.

51. *Soldiering On, Being the Memoirs of General Sir Hubert Gough* (London: Arthur Barker Ltd, 1954), p. 62.

52. 'IV Q.O. Hussars – Suggestions and Complaints, Bangalore Aug 12/97'. This original document containing the handwritten comments of Churchill and the other officers is preserved in the collection of the Queen's Royal Hussars Officers' mess and is quoted with the kind permission of the regiment.

53. OBI, CV2, pp. 697–8.

54. OBI, CV2, p. 701.

55. MEL, p. 123. Churchill's private university is the subject of Chapter IX of his autobiography.

56. OBI, CV2, p. 702.

57. OBI, CV2, p. 746.

58. OBI, CV2, p. 751. The bracketed language is supplied by the author.

59. OBI, CV2, p. 700.

60. OBI, p. 328.

61. OBI, CV2, pp. 710–11.

62. OBI, CV2, p. 717.

63. OBI, CV2, p. 720.

64. 'Historical Account of the 4th', *supra*, p. 163.

65. OBI, CV2, p. 726.

66. MFF, p. 168, Churchill was photographed in India wearing his khaki uniform and the colonial-pattern helmet referred to as the pith helmet in his history of the Malakand Field Force. A year later he was photographed in North Africa wearing a third style of helmet, the Wolseley pattern.

67. *Dress Regulations for the Officers of the Army* (London: War Office, 1900), p. 75.

68. Churchill's revolver is in the collection of The Imperial War Museum and is displayed at the Cabinet War Rooms museum in London on loan from Mr Winston Churchill.

69. *Brassey's Companion to the British Army* by Antony Makepeace-Warne (London: Brassey's, 1995), p. 5.

70. OBI, CV2, p. 727.

71. 'Historical Account of the 4th', *supra*, p. 163.

72. OBI, CV2, p. 731.

73. *ibid.*

74. *4th Hussar, supra*, pp. 228–9.

75. OBI, CV2, p. 748.

76. OBI, CV2, pp. 753–4.

77. OBI, CV2, p. 774.

78. OBI, CV2, p. 777. In *My Early Life*, at page 137, Churchill remembered hearing from Blood at Bombay but a review of his contemporary correspondence shows that he received Blood's letter at Bangalore a week after his return to India.

79. OBI, CV2, p. 779. The 346-page novel, entitled *Savrola, A Tale of the Revolution in Lauraria*, was published by Longman's, Green & Co. in New York in 1899 and London in 1900. It was inscribed to 'The officers of the IVth (Queen's Own) Hussars in whose company the author lived for four happy years.'

80. OBI, CV2, p. 780.

81. OBI, CV2, p. 781.

82. OBI, CV2, p. 783.

83. MFF, p. 2.

84. *Young Winston's Wars, The Original Despatches of Winston S. Churchill, War Correspondent 1897–1900*. Frederick Woods, ed. (London: Leo Cooper Ltd., 1972), p. 5. This quotation is taken from the first of the fifteen letters Churchill wrote for the *Daily Telegraph* between 3 September and 16 October 1897. The letters may also be found in *Winston S. Churchill, War Correspondent 1895–1900*, Fredrick Woods, ed. (London: Brassey's 1992). They do not appear in the *Collected Essays* and only letters four and eleven appear in the companion volumes to the official biography. The dates, all in 1897, and locations where Churchill wrote his dispatches from India, and dates of publication in the *Daily Telegraph* are:

1. 3 September, Malakand, October 6
2. 6 September, Khar, October 7
3. 9 September, Kotkai, October 8
4. 12 September, Nowagai, October 9
5. 17 September, Camp Inayat Kila, October 14
6. 18 September, Inayat Kila, October 15
7. 21 September, Shumshuk, November 6
8. 23 September, The Camp, Inayat Kila, November 2
9. 28 September, Inayat Kila, November 9
10. 2 October, Inayat Kila, October 26
11. 6 October, Inayat Kila, November 13

12. 8 October, Inayat Kila, November 16
13. 14 October, Nowshera, November 19
14. 15 October, Nowshera, December 3
15. 16 October, Nowshera, December 6
85. 'The Ethics of Frontier Policy', by Winston S.
Churchill, *The United States Magazine, August
1898*. Reprinted in *The Collected Essays, ibid*,
p. 32. The bracketed word is supplied by the
author.
86. *British Battles & Medals*, by E. C. Joslin, A.
R. Litherland and B. T. Simpkin (London:
Spink & Son Ltd., 1988)
87. There are many excellent histories about the
British experience on the North-West Frontier. See for example, *From Black Mountain to
Waziristan* by Colonel H. C. Wylly (London:
MacMillan and Co., Ltd., 1912), recently
republished by The Naval and Military Press,
Ltd.; *North-West Frontier, British and Indian
Army Campaigns on the North-West Frontier of
India 1849–1908* by Captain H. L. Nevill,
originally published in 1912, republished
(London: Tom Donovan Publishing, Ltd.,
1992); and *The Indian Borderland 1880–1900*
by Colonel Sir T. Hungerford Holdich
(London: Methuen and Co.), republished
(New Delhi: Asian Educational Services,
1996); *The Pathan Revolt in North-West India*
by H. Woosnam Mills (Lahore: The 'Civil and
Military Gazette' Press, 1897); *Indian Frontier
Warfare* by G. J. Younghusband (London:
Kegan Paul, 1898), reprinted (Delhi: Anmol
Publications, 1985); *The North-West Frontier,
British India and Afghanistan, A Pictoral
History, 1839–1947* by Michael Barthorp
(Poole, Dorset: New Orchard Editions, Ltd.,
1986); and *The Frontier Ablaze, The North-West
Frontier Rising, 1897–98* by Michael Barthorp
(London: Windrow & Greene, Ltd., 1996). I
am also indebted to Major Robert Henderson,
late of the 2nd Royal Battalion, The Sikh
Regiment, and to Sue Farrington for sharing
their experiences in India and for their guidance in the study of the British Raj.
88. MFF, p. 223. A splendid article on British
imperial policy and purposes and Churchill's
role in the 1890s is 'Churchill's Initial Experience with the British Conduct of Small Wars:
India and the Sudan, 1897–1898' by David
Jablonsky, in *Small Wars and Insurgencies*, Vol.
II, No. 1 (Spring, 2000), pp. 1–25, published
by Frank Cass, London. See also *Winston S.
Churchill on Empire* by Kirk Emmert
(Durham, NC: Carolina Academic Press,
1989).
89. RWI, pp. 34–5.
90. MEL, pp. 140–1.
91. MFF, p. 108. Although a variety of tribes and
sub-groups were involved in the uprising most
were Pushtu speaking and of eastern Afghan
origin, to which the general term Pathan was
applied. The 1897 uprising was often referred

to as the Pathan Revolt.
92. MFF, p. 40.
93. *Young Winston's Wars*, p. 8.
94. MFF, pp. 4–5.
95. MFF, p. 78. The 3rd Brigade was comprised
of The Queen's Own Regiment, 22nd Punjab
Infantry, 39th Punjab Infantry, No. 3
Company (Bombay) Sappers and Miners,
and No. 1 Mountain Battery, Royal Artillery.
See MFF, p. 135. Although Churchill spent
several days with the 3rd Brigade he only saw
combat with the 2nd Brigade.
96. MFF, p. 80. Churchill inscribed the book 'To
Major-General Sir Bindon Blood, K.C.B.,
under whose command, the operations therein
recorded, were carried out; by whose generalship they were brought to a successful conclusion; and to whose kindness the author is
indebted for the most valuable and fascinating
experience of his life.'
97. The VCs for Colonel Adams and Lt Fincastle
were gazetted 9 November 1897. Lt
MacClean was killed in the action and his
decoration was not gazetted until 15 January
1907, after the rules were changed to allow
the posthumous award of the Victoria Cross in
1902. These awards are significant to the
Churchill story as neither Fincastle nor
MacClean had an official position but were
attached as newspaper correspondents.
98. MFF, p. 161.
99. *Four Score Years and Ten, Sir Bindon Blood's
Reminiscences* by General Sir Bindon Blood
(London: G. Bell And Sons Ltd., 1933), p.
303. An ADC is an aide-de-camp, a junior
staff officer.
100. OBI, CV2, pp. 784–5.
101. *Young Winston's Wars*, p. 15.
102. As Churchill put it in *My Early Life* at page
146, while the politicos wanted to negotiate a
settlement, 'We on the other hand wanted to
let off our guns.'
103. *Sketches on Service During the Indian Frontier Campaigns of 1897* by Major E. A. P.
Hobday (London: James Bowden, 1898), pp.
86–7. See also MFF, pp. 151–3. Both
Churchill and Fincastle wanted to use
Hobday's pictures in their books. Fincastle
did.
104. MFF, p. 172.
105. MFF, p. 175-78. In *My Early Life* at page
157, Churchill recorded casualties of 'about
forty officers and men'.
106. *Four Score Years and Ten*, p. 303.
107. MFF, p. 180.
108. MFF, p. 183. The 35th Sikh Regiment was
raised in 1858, disbanded in 1882 and
reformed in 1887. After service on the North-
West Frontier, they remained in India and did
not leave the country in the First World War.
In 1922 the 35th became the training battalion
for the Sikh Regiment. See *35th Sikhs, Regi-*

mental Record 1887–1922, by Colonel J. C.
Freeland (Peshawar: Sham Lall & Sons,
1923). Sappers are Royal Engineers.
109. MEL, p. 155.
110. A Frontier Campaign, A Narrative of the
Malakand and Buner Field Forces on the North
West Frontiers of India, 1897–1898 by The
Viscount Fincastle (London: R. J. Leach &
Co., 1990), p. 174.
111. The subjects of hill fighting and retreats and
the difficulties of each are the subject of chapters in the excellent Small Wars, A Tactical Textbook for Imperial Soldiers by Colonel C. E.
Callwell which was first published by Her
Majesty's Stationery Office in 1896 and in
revised editions in 1899 and 1906. A modern
edition was published by Greenhill Books,
London and Presidio Press, Novato, CA in
1990.
112. The Operations of the Malakand Field Force
and the Buner Field Force, 1897–1898,
Compiled in the Intelligence Branch, Under the
Orders of the Quarter Master General in India
by Captain H. F. Walters (Simla: Government
Central Printing Office, 1900), p. 54.
113. MEL, p. 154.
114. Young Winston's Wars, p. 24.
115. OBI, CV2, pp. 792-3. I have based my
account of the action at Shahi-Tangi on
Churchill's writings. It was a relatively minor
action in a series of many such actions during
the campaign. The twelve-chapter Intelligence
Branch report gives the retreat a paragraph
and Fincastle's book covers it in a few pages.
The most reliable of the Churchill sources are
his contemporary newspaper articles and
correspondence and The Story of the
Malakand Field Force. My Early Life, written
thirty four years later, is an inaccurate recollection in some details. When it is in conflict
with Churchill's contemporary accounts, I rely
on the earlier version.
116. The Victoria Cross recipients were Lt
Thomas C. Watson, Royal Engineers, Lt
James M. C. Colvin, Royal Engineers, and
Corporal James Smith, East Kent Regiment
(The Buffs). There were four later VCs on the
North-West Frontier in 1897, all on 20
October for the assault on the Dargai Heights
by the Tirah Field Force. Three of the four
were for the rescue of wounded men under
fire. See The Register of the Victoria Cross
(Cheltenham, Gloucestershire, This England
Books, 1988).
117. The London Gazette, 11 January 1898, p.
151. The bracketed words were added by the
author.
118. OBI, CV2, pp. 833-4.
119. British Battles & Medals by E. C. Joslin, A.
R. Litherland and B. D. Simpkin. (London:
Spink & Son Ltd., 1988), pp. 177-9.
120. The India Medal, 1895, Public Record

Office, Reference Class W.O. 100/89, Folio
337.
121. Churchill's India Medal and other medals
earned as an officer in the British army are
owned by his family. They are currently on
loan to the Imperial War Museum and are on
display at the Cabinet War Rooms Museum in
London.
122. MFF, p. 207.
123. MFF, p. 206.
124. Memoirs of Brigadier-General E. W. S. K.
Maconchy, CB, CMG, CIE, DSO, 1860–1920.
Unpublished, typewritten manuscript in the
collection of the National Army Museum,
London. ACC No. 7908-62-1.
125. Diaries of Lt Col D. A. D. McVean,
1890–1930. In the collection of the Imperial
War Museum, London. Excerpt from the
entry for Saturday, 25 September 1897.
Reference No. 67/204/1-3. Colonel McVean
kept a diary every day for forty years in a neat
hand.
126. The anecdote was related to me by Major
Robert Henderson, 2nd Royal Battalion, the
Sikh Regiment. It was confirmed and repeated
to me by Colonel McVean's son Colin, himself
a retired British army colonel, in a letter dated
29 January 1995. As Colin McVean wrote:
'Whether Winston actually told my father that
in so many words or that my father deduced it
from talking to him I cannot say. Sharing a
tent together they would have talked a great
deal. My father was a keen soldier and a good
listener.' With the diary entry proving the two
soldiers shared a tent in the Malakand and
with two sources relating the same anecdote to
me in the same words, I accept the story as
true. And, for that matter, if it is not true the
comment attributed to Churchill certainly has
the characteristic ring of truth and so is
deemed worthy of inclusion.
127. The Operations of the Malakand Field Force
and the Buner Field Force, supra, p. 66. The
31st Punjabis were originally raised at
Ferozepore in 1857 to fight against the muti-
neers of the Bengal Army. In the 1922 reorganisation of the Indian Army it became the
2nd Battalion, 16th Punjab Regiment. The
regimental history is Van Courtland's Levy,
Afterwards Called Bloomfield's Sikhs, 23rd
Punjab Regiment, 35th Punjab Infantry, 31st
Punjabis, 2nd Bn 16th Punjab Regt by
Brigadier-General A. G. Kemball (Bombay:
Thacker & Co, Ltd., 1926).
128. Four Score Years and Ten, p. 303. Bracketed
language added by the author.
129. MEL, p. 163–4.
130. OBI, CV2, p. 933.
131. MFF, p. 246.
132. MFF, p. 248. Colonel O'Bryen was buried
at the Jamrud Road Cemetery in Peshawar. A
plaque in his honour may still be seen at St

John's Church in Peshawar, reading, 'In Memory of Lieut. Col. James Loughnan O'Bryen Commandant 31st P. I. who was killed in action at the head of his regiment at Agrah in the Mamund Valley, Bajaur on the 30th Sept 1897, aged 43 years. Deeply regretted by his brother officers by whom this tablet is erected.' The other officer killed on 30 September, at Gat, 2nd Lt W. C. Clayton Browne, Royal West Kent Regiment, is buried at the Malakand Cemetery. I am indebted to the kind assistance of Ms Sue Farrington of the Council of the British Association for Cemeteries in South Asia in locating graves and memorials of those killed while serving with the Malakand Field Force.

133. OBI, CV2, pp. 796–7. The bracketed language was added by the author. In *The Story of the Malakand Field Force*, at pp. 272–3, Churchill detailed final casualty figures as follows (bracketed information supplied by the author):

British officers killed	7
British officers wounded	17
British other ranks killed	7
British other ranks wounded	41
Native officers killed	0
Native officers wounded	7
Native other ranks killed	48
Native other ranks wounded	147
Camp Followers wounded	8
[23.5% of 1,200]	282
Tribesmen killed	350
Tribesmen wounded	700-800 est.

134. MEL, p. 162.
135. OBI, CV2, p. 830. Even after he left the forward area Churchill was not completely out of danger. As he wrote to Lord William Beresford on 2 November 1897: 'Indeed on the last day I was up there I was nearer killed – by a subaltern who forgot his pistol was loaded – than at any other time. It would have been an irony of fate.' See OBI, CV2, p. 822.
136. OBI, CV2, p. 804. In a 2 November 1897 letter he wrote: 'I find I was on seven occasions under armed fire for periods of from 4 to 13 hours at a time: and twelve nights of desultory shooting besides.' See OBI, CV2, p. 815.
137. *Young Winston's Wars*, pp. 57–63.
138. *Young Winston's Wars*, pp. 64–6.
139. OBI, CV2, p. 807.
140. A brief recent history of the Malakand area is *Malakand, A Journey Through History* by Muhammad Nawaz Kahn (Peshawar: Gandhara Markaz, 1995).
141. MEL, p. 165.
142. OBI, CV2, p. 805.
143. 'Historical Account of the 4th', *supra*, p. 164.
144. OBI, CV2, p. 811.
145. OBI, CV2, p. 813.

146. OBI, CV2, pp. 863–4.
147. OBI, CV2, p. 839.
148. OBI, CV2, p. 853.
149. OBI, CV2, p. 854.
150. OBI, CV2, p. 856.
151. OBI, CV2, p. 883.
152. MEL, p. 172.
153. MEL, pp. 173–4. Lieutenant-General Sir William Lockhart, GCB, KCSI was born in 1841 and died in 1900. He served in the Bhutan Campaign (1864–6), the Abyssinian Campaign (1867–8), the Black Mountain Expedition (1891) and the Isazai Expedition (1892).
154. OBI, CV2, pp. 890 and 892.
155. OBI, CV2, p. 890.
156. *A Soldier's Saga, The Autobiography of General Sir Aylmer Haldane, G.C.M.G., K. C. B., D.S.O.* (Edinburgh and London: William Blackwood & Sons, Ltd., 1948), p. 119. It was to Haldane that Churchill owed his appointment to Lockhart's staff and the opportunity to accompany the general in his travels all over the area of operations. They would meet again, in South Africa in 1899.
157. OBI, CV2, pp. 903–6. The letter was published in *The Times* on 3 May 1898 and carried Churchill's by-line.
158. MEL, p. 175.
159. OBI, CV2, p. 908.
160. OBI, CV2, p. 913.
161. *The Times*, 7 April 1898.
162. MEL, pp. 170–1 and OBI, CV2, pp. 930–1.
163. OBI, CV2, p. 922.
164. OBI, CV2, p. 922. In 1961 Cassell and Co. Ltd in London and Dodd, Mead & Co in New York published *The American Civil War* which was excerpted from Churchill's *A History of the English Speaking Peoples*, four volumes (London: Cassell & Co Ltd., 1956-8).
165. In due course, both biographies were written. *Lord Randolph Churchill*, two volumes (London: MacMillan and Co. Ltd, 1906) and *Marlborough, His Life and Times*, four volumes (London: George G. Harrap & Co, Ltd., 1933–8).
166. MEL, p. 176.
167. OBI, CV2, p. 936. Although Churchill could have resigned his commission and gone to the Sudan as a civilian war correspondent he did not want to do so. He wrote to Lady Randolph on 25 April 1898: 'I have no present intention of leaving the army until I am sure of a seat in parliament.' See OBI, CV2, p. 923.
168. MEL, p. 177.

CHAPTER SIX: THE WAR ON THE NILE:
1. OBI, CV1, p. 103.
2. *England in Egypt* by Alfred Milner (London: Edward Arnold, 1892). *Ten Years Captivity in*

the *Mahdi's Camp* by Father Joseph Ohrwalder
translated by F. R. Wingate (London:
Sampson Low, 1893). *Fire and Sword in the
Sudan* by Rudolph C. Slatin, translated by F.
R. Wingate (London: Edward Arnold, 1896).
F. R. Wingate was Colonel Francis Reginald
Wingate, Director of Military Intelligence for
the Egyptian army during the 1896–8 Sudan
campaign.

3. OBI, CV1, p. 627.

4. OBI, CV2, p. 949.

5. MEL, p. 177.

6. MEL, p. 356.

7. OB1, CV2, p. 949.

8. OBI, CV2, p. 971.

9. OBI, CV2, p. 926.

10. In the book Churchill quoted Lord Salisbury
on the title page thus: 'They (Frontier Wars)
are but the surf that marks the edge and
advance of the wave of civilisation.' This, no
doubt, would have caught even a casual
reader's eye. Churchill's history of the Sudan
campaign was later dedicated to Lord Salisbury.

11. MEL, p. 179.

12. MEL, p. 182-3.

13. MEL, p. 182.

14. OBI, CV2, p. 956.

15. *The River War, An Historical Account of the
Reconquest of the Soudan*, by Winston Spencer
Churchill (London: Longmans, Green and
Co. 1899), Volume I, p. 201. Published in two
volumes, references to this work hereafter will
be abbreviated as RWI and RWII for the
respective volumes. There is much variety in
the spelling of place names in Egypt and the
Sudan. I have used Churchill's throughout.

16. *The Vedette, The Regimental Magazine of the
21st (E. of I.) Lancers*, No. 109, July 1–31
December 1898 (Cairo: Boehme & Anderer
Printers, 1899), p. 21. Provided by the courtesy of the Queen's Royal Lancers Archive
and Museum and Captain J. M. Holtby.

17. *The Last Charge, The 21st Lancers and the
Battle of Omdurman, 2 September 1898*, by
Terry Brighton (Ramsbury, Marlborough,
Wiltshire: The Crowood Press, 1998), pp.
122–3. Other officers attached to the 21st
Lancers and serving in the campaign were
surgeon Major Pinches, Royal Army Medical
Corps; Captain the Marquis Tullibardine,
Royal Horse Guards, as an ADC to Kitch-
ener; and Captain Drage and Lt Smith, Army
Veterinary Department.

18. RWI, p. 201.

19. Brighton, Assistant Curator of The Queen's
Royal Lancers Regimental Museum at Belvoir
Castle, has written the best history of the 21st
Lancers. See also *A Short History of the
17th/21st Lancers, 1759–1959* by R. L. C.
Tamplin (1959) and *The 17th/21st Lancers
1759–1993* by R. L. V. French Blake (1993).

20. *The Last Charge, supra*, pp. 9–36. The regiment's later history was similarly unremark-
able, making the charge at Omdurman its one
brief, shining moment of glory. The 21st
remained in Egypt for a year following the
battle. They served in Ireland from 1899 to
1903 and in England from 1903 to September
1910. Following two years' duty in Egypt the
regiment was posted to the North-West Frontier of India in 1912 where they saw some
active service and remained all during the
First World War. For this the 21st received the
battle honour 'N.W. Frontier, India,
1915–1916.' One service battalion drawn from
its ranks served on the Western Front in
1916–1917. The regiment was returned to
India where it was amalgamated with the 17th
(Duke of Cambridge's Own) Lancers to form
the 17th/21st Lancers. This new formation
was further amalgamated with the 16th/5th,
The Queen's Royal Lancers in 1993 to form
the present-day The Queen's Royal Lancers,
one of only two remaining Lancer regiments
in the British army.

21. *The Last Charge, supra*, pp. 37–41.

22. *The Vedette, supra*, p. 2.

23. *With Kitchener to Khartoum* by George W.
Steevens (Edinburgh and London: William
Blackwood and Sons, 1898), pp. 11–16.

24. RWI, p. 156.

25. The Khedive's Sudan Medal, authorised by
Special Army Order, Cairo 12 Feb. 1897,
would eventually cover the period from
1896–1908 with a total of fifteen clasps:
'Firket', 7 June 1896; 'Hafir', 16–26 Sept.
1896; 'Abu Hamed', 7 July 1896; 'Sudan
1897', 15 July–6 Nov. 1897; 'The Atbara', 8
April 1898; 'Khartoum', 2 Sept. 1898;
'Gedaref', 2 Sept.–26 Dec. 1898; 'Gedid', 22
Nov. 1898; 'Sudan 1899'; 'Bahr-el-Ghazal
1900–2', 13 Dec. 1900–28 April 1902; 'Jerok',
Jan.–March 1904; 'Nyam-Nyam', April 1908;
'Nyima,' 1–21 Nov. 1908. *British Battles &
Medals* by E. C. Joslin, A. R. Litherland, and
B. T. Simpkin (London: Spink & Son, Ltd.
1988), pp. 181–3.

26. RWI, p. 233. The casualty figures used are
Churchill's. The word 'battle' as applied to
Firket shows how variable the term can be.
This brief firefight or skirmish rated a clasp
on the Khedive's Sudan Medal. By way of
contrast, the General Service Medal instituted
in 1962 has a clasp, 'Northern Ireland',
covering the period from August 1969 and
still open.

27. RWI, pp. 253–4.

28. RWI, pp. 266. Nonetheless, Hafir also rated a
clasp on the Khedive's Sudan Medal.

29. RWI, pp. 260–5.

30. RWI, p. 277. The railway built for the
campaign is still in operation between Wadi
Halfa and Khartoum. The once-weekly service

leaves Wadi Halfa each Wednesday at 8.40
p.m. and arrives at Khartoum the next day at
8.40 p.m. The train features first-class
sleeping compartments and a dining car.

31. RWI, p. 253.

32. RW, pp. 329–30.

33. RWI, p. 334. The action at Abu Hamed rated
a clasp on the Khedive's Sudan Medal.

34. RWI, p. 427.

35. RWI, pp. 447–8. Steevens, in *With Kitchener
to Khartoum*, gives the figures of British army
24 killed and 104 wounded (of whom twenty
later died), Egyptian army fifty-seven killed
and 365 wounded (including four British officers, two British NCOs and sixteen Egyptian
officers) at pp. 155–7.

36. No complete Dervish casualty figures for the
Atbara are available. Donald Featherstone, in
*Omdurman 1898, Kitchener's Victory in the
Sudan* (London: Osprey Publishing Ltd.,
1993) at p. 53 estimates 1,000 Dervishes were
killed and 'many captured'. Steevens, who was
present, estimates that 3,000 Dervishes died,
writing that an 'A. D. C. to the Sirdar counted
over 2,000 before he was sick of it'. One
reason no one gives figures of Dervish
wounded is that, according to Steevens, they
were given no quarter. Churchill reported
2,600 Dervish dead were counted in and
around the *zariba* and that 'several hundred'
prisoners were taken. RWI, pp. 444–5.

37. RWI, p. 460.

38. RWI, pp. 308–9.

39. MEL, p. 183. Two of Grenfell's brothers,
Francis and Riversdale, were killed in action in
the First World War. Francis was awarded the
Victoria Cross for a cavalry action at Audrég-
nies, Belgium in 1914, nine months before his
death.

40. *The Last Charge, supra*, pp. 69 and 73.

41. After 1898 there were three variants of the
badge, one with a pair of upright lances, two
with crossed lances and all featuring the
cypher 'VRI' of Queen Victoria as Empress of
India.

42. *The Last Charge, supra*, p. 31.

43. *With Kitchener to Khartoum, supra*, p. 69.

44. RWI, p. 366.

45. RWI, pp. 366–7.

46. MEL, p. 183.

47. *The Vedette, supra*, p. 3.

48. *With Kitchener to Khartoum, supra*, p. 173.

49. OBI, CV2, p. 957.

50. OBI, CV2, p. 963.

51. See 'Young Winston's Addisonian Conceit, A
Note on The War on the Nile Letters', by
Keith Wilson in *Sudan The Reconquest Reap-
praised*, Edward M. Spears, editor (London:
Frank Cass Publishers, 1998), p. 223. The
letters, fifteen in all, were reprinted in *Young
Winston's Wars*, Frederick Woods, editor
(London: Leo Cooper, Ltd., 1972) and

*Winston S. Churchill, War Correspondent
1895–1900*, Frederick Woods, editor (London:
Brassey's, 1992).

52. *Extracts from The Diaries and Letters of Hubert
Howard* (Oxford: Horace Hart, printer to the
University, 1899), p. 246.

53. RWII, p. 9.

54. RWII, p. 22.

55. RWI, p. 290.

56. *Winston Churchill, An Informal Study in
Greatness*, by Robert Lewis Taylor (Garden
City, New York: Doubleday & Company, Inc.,
1952), p. 145.

57. Churchill's own definition is best. 'A khor is a
watercourse, usually dry. In India it would be
called a nullah; in South Africa a donga; in
Australia [and the United States] a gully.'
RWII, p. 40. The bracketed language was
added by the author.

58. *Khartoum Campaign 1898 or the Re-Conquest
of the Soudan*, by Bennet Burleigh (London:
Chapman & Hall, Limited, 1899), pp. 78-9.

59. RWII, p. 45.

60. OBI, CV2, p. 968.

61. OBI, CV2, p. 967.

62. RWII, p. 47. The bracketed language was
added by the author.

63. RWII, pp. 55–6. Churchill's listing of the
Anglo-Egyptian order of battle appears to be
accurate and complete. More recent lists are
substantially in accord. See, for example,
*Omdurman 1898, Kitchener's Victory in the
Sudan, supra*, p. 61. See also *The Last Charge,
supra*, p. 46. I have supplemented the name
information from *The Army List*.

64. *The Last Charge, supra*, pp. 122–3. There is
much dispute about the number of chargers.
At various times Churchill stated there were
310 (OBI, CV2, p. 979 and MEL, p. 210) and
'Less than 400' (RWII, p. 138). Major Finn
wrote 'about 350'. Lt Smyth said 300. *The
Vedette* (p. 10) noted 'less than 400'.

65. *Extracts from the Diaries and Letters of Hubert
Howard, supra*, p. 275.

66. *Winston Churchill War Correspondent, supra*, p.
114.

67. OVI, CV2, p. 969.

68. MEL, p. 195.

69. Douglas Haig (1861–1928) had a distinguished, if controversial, career. Passing out of
Sandhurst first in his class he was commissioned into the 7th Hussars in 1885, which he
later left to command the 17th Lancers. He
served in the Boer War and in a series of staff
positions in England and India. At the outset
of the First World War he commanded I
Corps at Aldershot. He later commanded First
Army and by December 1915 as Field
Marshal Sir Douglas Haig became
Commander-in-Chief of the British Expeditionary Force in which capacity he served
until the war's end.

70. *Winston S. Churchill War Correspondent, supra*, p. 114.

71. MEL, p. 188.

72. *With Kitchener to Khartoum, supra*, p. 219.

73. RWII, p. 70.

74. George W. Steevens, 'The Downfall of Mahdism', A Lecture to the Aldershot Military Society, 22 November 1898 (London: Edward Stanford, Publisher, 1898), p. 13.

75. RWII, p. 73.

76. RWII, pp. 72–3.

77. RWII, p. 78. The bracketed language was added by the author.

78. RWII, p. 79.

79. *Khartoum Campaign 1898, supra*, pp. 119–20.

80. *The Vedette, supra*, p. 6.

81. RWII, p. 110.

82. *The Vedette, supra*, p. 6.

83. MEL, p. 189.

84. *Khartoum Campaign 1898, supra*, p. 131.

85. *Young Winston's Wars, supra*, p. 101. The bracketed language was added by the author.

86. RWII, p. 87.

87. Donald Featherstone, in *Omdurman, 1898*, p. 63, outlines the Dervish order of battle in great detail based on Appendix 13 of Intelligence Report No. 60, dated Cairo, January 1899. Churchill's order of battle numbers found at RWII, p. 89, are rounded-off numbers and vary by several thousands from Featherstone.

88. MEL, p. 190.

89. MEL, 192.

90. MEL, p. 193.

91. MEL, p. 194.

92. *Omdurman Diaries 1898, Eyewitness Accounts of the Legendary Campaign*, edited by John Meredith (London: Leo Cooper, Ltd., 1998), p. 180.

93. David Beatty (1871–1936) entered the navy at the age of thirteen; he was awarded the Distinguished Service Order for the Sudan campaign. He later served in the Boxer Rebellion (1900) and in 1910 became the youngest rear admiral in one hundred years. He served as Churchill's Naval Secretary when Churchill was First Lord of the Admiralty. He was the flag officer of the Battle Cruiser Squadron at the battle of Jutland (1916) and ended the war as Commander of the British Grand Fleet. He served as First Sea Lord before his retirement.

94. RWII, p. 106.

95. *Omdurman 1898: The Eye-Witnesses Speak*, edited by Peter Harrington and Frederic A. Sharf (London: Greenhill Books, 1998), p. 154.

96. National Army Museum, Cameron MSS, Cameron to S. W. Cameron 4 Sept. 1898, quoted in *Sudan the Reconquest Reappraised*, edited by Edward M. Spiers (London: Frank Cass, 1998), p. 69.

97. RWII, p. 108.

98. *Karari, the Sudanese Account of the Battle of Omdurman* by Ismit Hasan Zulfo (London: Frederick Warne (Publishers), Ltd., 1980), pp. 157–62. This is a valuable book presenting, as the subtitle suggests, the Dervish perspective. First published in Arabic in 1973 by Zulfo, an officer in the Sudanese army, it was translated into English by Dr Peter Clark for the 1980 edition. It must be read in tandem with the British accounts because its facts are often at variance with the reports of eyewitnesses on the other side of the conflict. The Dervish order of battle figures given in this section, however, are Zulfo's.

99. MEL, p. 197.

100. OBI, CV2, p. 972.

101. OBI, CV2, p. 972.

102. MEL, p. 199.

103. MEL, p. 200.

104. OBI, CV2, p. 977.

105. *With Kitchener to Khartoum, supra*, pp. 263–4. The bracketed language is supplied by the author.

106. *The Vedette, supra*, p. 9. This is the exact wording of the order, a copy of which is in the collection of The Queen's Royal Lancers.

107. The best and most detailed information of the arrangement of the regiment for the charge is found in Terry Brighton's *The Last Charge* at page 79. Churchill's account in *My Early Life* (at page 204) also places him in the second from the right troop.

108. This aptly descriptive phrase, 'deceitful ground', was used by Lionel James, correspondent for the Reuters Agency and is quoted in *Omdurman 1898: The Eye-Witnesses Speak, supra*, at p. 104.

109. MEL, p. 210.

110. MEL, p. 204. The story of how the Mauser pistol allowed him successfully to survive the charge is one that Churchill often retold in later years. See, for example, *Sketches from Life of Men I Have Known*, by Dean Acheson (New York: Harper & Brothers, 1961), pp. 79–80.

111. Private Thomas Byrne's VC was announced in the *London Gazette* on 15 November 1898. Born in Dublin in 1866, he served in the British army for twenty-two years including service in the Boer War. He died in 1944. See *The Victoria Cross 1856–1920* by O'Moore Creagh and E. M. Humphris (Polstead, Suffolk: J. B. Hayward & Son, 1985), p. 110. See also *The Register of the Victoria Cross* (Cheltenham: This England Books, 1988). Byrne's duplicate Victoria Cross was sold at auction by Spink in London in March 1996 together with his Queen's Sudan Medal, Queen's South Africa Medal (clasps Cape Colony, Orange Free State, and Transvaal), British War Medal, 1935 Jubilee Medal, 1937 Coronation Medal, Army Long Service and

Good Conduct Medal and Khedive's Sudan Medal (clasp, Khartoum) for £6,500. The author expresses his thanks to B. T. Simpkin of the Medal Department at Spink for the auction information.

112. Lieutenant de Montmorency's VC was announced in the *London Gazette* on 15 November 1898. Born in Montreal, Canada in 1867, de Montmorency joined the 21st Lancers in 1887 and served with them until the Boer War in which he organized then commanded Montmorency's Scouts from December 1899 until he was killed in action on 23 February 1900 near Stormberg in Cape Colony. See *The Victoria Cross 1856–1920, ibid*, at p. 110 and *The Register of the Victoria Cross, ibid*, at p. 88.

113. Captain Kenna's VC was announced in the *London Gazette* on 15 November 1898. Born in Lancashire in 1862, Paul Aloysius Kenna was educated at Sandhurst and had a long and honourable career. He received the Distinguished Service Order in 1902. He was promoted brigadier general in 1914. He commanded a division at Gallipoli in the First World War where he was killed in action on 30 August 1915. See *The Victoria Cross 1856–1920, ibid*, at p. 109 and *The Register of the Victoria Cross, ibid*, at p. 176. His medal is in the collection of the Queen's Royal Lancers, Home Headquarters.

114. The DCMs were announced in the *London Gazette* on 15 November 1898. (War Office Record 146/1, 12856). Swarbrick's medal is in the collection of the Queen's Royal Lancer's Home Headquarters. Sergeant Chalmers DCM, together with his other medals, were sold at auction by Sotheby's in July 1996 for £5,980. The author expresses his thanks to Edward Playfair of Sotheby's for this information. Lance Corporal Harold Penn's DCM, Queen's Sudan Medal and Khedives Sudan Medal (clasp, Khartoum) were sold at auction by Dix, Noonan, Webb in November 1996 for £3,565. The author expresses his thanks to Nimrod Dix for this information. Clearly, there is great interest in the charge over a century later.

115. MEL, pp. 206–7.

116. OBI, CV2, p. 981.

117. MEL, p. 208.

118. Norris is quoted in *Winston Churchill, the Era and the Man* by Virginia Cowles (London: Hamish Hamilton, Ltd., 1953), p. 154.

119. *The Vedette, supra*, p. 11.

120. *Young Winston's Wars, supra*, p. 112.

121. *Khartoum Campaign 1898*, p. 177. This episode was also reported to Jack Churchill by Cecil Grenfell whose brother Harold had taken part in the campaign and returned to London in late September. As Jack related Grenfell's account of Churchill's act of valour,

'When he was through [the Khor] he turned back and rescued his troop non-com.' See OBI, CV2, p. 983. Neither Churchill's letters to his mother and to General Ian Hamilton describing the battle nor his accounts of the battle in the *Morning Post, The River War* or *My Early Life* mention the episode. The major biographies do not report it. Some biographies do mention, even embellish it, but, alas, without a single footnote: *Winston Churchill* by 'Ephesian' (Bechofer Roberts), second edition (London: Mills Boon, Ltd.), p. 47. *The Young Churchill, a Biography* by Stanley Nott (New York: Coward-McCann, Inc., 1941), p. 177, *Winston Churchill, An Informal Study in Greatness*, by Robert Lewis Taylor (Garden City: Doubleday & Company, Inc., 1952), p. 154. Based on the contemporary accounts of Burleigh and Grenfell, one must conclude this act of bravery did occur even though it was not recognised by the authorities. It is reminiscent of Churchill's rescue of a wounded sepoy in combat on the North-West Frontier of India in September 1897 which also went without official notice.

122. *Long Sunset, Memoirs of Winston Churchill's Last Private Secretary*, by Anthony Montague Browne (London: Cassell Publishers, Ltd., 1995), p. 151. In fact, none of the seven attached officers who rode with the 21st Lancers in the charge was decorated. Although one was killed (Lt Grenfell) and two wounded (Lt J.C. Brinton and R. Molyneux), Lt Molyneaux was the only attached officer to be mentioned in dispatches.

123. These figures are from Terry Brighton's *The Last Charge* at pp. 122–3 and show a total of sixty-nine casualties based on his review of contemporary records. With Brighton's estimate, there were 447 chargers, this would be a casualty rate of 15 per cent. Churchill in *The River War* (RWII, p. 198) stated there were seventy-one casualties, twenty-one killed and fifty wounded. Compared to his estimate that there were 310 chargers (OB1, CV2, p. 979), the casualty rate would be 23 per cent.

124. Captain Haig to Wood, 7 September 1898, Haig MSS, LLS, ACC 3155, quoted in *The Late Victorian Army* by Edward M. Spiers (Manchester and New York: Manchester University Press, 1992), p. 293.

125. Lt Smyth is quoted in *The Last Charge, supra*, p. 95.

126. 'The Downfall of Mahdism', *supra*, p. 22. In his book on the campaign which came out before this lecture, *With Kitchener to Khartoum*, at p. 293 Steevens referred to the charge as a 'gross blunder'.

127. *Long Sunset, supra*, p. 22. There is considerable debate on whether this was the last cavalry charge of the British Empire. Other 'last charges' cited are the British at Huj,

Palestine on 8 November 1917, the Canadian Cavalry Brigade at Moreuil Wood, France on 30 March 1918, and the Central India Horse at Toungoo, Burma 1942. See *Finest Hour* numbers 74, 76, 79. Apparently the quest for glory on horseback died a lingering death.

128. *With Kitchener to Khartoum, supra*, p. 276.

129. *ibid*, p. 278 and p. 281.

130. *Young Winston's Wars, supra*, p. 115.

131. Howard was not the only correspondent to be a casualty. Colonel Frank Rhodes, serving as a correspondent for *The Times* was shot in the shoulder, and Mr C. Williams of the *Daily Chronicle* was also wounded. See RWII, p. 198.

132. *With Kitchener to Khartoum, supra*, p. 309.

133. *The Vedette, supra*, pp. 13–14.

134. OBI, CV2, p. 973.

135. OBI, CV2, p. 974.

136. RWII, pp. 198–9.

137. RWII, p. 200.

138. *Omdurman 1898: The Eye-Witnesses Speak, supra*, p. 84.

139. 'Campaigning Under Kitchener' by Edward M. Spiers in *Sudan the Reconquest Reappraised, supra*, p. 74, in particular Spiers's footnote 106 at p. 81.

140. *Karari, The Sudanese Account of the Battle of Omdurman, supra*, pp. 179–89, 217, 228.

141. RWII, p. 200.

142. *Karari, The Sudanese Account of the Battle of Omdurman, supra*, p. 243.

143. RWII, p. 301–21. For a more complete treatment see David Levering Lewis, *The Race to Fashoda* (New York: Weidenfeld & Nicholson, 1987).

144. RWII, p. 195.

145. *Young Winston's Wars, supra*, p. 114.

146. RWII, p. 214.

147. OBI, CV2, p. 979.

148. *Young Winston's Wars, supra*, p. 126.

149. *The Vedette, supra*, p. 16.

150. *The Vedette, supra*, p. 21.

151. *The Vedette, supra*, p. 21.

152. *The Vedette, supra*, p. 22.

153. *British Battles & Medals, supra*, pp. 180–1. See also *The Orders, Decorations and Medals of Sir Winston Churchill, supra*, pp. 24–8. Medals to the 21st Lancers are highly sought after by collectors. A 'charger's pair' of the Queens Sudan Medal and the Khedive's Sudan Medal named to Private G. Western of B Squadron who was wounded was listed for sale by Harpers Military Medals in London for £1,200 in 1997.

154. MEL, p. 212.

155. OB VII, pp. 1156–7.

156. MEL, p. 186.

157. *Young Winston's Wars, supra*, p. 123.

158. The most recent accounts of the battlefield today are found in *The Last Charge, supra*, p. 121, and 'Let The Ghosts of Omdurman

Sleep', by Lord Deedes in *Finest Hour*, No. 99, Summer 1998, p. 33. I have also benefited from photographs of the Mahdi's tomb, the Khalifa's house and the 'Melik' by Ray Currie.

159. OB1, CV2, p.979.

160. OBI, CV2, p. 973.

161. Churchill returned to Omdurman only once in 1908 as Under Secretary of State for the Colonies. During his visit there his valet, George Scrivings, was stricken with 'choleraic diarrhoea' (enteric fever) and died. See *My African Journey* by Winston S. Churchill (London: Hodder and Stoughton, 1908), pp. 207–8.

162. This document is in the archives of The Queen's Royal Lancers and is reproduced with their permission through the courtesy of Captain J. M. Holtby.

CHAPTER SEVEN: THE SOUTH AFRICAN WAR: CAPETOWN TO PRETORIA

1. MEL, p. 213.

2. MEL, p. 217.

3. MEL, p. 220. In *My Early Life* Churchill recalled giving his first political speech during the autumn of 1898 at Bath. That maiden speech was, in fact, given on 26 July 1897, during a previous period of leave over a year earlier. He also recorded in his memoir that he first went to the Conservative Party offices in 'early November' when, in fact, it must have been early October as the speaking engagements they arranged for him took place in October 1898.

4. OBI, CV2, p. 994.

5. OBI, CV2, p. 995.

6. OBI, CV2, pp. 1010 and 997. The bracketed word is added by the author.

7. OBI, CV2, p. 1004. Watson later skirted this prohibition by giving Churchill information verbally, rather than in writing, when Churchill visited Cairo in April 1899.

8. OBI, CV2, p. 1007. In *My Early Life* it was both ankles sprained; in this contemporary letter only one.

9. *4th Hussar, The Story of a British Cavalry Regiment*, p. 231.

10. In *My Early Life* (at pages 224–5) and in a 2 March 1899 letter to Lady Randolph (at OBI, CV2, p. 1011) Churchill claimed three goals. In the official biography (at OBI, pp. 416–17) Randolph Churchill compared these sources to a contemporary account in the *Pioneer Mail* which attributed two goals to Albert Savory and one each to Reginald Hoare and to Churchill. The biographer, after consulting an authority on polo on the difficulty of noting the actual scorer on a dusty field filled with moving horses, sided with Lt Churchill who would not 'so soon after the match have assumed the role of hero when he could easily

have been exposed as a braggart'.

11. *Memories of India, Recollections of Soldiering and Sport*, by Lt General Sir Robert Baden-Powell KCB (Philadelphia: David McKay Publisher, 1915), pp. 35–6.

12. I am grateful to the Lady Soames for the story of the unpaid bill and for providing a copy of the sub-committee minutes. These had earlier been sent to her by Lieutenant Colonel C. R. D. Gray, vice-president of the Indian Cavalry Officers Association.

13. OBI, CV2, p. 1009.

14. MEL, p. 225.

15. MEL, p. 227.

16. 'The Youngest Man in Europe: Churchill at Twenty-four', by G. W. Steevens, reprinted in *Churchill by His Contemporaries*, edited by Charles Eade (New York: Simon and Schuster, 1954), pp. 43–7.

17. The *London Gazette*, 2 May 1899, p. 2806.

18. MEL, p. 235.

19. Quoted in OBI, CV2, p. 1036. The election results showed the two prevailing Liberal candidates with 12,976 and 12,770 votes, respectively, Churchill with 11,477 and his losing Conservative colleague with 11,449.

20. OBI, CV2, p. 1049. It was, Churchill thought, the highest amount ever paid to a British war correspondent. See MEL, p. 244.

21. OBI, CV2, pp. 1052

22. OBI, CV2, pp. 1055–6.

23. OBI, CV2, p. 1056.

24. MEL, p. 246.

25. Commonly referred to as the Boer War, the conflict between Britain and Boer in 1899–1902 is also referred to as the Anglo-Boer War and by some historians as the Second Anglo-Boer War and by many South Africans as the War of Independence. The most complete accounts of the conflict are *The Times History of the War in South Africa* (seven volumes), edited by L. S. Amery (London: Sampson Low, Marston and Co. 1902–9) and *Official History of the War in South Africa* (four volumes) edited by F. Maurice, H. Grant and others (London: Hurst and Blackett, 1906–1910). I have relied on two excellent one-volume studies: *The Great Anglo-Boer War* by Byron Farwell (New York: Harper & Row, Inc., 1976) and *The Boer War* by Thomas Packenham (New York: Random House, Inc., 1979). All of these contain useful bibliographies.

26. The estimated white population of the Transvaal was 300,000 and of the Orange Free State 145,000. By comparison, the population of the United Kingdom including Northern Ireland was 44,500,000. See *The Boer War* by Eversley Belfield (London: Leo Cooper, 1993), pp. 165–6.

27. OBI, CV2, p. 1082.

28. *The Notes of a War Correspondent* by Richard Harding Davis (New York: Charles Scribner's Sons, 1914), pp. 140–1.

29. *The Times* history used the lower number; the official history used the higher number. I have relied on Eversley Belfield's *The Boer War* which summarises both sources in Appendix V at pp. 165–8.

30. See *The Phases of the Anglo-Boer War* by Andre Wessels (Blomfontein: War Museum of the Boer Republics, 1998). This is an excellent brief summary of the military operations of the war by Professor Wessels, Department of History, University of the Orange Free State. I have accepted his analytical framework for describing the progress of the war.

31. *London to Ladysmith via Pretoria* by Winston S. Churchill (London: Longmans, Green, and Co., 1900), p. 10. This, the first of Churchill's two books of dispatches from South Africa, was comprised of twenty-seven letters written between 29 October 1899 and 10 March 1900. Some, but not all, of the letters were reprinted in *Young Winston's Wars*, Frederick Woods, editor (London: Leo Cooper, 1972) and *Winston S. Churchill, War Correspondent, 1895–1900*, Frederick Woods, editor (London: Brassey's, 1992). Edited versions of the letters also appear in *Frontiers and Wars* by Winston S. Churchill (London: Eyre & Spottiswoode, 1962) and (New York: Harcourt, Brace & World, Inc., 1962).

32. OBI, CV2, p. 1058.

33. *The Relief of Ladysmith* by J. B. Atkins (London: Methuen & Co., 1900). Like Churchill, Atkins had also observed the fighting in Cuba. He was the author of *The War in Cuba: The Experiences of an Englishman with the United States Army* (London: Smith, 1899). Churchill, however, had got there first.

34. *Incidents and Reflections* by J. B. Atkins (London: Christophers, 1947) p. 122.

35. *ibid.*, p. 126.

36. *ibid.*, p. 125.

37. The Mount Nelson Hotel is still in operation as a first-class hotel at 76 Orange Street in Cape Town, its pink stucco façade beautiful when viewed against the dramatic backdrop of nearby Table Mountain.

38. MEL, p. 256. In *London to Ladysmith via Pretoria*, Churchill wrote of seeing Barnes in Durban. See also OBI, CV2, p. 1058 for a 10 November 1899 letter to the same effect. In *My Early Life* he recalled seeing Barnes in the hospital at Pietermaritzburg, sixty miles from the coast. The author relies on Churchill's contemporary letters.

39. MEL, p. 256 and *London to Ladysmith via Pretoria*, p. 51. The Royal Dublin Fusiliers were regular infantry of the British army originally raised in India as the 102nd (Royal Madras) Fusiliers and the 103rd (Royal Bombay) Fusiliers. They were disbanded in

1922. The Border Regiment were also regular infantry created in 1881 from 34th Foot and 55th Foot. The two battalions had a long history of service including the Seven Years' War (1756–63), the American War of Independence (1775–8), the Peninsular War (1808–14), the Crimean War (1854–6) and the Indian Mutiny (1857–8). See *Regiments and Corps of the British Army* by Ian S. Hallows (London: New Orchard Editions, 1994), pp. 114–15 and 284. The Imperial Light Horse was a volunteer cavalry regiment raised from the uitlanders who fled from the Transvaal into Natal just before the outbreak of the war. It was considered one of the finest colonial regiments to serve in the conflict and numbered about 500 officers and men. The Natal Carbineers was a volunteer force of mounted infantry raised in Natal and mobilised in September 1899 with a strength of 508 officers and men. Over 300 of these were besieged in Ladysmith by the end of October. The Durban Light Infantry was a volunteer infantry regiment raised in Natal and mobilised as part of the Natal Volunteers at the end of September 1899. They were stationed at Colenso at the outbreak of the war with a strength of 416 officers and men. See *The Colonials in South Africa 1899–1902* by John Sterline (Polstead, Suffolk: J. B. Hayward & Son, 1990), pp. 1–49. This fine book was originally published in 1907 by William Blackwood & Sons.

40. All of these would write about their experiences in South Africa. As noted above, Amery was the editor of *The Times* multi-volume history of the war. Haldane covered the Boer War years in both *A Soldier's Saga* (Edinburgh and London: William Blackwood & Sons, Ltd., 1948) and *How We Escaped from Pretoria* (Edinburgh and London: William Blackwood and Sons, 1901). Burleigh wrote *The Natal Campaign* (London: Chapman & Hall, Ltd., 1900).

41. *London to Ladysmith via Pretoria*, pp. 52–3.

42. MEL, pp. 257–8.

43. MEL, p. 258.

44. *The Relief of Ladysmith*, p. 72.

45. *Incidents and Reflections*, p. 128

46. There are several contemporary accounts of the configuration of the armoured train including Churchill's seventh letter to the *Morning Post* written in Pretoria on 20 November; Churchill's autobiography; Haldane's official report written in Pretoria on 30 November 1899 and included in full in OBI, CV2, pp. 1064–7; a telegram report from Petrus Joubert, commander of the Boer commando which attacked the train, see OBI, CV2 at p. 1062; Bennet Burleigh's account in *The Natal Campaign*; and the sketchbook of Lt Thomas Frankland of the Royal Dublin

Fusiliers who was on the train and made a prisoner-of-war. All of these accounts are in agreement that there were five trucks in addition to the engine and tender except *My Early Life* which states there were six trucks. It appears this is in error as is Churchill's diagram of the train at page 263 of *My Early Life* which shows an extra armoured truck in front of the engine. Similarly, there is much variation in description of the size of the gun mounted in the flat truck. Churchill said it was a six-pounder in *My Early Life* and a seven-pounder in *London to Ladysmith via Pretoria*. Doyle and Burleigh wrote it was a seven-pounder while Haldane's official report describes it as 'a 9-pr muzzle-loading Naval gun'. See OBI, CV2, p. 1065.

47. See Churchill's account in *London to Ladysmith via Pretoria* at p. 78, Haldane's account at OBI, CV2 at p. 1065, Burleigh's account in *The Natal Campaign* at p. 75. Churchill gives no number of the men on the train in *My Early Life* in which he wrongly states at p. 258 that the sailors were from HMS *Terrible*. In his contemporary letter he correctly notes their ship was HMS *Tartar*. Arthur Conan Doyle's account of the incident in his *The Great Boer War* (London: Smith, Elder & Co., 1900) at pp. 214–15 lists 183 men on the train but is discounted by the author because he was neither on the train nor at the scene of the ambush any time soon after.

48. *A Soldier's Saga*, p. 142.

49. *The Great Boer War*, p. 215.

50. *A Soldier's Saga*, pp. 143–4.

51. *Incidents and Reflections*, p. 129.

52. MEL, p. 262.

53. MEL, p. 265.

54. *The Natal Campaign*, p. 80.

55. *London to Ladysmith via Pretoria*, p. 96.

56. *ibid.*, p. 96–7.

57. Casualty figures are difficult to state with accuracy and the accounts vary a good deal. Except for the wounded who escaped on the train and about which he had no knowledge, I have relied on Haldane and his 30 November 1899 report to the Chief-of-Staff. See OBI, CV2, pp. 1064–7. Burleigh stated that there were three British killed and twelve wounded (not including those who escaped on the engine), two officers and forty-five Dublin Fusiliers and twenty-four Durban Light Infantry captured and four plate-layers and Churchill missing. See *The Natal Campaign*, p. 81. Conan Doyle listed two killed, twenty wounded and eighty prisoners of war. See *The Great Boer War* at p. 81. Boer Commandant-General Petrus Joubert stated that the Boers had 'five slightly wounded and a few more serious' and that the British lost two killed, ten wounded and fifty-six taken prisoner in his 15 November 1899 report. See OBI, CV2, p.

1062. Celia Sandys, in *Churchill: Wanted Dead or Alive* (London: HarperCollins, 1999), at p. 55, states the British casualties were six killed (four at the scene and two dead later of wounds), sixteen wounded who escaped on the engine, ten wounded who were taken to the hospital at Ladysmith, three wounded kept in Boer field ambulances, and seven slightly wounded taken prisoner. Ms Sandys's figures, based in part on *London to Ladysmith via Pretoria*, put the British casualties at thirty-five per cent of the armoured train force killed or wounded. Churchill's letter to Haldane is found at OBI, CV2, p. 1180.

58. OBI, CV2, p. 1063 quoting the *Natal Witness* of 17 November 1899.

59. OBI, CV2, p. 1064.

60. OBI, CV2, p. 1069.

61. *Black & White Magazine*, London, 23 December 1899, quoted in *Finest Hour* No. 55, Spring 1987, p. 5.

62. OBI, CV2, pp. 1066–7.

63. *British Gallantry Awards* by J. M. A. Tamplin and P. E. Abbott (Garden City, New York: Doubleday & Company, Inc., 1972), pp. 310-16.

64. OBI, CV2, p. 1058.

65. OBI, CV2, p. 1057.

66. OBI, CV2, p. 1059.

67. *British Gallantry Awards*, pp. 47–58. By warrant of 1971, surviving holders of the Albert Medal could exchange it for the George Cross which was created in 1940 and is the current highest award for gallantry for civilians and for non-combat gallantry for service members.

68. OBI, CV2, pp. 1071–2.

69. The *London Gazette*, 14 June 1910, p. 4172 (PRO 1/588).

70. OBI, CV2, pp. 1069–70.

71. MEL, p. 272.

72. *London to Ladysmith via Pretoria*, pp. 133–4.

73. *London to Ladysmith via Pretoria*, p. 100. Churchill's own civilian hat had been found on the ground during the armoured train fight by Haldane, who tossed it on the tender. See *A Soldier's Saga*, p. 146. Churchill was not, as some have suggested, in uniform during the battle. The Irish Fusiliers cap is what Churchill was wearing when photographed at the rail station in Pretoria.

74. OBI, CV2, p. 1133. The plaque was unveiled on 20 May 1963. The school is remarkably unchanged and when visited by the author in August 1999 one could observe the room layout was intact and both Lt Frankland's wall map of Natal and Captain Haldane's trap-door, used to gain access to the crawl space under the floor for his eventual escape, are still in place, the former under plexiglass.

75. MEL, p. 273.

76. OBI, CV2, p. 1084.

77. The Churchill letters to De Souza and the Boer telegrams and messages concerning his status appear at OBI, CV2, pp. 1062–86.

78. It is clear from Haldane's diary (see OBI, CV2, p. 1087) and his memoirs (see *A Soldier's Saga*, pp. 152–3) that the plan was originated by Haldane and Brockie and that they carefully gathered information from local newspapers about train schedules. In *My Early Life*, and in other accounts of his escape, Churchill takes credit for the plan and even states at one point incorrectly that Haldane's plan was to walk to Delagoa Bay by night, hiding by day. It must be remembered that Churchill asked to join Haldane's venture, not vice versa.

79. *A Soldier's Saga*, p. 155. Haldane in his book tells the story of his failed escape attempt of December 1899. His later successful escape in March 1900 is the subject of *How We Escaped from Pretoria*.

80. MEL, p. 285.

81. OBI, CV2, pp. 1086 and 1101.

82. This issue is covered in detail by Celia Sandys in *Churchill: Wanted Dead or Alive* at pp. 98–115. Those interested in the accounts of Churchill and Haldane in their own memoranda and diary entries are referred to OBI, CV2, pp. 1087–8, 1094–1112.

83. OBI, CV2, pp. 1104–5.

84. OBI, CV2, p. 1115.

85. In 1900 he initiated legal action against William Blackwood and Sons, a publisher, concerning Lord Rosslyn's book *Twice Captured: A Record of Adventure During the Boer War* in which he wrote Churchill's escape 'followed the principles of sauve qui peut rather than "shoulder to shoulder" '. Churchill's attorneys got Blackwood and Sons to remove the offending passage from subsequent editions. This dispute is the subject of Ryno Greenwall's article, 'Lord Rosslyn and His Controversial Book *Twice Captured: A Record of Adventure During the Boer War*', *Quarterly Bulletin of the South African Library*, Vol. 44, No. 1, September 1989.

86. *A Soldier's Saga*, p. 156. Churchill's and Haldane's are the only written accounts extant. Brockie died in a mining accident soon after the war. Le Mesurier was killed in action at Ypres on 25 April 1915. Frankland was killed in action at the Gallipoli landings on 25 April 1915. Brockie apparently bore no hatred for Churchill for in 1902 he wrote to Churchill asking for money and Churchill sent him £10 regretting he could not send more as 'I am not a rich man and have to earn by writing all I spend.' I am indebted to Brockie's granddaughter, Vera Gallony, for sharing with me Churchill's 21 September 1902 letter to Brockie which she had kept for fifty-four years.

87. OBI, CV2, pp. 1098–9.

88. MEL, p. 288.

89. MEL, p. 289.

90. MEL, p. 296. In the case of Churchill's escape, the later sources are the best because he did not tell the whole story in his contemporary accounts for fear of exposing those who assisted him. There is much variety in the details of his many accounts, both the early and the later ones.

91. OBI, CV2, p. 1085.

92. *The Biograph in Battle, Its Story in the South African War* by W. K-L. Dickson. Facsimile reprint edition (Trowbridge, Wiltshire: Flick Books, 1995), p. 204. Originally published by T. Fisher Unwin, London, 1901.

93. OBI, CV2, p. 1091. There is some dispute as to whether a wanted poster was circulated. Churchill mentions it in *My Early Life* and uses it as an illustration at p. 305. The note on that page states, 'NOTE: The Original Reward for the arrest of Winston Churchill on his escape from Pretoria, posted on Government House at Pretoria, brought to England by the Hon. Henry Masham, and is now the property of W. R. Burton.' In *Finest Hour* No. 45, H. Ashley Redburn wrote: 'Every modern historian except Mr [Piers] Brendon knows the £25 reward poster for fugitive Churchill was a spoof.' See p. 6. Perhaps the best discussion of the wanted poster is by Dal Newfield in *Finest Hour* No. 32. He concludes the poster was a prank. An examination of the poster from the Churchill Archives Centre at the 2004 exhibit, 'Churchill and the Great Republic', in Washington, D.C. clearly shows that the top part of the poster, handwritten in Dutch, and the lower printed part of the poster printed in English, are separate pieces of paper, but framed together.

94. OBI, CV2, pp. 1135–6. See also *Churchill: Wanted Dead or Alive*, pp. 140–1 for the latest on the watches including a photograph following p. 129 and also *The Capture and Escape of Winston Churchill During the South African War* by Alexander J. P. Graham (Salisbury, Rhodesia: Edinburgh Press, 1965), pp. 13–15.

95. *The Medal News*, Volume 40, No. 6, June/July 2002, p. 11. The flask and the pistol, a six-shot, 9mm, double-action frame, pin-fire revolver and a specially-made box brought £32,000 at auction by Wallis & Wallis in London in April 2002.

96. MEL, p. 311.

97. *The Natal Mercury*, 25 December 1899, p. 5.

98. The text of the plaque is in Afrikaans and English, the latter reading, 'In commemoration of the speech delivered by Winston Churchill War Correspondent from the steps of this building on 23 December 1899 this plaque has been erected by A. H. Smith, O. B. E., of Durban.' A photograph of the plaque is contained in *An Eightieth Year Tribute to Winston Churchill*, edited by Bruce Ingram (London: *The Illustrated London News*, 1954), p. 25.

99. MEL, p. 313. To give a sense of just how widespread the press coverage was, the author notes that there was an article with an illustration of the armoured train fight in the 21 January 1900 issue of the *Daily Iowa State Press* newspaper in Iowa City, Iowa, a small county seat town, population 7,987, west of the Mississippi river and 230 miles from Chicago.

100. *Churchill, A Life* by Martin Gilbert (New York: Henry Holt and Company, 1991), p. 121.

101. The father, Lord Roberts, had won the VC in 1858 during the Indian Mutiny and is buried in the crypt at St Paul's Cathedral in London. The son is buried in the Chieveley Military Cemetery in Natal where his grave is marked by a tall Christian cross of white stone inscribed, 'In loving memory of Frederick Sherston Roberts, VC Lieutenant, King's Royal Rifles, only surviving son of Field-Marshal Lord Roberts and Nora, his wife, who fell mortally wounded in an attempt to save the British guns at the Battle of Colenso on the 15th December 1899, and died two days afterwards aged 27 years and 11 months. "Blessed are the pure of heart for they shall see God." '

CHAPTER EIGHT: THE SOUTH AFRICAN WAR: THE RELIEF OF LADYSMITH

1. *London to Ladysmith via Pretoria*, p. 221.

2. *ibid*, pp. 250–1.

3. MEL, pp. 318–19.

4. OBI, CV2, p. 1093.

5. MEL, p. 320.

6. OBI, CV2, p. 1143.

7. OBI, CV2, p. 1141.

8. MEL, pp. 320–1.

9. MEL, p. 321. In *London to Ladysmith via Pretoria* at page 176, Churchill noted the regiment included an American who had served in the Civil War under General Phil Sheridan, who held a command in the Union army, not the Confederate army. Among the regular British army officers who served with the South African Light Horse was his polo team-mate Captain Albert Savory who died of wounds received in action near Dalmanutha in the Transvaal on 23 August 1900, and Lt Edmund Clutterbuck, also of the 4th Hussars.

10. MEL, pp. 320–1. The six squadrons and 700 men are Churchill's figures. In *The Colonials in South Africa 1899–1902* (Edinburgh and London: Wilham Blackwood & Sons, 1907), reprinted (Polstead, Suffolk: J. B. Hayward & Son, 1990), author John Stirling notes that

eight squadrons were raised with six sent to Natal and the balance kept in Cape Colony 'to form the nucleus of Roberts's Horse and Kitchener's Horse'. See the 1990 edition at p. 50. *Byng of Vimy* by Jeffery Williams (London: Leo Cooper, 1983), at p. 29, lists eight squadrons and 600 men, citing the Byng papers.

11. I am indebted to Major General Philip Pretorius of the South African National Museum of Military History for providing research materials on the uniforms and badges of the South African Light Horse. See *The Armed Forces of South Africa* by G. Tylden (Johannesburg: Africana Museum, 1954), pp. 169–70. See also 'The South African Light Horse of 1899–1902, Its Badges and a Brief History', by Mike Lukich in *The Bulletin of the Military Historical Society*, February 1984. Reference was also made to a drawing of the uniform and its badges in the collection of the National Army Museum, London. 'ACC No. 8102–15, Box 132, Envelope 15. © National Dept. of Photographs, Canada.'

12. See MEL, p. 320 and *Churchills in Africa* by Brian Roberts (London: Hamish Hamilton, 1970), frontispiece; *Winston Churchill An Illustrated Biography* by R. G. Grant (New York: Gallery Books, 1989), pp. 36–7; *Young Winston's Wars*, p. 161; and *The Young Churchill* by Stanley Nott (New York: Coward-McCann, Inc., 1941), frontispiece.

13. *London to Ladysmith via Pretoria*, pp. 98–9.

14. A drift is a ford, a place of shallow water.

15. *My Army Life* by Lieutenant General The Earl of Dundonald (London: Edward Arnold & Co., 1926), p. 118. Captain William Birdwood recorded the episode in his memoirs in similar terms, calling Churchill's ride 'a very gallant effort, considering the likelihood of encountering parties of Boers'. *Khaki and Gown* by Field Marshall Lord Birdwood (London: Ward, Lock & Co., Limited, 1941), p. 98. Churchill makes no mention of this in his own writings.

16. *London to Ladysmith via Pretoria*, p. 283.

17. *ibid*, p. 291.

18. *ibid*, p. 292.

19. MEL, p. 323.

20. MEL, p. 324.

21. *The Natal Campaign*, p. 332.

22. *London to Ladysmith via Pretoria*, p. 306.

23. *ibid*, pp. 307–9.

24. MEL, p. 327.

25. *ibid*, p. 328.

26. *Soldiering On*, p. 69.

27. *Commando, A Boer Journal of the Boer War* by Deneys Reitz (London: The Folio Society, 1982), p. 59. First published by Faber & Faber Limited in 1929, this is one of the finest memoirs of the war.

28. *The Last Post*, p. 13. Awdry was one of eight members of the Royal Military College intake of September 1893 killed in South Africa. See Appendix A.

29. There are no agreed figures for the casualties at Spion Kop for either side. I have used Byron Farwell's figures from *The Great Anglo-Boer War* at p. 184. Thomas Pakenham in his *The Boer War* states at p. 320 that 243 British were killed in the battle while the Boers 'lost' 335. In his *The Boer War* Eversley Belfield reports at p. 75 that the British 'lost nearly 1,300 of whom 350 were killed, and the Boers about 300'.

30. *The Boer War Generals* by Peter Trew (Wrens Park Publishing, 2001), pp. 168–71.

31. Leo Cooper's introduction to *Commando, A Boer Journal of the Boer War* (London: The Folio Society, 1982), pp. ix–xii.

32. *An Autobiography or The Story of My Experiments With Truth* by M. K. Gandhi (Ahmedabad: Navajivan Publishing House, 1945), pp. 264–8. There is a statue of Gandhi at Ladysmith, but none at Spion Kop.

33. MEL, p. 329.

34. *The Colonials in South Africa*, p. 52.

35. Pakenham in *The Boer War* at p. 318 wrote: 'Then, out of the darkness and confusion, appeared one man, one self-appointed messenger who might have turned the balance in favour of the British. It was young Winston, not content with his double job as *Morning Post* correspondent and lieutenant in the South African Light Horse, instinctively taking over the role of general.' With this I cannot concur. Celia Sandys is of a different opinion, entitling her chapter about Spion Kop in *Churchill Wanted Dead or Alive*, 'A General on Spion Kop', and referring to Churchill's role as 'his self-appointed mission to turn the tide of battle' at p. 166.

36. OBI, CV2, p. 1146.

37. The most complete account of the *Maine* is found in *The Reminiscences of Lady Randolph Churchill* by Mrs George Cornwallis-West (New York: The Century Company, 1908) pp. 396–463. The information about the ship is all taken from a commemorative coin in the author's collection depicting the ship on one side and crossed British and American flags on the other. The coin was probably a token given as part of the fund-raising effort or perhaps as a shipboard souvenir. See also *Churchills in Africa* by Brian Roberts (London: Hamish Hamilton, 1970), pp. 272–91.

38. *My Army Life*, p. 136. Gough's opinion of Dundonald was less favourable. In his memoir Gough wrote: 'Dundonald was another of Buller's weak subordinates. Known among us as Dundoodle, he was hesitating, vacillating and vain.' See *Soldiering On* at page 70.

39. MEL, p. 332.

40. MEL, pp. 334–5.

41. *London to Ladysmith via Pretoria*, p. 376. In *My Early Life* at page 335 Churchill wrote that both men were in the prone position.

42. The reporter is Martin Gilbert, as narrator of the 1991 BBC series 'The Complete Churchill, Volume I, Maverick Politician'.

43. MEL, p. 336. 'This was a sound and indeed fairly obvious plan, and there was no reason why it should not have been followed from the very beginning. Buller had not happened to think of it before.'

44. *London to Ladysmith via Pretoria*, p. 396.

45. *ibid*, p. 401.

46. MEL, p. 338.

47. *London to Ladysmith via Pretoria*, p. 405.

48. *ibid*, pp. 414–15.

49. *ibid*, p. 420. Iniskilling Hill was named for the Royal Iniskilling Fusiliers, an Irish infantry regiment which led the assault and suffered heavy casualties.

50. OBI, CV2, pp. 1151–2.

51. *My Army Life*, p. 147.

52. OBI, CV2, pp. 1148 and 1174.

53. *London to Ladysmith via Pretoria*, p. 435.

54. *London to Ladysmith via Pretoria*, pp. 447–8.

55. *Soldiering On*, p. 73.

56. *My Army Life*, p. 151.

57. *ibid*, pp. 151–2.

58. *London to Ladysmith via Pretoria*, pp. 463–5.

59. MEL, pp. 340–1.

60. *Khaki and Gown, An Autobiography*, by Field-Marshal Lord Birdwood (London: Ward, Lock & Co., Limited, 1941), p. 106. The preface to the memoir was written by Winston S. Churchill.

61. *Soldiering On*, p. 78. The relief of Ladysmith is covered on pp. 72–82. Gough's memoir written in 1954 did not withhold criticism of the young Churchill in India or in South Africa, which bolsters the credibility of his recollections. His final judgment on Churchill, at page 81, is both insightful and favourable. 'The incidents which I have related of Churchill's early days may not show him as a very pleasant and popular young man, but one can recognise in them his energy, his capacity for emotional excitement, which could stir him so deeply and which were the foundations of his power for leadership. That quality eventually was to make him the greatest war leader, not only of his time, but perhaps of all time. Certainly no one can call a whole people to great emotional resolutions and courageous effort unless he himself is fired by deep emotions, as Churchill is.'

62. *My Army Life*, p. 153.

63. Steevens's last book of dispatches was published posthumously. *From Cape Town to Ladysmith, An Unfinished Record of the South African War* (New York: Dodd, Mead and Company, 1900). It contains a tribute by Churchill in its final chapter.

64. OBI, CV2, p. 1153. A similar anecdote was sent to Randolph Churchill in 1963 as he was preparing the first volume of his biography of Sir Winston by Miss K. M. Clegg of Durban. 'During the siege of Ladysmith my Grandfather, Mr R. E. Clegg, was the Station Master of Estcourt, at that time the Railhead of the British Army, and the station from which the armoured train operated and my Father, George Clegg, was one of the armoured train crew. At that time Estcourt was crowded with refugees, including my Mother and her family and your Father could not find accommodation, so he was allowed to pitch his tent in my Grandfather's back yard. Many evenings over the camp fires and in the bar your Father would tell of his adventures as a reporter in India and Egypt. These tales were often so fantastic that my Father and his Friends did not believe half of them and would laugh and Accuse your Father of telling "tall stories" to impress them. Then one day your Father said, "Mark my words, I shall be the Prime Minister of England before I'm finished," only to be greeted by more laughter. The years passed and World War II was upon us, then one Morning my Father read in the head lines of the *Natal Mercury* – Winston Churchill – Prime Minister – and suddenly he exclaimed, "By jove, he's done it." Then he told us the story that I have just written. . . .' See the Official Biography, Volume I, Companion Volume 2, at page 1152.

65. *London to Ladysmith via Pretoria*, pp. 470–1.

66. The names listed on the tablet are as follows:
Major [Charles] Childe
Trooper W. G. Core
Captain [Harold Wake] de Rougemont
Trooper E. A. Cullum
Q. M. Sgt. J. Tregonning
Trooper X. DeVilliers
Sergeant H. S. Maddocks
Trooper H.C. Gillbanks
Corporal F. Snowdon
Trooper G. Godden
Lce. Corpl. J. Eustace
Trooper F. Gornall
Trooper A. Alard
Trooper T. Jollife
Trooper A. Baker
Trooper B. S. O. Julyan
Trooper G. Bolderstone
Trooper W. G. Levoir
Trooper J. Bray
Trooper C. Lewis
Trooper H. Brooks
Trooper W. McLean
Trooper A. W. M. Brown
Trooper N. Wright

67. *Ian Hamilton's March* by Winston Spencer Churchill (London: Longmans, Green and

Co., 1900), p. 3. This is the second of Churchill's South Africa books and contains the final seventeen letters to the *Morning Post* plus an appendix setting out the order of battle of Lt General Ian Hamilton's force and certain extracts from the prisoner of war diary Lt Frankland kept in Pretoria. Its first chapter is entitled, 'A Roving Commission', which would serve as the subtitle for Churchill's 1930 autobiography, *My Early Life* and as the title of the American edition of the book. *Ian Hamilton's March* is dedicated to 'Lieut. - General Ian Hamilton, C. B., D. S. O., with whose military achievements it is largely concerned.' Six of the *Morning Post* letters are reprinted in *Young Winston's Wars* and *Winston S. Churchill, War Correspondent 1895–1900*.

68. The letter appears at OBI, CV2, pp. 1162–4. It also appears in *The Collected Essays of Sir Winston Churchill, Volume I, Churchill and War* at p. 42 as 'A Plea For Magnanimity'. Jack Churchill's 3 April 1900 letter to Lady Randolph on the subject said: 'Winston is being severely criticised about his Peaceful telegrams – and everyone here in Natal is going against his views. They say that even if you are going to treat the Boers well after their surrender, this is not the time to say so. For knowing they will lose nothing and may gain a lot, they may go on fighting.' OBI, CV2, pp. 1165–6.

69. OBI, CV2, p. 1163.

70. MEL, p. 343. Although Lieutenant Colonel Byng's certificate (see OBI, CV2, p. 1141) states Churchill served with the SALH from 2 January 2 to 23 March 23, 1900, a letter he wrote to Churchill on 29 July 1905, states: 'I think the best thing I can do is to give you the enclosed certificate, asking you to fill in the date of joining the Light Horse & the date of your leaving S. A. as I consider you belonged to us all that time.' (See OBI, CV2, p. 1141.) Further support for the fact that Churchill retained his commission until he left South Africa in July 1900 is that the War Office awarded him clasps for his Queen's South Africa Medal for Orange Free State, Johannesburg and Diamond Hill, all for events after he left the SALH in Natal.

71. The *Cape Times* of 3 March 1899 reported on the then newly opened Mount Nelson: 'Such a triumph of construction, of decoration, so perfect a blending of every one of the many essentials of a first-class modern hotel, South Africa would try vainly to even distantly imitate, and there is no exaggeration in the statement that London, the capital of the world, would not be able to produce anything superior.'

72. *London to Ladysmith via Pretoria*, pp. 345–7.

73. OBI, CV2, p. 1168.

74. MEL, p. 342. Indeed, Roberts had known

Winston Churchill as a child.

75. *The Great Anglo-Boer War*, p. 192. There is much variety in the reports of the strength of Roberts's force. I have used Farwell's numbers which are those provided by an American military attaché accompanying the force. *The Times History* listed 'roughly 37,000 men' including 30,000 combatants. See Farwell for other estimates.

76. *The Great Anglo-Boer War*, p. 239, quoting *The Letters of Queen Victoria*, third series, Vol. 3, p. 511f.

77. *Ian Hamilton's March*, p. 42.

78. MEL, pp. 349–50.

79. OBI, CV2, p. 1177.

80. This corps of scouts was raised in December 1899 by Captain the Honourable Raymond de Montmorency who had received the Victoria Cross for his actions in the charge of the 21st Lancers at Omdurman on 2 September 1898. He was killed in action in a skirmish at Dordrecht, near Stormberg, in Cape Colony, on 23 February 23 1900.

81. *Ian Hamilton's March*, p. 65.

82. *ibid.*, p. 66.

83. OBI, CV2, p. 1172.

84. The MID is noted in *The Colonials in South Africa 1899–1902*, p. 125. The DCM was announced in the *London Gazette*, 19 April 1900 (PRO, ZJ 1/486, pp. 2707 and 2709). The *London Gazette* erroneously lists Roberts's unit as Montgomery's Scouts. Churchill was in error to refer to the Distinguished Service Medal. Clement Roberts received the Distinguished Conduct Medal.

85. *ibid*, and see also *British Gallantry Awards* by P. E. Abbott and J. M. A. Tamplin (Garden City, New York: Doubleday & Company, Inc., 1972), pp. 78–100. Roberts's DCM was one of 2,050 awarded in the South African War. Although earned and gazetted before Queen Victoria's death on 22 January 1901, Roberts's DCM had the obverse of King Edward VII. Roberts also received the Queen's South Africa Medal with three clasps and the King's South Africa Medal with clasps, 'South Africa 1901' and 'South Africa 1902'. I am deeply indebted to Doris Maud, Clement Roberts's granddaughter, for sharing with me photographs of the medals and copies of news clippings and correspondence concerning the DCM.

86. CV2, p. 1171.

87. Unpublished private letter from Churchill to Roberts, a copy of which was provided to the author by Clement Roberts's granddaughter, Doris Maud, and is used with her permission. In fairness to Trooper Roberts and by way of comparison, Churchill's old Harrow friend, John Peniston Milbanke, won the VC in South Africa on 5 January 1900, as a lieutenant in the 10th Hussars in an action where he rode

out under fire to rescue a man whose horse was exhausted, placed the man upon his own horse under heavy fire and took him to safety. Milbanke was wounded, however, while Roberts was not. See *Register of the Victoria Cross*, p. 224.

88. *Ian Hamilton's March*, pp. 403-408 and MEL, p. 358.

89. MEL, p. 359.

90. OBI, CV2, p. 1178.

91. *In Search of Churchill*, by Martin Gilbert (London: HarperCollins, 1994), p. 311.

92. MEL, pp. 361-2. Churchill got the date wrong in his memoir, recording the action at Florida as 2 June rather than 29 May. Lieutenant General Horace Smith-Dorrien was no stranger to narrow escapes. He was one of the very few British survivors of the battle of Isandlwana on 22 January 1879, in the Zulu War. See *Memories of Forty-Eight Years' Service* by General Sir Horace Smith-Dorrien (New York: E. P. Dutton and Co., 1925).

93. MEL, pp. 362-363.

94. MEL, p. 364. In his contemporary account, Churchill opined that his French 'might be good enough to deceive a Dutchman'. See *Ian Hamilton's March*, p. 271.

95. *Ian Hamilton's March*, pp. 294-5.

96. OBI, CV2, p. 1178.

97. *Listening for the Drums* by General Sir Ian Hamilton (London: Faber and Faber, Ltd., 1944), p. 248. The battle is called Diamond Hill by the British, Donkerhoek by the Boers.

98. *ibid*, p. 249. 'Bobs' was Lord Roberts. 'K' was Lord Kitchener.

99. *My Army Life*, p. 147.

100. OBI, CV2, p. 1160.

101. *British Battles & Medals*, pp. 187–92.

102. Queen's South Africa Medal, Public Records Office reference, Class W. O. 100/274, Folio 11, South African Light Horse. The periods of operational service for which the clasps were given are: Cape Colony – 11 October 1899, to 31 May 1902; Tugela Heights – 14–27 February 1900; Orange Free State – 28 February 1900 to 31 May 1902; Relief of Ladysmith – 15 December 1899 to 28 February 1900; Johannesburg – 31 May 1900; Diamond Hill – 11–12 June 1900. See *British Battles & Medals*, pp. 188–92 for details.

103. *The Orders, Decorations and Medals of Sir Winston Churchill*, pp. 34-5.

104. OBI, CV2, p. 1178. The bracketed word was added by the author.

105. MEL, pp. 366-7.

106. OBI, CV2, p. 1183. The next book based on his *Morning Post* articles from South Africa, *Ian Hamilton's March*, was published on 12 October 1900, and by the end of the year had sold 8,000 copies in Great Britain and 1,500 copies in the United States. See *Churchill: A Life* by Martin Gilbert (New York: Henry Holt

and Company, 1991), pp.131 and 136.

107. *The Boer War* (Belfield), pp. 165–8. Belfield reviews and compares the figures given in the *Official History of the War in South Africa* and *The Times History of The War in South Africa*. See also *The National Army Museum Book of the Boer War* by Field Marshal Lord Carver (London: Sidgwick & Jackson, 1999), p. 252 which is generally in accord on casualty figures. Other secondary sources vary widely.

CHAPTER NINE: BETWEEN WARS

1. OBI, CV2, p. 1191.

2. MEL, p. 371.

3. OBI, CV2, p. 1203. In *My Early Life* at page 373 Churchill remembered the margin as 230 votes.

4. OBI, CV2, p. 1205.

5. *The Young Winston Churchill*, by John Marsh, foreword by The Rt Hon. L. S. Amery, CH (London: Evans Brothers Limited, 1955), pp. 11-12. Churchill's similar statement in *My Early Life* is found at page 271.

6. MEL, p. 74. The British lecture tour took Churchill to thirty venues in a month. The lectures in Great Britain, Canada and the United States, together with his pay from the newspaper and book royalties, earned him £10,000 in a two-year period. *The Story of the Malakand Field Force* was published on 14 March 1898, and the two-volume *The River War* on 6 November 1899. His only novel, *Savrola, A Tale of the Revolution in Laurania* was published in November 1899. The two books on South Africa, *London to Ladysmith via Pretoria* and *Ian Hamilton's March* were published respectively on 15 May and 12 October 1900.

7. OBI, CV2, p. 1229.

8. For Churchill's speeches both in and outside Parliament, see *Winston S. Churchill, His Complete Speeches, 1897–1963, supra*. For Churchill's essays and magazine articles, see *The Collected Essays of Sir Winston Churchill, supra*, in which *'Some Impressions of the War In South Africa'* appears in Volume 1, pp. 68–80.

9. OBI, CV2, p. 867.

10. One of the most notable memoirs of service with the Imperial Yeomanry in the South African War is *Trooper 8008, IY* by Hon. Sidney Peel (London: Edward Arnold 1902). Peel, an Oxford-educated barrister-at-law, served as a trooper in the Queen's Own Oxfordshire Hussars before the war and in the 40th (Oxfordshire) Company, 10th Battalion of Imperial Yeomanry in South Africa. In the dedication of the book at page vi he voiced a sentiment with which the author is in wholehearted agreement: 'Collectively, indeed, privates are of the utmost importance.'

11. OBI, CV2, pp. 925–6.

12. MEL, p. 321.

13. Holdings of the Oxfordshire Yeomanry Trust, Order Book, Catalogue number 120. The holdings of the Oxfordshire Yeomanry Trust to which reference is made in this chapter were made available through the courtesy of the Trust and its Chairman, Colonel T. L. May CBE, TD, DL, and are used with the permission of the Oxfordshire Yeomanry Trust. The Valentia album is owned by Gerald Flint Shipman and is used with his kind permission.

14. The *London Gazette*, 3 January 1902, p. 10.

15. *Forward Everywhere: Her Majesty's Territorials*, by Stanley Simm Baldwin (London: Brassey's (UK) Ltd., 1994)), pp. 7–21. This book is an excellent recent history of the auxiliary forces. A more contemporary description is contained in *The Army Book for the British Army, supra*, at pages 359–9.

16. *Forward Everywhere*, pp. 22–45.

17. *The Development of the British Army 1899–1914* by Colonel John K. Dunlop (London: Methuen, 1938), pp. 52–5. This is a most interesting and useful reference work as indicated by its sub-title, 'From the eve of the South African War to the eve of the Great War, with special reference to the Territorial Force.'

18. *Forward Everywhere, supra*, at page 55, puts the 1901 establishment of a Yeomanry regiment at 596 officers and men plus one officer and sixteen men for the machine-gun detachment but gives no source reference. *The Regulations for the Territorial Force 1908* (London: HMSO), reprinted by the Naval and Military Press in a facsimile edition, listed at page 140 the authorised strength for a Yeomanry regiment at 449 officers and men, 106 per squadron plus a sixteen-man machine-gun section.

19. *The Story of the Oxfordshire Yeomanry, Queen's Own Oxfordshire Hussars, 1798–1998*, by David Eddershaw (Oxford: Oxfordshire Yeomanry Trust, 1998), p. 24. This excellent, brief history was commissioned by the Oxfordshire Yeomanry Trust to accompany its bicentenary exhibit at the Oxfordshire County Museum in Woodstock.

20. 'Queer Objects on Horseback' was the title of the regiment's bicentenary exhibit in 1998. This is an indication that the nickname is used by the regiment and not only about them by outsiders.

21. An excellent collection of Queen's Own Oxfordshire Hussars uniforms is displayed at the regimental museum of the Oxford and Buckinghamshire Light Infantry at the TA Centre at Slade Park, Headington in Oxford. The Ninth Duke's busby and shabraque are still maintained at Blenheim Palace.

22. *The Oxfordshire Hussars in the Great War (1914–1918)* by Adrian Keith-Falconer (London: John Murray, 1927), pp. 11–12. The first chapter of the book, entitled 'Introductory', contains an excellent brief history of the regiment before the First World War.

23. *His Majesty's Territorial Army, A Descriptive Account of the Yeomanry, Artillery, Engineers and Infantry With the Army Service and Medical Corps Comprising The King's Imperial Army of the Second Line* by Walter Richards (London: Virtue & Co. (undated, 1909–11) in four volumes), p. 183.

24. *The Glitter and the Gold, An Autobiography*, by Consuelo Vanderbilt Balsan (New York: Harper & Brothers Publishers, 1952), p. 84.

25. Holdings of the Oxfordshire Yeomanry Trust, Henley Album 2, F36. The strength of the four squadrons was given as Henley 70, Oxford 130, Woodstock 77 and Banbury 84.

26. The F. E. Smith anecdote was provided to the author in a 9 January 1995, letter from T. E. Nicholls, Honorary Secretary of the Oxfordshire Yeomanry OC Association.

27. OBII, CV1, pp. 253–4.

28. Churchill's letter is dated 6 May 1904. Holdings of the Oxfordshire Yeomanry Trust, Letter Book, Catalogue No. 121, F131.

29. Holdings of the Oxfordshire Yeomanry Trust, Order Book, Catalogue No. 122.

30. The *London Gazette*, 30 May 1905, p. 3866.

31. Holdings of the Oxfordshire Yeomanry Trust. For orders moving the squadron to permanent duty, see the examples at the Henley Album at F2 for 1907, at F71 for 1908, F77 for 1909, F86 for 1910, F101 for 1911. Again, orders of this type for the period from 1912 and after are no longer extant.

32. Holdings of the Oxfordshire Yeomanry Trust. For detailed squadron orders, see the examples in the Henley album at F57 for 1905, F62 for 1906, F68 for 1907, F78 for 1908, F84 for 1909, F99 for 1910. The squadron orders for the period from 1912 and after are no longer extant.

33. *Mr Brodrick's Army* by Winston Spencer Churchill, MP (London: Arthur L. Humphreys, 1903). This is, in 2004, the rarest of Churchill's books. It was originally bound in red card wrappers, a paperback book which was by its nature fragile. It is not known how many copies were produced but few survive. In his *A Connoisseur's Guide to the Books of Sir Winston Churchill*, Richard Langworth notes copies have recently sold for tens of thousands of dollars, a far cry from the original price of one shilling. A facsimile edition was published by Dalton Newfield's The Churchilliana Company in Sacramento, California in 1977. This, the American first edition, is available for about $35.00.

34. *Mr Brodrick's Army*, p. 23 (Churchilliana edition).

35. 'The German Splendour,' in *Thoughts and Adventures*, by The Rt Hon. Winston S. Churchill (London: Hornton Butterworth Ltd, 1931), pp. 76–7.

36. OBII, CV1, p. 582.

37. *ibid.*

38. *The End of a Chapter*, by Shane Leslie (New York: Charles Scribner's Sons, 1917), p. 123. Shane Leslie, Churchill's cousin, was presumably present to overhear this remark.

39. OBII, CV2, p. 685.

40. OBII, p. 215.

41. OBII, CV2, p. 893.

42. 'The German Splendour,' *supra*, p. 81.

43. OBII, CV2, pp. 911–12.

44. Holdings of the Oxfordshire Yeomanry Trust, Henley Album F85 for the pre-camp drills and F86 for the Orders to move to camp.

45. Holdings of the Oxfordshire Yeomanry Trust, Henley Album, F91.

46. Holdings of the Oxfordshire Yeomanry Trust, Henley Album, F99 and F100.

47. OBII, CV2, p. 1087. How fitting a camp for the span of Churchill's life, for he was born in Blenheim Palace and is buried at Bladon churchyard. It is also noted that Churchill's reference to suffering from the sun refers to an ongoing problem he had getting badly sunburned when out of doors for long periods. He suffered similarly in India. A number of photographs of Churchill in the QOOH show him wearing a cloth sunshade, French Foreign Legion style, suspended from his service cap to protect his neck from the sun.

48. OBII, CV2, p. 1089. The bracketed language was added by the author.

49. Holdings of the Oxfordshire Yeomanry Trust, Henley Album F102.

50. Holdings of the Oxfordshire Yeomanry Trust, Henley Album F104.

51. The records of the Oxfordshire Yeomanry Trust are incomplete as to Churchill's role in the regiment after 1912.

52. *The Oxfordshire Hussars in the Great War*, pp. 16–17. Among the other officers on the strength of the regiment in July 1914 were Lt Adrian Keith-Falconer, the author of the book to which this footnote refers and Second Lt P. Fleming, the father of author Ian Fleming of James Bond fame.

53. *ibid*, p. 19.

54. *ibid*, p. 25.

55. *ibid*, p. 25–6.

56. *ibid*, p. 30.

57. *ibid*, p. 32 and pp. 366–8.

58. *ibid.*, p. vii.

59. *ibid*, see Appendices A, B, C and E, pp. 350–68 which name all the officers and all the casualties individually. The author's note to the appendices at page 348 states that the casualties were actually higher than listed

because the regimental diary had a gap from July 1917 and March 1918, during which period it is known casualties were incurred but none were listed.

60. *ibid*, see Appendix D, pp. 361–4. No doubt Jack Churchill would agree with Field Marshal Bernard Montgomery who is said to have remarked about staff rather than front line service in the First World War, 'Staff is the bread of life.'

61. This record was provided to the author with the permission of the Churchill family by the courtesy of Mr Joseph E. Kelly, Head of Ministry of Defence Archives.

62. Royal warrant quoted in *The Territorial Decoration 1908–1930* by J. M. A. Tamplin (London: Spink & Son, Ltd., 1983), pp. 2–3.

63. The *London Gazette* of Tuesday, 10 April 1923, p. 2648.

64. This anecdote is attributed to Sir John Thompson, a former commander of the regiment and former Lord Lieutenant of Oxfordshire as told to Colonel Tim May, President of the Oxfordshire Yeomanry Trust. It was related to me by T. E. Nicholls, Honorary Secretary of the Oxfordshire Yeomanry OC Association, of which Colonel Sir John Thompson was President, in a letter dated 9 January 1995. It is also included in *The Story of the Oxfordshire Yeomanry* at page 65.

65. The *London Gazette*, 5 August 1924, p. 5891.

66. The *London Gazette*, 31 October 1924, p. 7861.

67. The recitation of the later history of the regiment is based on David Eddershaw's *The Story of the Oxfordshire Yeomanry* and typewritten documents provided by T. E. Nicholls of the Oxfordshire Yeomanry OC Association and an article, 'The Queen's Own Oxfordshire Hussars', reprinted from the *Territorial Magazine*, April 1957. Churchill became Honorary Colonel upon the death of Queen Mary. His letter to Q Battery is in the Holdings of the Oxfordshire Yeomanry Trust, C127, Box 9, Battery Album. I must also express my appreciation to Ray Westlake for sharing excerpts from books in his collection concerning the Territorial Army and Churchill's Yeomanry regiment which provide helpful background and information.

68. I am deeply indebted to Colonel Tim May for sharing with me his recollections of Churchill's funeral and his outlines of the Holdings of the Oxfordshire Yeomanry Trust of which he is President. The details of Churchill's funeral in this chapter and in the introduction to this book are based on 'Ceremonial To Be Observed At the Funeral of The Right Honourable Sir Winston Leonard Spencer Churchill KG, OM, C H, 30 January 1965.' Printed by Her Majesty's Stationery Office.

CHAPTER TEN: THE GREAT WAR

1. OBII, CV3, p. 1999.
2. *Winston Churchill As I Knew Him*, by Violet Bonham-Carter (London: Eyre & Spottis-woode and Collins, 1965), p. 237. There are a number of books about Churchill's service at the Admiralty in both World Wars. See the bibliography.
3. OBII, CV3, pp. 1989–90.
4. *The World Crisis, 1911–1914* by the Rt. Hon. Winston S. Churchill, CH (London: Thornton Butterworth Limited, 1923), pp. 212–13. Churchill's magisterial history of the First World War appeared as five volumes in six books between 1923 and 1931. The subsequent volumes are: *The World Crisis, 1915* (1923); *The World Crisis, 1916–1918, Part I* (1927); *The World Crisis, 1916–1918, Part II* (1927); *The World Crisis, The Aftermath* (1929); and *The World Crisis, The Eastern Front* (1931).
5. 'Antwerp: The Story of Its Siege and Fall,' by Winston S. Churchill, *The Sunday Pictorial*, 19 November, 1916, reprinted in *The Collected Essays of Sir Winston Churchill, Volume I, Churchill and War* (London: ibrary of Imperial History, 1976), p. 172.
6. *Adventure* by Major-General the Rt Hon. J. E. B. Seely (London: William Heinemann, Ltd., 1930), p. 189. John Edward Bernard Seely (1868–1947) had been at Harrow and in the South African War with Churchill.
7. OBII, pp. 111–12. Runciman was the same Walter Runciman whom Churchill had defeated to win his seat in Parliament in 1900.
8. OBIII, p. 111.
9. *The Royal Naval Division* by Douglas Jerrold (London: Hutchinson & Co. (Publishers) Ltd., second edition, 1927), p. 39. This edition includes an introduction by the Right Hon. Winston S. Churchill.
10. *Adventure*, pp. 187–8 and 1967. The bracketed number, though Seely's own, was added by the author.
11. *Alarms & Excursions, Reminiscences of a Soldier* by Lt Gen. Sir Tom Bridges, KCB, KCMG, DSO, LL.D (London: Longmans Green and Co., 1938), p. 110. The foreword is by Winston S. Churchill. He and Bridges were good friends and served together in Lord Dundonald's brigade in the relief of Ladysmith.
12. Churchill's own views on Antwerp are set out in *The World Crisis, 1911–1914* and in two 1916 magazine articles: 'Antwerp: The Story of Its Siege And Fall', *The Sunday Pictorial*, 19 November 1916, and 'How Antwerp Saved the Channel Ports', *The Sunday Pictorial*, 26 November 1916. These were reprinted in *The Collected Essays of Sir Winston Churchill, Volume I, Churchill and War* at pp. 172–82.

13. *Thoughts and Adventures*, pp. 16–17. The bracketed language was added by the author.
14. OBIII, CVI, p. 344.
15. OBIII, CV1, p. 377 and OBIII, CV1, pp. 552–3.
16. Churchill's *The World Crisis* fully details his actions and views, in effect his defence. Two useful histories are *Gallipoli* by John Masefield (New York: The MacMillan Company, 1917), which was written soon after the events, and *Gallipoli* by Alan Moorehead (New York: Harper & Row Publishers, 1956). Martin Gilbert's *Winston S. Churchill, Volume III, 1914–1916*, is comprehensive on Churchill's military service in the First World War. Two studies of political as well as the military aspects of the campaign are *Winston Churchill and the Dardanelles* by Trumbull Higgins (New York: The Macmillan Company, 1963), and *Fisher, Churchill and the Dardanelles* by Geoffrey Penn (London: Leo Cooper, 1999). See also the report of the Dardanelles Commission in abridgements published as *Lord Kitchener and Winston Churchill: The Dardanelles, Part I, 1914–15* (London: The Stationery Office, 2000) and *Defeat at Gallipoli: The Dardanelles, Part II, 1915–1916* (London: The Stationery Office, 2000). For an early critique of Churchill's history of the First World War, see *The World Crisis by Winston Churchill, A Criticism* by Sydenham of Combe, The Lord, *et al.* (London: Hutchinson & Co. (Publishers) Ltd, 1928),
17. OBIII, CV2, p. 921.
18. OBIII, CV2, p. 932.
19. OBIII, CV2, p. 927. The bracketed language was added by the author.
20. *The World Crisis, 1915*, pp. 374–5.
21. OBIII, CV2, p. 940.
22. OBIII, CV2, pp. 1095–1101.
23. OBIII, CV2, p. 1098. The letter was written from the Duchy of Lancaster office on 17 July 1915 before his planned trip to Gallipoli and was placed in an envelope labelled, 'To be sent to Mrs Churchill in the event of my death.'
24. *In Search of Churchill*, p. 64.
25. *Winston Churchill, His Life as a Painter, A Memoir by his Daughter Mary Soames* (London: William Collins Sons & Co., 1990), p. 24.
26. OBIII, CV2, p. 56.
27. OBIII, CV2, p. 927.
28. OBIII, CV2, p. 987.
29. OBIII, CV2, p. 1017.
30. OBIII, CV2, p. 1119. Archibald Sinclair (1890–1970) was educated at Sandhurst and commissioned in the Life Guards in 1910. He was returned to Parliament in 1922 and served as leader of the Liberal Party and as Secretary of State for Air in Churchill's Cabinet in the Second World War. He became 1st Viscount Thurso in 1952. See *Liberal*

Crusader, The Life of Sir Archibald Sinclair, by
Gerard J. DeGroot (London: Hurst &
Company, 1993).
31. OBIII, CV2, p. 1171.
32. *Thoughts and Adventures*, p. 99. Churchill's
army personnel file indicates he was embodied
for service in the rank of major and restored
to the establishment of the Queen's Own
Oxfordshire Hussars, Territorial Force, on 17
November 1915. Churchill's resignation
speech was given in the House of Commons
on 15 November 1915 and may be viewed as
a summary of his defence of his tenure at the
Admiralty that was fully developed in *The
World Crisis*. The speech is well worth reading
and is printed in its entirety in *Winston S.
Churchill, His Complete Speeches, 1897–1963*,
Vol. III, pp. 2390–2403.
33. *Great Contemporaries*, p. 90.
34. *Thoughts and Adventures*, p. 100.
35. *ibid.*
36. *Regiments and Corps of the British Army*, pp.
86–7. See also R. H. Whitworth, *The Grenadier
Guards* (London: Leo Cooper, 1974) and Sir
Frederick Ponsonby, *The Grenadier Guards in
the Great War of 1914–1918* (London:
Macmillan, 1920).
37. *Marlborough, His Life and Times, Volume I*,
unnumbered page following the verso of the
title page.
38. OBIII, CV2, p. 1282.
39. *Thoughts and Adventures*, p. 101.
40. Churchill's Colt .45 is currently on display at
the Imperial War Museum, Cabinet War
Rooms in London on loan from his grandson
Winston S. Churchill.
41. The oil portrait, a gift to Churchill from the
officers of the armoured car squadrons, is
hung in a stairwell at Chartwell below which is
hung Churchill's helmet mounted on a
wooden plaque.
42. OBIII, CV2, p. 1286.
43. OVIII, CV2, p. 1289. This letter was written
on 26 November 1915, the day after the
events described. The episode was also related
in Churchill's essay 'With the Grenadiers' in
the 1932 book *Thoughts and Adventures* at pp.
99–110. The American edition, *Amid These
Storms* (New York: Charles Scribner's Sons,
1932) contains the essay at pp. 99–120. The
later version of the story is a bit more detailed
than his contemporary letter, including much
recalled dialogue and having the lethal shell
arrive five minutes after Churchill's departure
rather than fifteen, making it a somewhat
nearer miss. It is not uncommon for war
stories to improve over time.
44. OBIII, CV2, p. 1288.
45. OBIII, CV2, p. 1290.
46. OBIII, CV2, p. 1316.
47. OBIII, CV2, pp. 1303–8.
48. OBIII, CV2, p. 1322.

49. OBIII, CV2, p. 1333. It was clearly a political
decision by Asquith overruling a military decision by French.
50. OBIII, CV2, p. 1334.
51. *Adventure*, pp. 237–8. Seely was incorrect to
state Churchill had already commanded a
battalion or been promoted to lieutenant
colonel. In 1915 Churchill was still a major
and had held no command in France.
52. OBIII, CV2, pp. 1339–40. In another letter
home in which he thought of what he could
do in London he wrote: 'God for a month of
power & a good shorthand writer.' See OBIII,
CV2, p. 1354.
53. *Regiments and Corps of the British Army*, pp.
161–2. The relevant regimental histories are
*The History of the Royal Scots Fusiliers,
1678–1918* by John Buchan (London: Thomas
Nelson and Sons, Ltd., 1925) and *The History
of the 9th (Scottish) Division, 1914–1919* by
John Ewing, MC (London: John Murray,
1921).
54. OBIII, CV2, pp. 1354 and 1358.
55. Supplement to The *London Gazette* of 24
March 1916, dated 25 March 1916, p. 3260.
56. Churchill was photographed in this uniform
with the other officers of the battalion in April
1916 at Ploegsteert, Belgium. The picture
appears as the frontispiece photograph in
Winston S. Churchill, Volume III, 1914–1916 by
Martin Gilbert (London: William Heinemann,
Ltd., 1971).
57. OBIII, CV2, pp. 1326-7. This letter was
dated 12 December 1915. In an 8 December
letter he told her that the helmet 'will perhaps
protect my valuable cranium'. See p. 1318.
58. OBIII, CV2, cp. 1376 and 1397.
59. OBIII, CV2, p. 1365.
60. OBIII, p. 632.
61. *With Winston Churchill at the Front* by
Captain X (Andrew Dewar Gibb) (London
and Glasgow: Cowans & Gray, Ltd., 1924),
pp. 21, 23. This little, 3½ by 6½ inch, 112-
page paperback is the only contemporary
account of Churchill's service with the 6th
Royal Scots Fusiliers in book form.
62. OBIII, CV2, p. 1369. In current parlance, a
grenade would be classified as a dumb rather
than a smart bomb.
63. *With Winston Churchill at the Front*, p. 24.
64. OBIII, CV2, p. 1385.
65. An excellent guide to this area of Flanders is
*A Walk Round Plugstreet, Cameos of the Western
Front, South Ypres Sector 1914–1918* by Tony
Spagnoli and Ted Smith (London: Leo
Cooper, 1997)
66. OBIII, CV2, p. 1397.
67. OBIII, CV2, p. 1399.
68. *With Winston Churchill at the Front*, p. 56.
69. *With Winston Churchill at the Front*, p. 59.
70. OBIII, CV2, p. 1456.
71. OBIII, CV2, p. 1400.

72. OBIII, CV2, p. 1412.

73. OBIII, CV2, p. 1419.

74. OBIII, CV2, p. 1427.

75. OBIII, CV2, p. 1433. In *Thoughts and Adventures* at page 117 Churchill voiced a similar sentiment: 'When one has been under shell fire every day for a month, one does not exaggerate these experiences. They were the commonplaces of the life of millions in those strange times.'

76. OBIII, CV2, p. 1421. The bracketed words were added by the author.

77. 'The Death of Lt Col Ian Hogg DSO 4H' by Major R. A. Noone, *The Cross Belts, The Journal of The Queen's Royal Hussars*, Vol. 1, No. 2, 1994–5, pp. 101–2.

78. *The 4th (Queen's Own) Hussars in the Great War* by Captain H. K. D. Evans, MC, and Major N. O. Laing, DSO (Aldershot: Gale & Polden Limited, 1920), pp. 179–99. This is the best source listing each man and the date of injury, death or capture. This history features a foreword by the Right Hon. Winston Churchill, PC. Daniell's *4th Hussars* at page 278 list the regiment's First World War casualties as 400 wounded in action and 149 killed in action including twenty of the 115 officers who served. *Officers Died in the Great War 1914–1919*, first published 1919 by HMSO, new enlarged edition (Polstead, Suffolk: J. B. Hayward & Son, 1988), p. 21 lists eighteen 4th Hussars officers killed. There are a number of discrepancies among the sources as to the names of the officers.

79. *The 4th (Queen's Own) Hussars in the Great War*, frontispiece.

80. OBIII, CV2, p. 1386.

81. OBIII, CV2, p. 1425.

82. OBIII, CV2, p. 1467.

83. OBIII, p. 658.

84. *With Winston Churchill at the Front*, pp. 67–8.

85. *ibid.*

86. OBIII, CV2, p. 1436 citing War Office Papers 95/1769.

87. OBIII, CV2, pp. 1290–1 and p. 1391.

88. OBIII, CV2, p. 1453.

89. OBIII, CV2, p. 1320.

90. OBIII, CV2, p. 1460.

91. OBIII, CV2, p. 1502.

92. *With Winston Churchill at the Front*, pp. 108–9. The bracketed language was added by the author.

93. *Adventure*, p. 236.

94. OBIII, p. 635.

95. *With Winston Churchill at the Front*, pp. 109–10. Andrew Dewar Gibb was educated at Glasgow University where he received his LL.B. in 1913. He was later an MP for the Scottish Universities and Chairman of the Scottish National Party. From 1934 he served as Regius Professor of Law at the University of Glasgow.

96. Record of the award of the 1914–1915 Star to Churchill is found in the supplementary roll of the Queen's Own Oxfordshire Hussars which indicate that his medal was authorised on 10 October 1919. Public Record Office reference, Class W. O. 329/2944, no folio number. For details about this medal see *British Battles & Medals*, p. 227.

97. For details of the British War Medal see *British Battles & Medals*, pp. 228–9.

98. Record of the award of the British War Medal and the Victory Medal to Churchill is found in the 'Medal Roll of Individuals, Staff' which indicate that he was issued the former on 13 October 1919 and the latter on 4 June 1920. Victory Medal and British War Medal, Public Record Office reference, Class W. O. 329/2138, folio 8, Staff. For details about the Victory Medal see *British Battles & Medals*, pp. 230–1.

99. The *London Gazette* of Friday, 2 June 1916, p. 5471.

100. My thanks to Charles D. Platt for sharing his Plugstreet photographs with me.

101. *Winston S. Churchill, His Complete Speeches, 1897–1963*, Volume III, p. 2439.

102. *ibid*, p. 2466.

103. Moorehead, *Gallipoli* (1985 edition), p. 361 and OBIII, CV2, p. 1328.

104. Churchill's service as Minister of Munitions is the subject of *Churchill, Munitions, and Mechanical Warfare, The Politics of Supply and Strategy* by Eugene E. Beiriger (New York: Peter Lang Publishing, Inc., 1997).

105. General Orders No. 62, War Department 10 May 1919 (Washington, D.C.: Government Printing Office, 1919). See also 'Congressional Medal of Honor, The Distinguished Service Cross and The Distinguished Service Medal,' compiled by the Office of the Adjutant General of the Army, 1919 (Washington, D.C.: Government Printing Office, 1920), p. 9.

106. *The Times*, 17 July 1919, p. 3. *The New York Times*, 17 July 1919, p. 14.

107. OBIII, p. 641.

108. The most recent edition is *The World Crisis, An Abridgement of The Classic 4-Volume History of World War I* by Winston S. Churchill (New York: Charles Scribner's Sons, 1992). The edition does not include the final two volumes, *The Aftermath* and *The Eastern Front*. To pursue an interest in Churchill's career as an historian of the First World War see *Churchill as Historian* by Maurice Ashley (London: Martin Secker & Warburg, Limited, 1968), *Churchill's World Crisis as History* by Robin Prior (London: Croom Helm, Ltd., 1983), and *Churchill's Military Histories, A Rhetorical Study* (Lanham, MD: Rowman & Littlefield Publishers, Inc., 2002).

109. *The World War Source Book* by Philip J.

Haythornthwaite (London: Arms and Armour Press, 1997), pp. 52–5. Further killed in action totals are: Germany 1,800,000; Russia 1,700,000; France 1,300,000; Austria-Hungary 922,000; Italy 460,000; Bulgaria 75,000; USA 50,500. It is estimated that more than 70,000 American soldiers died from disease, particularly influenza, during the conflict. The breakdown for the war dead of the British Empire included India 72,000; Canada 65,000; Australia 62,000; New Zealand 18,000 and South Africa 9,300. In addition, approximately 2,000,000 men of the British Empire were wounded.

110. The poem, in Churchill's hand, is in the collection of the Harrow School Archive and was made available to the author through the courtesy of Alisdair Hawkyard and Rita M. Boswell Gibbs.

CONCLUSION

1. David McCullough, 'Harry S. Truman' in *Character Above All, Ten Presidents from FDR to Bush*, Robert A. Wilson, editor (New York: Simon & Schuster, 1995), p. 56.

2. *In Search of Churchill*, p. 215.

3. *Sixty Minutes With Churchill*, by W. H. Thompson (London: Christopher Johnson, 1957), pp. 53–4.

4. OBVII, p. 217.

5. It is this aspect of Churchill's character that Martin Gilbert emphasised when the *Daily Telegraph* asked him to describe Churchill in a single sentence. He said: 'He was a great humanitarian who was himself distressed that the accidents of history gave him his greatest power at a time when everything had to be focused on defending the country from destruction, rather than achieving his goals of a fairer society.' Quoted in *Finest Hour*, No. 101, Winter 1998–9.

6. These personal anecdotes concerning Churchill's interest in medals were provided to the author by the Lady Soames.

7. Although numerous statesmen have received the Nobel Peace Prize, Churchill is notable for having received the Nobel Prize for Literature in 1953 for the body of his writing.

8. See for example, 'The Cavalry Charge at Omdurman,' in *Men at War, The Best War Stories of All Time*, edited by Ernest Hemingway (New York: Crown Publishers, 1942) and 'Escape' in *The Mammoth Book of War Correspondents*, edited by Jon E. Lewis (New York: Carrol & Graf Publishers, Inc., 2001).

9. In March 1943 the Air Council, with the approval of King George VI, awarded honorary wings, the flying badge of the Royal Air Force. This was a signal honour and explains why Churchill wore the wings on his air commodore's uniform even though he was not a qualified pilot. See *Onwards to Victory* by Winston S. Churchill (London: Cassell and Company, Ltd., 1944), p. 67.

10. Churchill's honorary military positions and dates of appointments are: Honorary Air Commodore, No. 615 (County of Surrey) Squadron, Royal Auxiliary Air Force, 4 April 1939; Honorary Colonel, 63rd (Oxfordshire Yeomanry) Anti-Tank Regiment, Royal Artillery, 21 October 1939; Honorary Colonel, 6th Battalion, the Royal Scots Fusiliers, 24 January 1940; Colonel, 4th (Queen's Own) Hussars, Royal Armoured Corps, 22 October 1941; Honorary Colonel, 5th (Cinque Ports) Battalion, the Royal Sussex Regiment, 14 November 1941; Honorary Colonel, 89th (Cinque Ports) Battalion, Heavy Anti-Aircraft Regiment, Royal Artillery, 20 February 1942; Honorary Colonel, the Essex Regiment, Territorial Army, 21 January 1945; Honorary Colonel, 6th (Cinque Ports) Cadet Battalion, the Buffs, 29 August 1946; Colonel, the Queen's Royal Irish Hussars, 24 October 1958. Sources: The *London Gazette* and Churchill's army personal file, Ministry of Defence.

11. *The Second World War, Volume I, The Gathering Storm* by Winston S. Churchill (London: Cassell & Co., Ltd., 1948), pp. 526–7. It is beyond the scope of this study to enter into the debate about Churchill's abilities as a military strategist in either world war. Whether he was an amateur meddler in the work of the admirals and generals, or a necessary prod or brake, is a topic of vigorous, ongoing debate among historians. I have included a number of the many books on the topic in the bibliography for those who wish to read further.

Select Bibliography

THE OFFICIAL BIOGRAPHY
(London: William Heinemann, Ltd.)

Volume I: *Youth, 1874–1900*, by Randolph S. Churchill, 1966.

Volume II: *Young Statesman, 1901–1914*, by Randolph S. Churchill, 1967.

Volume III: *The Challenge of War, 1914–1916*, by Martin Gilbert, 1971.

Volume IV: *The Stricken World, 1916–1922*, by Martin Gilbert, 1975.

Volume V: *The Prophet of Truth, 1922–1939*, by Martin Gilbert, 1976.

Volume VII: *Road to Victory, 1941–1945*, by Martin Gilbert, 1986.

Companion Volume 1, Part 1, 1874–1896, edited by Randolph S. Churchill, 1967.

Companion Volume I, Part 2, 1896–1900, edited by Randolph S. Churchill, 1967.

Companion Volume II, Part 1, 1901–1907, edited by Randolph S. Churchill, 1969.

Companion Volume II, Part 2, 1907–1911, edited by Randolph S. Churchill, 1969.

Companion Volume II, Part 3, 1911–1914, edited by Randolph S. Churchill, 1969.

Companion Volume III, Part 1, July 1914–April 1915, edited by Martin Gilbert, 1972.

Companion Volume III, Part 2, May 1915–December 1916, edited by Martin Gilbert, 1972.

Companion Volume IV, Part 1, January 1917–June 1919, edited by Martin Gilbert, 1977.

Companion Volume IV, Part 2, July 1919–March 1921, edited by Martin Gilbert, 1977.

Companion Volume IV, Part 3, April 1921–November 1922, edited by Martin Gilbert, 1977.

Companion Volume V, Part 1, *The Exchequer Years*, 1922–1929, edited by Martin Gilbert, 1981.

Companion Volume V, Part 2, *The Wilderness Years*, 1929–1935, edited by Martin Gilbert, 1981.

Companion Volume V, Part 3, 1936–1939, edited by Martin Gilbert, 1982.

WORKS BY CHURCHILL

'A Grave In Flanders' (poem), Harrow School Archive document.

'Antwerp: The Story of its Siege and Fall', *The Sunday Pictorial*, 19 November 1916.

Blenheim (London: The British Publishers Guild by George G. Harrap & Co., Ltd., 1941).

'British Cavalry', *The Anglo-Saxon Review*, March 1901.

Great Contemporaries (London: Thornton Butterworth, Ltd., 1937).

'How Antwerp Saved the Channel Ports', *The Sunday Pictorial*, 26 November 1916.

Ian Hamilton's March (London: Longmans, Green and Co., 1900).

'Influenza' (poem), Harrow School Archive document.

London to Ladysmith via Pretoria (London: Longmans, Green and Co., 1900).

Marlborough, His Life and Times (4 Volumes) (London: George G. Harrap & Co., Ltd., 1933–8).

Mr Brodrick's Army (Sacramento, CA: The Churchilliana Co., 1977).

My Early Life, A Roving Commission (London: Thornton Butterworth Ltd., 1930).

'Officers and Gentlemen', *The Saturday Evening Post*, 29 December 1900.

Savrola, A Tale of the Revolution in Laurania (London: Longmans, Green and Co., 1900).

'Some Impressions of the War in South Africa', *Royal United Services Institution Journal*, July 1901.

The Collected Essays of Sir Winston Churchill (4 Volumes) (London: Library of Imperial History, 1976).

'The Engagement of 'La Marais' July 7th, 1914' (essay), Harrow School Archive document.

'The Ethics of Frontier Policy', *The United Service Magazine*, August 1898.

'The Fashoda Incident', *The North American Review*, December 1898.

The River War, An Historical Account of the Reconquest of the Soudan (2 Volumes) (London: Longmans, Green and Co., 1899).

'The Royal Military College Sandhurst', *Pall Mall Magazine*, December 1896.

The Story of the Malakand Field Force, An Episode of Frontier War (London: Longmans, Green and Co., 1898).

'The Tirah Campaign', *The Times*, 3 May 1898.

The World Crisis (6 Volumes) (London: Thornton Butterworth Ltd., 1923–31).

Thoughts and Adventures (London: Thornton Butterworth Ltd., 1931).

Winston S. Churchill, His Complete Speeches, 1897–1963 (8 Volumes), edited by Robert Rhodes James (New York: Chelsea House Publishers, 1974).

Winston S. Churchill, War Correspondent, 1895–1900, edited by Frederick Woods (London: Brassey's, 1992).

Young Winston's Wars, edited by Frederick Woods (London: Leo Cooper, Ltd., 1972).

GENERAL WORKS

Abrams, M. H., General Editor, *The Norton Anthology of English Literature*, Volume 2 (New York: . W. W. Norton & Company, Inc., 1968).

'A British Officer,' *Social Life in the British Army* (London: John Long, 1901).

Addison, Paul, 'The Three Careers of Winston Churchill,' *Transactions of The Royal Historical Society*, Sixth Series, XI, Cambridge (University Press, 2001).

Alford, Henry S. L. and Sword, W. Dennistoun, *The Egyptian Soudan, Its Loss and Recovery* (London: MacMillan & Co., Ltd., 1898).

Amery, Leo S, Foreword in *The Young Winston Churchill*, by John Marsh (London: Evans Brothers, Limited, 1955).

— *My Political Life, England Before the Storm, 1896–1914* (Volume 1), London: Hutchinson, 1953).

Arnold, Guy, *Held Fast for England: G. A. Henty Imperialist Boy's Writer* (London: Hamish Hamilton, 1980).

Atkins, J. B., *Incidents and Reflections* (London: Christophers, 1947).

— *The Relief of Ladysmith* (London: Methuen & Co., 1900).

Baden-Powell, Sir Robert, *Memories of India: Recollections of Soldiering and Sport* (Philadelphia: David McKay (1915)).

Baker, B. Gránville, *Old Cavalry Stations* (London: Heath Cranton Limited, 1934).

Baldwin, Stanley Simm, *Forward Everywhere: Her Majesty's Territorials* (London: Brassey's, 1994).

Balsan, Consuelo Vanderbilt, *The Glitter and the Gold* (New York: Harper & Brothers Publishers, 1952).

Barnett, Correlli, *Britain and Her Army, 1509–1970, A Military, Political and Social Survey* (Harmondsworth, Middlesex: Penguin Books, Ltd., 1974).

Barthorp, Michael, *The Anglo-Boer Wars: the British and the Afrikaners, 1815–1902* (Poole, Dorset: Blandford Press, 1987).

— *The Frontier Ablaze, The North-West Frontier Rising, 1897–98* (London: Windrow & Greene, Ltd., 1996).

— *The North-West Frontier, British India and Afghanistan,* A Pictorial History, 1839–1947 (Poole, Dorset: New Orchard Editions, Ltd., 1986).

— *War on the Nile: Britain, Egypt and the Sudan, 1882–1898* (Poole, Dorset: Blandford Press, 1984).

Beiriger, Eugene Edward, *Churchill, Munitions and Mechanical Warfare: The Politics of Supply and Strategy* (New York: Peter Lang Publishing, Inc., 1997).

Belfield, Eversley, *The Boer War* (London: Leo Cooper, 1975).

Ben-Moshe, Tuvia, *Churchill, Strategy and History* (Boulder, CO: Lynne Rienner Publishers, Inc., 1992).

Birdwood, Field-Marshal Lord, *Khaki and Gown* (London: Ward, Lock & Co., Ltd., 1941).

'Black & White Budget,' (magazine), London: Black and White Publishing Company, February 10, 1900.

Blake, Robert and Louis, William Roger, *Churchill, A Major New Assessment of His Life in Peace and War* (New York: W. W. Norton & Company, 1993).

Blood, General Sir Bindon, *Four Score Years and Ten, Sir Bindon Blood's Reminiscences* (London: G. Bell and Sons, Ltd., 1933).

Blow, Michael, *A Ship to Remember: The Maine and the Spanish-American War* (New York: Morrow William & Co., 1992).

— 'The Trochas,' *Military History Quarterly,* Vol. 10, No. 4, Summer 1998.

Bonham Carter, Violet, *Winston Churchill as I Knew Him* (London: Eyre & Spottiswoode and Collins, 1965).

Bonsor, N. R. P. and Isherwood, J. H., *North Atlantic Seaway, Volume 1* (New York: Arco Publishing Company, Inc., 1975).

Bourquin, S. B. and Torlage, Gilbert, *The Battle of Colenso, 15 December 1899* (Randburg, South Africa: Ravan Press, 1999).

Bowling, A. H., *British Hussar Regiments, 1805–1914* (London: Almark Publishing Co., Ltd., 1972).

Bridges, Lieut. Gen. Sir Tom, *Alarms and Excursions, Reminiscences of a Soldier* (London: Longmans, Green and Co., 1938).

Brighton, Terry, *The Last Charge, The 21st Lancers and the Battle of Omdurman, 2 September 1898* (Ramsbury, Wilts: The Crowood Press, Ltd., 1998).

Burleigh, Bennet, *Khartoum Campaign, 1898, Or The Reconquest of the Sudan* (London: Chapman & Hall, Ltd., 1899).

— *The Natal Campaign* (London: Chapman & Hall, Ltd., 1900).

Buzzell, Nora (compiler), *The Register of the Victoria Cross* (Cheltenham, Gloucestershire: This England Books, 1988).

Callwell, C. E., *Small Wars: A Tactical Textbook for Imperial Soldiers* (London: Greenhill Books, 1990).

Carver, Field Marshal Lord, *The*

National Army Museum Book of The Boer War (London: Sidgwick & Jackson, 1999).

'Ceremonial To Be Observed At The Funeral of The Right Honourable Sir Winston Leonard Spencer-Churchill' (London: HMSO, 1965).

Chaplin, E. D. W. (as collected by) *Winston Churchill and Harrow, Memories of the Prime Minister's Schooldays, 1888–1892* (Harrow: Harrow School Bookshop, 1941).

Childs, Lewis, *Battleground South Africa, Ladysmith, Colenso/Spion Kop/Hlangwane/Tugela* (London: Leo Cooper, 1998).

Churchill, Sarah, *A Thread in the Tapestry* (London: Andre Deutsch Ltd., 1967).

Cohen, Eliot A., *Supreme Command, Soldiers, Statesmen and Leadership in Wartime* (New York: The Free Press, 2002).

Cole, Lt Col Howard N., *The Story of Aldershot, A History and Guide to Town and Camp* (Aldershot: Gale & Polden Limited, 1951).

Cornwallis-West, Mrs George, *The Reminiscences of Lady Randolph Churchill* (New York: The Century Co., 1908).

Cosgrave, Patrick, *Churchill at War, Vol. I, Alone 1939–40* (London: William Collins Sons & Co., Ltd., 1974).

Cowles, Virginia, *Winston Churchill, the Era and the Man* (London: Hamish Hamilton, 1953).

Creagh, Sir O'Moore and Humphris, E. M. (editors), *The Victoria Cross, 1856–1920* (Polstead, Suffolk: J. B. Hayward & Son, 1985).

Daniell, David Scott, *4th Hussar, The Story of a British Cavalry Regiment* (Aldershot, Gale & Polden, Ltd., 1959).

Dardanelles Commission, *Lord Kitchener and Winston Churchill: The Dardanelles, Part I, 1914–1915* (London: The Stationery Office, 2000).

— *Defeat at Gallipoli: The Dardanelles, Part II, 1915–1916* (London: The Stationery Office, 2000).

Davis, Richard Harding, *Real Soldiers of Fortune* (New York: Charles Scribner's Sons, 1914).

De Groot, Gerard, J., *Liberal Crusader, The Life of Sir Archibald Sinclair* (London: Hurst & Company, 1993).

Dickson, W. K. L., *The Biograph in Battle, Its Story in The South African War* (Trowbridge, Wilts: Flicks Books, 1995).

Dooner, Mildred G., *The Last Post* (Polstead, Suffolk: J. B. Hayward & Son, 1980).

Doyle, Arthur Conan, *The Great Boer War* (London: Smith, Elder & Co., 1900).

Dundonald, Lieut Gen. The Earl of, *My Army Life* (London: Edward Arnold & Co., 1926).

Dunlop, Col. John K., *The Development of the British Army 1899–1914* (London: Methuen, 1938).

Dupuy, Trevor N., *The Military Life of Winston Churchill of Britain* (New York: Franklin Watts, Inc., 1970).

Eade, Charles (editor), *Churchill By His Contemporaries* (New York: Simon and Schuster, Inc., 1954).

Eddershaw, David, *The Story of The Oxfordshire Yeomanry, Queen's Own Oxfordshire Hussars 1798–1998* (Oxford: The Oxfordshire Yeomanry Trust, 1998).

Edwards, Major T. J., *Military Customs* (Aldershot: Gale & Polden, Ltd., 1954).

Ellis, John, *Eye-Deep In Hell: Trench Warfare in World War I* (Baltimore: The Johns Hopkins University Press, 1989).

Emmert, Kirk, *Winston S. Churchill on Empire* (Durham, NC: Carolina Academic Press, 1989).

Evans, Capt. H. K. D., *The 4th (Queen's Own) Hussars in the Great War* (Aldershot: Gale & Polden, Ltd., 1920).

Ewing, John, *The History of The 9th (Scottish) Division* (London: John Murray, 1921).

Ezell, Edward Clinton, *Small Arms of the World* (New York: Barnes & Noble, 1983).

Falls, Cyril, 'Sir Winston Churchill In War', in *The Illustrated London News, An Eightieth Year Tribute to Winston Churchill*, 1954 (edited by Bruce Ingram).

Farwell, Byron, *Armies of the Raj* (New York: W. W. Norton & Co., 1989).

— *Eminent Victorian Soldiers* (New York: W. W. Norton & Co., 1985).

— *Mr Kipling's Army, All the Queen's Men* (New York: W. W. Norton & Co., 1981).

— *Prisoners of the Mahdi* (New York: W. W. Norton & Co., 1989).

— *Queen Victoria's Little Wars* (New York: Harper & Row Publishers, 1972).

— *The Great Anglo-Boer War* (New York: Harper & Row Publishers, 1976).

Featherstone, Donald, *Khaki & Red, Soldiers of the Queen in India and Africa* (London: Arms and Armour Press, 1995).

— *Khartoum 1885, General Gordon's Last Stand* (London: Osprey/Reed Consumer Books, Ltd., 1996).

— *Omdurman 1898, Kitchener's Victory in the Sudan* (London: Osprey/Reed Consumer Books, Ltd., 1993).

— *Victorian Colonial Warfare, Africa, from the Campaigns Against the Kaffirs to the South African War* (London: Blandford Press, 1993).

— *Victorian Colonial Warfare, India, from the Conquest of Sind to the Indian Mutiny* (London: Blandford Press, 1993).

— *Victoria's Enemies, An A-Z of British Colonial Warfare* (London: Blandford Press, 1989).

— *Weapons & Equipment of the Victorian Soldier* (London: Arms and Armour Press, 1996).

Fincastle, The Viscount and Eliot-Lockhart, P.C., *A Frontier Campaign* (London: R. J. Leach & Co, 1990).

Fowler, Marian, *Blenheim, Biography of a Palace* (London: Viking, 1989).

Frankland, Thomas, Sketchbook in the collection of the Winston Churchill Memorial and Library, Fulton, Missouri.

Gandhi, M. K., *An Autobiography* (Ahmedabad: Navajivan Publishing House, 1945).

Gardner, Brian, *Mafeking: A Victorian Legend* (New York: Harcourt, Brace & World, Inc., 1967).

Gibb, Andrew Dewar ('Captain X'), *With Winston Churchill at the Front* (Glasgow: Cowans & Gray, 1924).

Gilbert, Martin, *Churchill, A Photograph Portrait* (Boston: Houghton Mifflin Company, 1988).

— *Churchill A Life* (New York: Henry Holt and Company, 1991).

— *First World War Atlas* (London: Weidenfeld and Nicolson, 1970).

— *In Search of Churchill* (London: Harper Collins Publishers, 1994).

— *The First World War, A Complete History* (New York: Henry Holt and Company, 1994).

— *Winston Churchill's War Leadership* (New York: Random House, Inc., 2003).

Golland, Jim, *Not Winston, Just William?, Winston Churchill at Harrow School* (Harrow: The Herga Press, 1988).

Goodenough, Lieut General W. H. and Dalton, Lieut Colonel J. C., *The Army Book for the British Empire* (London: HMSO, 1893).

Gough, General Sir Hubert, *Soldiering*

On (London: Arthur Barker, Ltd., 1954).

Graham, Alexander J. P., *The Capture and Escape of Winston Churchill During the South African War* (Salisbury, Rhodesia: Edinburgh Press, 1965).

Green, David, *Sir Winston Churchill at Blenheim Palace, An Anthology* (Oxford: Alden & Company, 1959).

Gretton, Vice-Admiral Sir Peter, *Former Naval Person: Winston Churchill and the Royal Navy* (London: Cassell & Company, Ltd., 1968).

Grierson, J. M., *The British Army* (by a Lieutenant-Colonel in the British Army) (London: Sampson Low, Marston & Company, 1899).

Griffith, Kenneth, *Thank God We Kept the Flag Flying, The Siege and Relief of Ladysmith 1899–1900* (New York: The Viking Press, 1974).

Guggisberg, Captain F. G., *The Shop, The Story of The Royal Military Academy* (London: Cassell and Company, Ltd., 1900).

Haldane, Captain Aylmer, *How We Escaped from Pretoria* (Edinburgh and London: William Blackwood and Sons, 1901).

Haldane, Sir Aylmer, *A Soldier's Saga: The Autobiography of General Sir Aylmer Haldane* (Edinburgh & London: William Blackwood & Sons, Ltd., 1948).

Halstead, Murat, *The Story of Cuba, Her Struggles for Liberty, the Cause, Crisis and Destiny of the Pearl of the Antilles* (Akron, OH: The Werner Company, 1898).

Hallows, Ian S., *Regiments and Corps of the British Army* (London: Arms and Armour Press, 1991).

Hamilton, General Sir Ian, *Listening for the Drums* (London: Faber & Faber, Ltd., 1944).

Hamley, Edward Bruce, *The Operations*

of War, Explained and Illustrated (Edinburgh and London: Blackwood and Sons, 1878).

Handbook For Travellers in India Burma and Ceylon (London: John Murray, 1938).

Harfield, Alan, *The Indian Army of the Empress, 1861–1903* (Tunbridge Wells, Kent: Spellmount, Ltd., 1990).

Harries-Jenkins, Gwyn, *The Army in Victorian Society* (London: Routledge & Keegan Paul, Ltd., 1977).

Harrington, Peter, *British Artists and War, The Face of Battle in Paintings and Prints* (London: Greenhill Books, 1993).

Harrow School Bill Books (Harrow School Archive)

Harrow School Songs (Henley on Thames: The Gresham Press, 1993).

Hasan, M. Fazlul, *Bangalore Through the Centuries* (Bangalore, India: Historical Publications, 1970).

Haythornthwaite, Philip J., *The Colonial Wars Source Book* (London: Arms and Armour Press, 1995).

— *The World War One Source Book* (London: Arms and Armour Press, 1997).

Heathcote, T. A., *The Indian Army, The Garrison of British Imperial India, 1822–1922* (London: David & Charles, 1974).

— *The Royal Military Academy Sandhurst, An Illustrated Guide to the Buildings and Grounds* (Camberley: The Royal Academy Sandhurst, no date).

Herbertson, A. J. and Howarth, O. J. R. (editors), *The Oxford Survey of the British Empire* (6 Volumes) (Oxford: Clarendon Press, 1914).

Higgins, Trumbull, *Winston Churchill and the Dardanelles* (New York: The Macmillan Company, 1963).

Hobday, Major E. A. P., *Sketches on*

Service During the Indian Frontier Campaigns of 1897 (London: James Bowden, 1898).

Hogg, Ian V., *Military Pistols and Revolvers* (Poole, Dorset: Arms and Armour Press, Ltd., 1987).

Holdich, Col. Sir T. Hungerford, *The Indian Borderland 1880–1900* (London: Methuen and Co., 1900).

Holmes, Richard, *The Little Field-Marshal, Sir John French* (London: Jonathan Cape, 1981).

Holt, Tonie and Valmai, *Battlefields of the First World War, A Traveller's Guide* (London: Parkgate Books, Ltd., 1995).

Hough, Richard, *Former Naval Person: Churchill and the Wars at Sea* (London: Weidenfeld and Nicolson, Ltd., 1985).

— *The Great War at Sea 1914–1918* (Oxford: Oxford University Press, 1983).

Howarth, David and Stephen, *The Story of the P & O* (London: Weidenfeld and Nicolson, 1966).

Issar, T. P., *The City Beautiful, A Celebration of the Architectural Heritage and City-Aesthetics of Bangalore* (Bangalore: Bangalore Urban Arts Commission).

Jablonsky, David, 'Churchill's Initial Experience with the British Conduct of Small Wars: India and the Sudan, 1897–98,' in *Small Wars and Insurgencies*, Vol. II, No. 1 (Spring 2000), pp. 1–25. Published by Frank Cass & Co., Ltd, London.

— *Churchill, The Great Game and Total War* (London: Frank Cass & Co., Ltd., 1991).

— *Churchill: The Making of a Grand Strategist* (Carlisle Barracks, PA: Strategic Studies Institute, U S Army War College, 1990).

James, Lawrence, *Raj: The Making and Unmaking of British India* (New York: St Martin's Press, 1998).

— *The Rise and Fall of the British Empire* (London: Little, Brown & Company, 1994).

Jerrold, Douglas, *The Royal Naval Division* (London: Hutchinson & Co. (Publishers), 1927)).

Jog, Narayan Gopal, *Churchill's Blind Spot: India* (Bombay: New Book Company, 1944).

Joslin, E. C., Litherland, AR, and Simpkin, B.T., *British Battles & Medals* (London: Spink & Son, Ltd., 1988).

Khan, Aga, *The Memoirs of Aga Khan, World Enough and Time* (London: Cassell and Company, Ltd., 1954).

Khan, Muhammad Nawaz, *Malakand, A Journey Through History* (Peshawar: Gandhara Markaz, 1995).

Keegan, John, *Fields of Battle, The Wars of North America* (New York: Alfred A. Knopf, 1996).

Keith-Falconer, Adrian, *The Oxfordshire Hussars in the Great War (1914–1918)* (London: John Murray, 1927).

Knight, Ian, *Colenso 1899, The Boer War in Natal* (London: Osprey/Reed Consumer Books, Ltd., 1995).

— *Go to Your God Like a Soldier, The British Soldier Fighting for Empire, 1837–1902* (London: Greenhill Books, 1996).

Kraft, Prince Zu Hohenlohe Ingelfingen, *Letters on Cavalry* (London: Edward Stanford, 1893).

Laffin, John, *A Western Front Companion, 1914–1918* (London: Sutton Publishing, Ltd., 2000).

Lamb, Richard, *Churchill as War Leader, Right or Wrong?* (London: Bloomsbury Publishing, Ltd., 1991).

Langworth, Barbara, 'Churchill and Polo, The Hot Pursuit of His Other Hobby' in *Finest Hour*, No. 72, 3rd Quarter 1991.

Langworth, Richard M., *A Connoisseur's Guide to the Books of Sir Winston Churchill* (London: Brassey's, 1998).

Leaf, John, *Harrow School* (London: Pitkin Pictorials, Ltd., 1990).

Lehmann, Joseph, *The First Boer War* (London: Jonathan Cape, Ltd., 1972).

Leslie, Anita, *The Marlborough House Set* (New York: Doubleday & Company, Inc., 1973).

Leslie, Shane, *The End of a Chapter* (New York: Charles Scribner's Sons, 1917).

Lewin, Ronald, *Churchill as Warlord* (New York: Stein & Day Publishers, 1973).

Lewis, David Levering, *The Race to Fashoda* (New York: Weidenfeld & Nicolson, 1987).

Liddell Hart, B. H., *History of the First World War* (London: Pan Books, 1973).

Maber, John M., *The Ships, Channel Packets and Ocean Liners 1850–1970* (London: HMSO, no date).

Maconcly, Brig.-Gen. E. W. S. K., Memoirs 1860–1920, typewritten manuscript in the National Army Museum Collection, Acc No. 7908-62-1 and 7908-62-2.

Macaulay, Lord, *Lays of Ancient Rome* (Washington, D.C.: Regnery Publishing, Inc., 1997).

MacGregor-Hastie, Roy, *Never to Be Taken Alive, A Biography of General Gordon* (New York: St Martin's Press, 1985).

MacKay, James, and Mussell, John W. and the editorial team of *The Medal News*, *The Medal Yearbook 1997* (Honiton, Devon: Token Publishing, Limited, 1997).

Magnus, Philip, *Kitchener, Portrait of an Imperialist* (London: John Murray, 1958).

Maitland, Francis Hereward, *Hussar of the Line* (London: Hurst & Blackett, Ltd., 1951).

Makepeace-Warne, Antony, *Brassey's Companion to the British Army* (London: Brassey's, 1995).

Manchester, William, *The Last Lion, Visions of Glory 1874–1932* (Boston: Little, Brown and Company, 1983).

Masefield, John, *Gallipoli* (New York: The MacMillan Company, 1917.

Mason, David, *Churchill 1914–1918* (New York: Ballantine Books, Inc., 1973).

Mason, Philip, *A Matter of Honour* (New York: Holt Rinehart Winston, 1974).

— *The Men Who Ruled India* (New York: W. W. Norton & Company, 1985).

Masters, John, *Bugles and a Tiger* (London: Michael Joseph, 1956).

May, Col. T. L., 'Particulars of The Association of Sir Winston Churchill and The Queen's Own Oxfordshire Hussars, 1901–1965'. Archive Document, Oxfordshire Yeomanry Trust.

— 'The Queen's Own Oxfordshire Hussars and the Funeral of Sir Winston S. Churchill'. Archive Document, Oxfordshire Yeomanry Trust.

— 'Sir WLS Churchill and the Queen's Own Oxfordshire Hussars'. Archive Document, Oxfordshire Yeomanry Trust.

McCullough, David, 'Harry S. Truman' in *Character Above All, Ten Presidents from FDR to Bush*, Robert A. Wilson, editor (New York: Simon & Schuster, 1995).

McVean, Lt-Col D. A. D, Diary for 1897 (Archive Document), Imperial War Museum, Ref: 67/204/1-3.

Menpes, Mortimer, *War Impressions* (London: Adam & Charles Black, 1903).

Meredith John, editor, *Omdurman*

*Diaries 1898, Eyewitness Accounts of
the Legendary Campaign* (London:
Leo Cooper, Ltd., 1998).

Mills, H. Woosnam, *The Pathan Revolt
in North-West India* (Lahore: The
'Civil and Military Gazette' Press,
1897).

Mockler-Ferryman, A. F., *Annals of
Sandhurst: A Chronicle of the Royal
Military College from Its Foundation
to the Present Day* (London: William
Heinemann, 1900).

Mollo, Boris, *The Indian Army* (Poole,
Dorset: New Orchard Editions, Ltd.,
1986).

Montague Browne, Anthony, *Long
Sunset* (London: Cassell Publishers,
Ltd., 1995).

Moorehead, Alan, *Gallipoli* (New York:
Harper & Row Publishers, 1956).

Moorhouse, Geoffrey, *India Britannica*
(New York: Harper & Row,
Publishers, 1983).

Morris, James, *Farewell the Trumpets*
(London: Faber and Faber, Ltd.,
1978).

— *Heaven's Command, An Imperial
Progress* (London: Faber and Faber,
1973).

— *Pax Britannica, The Climax of
Empire* (London: Faber and Faber,
Ltd., 1968).

Morris, Jan, *Stones of Empire, The
Buildings of the Raj* (Oxford: Oxford
University Press, 1983).

National Geographic (Churchill Funeral
Issue), Vol. 128, No. 2, August,
1965.

Neillands, Robin, *The Dervish Wars,
Gordon & Kitchener in the Sudan
1880–1898* (London: John Murray
(Publishers) Ltd., 1996).

Nelson, James (editor), *General Eisen-
hower on the Military Churchill* (New
York: W. W. Norton & Company,
Inc., 1970).

Nevill, H. L., *North-West Frontier,
British and Indian Army Campaigns
on the North-West Frontier of India,
1849–1908* (London: Tom Donovan
Publishing, Ltd., 1992).

*Officers Died in the Great War
1914–1919* (Polstead, Suffolk: J. B.
Hayward & Son, 1988).

Pakenham, Thomas, *The Boer War*
(New York: Random House, 1979).

Parker, R. A. C., *Winston Churchill,
Studies in Statesmanship* (London:
Brassey's, 1995).

Peel, Sidney, *Trooper 8008 I.Y.*
(London: Edward Arnold, 1902).

Penn, Geoffrey, *Fisher, Churchill and
the Dardanelles* (London: Leo
Cooper, 1999).

Perez, Louis A. Jr., *Cuba Between
Empires 1878–1902* (Pittsburg:
University of Pittsburg Press, 1983).

Pilpel, Robert H. *Churchill in America
1895–1961, An Affectionate Portrait*
(New York: Harcourt Brace
Jovanovich, 1976).

Pitt, Barrie, *Churchill and the Generals*
(Newton Abbot, Devon: David &
Charles Publishers, Inc., 1998).

Powell, Geoffrey, *Buller: A Scapegoat?*
(London: Leo Cooper, 1994).

Prior, Robin, *Churchill's 'World Crisis'
as History* (London: Croom Helm,
Ltd., 1983).

Queen's Royal Hussars, 'Historical
Account of the 4th, THE QUEEN'S
OWN, Historical Papers, 1801-
1921, 4th Hussars', (Archive Docu-
ment, The Queen's Royal Hussars
Collection).

Queen's Royal Hussars. 'The Queen's
Royal Hussars (The Queen's Own
and Royal Irish)', Undated
pamphlet, no author noted.

*Regulations for the Territorial Force
1908* (London: HMSO). Reprinted
by The Naval & Military Press,
Ltd., 2004.

Reitz, Deneys, *Commando, A Boer
Journal of the Boer War* (London:
Faber and Faber, Ltd., 1929).

Richards, Walter, *Her Majesty's Territorial Army* (4 volumes) (London: Virtue & Co., 1909–11).

Roberts, Brian, *Churchills in Africa* (London: Hamish Hamilton, Ltd., 1970).

Robson, Brian, *Swords of the British Army, The Regulation Patterns 1788–1914* (London: The National Army Museum, 1996).

Roskill, Stephen, *Churchill & the Admirals* (London: William Collins Sons & Co., Ltd., 1977).

Routledge, Edmund (editor), *Routledge's Every Boy's Annual Illustrated* (London: George Routledge & Sons, 1884).

Royal Military College Sandhurst, The Register of Gentlemen Cadets, Vol. 4, 1890 Feb. to 1897 Jan. (Archive Document, National Archives, Kew).

Russell, Douglas S., *The Orders, Decorations and Medals of Sir Winston Churchill* (Washington, D. C.: The Churchill Centre, 2004).

Sandys, Celia, *Chasing Churchill, The Travels of Winston Churchill* (New York: Carroll & Graf Publishers, 2003).

— *Churchill Wanted Dead or Alive* (London: HarperCollins Publishers, 1999).

Schoenfeld, Maxwell, P., *The War Ministry of Winston Churchill* (Ames, IA: The Iowa State University Press, 1972).

Seely, Major General J. E. B., *Adventure* (London: William Heinemann, Ltd., 1930).

Sharf, Frederica and Harrington, Peter (editors), *Omdurman 1898: The Eyewitnesses Speak* (London: Greenhill Books, 1998).

Shepperd, Alan, *Sandhurst, The Royal Military Academy and Its Predecessors* (London: Country Life Books, 1980).

Sheridan, Claire, *Naked Truth* (New York: Harper & Bros., 1928).

Smalley, George W., *Anglo-American Memories* (London: Duckworth & Co., 1912).

Smyth, Sir John, *Sandhurst* (London: Weidenfeld & Nicolson, 1961).

Soames, Mary, *Clementine Churchill* (London: Cassell and Company, Ltd., 1979).

— *Family Album* (Boston: Houghton Mifflin Company, 1982).

— *Winston Churchill, His Life as a Painter* (London: William Collins Sons & Co., 1990).

Spagnoly, Tony and Smith, Ted, *A Walk Around Plugstreet, Cameos of the Western Front, South Ypres Sector 1914–1918* (London: Leo Cooper, 1997).

Spiers, Edward M. ed., *Sudan, The Reconquest Reappraised* (London: Frank Cass & Co., Ltd., 1998).

— *The Late Victorian Army, 1868–1902* (Manchester and New York: Manchester University Press, 1992).

Staley, Elizabeth, *Monkey Tops, Old Buildings in Bangalore Cantonment* (Bangalore: Tara Books, 1981).

Stansky, Peter (editor), *Churchill, A Profile* (New York: Hill and Wang, 1973).

Steevens, George W., *Egypt in 1898* (New York: Dodd, Mead & Company, 1899).

— *From Capetown to Ladysmith: An Unfinished Record of the South African War* (New York: Dodd, Mead and Company, 1900).

— *In India* (Edinburgh and London: William Blackwood and Sons, 1900).

— *With Kitchener to Khartoum* (London: William Blackwood and Sons, 1898).

Stirling, John, *The Colonials in South Africa 1899–1902* (Polstead, Suffolk: J. B. Hayward & Son, 1990).

Strawson, John, *Gentlemen in Khaki: The British Army 1890–1990* (London: Secker & Warburg, Limited, 1989).

Tamplin, J. M. A. and Abbott, P. E., *British Gallantry Awards* (Garden City, NY: Doubleday & Company, Inc., 1972).

Taylor, A. J. P. (and others), *Churchill Revised, A Critical Assessment* (New York: The Dial Press, Inc., 1969).

Terraine, John, *Douglas Haig: The Educated Soldier* (London: Leo Cooper, 1990).

The Harrovian, Harrow School Archive documents.

'The Order of Service for the Funeral of the Right Honourable Sir Winston Leonard Spencer-Churchill', (London: HMSO, 1965).

'The Queen's Own Oxfordshire Hussars', in *Territorial Magazine*, County of Oxford Supplement (reprinted April 1957 issue).

Thompson, R. W., *Generalissimo Churchill* (New York: Charles Scribner's Sons, 1973).

Torlage, Gilbert, *The Battle of Spion Kop 23–24 January 1900* (Randburg, South Africa: Ravan Press, 1999).

Torlage, Gilbert and Watt Steve, *A Guide to Anglo-Boer War Sites of Kwazulu-Natal* (Randburg, South Africa, Ravan Press, 1999).

Trask, David F., *The War with Spain in 1898* (New York: Macmillan Publishing Co., Inc., 1981).

Trew, Peter, *The Boer War Generals* (Thrupp, Gloucestershire: Sutton Publishing, Ltd., 1999).

Valiunas, Algis, *Churchill's Military Histories, A Rhetorical Study* (Lantham, NJ: Rowman & Littlefield Publishers, Inc., 2002).

Van Hartesveldt, Fred R., *The Boer War* (Thrupp, Gloucestershire: Sutton Publishing, Ltd., 2000).

Walter, John, *Rifles of the World* (Northbrook, IL: DBI Books, Inc., 1993).

Walters, Capt. H. F., *The Operations of the Malakand Field Force and the Buner Field Force, 1897–1898* (Simla: Government Central Printing Office, 1900).

Walton, Lt Col P. S., *Simkin's Soldiers, the British Army in 1890*, Volume I (Dorking, Surrey: The Victorian Military Society, 1981).

Warner, Philip, *Army Life in the 90s* (London: Country Life Books, 1975).

—, *Dervish, The Rise and Fall of an African Empire* (London: MacDonald & James, 1973).

War Office, *Dress Regulations for Officers of the Army* (London: War Office, 1900).

—, *Regulations for the Instruction and Movements of Cavalry* (London: HMSO, 1885).

—, *Regulations for the Supply of Clothing and Necessaries to the Regular Forces (1894)*, reprint edition (Newport, Gwent: Ray Westlake Military Books, 1987).

—, *The Official Army List*.

Watt, Steve, *The Siege of Ladysmith 2 November 1899–28 February 1900* (Randburg, South Africa: Ravan Press, 1999).

Weidhorn, Manfred, *A Harmony of Interests, Explorations in the Mind of Sir Winston Churchill* (London: Associated University Presses, 1992).

— *Sword and Pen, A Survey of the Writings of Sir Winston Churchill* (Albuquerque, NM: University of New Mexico Press, 1974).

Wessels, Andre, *The Phases of the Anglo-Boer War 1899–1902* (Bloemfontein, S. Africa: War Museum of The Boer Republics, 1998).

Williams, Jeffery, *Byng of Vimy, General and Governor General* (London: Leo

Cooper, 1983).

'With The Flag To Pretoria, Part 10',
Dec, 1899 (magazine) (London:
Harmsworth Brothers, Ltd., 1899).

Woods, Frederick, *Artillery of Words,
The Writings of Sir Winston Churchill*
(London: Leo Cooper, 1992).

Wylly, Colonel H. C., *From Black
Mountain to Waziristan* (London:
MacMillan and Co., Limited, 1912).

Yardley, Michael, *Sandhurst: A Docu-
mentary* (London: Harrap, Ltd.,
1987).

Younghusband, George C., *Indian
Frontier Warfare* (Delhi: Anmol
Publications, 1985).

Ziegler, Philip, *Omdurman* (New York:
Dorset Press, 1973).

Zoller, Curt J., *Annotated Bibliography
of Works About Sir Winston S.
Churchill* (Armonk, NY: M. E.
Sharpe, Inc., 2004).

Zulfo, Ismat Hasan, *Karari: The
Sudanese Account of the Battle of
Omdurman* (London: Frederick
Warne (Publishers) Ltd., 1980).

Index